NANJING 1937

MEMORIES OF A MASSACRE

HE JIANMING

ACA PUBLISHING LTD

Published by
ACA Publishing Ltd.
University House
11-13 Lower Grosvenor Place,
London SW1W 0EX, UK
Tel: +44 20 3289 3885
E-mail: info@alaincharlesasia.com
Web: www.alaincharlesasia.com

Beijing Office
Tel: +86 (0) 10 8472 1250

Author: He Jianming
Translator: Miles Craven, Lisa Murphy, Jiang Lin

Published by ACA Publishing Ltd in association with the China Translation & Publishing House

Original Chinese Text © 南京大屠杀 *(Nan Jing Da Tu Sha)* 2017, China Translation & Publishing House, Beijing, China

English Translation © 2020, ACA Publishing Ltd, London, UK

ALL RIGHTS RESERVED. NO PART OF THIS PUBLICATION MAY BE REPRODUCED IN MATERIAL FORM, BY ANY MEANS, WHETHER GRAPHIC, ELECTRONIC, MECHANICAL OR OTHER, INCLUDING PHOTOCOPYING OR INFORMATION STORAGE, IN WHOLE OR IN PART, AND MAY NOT BE USED TO PREPARE OTHER PUBLICATIONS WITHOUT WRITTEN PERMISSION FROM THE PUBLISHER.

The greatest care has been taken to ensure accuracy but the publisher can accept no responsibility for errors or omissions, or for any liability occasioned by relying on its content.

Paperback ISBN: 978-1-910760-43-7
eBook ISBN: 978-1-83890-005-2

A catalogue record for *Nanjing 1937: Memories of the Massacre* is available from the National Bibliographic Service of the British Library.

CONTENTS

1. The Decisive Battle Before the Massacre   1
2. The First Day of the Massacre   126
3. Nanjing is Suffocated   177
4. Rape: Screams on Mochou Lake   211
5. John Rabe and the International Safety Zone   271
6. A Foreign Lady Clings to the Island of Life   432
7. Trials and Testimonies   486
8. Another Unresolved Injustice   541
9. Between Man and Devil: The Confessions of the Japanese   552

About the Author   593

1

THE DECISIVE BATTLE BEFORE THE MASSACRE

In addition to their political, military, cultural and economic significance, the capitals of almost every country that have made a significant contribution to the development of human civilisation boast another feature: a role in the history of warfare. For instance, the fierce fighting and military campaigns in battles like the siege of the Acropolis in Athens, the capital of Greece, and the battle of Moscow, the capital of the former Soviet Union, have been enthusiastically read about and studied by later generations. Now, the Battle of Nanjing, which was fought before the massacre and featured an intensity of fighting rarely seen in modern Chinese history, should be given the same level of attention. Though the battle resulted in failure for the Chinese forces and it later led to the death of 300,000 of their countrymen in Nanjing, the integrity of the city still remains and, with it, our duty to preserve the records of what really happened then.

At the time of the battle, Nanjing was the capital of the Chinese Nationalist government. The battle fought before the massacre took place is a tragedy in its own right with a legacy that hangs heavy in the history of the entire Chinese nation. With this in mind, I hope that today, all Chinese, regardless of their background and political beliefs, can put their prejudices to one side and objectively approach the historical facts of the matter.

Chiang Kai-shek Made Relatively Serious Efforts Before and After the Fall of Shanghai

"Relatively serious efforts" was how Mao Zedong described his longstanding adversary Chiang's actions. To understand why Chairman Mao would ever say anything like this about his mortal enemy, we need to focus on the Japanese invaders' massacre at Nanjing.

When understanding the Nanjing Massacre and the resulting problems between China and Japan, we have to look back at the Marco Polo Bridge Incident, which took place on 7 July 1937.

Wars between countries often resemble conflicts between individuals, and while some fight by the rules, others certainly do not. Ever since the Mukden Incident on 18 September 1931 when Japan captured the three provinces of northeastern China, namely Heilongjiang, Jilin and Liaoning, it had its sights set on more Chinese land and had been scheming ways of launching a larger scale invasion to the south. Then, one night on 7 July 1937, the Japanese army stationed on the Marco Polo Bridge held a 'military exercise' near the Chinese garrison without notifying the local authorities. They falsely claimed that a Japanese soldier had gone missing and asked to enter Wanping in Beiping, the former name for Beijing, to search for him. Their request was met with a flat refusal by the Chinese side, leading to an immediate attack from the Japanese troops, with the 219th regiment of the 37th division from the 29th army of the Chinese garrison swiftly and resolutely striking back. Using this incident as an excuse, Japan quickly drafted a plan to invade north China and deployed 400,000 armed forces with a full declaration of war on China.

The day after the Marco Polo Bridge Incident, the CPC Central Committee in Yan'an made a nationwide public announcement, calling for solidarity between soldiers and civilians all over the country to unite against and resist the Japanese invasion. At the time, however, the Chinese government was located in Nanjing, with Chiang Kai-shek the commander-in-chief of the armed forces and responsible for directing the army in battle on the front lines.

In June 1937, Chiang Kai-shek came to Lushan (Mount Lu) to organise a central military academy teaching corps and designated himself as the regimental commander, targeting "civil and military comrades from all walks of life" and "public officials nationwide". According to the address titled *Points and Purposes of the Nation-Building Training* that Chiang delivered on 27 June to officers ranked captain and above, the reason for the training was:

> Following the resolute central policy of collectively resisting the foreign invasion and guarding against subjugation to ensure our survival, it is everyone's duty to be both enthusiastic about building our nation and responsible for its survival and downfall so as to achieve our common goals through our own efforts and devotion. Everyone is expected to fulfil their duties through self-reliance and struggle, morality and being prepared to make sacrifices to rejuvenate our nation at any time. This is the policy we need to uphold and the only goal we will pursue through this training.

The Mukden Incident in 1931 further highlighted the dangers of Japan's aggressive ambitions to Chiang Kai-shek, but he still clung on to his policy of resisting foreign aggression after stabilising the country and focused much of his energy on the "encirclement and suppression of the Communist Party of China (CPC)". In Xi'an on 12 December 1936, what became known as the Xi'an Incident took place. Zhang Xueliang and Yang Hucheng, Kuomintang (KMT) generals influenced by the CPC's policy of creating an anti-Japanese national united front, imprisoned Chiang Kai-shek and demanded that he cease the civil war and unite with the CPC in the fight against the Japanese invaders. Japanese aggression continued after the incident's resolution, and Chiang began to feel let down by his former allies and somewhat toned down his anti-communist stance while gradually becoming more determined to "fight off the Japanese invaders". In April 1937, Chiang Kai-shek took a two-month leave to recuperate at home and returned to Nanjing in May for training at Lushan. During this period, Wang Jingwei, the later president of the Japanese puppet state in China, secretly colluded with the Japanese in Nanjing while Sino-Japanese relations were at breaking point following the Japanese foreign ministry's three demands on China:

> First, China should recognise the existence of the Japanese puppet state Manchukuo in northeast China and its loss of Manchuria to make up the territory.
>
> Second, China should sign special treaties with Japan to ensure Japanese interests in China. In the event of any wars in the Far East, China should be friendly to Japan and remain neutral.
>
> Third, China should agree to the privileges entitled to Japan in north China. China should also comply with Japan's wishes in regard to the issue of Inner Mongolia.

"Damn it!" Chiang was furious now. He wrote in his diary that: "The flagrant aggression of the Japanese has come to its limit. Once a certain limit has been reached, a change in the opposite direction is inevitable, so Japan's failure is on the horizon."

Several days before the Marco Polo Bridge Incident, Chiang Kai-shek, still in the mountains, was unaware of the full details of the situation. It was He Yingqin, Chiang's military right-hand man, who first received news of the development on the front.

He Yingqin was in Chongqing at the time for discussions with Liu Xiang, a high-ranking official in the Sichuan army, over the issue of military downsizing at Chiang's behest.

"Consolidating the army is just a load of nonsense! Chiang disarmed a third of our forces two years earlier and now he has sent He Yingqin to deal with us with only one purpose in mind: he wants to annex the Sichuan army! Just stay away from the damned meeting!" Liu Xiang's subordinates complained, dissuading him from meeting He Yingqin, Chen Cheng, Gu Zhu and other high-ranking government officials in Chongqing.

Smoking a water pipe, Liu Xiang replied slowly with his eyes half closed: "Not going to the meeting means that Chiang's henchmen from Nanjing will have the chance to manipulate everything, which is more detrimental to our army."

The generals then bit their lips and agreed to attend the Chongqing military rectification conference. The conference required the presence of officials at the divisional level and above, so Rao Guohua, the commander of the 145th division, who later died in the Battle of Nanjing, was among the attendees.

The generals at the conference had been arguing for two days without much progress since the meeting had begun on 6 July. On the morning of 8 July, the meeting started for a third day. All the generals were present with the sole exception of He Yingqin, who later rushed in with a telegram in hand, hastily taking to the podium while the others were wondering where he had been. He whispered to Liu Xiang and others sitting nearby before standing up and announcing solemnly: "My fellow officers, I have some very bad news. This morning, I picked up an emergency call from the Central Military Commission and just received an urgent telegram from the foreign ministry, both informing me that fierce fighting broke out around midnight between the Japanese expeditionary forces in north China stationed in the Fengtai district of Beiping and our 29th army in Nanyuan in the Beiping-Tianjin region defending the Marco Polo Bridge. Both sides have reported casualties with the scale of hostilities still increasing."

"These little Japanese devils are way out of line! They've insulted us for the last time! First it was northeast China, and now they want to devour the north!"

"Let's fight! Let's fight them to the end!"

The news immediately sparked outrage among the generals, appalled by Japan's aggression. Commander Rao Guohua stood up and asked: "Does the Central Military Commission have any plan to send reinforcements to north China?"

"It happened so suddenly that we had no time to work out a plan," He Yingqin replied.

"Then just get on with a plan!"

"Yes! The Japanese want to fight us bitterly every step of the way and force us to surrender. They won't have their way this time!"

"Yes! They'll never get their way!" The generals were burning with a passion to defend their homeland.

"Please calm down and listen to me first..." He Yingqin said morosely on the podium: "War is more about military strength and savvy than blind emotion. Many of you have never been to Japan and can't imagine the scale of their advantages in military strength and equipment. To fight the Japanese with our current national and military strength would be to invite disaster by overreaching ourselves."

His words were met with uproar around the room as the appalled generals responded: "The Japanese are no more special than anybody else. They're not bulletproof."

"I agree. I'll kill them with my sword and cut the bastards to pieces!" He Yingqin's face twisted into an uncomfortable mix of awkwardness and emotion as the generals around him gesticulated in anger.

"Mr He, we in the Sichuan army will be the first to respond if any reinforcements are needed on the front. All the officers and soldiers from the 145th division will fight the Japanese to the death!" Rao Guohua promised.

"Same here. My fellow officers and men from the 45th army will never back down!" declared Deng Xihou, head of the 45th army, taking up where Rao left off.

"Good to hear. I'm very touched by your determination, my fellow officers," He Yingqin said as he nodded repeatedly.

Liu Xiang, sat next to He, felt it was time for him to talk: "Mr He, I think you should tell Chiang that it's imperative for the central government to change course and put an end to the civil war and mobilise the entire country to resist the foreign invasion together. If needed, I'm willing to march to the frontline with my troops straight away."

He Yingqin continued to nod at Liu Xiang and the other generals, not saying anything else. He wondered if Chiang's plans of streamlining the entire Sichuan army would have to stop as resistance against the Japanese now seemed to be the top priority.

He hurried back to Nanjing that afternoon for a high command military meeting at Chiang Kai-shek's request, with the military arrangement about the volatile situation in north China in hand.

On 11 July, the first briefing of the high command was convened to deliberate 11 issues. According to Chiang Kai-shek's instructions, staff should be dispatched to Beiping to inspect military preparations. If the situation with Japan escalated, regions north of the Yellow River would act as a strategic bridgehead against the Japanese. In short, China would move to restrict the battlefield to north of the Yellow River once the war against Japan opened up on all fronts.

Over the course of 22 days, from 11 July to 1 August, 22 military conferences were held by the KMT military department high command, reviewing the situation and making preparations to fight against the Japanese invasion day and night. Although these meetings were chaired by He Yingqin, Chiang Kai-shek's instructions were sternly implemented without even the slightest change: "Chiang Kai-shek took an 'unyielding and non-expanding' attitude to the situation then" (*Memoirs of Chen Bulei*, p. 69).

The Chinese military leaders' unyielding attitude allowed the troops on the frontline to win some extraordinary victories. The 29th army of the KMT, which fought the Japanese at the Marco Polo Bridge, used to be the nationalist army led by the warlord Feng Yuxiang. Poorly equipped, Chiang Kai-shek considered the troops to be inferior, yet they were known for their brave soldiers, especially the so-called "big sword unit", which terrified enemy forces. They had fought bravely in Xifengkou, forcing the well-equipped Japanese forces to flee, leaving a total mess. The prestigious musician Mai Xin dedicated a piece of music titled *The Sword March* to the warriors who'd fought so bravely in the battle:

Swing your sword towards the Japanese;
My brothers in the 29th army!
The day has come for resistance;
The day has come for resistance!
At the forefront are our volunteers from the northeast;
Followed by the whole nation.
We in the 29th army are not alone;
Target the enemies;
And wipe them out, wipe them out!
Swing your sword towards the Japanese!
March and fight!

The song was formerly dedicated to the big sword unit and later, some modifications were made to its lyrics, making it the battle song of the national anti-Japanese campaign. Over the next 70 years, it became one of the most famous war songs in the Chinese military.

Chiang Kai-shek had been indecisive about fighting the Japanese. Following his no surrender policy was the non-expansion policy, namely, preventing the war from spreading and trying as much as possible to control it. However, the Japanese, hell-bent on conquering China, didn't do as Chiang

Kai-shek had hoped. Instead, they became enraged and pressed on relentlessly, eventually bringing the regions of Beiping and Tianjin under their heel.

The loss of the Beiping-Tianjin area made it clear to Chiang Kai-shek, being a graduate from the imperial Japanese army academy, that the Japanese would never show any sign of leniency, and it was just a matter of time until they seized more land. On 1 August, he returned from Lushan to Nanjing. While attending activities at the central officer military academy, Chiang Kai-shek noted in a rousing speech, *Prepare for National Retaliation*, that: "Now it is time for us to sober up as one shall stand and one shall fall in this war! We cannot be fooled by the Japanese once again, nor shall we ask for the insult of pleading for peace."

Beiping and Tianjin in the north successively fell into enemy hands. The deaths of Tong Linge and Zhao Dengyu, the respective deputy commander and divisional commander of the 29th army, not only shocked the entire nation but also forced Chiang Kai-shek's government to increase the scale of fighting against the Japanese. In the following years, Chiang Kai-shek "made relatively serious efforts" to resist the Japanese, as was described by the leader of the CPC Mao Zedong, who was far away in Yan'an at the time. Mao went on to say that: "In this period, the Japanese troops brought total war in their invasion of China, while the Chinese retaliated with an ever-growing sense of nationalist outrage, both of which forced the KMT to prioritise the resistance against Japanese aggression. By doing so, they took the nationwide war of resistance against Japanese aggression to new heights with a reinvigorated spirit." (*Selected Works of Mao Zedong*, People's Publishing House, 1956, vol. 3 p. 1037)

There's no doubt about the evil of the actions of the Japanese invaders. Although military aides and staff back in Japan temporarily opposed the expansion of the war against China by "doing whatever they could to avoid military deployments in central and south China", the Japanese military deployed at the front were incredibly arrogant and had long coveted the economic jewel of Shanghai in particular. They then decided to try an old tactic again. On 9 August, Lieutenant Isamu Daisen and his subordinate Yozō Saitō from the Japanese marine corps stationed in Shanghai ignored Chinese warnings and were shot dead after attempting to storm Hongqiao Airport to deliberately cause an incident. Taking advantage of the developments, the Japanese amassed several warships and ordered their marines to land in a huge show of force and even tried to force the Chinese guards defending Shanghai to retreat and dismantle the fortifications, which they resolutely refused to do. The Japanese were now targeting Shanghai for revenge.

While writing this book, I happened to read *Gold Warriors* by American writers Sterling and Peggy Seagrave, which revealed every last nauseating aspect of the Japanese invasion of China during the Second World War. On 28 January 1932, five young Japanese men dressed as monks from the aggressive and nationalist Nichiren Buddhist sect paraded down a busy street in Shanghai chanting in celebration of their victory in Manchuria in an obvious attempt to provoke the Chinese. This was in fact an elaborate Japanese scheme, which the Chinese locals were totally unaware of as they assaulted them, beating one to death on the spot. These monks were actually secret agents hired by Major Yoshi Tanaka of the Japanese secret service in Shanghai. The death of a Japanese citizen provided an opportunity for the major to follow a plan that had been previously proposed by Japanese senior officials. The secret service then launched a military intervention under the guise of protecting Japanese citizens in Shanghai. Tokyo liked to play the victim and so Japan sent more troops to Shanghai. Meanwhile, the Japanese secret service in the city rallied hundreds of thugs from the 30,000 Japanese expatriate population. Calling themselves "ronin" (a samurai without a master) and armed with guns, knives and clubs, they joined the Japanese marines in provoking Chinese troops, with the 19th route army left with no choice but to strike back. The Japanese emperor then immediately sent reinforcements with as many as 90,000 troops arriving to support their forces in Shanghai. Fierce fighting took place over 34 days with over 18,000 civilians and thousands of Chinese soldiers killed as the Japanese troops collaborated with the so-called *ronin*. However, the Japanese then suddenly announced a unilateral ceasefire. On the surface, it looked like Japan was acting out of humanity, but this was actually to gain a firm foothold in Shanghai before completely devouring the city and China. Five years later in 1937, the Japanese decided to finish off Shanghai, staging another incident of self-harm by using two of their soldiers to cause yet more trouble in a bid to take a bigger piece of the pie. There's no doubt that the Japanese rulers in the country's militaristic period were capable of acts of extreme evil.

However, this time, China seemed to have seen through Japan's smokescreen as Chiang Kai-shek and his military aides proved not to be so utterly useless after all. General Zhang Zhizhong, the appointed commander of the Beiping Shanghai garrison corps, had secretly telegraphed Chiang before the Hongqiao Incident on 9 August. He revealed that the number of Japanese troops stationed in Shanghai had recently been growing. In total, there were about 5,000 marines, 3,000 well-organised soldiers and 3,500 able bodied volunteers. Details about their weapons were as follows: over 30 heavy and light cannons of all kinds; eight antiaircraft guns; 20 tanks and 20 armoured vehicles. On top of that, nine Japanese warships had arrived in Shanghai from the upper reach of the Yangtze River. This number rose to 12 if three other warships already anchored in the city were included. A further 3,000 marines were ready to land at any time.

A couple of days later, General Zhang Zhizhong telegraphed Chiang Kai-shek again, informing him that the Japanese army had not only increased the size of its fleet but had also approached Shanghai from Longgang. "Unidentified" planes had also been seen continuously circling in the air above Hongqiao Airport. A report from the intelligence service read: "It's said that the Japanese army mobilised their reserve soldiers under 53 years old at 4 o'clock this morning." Chiang was shocked to the core as he realised that the Japanese were moving to take Shanghai.

China didn't just sit by idly doing nothing about Japan's military offensive. Chiang Kai-shek and his aides took the correct course of action this time; he secretly ordered Zhang Zhizhong to rapidly deploy troops in Jiangsu and to prepare to blockade the Yangtze River in Jiangyin while three armoured divisions and two artillery regiments would be sent to march towards Shanghai. The equipment had been made in Germany and could certainly match the quality of the Japanese, with one regiment using 100mm calibre guns and another using 150mm calibre howitzers. Zhang Zhizhong moved his headquarters to Nanxiang on the evening of 11 August. The next day, he swiftly deployed his troops and reported to Chiang that:

1. The main forces of the army in Shanghai are stationed to guard Zhenru, Zhabei, the central district of Jiangwan and Wusong. Another unit is observing the west and south of Shanghai, providing cover for the advancing troops.
2. One unit from the 87th division is well positioned to hold Wusong while the main force is being sent to the frontlines to the north in Dachang and Jiangwan before marching to the central district of Jiangwan to attack. Another strong unit is to be dispatched to Luodian and Liuhe.
3. One regiment from the 88th division is to be sent to the frontline for deployment in Zhenru and Dachang before marching to Zhabei and Jiangwan for a counter attack.
4. The first battalion of the 10th artillery regiment and the 8th artillery regiment are to march towards Zhenru and Dachang to occupy the position.
5. Zhong Song's unit in the first regiment is to be transferred from the Sujia Road to Nanxiang to stand by.

6. The 56th division is to be sent to Kunshan before marching into Zhitang, Taicang to stand by.
7. The 527 regiments of the 88th division are also to be sent to Nanxiang to form reserve forces.

Zhang Zhizhong's aim was to concentrate their superior forces to: "Stage a fierce attack against the Japanese and gradually gain ground before wiping them out near Jiangwan and Pengpu." (*Chiang Kai-shek during the War of Resistance Against Japanese Aggression* by Yang Shubiao and Yang Jin, Sino Culture Press, 2014, p. 91)

Chiang Kai-shek approved Zhang's military deployments that same day. On the evening of 12 August, under the leadership of two commanders, Wang Jingjiu and Sun Yuanliang, the 87th and 88th divisions arrived in Jiangwan in Shanghai and were stationed in Wusong, blockading the Yangtze River waterway. However, Tokyo had learned about the Chinese plans and its cabinet immediately decided to organise expeditionary forces for battle that very night.

General Zhang Zhizhong swore vehemently to his subordinates before the war: "My fellow officers and soldiers, today our nation is in crisis and we now fight for our survival! A bloody curtain will soon rise to mark the start of a life-and-death battle for our glorious nation. It is my sincere hope that you remember the message I am about to give you and that you face the hardships and challenges without fear and resolutely strive for the bright future to which we are destined."

Another vicious battle between China and Japan was about to arrive. The Japanese were convinced of victory as they had established headquarters for the emperor to command the battle in person just three days into the war. This was the third time that the Japanese had done this, having done so once in 1894 in the first Sino-Japanese war and again in 1904 when the Russo-Japanese war broke out. The establishment of such headquarters was the sign of the first national total war against China in modern history.

On 13 August 1937, the sound of the first shot of the Battle of Shanghai rang out, fired by the Chinese. When Sun Yuanliang's 88th division opened fire in unison at the hostile Japanese marines on the Bazi bridge, hatred and anger reached boiling point in the hearts of the Chinese, fury erupting like a volcano, shattering the Japanese forces as they were routed.

"The mountains and rivers strewn with our blood must be forever in our hands. The survival and glory of the nation can only be maintained by the flesh and blood of its people!" Our soldiers chanted and recited the famous address delivered a year earlier by Luo Jialun from the National Central

University when he visited soldiers on the frontlines in north China as they fired at the enemy.

The Battle of Shanghai lasted for three months until 12 November. Throughout the battle, the Chinese deployed 50 divisions with 700,000 soldiers. The Japanese increased their divisions to a total of 10, along with their marine corps, bringing their total of armed forces to 300,000. They also had about 300 artillery guns, 200 combat vehicles, 200 aeroplanes and dozens of warships at their disposal, boasting that "their military strength and power are unparalleled anywhere in the world". It would be unfair to say that Chiang Kai-shek didn't do his utmost in the battle as he commanded the whole battle in person and dispatched troops under his direct control in the battlefield. Chiang's final defeat was due to a major mistake, namely, a wasted combat opportunity. The situation could have been completely different if the war had broken out before 13 August when the Japanese were preparing for the invasion. The Chinese forces also lagged behind the Japanese in terms of military equipment and air and naval power. More importantly, in the third stage of the battle – the final skirmishes on 11, 12 and 13 November – the face of the conflict rapidly changed with the sudden emergence of Japan's 10th army surrounding Chinese forces on the south bank of the Suzhou river. On 11 November, Susumu Fujita's 3rd division stormed into Shanghai. Shanghai fell into enemy hands the next day.

Chiang Kai-shek's decision to fight the Japanese in Shanghai was based on three points. Firstly, he wanted to salvage his reputation in resisting the Japanese; secondly, he readily trusted those around him like T. V. Soong who provided him with false information that "Japan will be on the verge of breakdown and face revolution within three months"; thirdly, he hoped that the battle would help to gain support from the international community and possible military intervention from his allies. Out of the three points, it was the third that had really convinced Chiang. However, the Soviet Union and the US refused to help, but Germany contributed a great deal, albeit to make money. The Germans acted as Chiang's military advisers and sold him arms. Dozens of German military advisers were in Nanjing at the time, most of whom were retired generals and had signed private contracts with the Chiang Kai-shek government.

The Battle of Shanghai saw Japanese casualties of about 50,000, five times smaller than those of the Chinese side which stood at 250,000.

In spite of its failure, the battle still had significant positives for China. First and foremost, the Chinese national spirit still remained high and the Japanese plans of sweeping into Wuhan through north China before eliminating China altogether had been dashed. Secondly, the Chinese had bought themselves three months to move factories and supplies near the mouth of the Yangtze River, providing the material foundation for China's prolonged resistance against Japan in the future. Thirdly, the best of the Japanese forces had been wiped out, reducing the amount of Japanese force in the north China theatre of war and buying time for the later decisive battle in Shanxi. Last but not least, the Chinese determination and fierce spirit in fighting the Japanese to the death had undone the embarrassment felt by the Chinese army ever since the Mukden Incident and bolstered their confidence of victory.

Officers and soldiers displayed great courage at the Battle of Shanghai. Every hour saw thousands of soldiers bravely and gloriously sacrificing their lives, a rare happening in the Chinese history of wars against foreign invaders. Poorly equipped, the Chinese army still fought tenaciously with the Japanese for every last county and village, often repeatedly fighting for a position that the Japanese would seize in the day while the Chinese would take it back at night, with heavy casualties on both sides. Each division of the main forces of the KMT army has been reinforced four to five times as regiments behind the lines are sent into battle in large numbers. Two thirds of the junior officers and soldiers fell as casualties, as did half of the brigadiers and regimental commanders.

(*Chiang Kai-shek During the War of Resistance Against Japanese Aggression* by Yang Shubiao and Yang Jin, Sino Culture Press, 2014, p. 101)

The cream of the country's forces had been engaged in three months of fighting, only to result in the fall of Shanghai and a full withdrawal from the battlefields. How could Chiang Kai-shek face the citizens of Shanghai?

On 12 November, the Chinese government's military commission issued the *Message to Compatriots in Shanghai* in the *Shen Bao* newspaper under the name of the Office of Political Training of the Military Commission, which read:

> Dear Shanghai compatriots,
>
> In relation to our military strategy, our army is conducting a temporary retreat near Shanghai. However, we are trying our utmost to consolidate our position in the second battlefield to recover from our loss in Shanghai in the shortest period possible. Our retreat at this time is strategically planned, and it is absolutely not a defeat in the war. A real war of resistance against Japan in fact starts from this very moment, which is what our compatriots have produced and fought for with extraordinary skill. Our army will leave our Shanghai compatriots. Over the past three months of the anti-Japanese war, the Shanghai compatriots have taken risks both day and night to assist at the front

to provide everything we need. We suffered great losses on the battlefield, but the cooperation between the military and civilians has grown stronger. This kind of courage and enthusiasm is deeply rooted in the hearts of all officers and soldiers, and is a feeling that they will never forget their entire lives.

Although we are temporarily retreating, we shall never forget our compatriots. While our army retreats from Shanghai, the enemy will likely enforce all sorts of acts of oppression and temptation on our compatriots, which is a great source of sorrow and anxiety for us. However, we believe that while our patriotic compatriots in Shanghai may suffer a great deal now, they must remain determined. We sincerely hope that our compatriots in Shanghai always maintain their spirit of sacrifice and resistance to help encourage one another. Everyone is now a soldier fighting fiercely on the battlefield against the enemy. Our compatriots in Shanghai shall never forget the tragic casualties suffered by our army and our compatriots in the three-month long battle, and shall continue to celebrate the spirit of these martyrs. Shanghai is the centre of the Chinese spirit, and our compatriots there have to remain determined to serve as the great wall of our national spirit.

Our dear compatriots, our army will leave you for now, and your pain and sacrifice concerns us. We have no words to express our gratitude for your patriotic spirit. We will always remember your passion and shall continue to fight until the end. Even though we leave Shanghai, we still overlook Shanghai in the battlefields in Jiading and Nanxiang. Our soldiers' souls still remain in Shanghai, along with our determination to recover from our loss at the Battle of Shanghai as soon as possible. Our compatriots will always be connected with us, together forming a mighty force. We believe that we will win victory in the war of resistance against Japanese aggression to restore our nation's sovereignty. Our army must recover from the Battle of Shanghai as soon as possible to repay our compatriots. We shall never let our Shanghai compatriots down.

— OFFICE OF POLITICAL TRAINING OF THE MILITARY COMMISSION, 12 NOVEMBER

Several scholars in the political training office had rapidly written a few statements, but the citizens of Shanghai saw the sheer number of empty promises and quickly scolded Chiang Kai-shek's message for being "meaningless", and boldly proclaimed that "the Japanese are doomed to a painful death".

With the fall of Shanghai, the capital of Nanjing now also faced the enemy. It was at this point that China's real suffering began. "Fight! These *Shinajin* think we in the Japanese army are made of mud, and they're mad enough to think they can chase us out of Shanghai. They must be dreaming!" The word "Shinajin" (pronounced 'zhinaren' in Chinese, meaning 'Chinamen' and considered derogatory by the Chinese) is a slur used by the Japanese to refer to the Chinese. "We'll never withdraw our army, fight on to Nanjing! Capture Chiang Kai-shek." These were the words of a group of young Japanese officers chatting leisurely while drinking in the evening after they'd stormed the national government building in Shanghai. Amidst the celebrations following the victory, one individual smashed a bottle on a warship's deck and then sang the song *Sakura of the Same Period*:

We are sakura of the same period;
Blossoming in the same military school yard;
When the flowers blossom and fall;
We shall gloriously fall for the nation.
We are sakura of the same period;
Blossoming in the same military school yard;
Deep ties of brotherhood between us;
A common breath links us inseparably.
We are sakura of the same period;
Blossoming in the same military school yard;
Looking into the southern sky with a sunset glow;
One warplane does not return.
We are sakura of the same period;
Blossoming in the same military school yard;
The day of our oath to die hasn't come;
Why wither away before then?

There's no denying the great influence of this old Japanese military song, especially on the young sergeants. The sakura, or cherry blossom, is Japan's national flower, and when it blossoms, it becomes a symbol of a cold beauty and elegance. Japanese soldiers compared their lives to the sakura, an inconceivable concept for people from other countries. Their *bushido* ("the way of the warrior") philosophy, associated with the way of the samurai, is another macabre facet of Japanese culture. According to this code, Japanese warriors were to commit ritualistic suicide if they failed or were humiliated, and this philosophy was very popular among Japanese soldiers. It's a bizarre notion and its reasoning still remains unclear to me now. While writing this book, I watched a film called *The Last Samurai*, which tells the story of the American captain Nathan Algren's experiences after he was captured by a band of Japanese samurai in the 1870s. In the samurai group, the samurai leader, Katsumoto, tells Algren about the essence of their samurai spirit. The *bushido* spirit, he explains, is like sakura; every breath is like a withered petal, but also an awakening of life. Failure is shameful for a samurai, so they commit suicide as both suicide and being killed by the enemy are shameful, but dying in battle is glorious. This is the basic tenet of the *bushido* belief. After Japan embarked on a path to militarism, *bushido* became a spiritual pillar and a tool used in aggression as soldiers pledged loyalty to the emperor of Japan.

On the evening of 13 November 1937, hearts filled with joy from the victory and surrounded by the picturesque scenery of the Bund in Shanghai, young Japanese officers embraced the *bushido* spirit with great pride as the emperor's imperial military. They waved their swords or held bottles, hysterically shouting "occupy Nanjing", and defiantly shot their guns, as if they would be seeing the Japanese flag rising above Nanjing's Purple Mountain the next morning.

In fact, the Japanese army didn't initially have plans at this point to attack the Chinese capital in Nanjing. When the Battle of Shanghai had come to an end and the Chinese troops had withdrawn from Shanghai, the Japanese army had suffered enormous losses. The Shanghai Expeditionary Force commander Iwane Matsui and Commander Heisuke Yanagawa of the 10th army in Hangzhou Bay had also immediately been ordered to: "sweep away all hostiles near Shanghai, extend the frontlines to the east in Suzhou and Jiaxing". This clearly shows that they wanted to take a moment to catch their breath, waiting to punish China once again. However, the 10th army, led by Yanagawa, refused this order as they had just landed in Hangzhou Bay. There were many frenzied young Japanese officers among them who believed that it was unacceptable for soldiers to stop fighting when they'd just set foot on Chinese soil. Then, on 15 November, Yanagawa, without notifying the expeditionary force commander, Iwane Matsui, held a meeting, allowing middle-ranking subordinate commanders to attend. During the meeting, some young officers proposed ignoring old Matsui and that the 10th army could advance towards Nanjing and invade on their own.

"If we miss this chance, when can we go?"

"It's time to show our loyalty to the emperor! We can report it to the ministry after we arrive in Nanjing!"

Waving their swords, the young officers pledged themselves to Yanagawa.

"Very well, we'll advance towards Nanjing!" Yanagawa's eyes shone with the cold light of a sword.

The 10th army was originally supposed to cooperate with Matsui, but it had now become the main force for the long-distance attack on Nanjing. Despite not having enough food or ammunition to support them in battle, they were blinded by a sense of honour and the *bushido* spirit, and twisted this lack of supplies to become further sources of motivation: "If we're short on food, we'll take it from the locals. If we don't have ammunition, we'll fight hand-to-hand."

Yanagawa's army had now become a vicious horde that made bloodshed inevitable.

Five days later, on 20 November, the 10th army invaded Nanjing in a fit of insanity. The Japanese army headquarters deputy adviser in Tokyo, Hayao Tada, was shocked by the news that Yanagawa's army had gone to Nanjing, and immediately ordered them to cease their operations. But Yanagawa refused to listen.

After finding out that their "allies" in the 10th army had marched on to Nanjing, several senior officers in the expeditionary force of the Japanese main army in Shanghai constantly called upon Commander Matsui to attack Nanjing before Yanagawa's army: "General, Yanagawa's forces have gone to Nanjing. They want to claim victory for the emperor themselves before us. We can't give such a great honour to Yanagawa's army!"

In fact, Matsui, as the commander sent from the Japanese cabinet's headquarters to Shanghai, had already known that Yanagawa's army was advancing, but he had been struggling with the decision himself of whether to attack Nanjing or not. Those who knew him well understood that this was how he worked, although Matsui himself was clear that the policy for China was still being planned by the Japanese emperor and the imperial Japanese army general office. Without having a clear idea of what the next step would be after the Battle of Shanghai, he, as the commander of the Japanese army's central front in China, needed to carefully consider the strategy before action.

At this point, it is worth explaining more about Iwane Matsui to help readers understand the man. He was the commander of the Japanese army at the Nanjing Massacre and was later judged by the International Military Tribunal for the Far East as the principal culprit behind the Nanjing Massacre and hanged as a Class A war criminal. He had returned to his career in the army a couple of days before the start of the Second Sino-Japanese War and was appointed by the emperor as the commander-in-chief of the Japanese Shanghai expeditionary force. He was 59 years old at the time, a thin old man, and was actually a "China hand", meaning someone who was knowledgeable of the Chinese language, people and culture. Matsui was born in 1878 in the Aichi Prefecture, the son of a famous sinologist Takekuni Matsui, whose ancestors were famous Japanese generals. Iwane Matsui graduated from the imperial Japanese military academy, and then entered the Japanese army war college, getting the top grades. He once had a close relationship with China, and kept in contact with Sun Yat-sen, who'd gained a lot of support from Matsui while he'd been in Japan.

In fact, many of China's leaders during the republican period kept in close contact with Matsui, even Chiang Kai-shek, his mortal enemy in the anti-Japanese war. He had been helped by Matsui while studying in Japan, and it is even rumoured that Chiang had lived in Matsui's home for two years, showing the once close relationship between the two. In 1915, Matsui served as a military attaché in Shanghai. In 1922, he was made the head of the secret service in Harbin, being promoted to major general the following year, and becoming a lieutenant general in the Japanese army five years later. In 1933, Matsui was designated Taiwan garrison commander, and promoted to army general the same year. Due to internal conflicts in the Japanese army, in August 1934, Matsui withdrew from the military and went into politics.

When Matsui left the military, the Manchurian Japanese puppet state of Manchukuo, established after Japan occupied the three provinces in northeast China, was not acknowledged by the international community. The Japanese government was frustrated with the diplomacy surrounding the Manchurian controversy. Matsui then claimed to the prime minister that he was close to the Chinese authorities and that he'd be able to make the Chinese government recognise the existence of Manchukuo. This would mean that the Japanese puppet state would be recognised by the international community. The Japanese government agreed to the plan, so Matsui, a retired general and China hand, began to return to life in the military. In early 1936, Matsui began a many-month long process of lobbying in China, with in-depth communication with Chiang Kai-shek. At the same time, Japan repeatedly violated China's territorial rights and provoked conflict, putting his "old friend" Chiang in a difficult and humiliating position. When the issue of Manchukuo was raised, Chiang furiously replied to Matsui: "Recognising Manchukuo means abandoning my ancestors to foreigners, or slapping myself in the face! When the Mukden Incident happened, I was the leader of the Chinese national government, but you occupied our three provinces in the northeast. I hated Japan for it, but I have also often been criticised by the CPC for being a traitor putting up no resistance. If you were me, would you ever bring yourself to recognise Manchukuo?"

Chiang Kai-shek had been so frank with Matsui that he thought there was no way he'd be able to succeed in his mission. On the day he left Nanjing, he wrote in his diary: "Chiang is aware of my activities and avoiding giving an answer." Chiang had actually very clearly told the Japanese lobbyist his response, but Matsui didn't want to lose face in front of his government. He had thought that with the help of his "special relationship" with individuals in important circles in China, he could persuade the Chinese to acknowledge or at least not to oppose Japan on the international stage. However, Matsui's old Chinese friend refused to listen to him, an awkward position for Matsui, a man who regarded himself as a "friend of the Chinese revolution". He thought the Chinese had been ungrateful and bore a grudge that he intended to repay. On his way back to Japan, Matsui repeatedly said in public and private that the current leader of the republic of China had already forgotten how he and Japan had once supported Sun Yat-sen in the revolution. With this in mind, he intended to punish the unfriendly government and state for this ingratitude sooner or later.

When the first shots of the Marco Polo Bridge were fired, it was clear that the Second Sino-Japanese War was imminent. After the Battle of Shanghai had begun, the Japanese authorities made a quick decision to appoint a China expert as the commander-in-chief of the forces there. At this point, Matsui was recalled to the military by the Japanese cabinet as the commander of the Japanese army in Shanghai leading the 3rd and 11th divisions to support the Japanese marines in Shanghai. One reason why the Japanese government sent the retired general was that once war broke out in Shanghai, the international community would react in fury, thinking that the Soviets may even march to the northeast of China, which would endanger Japan's ambitions for a Greater East Asia Co-Prosperity Sphere. This was unacceptable to the Japanese government, so Shanghai had to be occupied without agitating the "laomaozi" (Russkies) and the international community.

The Japanese government, unwilling to risk angering the Soviet military, assigned Matsui the following mission: "Clear all hostiles near Shanghai, to occupy the key battle sites, and to protect the lives of expatriates in Shanghai." A military command like this clearly limited the range of the Shanghai expeditionary force, restricting them to fighting around the Suzhou and Jiaxing front. But before setting off on a train from Tokyo, Matsui said the following to the Japanese prime minister Fumimaro Konoe, who had come to see him off: "With troops in China anyway, we should take Nanjing this time." The prime minister and other important officials were stunned, and diplomats advised him in a hushed tone: "Look before you leap General!"

"I know more about China than any of you," Matsui arrogantly replied.

Matsui indeed knew more about China and the Chinese people than anyone else. Over the three months of fighting in the Battle of Shanghai, although the Chinese army was courageous, they couldn't fight off the Japanese, especially towards the end, and it had become a catastrophe. Matsui then came to the conclusion that as long as Chiang Kai-shek led the country and commanded the Chinese military, Japan would win.

When he heard the news that Yanagawa's army had moved to Nanjing, Matsui spent several days debating whether to send his troops, and he wrote the poem below before his departure, and flatly decided: "To occupy the capital of the enemy, and to force China to yield."

> My military uniforms have been drenched with sweat during my fighting for four decades;
> The rise and fall seems to be a dream finally vanishing in the river.
> I've got old before repaying the grace of the Mikado;
> With a sword in my hand, I come from afar again to conquer that place.

For a soldier fighting in a foreign theatre of war, there is no kind of victory that has a higher honour than occupying the enemy's capital. Matsui, who had been in the army for over 40 years, knew that this was his last chance as a soldier to pledge loyalty to the emperor and his country, so in the end he decided to attack Nanjing and take the capital of China.

Since the soldiers on the frontline were determined to advance and win, why would the commanders stop it? The Japanese high command quickly made arrangements to approve Matsui's request, and appointed Emperor Hirohito's uncle Yasuhiko Asaka as the commander of the Shanghai expeditionary force and Matsui as the commander-in-chief of the central China army, including the Shanghai expeditionary force and Yanagawa's 10th army that had attacked Nanjing. Yasuhiko Asaka was actually the leading war criminal behind the Nanjing Massacre, but he escaped the postwar war crimes trial and lived to the old age of 93 because of his relationship with the emperor. The Japanese royal families and their relatives were not investigated for war crimes, which was one of the major drawbacks of the Tokyo trials. This also laid the foundations for the Japanese militaristic renaissance that can be seen among so many right-wing politicians in postwar Japan today. This, however, is another story for another time.

Japanese headquarters, according to a report by Matsui, made comprehensive military deployments and adjustments in preparation for the attack on Nanjing, respectively establishing four divisions from the Shanghai expeditionary forces led by Yasuhiko Asaka and four from the 10th army led by Yanagawa. These included: the 9th division led by Yoshizumi Ryosuke, the 16th division led by Kesago Nakajima, the 13th division led by Rippei Ogisu and the 10th division led by Amatani Naojiro, all under the command of Prince Yasuhiko Asaka. Meanwhile, the 6th division led by Hisao Tani, the

114th division led by Maimatsu Moji, the 18th division led by Sado Ushijima, and the 9th brigade led by Noboru Kunisaki were under Yanagawa's command.

Out of these troops, the Japanese armies led by Kesago Nakajima and Hisao Tani were the main military force in the Nanjing Massacre, as well as the Japanese central China army's elite troops. There were approximately 100,000 Japanese soldiers and dozens of ships ready to assault Nanjing.

This is a good opportunity to analyse the situation of China following the Battle of Shanghai.

There was only a month between the loss of Shanghai and the end of 1937. Many great rivers and mountains had been lost, as had the battle of Beiping-Tianjin and the Battle of Shanghai. A few of the best cities in China had been occupied by the Japanese in under a year. After the plan to attack Nanjing had been approved by high command, the Japanese invaders became incredibly aggressive and arrogant. The Japanese soldiers had become increasingly bloodthirsty as the war went on and now Nanjing was at risk, a terrible mix that would have disastrous consequences.

Nanjing was in danger as it was only two hours by train from Shanghai. By river, if moving with the current, it would take around two days, and if going against it, it would take around a week. Even by foot, the journey was, at most, a dozen days. To make matters worse, all the roads from Shanghai to Nanjing were very flat. It would take less than a day for tanks and armoured transport to arrive at the nearby Purple Mountain. The idea of enemy troops occupying the Chinese capital was inconceivable, but faced with Matsui and Yanagawa's frenzied assault, how could Japan be defeated?

Everything depended on Chiang Kai-shek. Chiang and Matsui had been old friends, with Matsui even acting as Chiang's mentor. As mentioned previously, Chiang Kai-shek had once lived in Matsui's home for quite a long time during his overseas studies in Japan. His reverence for Japan in his youth fostered his future position as the leader of China. When he studied at the imperial military academy in Japan, Chiang Kai-shek became close to Chen Qimei, a close friend who greatly influenced him. It was Chen who introduced him to Sun Yat-sen who put him in an important position later and promoted him to rank of commander of the northern expeditionary army. Chiang Kai-shek became the KMT leader after Sun Yat-sen passed away and the head of the national government afterwards. As a result, he described Japan as his "second homeland".

Now, it was his former mentor and China hand that was attacking Nanjing, and Chiang who had to fight against the Japanese troops to defend Nanjing. The Sino-Japanese war between Matsui and Chiang had very dramatic beginnings and, of course, ended with a tragedy. Even now, 70 or 80 years after the war, China and Japan still blame each other and have a strained relationship. Needless to say, Japan's actions show that it was to blame.

Expecting to win the last "supreme honour" of his life, Matsui aimed to violently attack his old friend with no consideration for him. While marching on Nanjing, Matsui thought to himself: "When I graduated from the Japanese army college, little Chiang was still being breastfed!"

However, Chiang was no longer the Chinese bumpkin Matsui had thought him to be. He was now the head of the Chinese government and the commander-in-chief of the millions of troops in the Chinese army. He could never tolerate the small island nation of Japan conquering the vast lands of China.

Chiang Kai-shek wrote the poem below to his cousin Shan Weize when he graduated from the imperial Japanese army academy at the age of 23. The poem expresses Chiang's desires and shows that while Chiang worshipped Japan when he was young, he also hated Japanese brutality in China.

> *The seething murderous look prevails all over the world;*
> *How can the conquered permit that?*
> *I will recover the divine land and fulfil my responsibility;*
> *I do not aim for a rank in nobility.*

In 1907, Chiang Kai-shek attended accelerated courses at the Baoding military academy, an initiative launched by the Qing Dynasty government. One day, while a Japanese surgeon was giving a lecture about microorganisms, he pointed to a piece of soil on the podium and said: "The soil covers about one cubic inch, which contains about 400 million microscopic worms." He then continued: "We can compare it to China, since China has a population of 400 million just like the mud..."

"Teacher, how can you say that!"

Suddenly, a young student in the class rushed to the podium, dividing the soil into eight pieces, and angrily stated: "Japan has a population of 50 million, which is also comparable to these microscopic worms living in one eighth of a cubic inch of soil!"

The Japanese surgeon turned bright red and the Chinese students burst into laughter. At the time, anyone who dared to argue against Japanese teachers could be expelled, but the school principal later recognised that the student had said this out of a sense of patriotism, and settled the incident in secret without punishing him. This event made the student famous, and it was none other than Chiang Kai-shek.

Chinese people today generally see Chiang Kai-shek in a mostly negative light. During the anti-Japanese war period, Chiang Kai-shek was China's leader, and the commander-in-chief on the central Chinese battlefield, representing China's international image, with a close relationship to the state's successes and failures and glory and shame. We should understand Chiang's role in the survival of the Chinese nation and his performance in the Sino-Japanese war in an objective manner in order to provide a fair overview of his role in our national history.

It would be both wrong and unfair to suggest that Chiang Kai-shek didn't want to resist Japanese aggression, or that he feared Japan. Thanks to several years' experience in the military in Japan and one year in the 19th field artillery regiment, Chiang was familiar with the Japanese army, and it had profoundly impressed him with its focus on discipline, flawless management styles, *bushido* spirit, loyalty to the emperor, tough training and advanced equipment. It was the Marco Polo Bridge Incident that made Chiang realise that the Japanese would never respect him and that they had their sights set on a conquest of China. It was a tragic shame that the Chinese army was shambolic at the time, and the major warlords were fighting amongst each other, ignoring Chiang's commands. He felt powerless about how to protect China, and had been looking for support from Stalin in the Soviet Union and Roosevelt in the US. To help gain support, he sent his wife Soong Mei-ling to the US for help and ordered his son to negotiate with Stalin. He had plans to persuade the two countries to help. For the US, he planned to offer access to the huge Chinese market in return for assistance while he would cede Outer Mongolia to the Soviets, which they had long coveted. Although Chiang was reluctant to give up any Chinese land, it was better than the entire country being occupied by the enemy, trading personal and state power with land to protect his reputation.

In early 1937, Chiang Kai-shek had just recovered from the Xi'an Incident and the subsequent political crisis. When the country was already riddled with troubles, both internally and externally, the Japanese further provoked China at the Marco Polo Bridge Incident. It would be understandable then for Chiang to lose himself in anger.

However, at that point, Chiang was relatively rational and prepared in his thinking, saying: "The Japanese still seek to destroy China, we have to be ever vigilant." The preparations Chiang presided over were relatively thorough and advanced. With the Chinese Civil War having raged for many years and the country's citizens divided with the warlords leading their own factions,

Chiang knew Japan would see their advantage and had busied himself with preparations a couple of years before Japan officially declared war. One preparatory activity he conducted was employing a group of German military advisors. Another was using Weng Wenhao, also from Chiang's homeland in Zhejiang, to work on importing weapons from Germany.

According to KMT data, a couple of years before 1937, China had begun to purchase weapons, ordnance and heavy industry equipment from Germany, with weapons making up the majority of the purchases. Chiang established a military unit under his direct command consisting of his relatives. These troops made a great contribution to the Battle of Shanghai, playing a vital role in undermining the Japanese forces' confidence. It is also worth noting that Chiang focused a great deal of attention on the military and commercial relationship with Germany, meaning that there were many Germans in Nanjing, the capital city of China, before the anti-Japanese war. Many of these German nationals protected hundreds of thousands of Chinese citizens, which shall be discussed in more detail later. For now, let's discuss the role of the German military advisors.

Around the time of the anti-Japanese war, a couple of key German military advisors worked for Chiang Kai-shek, one of whom was very famous, called Alexander von Falkenhausen. He was the leader of the military advisors. The famous strategy of "luring the enemy in deep", used at the Battle of Tai'erzhuang in 1938, had been his idea. The German advisor once directly criticised Chiang for being passive in resistance to Japan. He'd warned Chiang Kai-shek many times: "North China, including Shandong, will be lost if China doesn't do whatever it can to fight." More importantly, although Falkenhausen was a military advisor dispatched by Hitler's government, he greatly opposed Nazism. In 1938, he returned to Germany and had to serve Hitler and was suspected and monitored by the Gestapo for a long period of time. After the Second World War, Falkenhausen took up the post of chairman of the Sino-German cultural association. He died at 88 years old in Berlin, 1966.

Falkenhausen was a professional soldier. He arrived in China in 1900 during the siege of the international legations as part of the Boxer Rebellion. Later, as a military diplomat who knew Chinese well, he was appointed to the post of military attaché at the German embassy. After the First World War, he became the president of the German infantry school and a military advisor to Chiang Kai-shek in 1933. Germans generally have a reputation of being serious and cautious, and Falkenhausen fit the stereotype well, a professional soldier who'd been the president of an infantry school as well as familiar with Chinese and Japanese military and culture. While he recommended that the

KMT purchase advanced weapons from the Germans, he also insisted on the importance of training the KMT army and creating military plans to fight against Japan. Chiang's army was reorganised and improved with the assistance of these military advisors. In 1934, Falkenhausen advised Chiang to plan for the protection of Nanjing to guard against the increasing ambitions of the Japanese to annex China. Chiang took his advice and ordered Gu Zhenglun, the Nanjing chief of police, to implement the scheme. On 17 August that year, Falkenhausen showed his admiration of Gu's plan, saying:

> In my humble opinion, I completely agree with Gu Zhenglun's plan to dig a long channel and build a high wall with the mud from the channel around the Rain Flower Terrace and from the Tianbaocheng fortifications to the road outside the Taiping gate.
>
> I do not believe that there is any need to construct huge fortifications if the aim is just to protect Nanjing. This large-scale programme will be enormously expensive, and will take a long time and a lot of labour. So it is better to apply a new and more efficient programme. We can try to assess the soil here and find the correct material for this.
>
> These fortifications, used for defending against tanks, are very useful, however they are not needed if tanks are not being used, and light assault infantry is involved instead.
>
> If fighting against constant besiegers, this fortification is fragile and could be destroyed immediately by several grenades, at just 15cm thick. In my humble opinion, I suggest strengthening field fortifications (supporting point for infantry, machine gun positions and observation points), and then we can prepare other barriers at possible fronts, such as activated mines, becoming more intense deeper into the region.
>
> I think this plan is better as it is more powerful, has a broader range and more uses. It is quick and cost effective.
>
> — (COLLECTION OF NANJING MASSACRE HISTORICAL DATA, JIANGSU PHOENIX PUBLISHING GROUP, 2005, VOL. 2 P. 11)

Thanks to his agreement with the plan, the KMT military leaders implemented the first Nanjing defensive plan in 1934. This plan was organised from eight perspectives: analysis of the enemy's situation; defence policy; outline of instructions; military deployment; artillery barrage; air defence; transposition and communication. The outline of the instructions stipulated the following:

First attack the enemy warships with artillery with a mobile light and heavy artillery force deployed on the southern bank of the Yangtze River, with a unit on the north bank and cooperation with other fixed artillery points and an artillery captain in charge of the operation. They should concentrate their fire in a surprise attack when the enemy warship is in range. The fire of the mobile artillery has to focus on closer targets. Second, when fighting against the Japanese marines, every fixed and mobile artillery unit needs to focus on destroying the enemy warships at the front to prevent them from landing. At the same time, troops should be deployed at strategic points to violently attack the enemy units that have already landed, and destroy the enemy forces still in the river. Third, when fighting against the enemy air force, all the air defence forces should be under the control of the air defence commander. Every strategic point should be equipped with lookouts to spy on the enemy's activity. The air defence group should immediately launch into action whenever the siren is sounded to shoot down enemy planes outside the city. Antiaircraft guns and artillery should be prepared to annihilate enemy forces as soon as possible. Fourth, reserves in the garrison command and field army should be centralised to fight against the enemy army and destroy them on a front far away from Nanjing. Regardless of the route the enemies choose, be it the Beijing-Shanghai road, the Beijing-Hangzhou highway or the Jiangbei district, the terrain can be used to attack to the Chinese troops' advantage, exploiting the enemy's weak points. Fifth, if the Yangtze River can be blockaded and there are no enemy warships in the upper reaches of the Yangtze, then removable artillery and garrisons in Nanjing, Hankou and Chongqing can be moved to another place during the war. Sixth is the outlines for preparations:

1) When the war is about to begin, the Nanjing garrison should enforce martial law.

2) Begin the preparations and operations of the military police and the army in Beijing.

3) Decide whether the garrison should join the field army or should be an independent defence force.

4) Decide what kind of army should be in the garrison reserves and what kind of air force it should include.

The general strategy chosen in the defensive plan was relatively appropriate for the situation. However, the problems lay in the situation having changed, and problems caused by the people who implemented the plan. For example, during the most intense fighting in the Battle of Nanjing, one unit sheltered in the cement defence bunkers. It turned out that they were actually made of bamboo, apart from the cement on the surface. This couldn't even stop bullets, let alone the Japanese tanks. This naturally caused anger among the soldiers defending the city, cursing Chiang Kai-shek and his officers, thinking that they'd sacrificed the lives of their citizens for their own interests.

This wasn't even the biggest problem. After the Marco Polo Bridge Incident in 1937, Chiang Kai-shek and his associates had been indecisive about their strategy in the war against Japan. As a result, their preparations were inadequate for resisting the enemy when they came, which caused widespread chaos.

Before the Battle of Shanghai, the Chinese military included: 182 divisions and 46 independent brigades in the infantry; nine divisions and six independent brigades in the cavalry; four brigades and 20 independent regiments in the artillery; 110,000 tonnes of firepower in the navy; and about 600 aircraft of all kinds (including 305 fighters) in the air force. In fact, the total military force that could be deployed by the National Revolutionary Army for frontline fighting in the preliminary stage only consisted of 80 divisions and nine independent brigades in the infantry, nine cavalry divisions, two brigades and 16 independent regiments of artillery. In stark contrast, the Japanese military had: 4.48 million soldiers (1.99 million combat troops); 1.9 million tonnes of naval firepower and about 2,700 aircraft in the air force (1,480 army aircraft and 1,220 naval aircraft). Faced with the scale of the Japanese military, Chiang took Falkenhausen's advice of conducting protracted warfare, meaning dragging Japan down in guerrilla warfare in a large territory causing logistical problems. In terms of the deployment of troops and tactics, the battlefields were divided into five theatres of war, including Jiangsu Province, Zhejiang Province and Shanghai in the east. While the capital in Nanjing was the seat of the government, it was not suitable for a profound and long lasting defence as it was located so close to the Japanese landing zone. Chiang Kai-shek had planned to retreat from Nanjing for a long time. Nevertheless, abandoning Nanjing was unacceptable to the citizens of China as Nanjing was its capital city, so Chiang had declared that he would: "Protect Nanjing with all of his might."

In the 22 days from 11 July to 1 August, high command held 22 military meetings consecutively, analysing the enemy's situation every day. The Japanese army was causing problems for China in the east and high command was now working on war preparations in cities along the Yangtze. The frenzied Japanese army harried the KMT at every step, and looked to invade Nanjing, the country's military and political centre.

On 12 August, Shanghai was laid under siege and needed aid. Chiang

Kai-shek and other leaders then held a KMT high command meeting to discuss the war plan to relieve the city. Chiang was named generalissimo of all the armed forces at the meeting, prompting Chiang to say: "What's the point of these titles in times of crisis? Just get on with it!"

The other delegates enthusiastically agreed, and He Yingqin was named chief of the general staff. At that point, high command set out the plans for the war against the Japanese: "One KMT force is to be deployed in north China to resist the invasion, with special attention to be paid on Tianding Fortress in Shanxi Province. The main KMT forces are to be deployed in east China, fighting against the enemy in Shanghai and protecting Nanjing" (Wu Xiangxiang, *Second Sino-Japanese War*, vol. 1 p. 388). The frontline in Shanghai tragically fell three months after the plan was established and the goal of strengthening Nanjing looked even harder to achieve. Nanjing was now in danger, great danger.

Airstrikes Begin in August

Nanjing is my hometown, as well as Zhu Chengshan's, the man who made the Nanjing Massacre memorial hall famous both in China and around the world thanks to his dedication to Nanjing. His grandfather worked in a bank located in Xinjiekou, the city centre: "When the Japanese came, my grandpa escaped to his hometown Liuhe. My grandpa always told me how the Japanese killed people like flies." Several days later, his grandfather could see corpses piled up in the city's streets. Zhu grew up in Nanjing and then became a soldier in the area. He later became the curator of the Nanjing Massacre memorial hall, being a Nanjing native with an intense connection to the Nanjing Massacre.

To write this book, I met a great deal of people who recalled the stories told by grandparents about the many crimes committed by the Japanese soldiers.

The air raid campaign in Nanjing began in August and was followed by the first war crimes committed there by the Japanese. It also marked the beginning of the defence of Nanjing.

On 15 August, the third day of the Battle of Shanghai, Japan began the bombing campaign. On 4 August, nine days before the Japanese commitment to the plan to bomb Nanjing, the deputy minister of the Japanese military commanded the 3rd fleet in China to attack Nanchang, Nanjing, Jurong, Bengbu, Guangde and Hangzhou. It was the Kisarazu squadron of the 1st fleet that launched the first attack on Nanjing.

At the beginning of the conflict in Shanghai, the Japanese air force had planned to directly go to Nanjing. A lieutenant colonel called Oshino wrote a book called *Record of War in China: Naval and Air Attacks*, describing the scene when Japan first invaded Nanjing:

The First Attack on Nanjing Across the Ocean

On 14 August 1937, Japan launched its first attack on Nanjing across the ocean. The first targets included Hangzhou and Guangde in Anhui Province. We expanded operations to Nanchang and Nanjing the next day. This action of attacking Nanjing, China's capital city and military hub, was a great success.

At about 9 o'clock that day, as planned, we crossed the ocean, suddenly appearing in the skies above Nanjing. The city found itself on the verge of collapse in this fierce storm of fire. It was a rainy day; the loud roar of thunder could be heard in the sky. Then, a multitude of bombs fell from the clouds. The enemy had been destroyed like rats; the people were unsurprisingly too shocked to say a word.

Our planes dived from the clouds into Nanjing, strafing through the city's streets. We aimed at important military facilities and unleashed a fierce attack. Sirens sounded everywhere. From Purple Mountain to the antiaircraft positions, the Chinese army shot at our planes haphazardly. The sound of artillery and bombs exploding mixed with the patter of the rain, with several Chinese planes defending the city in the storm. A heroic dogfight unfolded in the skies above Nanjing.

At that point, we bombed the hangar in the Nanjing air base, showing the world our power in the skies. However, our forces made great sacrifices for this spectacular result. Eight planes were destroyed and many aviators died on that cloudy day, counterattacked by the enemy during their bombing runs.

Their heroic actions stunned the world. The bad weather meant that there was a risk of innocent people and non-combatants being injured, and so with the Japanese army's humanitarian and international concerns, we seriously considered the possible outcomes of the fighting.

The first attack was inspiring and we would show our highest respect to those heroes whose planes are never to return. And what about discussion of this battle? Here are some comments from fellow officers and soldiers. A commander said: "The first bombing was most impressive, with an unprecedented air raid on the city despite the risk from the violent typhoon. On 13 August, the Chinese air force arrogantly showed off in the skies above Shanghai, a lamentable act of violence. Everyone here has acted with heroism that is difficult to describe. In my opinion, we did a marvellous job and we can never forget the tremendous sacrifices of our men."

Another aviator at the battle described the scene:

We devoted ourselves to the war as soon as we got the orders. The dark clouds made for extremely poor vision so we flew the planes at an altitude of 70 metres, soaring just above the ocean surface. Despite the strong winds, the wings were firm enough to not break.

We arrived at the mainland before we knew it. The plane was at an altitude of 300 metres when we arrived at Lake Tai. Three planes came to fight us. After 30 minutes, one plane fell into the lake and another plane was forced to land in the fields.

We then flew to the Yangtze River, dropping to an altitude of 200 metres, heading straight for Nanjing over a road. The clouds were still thick, making us fly at an altitude of 400-500 metres, below the clouds.

Y squadron bombed the Ming Palace airport; several planes from the squadron flattened Dajiaochang Airport, bombing many planes on the runway. They all returned when the objectives had been achieved.

The antiaircraft artillery and machine guns shot at us violently over Xiaguan Port, Purple Mountain and the airports. I was in the first plane of the squadron. After the bombing, I encountered five enemy planes. Two planes were destroyed during the battle. The fourth plane in our squadron may have been shot. It began to separate from us at first, and then was attacked by the enemy and finally destroyed.

At that point, my plane was also shot, and the scout, Watanabe, died from the wound. One of our engines had been shot. We carried on with just one engine, causing the plane to drop suddenly. We had to abandon any heavy equipment we had on board, flying the plane at an altitude of just 100 metres.

"To protect the squadron leader's plane, the second and the third plane in our squadron flew over several times, although I ordered them to return. Our entire squadron could be lost if we didn't do something. So I told the planes on the wing to return first and I returned alone to the base with a single engine, flying at half speed.

"The radio was useless after being shot, making me distressed and anxious. After seeing my subordinates complete their own missions, I was determined to make it to the end.

"When landing on Jeju Island, I was profoundly grateful for my training and the trust my subordinates had in me. After hearing of our survival, the commander said: 'You reported that you were "flying with a single engine at a speed of…" and then you just cut out. I thought you'd died like the fourth plane.' He then laughed."

Heavy losses were also suffered by T and H squadrons that day. The leader of H squadron said: "We couldn't see anything when we arrived on the mainland so we were separated from the other planes. At that moment, I saw the streets in Wuhu through the clouds and thought about bombing the airport there. However, at second thought, Nanjing was the priority. Then, I saw the Ming Palace airport, and bombed our enemy's planes at an altitude of 500 metres. Fierce antiaircraft fire was launched from Purple Mountain. We hovered above Nanjing and found Dajiaochang Airport. Then we dropped bombs destroying four planes on the ground. Then, five or six enemy planes came, of which we destroyed three. At that moment, the fourth plane got hit with a bullet and caught fire. It fell to the ground and exploded. The second plane was also on fire. Completing our mission, I believed that it was unnecessary to remain there and flew into the clouds. I couldn't see anything in the clouds and was separated from the third plane. Though I received the news that they were safe and sound, it was still difficult for me to fly for three hours without being able to see. Our losses were twice those of the other squadrons. Remembering the destruction of the plane on the wing, I am determined to take revenge next time!"

The commander continued: "The first bombing raid on Nanjing was a successful strike despite the bad weather, but our losses were severe. The second bombing raid was for revenge and to vent our anger."

This was the reality during the first air raid on Nanjing.

The War Journal [p. 236-237, 28 January 1938], filed in the *Second Historical Archives of China*, featured an article called *Light Bombing in Nanjing*. This article was translated from a Japanese article about the experiences of Captain Hiramoto, a leader in the Japanese air force during the first attack on Nanjing:

It was the morning of 15 August when we unexpectedly received an order to fly across the ocean to bomb Nanjing. This was the great adventure of our lives and a golden opportunity that we had long awaited.

Each detachment stood in formation in front of giant fighter planes. As I walked in front of each aviator, I received their war preparation reports and immediately relayed the information to the commander of the air force base. He curtly ordered: "Set out to bomb Nanjing at once." Abuzz with excitement, all the crewmen climbed into the giant aeroplanes, carrying the fate of Japan in the Far East with them. The planes immediately left after the servicemen had started the propellers, quietly flying up into the sky one by one. My plane led the way. Now in the skies, each plane headed towards the sea in formation. The sky was dark, covered by stratus clouds in low-pressure areas. We could see nothing when we looked down. We knew that a typhoon was heading towards

Shanghai as we flew towards the centre of a heavy storm. White, raging billows floated on the ocean surface beneath us and we were flying above it at a height of 70 metres. We soon felt the tempest upon us from the south and our wings constantly oscillated. We did not know whether we would arrive safely. We ran the risk the entire way in the bad weather.

We had never encountered any circumstances like this in our countless past training sessions, namely flying while struggling against a typhoon on the ocean and trying to drop bombs at the same time. We set aside our concerns about the danger created by the storm simply because of one issue that lingered in our minds. One day before, namely 14 August, the Chinese air force had slaughtered unarmed Japanese, Chinese and European people in the busiest part of Nanjing Street in Shanghai, and had bombed Cathay Hotel and Palace Hotel. China's air force, just like its army, was composed of bandits. We were determined to take revenge just for that reason. We had eagerly awaited for this opportunity. We were now on our way to teach the arrogant air force a lesson. We flew over the top of the humid mountains for hours and eventually saw Shanghai in the misty horizon. Soon afterwards, we saw a large lake below the clouds, which was Lake Tai. We later flew up to the sky at an altitude of 300 metres.

Five enemy planes suddenly appeared out of nowhere and boldly charged towards us. The sounds of machine guns from both sides created a chorus. Aeroplanes danced in a circle on both sides. As quickly as we could, we shot down two enemy planes. I saw one of the enemy planes fall into the lake with its tail smoking and another spiral down into the field on fire. The other enemy planes pulled away from us. It was my first air battle. I had been unsatisfied with the transient battle. I was deeply saddened by the sight of the falling enemy planes. However, everything vanished into smoke like a dream. We turned around and flew towards Nanjing. We soon saw Nanjing from the sky. Our enemies must have been informed of our assault. They surrounded and protected the mountain stronghold of this ancient city and opened fire with their antiaircraft guns. The roar of gunfire on Purple Mountain resounded strongly, seeming to lead the chorus of destruction.

We hovered to and fro amidst the numerous antiaircraft attacks, many of which were positioned in the city. But as we hovered ever lower still under attack by the Chinese antiaircraft, we saw many frightened Nanjing citizens run to shelter. Eventually, we found the correct targets. We could clearly see the situation on the ground in detail. The following is a description of the assaults on the Senior Colonel Military airfield and the Imperial Palace airport.

Our bombers dropped bombs on the targets like carrier pigeons. We flew at a low altitude and could even feel the vibration of the explosions. The giant roof of the hangar flew into the sky and then back onto the crater like a magic carpet, with red and yellow fiery smoke gushing out of it. A thunderstorm of bombs smashed the hangar and the surrounding areas. There were about 20 aeroplanes there. When the smoke and fire stopped, the great military airfield had been left dilapidated.

After finishing our task there, we focused our attention on the second target, namely the air force base at the Imperial Palace airport. After we fulfilled our mission of dropping our bombs, we flew back to Japan. It was about 3pm then. During that period, we became the targets of the antiaircraft positions in the mountains both inside and outside the city. It lasted 30 minutes in total. Some of our airplanes were hit.

When we left Nanjing, five enemy planes arose from the clouds. We immediately exchanged machine gunfire. In a flash, we knocked down two enemy planes, with the rest fleeing at once at a speed we had never seen before. I noticed that something was wrong with Aeroplane No.4. Its engine was out of control. As it had fallen behind and could not return to the formation, the enemy planes took the opportunity to centralise their aim and shoot at it. I saw it fall amidst smoke and fire.

We were flying the guiding aeroplane, so we paid attention to everything as commanders. First Class Aviator Watanabe was immediately killed in action. A bullet damaged our radios and another completely destroyed one of our engines. We flew at half our speed and gradually lost climbing capacity. Anything that could be discarded was thrown out of the plane to reduce the weight. We fought against the atrocious weather and returned over the sea, supported by just one engine. When we reached the local port at last, many Japanese soldiers worried about us, acting like hysterical schoolchildren and welcoming us enthusiastically. "Thank goodness!" the commander of the air force shouted loudly, "I thought you'd suffered the same lot as Aeroplane No.4. We hadn't received any information for a good seven hours, when you sent out a message that you were flying with one engine. We thought you must have been done for." Later, I climbed out of my faithful plane with great care.

I counted that there were 48 holes from enemy bullets and flak cannons. Since we'd been flying at an extremely low altitude in our first bombing of Nanjing, we'd dropped our bombs with extraordinary accuracy. Nonetheless, for this reason, we'd also paid more - our losses were greater than in any subsequent bombing of Nanjing.

The article showed that the Japanese had acted like bandits when attacking Nanjing. Every emotion under the sun can be found in the article, from thrill to fear and victory to defeat. If we look at what the article is really saying, we can conclude that the Chinese army made great efforts in the war, especially in its aerial resistance, inflicting a great deal of damage on the Japanese. This was largely due to the previous air defence planning in the capital. According to the materials that I've found, the planes involved in the bombing raid on Nanjing all together totalled 20, and were led by Captain Hayashida from the Kisarazu air force. At 9 o'clock, the plane team took off from the Omura air base near Nagasaki, crossing the East China Sea to reach Nanjing. Between 14.50 and 15.30, the aerial force conducted a bombing raid aiming to destroy Nanjing's airports, and at 21.20, it returned back to the mainland, shooting down four Chinese planes in the process.

On 16 August, the Japanese army planned to attack Nanjing for a second time. They changed the strategy to bomb Suzhou Airport due to the bad weather. The Japanese suffered huge losses over the course of the two-day air battle. The Omura air force lost 12 of their 20 planes, with a Japanese official saying: "It is because we insisted on attacking at a low altitude due to the bad weather." The huge losses also inflicted a psychological wound upon Japan, making them consider the effectiveness of attacks across the ocean. As a result, the Japanese high command adjusted their strategy. They transferred their planes from Japanese airports to Taiwanese airports to carry out the task of attacking at a low altitude over the ocean.

At that point, the Chinese air force was still in a strong position. It had hit back against Japan and attacked the Japanese army in the Shanghai garrison when Japan launched the bombing raids on Nanjing. In those days, there were also unprecedented battles in the skies above Beijing, Shanghai and Hangzhou, resulting in a stalemate until 18 August. Although China had suffered great losses, it had greatly weakened the effectiveness of the Japanese forces. However, after 19 August, the situation rapidly went from bad to worse. As the Japanese army had partially decoded Chinese air force messages, it enabled the Japanese to learn information from the Chinese air force, such as their movements and objectives. The Japanese military then began to bomb Nanjing city that afternoon. They then bombed the military school and armoury at dusk, while also attacking the KMT general staff. The good thing was that the Chinese government still had the power to fight back and hadn't been totally destroyed.

The Japanese were incredibly proud of the attack. Here is Hiramoto's description. He described the scene to a war correspondent after he set off on the second raid on Nanjing:

> We took our revenge four days later. It was sunny that day. The plan was to bomb Nanjing after sunset. Like the first time, we arrived at Nanjing with ease.

We hovered above the city several times and chose our targets carefully. All the antiaircraft cannons were turned towards us, from Purple Mountain to the city wall and inner city. The night was filled with antiaircraft artillery and machine gunfire. The city stank with the smell of death.

But these bullets exploded in the air all over the city like tens of thousands of colourful stars, resembling the wonderful annual firework display in Tokyo, which was enjoyed by the Japanese children. However, compared with these explosions, the firework display in Tokyo was nothing more than the last embers of a matchstick. Red, blue and orange flames exploded in the night sky of Nanjing.

Around 8 o'clock that night, as we found the Nanjing central military academy compound, we dropped 10 bombs on them, immediately turning the buildings to ash. Then, we turned our attention to the general staff headquarters, dropping a further 10 bombs on the target. Once we completed those easy tasks, we returned to our base, with a bright and round moon over us and the endless sparkling sea below. The most wonderful thing was that we didn't lose any planes in the second raid on Nanjing.

The Japanese Sea Eagle plane remained intact. Inside the aircraft, the four crew members, apart from the pilot, were blessed with sweet dreams...

As bandits flew in the air, Nanjing, the capital of China, suffered from bombardment every single day. A terrible scene. Since the bombardment of the Japanese army on 15 August, the ancient and beautiful city of Nanjing had been turned into a sea of fire and ruins, bringing untold suffering to the people.

Sorrow weighed heavily on my heart;
I want to make a sacrifice in a heroic way.
But not like this.
Not like this!

While this poem may not be one of the greats, it says a great deal about the raids at the time. Picture the scene: the poet clenching his fists, desperate to fight the Japanese to the death. This poet was Feng Yuxiang, a famous patriotic general. Faced with the enemy's bombardment, General Feng, a tall and big man, was tormented by his feeling of powerlessness.

For three months after the Battle of Shanghai, from August to 13 November, the Japanese army bombarded Nanjing almost every single day, apart from on rainy days and typhoons. The suffering and helplessness of the people of Nanjing during this time is something we can never really imagine.

As for the horrors committed by the Japanese, I'd like to see how the sympathetic authorities and academic community tries to rationalise or justify it. While writing this book, I happened to read a piece by Guo Moruo, a great writer, from late September 1937, written during his visits to Nanjing. I felt so moved that I have quoted some of his book here:

> I left Shanghai on the evening of 20 September 1937 and went to another location. When I was just about to visit Chen You, Chen Cheng came along with a section chief and told me he was going to give a motivational talk to a division. I then got into his car and headed there with him.
>
> Chen Cheng told me in the car that the division had had the most military success and had made full preparations to join the front, so he rallied the military officers and gave them a motivational talk.
>
> I felt that it was somewhat risky to give a motivational talk to the military officers of the entire division, even though it was at night. Even Chen Cheng felt it was risky too. After a long silence, he suddenly said to me: "I wish everything goes smoothly because of you." I didn't get it. Chen Cheng then explained that I'd said that I was lucky in an article. I then realised that he'd read my article *Return from Japan*, written when I was a lucky man at the age of 46. It was a hazy night, with the moon somewhat hidden amidst the clouds. When we reached our destination, colourful illuminating balls were rising up towards the sky. They were signals released by traitors. Many aeroplanes followed, however, with the planes seeming to be invisible.
>
> The petty officers gathered on the lawn and waited for a long while. Chen Cheng asked a section chief and me to give the motivational talk with him, but we refused and instead just listened by the road. The talk lasted for more than an hour because the army commander and division chief followed Chen Cheng to give talks. Halfway through, a bomb fell not far away from the venue, surely dropped by an enemy plane. But the petty officers stood still and didn't even move. After the talk, we got back into the car and returned. On the way, Chen Cheng said to me: "We have your luck to thank! Had the bomb been dropped on the men, it would have been a disaster!" Yes, I'd found myself believing in fate to some extent recently. My luck had blessed many people and I thought that it was the blessing of our country and nation. Auspicious omens seemed to foretell the prosperity of the country. It seemed reasonable to me, but I didn't have the time to think about it thoroughly.
>
> I parted from the section chief before he headed for Suzhou. He said he'd be returning to Nanjing the following afternoon. I wanted to take the opportunity of going there in his car, so I arranged to visit him in Suzhou the next day.
>
> It was past 2am when we reached the headquarters. I stayed in Chen

Cheng's house that night. I arrived in Suzhou on the evening of 21 September. By the time I phoned the section chief, he'd left. So, I decided to stay in Wuxian county that night. The sweet-scented osmanthus at the lodging gave off a strong sweet fragrance in the darkness. There were occasionally air raid sirens, but I remained undisturbed and slept soundly because of my comfortable clothes that had been made just before I went to Shanghai. The next day, since I had to wait for the car, I had enough time to enjoy some sightseeing in Suzhou before noon. The citizens were calm but the stores were closed. I found it somewhat ridiculous. Maybe the shop owners closed their businesses just as a precaution against the bombing. But there was no need to do so if the bombs didn't hit their stores. If the bombs did hit them, just shutting them wouldn't have helped in the slightest. It had more to do with stupidity than a lack of courage.

It was 6 o'clock in the evening and I could see the dripping rain. When we arrived at a place where two big trucks were parked, our car also stopped. The driver of the vehicle ahead told us that there was an air raid. When I listened carefully, there was a soft drone in the hazy night sky. I didn't know if it was the drone of the enemy planes or our planes. The drone stopped and the car started again. We drove in the car for the entire night and did not arrive in Nanjing until 5am on 22 September.

After I arrived in Nanjing, I paid a first visit to Division Head Zhao from the Beijing office of one of the armies. Then, guided by Zhao, I visited Zhou Zhirou. It was interesting for me to talk with friends in military service because of their candid attitude and determination in resisting aggression.

I voiced my opinions to Zhou Zhirou. I predicted that the Soviet Union may get involved in the war due to the situation brought about by Japan as Japan was most fearful of the aerial power of the Soviet Union's eastern forces. The Soviet Union could launch aerial raids from Vladivostok to bomb Japan's heartland, for instance, Tokyo, Yokohama, Osaka and Kobe. Their aeroplanes could fly there and back. The Japanese air force could bomb Vladivostok or the heavy industry belt around Lake Baikal. But these areas were not necessary for the survival of the Soviet Union. There was no way that Japan's air force could bomb Moscow or Leningrad. Japan intended to fight a quick battle for quick victories in their war against China. But the Chinese army fought with increasing determination and it was impossible for Japan to win a quick war. It made the Japanese restless with anxiety. The longer the war lasted, the more restless, aggressive and fearful of the Soviet Union the Japanese became. I thought that the Japanese army was going to attack the Soviet Union due to this fear.

Zhou Zhirou disagreed with me. He said that Japan would go all out to fight against the Chinese army while trying to keep the Soviet Union away from any involvement to succeed in its scheme. It wouldn't be stupid enough to fight two countries at the same time. Besides, it wasn't prepared for a war against the Soviet Union.

Zhou Zhirou's view was one of common sense. Thinking about things rationally, Japan would naturally do all it could to deal with the Chinese army to win the war. Nevertheless, the Japanese high command had lost all sense. If they had been making sane decisions, they would have first realised that encroaching into China would expedite their losses; secondly, they would have at least been aware that they should not have provoked conflict in the south while fighting in the north of China. But they were not conscious of these two points. Therefore, we can speculate that they would pre-emptively attack the Soviet Union believing that it would succeed as a military strategy.

In the yard amidst the dusk twilight, Zhenru told me an anecdote.

"The artillerist of the Shanghai Incident, Mr Wu, divorced his Japanese wife and went to the front in north China."

I thought that it was ideal material for a play. It could be used to provide some material for a play when dramatic societies were short of scripts.

"Mr Wu graduated from the Imperial Japanese Army academy; he was born in Guangdong, of a tall build and only about 30 years old. He had been the regimental commander of the former 19th army during the Shanghai Incident. When his Japanese wife gave birth to their first boy on the very night of the incident, he was firing his first missile at the Japanese soldiers in Zhabei.

"After the 19th army dissolved, he travelled to Europe and returned to Japan two years ago. I made acquaintance with him at that time. I met his wife several times. He and his wife loved each other very much. Soon afterwards, they returned to Guangdong.

"I returned to Shanghai this year when Mr Wu happened to come from Kushan Mountain to Guangzhou. We met in Shanghai, when he told me that he cared for his wife very much and his wife was going to give birth to their third child. He sent me a letter after he returned to Guangzhou to tell me that it was another boy.

"Soon after our parting, the anti-Japanese war broke out. Unexpectedly, in just two months, he divorced his wife and went to the front in north China."

They divorced, as Zhenru described, willingly. At their divorce banquet, Zhenru served as their witness and their two boys and daughter were brought there by their mother.

Ms Wu said at the banquet: "Wu, you are a soldier. It is your duty to bravely defend the territory of your country when it is exposed to disaster. Please don't worry about me. Although I was born in Japan, I'm completely opposed to the brutal aggression of the Japanese. I'll care for your children wholeheartedly and teach them to be like you. They'll be the children of China forever."

This was straight out of an opera.

Mr Wu could have stayed in Guangzhou to fulfil his duty. But he went to the front in north China in fine spirits.

Hearing this story in the vast darkness, I felt excited and contented in the knowledge that China shall never perish with the existence of such soldiers.

Ji Xing lived in a two-storey foreign-style house. Two air-raid shelters had been excavated in the lawn in the courtyard. When she took me upstairs, she pointed to a hill of a similar height from a window in the room and said to me: "We have also excavated a trench under the hill along the ridge of the mountain. With more than six metres of ground above, it can serve as our shelter when we hear the sirens."

She then told me what the sirens meant by whistling. The first siren was sounded before the enemy planes arrived; the second was for red alert when enemy planes drew near. Preparations had to be made to find shelter during the first siren, while we needed to enter the air defence trench during the second siren. The whistle after the enemy planes had left ended the sirens.

Hearing these sirens felt bizarre because it seemed like some sort of alien world to me.

I had supper with Section Head Zhao and other guests, having been invited by Zhou Zhirou. Zhou and I had met twice in total by then. He was of a tall and strong build and was interested in literature. He talked about Yu Dafu, Mao Dun and Yun Daiying. He said that Daiying wasn't just good at giving speeches but also at writing; unfortunately he died early but otherwise he would have had much more of a career in writing. He also mentioned the enemy bombing of Nanjing. The enemy had earlier declared that it was going to launch a massive bombing raid on Nanjing after midday of 21 September and it had asked the diplomatic personnel and residents of all countries to retreat. The clumsy, ruthless and tyrannical declaration manifestly revealed their extreme arrogance, bullying nature and fear of the strong. They thought that the Chinese were easy to handle and it didn't matter if they killed tens of millions of them, but the foreigners were not to be bullied! The Japanese were dwarfs before the foreigners but swaggered around before the Chinese. Was that their *bushido* spirit? Complete nonsense!

The enemy planes usually flew to attack the rear. This seemed better to us because it reduced the strain on the officers and men at the front while boosting our morale and devotion to the anti-Japanese War. This was what Zhou believed.

Zhou told us about the victory at Pingxingguan. I'd heard the news at midday, but we were all suspicious of it. It was proven then. However, the details of the fighting and the soldiers who'd fought in the battle had not been clearly reported.

After supper, I told Zhao that I was going to return to Shanghai in one or two days because of my urgent work.

Zhao said a car was available for me at any time to go to Shanghai. He added that he wanted to investigate the front too. He had asked the front for instructions by telegraph and it was possible that he was going to receive a reply the next day.

We agreed to leave Nanjing at about 3 or 4pm the next day, if everything permitted. Since I'd decided to return to Shanghai, I needed to report it to Mr Chiang. After leaving Zhou's home, I went to visit Zhang Qun and asked him to convey the message on my behalf. I also told him about the talk between Mr Chiang and myself and reiterated that I dared not accept the nomination.

Zhang Qun agreed to convey the message for me. He asked me whether I'd like to see Mr Wang. I said that I would go to see him if it was convenient for him. Zhang phoned Wang and made an appointment for us to meet at a specific location at 9am the next day. I told him about the victory at Pingxingguan and he asked the parties concerned for details.

It had indeed been a massive victory, killing 3,000 enemies and capturing 2,000, as well as enemy provisions, supplies and equipment. The enemy had been an elite unit called the Itagaki division, while the Chinese troops had been the 8th route army. In the battle, a battalion of soldiers had been tasked with disturbing the enemy's rear and luring the enemy into a deep valley to annihilate them in a single stroke.

Delightful! Even if it had been 10 years ago, I would have drunk a large bottle of brandy at the news.

25 September was a bright and sunny day in Nanjing. It was said in the early morning that Nanjing was expecting to be attacked by enemy aircraft today. As expected, at around 9 o'clock, when I was about to visit Wang by car, my roommate told me that the air raid siren was sounding, not that I noticed due to me being half deaf.

The red alert followed shortly so the people living together rushed for the trench at the foot of the mountain to take shelter. They were deeply concerned about me and asked me to sit deep inside the trench. The trench had been dug along the mountain and there were no air holes apart from the entrance. I was crammed into the trench like a sardine for a while. It felt stuffy in there so I moved close to the entrance, with the antiaircraft guns rumbling all around.

Ji Xing and Mingde went to the newspaper office. Ji Xing had a brother called Youhai who was studying at a senior high school. He was a lovely boy dressed in a yellow canvas Chinese tunic suit. He carried a black, horn-shaped listening device and stood on the stairs of the entrance, monitoring the situation in the skies and reporting it to those inside the trench. Someone inside told me: "Youhai is our sentry."

"It looks interesting. I'll take the place of you two as the sentry." With that, I stood on the stairs.

"Mr Guo, come down. It's dangerous!" warned the people inside the trench.

"Mr Guo, get into the trench. It's dangerous!" warned Youhai.

I didn't follow their warnings and asked Youhai for the device. Youhai gave it to me, which made it clearer for me to hear the chorus of the antiaircraft guns and enemy planes.

I saw, at first, 21 enemy planes flying towards us, spreading from the south to the eastern part of the city. Antiaircraft guns hidden all around the city began to roar into action, leaving the enemy's planes in clouds of smoke. It was very difficult to distinguish between smoke, cloud and planes as they all weaved together.

With the deep rumble of an explosion, a plane plummeted like a comet with a tail of black smoke.

"Excellent! Excellent! A plane has fallen!" Youhai joyfully shouted from the trench.

With one plane shot down, others danced around the sky. Fire from the antiaircraft guns chased them for a while, and then the planes escaped, leading to an uneasy truce in the sky. Youhai and I left the trench for a mound. Looking out from the position, we saw that there were no pedestrians, apart from soldiers, on the street and communication was nowhere to be found.

Despite the silent streets, a sound rumbled in the air. After a short while, another 15 planes arrived, still flying from the south but spreading to the northwest of the city. Heavy fire from the antiaircraft guns chased the planes once again. Suddenly, with another explosion, a plane, glowing bright red, fell like a comet again with a black plume of smoke behind it.

"Good job! Very good job!" Youhai jumped with joy and shouted from the trench.

"How come there was red light?" I asked.

"The engine must have been hit," Youhai said confidently.

The hit plane crashed into the northwest of the city with smoke and fire.

Other planes scrambled to get away.

Both the sky and the ground enjoyed a respite of silence.

"Fantastic! We saw a battle in the sky in person during our stay here, and saw two Japanese planes being hit by antiaircraft fire!" I enthusiastically said to Youhai.

"It's not easy for antiaircraft guns to hit a plane. It was also my first time seeing it myself."

"Where are our planes?"

"Our planes are fighting outside of the city, intercepting enemy planes. If they flew into the city, we'd hit them with our antiaircraft fire. It'd be dangerous for the citizens if they fight inside the city, with bombs going off everywhere."

Youhai explained it like he knew the inner workings of modern war, but I was in no position to know whether what he was saying had any truth to it. It was just a conversation between two people, and I've noted it down here.

As the siren continued to sound, I lost my patience under the hot sun.

"I guess it's about to be all clear, shall we go back?" I urged Youhai. "It's likely okay now."

When Youhai came with me back home, he said: "Wow, you were right, it's all clear now."

He heard the signal whistle, but I didn't. In an instant, ecstatic people returned from the shelters. We then received a call from the *Xinmin* newspaper, which made us happier than ever.

We heard that our planes had intercepted the enemy outside the city, while some of theirs had managed to find their way in. Antiaircraft fire had hit three planes in a row at Pukou, firing at and hitting an enemy plane which then exploded, destroying another two as they all fell together.

Killing three planes with one bomb was going to become a new proverb, more modern and catchier than killing two birds with one stone.

The Japanese had warned that they would turn Nanjing to ashes.

Instead, I saw that the enemies were being turned to ashes themselves in Nanjing.

After an all clear, cars returned to the streets once again. A driver was so excited that he told me while driving: "Fantastic! Didn't the antiaircraft gunners do well?!" He had also seen the two planes being hit.

People on the street were all beaming with joy, showing that they were relieved from their fear, not to mention their joy at the success of the Chinese defences. The joy made the people of Nanjing closer, which we would harness as a kind of power to bring all of the Japanese planes down!

— (AGE OF REVOLUTION BY GUO MORUO, PEOPLE'S LITERATURE PUBLISHING HOUSE, 1979, PP. 458-488)

As a romantic poet, Guo Moruo felt a sense of pride in the Chinese military and the people's resistance against the Japanese. There was a clear and profound contrasting mix of love and hatred in Guo's heart.

Before the Nanjing Massacre, Chiang Kai-shek had paid a great deal of attention to enemy airstrikes in Nanjing. In addition to the creation of air defence precautions, an air defence law was drafted, showing that at this point, the national government had been making some form of preparations. The following is Chiang's secret air defence order:

> The municipal government and garrison headquarters are all to be conducted by Ting Mi, the commander of the garrison and air defence force. As we fight against the Japanese forces, when the enemy's planes sporadically attack, all officers should prioritise local security and the public's safety. All provinces and locally affiliated areas should do their utmost to immediately provide air defence facilities. Civilians should especially be guided and assisted in digging trenches six *chi* high [about 1.9 metres] and two *chi* wide [about 64 centimetres], covered by a wooden board and buried under soil. These trenches should be dug in as many places as possible. Do not make the public panic but prepare the people for alarm. The public must depend on the officers to guide them and they must obey the rules; the county leaders must also take responsibility. In the event of dereliction of duty, or if local officers cower and flee, or delay in defending against the airstrike, break orders, or cause more casualties, once found out, they will be punished according to martial law. Do not break these orders!

Influenced by the government and army, civilians and soldiers in Nanjing during the Japanese airstrikes experienced a wide range of emotions, from fear and helplessness, to calmness and even mocking them, which is understandable in a country as large as China. Below are some interesting reports written at the time by three reporters from China and abroad, showing the mentality of the people of Nanjing. First is an extract from a reporter from the Ministry of War:

A GLIMPSE OF THE POWERFUL CHINESE AIR FORCE

As the capital of the Republic of China, Nanjing, with its wonderful profile, enjoys both ancient palatial architecture and modernity with the most sophisticated Western style architecture. It's a bustling metropolis. Nanjing is just as grand as the prosperous New York, as great as the glamorous Paris and as vital as the powerful London.

On a muggy autumn day the day before yesterday, I left for the capital. It was so hot that the asphalt road was on the verge of melting. When I looked around the city, I knew that Nanjing was ready, preparing for war. On Xuanwu Lake, I couldn't see any of the lake's usual layabouts, and there wasn't even a boat seller in sight. Just sheer silence accompanied by the usual moored boats.

Singing from the Fuzimiao Confucian Temple could be heard no more due to the fighting against Japan, which had even startled the local wildlife.

No crows could be heard anymore from Jiming Temple, despite its name meaning the caw of a crow in Chinese. In the same way, Mochou Lake, literally meaning "the lake of no worries" had an air of panic.

The Dahua theatre, where the operatic maestro Mei Lanfang used to perform, was now boarded up with wooden planks and had been turned into a makeshift shelter. This was rather symbolic of this tragic period. The basements along Zhenghong Road had also been prepared for the war.

At night, on the central streets of Xinjiekou, the neon lights at the town gates in the Huapailou neighbourhood didn't work, let alone the lights in other parts of the city. Even the two gourd-shaped lights on the roof of the Bank of China had been covered with blue cloth.

It was a completely different scene when walking down Jiankang Road: the national flag was flying outside a hospital. With the constant fighting against the Japanese invasion, the atmosphere in Nanjing was incredibly intense.

When I was eating at a small eatery that advertised "home-made food and simple snacks", an alarm suddenly sounded, so the owner approached me for the bill and asked me to leave at once. He said to me seriously: "To visit Nanjing now you have to have a hotel to stay at, especially when the alarm sounds, no shops dare to let people stay." I had no choice but to walk outside in fear. No pedestrians could be seen in the streets. Instead, the streets were heavily guarded, with police officers patrolling with guns and bayonets. Trucks carrying military police were also patrolling around the city. Iron gates were closed down in front of the wooden boards that covered shops. Approaching planes could be heard rumbling overhead: I got lost, like a lamb, and for a short moment, I was brought into a truck by military police, heading to a shelter inside the Xinmin theatre. The aerial defence of the city was in incredibly good order, which was rarely seen in other places.

I didn't expect to find so many other compatriots at the shelter too, from important governors wearing round badges and professors to leather tanners and poor tailors. Sharing the same atmosphere, the fear in the shelter was infectious.

As I looked up, Chinese planes, like iron birds, were soaring in the clear skies, protecting our land with loyalty and great courage. There's no other way to describe them than heroes.

We were pretty sure that the aerial defence network here was tight, so we were happy and encouraged even in the heart of the conflict. People in the capital had accepted these air strikes as part of life and knew how to resist them. It had to be a sign of progress for China that people here remained brave in the face of the violent attacks in their darkest hour.

About half an hour later, an all-clear sounded, signalling that we could leave the intense atmosphere inside the shelter. When running back onto the streets, I saw the Chinese iron birds returning to the roost after chasing off the enemy's planes.

I only stayed for one night in the capital, but the powerful Chinese air force had left an impression on me.

— *Huamei Evening News*, 20 September 1937

This following report was written by a foreign journalist and translated by Xu Zhilin:

NANJING, UNDER THE AIR STRIKE

Nanjing's residents were extremely used to Japanese airstrikes. Almost every day, as the alarm went off, they would take shelter in trenches or cellars without any panic.

During the battle in Shanghai, Japanese planes flew here almost every single day, even four or five times a day. Back then, after the residents ran into cellars, they were extremely scared; even when walking out of the cellars, they would whisper to each other about whether it was still dangerous or not. But now, as the alarm sounded, they would go into the shelters with smiles on their faces, guessing how many Japanese planes were going to be shot down.

Obviously, Nanjing's aerial defence capacity was pretty advanced, being one of the strongest out of all the cities in China. Nanjing boasted several fighter aircraft. The specific number was unknown, but it was large. Fighters were used to intercept bombers. Antiaircraft guns were used for shooting down Japanese planes that escaped from being intercepted, which were all around and inside the city.

Whenever any Japanese plane appeared in the sky, the alarm would immediately sound so residents would have enough time to hide in public or private shelters. Public shelters were dotted around the city, as common as toilets in other cities. When the alarms sounded, pedestrians would be directed by the army and police responsible for air defence to go inside or into shelters.

As a result, the streets would be abandoned. Everything returned to normal when the Japanese planes flew away.

When Japanese planes attacked at night, when the alarms went off, no lights were allowed. The aerial defence forces would patrol the streets to see whether there were any lights that could still be seen. The residents were all very obedient, and would turn their lights off. Another reason for patrolling was to check if there were any traitors giving signals to Japanese planes. Thanks to the efforts of the people of the city, it was far from easy for the Japanese to flatten Nanjing as they had planned.

While the journalist was in Nanjing, he experienced what it was like to be in an airstrike. The alarm sounded before the Japanese planes had even appeared. People on the streets promptly ran into shelters, leaving the streets empty. With no Chinese planes in the sky, the antiaircraft guns stormed into action:

The sound of the antiaircraft guns we heard here was rather different to those of the Japanese warships shooting down Chinese planes over the Huangpu River in Shanghai, which had been incredibly loud. The shots fired by the Chinese had been rather accurate, each one coming incredibly close to the Japanese planes. One plane was hit, almost crashing down, but it escaped in the end, one hour later than the other two. It was said that it was repaired after landing. All of this was due to a drill beforehand that made the air force so good and the citizens so calm.

Although Japan launched air strikes incredibly frequently, everything carried on as it had before. When it came to the government, everything from the police, the leadership, legislators and judicial regulators to examiners were all working as usual, with no staff leaving their posts and fleeing Nanjing. There were special circumstances, so office hours were extended and no shops closed. Tea houses, taverns and other recreational amenities were closed in the Fuzimiao Temple neighbourhood as there was no interest in visiting them.

Amid such a peaceful environment, for a visitor who'd just arrived at the city, if you didn't see the air defence shelters scattered along the streets, you'd never believe that the city had been attacked countless times over the past weeks, and the ruined roads were repaired at night. The ruins of the central communist department and areas in Xiaguan were still there, with broken walls remaining.

We visited some other ruined places, which used to be crowded, but now were reduced to tiles and bricks. Although Nanjing had suffered from constant bombing, its residents were as calm as the people in foreign concessions in Shanghai.

— *Damei Evening News* English language newspaper, 23 October 1937

Here is another interesting report entitled *Anecdote* by Tao Jinghuan, published in the *Xin Bao* newspaper on 19 October 1937:

> There were five kinds of air defence sirens in Nanjing, all different from each other: the air strike alarm, the emergency alarm, the all clear, the toxic gas alarm and the fire alarm.
>
> The capital of Nanjing suffered from its first ever airstrike on 15 August, and was attacked for the first time at night on the 25 August and experienced the heaviest bombardments from 19 to 26 September. After launching 825 airstrikes at night, the enemy didn't risk attacking any more.
>
> The week from 19 to 26 September saw heavy attacks on Nanjing; all shops were at risk, and the staff had to hide in shelters, closing their businesses as a result. However, three restaurants and taverns, which were the Lingnan restaurant on Zhongshan North Road, Houdefu at the Zhongyang department store and Bieyoutian near the Fuzimiao Temple, were exceptions, conducting business as usual. Foodies risked their lives for culinary delicacies and flocked to the restaurants, but none of them made a handsome profit.
>
> The capital's air defence force specialised in shooting down planes. I witnessed two Japanese planes being shot by antiaircraft guns. One attacked plane was on fire, crashing down with its tail in the air. It dropped so quickly that it crashed upon landing. The bomb on board the plane exploded, blowing it to pieces. The pilot on board had not evacuated, and his body could not be found by the Chinese Red Cross workers.
>
> It was on 25 September that an enemy plane was hit by our antiaircraft fire for the first time. The plane crashed into a house belonging to the Suo family in Wangfuyuan. The Suo family had left Nanjing at that time so no one was injured.
>
> Since the outbreak of total war against the Japanese, no one asked for rent in the city. The residents didn't pay rent or electricity bills, feeling that staying in the city wasn't that dangerous, and instead there were various benefits to enjoy.
>
> The well-known Qifangge tea house near the Fuzimiao Temple had been closed due to bombing fears, much to the annoyance of tea lovers.
>
> The wreckages of Japanese planes were publicly displayed. The first one was a heavy bomber, with parts displayed at the martyrs' cemetery. Tens of thousands of visitors went there each day, hitting record highs.
>
> It was recently suggested that using films could be one method of education. Since the outbreak of the war, all cinemas in Nanjing had been closed. Yet, due to the special need for propaganda, movies regarding revolution, battles, adventure, science, patriotism and other such topics should be staged at cinemas in an effort to raise people's patriotic awareness.

Mr Zhao, a marketing department employee, was meandering down the Guofu road with his wife as a Japanese plane bombed the street. The enemy then returned, so they hid in a public shelter for safety. After the alarm ended, they went back home, only to find they couldn't because their house had been bombed by the enemy. All they had was their clothes, and still they felt blessed.

One time, while the battle in the sky was raging, a Chinese plane was shot by the enemy and was plummeting to the ground. I thought the pilot was in danger, but a man jumped from the plane, opening up a huge white thing behind him, which became bigger and bigger. The jumping guy was dropping slowly under the white object, which turned out to be a parachute. I found out afterwards that the parachutist was our brave aviator Le Yiqin who had successfully shot down several enemy planes. Le suffered some slight injuries, but after he recovered, he went back to battle.

It's rained a lot this month. Every time it was raining, the residents here would joke that the enemy's planes wouldn't come so they could have a day to relax. Some people even bet on whether the enemy would come or not. They knew that the Japanese played dirty and were afraid to die, not like our army who devoted their lives to protecting our country.

Enjoying life in adversity is what shaped China. However, we need to find other styles of description to learn how the war hurt the residents and soldiers in the city, as well as many foreigners. In the vast sea of files collected at the Second Historical Archives of China in Nanjing, I was overjoyed to find a copy of Dr Robert Wilson's diary, who worked at the Nanjing Gulou Hospital at the time. The original version of this precious document was kept at Yale University. On the 100th anniversary of the founding of Gulou Hospital, a Japanese man named Eisei Kato donated the copy of this diary and a video cassette to the hospital. By risking his own life, Dr Robert Wilson provided a record from a doctor's perspective of how he and his colleagues aided the injured while avoiding the bombing, and living there several months after Nanjing was occupied. The following is from his journal, which recounted the violence shown by the Japanese army:

13 August

I hope last week's letter made the grade but there is some reason to doubt it. I will start this one as a sort of diary letter and add a little now and then until such time as we think it might go through.

Today we had a genuine thrill: the first air raid any of us have ever experienced. It will probably not be the last. I was down at Socony hill seeing two patients and incidentally had an opportunity to listen to the English broadcast from Shanghai which went into detail about the fighting there, which I will describe later. On my return, I noticed that people were collecting in groups in front of their houses and looking at the sky toward the north. Those not near houses were all running for shelter. The noise of the Ford I was driving was sufficient that I didn't hear the sirens which apparently had been going for some minutes in various parts of the city.

Arriving home there was some excitement among the servants and Marjorie was so grateful for my return though she was not at all panicky. The sirens sounded and soon we heard firing north of us and then the noise of airplanes. They came almost directly over our house, flying low because of the low ceiling and being shot at all around us. The ministry of justice about three hundred yards away had machine guns sticking out of windows. The minister of war, Ho Ying Ching, lives only a couple of hundred yards away and from the sound, I guess his place bristles with antiaircraft weapons.

We weren't sure whether we heard any bombs discharged or not. At least none dropped near us. The siren warns us and when we hear airplane motors, we head for the cellar where we were safe from anything but a direct hit right on the house. The warning was repeated several times during the afternoon and another time two airplanes passed almost directly over us. By this time, however, the Chinese airplanes had also taken to the air and the Japs were driven away. The rumours have it that from two to four planes were shot down.

Later news indicated that they had bombed the commercial airport near the Central Hospital. No mention was made of the military airport. One wounded man was sent to University Hospital after having been shot by a machine gun from the airplanes. He was near the reservoir, Tsing Liang Shan. Central Hospital also called up saying they had wounded from the airport and wondering if we had any room for them.

The Hospital has been organised on an emergency basis. For two days, I have been busy straightening out the inpatients so that those who can not walk are given a bed on the lower floor while those that can are put on the upper floors and expected to walk down themselves when the siren blows. I called up later to see if there is anything I could do at the hospital but the system worked perfectly and there was no need for me to leave Marjorie and Elizabeth. Dr Cheng's family is away and Dr Theodore Hsu is a bachelor so they can take direct responsibility without having to think about two places. There is some discussion of our moving into the hospital but for the present we are planning to stay here. The advantage there is three cement floors overhead so even a direct hit by anything but poison gas is relatively safe.

(Over the phone, just now, another report comes in that eight Japanese planes were sighted during the air raid and that no less than five were brought down by antiaircraft guns. At this rate we should not have to fear much but it sounds a little too good to be true.)

Probably the news you get from the Shanghai quarter is more accurate than ours. We get one-side news from the Chinese papers, usually over-optimistic and occasional reports from the Shanghai Broadcasting Station. I wish we had a radio. Last week I wrote about the incident at the Hungjiao Airdrome. The upshot of that was that the entire Third Fleet of the Navy invaded the Woosung River. Forty men of war. That, combined with the heavy-handed way they were acting in Shanghai, was a little too much and the Chinese decided to open up. All day yesterday the Chinese planes bombed the vessels. Several old river steamers have been sunk to shut off their retreat. In the first bombing, a fair proportion of the reserve supply of gas was burned and a number of ammunition dumps. The Japanese set up antiaircraft guns in the International Settlement on the Bund. The Chinese authorities gave a vigorous warning that unless those were immediately removed they would be bombed by Chinese planes.

A late report today, probably a wild rumour, has it that the Japanese have been driven boldly out of Shanghai. Tomorrow is another day and we shall see what it has in store for us.

17 August

Franklin's birthday. Many happy returns. My last statement seems quite a while ago by now. 'Tomorrow' was another day, only it was yesterday. We were awakened by the siren at six-fifteen and jumped into our dressing gowns. The siren system is all worked out now so that the first signal means that planes have been sighted. The next signal given in a series of wails indicates that they are near and it is time to dive for cover. After the second signal no one is allowed to move on the streets and the place looks like a long deserted city. As long as the raid is on there is absolute silence from below unless a Japanese plane is overhead in which case there is a veritable bedlam of machine gun and antiaircraft firing from places nobody seems to see. The third signal is a prolonged one indicating that the raid is over and the street appears miraculously full of people.

That process was repeated five times yesterday. In the morning I went to the hospital between the first and second raids. The Japanese planes did not reach the city in the first raid. The siren sounded for the second just as we had injected a spinal anaesthesia for a rather minor operation. We moved the patient and impedimenta to the x-ray room where there were two cement floors above us. The Jap planes broke through and dropped a few bombs, one falling not far (about three hundred yards) from our house and making Marjorie for the first time a little nervous. We finished our case and were about to call it a day and get home, having phoned in the meantime and found out that everything was all right, when the third air raid began and we were kept in suspense for about two and a half hours before the releasing siren sounded. That brought it to after two o'clock and I was able to get home. No bombs were dropped in that time and we were coming to realise more of what was going on, namely that our planes were meeting the Jap planes before they got to the city and engaging them. We had no more than finished dinner when the fourth raid came. The defence seemed to be better organised every time. From our upstairs window after the first siren blew we could see the Chinese planes rising from the airport outside of Tung Chi Men, to the southeast, in twos and threes and head off usually toward the north sometimes passing quite close to us. Then, after an indefinite period, they would come back in about the same formations, circle for a while and then settle on the airfield.

It was during this attack that Mr Marx called up and said that the US embassy had advised all women and children to go to Kuling or Hankow and that they had reserved space (not berths) for twenty five on the *Woosung*, a Butterfield and Swire boat that left at midnight. We got in touch with the Bradys and also called Hall Paxton, second secretary of the embassy in charge of getting the people out. Marjorie was not keen to go because we seemed to be relatively safe but an embassy invitation is more or less of a command and so we packed up. The Bradys decided to go too. We were to gather at the embassy at about eight o'clock. We divided our time between packing, listening for Japanese planes and watching Chinese planes circling about, when at five-thirty another alarm sounded and was kept going until about ten after eight. I had just finished telephoning Hall for instructions, being told to come over to the embassy as soon as the final siren blew, when it did blow, we piled over to the embassy.

Elizabeth had lost a little sleep during her numerous trips to the cellar but slept quietly during the ride down. The chief officer of the *Woosung* took one look at her and piloted us into his cabin. Everyone else slept on the deck around the captains and officers' quarters. The rest of the boat was filled to standing room only with Chinese. Marjorie and Elizabeth's necessities were all in one corey and one suitcase and with the Trimmers now at Kuling and a good many old China hands on board, including Mr Rugh, who Marjorie had met at Yenching last fall, I felt that she would be well taken care of. She bore up like a Trojan and I'm hoping that the next word will say that she is safe in Methodist Valley. One of my final instructions was to be sure and make the August 21 trip to the cemetery.

Our amah was allowed to go with her little boy and she was tickled to death to get out. I am left with a substitute cook and a substitute coolie, both Nankingites who are about the most cool and collected and unconcerned people in town. We came back with the aid of an embassy pass. Dick Brady was seized the day before with a terrible intestinal upset and I had been attending him. He took a decided turn for the better and was able to help with getting his family off. I drove his car and our duffle was divided between his and an embassy car. The Daniels had left a camp cot which we sent along to let the chief officer sleep on. I returned to a deserted house shortly after midnight and got a few hours' sleep.

We heard quite a bit of news while down at the boat. One of the families leaving was the Lancaster mother and daughter. I have probably mentioned them before. He (Lancaster) is employed by the Chinese government and is located at the big military airport outside of Tung Chi Men. The figures he gives as authentic for the aerial combats of Friday and Saturday were almost fantastic. (I mean Saturday and Sunday) It seemed that the Chinese here are equipped with the latest type American pursuit planes with some large caliber machine guns which make havoc of anything they hit. The Japanese planes involved in these raid have been of a German, Junker, model with smaller guns. The Chinese pilots actually downed on those two days twenty-six Japanese bombers with a loss of only three of their own planes. In the second raid when some of the Japs broke through they dropped a bomb on the airport which destroyed three more, a total of six. Practically no other damage was done in the whole Nanking area and vicinity. On the Japanese pilots in their planes were found maps with about forty places listed for bombing. The above figures do not seem entirely credible but it gives a general idea of the fact that the Chinese are on their toes. Lancaster says there is no doubt of the figures and that the Chinese are not publishing them for fear the people will get overconfident and relax precautions. Japan would not give up easily and a few raids are only a sample of what they are bound to do, if for nothing else than to make up some of their lost face…

17 August continued.

Only two air raids disturbed our equanimity today. The first caught me again in the operating room; this time doing a colostomy on a young woman of thirty who had an inoperable cancer of the rectum which had nearly closed off the lower end of her intestinal tract. How I wish we could have seen her a few months ago! The cancer had by now involved the uterus, one tube was fixed to the sacrum. The operation will relieve the very distressing obstruction but will not be able to be followed by a removal of the tumor. We didn't bother to get out of the operating room and in about fifteen minutes the second signal came, only this time instead of the wails, indicating danger, a long triumphant blast indicated that the planes had never even approached the city.

Shortly after finishing lunch, continuing our new system of eating Chinese food every noon, the siren again blew. The cook, coolie and I watched plane after plane rise from the southwest and head northwards. The danger signal sounded but we didn't see any Japanese planes and at about quarter to three, the final blow announced that again they had been turned back. Our planes continued to circle around for about half an hour. Returning to the hospital I found that the clinic had been practically non-existent. There seemed to be plenty to do, however. One of our aviators had been admitted on my ward. He had only a few scratches, including one on the eyelid that had to be sutured. We promised him that he would be fit as a fiddle in a few days and could get up in the air again soon. He was a pilot of one of our pursuit planes.

The planes have not returned so far, it being eleven pm. No Japanese plane has even reached the city for the last four raids and if their mortality continues at the rate of Saturday and Sunday they cannot afford to keep trying to bomb Nanking. The change in the countenances of the Chinese from a rather deep gloom on Sunday has changed to a look of hope and returning confidence.

The Shanghai news is not quite so encouraging but even there the Chinese are making definite progress. Their bombers are being used with telling effect. Quite a few, probably twenty or so, have been brought down but to show for it they have actually driven the powerful line-up of Japanese vessels out of the Woosung river. One boat, a battleship, is actually sinking and their flagship was so badly damaged that it had to be towed away. Another ship was also put out of commission. With their main support taken away from them the Japanese are losing ground on the land also and their headquarters was taken by the Chinese today. They have a large aircraft carrier some miles off the mouth of the Yangtze. It is completely surrounded by battleships making it impossible to approach from the air. A squadron of twenty six bombers was sent yesterday to make the attempt by a certain man named Ting who is probably the best ace of the Chinese air force

Dr Cheng was called over to see Madame Chiang yesterday evening as she had an infection in her finger. He had to attend her during a meeting of military officials. The same change in atmosphere was also noticeable about these officials. The generalissimo was in good spirits and a quiet confidence was beginning to take the place of the anguish of the previous weeks when the cruel dilemma confronted him of a peace with dishonour and loss of her place as a sovereign state, or a war in which he felt that China was still inadequately prepared and would hence lead to the total destruction of all he had been building up for the last ten years. China is better fitted for a prolonged struggle than Japan, unless her air force gives out. In that case, the Japanese would proceed systematically to bomb intensively every place of importance in the country. Today for the first time they used poison gas bombs, the result is not known. It was at a place called Haining and I don't even know where that is. From present indications, it does not seem too much to hope that the Japanese air force will be the first to succumb in which case there will be a speedy cessation of fighting as the Chinese people have no greater desire than to be left alone to develop as they are now developing.

But to return to Colonel Ting's story which Cheng heard at the generalissimo's. It seems that he, Ting, had orders to get the aircraft carrier or die in the attempt. With his 26 bombers he started from Nanking, avoided Shanghai and headed to sea, where they soon sighted the Japanese battleships surrounding the carrier. A perfect hell of antiaircraft bombs from all around the carrier kept a steady barrage and made it impossible to get close enough even to attempt to get at the carrier. Ting then ordered his men to return to Nanking, rather than sacrifice all their planes (and incidentally lives) while he could circle around and watch for his chance. They turned around and at Yangchow met some Japanese planes bringing down two. They landed there and phoned for instructions which were in no uncertain terms to get back to their commander. They found him still circling out of reach of the guns. The fire was too fierce to penetrate, however, and they turned around. At Chingkiang, Colonel Ting himself shot down two more Japanese planes and then every one of the twenty-six returned to Nanking. In view of their shooting down of four planes, they were forgiven for not getting the carrier but something tells me that we are going to hear more about that carrier.

A tale of true heroism was also reported today. A young gunner in his machine was engaged in a fierce encounter with Japanese planes, shooting down two. Suddenly, his plane didn't seem to be acting right and to his dismay he saw that his pilot had been shot. He crawled out of his cockpit and to that of the pilot, whom he found dead. There was not room for two so he draped the dead man around the back of his neck and brought the plane safely back to Nanking.

Last night, the Marx's were listening to a Japanese broadcasting station giving news in English. The Japanese it seems were about to call on the British, French and Americans to force the Chinese to stop picking on them.

In the north, the Chinese are closing in on Tientsin. The Japanese are trying desperately to take the Nankow Pass. So far they have been unsuccessful and have lost upwards of five thousand men and over forty tanks in the attempt. I didn't know how many the Chinese have lost there but as they are not as well equipped as the armies down this way the chances are that their losses are heavy. However, being on the defensive, their losses may not be too heavy.

Ms Hynds has ceased to be a pacifist and is heart and soul for the Chinese as we all are. The Lord's will be done but we can't help but hope and pray that all the progress that we can see about us will not be destroyed by a power that to us at least seems to be some sort of reincarnation of Lucifer himself.

18 August

A breath of relief today. Not a single air raid. The air is filled with rumours. The German ambassador today told all German nationals to secure gas masks. I now carry mine around with me even though the possibility of having to use it is very remote. The kind that fits over one's head and looks like the head of some futuristic monster costs too much and the supply is too limited for general distributions. We each carry around a face mask with twenty thickness of gauze and a small bottle of a chemical solvent. When the warning comes we are to pour the solution on the mask and place it over our mouths and nose until the danger is over. For the deadly mustard gas, which cuts holes right through the flesh, we have to take our chances. The supply of bleaching powder is small and that is supposed to be the most effective antidote. The solution we have is calculated to neutralise phosgene, chlorine and several of the other possible gases.

The Shanghai situation is by no means clearing. Americans, British and others are leaving by the hundreds. Again a slow but steady advance seems to be under way in every sector and the Japanese are gradually getting with their backs to the river. The advance is made at frightful expense to Chinese lives as every street gained means a drive right into the worst kind of machine gun fire and sniping. Two divisions are said to have suffered very heavily. While some Japanese gunboats left, apparently all did not go as there are thirty still reported in the river.

The Nankow battle is still fierce. The only ulterior motive seems to be a severance of the shortest route between China and Russia. One Chinese division of 1500 men was reported to have been virtually wiped out in a terrific attack by the Japanese with numerous tanks. Their stand gave sufficient time however for their reinforcements to come up and in an equally severe counter attack with fresh troops the Chinese gained back all the lost territory and captured a number of the tanks.

The hospital is quieting down and we have quite a few empty beds. We do not know when they will begin to fill up with wounded. Three Japanese aviators are patients in the Central Hospital. They are being given every consideration and have been allowed to send messages to their families. We are writing to the American Red Cross to see if anything in the way of money or supplies can be sent in to help us out.

Dick Brady and I are making it a nightly practice to go over to Mr Marx's house where we listen to the evening broadcasts from Shanghai, Nanking and Manila. The Japanese run as much interference as they can on the Chinese wave length and tonight for the first time we found that the Chinese were starting to do the same with the Japanese broadcasting station in Manchuria. I got a letter from Dave Rowe from Shanghai today. He arrived there on August 12 and wrote on August 13, just before the trouble started. He is marooned there now.

20 August

The recovery from Wednesday has taken a while. The siren is still sounding while I write this. We kept quiet for two hours and could hear the sound of countless planes diving. We could barely see any planes under the bright and clear moon, but we were told that the pilots could see other planes easily in the sky. Obviously, the Japanese planes haven't arrived at the city, and that's why there aren't any bombs. By the time the last alarm rang signalling the end of the airstrike (it lasted from midnight to 2 o'clock), I was already in bed. As I said before, I've moved my bed to the living room as it's more convenient for running into the basement.

It was quiet yesterday morning and we had a relatively normal day: seeing to the ward, operating and other chores. I went home for lunch earlier than usual. At about 12.15pm, the siren sounded again because of the Japanese military aircrafts' arrival. We had a few defences in place to fight off the attack. But this time, a small aircraft dived from high in the air as soon as the siren went off. There were two military aircraft above us, and they dropped many incendiary bombs, including one about one mile south of our house, which caused a fire for about 15 minutes before it was put out.

The siren didn't stop until 2.45pm. When I rushed back to the hospital, I found a lot of patients in the clinic. A young pilot had a mild injury and he looked very depressed. The optimism of yesterday had already passed into an atmosphere of increased depression and a feeling of impending doom. He said that although in the Nanking area, the Chinese were faring somewhat better than the Japanese, this was not the case in Shanghai. The Japanese antiaircraft fire had been catastrophic for the Chinese planes: many of their best aircraft had been shot down and 10 aircraft from Shanghai had been destroyed which were a gift for Generalissimo Chiang's birthday.

Bai Ruide made two visits in the late afternoon. One was a meeting in the Hsiakuan district where there was a pessimistic atmosphere. He then went to the Soviet embassy, but he found the same atmosphere there. People were frightened and believed that we would hear more enemy airstrikes before the night was over. But we were used to that.

When I was having supper, the siren sounded again. It had no effect on me apart from reducing my appetite. After dinner, I went to the porch with the cook to see the Chinese aircraft flying northwest from the airport. About half an hour later, they came back and began to land. It was almost twilight when it began to rain. The clouds were very low and we could see the blue sky between the gaps. Suddenly, we heard a muffled and ominous hum from the northeast. From my front porch, I could see the first plane, which was in a group of three. Then another three came and then a third group. They came straight for us and then turned south. When they were about half a mile away from us, we heard the sound of antiaircraft fire. Shells and small projectiles were firing like raindrops from the He Yingqin residence and the ministry of justice. The shells were very interesting to watch as you could see and distinguish the direction of their fire. Apparently, the shells had missed as the planes kept coming. When I saw the third group of aircraft, two large explosions shook the earth. Before I saw another three aircraft in a fourth group, I noticed that the explosion was behind me, so I quickly hid in the basement. I ran out when the sound of their motors weakened, and saw that there were two fires burning half a mile away to the east and the north of the house. The fire in the east was an armoury, which continued to burn for about 15 minutes.

An hour later, the sirens finally stopped and I rushed to the hospital, imagining it would be full of casualties. But no one came, so Brad, Max and I went into Max's house together to listen to the radio to find out the day's news. There was no electricity so the radio didn't work. We could only sit around a candle. But this didn't last very long as the siren soon sounded again. We blew out the candle, preparing to go to the shelter, where there was a concrete roof. We sat on the stairs of the shelter waiting for the siren forecasting the aircrafts' arrival. We waited for about 45 minutes, but the alarm stopped. Still without electricity, we could get no news from the outside world. Max advised me to sleep there, but I wasn't willing to do so.

This morning, we found that about 12 people were killed and many more wounded. This was a day full of operations and when I started the first surgeries of the real war. A foot amputation, a finger amputation, and a very strange trauma treatment. A girl in her late teens saw a bomb and crouched down with her back to the explosion. Her hip had almost shattered. We treated the trauma until the infection was cleared and performed a skin graft on her. A man who'd suffered from a broken leg died in the evening due to internal injuries.

While doing the foot amputation, the siren sounded again, but we continued to operate. After half an hour, the siren stopped as the enemy aeroplanes had failed to arrive in the city. Now all kinds of reports and rumours were spreading here and there. Chinese newspapers reported that four aircraft had been shot down. Several sources spread rumours that our planes wanted to avoid battle, which gave an opportunity for the antiaircraft guns to show what they could do. If that's true, I hope they don't give them another chance...

25 September

A terrible day today. Mrs Dai Laisan was doing a shortwave broadcast in English for the national central broadcasting station. You may have heard of her. She, Brad, and Lewis Smythe had dinner together here. We helped her to create tonight's broadcast's opening phrases, which went like this: "Today, civilians shed gallons of blood. Nanjing has suffered three terrible airstrikes."

After breakfast, I went downstairs to get some films. Two weeks ago, before I went to Guling and Hankou, I had left them in the store. When I was in the store, I heard the first sound of the siren, so I went on a bicycle in a hurry to Dick's comfortable shelter. Lewis Smythe and Dick had already arrived. Smythe was there to help us fix the car for emergency rescues. We saw 14 Chinese fighters flying across the river. They had recently seldom fought with the enemy because it would likely mean their entire destruction. After they left for a little while, the Japanese bombers came in droves and started bombing. Our forces started shooting at them and we had already arrived in the shelter by that point, which shook every time a bomb exploded. Many people saw a bomber crashing to the ground, burning in front of the Young Men's Christian Association (YMCA).

After the air strikes, we went to the hospital because it was my turn to be on duty for a carbuncle operation. Just as we were about to have lunch, another air strike began, and the enemy started bombing us more violently. This time we were told to go opposite the Jiangsu Bank on Zhongshan East Road. We saw that all the windows had been shattered, and many houses belonging to the poor had collapsed. Two people had been bombed and died at the entrance of the underground shelter, their bodies bloodied. I clambered over the debris of the room, and saw a person lying on the floor who had been killed by the building's central beam. He'd been dead for a long time as his chest had been completely pierced. When I climbed out of the debris, I found a group of people who had already left for the hospital, so I began to walk back there as well. The siren then sounded again. After running for a while, I thought I should go to the best shelter prepared by the embassy. I turned back and ran over, and I found that it was close to my own house, but the door had been locked. The Japanese aircraft were gliding in the sky. Bombs fell around like rain, causing widespread damage again. We could see the smoke from the antiaircraft guns, but no one could see where it was coming from. The siren just stopped, but another soon followed. However, the bombers failed to reach the city this time.

It was 5 o'clock. I went to the hospital to meet the director of the Central Hospital, Dr James Shen, to prepare to transfer their staff and patients to our hospital. I'd heard that 20 bombs had exploded near the hospital, destroying their kitchen, laundry room and water tank, not to mention shattering all the windows in the operating rooms. It had also killed their electrician, damaged two of their four ambulances, and had injured four workers. Fortunately, the doctors and nurses had not been injured, and the building was in good condition apart from the broken windows. Dr Shen had hurried back only to see all this suffering.

At 5.30pm, Brad, Lewis, Mrs Dai Laisan and I went home to have a meal together because we could assist in nursing the wounded and transferring the patients from the Central Hospital. They had done well. Dick drove his car to transport the patients. Pearl Buck had donated her car, but it was unavailable because it was locked in the Ford dealership. When we took it out, I acted as a driver in addition to the other jobs. After we checked about 10 of the wounded, we found it unnecessary to do any immediate surgery, so that I was able to return home to write this piece. We only had candlelight tonight because the airstrikes in the morning had caused slight damage to the power plant, which couldn't be fixed due to the frequent airstrikes. We still had no power supply tonight. There were 39 airstrikes and sirens.

Wilson continued writing his diary every day. His diaries were sent by his wife to friends in the press to be published in the American newspapers at the time. They told the truth about the Japanese invasion of China to the world, creating strong international repercussions. Today, I cannot help but feel a mix of emotions while reading Mr Wilson's valuable diaries. On the one hand, I found myself with a growing resentment for the Japanese atrocities, while on the other hand, my heart was filled with a strong sense of gratitude. I, of course, would like to show gratitude to our foreign friends like Wilson who helped us in the war. They cherished human life and had faith in God to do their sacred work to help aid the Chinese soldiers and civilians affected by the war. While doing so, they were also able to write down the details of life during the Japanese invasion so diligently.

There are many things we Chinese should learn from such international allies. It was also because of the presence of these international allies and their contributions that Japan, which has never admitted to its crimes, has never been able to really escape punishment.

Japanese right wing forces still do not agree on the fact that about 300,000 people were killed in the Nanjing Massacre. Instead, they have kept silent and refuse to even talk about the disaster and the casualties they caused while bombarding Nanjing for four months before the massacre.

It is still unknown how many civilians and soldiers were killed or wounded during the bombing of Nanjing. Nanjing was already thoroughly subjugated by 13 December and then the Japanese soldiers decided to massacre the entire city. As a result, the early losses and casualties are hard to estimate. However, according to investigations after the war, hundreds of Chinese people had been killed in the bombing campaign, and one fifth of the city's ancient buildings were damaged.

"On 25 September alone, the Japanese troops deployed 94 planes to bomb Nanjing which had almost no air defence forces, drowning the city in a sea of fire..." A famous expert from the Second Historical Archives of China then took out a thick stack of old photographs depicting the slaughter. Looking at the scene of the dead bodies, collapsed walls and bridges, it was impossible to not become angry.

However, the crimes committed by the Japanese invaders go far beyond that. The bombing was just a prelude to the Nanjing Massacre.

Savage Fighting on the Shanghai and Nanjing Front

After the Battle of Shanghai was lost on 12 November, the Japanese forces under Matsui and Yanagawa invaded Nanjing from two directions. The Yanagawa forces in the front arrived in Jiaxing from Hangzhou, and then moved directly to Changxing along the northern shore of Lake Tai. They then divided into two units: one unit marched to Nanjing via Yixing and Liyang while another team went around Guangde and Wuhu in Anhui, and then moved towards Nanjing from the Yangtze River gate. Matsui's troops marched from my homeland in Kunshan and Changshu to Suzhou and Wuxi, and then directly entered Wujin and Zhenjiang. The other unit used the Yangtze River waterway to allow the land army and naval ships to advance at the same time. Transferring the army through the Baimao gate and attacking Jiangyin Fortress were the key battles on the east Nanjing and Shanghai front, with great advances made.

As mentioned earlier, the distance between Shanghai and Nanjing is under 300km as the crow flies, which is actually the distance between the two city centres. The closest distance between the edges of the two cities is just 250km. After the loss at the Battle of Shanghai, only the Yangtze River, Lake Tai and natural ridges served as natural barriers for the battlefield as there were no steep mountains or steep forts in the beautiful Jiangnan waterside towns. Faced with the invaders, beautiful and affluent Jiangnan was like a vulnerable and naked mother forced to bear the suffering of being trampled upon and raped by the Japanese bandits.

When I was a child, my grandparents often told me about the crimes of the Japanese. At that time, my primary school was a house with only one side of a wall as the others had been bombed by the Japanese soldiers when they started the conflict at Baimao gate. My schoolmate, Jin Chongliang, said that his grandfather had been killed in that airstrike.

My grandmother had said: "The Japanese were incredibly ruthless back then. They imprisoned the men they encountered to help in building bridges and cooking meals, and grabbed the women to sleep with them." When the Japanese arrived in the area, she and my grandfather had just been married for three years. She hid in the reed marshes near the river with her sisters: "There were many villages here with a lot of people, and few places for shelter, so the Japanese soldiers could easily catch people. So we had to blacken our faces with coal ash. But there was no stopping the Japanese soldiers. They thought we were not old women so they took us to the river and threw us into the water to clearly see our faces. The Japanese killed my brother Xu Guangquan and his wife with a sword." I didn't know the people who my grandmother was talking about, but one of my relatives was the captain of a guerrilla unit and was captured by the Japanese in an attack along with dozens of soldiers. The Japanese army ordered them to help in paving roads and building bridges. After that, they were chained up one by one and thrown under the rudder of the warship. All of them drowned in the river. Other civilians who were unwilling to help them loot or find "beautiful girls" were force fed several bowls of chaff and a lot of water. When their stomachs were so full that they couldn't bear the pain, the Japanese soldiers would put them into bags and violently beat them. When they were half dead, they then killed them. They would throw them into the river.

The Japanese committed many crimes in my homeland, but the bloodiest ones were in Suzhou and a few other cities.

Chiang Kai-shek's government established three defensive lines between Shanghai and Nanjing. The first was to link a chain of defence from Suzhou in the centre to Changshu in the north and Jiaxing in the south. Yanagawa's division promptly occupied Jiaxing on 10 November. After Matsui's troops saw their conquests, they immediately decided to attack Suzhou. How could the beautiful but sorrowful Suzhou be forced to withstand such horrors at the hands of the Japanese invaders?

Blood Rains on Suzhou

The Japanese knew of Suzhou's reputation. Like Hangzhou, it was known by the nickname "Heaven on Earth", but it was also regarded as the "Venice of China", just 50km away from Shanghai. When the Japanese invaded China, the city already had railways and modern roads for transportation. In the 1930s, the city had a population of around 350,000 permanent residents. After the Chinese army retreated from Shanghai, Suzhou became a completely undefended bastion. On 19 November, the beautiful city was stormed by the Japanese invaders. But the Japanese had been concerned that the Chinese military would put up a heavy resistance, so they conducted several large-scale airstrikes before taking the city. The poor unarmed civilians of the city were left weak and unable to resist, and were slaughtered by the Japanese in a rain of blood.

"Many bombs were dropped from the sky, violently exploding. Limbs, dust, bricks and coal flew in the air like a cascade, which was a horrifying scene. The scene was so appalling and unbelievable that we dared not look and wanted to flee. The Japanese aircraft were hovering overhead the entire day, bringing down their gifts of death," wrote a foreign tourist, who was travelling in Suzhou and had been unable to leave.

A few days later, the Japanese still refused to enter the city, thinking that there was a Chinese army that had not been annihilated, so they used a plane to drop leaflets over the city, warning: "Three days from now, the city will be bombed again."

"Damn it! We'll die if we don't leave now!" The citizens panicked. All sorts of people, old and young, men and women, left in droves, carrying their few belongings, from the city where they had lived for so long. This miserable and helpless scene is difficult to imagine. They didn't have enough wagons, rickshaws or other vehicles, and some families even used buckets to cross the river, carrying their children and the elderly as they crossed the rivers and lakes. The Japanese fired behind them as they laughed.

Many citizens couldn't leave Suzhou and the Japanese had now surrounded the entire city. They bombed it heavily for 12 hours, and then swept the entire city. At that moment, Suzhou was like a naked, beautiful lady, torn apart by thousands of swords; she was a sight too miserable to see.

An American war reporter witnessed the scene as civilians fled to a famous temple in Guangfu:

I went to enter the city in the morning. The scenes of death and destruction we have witnessed cannot be described with any words. I felt great sorrow and sadness in my heart. A Chinese pastor led 1,000 refugees in flight to Guangfu, which was the only positive news. However, that too was a miserable scene. Little children, old men, old women, the lame and the disabled, wounded by bullets and bombs, stumbled along with the pastor, who reminded me of Christ himself. Within two days, 5,000 refugees had fled from Suzhou to Guangfu.

We finally realised that the church had been robbed, with the front door, side door and back door knocked down, while the doors of schools and residential buildings had apparently been smashed with axes and swords. Big and small doors were all damaged. All kinds of boxes had been searched. Anything that wasn't needed had been thrown away. The floor was in a mess, and in my house, all the cups and bowls had been smashed to pieces. In a friend's home, a religious icon on the floor had been damaged beyond repair [this was inevitable as the Japanese soldiers didn't care about the holy temple].

I later went to examine Yancheng Middle School. The Japanese soldiers didn't know that I was going to go there so suddenly, so I saw them in the school. They were struggling to open a safe, while a soldier was hacking at its door with a pickaxe, and several soldiers attempted to crush it completely. The other soldiers were moving around the principal and provosts' tables. When I went looking for an interpreter, they sneaked away.

The next morning, we went to Yancheng Middle School again, only to find that the safe had finally been opened by the Japanese soldiers, who took about 400 yuan. But very interestingly, the gangsters had thrown an envelope containing 300 yuan on the floor, probably thinking that it was useless. Meanwhile, as we saw in our inspections, the other safes in several churches, shops and banks had all been damaged by Japanese soldiers who stole everything.

The Japanese took the contents of the safes, and countless antique shops also suffered from the havoc of their looting. Since 200 or 300 years after the establishment of the Ming dynasty, Suzhou had been a Chinese economic centre, known all over the world, and it was a place where different famous scholars gathered. It contained large amounts of redwood furniture in its royal gardens and the houses of wealthy families. The greedy Japanese soldiers painstakingly packed all of this great redwood furniture onto their ships and took it back to Japan. But this wasn't enough for these thieves. They intended to conquer the Chinese and ruin them.

After the Japanese soldiers had occupied Suzhou, the first time I went back, I saw that the streets were covered with dead bodies, which stayed there for 10 days. The most detestable thing was that the Japanese soldiers had attacked women of all backgrounds. It was impossible to estimate how many women had been raped by the vicious Japanese soldiers. I knew of many instances of such crimes as I had received a reliable report. However, there was really no need for an estimate, as whether there were 9,500 or 9,600 rapes, it was still such a monstrously evil act. It made it no better. One morning, I met a student from Dongwu University in Guangfu, and he told me with tears in his eyes that the Japanese soldiers had raped his beautiful sister. I also saw many villagers, sitting and shivering on the sidewalk because a group of armed Japanese soldiers had thrown them out and taken their wives and daughters.

That night, a Chinese man begged me to stay at his home to protect his daughter and several refugee girls. I agreed. At 11 o'clock that night, I was woken up by a flashlight; a light shot into the house from the small window above the door. Someone whispered in my ear: "The Japanese soldiers are here." I rushed into the next room with a flashlight in my hand. I saw three Japanese soldiers shining a light on over a dozen girls on the floor. My appearance had startled them. When I scolded them, the soldiers rushed downstairs. In the urgency of the moment, the host didn't leave my side...

It was extraordinarily fortunate for the man to have met a foreign ally like this when the soldiers arrived. However, the vast majority of people in Suzhou didn't have such an ally. They would have to suffer from the Japanese army's brutality.

The city had become a killing field, and blood flowing in the streets blocked the sewers, spilling down the alleyways and streets over to the nearby fields and villages.

The paddy fields, which should have been harvested in the autumn, were trampled under Japanese boots and tanks. Villages were set alight, and the cattle and sheep who had lost their masters were slaughtered by the thieves. After they had their fill, the Japanese started to rape and loot once again. Thinking of Suzhou and the plight of my relatives fills me with great sadness.

Was there anything in the beautiful Jiangnan waterside towns that could defeat the invaders? It seemed not, until a torrential downpour began.

The Japanese soldiers were shivering in the cold rain, and their legs were stuck in the mud, unable to move. It looked like God was smiling on the Chinese people, helping them in their hour of need.

As I mentioned earlier, the terrain between Shanghai and Nanjing was almost entirely flat for about 300 kilometres. It would be very easy for the invaders to quickly reach the capital. In a war against such a powerful foe, the Chinese couldn't bear the idea of Nanjing falling to the Japanese. The Chinese had only just been able to resist the Japanese army in the cities and the rivers and lakes, like the Yangtze River and Lake Tai. The turbulent Yangtze River was flowing violently to the east, but the Chinese didn't have strong ships to fight on it. Instead, the Japanese ships went upstream to slaughter the innocent people on both sides of the river. But the Japanese were currently unaware that the waterside towns of Jiangnan had been drenched by continuous autumn rains, and the paths were covered with mud, making it hard for them to advance. It would originally have only taken them a week to arrive in Nanjing, but now, as if by divine intervention, it seemed impossible for them to do so.

Kojiro Saito, a soldier in the signalling squadron of the headquarters of the 65th wing of the Japanese infantry, was a new recruit enlisted in Fukushima Prefecture in Japan after the Battle of Shanghai broke out. This Japanese soldier was ordered to go to the front in China on 10 September 1937. After travelling for days on the sea, he arrived in south Jiangsu, my homeland. At that point, the Battle of Shanghai was intense and the Japanese infantry didn't have even one fortuitous day, be it safe from the rain or wind or terror. After the end of the Second Sino-Japanese War, some non-governmental pacifist volunteers organised a collection of war diaries written by veterans. Saito's family donated his war diaries, which recorded his involvement in the Battle of Shanghai and the assault on Nanjing, which made it possible for me to truly understand many of the scenes the Japanese infantry faced, spending bitter rainy autumn days in the regions south of the Yangtze River.

6 October was cloudy. Kojiro Saito went out to battle with the troops that night and experienced three air raids, which were the counterattacks by the Chinese air force. For the entire night, he felt hungry and dizzy and arrived at their destination at midnight. The destination had only been a little more than a couple of miles away but it was very muddy. Although he tilled the land in his hometown in Fukushima, he had never travelled on foot with a gun. Most of the Japanese soldiers were actually farmers who had only just started to use guns. Nevertheless, they had received military training. Decades ago, the Japanese government launched compulsory systematic military training for the public, especially for the youth and students. Saito marched near the town of Yanghang, which had been destroyed. It had a pervasive stink of corpses. Here, he first participated in an atrocity, killing more than 10 Chinese captives. "The water quality is quite bad because of cholera. Take care!" his commanding officer warned them. "We pitched tents at night and slept with our family photos," wrote Saito, who missed his family to the east across the sea as he looked at the picture with a flashlight.

7 October was rainy. Saito woke up at midnight because it was too cold. He took out and put on his coat, popped his head out of the tent and looked

around, only to be met with rain on his face. He couldn't help missing his family far away. He went out 'suppressing' with the other troops during the day, returned to the tent, dried his wet clothes and unconsciously felt a pang of weariness in his heart. "At night, the sound of shots swarmed my ears, the rain didn't stop and raindrops fell from the tents. The horses were in a poor state with their bodies wet all over," recorded Saito.

8 October was also rainy. Saito began the day with a grumble: "Damn fighting in the rain. I'll have to put up with this on the battlefield with the help of the phonograph I brought from Shanghai. There was an air raid at the front at night. The artillery roared and it was completely dark everywhere. I slept with my muddy boots and clothes on at night but woke up freezing at 11pm."

The explosions left piles of ruins. The Chinese were unwilling to give way to the Japanese bandits and it made Saito, a normal man, feel the difficulties of being in this foreign country. It continued to rain on 10 October. He wrote: "When I was on duty in the stable at midnight, the rain continued. Shells from heavy artillery guns roared, flying overhead and exploding in the distance." After being woken up by the sound of artillery, Saito went out of his tent in indignation and into the rain. He noted: "It rained the whole day today and the road was like a muddy field. Maybe the children back home are giddy with the happy festive air? How are my parents and wife? The sounds of rifles, machine guns and artillery went on ceaselessly at night. I don't know which division was attacking so furiously. The rain did not stop. The canals and ditches in the field have been filled with water. Amidst the intense sound of gunfire, I sang the Sendai ballad *Oh, A Shower of Rain* with Kamio and some others." These Japanese soldiers, who were seeking joy amidst the sorrow, seemed unaware of the pain they were inflicting on the people of my hometown.

It was cloudy the following day and Saito followed his troop to support another Japanese division. He wrote later: "The road was muddy with the mud coming above our knees. We went there by horse. On the way, I saw the corpses of Chinese soldiers everywhere and the stink made us turn away unconsciously. Many of our poor horses fell. The rural paths had been destroyed beyond all recognition by the war and it was a truly miserable sight."

On 18 October, Saito went through many more difficulties in the rain and had diarrhoea, his pains being too serious for him to bear. He began to complain and hate the Chinese while he shouldn't have complained or hated anyone at all. He wrote: "I felt most astonished by the bad water quality in China. There were no wells that were up to standard. The rain poured directly into incomplete wells. Unexpectedly, the Chinese who lacked drinking water were suffering!"

He was wrong. The water in my hometown had served my ancestors until the 1960s and 1970s. We continued to use well water as our drinking water, which was generally clean, sweet and refreshing. After the Japanese aggression, my grandparents told me that it was the Japanese invaders who had intentionally polluted and even poisoned our well water. Kojiro Saito was lucky to just have diarrhoea.

Ten days later, his diarrhoea stopped. On 29 October, it rained torrentially. "I went to the clinic at 9am. I had almost recovered mentally by then. It seemed to have been raining today. Having rain on the battlefield was most undesirable. It rained before I returned to our encampment. Before noon, I fixed the houses in the station because the roofs had been bombed and damaged by bullets so rain could get in. Most of the enemies seemed to have retreated and almost no shots could be heard. I heard that some people in the same village had died in battle and my friends had been wounded. I was speechless when I heard this news. Now, the wing commander and lieutenant also prepared to die in battle and commanded the soldiers at the front. The 65th wing was positioned in the training grounds of Chiang Kai-shek's teaching corps, which was a firm and rather large battlefield. The wing suffered the most losses. Many soldiers died in battle, being left in a miserable situation too horrible to look at. I feel for the families of the dead and the wounded." Saito did not know what to do.

It did not rain but it was cloudy on 30 October. The commanders waved their swords, wearing murderous expressions to try to infect the Japanese soldiers with their violence. But Saito felt depressed because he had: "Heard the news that senior aide Lieutenant Wing Commander Tetsujirō died in battle on the spot when he was shot in the head. In the battle, after 5pm on 29 October, the aide who had taken good care of us like a parent died, being a severe blow to the entire wing. The second aide's hand was wounded. The battalion chief's face had been injured. Most of the officers in the army had been wounded or shot. It was self-evident how hard the two armies had fought against each other. A total of more than 1,000 high-ranking officers and soldiers had lost their lives. The fates of the people from our neighbouring village was still unknown. Yoshida had been wounded in his left arm. The lively atmosphere of the day before had been destroyed by the death of the aide, which made us feel like infants having lost their mother. We immediately became quiet. Dr Aota took out a photo of a child to show everyone and said: 'You have children like this, you shouldn't die!' He forgot he'd said it in front of his superior officer. He could not help but weep. There was a fire in Shanghai at night and you could clearly see the violent explosions of the artillery."

Saito knew that although more than 1,000 of his comrades-in-arms had died, more than 10 times as many Chinese soldiers and non-combatants had died.

It rained even more heavily. Autumn rains like this are rarely seen in south Jiangsu. My grandfather said that the autumn rain was heavier that year because even heaven shed tears.

"It was cloudy again today," Saito Kojiro wrote forlornly. "Wing command has transferred to Liujiaxing, relieving a garrison, taking in the dead from the battle and settling on the battlefield along with other troops. I could not help crying after hearing the tales of the men at the front. The muddy waters in the trenches went up to their waists. If they were visible, they would be spotted by the enemy and shot violently with machine guns. If anyone fell down during the assaults at night, it was because they had fallen over the corpse of their comrade. The corpses of their comrades who had died in battle reeked and attracted flies. But one fierce battle went after another. Although we lamented their deaths, we had no time to bury these poor dead soldiers and asked them to hold out until we'd repelled the enemy as if they were alive. We clenched our teeth, gripped ours guns and shot fiercely at the enemy, trying to crush them. It seemed to have worked. Despite their firm positions, the stubbornly resisting enemy fell apart. I snapped a twig and rubbed away the mud on it to offer a sacrifice to our comrades-in-arms. I felt somewhat comforted as I cried for them."

The Chinese people would not feel any sympathy for Saito because their tears had already been dried by the Japanese bullets. Saito continued writing his war diaries: "With the explosion of artillery, flashes shone like thunderbolts in the dark sky. Amidst the flashes, the rain continued. The rain on the battlefield was cruel and ruthless. After the end of my shift at 2am, I went to sleep. The bombed-out roof let in a lot of rain. Turning on the lamp, I saw my comrades-in-arms happily dreaming. It rained all day today. Although I did rest, I felt tired. The soldiers on duty today marched in the muddy water in desperation. Stained with muddy water below their waists and walking in the heavy rain, they were soaked from head to toe."

On 12 November, the Japanese army had occupied Shanghai and the Chinese were evacuating from the city to the surrounding areas. It continued to rain.

Saito wrote: "Reports came to the signalling squadron one after another this morning. I received the news that the enemy were withdrawing from the front, the 11th division had arrived a kilometre away from Nanxiang and that the enemy was marching towards Jiading. The 65th wing was ordered to pursue and attack them. Large and small pieces of luggage from the headquarters would be soon sent as supplies. After breakfast, we needed to immediately return to Cai Ning's house to prepare to set off. We set off at 12.30, when it started to rain again. We didn't like the rain. We started out from the headquarters at 3pm. Soon afterwards, it rained again. We arrived at our destination about a mile away to the north of the town of Luodian. Other troops faced sudden attacks by enemy planes on the way there, which killed more than 10 soldiers and three horses. The rain continued to fall and it soon got dark. Marching on rainy days at night was most difficult of all. Tonight, the headquarters was transferred to Yangjiaqiao. We took up quarters in a stable, where we slept on straw with blankets thrown over. It was impossible to dry our trousers and this upset us. It was better to take off our wet jackets and put on woollen and cotton shirts. We fell asleep quickly due to tiredness but did not have the time to dream."

It was good that it rained then. Otherwise, the Japanese army would have rushed to Nanjing to arrest Chiang Kai-shek and occupy China.

The rain served as protection from their arson, killing and robbing.

It rained again on 17 November. Saito wrote: "We got up early in the morning and busied ourselves with preparing to set off. Since the signalling squad had left their luggage behind, we asked four Chinese people to take it. It rained yesterday and the roads were in bad condition. It was the toughest march since we had landed, walking along paths that were neither dry land nor paddy fields. We arrived at the Wang family's house, a short march east of Yangjiaqiao, as ordered. The Qian family's house was our destination today. It was about a mile away. We started out at 9am and arrived at 3pm. There was a stream in front of the Qian family's house and the bridge was very dangerous. Isao Shigeno's horse slipped on one side of the bridge and it jumped in panic. Its hoofs got stuck between the bridge planks and it fell over. It died miserably after fracturing its hind leg. The sad scene made us shed tears. A soldier in front of me also fell into the river when he tried to cross the bridge. It was my turn and I prayed to the gods and Buddha as I walked ahead. Thanks to their protection, I managed to cross safe and sound, although I was covered with cold sweat. I thanked the gods and the Buddha in my mind. After arriving at the Qian family's house, I wiped my sweat off and rubbed off the mud. I had vegetable miso soup for supper. We covered the floor of the earthen house with straw and I rested my tired body. It didn't rain heavily today and my jacket wasn't too wet, so I felt pretty good when I went to sleep. Since some Chinese people were staying nearby, we set up a sentry just in case. The evening skies seemed to improve. Might it be a better day tomorrow? We cannot bear the hardship of marching in the rain."

Despite Saito's wishes, the next day was terrible too.

18 November was as rainy as ever. Saito wrote: "We got up at 5am and got ready to set off. It rained today too. Would the ditches and trenches slow down our march and would the people and horses sweat like pigs in the rain again today, just like yesterday? Although it didn't rain heavily, the march was still slow. We started out at 8.30am and went through the paddy field and dry farmland – there was no path. But it was much better than yesterday when even the horses had felt exhausted. I almost lost sight of the friendly troops before noon. It felt incredibly lonely to be taking actions far away from the other troops in this enemy country. We marched on something that resembled a road with great difficulty at about 2pm and saw soldiers from the south marching. This was the 101st wing from Tokyo. I thought that my comrades-in-arms would be happy to see us. After marching for half a day, I could see them just a stone's throw away. It was very surprising. We crossed a bridge that had been badly burnt beyond all recognition due to the war. On the way, I saw a multitude of Chinese corpses. Had they been the soldiers resisting our army? It didn't seem like the fighting had been that fierce. The rice had been nearly all harvested and the wheat had been planted. The farmers who'd fled the conflict were returning with their belongings on their shoulders. Toddlers walked barefoot and with stuff on their shoulders. I couldn't help but cry. This was the miserable plight of the nationals of a defeated country." Kojiro Saito's tears showed that he was human among beasts. Many Japanese invaders covered up their crimes after the war and only a few Japanese people like Saito released their diaries on their own initiatives to atone for their crimes before history.

It continued to rain on 19 November. That day, Saito wrote: "I woke up suddenly during the night. Rain was pouring. I thought that it was going to be a rainy day again. With my eyes open, I thought about all my troubles but I eventually fell asleep again. I got up and made breakfast at 5am. I then adjusted my equipment and got ready to set off. The ominous weather grew worse and it rained again. I was worried about the march today while I washed my face. When I was preparing the saddle, Dr Aota commanded us not to leave since it had been raining and the horses were tired after two days of arduous marching. We all felt relieved. But we now didn't have enough supplies for the soldiers and horses. Out of contact with the others and unaware of the positions of the other troops, we didn't know how long our march would last. Thinking about it, we couldn't relax, despite deciding to stay, especially in this enemy country that was so different with a language barrier. Although some Chinese people wore cloth that read 'We welcome the soldiers of the Japanese Empire', we never truly believed it.

"I didn't know when disaster would rear its head. Getting supplies was the most urgent problem. Both in the morning and afternoon, our comrades-in-arms set out and collected things like rice, horse fodder and chickens. We had some sweet potatoes before lunch to restore some of our strength. It rained like the plum rains for the entire day and there was cold north wind. The pack horses trotted with difficulty, burdened with heavy equipment. Although their saddle sores had healed, they worsened again. The trees revealed the arrival of late autumn, covered with red autumnal leaves. As we were short on supplies, we planned to march to Tusong the next day. In the afternoon, only Misaki Sato and I were left; the others had all gone out to collect supplies. They found chickens, ducks and a bottle of Chinese liquor. Thank goodness. We enjoyed ourselves and there was no trace of the war at all tonight. After drinking the liquor, I should have forgotten everything and fallen fast asleep in a drunken state. But I couldn't sleep, thinking about the attacks of the previous days. As long as I was in this enemy land, even if it was just a farmer, I shouldn't let down my guard. I was on sentry duty between 11 and 12 pm." It was not uncommon for Japanese soldiers like Saito to fear retribution.

"Although it wasn't raining heavily, it was annoying to have rain every day. We were due to go to Tusong and walked half a day on the path along the fields. White flags were draped in each household along the way, which was a rare sight on the battlefield. In the afternoon, we walked on a new road and as it had rained every day, it was too muddy to walk on. We had to return to the old path. The planks on the bridge over the mud broke when we crossed and one horse got stuck in the mud and we could not pull it out. We had to push the bridge planks out and the horse down and then pulled at it again. At that moment, a unit of 30 to 40 cavalrymen, equipped with machine guns, came over to us. The acting sub-lieutenant leading the unit said: 'We've come to mop up the remnants of the enemy forces.' I didn't hear what he said afterwards clearly. It was cold today and I didn't sweat after the formidable march. The cotton leaves had fallen and the tips of the trees near the foundations had been blown off by the autumn wind. The weather was so drastically different after just a couple of miles north towards Cai Ning's house. We arrived at our destination in Tusong at 4pm and came across a cavalry unit, but it was not the Japanese army. It was a lonesome march.

"Not many Japanese troops would be in the town of Tusong. Even so, I hoped we would be able to make contact. After we arrived, we found that command had left on 18 November, so we felt frustrated. When Dr Aota and

Sergeant Igarashi gave us instructions during the evening roll call, they said that due to a lack of supplies, we had to eat soup every day, avoid any food waste and try our best to collect supplies. We couldn't get in touch with headquarters and the guide said the map for our march only showed Tusong and nothing beyond that so we didn't know where to go next. We looked at each other in speechless despair and frustration. We didn't know where our army was and we didn't have enough supplies. What's worse, three men fell ill (Fukuji Kanno, Isao Shigeno and the leader of the infantry squadron). Many Chinese people lived there so it was hard to say when we would come across danger. There were several different views. Some argued that we should move on and make contact but the horse feed had to be replenished; others proposed catching up with the rest of the battalion as soon as possible and that it would be dangerous otherwise. All in all, we needed to set out before 8am tomorrow. After covering the horse manure-dotted ground with straw and stretching my tired legs, I fell asleep."

Saito then dreamed of Changshu, Suzhou, my hometown in China.

He continued to write: "The weather and road conditions are perfect for marching. But without a map at hand and without knowing the whereabouts of the troops, we don't know where to go next. We had to advance with the help of a compass and the footprints of the previous troops and horses. I felt so alone in the march. We heard some rifle shots on the way and stopped advancing out of fear that remnants of the enemy forces were ahead. An infantryman went ahead to find out more information. It turned out to be a friendly unit. We continued moving on safely. We went more than 500 metres from Tusong and arrived at the Shanghai-Nanjing thoroughfare where we then advanced towards the northwest. On the way, the corpses of the Chinese were scattered everywhere. Their houses on the side of the road had been burnt beyond recognition. At 3pm, we arrived in Baiyuan through the town of Zhitang and camped there. We saw marching troops, military vehicles, gun carriers and antiaircraft guns passing by on the road. The melancholy, lonely mood we'd had when we started out earlier vanished immediately."

Kojiro Saito felt happy but the people of China suffered tremendously.

He wrote: "During our march from Tusong, the commoners' houses on both sides of the Shanghai-Nanjing thoroughfare had been almost all burnt down and Baiyuan had been destroyed and burnt. The fire spread east in the wind. Today, two houses to the north of the commoner's house in which we'd camped continued to burn fiercely. How cruel this war was! I think it would have been hard to believe it if I hadn't fought in the war myself." Many Japanese soldiers in the war like Kojiro Saito recognised that their aggression brought great hardships for the Chinese people. But how many Japanese remember the crimes they committed to this day?

It rained heavily on 27 November. Kojiro Saito and several others carried their butcher's knives and assaulted the picturesque Chinese countryside: "When we passed the village of Guli, we saw evidence of fierce fighting, and trenches, forts and the enemy's guns dotted across the river. We also saw 17 or 18 armed young people who'd died in battle. The enemy's corpses were scattered here and there. The commoners' houses and bridges had been burnt down and it was all unrecognisable, leaving just a miserable view of death. We arrived in Changshu at 4pm. The streets had been fairly busy before but now only the Japanese military officers, soldiers and horses were there. We camped there."

It continued to rain heavily amidst the clouds.

But the invaders didn't stop their advance. After they left Suzhou, they moved towards Wuxi and Zhenjiang again, with the target being the capital, Nanjing. The other group of Japanese soldiers marched along the west bank of Lake Tai, extending their aggression towards Changxing and Guangde, attempting to surround and crush the defensive army in the capital.

The General Makes a Sacrifice

After occupying Jiaxing, Yanagawa's army rapidly advanced to the second defensive line in Changxing, southwest of Lake Tai. After Changxing fell, they advanced to the third defensive line, which was also the last border southwest of Nanjing. Obviously once Guangde and Wuhu were lost, Nanjing was to be attacked from the back.

The Chinese defenders in Changxing were under the command of Liu Xiang's division, who had walked over 2,000 miles to arrive there. Matsui knew that the cities occupied by his southwest division were outside of the national defensive line established by Chiang Kai-shek. Guangde was in Anhui, Si'an was in Zhejiang, and Changxing was in Jiangsu at the time. All of them were located west of Lake Tai and south of Nanjing. If his army advanced rapidly to take Wuhu behind Nanjing, they would be able to isolate the Nanjing garrison army so that the Japanese army could easily occupy the capital. Therefore, Matsui ordered Hisao Tani to lead two divisions to march from Wuxing south of Lake Tai, and also ordered Ushijima to lead the 18th division to move over Lake Tai, attacking the positions of the Chinese Sichuan soldiers who had just arrived. They attempted to occupy Changxing, Yixing and then Guangde, and finally occupied Wuhu to thoroughly block Nanjing's defenders from retreating.

The Decisive Battle Before the Massacre | 73

When Yanagawa's forces took Jiaxing and moved to Wuxing, Chiang Kai-shek had already realised that crisis would soon be upon Nanjing, so he immediately ordered the military commission to establish the seventh war zone, and appointed the leader of the Sichuan army Liu Xiang, the commander-in-chief, to direct the 23rd army in the eastern area of Wuhu, in order to distract and hold back the enemy forces attempting to attack Nanjing from Lake Tai.

On 23 November, the 145th division commander Rao Guohua led his army along with the 23rd army to arrive at Xuancheng. He knew the situation: about three Japanese enemy divisions had occupied Wuxing, and Hisao Tani was rapidly advancing with two divisions along the Nanjing-Hangzhou road to Changxing. As Nanjing was the capital at the time, this highway was known as the Jinghang Road (Nanjing-Hangzhou). Ushijima's regiment, which had occupied Suzhou, was robbing civilians of their ships to advance to the Dongting mountain region near Lake Tai, aiming to attack Yixing over the lake. The 23rd army leadership, led by Liu Xiang, considered the various aspects of the situation and quickly made the deployment plans below.

Guo Xunqi would lead the 144th division to tenaciously defend the area around the village of Jiapujin north of Changxing and the east bank of Lake Tai, monitoring the movements of the enemy in the Dongting mountains in Lake Tai in case they attacked behind the Chinese positions. An army unit was ordered to support the 146th division in Changxing and Xintang to jointly resist the enemy from Wuxing. Liu Zhaoli commanded the 146th division to defend Xintang and Lixian south of Changxing, and to keep in contact with the 144th division to the left, and the 148th division in the south of Changxing to the right. Chen Wanren led the 148th division to protect the southwest of Changxing, along the Rainbow bridge to the Lincheng line, and was to keep in contact with the 146th division to the left, and the 145th division to the right who defended Si'an and Jiepai. The 14th Independent Brigade organised a defence from the north of Lixian town to Lincheng, and was to fight along with the 146th and the 148th divisions. Yang Guozhen led the 147th division to be stationed in White Rock by Mount Emei and the Yellow River as reserves, and was to cooperate with the other friendly armies in fighting when required. The 13th Independent Brigade was stationed at the northern shore of the Mei river to the central region of Si'an, and made sure to keep contact with the 145th division. Rao Guohua's 145th division organised a defence in upper Si'an, middle Si'an and lower Si'an along the Changxing-Guangde highway to keep the airports and warehouses safe.

Guangde was key to the southern battlefield as once Guangde was lost,

Wuhu would fall to the Japanese. Si'an was a strategic position fought over by the Japanese and Chinese armies. Defending Si'an meant the security of four places: Wuxing, Yixing, Changxing and Guangde. Guangde and Si'an were defended by the 145th division, so Rao Guohua was bearing the most important and difficult task in the southern battlefield. They were the most successful forces in the fight against the Japanese army.

"I received orders to defend Sichuan, to annihilate powerful enemies, to restore our nation and rescue our compatriots from their suffering," Rao Guohua said to his aide-de-camp. "Fortunately, we were the first to be sent to the front line against the enemy, which made my blood boil and encouraged our soldiers to fight, itching to go." The Sichuan general was born into a poor family and joined the National Revolutionary Army at the age of 17 and fought in the north and south along with troops who had crusaded against Yuan Shikai. He was promoted from soldier to platoon leader, to sergeant, to battalion leader, to regiment commander, to brigade commander and then to division commander. The famous general was held in high esteem by Liu Xiang.

After the Marco Polo Bridge Incident, He Yingqin failed to raise an army in Chongqing, making the anti-Japanese war even more complex. With the changes in the situation of the war, Rao's request to fight on the front had been a foregone conclusion. In early September, Rao led his division along with Liu Xiang's 300,000 troops and left Sichuan to fight in the anti-Japanese war. From that day on, Rao had vowed to crush the Japanese army. On the way out of Sichuan, when the troops arrived in Maoyang, Rao went home to visit his old mother. The humble Rao had decided to celebrate his 70 year old mother's birthday, and swept his ancestors' tombs to pay his respects. When he left, he told his teacher Mr Wu Jun: "I now go to fight in the anti-Japanese war, for victory or death." At that point, his wife and five children were in their hometown. He said goodbye to them without hesitation, and led the army, wearing sandals, to walk more than 2,000 kilometres to reach the frontline.

As the 23rd army prepared for deployment, Guangde and Si'an, where the 145th division was stationed, were located to the right flank of the entire army, so their location was very important. However, there were no steep positions that would be useful for defence there due to its flat relief. Having just arrived at a waterside town south of Lake Tai, Rao felt the weight of his heavy responsibility. The deputy army commander Pan Wenhua directly ordered Rao: "Even if only a single soldier is left, you must stay put."

Rao firmly replied: "As long as I live, the battlefield will be secure."

Before the 145th division arrived in Guangde, it was the 11th division of the central army that was stationed there. When Rao received his orders, the 145th division, rushing to battle, had no machine guns and only a few small artillery guns. Most of the officers and soldiers were armed with old Mauser rifles and Hanyang 88s from the Qing Dynasty, and some soldiers even carried guns made in Sichuan, which were in such bad condition it was difficult to reload even if they'd had dozens of rounds of ammunition. Sichuan soldiers wore traditional bamboo hats and thin clothes with straw sandals, and they could hardly be called a decent army. After a long journey of thousands of miles, many of the soldiers' feet were bleeding, suffering from unbearable pain. In November, the south was very wet and cold, so the Sichuan soldiers chewed dried chilli they'd taken with them to resist the cold.

However, the 11th division of the central army, although having just routed from the front lines of the Battle of Shanghai, were wearing yellow and green military winter uniforms and black rubber shoes distributed by the military. They were also armed with German equipment. The 11th division commander Peng Shan couldn't bear to look at his friend's army, which was in such poor condition, and he ordered his quartermaster to give them some of the spare equipment from his division as soon as possible, as well as asking if they could spare some of the previously captured Japanese weapons to donate to their comrades from Sichuan. Rao was extraordinarily grateful. However, the 145th division soldiers saw the central army armed with German made rifles, machine guns and artillery, and how they were still defeated by the Japanese, and inevitably whispered: "If even the central army can't defeat the Japanese, it'll be impossible for us to win with our broken equipment."

"The chairman and commander-in-chief has ordered us to fight in the battle. Don't complain. We can complain after we defeat the enemy. The Japanese are not made of steel. Although our guns may not be advanced, our bullets will still kill them!" Rao said loudly after hearing their complaints. Then he took a brush to write down several characters on a piece of paper: "If we win, we live; if defeated, we die". He raised it high in front of the assembly and shouted with his eyes wide: "Are you brave enough to do this and fight against the enemy? Do you have it in you?"

"Yes!" All the Sichuan soldiers were full of passion and excitement.

"Good boys! Good!" Rao smiled.

At 3 o'clock in the afternoon on 26 November, the 435th brigade of the 145th division, which had been stationed around the Si'an area, suddenly noticed about 200 Japanese cavalry appearing on the battlefield, some holding carbines, some with handguns, charging from the east to the west about 600 metres in front of their lines. They occasionally fired, and when the Chinese fought back, they would escape quickly in different directions. On the same day, other divisions also encountered a small Japanese army. When the Sichuan army opened fire in response, the Japanese immediately retreated. It seemed that they were on scouting missions.

Rao realised that a great battle was on its way, so he ordered his troops to stay alert. In the evening, the army senior staff gathered all the divisions and brigades to negotiate the operation plans, and then predicted that the battle would start on 27 November.

At dawn on 27 November, the Japanese army indeed sent 10 planes to take turns bombing the position of Liu Xiang's Sichuan army. Then, Japanese foot soldiers, with the help of tanks, separately attacked their positions. The 146th division was defending the Nanjing-Hangzhou highway, which was the main obstacle for the enemy. The Japanese had failed yesterday and ferociously returned today.

"Just keep calm! Let the Japanese army think we lack the strength to fight and retreat." Division commander Liu Zhaoli, noticing the Japanese army's frenzied advance to Chinese positions, deliberately ordered soldiers to pretend to be defeated and flee to lure the Japanese into a trap that had been prepared in advance.

"Advance!" the Japanese commander, sword in hand, commanded his army to march on.

Division commander Liu Zhaoli shouted from the Chinese battle positions: "Open fire!" Many guns suddenly started to open fire on the enemy in unison.

Faced with the deafening sound, the Japanese army was reduced to chaos, with tanks and soldiers clustered together. At this point, the 146th division ordered the 875th and 876th regiments, hidden on both sides of the road in advance, to quickly attack the enemy. Suddenly, heavy machine gun fire, rifle fire and grenades were launched towards the enemy's positions, blowing them to bloody smithereens in the smoke.

The Japanese army had suffered a great defeat and they finally managed to retreat from the trap with air support. The 146th division had captured six Japanese soldiers, destroyed three tanks, four artillery guns, nine armoured cars, and had taken three mountain guns, one field artillery gun, 89 rifles, two machine guns and 17 army flags, with over 300 other supplies. Rao Guohua was incredibly happy with the success.

On the same day, another group of Japanese soldiers attacked Si'an. This time, they changed strategies to destroy Chinese fortifications first, and then Rao's position was attacked by thousands upon thousands of tonnes of shells.

The newly built fortifications were destroyed and many soldiers were killed. The Japanese army was well-pleased.

The Si'an positions were divided into three parts: upper Si'an, central Si'an and lower Si'an. The central Si'an and lower Si'an positions were defended by two regiments from the Meng Haoran brigade in Rao Guohua's division. But because the brigade had suffered many casualties in fighting against the Japanese army, brigadier Meng Haoran urgently asked Rao to move Tong Yi's 433rd brigade to the front to relieve them.

Rao agreed and ordered the Tong Yi brigade to move at full speed. Unfortunately, the Japanese army was determined to occupy central Si'an and lower Si'an in a single day, so the 433rd brigade was attacked by nearly 6,000 Japanese soldiers with air support when they had just arrived in the battle positions. Central Si'an and lower Si'an were lost.

At that point, the 144th division, which was garrisoned on the west bank of Lake Tai as the left wing of the entire army, had also fought against Ushijima's 18th division. The Japanese army sent planes to bombard the 144th division, and at the same time, they secretly used a dozen boats full of soldiers as well as many motorboats to cross Lake Tai to attack Chinese positions. Division commander Guo Xunqi decided that the officers and soldiers garrisoned along the lake should try to delay the Japanese forces on the lake, but the soldiers were attacked by the Japanese planes and suffered a great defeat. Guo Xunqi was almost captured by the enemy, but fortunately, the positions were not lost.

On 28 November, the Japanese 18th division vanguard commander thought that the Sichuan army couldn't recover from the previous day's fighting and was preparing to strike again. However, they didn't expect to be attacked by the Sichuan soldiers at dawn as gunfire surrounded them.

"Shit!" The Japanese commander burst into a fit of anger, waving his sword, having almost been killed by the Chinese army. When Hisao Tani, the butcher of the Nanjing Massacre, heard that their elite troops had been besieged, he sent an additional 20 planes to relieve them.

Ushijima's division also suffered great losses at Lake Tai and he almost lost his vanguard troops. The Japanese army was outraged about this and decided to take revenge on the Sichuan army who they considered to be mere farmers.

On the morning of 29 November, the Japanese army, with the help of their planes in the air, and tanks, artillery and light machine guns at the front, attacked the Sichuan army's positions from every direction. About 10,000 soldiers from the two armies fought in Si'an, which was a fierce battle with hand to hand fighting. During the battle, the division commander Rao

Guohua rushed into the battle to fight the enemy but was shot in the stomach and forced to retreat.

By 2 o'clock in the afternoon, upper Si'an, central Si'an and lower Si'an positions were lost one by one. At that point, the main Japanese army was moving directly towards Guangde along the Wujia highway. "Never allow the enemy to reach Guangde!", the wounded Rao was incredibly worried and rushed to about five miles in front of Guangde to organise the defence and wait for the enemy.

"This is the last position held by our division!" Rao had hoped for reinforcements, but had heard that other places had already been lost, with Guangde being the final frontier of the entire 145th division. The autumn night on Lake Tai was bitterly cold and windy. Rao and his colleagues didn't lose heart and were instead full of passion.

While inspecting the position, Rao said to his soldiers: "Our country trains its soldiers to protect the country and our people. People may die, some with a death heavier than Mount Tai while others die as light as a feather. Now it's time for us to repay our country, by defending it and being dedicated to the struggle for the interests of our country's people. If the position is secure, we live; if the position is lost, we die. I hope we do everything we can to protect our country and fulfil our duties. To win is to live; to fail is to die. Never bend our knees before the enemy, and never lose face. We shall never be afraid of death, willing to sacrifice ourselves and fulfil our duties."

At dawn on 30 November, the Japanese army suddenly appeared in front of Rao's 145th division with the momentum of an avalanche.

In the face of the fierce offensive, the 145th division collapsed in chaos. Rao Guohua, eager and furious, had risked his life to lead about 20 artillery soldiers to monitor the battle hundreds of metres away from the enemy, but the battle was still being lost.

Rao was forced to lead his division in retreat to a place called Cishan Gang, which was located in Guangde.

The outcome of the battle was obvious. Rao Guohua looked at what was left, just a few soldiers, still shouting: "We're all soldiers from Sichuan. We will live together and die together. Today, it's time for us to sacrifice ourselves for our country. If you're real soldiers, you'll shed your last drop of blood to fight against the Japanese army!"

The soldiers passionately replied: "We'll fight with the commander until no blood beats in our hearts!"

The Japanese army quickly advanced to Rao's positions and surrounded them at Shizipu. Suddenly, the enemy stopped. This was because after fighting for so many days, Hisao Tani respected Rao. He ordered his soldiers not to approach Rao, but to persuade him to give in.

"You must be joking. I, Rao Guohua, am a real Chinese soldier. My name is Guohua, and it means that I will never do anything to humiliate my country."

Rao, surrounded by the enemy, calmly told his soldiers to stretch their blankets on the bloodied ground. He then sat in the middle of the blanket, looking up to the sky: a wonderful night sky with a waning moon.

Many thoughts and feelings must have been rushing through his head. Why was China being ravaged by such a small country? The enemy was approaching, and the light of their swords was shining.

"General, if you put down your gun, you will be forgiven!" a Japanese soldier said in broken Chinese. "Put down my gun? And admit defeat?" Rao laughed coldly, and replied loudly: "Others were strong too but they also failed. You, small Japan, will die in the future."

Then, Rao glared angrily at the enemy, and suddenly pulled out his gun, pointing it to his head. Bang! The sound of the gun echoed in the night sky for an eternity.

The vast Lake Tai's waters seemed to ripple with a sadness at the time of his death: 2am, 1 December 1937. The famous patriotic general Rao Guohua had shot himself surrounded by the Japanese at the age of 43.

Rao Guohua's body was transported by the people of the Minsheng company back to Sichuan. On 12 December 1937, when Nanjing was occupied, Rao Guohua's body arrived in Chongqing. The Chongqing national government held a grand ceremony for him, and Chiang Kai-shek personally composed a memorial poem:

> *The enemies are frenzied, hearing drums for the brave generals; the capital needs defending, swords and arrows may still gain outstanding achievements.*
> *I fight with ambition, to defend our country and our people; full of benevolence in my heart, I will fulfil my duty, alive with reputation but dead with grief.*

The national government also posthumously awarded Rao Guohua the rank of general. But would this have been of any relief to the general? Would this save China, which had lost many of its mountains and lands, and was on the verge of total collapse?

I was once on a business trip to Chongqing and Chengdu. Someone had heard that I was writing about the Nanjing Massacre and came over to chat to me. His father had been one of the Sichuan soldiers that supported Nanjing against the Japanese army. "Mr He, there's a phrase used in mahjong in Sichuan: 'fight to the last drop of blood'. Do you know where it comes from?"

People from Sichuan are famous all over China for their skill in playing mahjong, but I had no idea about the origin of the phrase. "It originates from when we Sichuan people ran to Nanjing to fight."

"Really?" I was very surprised.

"Of course!" The Sichuan soldier's son then proudly said:

"When my father was alive, he often told me that Liu Xiang had persuaded them to go to Wuhu, Anhui Province, to fight against the Japanese, and it caused many casualties. These Sichuan soldiers had never fought in battle, and when the Japanese army opened fire, they were terrified and fled. Their officers were reprimanded severely by Liu Xiang, saying that they shouldn't allow themselves to be humiliated in Nanjing and not to lose face in front of the Japanese. Even if they were under fire from artillery shells and machine guns, they had to hold their positions. They could never lose face in front of the Japanese. The officers tried their best, but they didn't have any good ideas. However, someone did have a bad idea: 'I used to keep cattle on the landlord's estate. To make sure they didn't run away, I locked up their legs with chains so they did whatever you wanted.' An officer thought this was a good idea, so he sent someone to ask the local blacksmith for vast numbers of chains and used them to shackle all of the Sichuan soldiers' legs. The Japanese army began to attack with artillery and machine guns, blowing plants, stones and mud into smithereens overhead. But the Sichuan soldiers didn't run away and held their positions. The Japanese army was later defeated with scores of dead bodies surrounding the position.

"The commanders of Yanagawa's 10th regiment were confused. Were there communists in Liu Xiang's army? After a reconnaissance survey, they concluded that there were no communists in the army and the Japanese army commander ordered the armoured combat vehicles to assemble. More than 20 tanks, with artillery and aerial support, savagely bombarded the Sichuan army's position. The Japanese commander looked through the telescope and clearly saw the soldiers being killed one after another, but these officers and soldiers, even when decapitated, remained unmoved and orderly in the trenches, stood still neatly. The Japanese army was stunned. They sent death squads to storm the trench and found that the headless soldiers had had their legs chained.

"A Japanese translator asked a dying Sichuan soldier: 'Why are you chained up?'

"The Sichuan soldier stared at the Japanese translator, and said: 'We fight till the last drop of blood!'"

This was the origin of the phrase "fighting to the last drop of blood". Sichuanese people now use it in mahjong, showing disrespect to their ancestors somewhat. After I told this story to the people of Nanjing, several old men said that the Sichuan soldiers had shown incredible bravery in defending the peripheries of the Nanjing battlefield and many people had died.

Despite this, in December 1937, Nanjing was at risk of falling to the enemy. The war had turned Purple Mountain and the Yangtze River blood red.

Jiangyin Is Lost

Only Jiangyin Fortress in the area surrounding Nanjing could hold off the enemy, or so at least Chiang Kai-shek thought. As did the Japanese commander Matsui. A fierce fight looked to be descending upon Jiangyin Fortress.

Before the establishment of the PRC, Jiangyin had been under the jurisdiction of Suzhou, so it was also in my homeland. It's located near Changshu, and my father often took me to Jiangyin to see the river there when I was a child. This was the narrowest and the most dangerous point along the Yangtze River downstream of Nanjing, and was also where Jiangyin Fortress was located, the gateway to the waterway to Nanjing.

The Yangtze River flowed upstream from the Wusong gate. If you looked across the river in Nantong, Taicang or Changshu, you'd be forgiven for thinking it was a sea. As the river there is more than a dozen miles wide, it's hard to see the other side from the bank. I often saw the Yangtze River in my homeland, so when I went to the Sichuan and Chongqing areas of the Yangtze as a soldier, I thought that there was no way that it was the Yangtze River; it was the size of the small river in front of my house!

In this area, only the Jiangyin section of the Yangtze River was narrow. Here the river was thin with fast-flowing currents, forming a natural barrier in the great river's downstream along with Wolf Mountain and Fushan in Jiangyin. The small mountains of Huangshan and Junshan tightly locked the river like two iron clamps, forming a rare and solid natural downstream fortress. This position not only allowed for the Chinese to prevent the enemy from escaping, but it also prevented the enemy forces from attacking downstream targets.

On the night of the Battle of Shanghai, it was rumoured that five Japanese warships and dozens of merchant ships carrying supplies were in the river around the Wuhan area upstream of Nanjing. Chiang Kai-shek immediately ordered He Yingqin in secret to send troops to the southern fortress to prevent the enemy ships from fleeing downstream and put an end to their plans of joining the Japanese forces in Shanghai. Unfortunately, the secret military meeting records were stolen by Wang Jingwei's personal secretary and the traitor, Huang Jun, told the Japanese ambassador in China of the plans. On the morning of 13 August, under the orders of the admiralty, the 1st fleet commander Chen Jiliang led more than 10 ships, including the *Pinghai*, *Hairong*, and *Haichou*, to the Jiangyin section of the Yangtze. Suddenly, black fumes could be seen upstream through the fog. After a little while, it was clear that a ship called the *Hachiyama* was leading five Japanese warships and several merchant ships full speed towards Shanghai.

"Oh my God! It's the Japanese fleet! What's the matter? Are we attacking or not? Don't let them get away!" The Chinese naval officers and soldiers were extremely worried as they had left Nanjing in the middle of the night the day before for Jiangyin Fortress to prevent any fleeing enemy forces upstream from escaping. Now the Japanese ships had arrived earlier than expected while the Chinese fleet was still making its way to the Chinese military stronghold.

"Commander Chen, what do we do? Do we attack or not?" Every ship's commander went to ask Chen Jiliang for advice.

However, Chen Jiliang was also confused. The Chinese fleet's mission had been to prevent the Japanese fleets upstream from escaping. How could they have arrived before his fleet?

"Contact the headquarters in Nanjing immediately. Quickly now!" Chen Jiliang rushed into the communications room and ordered the communication officers to contact the Nanjing military commission over radio.

"What? The Japanese fleet has arrived in Jiangyin? How could they be so fast? Who leaked our military secrets? Kill whoever's responsible!" A sense of panic hung in the air as no one knew what to do. The military commission finally transferred the phone to He Yingqin, who angrily barked: "Block them off! Destroy all their ships! Don't let a single ship in the fleet escape!" Chen weakly replied: "Chief He, the Japanese fleet slipped away from us an hour ago."

"Why didn't you give the order to attack them? Why not?!" He Yingqin jumped out of bed, shouting at Chen Jiliang over the phone.

"I know, I know, but I didn't receive any orders!" Chen Jiliang replied as his voice trembled.

The Japanese ships that should have been intercepted and quickly destroyed joined the land, sea and air forces after they arrived in Shanghai, playing a vital role in the battle. This had been the only chance for Jiangyin Fortress to be used to defeat the Japanese.

After that, the Jiangyin Fortress was in a state of constant passive defensive resistance for three months, with only two tasks. One was to rally all the naval forces there to prevent the Japanese navy from attacking Nanjing. The second was, with the help of more than 100 artillery guns in the fort, for several divisions that had been transferred from Guizhou and other areas to defend both sides of the river, painstakingly blockading the Japanese naval forces on the river.

Defending Jiangyin Fortress was of paramount importance. If lost, Nanjing would be exposed and its survival near impossible.

Chiang and He Yingqin were very clear about the importance of the fortress. Therefore, during the Battle of Shanghai, preparing the defences in Jiangyin was high on the agenda and they established an office to prepare the defences with Liu Xiang as its commander-in-chief. He was also responsible for the original Jiangyin Fortress department, which controlled the artillery units at eight forts on both sides of the river. The development of the defences was also the responsibility of the 57th regiment, the 111th division, the 112th division and the 103rd division led by He Zhizhong, which were respectively stationed along both sides of the river as garrison forces. Later, as Wuxi lacked troops, the 111th division was transferred there for support. A third force with more than a dozen ships that the national government had bought from Germany with almost the entire national budget was also stationed there to fight against Japanese ships on the river.

"Jiangyin Fortress is our home! Jiangyin is where we belong! Brothers, this is why we must be ready to give our lives for Jiangyin!" Xu Kang, the Jiangyin Fortress commander, yelled at his soldiers as he usually did. Now, faced with the coming Japanese siege, his voice was hoarse from shouting.

The fortress's readiness for combat seemed to have been carefully prepared and the project construction team had been dispatched by the chiefs of staff. Before the Battle of Shanghai, the military department had bought eight dual-purpose semi-automatic guns from Germany, with them being deployed on Dongshan Mountain and Xiaoshan Mountain. These guns were dubbed "jia guns" (or alpha guns) in China, with a 9km range in elevated antiaircraft mode and a 14.5km range firing horizontally. They were considered some of the most advanced weapons in the world at the time. China imported a total of 20 from Germany, and Jiangyin alone was equipped with eight.

At this point, it might be going a bit over the top to say that the defences at Jiangyin Fortress were foolproof or impregnable, but there was no doubt that they'd been carefully and comprehensively planned out. Passionate soldiers chanted on the riverbanks: "Stay with the fortress!"

Seven warships - the *Tongji, Datong, Ziqiang, Desheng, Weisheng, Wusheng* and *Lisheng* - had been fighting against the surrounding Japanese and were ordered to scuttle their ships without any prior notice. The officers were outraged and several more senior crew members spoke out too: "We're not even going to fight the Japanese? We're just going to sink and drown ourselves in the river? Are they insane?!"

There was no other choice as the capital was in imminent danger of being besieged by Japanese warships, even against the current. They needed to stop the Japanese from advancing up the Yangtze.

The ships began to sink, the *Tongji, Datong* and *Ziqiang*, one by one, followed by the *Desheng, Weisheng, Wusheng* and *Lisheng*. They all sank without a fight.

"Who gave this damned order? He ought to be tried for this under martial law!" Chiang was livid after He Yingqin reported that the *Desheng, Weisheng* and other warships had sunk in Jiangyin. However, the decision to block the Japanese warships by scuttling the seven Chinese ships had actually been approved by Chiang Kai-shek. However, as the generalissimo of China, the loss of the warships weighed heavily on his mind. The seven ships had not achieved their purpose of sealing off the rapid-flowing river. The military immediately came to help by transferring commercial ships, such as the *Ningxing* and *Waking Lion*. At the same time, the *Haiqi, Haishen* and other military vessels were scuttled together in the river.

"It isn't working!" General Zeng Yiding, the commander of the 2nd naval fleet, found that after having scuttled so many warships and merchant ships, they had still been unable to block the water route. He was incredibly anxious having failed to find any sort of solution and had to hurriedly seek help from local officials.

"Are there any other vessels?" Zeng asked the magistrates in Jiangyin. They replied: "There are hundreds of salt transportation ships of different sizes moored in the Yizheng County port. It's the distribution centre for Huai salt, and Anhui, Jiangxi, Hubei, Hunan and other provinces transport their salt from there."

"Well, take me there right now!" Hearing this, he felt a flicker of hope.

The next day, two commissioners were sent to arrange the transportation of the ships. They called Ge Kexin, the head of Yizheng County: "Wait for us at the salt harbour." At that point, Ge was extremely busy and tried to refuse when he was asked to immediately commandeer the civilian vessels in the port, but the commissioners attacked him: "If you dare to refuse this military order, you risk being beheaded!" Ge could see no way out and went to the port. People in the county had no idea about what was going on and spent the night preparing their ships for the commissioners. All of the boats were owned by people who had families to support, so taking their ships created a hysterical atmosphere with the elderly yelling, children crying and women cursing. Ge still successfully completed the daunting task of seizing more than 130 boats.

A few days later, all of these civilian ships were filled with cement and gravel, lined up in the river and then scuttled as part of the effort to block the way for the Japanese ships. After hearing their boats had been sunk in the river, the owners were outraged and set out to show Ge what they thought of him, clubs and harpoons in hand. They forced the poor officials to continuously complain to Nanjing: "They are the people's possessions and they deserve some kind of compensation, or at least an explanation."

Their superiors responded: "We're not saying that we won't compensate them but there's a war on, the Japanese are almost at the capital. You must help in this hour of need!"

The war had caused a huge amount of chaos. With the old warships sunk, more Chinese warships upstream in the Yangtze River altered course to approach Jiangyin at full speed.

Suffering loss after loss was enormously frustrating. Why weren't Chinese forces taking advantage of the Japanese military's exposed position in Shanghai? Hot-blooded students from the naval academy made a bold proposal to the academy leadership: "God damn it, why don't we attack?!" The naval academy, located in Jiangyin Fortress, had recently been formed by the KMT army for defence. They had imported 13 torpedo boats from Germany and the UK two years earlier. The government had ordered the 6,000dwt aircraft carrier *Tan Lun* from Germany, but it hadn't been delivered yet and was currently in Hong Kong and unable to reach the defensive line on the Yangtze.

On 14 August, the third day of the Battle of Shanghai, Chinese forces sent out the ships the *Shiwu 102* and the *Wen 171*, which had been camouflaged. Starting from the Jiangyin port of Huangni, and via Lake Tai and the Songjiang River, on the night of 16 August, the two ships launched a surprise attack on the *Izumo*, the flagship of the Japanese 3rd fleet, in the upstream Huangpu River. The Japanese naval force was incredibly powerful though, which meant that a comprehensive victory wasn't possible. However, the move had surprised the Japanese. Two days later, a Japanese general commented: "This has been the only proactive assault by the Chinese navy."

The Japanese military had always looked down on the Chinese troops so they decided to take revenge on the Jiangyin stronghold for their bold move, especially on the naval academy. Not unexpectedly, on 22 August, the well-prepared Japanese sent out 12 planes and directly targeted the academy in an intensive bombing raid.

The academy's emergency siren sounded.

"Enemy aircraft approaching!" Officers and soldiers in the academy quickly ran to their positions. All of a sudden, antiaircraft machine guns and rifles opened fire on the swooping Japanese planes.

Bombs and bullets rumbled into action. All was chaos.

One by one, the enemy planes dived sharply over the academy, dropping their hellfire bombs through a torrential shower of bullets. Back on the ground, some were bleeding, others had been shot dead, but no one flinched. When the fifth enemy plane swooped down, a ground team of students at the academy took direct aim with their machine guns and rifles. They opened fire. The plane was destroyed, dragging a black plume of smoke behind it. It fell to the ground by the corner of the academy buildings. Seeing this loss, the rest of the enemy planes flew away.

"We won!" The siren ceased. Students rushed over to where the plane had crashed, marvelling at the fruits of their victory. This was the first Japanese Aichi D1A Type 94 bomber aircraft to be shot down by the Chinese navy. The registration number on the aircraft was 154.

"The courage of the naval academy students is truly remarkable!" said the commander of the Yangtze defences about the efforts that had brought down this enemy aircraft. He awarded the students of the 3rd group there with a banner reading: "Battle-tested."

The Japanese army would surely continue to prioritise attacks on Jiangyin, the most significant stronghold in Nanjing's defences. On 22 September, while bombing the naval academy, Japanese planes began to bombard the Chinese navy defending the river. At noon, 30, maybe 40, Japanese planes bypassed the forts, taking turns to bomb the Chinese warships. Bullets pierced the river with terrible explosions on the decks of the ships. The Chinese navy was well prepared with antiaircraft guns, machine guns and even pistols and rifles firing into the air. The leading plane in the squadron was hit and crashed into the river. The battle lasted for more than two hours and the Japanese finally retreated due to running out of ammunition. The battle had sunk a Chinese flat-topped naval ship and the crew's head Gao Xianshen and 10 other crew members were wounded. The crewmen Gao Pinhuan and Luo Hanlin had been killed.

The Chinese navy were still inspired, but how could the Japanese be made to surrender?

The Chinese navy forces' morale was high. The next day, the morning of 23 September, more than 10 patrol torpedo boats first set out from the naval academy. Young students operated the torpedo boats around the warships, which gave out a deafening noise. The scene in Jiangyin was jaw-dropping and it was clear that a fierce battle was about to begin. The seamen on each ship were positioned ahead of time with their eyes focused on the eastern sky, waiting for the enemy to appear.

Without fail, at about 10 o'clock, the eastern sky was filled with a dense cloud of planes flying towards Jiangyin, several times more than the day before.

Suddenly, bombs were dropped from the sky, alongside a storm of bullets firing into the seamen on the ships. All of Jiangyin Fortress was enveloped in bursts of light, smoke and roaring gunfire. When a bomb fell on the ship *Ninghai*, an enemy plane also crashed into the water. While Chen Hongtai, the captain of the *Ninghai*, was holding his head out of the cockpit to save the navigator Lin Renji, a shard of shrapnel hit his arm. Chen screamed, holding his bloody arm. He looked back only to find Lin was already dead, with his white brain matter strewn all over the command deck.

Captain Chen clenched his fists and shouted: "For Lin!" The river was full of light and fire, with columns of water appearing to reach and pierce the sky.

This time the Japanese had sent more than 100 warplanes to destroy the entire Chinese navy's guard ships and they attacked them at all costs. After the antiaircraft fire in Yixian had exhausted their ammunition, the soldiers continued fighting fearlessly with artillery and hit one target. Hours of ferocious fighting had depleted the enemy's forces and the Japanese fled. The sound of gunfire gradually became quieter. Five enemy planes had been shot down during the fight. Several Chinese warships had also suffered, and the *Ninghai* had been completely destroyed while other ships had been severely damaged. Dozens of sailors and officers had been wounded and even killed. The overall result "satisfied" Chiang Kai-shek and He Yingqin.

However, at that point, only four warships had the ability to fight. Soon, Nanjing moved the *Yingrui* and *Yixian* ships back to Nanjing to act as a garrison, leaving only the *Hairong* and *Haichong* in the naval blockade in Jiangyin Fortress. Later, the destroyers *Haiqi* and *Haishen* came to Jiangyin Fortress from Shanghai. However, the remaining four ships didn't face the enemy and the captains were instead ordered to block the river by scuttling their ships. When they heard their orders, the officers wept.

The Chinese warships in the Jiangyin Fortress shipyard had been stranded or transferred, while most had been deliberately sunk in the river. Ouyang Jingxiu, the captain of the *Hairong*, with decades of memories of his ship painfully said: "I had been on that ship for many years. My life was sailing and combat on the water and all I wanted to do was serve the country with my skills, but when I saw the destruction of all the naval ships and the loss of their weapons, I became disillusioned. I was also getting old. So after the Battle of Jiangyin, I applied for retirement. I'd had a naval career for decades, but the second that happened, it ended."

Mr Ouyang wasn't the only disappointed person. Sadder still, thousands of unarmed naval officers walked to Nanjing for reassignment. When they entered the city gates, they didn't realise that the Japanese had already surrounded Nanjing. These Chinese sailors became the first to be beheaded in the Nanjing Massacre.

The warships may have gone but the fortress was still there. The Japanese warships began their attack on Jiangyin Fortress in an attempt to break through the Chinese defences. As dawn broke on 1 October, the enemy dispatched three destroyers out of the 24 stationed in Shanghai up against the current to test the Chinese defences. A soldier deployed at Wushan Fort quickly spotted the enemy and the fort deputy director Chen Bingqing ordered every fort to open fire on them. Four artillery guns targeted the invading Japanese in unison. Out of the four forts, one collapsed as its defences hadn't been strengthened. Fortunately, no one was injured but this was still humiliating. The other three artillery guns fired simultaneously, and one missed the target. The remaining two hit an enemy ship. The Japanese ship suddenly tilted to one side amidst a plume of dense smoke. The other two fled after realising what had happened.

In mid-November, just as the Chinese sailors were eager and ready to fight the invading Japanese in a desperate battle, the commander of the Yangtze defences received an order from the ministry of defence in Nanjing: "For the time being, Jiangyin is to expect orders to retreat from Chiang Kai-shek." Shortly after the orders from Chiang, a specific order from the ministry of war was received: "Disassemble the new gun and place it in the back. As soon as the iron barge comes, load it up and leave." They were referring to the newly installed German artillery in Jiangyin Fortress for shipment elsewhere.

Nanjing's orders bewildered the entire company of officers and soldiers: "What? We're abandoning Jiangyin Fortress? We're not staying to fight the Japanese? We're letting them storm Nanjing up the Yangtze?" Thousands of soldiers in the fortress were outraged: "We'll never quit! Why should we withdraw without a fight? What does Chiang Kai-shek really want? Cannon fodder? No way! We'd rather die with Jiangyin Fortress!"

Xu Kang, the helpless commander of the fortress, reported the situation to Nanjing asking for orders. Nanjing remained silent. A few days later, the military called and everything had now changed: "Defend Jiangyin. Chiang Kai-shek."

This was baffling. As the head of the country, how could he change his opinion so much in just a few days? Although the officers and soldiers in the fortress received it as good news, they still thought it was strange to receive entirely different orders from the supreme leader at this crucial time. The senior authorities replied that the UK, the US, France and the Soviet Union had sided with the Chinese and had offered to help so that they could recover their strength.

So that was why. Chiang Kai-shek had gained the support of the international community.

The fort received another message from Nanjing: "Defend Jiangyin to the death. Chiang Kai-shek."

The officers and men were dumbfounded. Within days, they'd received three orders in a row from the generalissimo: withdraw, defend and defend to the death. Did he want them to fight or not? To put up a real fight or just a show?

Nobody understood. They were doomed to lose with an unclear strategy. The officers began to curse "damned Chiang". Low levels of morale would make stopping the aggressive and determined Japanese impossible.

In fact, "damned Chiang", the Chinese generalissimo during this period, was in a pitiable position. He wanted to use the loss of Shanghai as an excuse to gain the support of several international powers, so that he could sit down with Japan and negotiate to maintain the situation prior to the Marco Polo Bridge Incident. But each country had its own plans. They were also preoccupied with their own problems as Hitler's aggression toward Germany's neighbours seemed to grow by the day. The Second World War was on the verge of breaking out, so who was there for China?

The Japanese high command also recognised this so, without a second's hesitation, they set their sights on destroying the Chinese capital in Nanjing. They not only successfully stormed Suzhou and Changshu, but they'd also swiftly defeated a garrison in Wuxi. Another attack was then launched west of Lake Tai. Another unit there, although against stiff resistance, would later occupy Wuhu after seizing Changxing and Guangde. No wonder Chiang Kai-shek was giving such chaotic orders. He had no overarching strategy and this caused a great deal of misery for the military.

Wuxi fell on 25 November. The Japanese army began to invade via the Chengxi road right behind the fortress. The 111th division and 103rd division were engaged in several days of fighting, putting up a fierce resistance. Meanwhile, the Japanese army was bearing down on them in force and light tanks also appeared at the front. Initially, artillery had produced some successes in defending against the Japanese, but after a while, the two defensive divisions were struggling to resist the Japanese onslaught.

On 1 December, Jiang Fangxing, the new army commander of the Yangtze defences, called on the commander and the chief of each division of the Jiangyin Fortress to discuss the war strategy. The chief of the 111th division, Huo Shouyi, pointed out: "Our infantry has been fighting the Japanese for a week with heavy casualties. The army still hasn't come to take over nor has anyone come to support us, so we want to retreat." The leader of the 103rd division held the same opinion. The president of the naval academy, Ouyang, said that the choice was theirs.

"No! The Jiangyin Fortress is the gateway to Nanjing. If we withdraw, it means opening the door to Nanjing. We cannot withdraw!" Xu Kang howled angrily, banging at his desk.

While they were arguing over the matter, Nanjing called: "There is no need for this dispute, the high command has made the decision for you to withdraw with the following specific orders: first, from now on (8pm) to 12pm, the fortress artillery should fire at the west gate to cover the infantry as they break through, which means the infantry defenders must retreat within four hours; second, after 12pm, we shall destroy the fortress and the fort's soldiers at the rear should then finish the retreat from Zhenjiang to Jingjiang; third, the department of the Yangtze defences will prepare boats and vessels to pull back to Nanjing. All troops are to act as soon as the order is received."

The fortress's soldiers wept and swore when they heard the command, but still most soon started to get ready for the withdrawal. Another important task for the officers and their men at the fort was to disassemble the valuable German guns that had only served for a short time. They couldn't fall into enemy hands. All the parts were removed or destroyed.

Poor "impregnable" Jiangyin Fortress; it had withstood the Japanese attacks but was finally brought down with sledge hammers by the Chinese army itself.

Jiangyin Fortress had fallen. Chinese officers and men had destroyed it. They could now escape towards Wuhu or retreat to the capital where an even more tragic fate would await them.

Xu Kang, the commander of the Yangtze defences, originally wanted to withdraw to Nanjing but was struck by the Japanese on a beach when arriving in Yizheng, where he almost lost his life. Under the covering fire of his subordinates, he instead made his way to Wuhan. It was said that when he arrived in Wuhan, the dignified Xu looked like a drowned rat. Xu himself said: "It's better to look like a drowned rat than to be dead. There are worse fates." This is true. Most of his subordinates had been killed by the Japanese: "There was no trace of the commander and chief of staff. The colonel was killed and the deputy commander beheaded, inspiring me to fight again in Zhenjiang for two days. Then Zhenjiang fell. After that we withdrew to Nanjing."

Wan Shijiong, the colonel of the 618th division recalled:

> On 12 December, we arrived in Xiaguan next to the Nanjing river. The confusion there was to be expected and there were people running everywhere looking for equipment. The officials didn't tell the soldiers anything and the soldiers didn't listen to their superiors' commands. The same situation could be seen in my regiment and I only had Wu Kai on my side. Seeing this, we knew that we couldn't cross the river so we turned back to the south following the flow of people across the Qinhuai River. When we walked to Dangshe, we were blocked by the enemy and the situation was extremely critical. An idea occurred to me and I shouted: "Brothers, I'm Wan Shijiong, the head of the 103rd division, I want to get you out of here but you have to be organised!" They agreed to do so in unison. I grouped them into two teams, one led by Wu Kai and another by myself. We moved along the road. The enemy then launched a counterattack. Faced with a hail of bullets, our group was frightened and it dispersed while I was at the back. Seven or eight Japanese soldiers carrying bayonets lunged towards me. Fortunately, I had studied martial arts before. After killing four of the enemy, I rushed to escape back to the riverside and found Wu Kai, who was looking for a boat. We got on a raft and my life was spared.

Wan was fortunate enough to survive but most soldiers in the division weren't lucky enough to find a boat. They later became the first victims of the massacre.

The Plaintive Cry of an Isolated City

It remained unclear whether Chiang knew that Nanjing would fall or whether he had deliberately decided on a fight to the death with the Japanese. Since the defeat at the Battle of Shanghai, Nanjing was in chaos. The Japanese had attacked Nanjing from three sides, with Nanjing having to fight on three fronts accordingly. Despite the soldiers on the frontline putting up a bitter and bloody resistance, the loss of Nanjing was inevitable due to weapon shortages and lack of a central force. However, as the national leader, conceding the loss of the capital would be cause for unimaginable shame for Chiang, not to mention it being a great failure for the state. As a consequence, Chiang Kai-shek and the Nationalist government were determined to hold fast until the last minute.

Only one month separated Shanghai's fall on 12 November 1937 and the loss of Nanjing on 13 December. Had Chiang and his colleagues really done nothing over the course of this month to defend Nanjing?

Despite some apparent effort, they hadn't done all they could in its defence. After the Marco Polo Bridge Incident, Chiang Kai-shek clearly instructed his colleagues to prepare for a prolonged war and indicated that they would pull back to Sichuan if needs be.

"Don't you dare come back! You deserve to die with the soldiers in Shanghai!" Chiang Kai-shek cursed furiously from his impromptu office in the Sun Yat-sen Mausoleum in Nanjing. The situation in Shanghai was critical at the time and Chiang spent every day enraged, even cursing himself: "If you can't do the job, I'll go to Shanghai to fight Matsui myself. I don't doubt I'll lose to the bandit."

It was 13 November and Chiang Kai-shek continued to fume in his office. It was just Chiang Kai-shek and his closest aides in the room: He Yingqin, Bai Chongxi, Xu Yongchang and Liu Fei, the director of the operational department. Chiang was standing in front of the window, brooding in anger. Liu hypothesised: "Since we were unsuccessful in our strategy of diminishing the strength of the enemy in Shanghai, nor did we succeed in readjusting the front or preserving our forces, now we need to avoid getting into a stalemate with the Japanese in the Yangtze River delta. Take a look at that so-called Nine-Power Treaty. All the countries that have always been 'good' to us show no intention of helping us. That's why we're in this position today. So, I think we should continue with the implementation of the long-term strategic plan proposed by the generalissimo. We should focus on the overall strategy through a comprehensive and long war of attrition with the enemy instead of trying to win back the lost city. If we can make the war last until it takes a battalion of troops to hold each occupied county, then, even if the Japanese gain some kind of tactical victory, they will lose the war."

After Liu Fei finished saying this, he was mocked by Xu Yongchang: "You sound like Mao Zedong!"

"The... the concept of protracted warfare wasn't put forward by Mao Zedong. It comes from the Generalissimo Chiang Kai-shek!" Liu Fei responded, red with anger.

"I think Director Liu's plans make sense." Bai Chongxi waved a hand at Xu Yongchang, and then pointed at Liu Fei, saying: "Tell us how to deal with the battle in Nanjing. This is what the generalissimo wants us to discuss today."

Liu Fei straightened himself after he gained Bai Chongxi's support and continued: "In light of the previous assumptions, it's unlikely and inappropriate for us to concede our capital Nanjing without a fight. But we shouldn't fight for every town and city with too many troops. It makes more sense to retreat after a certain level of resistance from a symbolic defending force. As for the armed forces to be deployed, 12 regiments are enough, 18 at most. It would be inconvenient to deploy too many fresh troops to be depleted there."

He Yingqin added: "Mr Liu's ideas make sense. This seems to be the best strategy for dealing with the battle in Nanjing. Only the defending troops and citizens of Nanjing would suffer that way." He sighed deeply and turned to Chiang Kai-shek, asking: "Commander, does this make sense to you?" Chiang didn't reply straight away, seeming to still be lost in anger.

At that point, the entire Sun Yat-sen Mausoleum seemed to be in silence as the fate of the ancient city, which had gone through so many hardships in its history, and the destinies of its hundreds of thousands of unarmed citizens, fell on the shoulders of the appalled Chiang: "I guess there's no other way out, but look, all of you, we can't tell them that we're not fighting for Nanjing. How else would we persuade the citizens, armies and leadership to stay here?" He paused as he turned to look around at the shining white beauty of the Sun Yat-sen Mausoleum, which would be at risk, and continued: "How can we face them?"

Chiang appeared to be lost in despair and bewilderment after he'd finished talking, leaving He Yingqin to conclude the meeting: "Listen, what the generalissimo said then is very important, remember to keep it in mind."

Bai Chongxi, Xu Yongchang and Liu Fei nodded together and replied: "Yes, sir!"

The second conference for the senior officials was held once again in Chiang Kai-shek's office in the Sun Yat-sen Mausoleum on 15 November.

More people attended the meeting this time in addition to those mentioned previously, and Tang Shengzhi, the director of the military commission's enforcement division, and Gu Zhenglun, the garrison commander of Nanjing, were also present. The meeting still focused on the issue of Nanjing. Chiang Kai-shek was open to suggestions after Liu Fei briefed the attendees on the last meeting.

"I think this is simply inappropriate, we have to defend Nanjing to the last!" Tang Shengzhi was first to respond, his voice drenched in emotion: "Nanjing is our capital, not to mention a city of international importance and the home to the father of the nation's mausoleum. If we abandon Nanjing, how would we ever face Dr Sun? I don't agree with Director Liu. Not in the slightest." He stared at Chiang Kai-shek when he finished, wondering what was on his mind.

Nobody else made a sound since they all knew what was on his mind, apart from Gu Zhenglun. "Mengxiao's words make sense and are worth considering. We'll discuss the matter again later," Chiang said. Mengxiao was Tang's nickname. No formal solution was reached in that meeting.

The conference continued in the Sun Yat-sen Mausoleum the next evening. This time, Tang Shengzhi's proposal had unexpectedly gained the most support because anyone who advocated a withdrawal from Nanjing faced being accused of failing Dr Sun. Just who was Tang Shengzhi? Tang had always been an old rival of Chiang's who'd once stood against him. Having failed to do so, he'd pled that he was unwell so Chiang never dealt with him seriously. Tang Shengzhi had been bitter about his loss of military power for all that time and had been contemplating a comeback. It's said that "sickly" Tang's fiery passion for defending Nanjing came from his intention to take back some military power from Chiang Kai-shek. Whether this was true or not, Chiang had a clear idea about his intentions.

Chiang Kai-shek had already made up his mind before the third conference that since Tang had proposed the defence, it was Tang's duty to implement it. But as the Chinese saying goes, old ginger is hotter than new, so Chiang still followed procedure and asked the senior officials for their opinions on how to proceed.

Tang Shengzhi responded first, eager to see the city defended. Chiang glanced at He Yingqin and the others, asking: "What about you?" Nobody replied.

Chiang continued with an apparent seriousness: "I'm with Mengxiao." Suddenly, he asked: "Then who should be responsible for defending Nanjing?"

Everybody threw a glance at He Yingqin, who sneered without saying anything, thinking to himself: "I'm the chief of the general staff. It'd be somewhat odd for me to stay behind."

Xu Yongchang shook his head and said nothing.

Gu Zhenglun stretched his neck and wanted to step forward bravely. But he knew he wasn't cut out for this and so he cast his gaze at Liu Fei, who was certain that as someone who supported a retreat, the chairman and generalissimo wouldn't leave him behind.

"Tell me, who should defend the city?" Chiang asked again. Silence still. Chiang became irritated and said: "Since nobody is willing to defend Nanjing, I'll do it!"

Tang Shengzhi panicked and stood up, dissuading him: "Chairman, you're head of the nation and chief of the military. You shouldn't fight personally and defend the city alone at this time. I'll accept the burden if nobody wants to assume responsibility and I can assure you all that I'll defend the city to the death!"

Chiang looked thrilled by what Tang had said. He approached him and vigorously patted the shoulders of his old rival, who had once wanted to cut him to pieces, saying: "Incredibly commendable indeed! You've shown the right spirit. Very well, then it's all up to you!" Chiang turned around and spoke to He Yingqin: "That's all settled then, just go ahead and prepare anything that's needed. Mengxiao can assume the role as soon as the order is given."

"Yes sir," He replied, wondering if the 'sickly' Tang was the right person for the role.

The dust had finally settled on the issue of Nanjing. Days later, the appointment of Tang Shengzhi as commander of the defending troops in Nanjing was announced in the army and in the *Central Daily* newspaper. In fact, Nanjing was already in chaos at the time partly because of the continuous bad news from Shanghai and partly because of an editorial titled *To the Citizens of Nanjing* published in the *Central Daily* the day Shanghai had been occupied by the Japanese, publicly announcing the government's decision to move the central government to Chongqing. The editorial was as follows:

> The reason for relocating the central government to Chongqing is to adapt to the current tactical situation. It is to gain mastery over, rather than fear of, the enemy, which was made clear in yesterday's editorial. The municipal party committee and government of Nanjing and anti-Japanese organisations from all walks of life issued a message to all compatriots yesterday, hoping that everyone can hold on tight without panic and fight for the rejuvenation of the nation and the independence of the country. Here, we need to clearly address some key issues.
>
> Firstly, the government is the top organ that deals with national affairs. It should enjoy utmost freedom in exercising its powers, immune from any threat or restriction. As a result, the location of our government must be in such an environment instead of being at the frontlines. As for the local authorities in Nanjing, apart from the established municipalities and police organs which are

still in service, the commander of the defending troops has also been appointed to lead the military, civil organs and all citizens in the defence against the Japanese.

Secondly, protracted warfare does not depend entirely on one city or one time. More often than not, victory or defeat in a war is more about lasting strength behind the lines than about military actions at the front, so civilians behind the lines are more important than the soldiers at the front. Nanjing sits behind the frontline; it has a clear idea of the frontline's needs. As for the aid coming from the rear, we shall concentrate more on support through coordinated action. Therefore, we are more concerned with the enhancement of the frontline and assisting the people behind it than the safety of the city.

Thirdly, the defence of the capital is the responsibility of the organs that also guarantee the security of the city, in addition to addressing other issues like sufficient food supplies and daily necessities, all of which are important in a war. At this point, national strength rests totally on the financial resources of the people. The more the people contribute, the more calmly the government can resist the enemy and turn the tide. This also provides a good opportunity for our people to serve the country. Now, citizens of Nanjing should set an example to everyone in the country by showing them how to fulfil the duty that has fallen on their shoulders. Following an affirmative resolution and a relentless struggle, we expect a bright future as a result of our efforts, the strength of which should not be underestimated nor insulted.

With Chiang Kai-shek leaving the city, the people in Nanjing were left with nowhere to turn. Upon confirming the news of moving the capital to Chongqing, people descended into total panic. "The battle hasn't even begun and the Japanese haven't come yet. Is it normal for a country's capital to be so chaotic?" Chiang said, enraged by a report from Dai Li, Chiang's spymaster.

Chiang Kai-shek decided to hold a press conference, expounding his views on the city of Nanjing and the current situation. Then on 26 November, *Reuters* reported:

Nanjing: In a press conference this evening, Chairman Chiang told foreign reporters that: "We firmly believe that justice will prevail; we have always believed in our might and fighting to the last clump of soil and resisting to the last person." Together with his wife, Mr Chiang entered the conference room with confidence and resolution rather than any sense of defeat. Chiang continued that: "China will maintain its policy of resolutely fighting the Japanese. We will defend Nanjing from afar and protect the foreigners' lives and property in an appropriate manner. The rumours that everything will go up in smoke if Nanjing falls into enemy hands are without basis." As for the possibility of a ceasefire, Chiang said that it was up to the Japanese. He then mentioned that lately a Japanese plane had dropped a box containing an anonymous letter, informing them that they hoped for a ceasefire soon and that the Japanese wouldn't include any harsh requirements except for cooperation with them against the communists. This rumour was untrue. Reporters asked when a peace negotiation would be possible; Chiang said that it was too early to discuss the matter because the Japanese must first come to their senses. Reporters continued, asking if they anticipated assistance from the Soviet Union and Chiang said that he anticipated assistance stipulated by the League of Nations. Reporters asked if assistance from other sources was expected since the Washington Conference had done nothing to help China. Chiang answered that he was sure the signatory states of the Nine Power Pact would assist China. If assistance was compromised, all treaties would be invalid and it would be a violation of the treaty.

At this crucial moment, Chiang continued to make a fool himself and others. His actions were merely to pacify the people and the public would have likely described him as a baseless and evil liar.

Still, preparations were needed. On the same day, Chiang Kai-shek secretly telegraphed Tang Shengzhi and deployed the battle array for the garrison troops in Nanjing:

1. Tang Shengzhi is the commanding officer, with Luo Zhuoying and Liu Xing acting as deputy commanders and Zhou Lan as chief of staff.
2. The main forces include Sun Yuanliang's troops from the 72nd army, Song Xilian's troops from the 78th army, Gu Zhenglun's troops, the teaching corps, military police from the capital defence corps, and the 112th and 103rd divisions who are retreating to Nanjing from the front, as well as armed forces such as the air defence artillery corps.

Afterwards, Chiang Kai-shek transferred Ye Zhao's 66th army, Wang Jingzhi's 71st army, Sun Yuanliang's 72nd army, Yu Jishi's 74th army and Deng Longguang's 83rd army to Tang Shengzhi. Their troops numbered more than 100,000 in total.

Government authorities and public officials were busy relocating their homes and belongings, but what about the civilians? What about the morale of the troops? As the commander of the defending troops, Tang Shengzhi seemed to be in high spirits, publishing an announcement entitled *Rise and Fall with Nanjing* in the newspaper on 27 November, reading: "Our capital may well become a battlefield in the near future. The top military authority has determined to defend the city to the death. We Chinese have to sacrifice for our country and I have decided to do so in two ways: first, as a Chinese soldier, I'll lay down my life for the motherland; second, I'll sacrifice myself for all of you, wiping out the enemy." He then boldly proclaimed that: "I will rise and fall with Nanjing!"

Bold words indeed. But the civilians and the defending troops were somewhat perplexed by his words as they saw that Chiang Kai-shek was withdrawing from Nanjing with his elite troops while replacing them with new recruits. Meanwhile, the Japanese were attacking from three directions with ever stronger momentum. The war was gradually spreading to Nanjing.

How much longer could Nanjing hold its ground? Only heaven could tell.

> Your excellency, according to a journalist from the *New York Times* in Nanjing: On the evening of 26 November, all important officials except for Chiang Kai-shek and his wife embarked on a ship to Hankou in a hurry. Judging from their perturbation, Nanjing appears to be under imminent threat of falling. Right now, troops and supplies are moving to Nanjing, with refugees fleeing in chaos.

This was a secret telegraph sent to the Japanese high command by Consul General Okamoto. His secret telegraph was numbered *code 2441* with every detail in Nanjing being explicitly recorded and sent to Tokyo. Secret agents like him lurking in China numbered in the hundreds.

It's worth mentioning that the Japanese were very diligent in their duties. They carefully planned and prepared before every invasion and slaughter, and I doubt the Chinese could ever best them in this. Chiang Kai-shek was still immersed in the fantasy of international assistance while the Japanese had already researched every detail of how to invade China with a great deal of accuracy.

At the time, the Chinese defending army was extremely busy as general commander Tang Shengzhi inspected the Zhonghua gate to check if the fortifications were adequate before going to the Rain Flower Terrace to motivate the defending forces. He also imposed a curfew on the city, requiring everyone coming in and out of important departments and military sites to wear an armband, reading "Garrison Department Officer". Another order was dispatching soldiers and military police to put up notices everywhere in the streets and alleyways. Most importantly, an air-raid siren system was installed and all lights were blacked out simultaneously in the evening, an indication of the wartime state of emergency.

One day, after an inspection at the Rain Flower Terrace, Tang Shengzhi dropped by at the education secretary Wang Shijie's house as he'd heard that he lived nearby. His officers all gathered around and Tang Shengzhi announced to them: "Commander Gu Zhenglun tendered his resignation as the commander of Nanjing's defence, so I now take full responsibility for the defence and security of the city." He spoke about the matter in a deep voice and let out a long sigh, continuing solemnly: "As the commander, I'm responsible for defending Nanjing and determined to rise and fall with it. I will lay down my life if Nanjing falls. As my officers, you are still young and in a different situation to me, there is no need for you to die with me and you can still withdraw once the city is besieged."

Tang Shengzhi then closed his eyes and whispered: "I only hope that you can stick to the end as long as I'm alive."

"Commander Tang, please don't say that. We swear to fight alongside you to the end and never to back down!" Junior officials like Cheng Kuilang were moved by Tang's words and committed themselves one after another. Tang Shengzhi nodded his head, his eyes glistening.

The transport minister, Qian Dajun, called him: "Mengxiao, I'm Dajun. Chairman Chiang has invited you to his place at 4pm."

Tang Shengzhi arrived at Chiang's official residence that day, thinking he was going to be leaving Nanjing, yet Chiang asked him to inspect the troops and fortifications with him.

"Chairman, it's dangerous outside, but you still want to make the inspection rounds. I'm touched," Tang said as he was close to tears.

Chiang Kai-shek, wearing his gloves, smiled and said: "I know, and I deeply appreciate your commitment to defending the city. As head of the military and state, I cannot leave you alone with such a heavy burden. I'll support you as much as possible."

"Thank you, sir," Tang said and wiped his eyes without thinking.

Obviously, Chiang's inspection was partly to encourage Tang Shengzhi and his troops and partly to get some credit for himself, which was the main reason for him making a public appearance before the battle. According to an article in *Shen Bao* the next day, Chiang Kai-shek was "quite satisfied" with the fortifications and order of the city and he intentionally disclosed that he and his wife were still in Nanjing.

The citizens and soldiers thought: "We'll be safe as long as the chairman and first lady are still in Nanjing."

Tang Shengzhi suddenly called the transport minister Qian Dajun and asked: "Dajun, do you know when Chairman Chiang will actually be leaving Nanjing?"

"I don't see any signs of him leaving," Qian replied.

"He'll be in great danger if he stays any longer!" Tang Shengzhi got angry.

"What's happened, Mengxiao?"

"You have no idea. Today my troops discovered that Japanese undercover agents have already entered the city. We wouldn't know if the soldiers weren't so vigilant."

Qian Dajun exclaimed: "Mengxiao, please take care. Remember to turn to Chairman Chiang if you can't hold out any more."

Tang Shengzhi sneered and said: "I've already committed myself to the city. There's only one way out. The Japanese will have to bury me."

"A true martyr!"

Tang Shengzhi hung up the phone and thought: "Whether I'm a martyr depends on Chiang and the Japanese. I'm just a nobody going with the tide."

Tang Shengzhi knew that as head of the defending army, he was a poor strategist when compared with Chiang Kai-shek. He couldn't understand why Chiang, who had washed his hands of the matter, was still staying at the Sun Yat-sen Mausoleum at risk from the enemy's bombs instead of leaving for Wuhan immediately with his beautiful wife Soong Mei-ling.

"I've told you that Mengxiao is incredibly naive and you won't believe me!" Chiang Kai-shek mockingly told his wife several times. "Obviously, I'm staying in Nanjing for a reason!" he said. However, Chiang didn't disclose his secret plans to the commander of the defending troops at this time. What was the conspiracy? Waiting for Dochterman, the German ambassador to China, to negotiate peace talks with the Japanese.

As early as October and November, the Nationalist government had been privately negotiating with Japan for peace talks. Wang Jingwei, the president of the Japanese puppet state in China, had first come up with the idea and was also naturally connected with Japan, so he proposed "a peace talk", namely, a surrender following Japan's launch of the Battle of Shanghai. Chiang Kai-shek was unhappy with the idea at first, but he felt that failure was inevitable as the war continued and he eventually agreed to hold "a peace talk" with Japan. Negotiations like this were naturally dominated by the stronger side. Japan had already wanted to devour China and was in an excellent negotiating position, so they proposed six terms to Chiang Kai-shek.

"Absolutely not! They want me and my country to be humiliated!" Chiang Kai-shek was outraged and broke his glass when he saw the Japanese proposals for the national government to recognise the independence of

Manchukuo and Mengjiang, the Japanese puppet states in Manchuria and Inner Mongolia.

The message from the Japanese was clear: the Japanese Empire wanted to humiliate China.

A "peace talk" was now impossible, so Wang Jingwei simply gave up and went to Wuhan, leaving Chiang Kai-shek alone in Nanjing.

"Power is respected by all." Ever since his beginnings as a soldier, Chiang Kai-shek had known this truth, and with that in mind, he would show the Japanese China's power. Chiang wondered if they would fight to the death in the Battle of Nanjing and knew that he could show that even without much strength, China could still intimidate Japan with its vast land and large population.

Once they had been intimidated, they could go back to the "peace talks" and they wouldn't force China to accept or cede anything. Chiang Kai-shek finally put his cards on the table. An intermediator would obviously be needed as peace talks were being held between China and Japan, which were deadly enemies. Under these circumstances, Chiang decided to stay in Nanjing and wait for his old friend, the German ambassador Mr Dochterman, while the decision was being made to relocate the capital to Chongqing and to leave Tang Shengzhi in charge of Nanjing.

"The Japanese will not keep their word and the Soviet Union and the US are not trustworthy. I trust you Germany. Germany and you are our friends. And we hope that you can always act as an intermediator between China and Japan and we look forward to good news." Chiang Kai-shek held a long and secret talk with Dochterman who hurried to Nanjing on the evening of 2 December deliberating on terms that would be acceptable to Japan. These terms were discussions regarding principled compromises based on the six terms proposed by Japan.

"Chiang just won't leave. How could I ask him to?" Qian Dajun told Tang Shengzhi awkwardly when asked several times why Chiang wasn't leaving Nanjing.

Had Dochterman managed to get something beneficial for Chiang from Japan? No. Not in the slightest. On the day Chiang entrusted Ambassador Dochterman to negotiate with the Japanese, the Japanese general Iwane Matsui issued a combat order to all the troops at the behest of the high command. The order dictated that the 10th regiment on the western front was to attack Nanjing on 3 December, while troops on the eastern front and along the Yangtze River were to attack on 5 December. Once the order was issued, troops from the three routes would "press forward day and night like wild bulls aimed at Nanjing".

"My dear committee head and friend, the Japanese didn't agree to your revisions and they have stuck to the original six terms without any alterations." Dochterman telegraphed a message from the Japanese to Chiang Kai-shek again without even coming to the Sun Yat-sen Mausoleum.

"Damn it! Damn it! I knew the Japanese wanted to humiliate me! I will never expect any form of negotiation in the future!" Chiang swore as he read Dochterman's telegram and had an irresistible urge to smash the glass doors at both ends of the living room like a vicious lion.

In the evening, Chiang Kai-shek was sitting on the couch with a glum expression on his face. He hailed the captain of the guard, Yu Jiemin, in a glum voice, asking: "How many of you are still here?" He meant how many of his own guards and officers. Yu answered that dozens of them were there. Chiang said: "Make a personnel roster and hand it in to the guards office." He then let out a deep sigh, continuing: "You are the vanguard of our nation and party as well as my most loyal soldiers. With national chaos on the horizon, I should stay in Nanjing as the head of the state and the military, but I have to leave here as the war won't end any time soon. Nanjing is our capital and where my dignity lies, so I should defend it, but my hands are tied. So, I want to help as much as I can. You can lead the troops, and I want you to stay in Nanjing for the moment with two teams of armed guards and await Tang Shengzhi's orders. Your main task is to guard the small warships anchored in Xiaguan." Chiang continued: "Don't underestimate those warships; they'll boost the morale of the defending troops."

"I understand. I will do as you say." Yu Jiemin clearly understood what he meant as a small warship coming downriver was a special ship for Chiang Kai-shek. He would be assumed to be present if the troops could see it, a sort of a visual motivation for the citizens and troops defending the city.

"I'm going to head for Commander Tang's home. Let's go!" Chiang Kai-shek then left.

Tang Shengzhi later recalled this and said: "On the evening he left Nanjing, Chiang Kai-shek came to my home with Soong Mei-ling. He said to me: 'I can't help but feel saddened; you're still unwell and are due to defend Nanjing.' I answered: 'It's what a soldier should do! I'd like to repeat what I said to you several days ago, that I would be calm in the hour of need and unselfish in the face of disaster. I will never retreat without your orders'."

This time Chiang Kai-shek was determined to leave.

On 7 December, the rays of the morning sun shone down on a group of vehicles speeding towards the Sun Yat-sen Mausoleum under heavy security. The vehicles pulled up in front of the Sun Yat-sen Mausoleum and Chiang Kai-shek walked out from the vehicle with the help of Soong Mei-ling.

With a glum expression on his face, Chiang Kai-shek went around the Sun Yat-sen Mausoleum and then bowed three times. Afterwards, he shook hands with the officials staying to defend Nanjing one by one. When he shook hands with Tang Shengzhi, Chiang Kai-shek nodded his head, saying: "We're counting on you, Mengxiao." After this, Chiang Kai-shek looked into the distance, cast a final glance at Nanjing city and silently closed his eyes.

The motorcade immediately headed for the airport. As soon as Chiang Kai-shek and Soong Mei-ling boarded their special plane, the Mei-ling, which had arrived at the airport earlier, it instantly roared down the runway and took off. A group of defending planes took to the skies afterwards and they soon left Nanjing.

"Now we're the only people left," Tang Shengzhi lamented with a sigh.

Nanjing began to weep. The Japanese bayonets had started to murder the people of the city.

Chiang Kai-shek had left. However, that didn't mean that Tang Shengzhi didn't have to report on the city's defence, so Tang Shengzhi sent Chiang comprehensive daily reports on the situation of the battle. From the secret files left behind by the Nationalists when they left Nanjing and escaped for Taiwan in 1949, we can better understand how Tang Shengzhi reported the situation, both good and bad, to Chiang Kai-shek. The reports are as follows:

7 December

At 10am, according to the uncertain intelligence from the 66th army, enemy forces occupying Mengtang and Dahushan suddenly disappeared and it seemed that they had advanced for the north side and intended to attack Longtan. As a result, the first platoon of the 36th division was ordered to temporarily lay in an ambush position next to Qilingmen to await further instructions. The 41st division held their positions as usual and advanced towards Mengtang to make contact with the left flank troops of the 66th army. The 71st army directly went to the areas surrounding Gaoqiaomen and awaited further instructions. After dawn, it was rumoured that the enemy forces staying near Dahushan still held the area and had not left, so all troops were ordered to advance and destroy the enemy as soon as possible. Eventually, due to difficulties in communications and enemy harassment, all of the troops failed to advance together and did not achieve the goal of a quick victory over the enemy. On this day, after being attacked by enemy forces with a comparative advantage in a battle in the artillery barracks, the Chinese frontline positions in front of Tangshui town were occupied by enemy forces from all directions. The Chinese military was forced to withdraw to the second line position after sunset and stubbornly defended the towns of Tangshan and Tangshui. On the same day, traces of the enemy in areas near Longtan, Baijingtai and Baoguoshan were found and enemy forces also fought with the 41st army, resulting in casualties and deaths on both sides.

Enemy forces in Chunhua town also made frenzied attacks on Chinese positions by using infantry, artillery and planes. More than 10 Chinese armoured vehicles were destroyed. The defending Chinese troops in the 51st division fought courageously and killed many of the enemy. Chinese positions were lost and gained several times, but the casualties and deaths sustained by the Chinese troops were severe. As a result, the division's reserves were deployed as reinforcements, holding the original positions after the sun had set.

The enemy forces in front of Molingguan attacked from two directions and they occupied positions like Duqiao and Yangshan. It looked as if they would be staying around the mountain to the east of the Chinese forces.

The 48th division also reached Nanjing that day and were ordered to occupy the positions alongside Yangfangshan and Wulonghshan and to proceed with defensive preparations. The 1st regiment of the 87th division reached Gaoqiaomen in vehicles and were prepared to take over the second line positions originally held by the 51st division, including Hedingqiao, Shangfangmen and Gaoqiaomen.

The 154th division on Dongchang Street also attacked and advanced, reaching areas near the towns of Baitu and Hangxiang. However, due to the changes in Tangshan, the advance was suspended.

8 December

On this day, the enemy forces attacked the defending troops on the second line of defence in Tangshan by using their main force with artillery and mechanised infantry. By 8 o'clock, the outcome of the battle in Tangshan town hung in the balance. Fortunately, Tangshan and the highlands on both sides were controlled by Chinese troops. The 156th division, which had advanced from Zhenjiang and had arrived in Qilingmen on the evening of 7 December under the command of the 66th army's commander, sent troops to take over the positions in Zhushan and Qinglongshan behind Tangshan. Their positions were gradually reinforced. Having occupied Dahushan and Gaojiazhuang and after receiving reinforcements the previous night, enemy forces fiercely attacked Chinese troops and deployed their main force to surround Chinese forces by Qixiashan. The Chinese 41st division and the 1st regiment of the 36th division repeatedly counterattacked and killed many enemy troops. However, eventually, due to the bombardment of the enemy aircraft and the danger posed by their artillery, the Chinese forces were overwhelmed and unable to eliminate the enemy forces and consequently, the losses suffered by the Chinese forces were colossal.

As for Chunhua town, the enemy attacked with increasing aggression and surrounded Chinese forces in areas near Dongqiao village and Xizhuang, attempting to cut off any route for retreat. The troops in the Chinese 51st division fought courageously. The Chinese troops suffered enormous losses; the officers and soldiers of the 5th battalion nearly all died a hero's death. Without prompt reinforcement, the town eventually fell into enemy hands at 4 o'clock.

Enemy forces attacking Niushoushan swarmed into areas near Jiangjun Mountain this morning, assisted by more than 40 vehicles. Six enemy vehicles were destroyed by the Chinese defenders' combat vehicles and bombs. They quickly retreated and the battlefield remained uneventful for the rest of the day. Only the forces on the right flank were heavily attacked by the Japanese and they seemed to be unable to hold out, so they automatically retreated to Banqiao town.

In the evening, most of the troops of the 87th division managed to reach their designated positions. The remnants of the 156th division and the 154th division are also en route to Nanjing.

Given the above and the need to concentrate Chinese forces to strengthen Nanjing, an order was given to allow the troops to pull back and defend the positions in Fuguo. The deployment positions were as follows:

The right flank detachment stubbornly defended the position of the large mountain in Banqiao town.

The 74th army defended the position in the stronghold around Niushoushan Mountain to Heding bridge.

The 88th division defended the Rain Flower Terrace.

The 87th division of the 71st army defended the line from Heding bridge to Haizili on the north side of the Jiangnan railway, and to its east, made contact with the 88th and 51st armies. To its west, it made contact with the teaching corps, which defended Purple Mountain.

The 2nd army group defended the line from Yangfang Mountain to Wulong Mountain and the Wulong Mountain fortress.

The 36th division defended the area of Hongshan Mountain and the Mufu mountains.

The 66th army amassed near Dashuiguan and awaited further directions.

The 156th division and the 1st regiment of the 36th division of the 83rd army covered the withdrawal on the Qinglong Mountain and Longwang Mountain line.

The 103rd and 112th division stayed in Zhenjiang and fell back to Nanjing.

9 December

The enemy forces took advantage of the 51st division's retreat, and out of all the troops in the 87th division, only two regiments arrived as Chinese efforts to hold their positions were overwhelmed. Gaoqiao gate, Qiweng bridge and Zhonghe bridge were lost. The Japanese occupied those positions and they moved to areas outside of the Guanghua gate before dawn, occupying the Dajiaochang and Tongguang barracks with a force of about 2,000 foot soldiers and more than 10 tanks. At that point, due to the fact that the positions near the Guanghua gate only had a teaching corps and a few defending soldiers, the gate to Nanjing was closed as the situation grew ever more urgent. The enemy then began to bombard the areas neighbouring the Gaoqiao gate and attacked the Guanghua gate. For a short while, there were two gaps in the gate and a small portion of the enemy forces suddenly broke through only to be killed by Chinese troops. The defences later proved insufficient as Chinese forces were outnumbered three to one. China mainly depended on attacks by the supporting forces from the 87th division and the reinforcement of elite troops and until 4pm, the enemy was held at Dajiaochang. A small portion of the enemy forces had settled in Tongguang barracks as the gaps in the gate continued to be stubbornly defended.

On Niushou Mountain, the 58th division fought with the enemy for several days. As the troops on the right flank deployed by the 88th division had pulled back too early, the first group of Japanese forces broke through and occupied Dashengguan. It appeared that the Japanese were trying to attack Chinese positions on the north bank of the river. The position was being held by the 58th division, who were ordered to withdraw after sunset and cooperated with the 51st division to jointly act as the defending troops in Shuangjian town and Songliao on the extensive line of the 88th division's right flank.

10 December

Enemy forces simultaneously attacked the Rain Flower Terrace, the Tongji gate, Guanghua gate and Purple Mountain's third summit, with even fiercer fighting than on 7 December. The enemy broke through the Guanghua gate twice. However, the enemy forces attempting to break into the city were entirely destroyed. The 156th division reinforced the Tongji gate and Guanghua gate and acted as the city's garrison. The troops worked hard on the defensive constructions. The 159th division controlled the areas near the Ming Palace. The 156th division was prepared to fight against the enemy. In addition to this, the 103rd division, having retreated from Zhenjiang to Nanjing, were appointed to act as the defending troops in the positions near the Zhongshan gate under the command of General Gui Yongqing. In the evening, the 156th division chose a so-called dare-to-die, or suicide, corps to enter the city to kill the few enemy forces hiding in the gaps of the city gate and eliminate the enemy troops settled in Tongguang barracks, and as a result, the areas near the Guanghua gate and Tongji gate looked to be out of danger for a while. However, in the Yuhuatai district, which was the position of the 88th division, their right flank had broken down somewhat and three strongholds in front of the position were lost. As for the 2nd army group, the situation wasn't as perilous on this day. Only the 41st division from the 2nd army encountered any difficulties, and it had withdrawn following the fierce attack on Mengtang.

11 December

The Japanese forces deployed their main force to attack Purple Mountain and the Rain Flower Terrace, while also deploying a part of their troops to occupy Yangfang mountain and Yinkong mountain. Another portion of their troops moved from Dashengguan to Jiangxin Island by crossing the river so they could shoot at the right flank of the Chinese 74th army. By 2pm, the right flank positions of the 88th division, the Rain Flower Terrace, were occupied by the Japanese forces and the Zhonghua gate was also destroyed by Japanese bombs. Some enemy troops broke through but were killed by the Chinese forces. Due to the loss of Yinkong mountain, the Chinese 2nd army group had no way of making contact with the troops in the city and their combat status remained unknown that afternoon. In the evening, the 88th division was ordered to shorten the position lines and to defend the main positions outside the city. To its east, it was in close proximity to the 74th army and to its west, it was in close proximity to the 87th division. The task of defending the city, except for the areas near the Zhonghua gate and the Rain Flower Terrace, was shared by the 156th division and the 74th army. Originally, there were plans to alter the battle plans of the troops in the 66th army or the 83rd army, but given the fact that they were exhausted and were therefore unable to fight, the battle weary 112th division and 103rd division retreated from Zhenjiang.

During this fierce battle, both the Chinese and Japanese sides kept their own daily military reports, which were later disclosed after the war. The daily military reports concerning the Japanese troops' attack on Nanjing were published in the *Japanese International Pictorial Report* in February 1938, which can now be found in the Nanjing archives. Here I include an excerpt of some of the Japanese military reports published several days before the Nanjing Massacre, offering a comparison between the records kept by the Japanese and the Chinese troops. These materials are of unquestionably high historical value.

7 December

The attack on Nanjing began. The troops responsible for attacking, the Sukegawa, Kitagiri, Ono, Wakisaka, Fujii, Hotomi, Shimoeda, Chiba and Yamada units, swept away all the obstacles, surrounded the Chinese troops in the east and south and advanced towards the enemy gates. At 1pm today, the coordinated attack on Nanjing began with the sound of bombs. Some of the enemy troops surrounding the city desperately fought and resisted. The houses near the roads between the Zhongshan gate in the east of Nanjing and the suburban Waigaoqiao gate were on fire. In addition to the navy's air force, the ground troops' air force and the amphibious assault troops crossing the river were all dispatched. They have launched coordinated attacks on the city since last afternoon and have fiercely bombed the stubborn enemy in the suburbs of Nanjing. The life and death struggle for Nanjing is in progress.

8 December

These are the last days of Nanjing. Gu Zhutong has also assisted Tang Shengzhi in commanding and they seem to have put up a fierce resistance. Now, there is a vicious battle in the suburbs of Nanjing. To the east, the enemy stayed on Tangshan Mountain, occupying the highlands and continuously resisting. As a result, troops such as the Noda, Kitagiri and Ono units have laid siege to them. The Sukekawa troops advanced early and began to fight the enemy forces on Purple Mountain. The buildings near the Sun Yat-sen Mausoleum at the bottom of the mountain were ignited by enemy troops. To the south, at 3pm, our troops broke through Suoshu town near Jurong and repelled the enemy troops holding Chunhua town, which is the gateway to Nanjing. They occupied the town and continuously attacked the highlands near Qinglong Mountain. To the southwest, troops like the Chiba and Yamada units attacked Nanjing's Lishui district, overcoming the obstacles in Molingguan and fiercely fighting in the mountains against the enemy troops positioned in Niushou Mountain. In this historic offensive, our lieutenant general Nakashima was gloriously wounded in battle on the afternoon of 7 December.

9 December

The best possible news that all citizens have been expecting has come, and now, the attack on Nanjing is at its height. Troops like the Ono, Noda and Kitagiri units attacking Purple Mountain by Tangshan Mountain, acting as pioneers on the eastern flank, arrived at Qiling gate, only a kilometre from Purple Mountain. Because the enemy troops began to retreat in the evening, this territory has been entirely controlled by our troops since yesterday morning. Our troops were only 1.25 kilometres from Nanjing, and troops like the Kitagiri and Sukekawa units continuously advanced to attack the enemy troops near the Sun Yat-sen Mausoleum before gradually moving to attack the Zhongshan gate, which is regarded as Nanjing's eastern gate. Troops such as the Wakisaka, Shimoeda, Fujii and Isa units attacked in a south-eastern direction. They attacked the enemy forces positioned in both sides of the highlands as they advanced to Nanjing. They reached the famous Dajiaochang Airport, which is located on the outskirts of Nanjing and in the afternoon, they advanced to the Guanghua gate in the south-eastern corner of Nanjing. Troops like the Hasegawa and Takeshita units on the southern side eventually occupied Niushou Mountain and the nearby areas after a night of fighting. The tanks managed to get close to the Tongji gate. The artillery positions fiercely bombarded the Rain Flower Terrace, which is near the Zhonghua gate. By doing so, we surrounded Nanjing in three directions and reached the city walls. Yesterday afternoon, the senior commander, Matsui, sent terms of surrender to Tang Shengzhi, the commander responsible for the defence of Nanjing. He instructed us to wait for a reply so our troops temporarily stopped the attack before noon on 10 December. As for Xuancheng, troops including the Fujiyama, Nozoe, Kataoka and Chiba units reached the southern suburb of Wuhu yesterday morning and after a frontal assault, they eventually occupied Wuhu at 5pm. The quick strike forces in the Nagano and Yamada units reached the eastern side of Dangtu county last night. Special thanks is owed to the Okamoto troops for taking the vital communication line to Wuhu and occupying the Xishan bridge, which is close to Nanjing and other important places nearby. The path for enemy troops in Nanjing to retreat from the city has now been cut off.

10 December

The defending troops in Nanjing not only refused to listen to our proposals for a surrender but they have also continued to resist. Our troops are now attacking in all possible ways and every unit has begun to fiercely attack the city walls. Troops like the Fujiyama, Kataoka, and Nozoe units from Guangde occupied Wuhu, meanwhile, the Nagano and Yamada troops occupied Dangtu county, which is not far away from Nanjing. In the evening, two units crossed the Yangtze River there. The Wu River was attacked yesterday morning after landing and it was occupied. Soon afterwards, they rapidly advanced towards the Jinpu line. Therefore, the path for the defending troops in Nanjing for a possible retreat has been cut off thanks to their loss of Dangtu and Wuhu, while escape to the north of the Yangtze River has also been stopped. They have nowhere to run.

11 December

On the first day of the full-scale assault, our Wakisaka troops took the Guanghua gate, which is located in the eastern corner of Nanjing. A rising sun flag was erected above Nanjing. We then repelled the enemy forces who attacked at night to recapture the city gate and reinforced the position. On the second day, after brave fighting, all of the attacking forces took advantage of the results of the battle. The Isa unit near the Banxie troops occupied the highlands by the south-eastern corner of the Guanghua gate at around 1pm and had a short-range gunfight with the defending troops on the city wall. The Shimoeda troops also approached the south-eastern corner of Nanjing. Troops like the Noda, Ono, Kitagiri and Sukekawa units attacking the city walls from the north-eastern side of Purple Mountain had been fiercely fighting since Qingping and later approached the Heping gate and Taiping gate. Part of the Date unit occupied the Sun Yat-sen Mausoleum in the foothills of Purple Mountain and soon afterwards, along with Fujii troops and under the cover of the tanks, they fought the defending enemy troops on the Zhongshan gate. Troops from the Hasekawa and Okamoto units attacking the Zhonghua gate in the south had been continuously fighting in the region since yesterday morning. The Takeshita troops continuously attacked the southwestern corner of Nanjing. Along with the Takeshita troops, the Okamoto troops fought by Mochou Lake in the west of the city. Shells rained down from the group of artillery in the highlands near Purple Mountain, hitting all their targets and showing their terrifying and formidable power. In both the morning and the afternoon, in the skies over the city district, the navy's air force unleashed a barrage of destructive bombs on the enemy troops.

The daily reports from the days before Nanjing fell provide a general description of the initial phase of the Imperial Japanese Army's attack on Nanjing. Two events from this period should be highlighted.

One is on 7 December. The Japanese lieutenant general Kesago Nakajima was hit by the Chinese army and seriously injured.

Another is on 9 December. Iwane Matsui was laying siege to Nanjing and he issued an ultimatum to Tang Shengzhi demanding the surrender of the defending army.

The first incident took place in a fierce battle when a Japanese lieutenant general was wounded, which greatly boosted the morale of the Chinese army, including Tang Shengzhi. As the commander of the 16th division of the Imperial Japanese Army, Kesago Nakajima was one of the commanders of the Japanese army's four frontline assaults, whose troops conducted the main attack on the first line on the southern side. At 3.40pm on 9 December, he was hit in the waist by a pilot from the Soviet Union's volunteer army during a bombing raid. After the information was relayed to General Tang, a brief smile returned to the faces of all of the Chinese defending soldiers.

But General Tang and the other soldiers became outraged once again soon after when they heard another message: a ceremony featuring 800,000 people to celebrate the occupation of Nanjing was being prepared in Tokyo.

"How dare they! Our great army, with nearly 200,000 soldiers, is still here standing our ground in Nanjing, why do they think victory is theirs?" General Tang gave an order to his officers: "All defending troops must safeguard the city gates and we shall not allow their plot to prevail."

On that day, the Nanjing commander delivered two orders to defend to the death: "First, the current position of our army is the final front for defending Nanjing. All troops must stay determined to die or survive with the land. We shall defend it with all our strength and shall never abandon an inch of land. If anyone doesn't observe this command or withdraws without authorisation, they are then subject to the serious collective punishments as ordered by the generalissimo. Second, all ships must be kept by their respective transportation commander and unauthorised use is not allowed. The commander of the 48th army Song Lian is hereby appointed to command the military police along the river. No soldiers are allowed to cross the river without authorisation. Violators shall be arrested and prosecuted; if they disobey, they shall be stopped by force."

As soon as the orders were issued, an officer trembled as he handed a piece of colourful paper to Tang.

Tang skimmed through it and became extremely angry, tearing it to pieces. "Absolutely not! Does Matsui think I'm a pushover? Tell them: 'As long as Nanjing survives, I, Tang Shengzhi will never surrender!'"

What the officer had given Tang was a leaflet demanding surrender that had been dropped from planes as ordered by the Japanese supreme commander Iwane Matsui. It read:

> Millions of Japanese soldiers have occupied the Jiangnan region and the Japanese army lays siege to Nanjing. As the war stands, future fighting will do nothing but end in tragedy for you. Nanjing is the ancient capital of China and the capital of the Republic of China. It holds the tomb of Ming Xiaoling, the Sun Yat-sen Mausoleum and numerous historic sites. Nanjing is a place that unites East Asian culture. The Imperial Japanese Army will kill anybody who resists while they shall be generous to innocent citizens and non-hostile Chinese soldiers and guard their safety. However, if you still resist, the essence of 1,000 years of culture will be destroyed in one day. Years of development will be reduced to nothing. As

commander, I, representing the Japanese army, hope to receive the ownership of Nanjing transferred from you peacefully according to the following procedures.

Your response is due at noon on 10 December at the warning line from Zhongshan Road to Jurong Road. One commander representative from your side and one from our side will make necessary concerted preparations to transfer the ownership of Nanjing. Without any response before the stated time, our army will open fire immediately.

— SIGNED BY THE COMMANDER OF THE IMPERIAL JAPANESE ARMY,
IWANE MATSUI.

"Repeat my order: never surrender! Resist to the death!" Tang said. On the night of 9 December, a subordinate came to check on his plans and was angrily criticised by Tang: "Anyone who wants to be a traitor, just surrender to them! I will never make you do so!" At that point, Tang decided to cut off all means of retreat. On the day of the ultimatum, 10 December, the Chinese army didn't stop defending the city gates and followed the order to use anything they could to defend the city, like sand, stones, cement, wood, bricks, and even doors. They used whatever they could to defend and block off the gates. They gathered petrol so that once the enemy attacked the gate, they could burn them to death.

On 10 December, finding that the Chinese army had no plans to surrender, the Japanese army launched a full-scale attack on the Rain Flower Terrace, the Tongji gate, the third peak of Purple Mountain and other positions. The fighting was much fiercer than before, especially on the south-eastern side. Due to the loss of the final front, the Japanese army directly attacked the city walls. Nanjing was in extreme danger. On that day, in order to outflank the defending Chinese army, the 18th division of the Japanese army occupied Wuhu. Nanjing was surrounded by enemies in three directions and in an extremely dangerous situation.

Nanjing was now isolated and they had only two choices: wage a desperate struggle against the enemy or die.

"For glory! For Nanjing!"

"Advance!"

Among the defending soldiers, some were shouting angrily, some were shouting with tears streaming down their faces, some were shouting insanely while pulling out their hair and some were throwing down their guns and weeping silently.

This is war.

Bloody Double 12

The day was 12 December.

On that day, an editor's note appeared in a Japanese newspaper: "On this day last year, the Xi'an Incident took place and Chiang Kai-shek was at death's door. One year later, our army has invaded Nanjing."

The Japanese wanted to humiliate Chiang Kai-shek. They appeared to have total confidence in victory and were determined to win.

> *Why? Why can't we see the blue sky and bright light?*
> *Why? Why does the broken bayonet still bleed?*
> *Look at my comrades' bodies piled up like a mountain all around;*
> *Touch my useless arms;*
> *Fire in my eyes, fire in my heart;*
> *Fire of thousands and millions of brothers and sisters behind me;*
> *They await the invading bandits' arrival.*

This isn't a poem, but the last cry of the Chinese soldiers who defended Nanjing in the final resistance on 12 December 1937.

Iwane Matsui's final military deployment and orders to invade Nanjing had now been officially issued. We are able to read this order for ourselves in the military records left by the Japanese army:

1. Two armies have marched to the battlefront under the order of China Operation 27 and have prepared for siege warfare.

2. If the commander-in-chief of Nanjing or the municipality still remains in the city, we ought to persuade them to open the city gates and provide a peaceful entrance for our army. At this point, each division and regiment should first let the group of selected infantry enter the city as the initial forces and then sweep the city by region.

3. If the remnants of the enemy put up a last-ditch resistance, all artillery guns arriving at the battlefront are to commence shelling to capture the ramparts. Each division and regiment is to sweep the city with one company as an initial force.

The rest of the principal force is to rally at the planned point outside the city.

4. The mopping-up operation inside the city must be conducted in designated areas to avoid the accidental injury of friendly forces, and each side ought to be crystal clear about the responsibilities of their activities.

5. The combat zones for the two armies are as follows:

Republic gate, Park Road, Zhongzheng Street, Zhongzheng Road, Hanzhong Road.

6. City gates assigned to each army:

Expeditionary army: Zhongshan gate, Taiping gate, Peace gate.

The 10th army: Republic gate, Zhonghua gate, Shuixi gate.

The six city gates of Nanjing selected by Iwane Matsui would be both routes leading into Nanjing and a critical combat area guarded by a large group of Chinese soldiers. Matsui designated the toughest assignment to Yanagawa and the 10th army. They seemed to have a blood feud with the Chinese army and fought fierce battles with the Chinese defending troops after accepting their mission.

The first targets of the Japanese 10th army were Purple Mountain and the Rain Flower Terrace, which were peripheral barriers leading to the Zhonghua gate. Taking these two positions would mean winning a breakthrough and occupying Nanjing. As a result, the Chinese ordered massive amounts of forces to defend these two places, including the 88th division led by Sun Yuanliang and Chiang's crack guards regiment, which had the most sophisticated equipment and many soldiers. Sun Yuanliang was the commander of the 72nd army, as well as the adjutant commander of the 88th division. The guards regiment, with three brigades and corps troops, consisted of about 300,000 soldiers. With two such excellent quality units guarding the Purple Mountain and the Rain Flower Terrace, their significance had already been proven.

Before 12 December, a couple of duals to the death had been fought between China and Japan at these two strongholds. The Japanese army first attacked and seized Qilin gate, which was a weak position for the Chinese defensive army. After this, they concentrated their forces on Tiger Cave in Purple Mountain. Due to the geological characteristics of the cave and its vulnerability to artillery fire, the Chinese defenders abandoned it after an entire day of being attacked and withdrew to the second peak of Purple Mountain. Believing that the Chinese defending army was vulnerable, the Japanese army marched towards the second peak of Purple Mountain with delight. However, they never imagined that the guards regiment, Chiang Kai-shek's crack troops, had been stationed there for four years and had trained there every day, which meant they were familiar with the terrain and had established strong fortifications. Due to this, the Japanese suffered a tremendous defeat in their first battle, leaving piles of corpses. After that, the Japanese army swiftly dispatched their forces to Purple Mountain and the western hills, where they fought a rapidly fluctuating battle with the Chinese defending troops. Heavy gunfire roared across the valleys and forests and the positions were still held by the Chinese defenders, even though the numbers of casualties in both the Chinese and Japanese armies were high. The continuous defeats angered the Japanese army, who increased the number of troops and dispatched artillery and armour piercing bullets to shoot at the Chinese positions. Constructions made of cement and gigantic stones were destroyed, flying into the sky with a deafening explosion. But what the Japanese army couldn't believe was that after several rounds of bombing, another attack with tanks and attacks by assault squads, they had been defeated by the Chinese army. On 11 December, after several series of attacks, Purple Mountain, whose plants had been uprooted as the mountain itself appeared to bleed, still held its head high.

On the dawn of 12 December, following an aerial bombing raid by several newly-dispatched squadrons, the Japanese army attacked the northern highlands of Purple Mountain from both the east and west. Blazing fires and broken stones immediately filled the hills, which echoed with the sounds of screams and slaughter.

"Hold on, comrades! In a few hours when our reinforcements arrive, we'll be able to defend Purple Mountain." After being pushed out of the fortifications, Li Kaixi, the colonel of the 3rd guards regiment, shook the dirt off his head, counted the soldiers around him and then led his dozens of troops to the ruined positions, ready to fight the enemy to the death.

"Colonel, our reinforcements aren't coming! They say we've lost the Zhonghua gate. Our regiment is being attacked from the front and the rear. What should we do?!" a subordinate asked Li Kaixi for advice.

"I'll call the brigade commander." Li Kaixi picked up a phone and dialled, but only to find out that nobody answered: "Brigade commander! Brigade commander! I need reinforcements! Reinforcements!"

"Colonel, there's no use. The brigade commander has already run away."

"They've run away before finishing the battle?" Li Kaixi couldn't believe it, and now faced with no answer on the phone, no reinforcements and their allies panicking, he had to accept reality: "My God. How can we win the battle? Nanjing, my poor Nanjing..." Colonel Li and his subordinates had been abandoned. He kowtowed three times, getting on his knees and bowing so his head touched the ground, a traditional sign of respect to the hundreds of corpses of his comrades-in-arms surrounding the position. He then quickly left the position on the north side of Purple Mountain.

"Why haven't they withdrawn from the position?" Major General Sasaki was the commander of the 30th brigade from the 16th division, which was an elite unit in the Japanese army that had been directed by Sasaki to attack the Purple Mountain positions. The Japanese army had failed to take the northern position on Purple Mountain even after two days of fighting. Sasaki was puzzled. He warned his subordinates: "Be cautious! We can't embarrass the commander-in-chief on the glorious final assault on Nanjing!"

He later dispatched several forces to a nearby small highland village called Xingwei and prepared to attack Purple Mountain from the west flank.

"We need to annihilate the main peak today!" Although Lieutenant General Kesago Nakajima, Sasaki's superior, was wounded, the crazed killer still held power over the 16th division and wouldn't give up on his greatest goal of "annihilating Nanjing".

"Have the heavy mortars been transported here? We can't break through Purple Mountain without them, not to mention the city gates!" Sasaki shouted.

Nakajima answered: "Dispatch two heavy mortar squadrons and the 33rd division will provide aid in your attack. We all eagerly await your annihilation of Purple Mountain."

Sasaki hadn't expected the following attacks. He recalled in his diary: "The position had become a sea of fire when suddenly a flurry of gunfire was heard from the rear. I rushed out asking what had happened. A subordinate answered: 'We've just defeated the enemy, how could a group of soldiers attack from the peak?'" Sasaki couldn't believe it and asked if they had been previously defeated troops, but the subordinate said no. Sasaki then personally directed the battle for a while and when he was just about to rest, his subordinates shouted out again. Sasaki recorded this, writing: "Enemy troops charged down from Purple Mountain, crowd after crowd of them everywhere we looked. They were all the soldiers from the guards regiment stationed on the peak of Purple Mountain. They tried to break through the gaps of our positions and launch a counterattack. This unit was Chiang Kai-shek's personal favourite, as well as the most valiant troops. They bravely fought to the end."

Shoji Iwasaki, a private first class in the 1st wing of the independent sappers in the Japanese expeditionary army, had praised the Chinese soldiers in his letters to his family: "They deserve to be the regular Chinese army. They sacrificed themselves with dignity and some even directly charged towards our guns before they died with a smile. If such men account for even 10% of China's population, this confrontation between Japan and China will be quite an arduous affair indeed."

The Rain Flower Terrace, located in hilly terrain at an altitude of around 60 metres, is one mile away from Nanjing's Zhonghua gate, which lies to the south. It is a mountain pass in southern Nanjing that has been referred to as "the southern gate of Jinling" - Jinling being a historic and poetic name for Nanjing. The Rain Flower Terrace has long been a place where many heroes have shed their blood: Yang Bangyi of the Southern Song Dynasty fought Jin Dynasty soldiers here before his heart was torn out by his enemies; Yin Junxiong, the heroine of the Xinhai Revolution, fought against the armies of the Qing Dynasty for 10 days at the Rain Flower Terrace, which won a final victory for the revolutionary army and her eternal place in Chinese history. During the Chinese Civil War, early Communist Party leaders like Yun Daiying fought there but were killed by KMT reactionaries. The Rain Flower Terrace has always been covered with blood. The Japanese army attempted to break through the southern gate of Nanjing but never expected the tenacious resistance of the Chinese defending army.

On 9 December, Japan dispatched a force to attack the Rain Flower Terrace but suffered a serious defeat, which led to another force being called upon to aid in the attack. The 527th and 528th regiments of the 88th division took up the positions of the fallen and rose to fight one after another. They fought hand-to-hand with the Japanese army at the position, along a front of nearly two miles. Another victory was won by the Chinese defending soldiers and the Japanese army withdrew, leaving more than 600 of their comrades dead.

On 10 December, the Japanese army dispatched aeroplanes and tanks to attack the Rain Flower Terrace and wipe out the Chinese defenders. Nevertheless, Chinese soldiers fought even more courageously this time around and the Japanese army once again failed to seize the position.

On 11 December, the Japanese dispatched their main force to the south and also surrounded the Zhonghua gate at the back of the Rain Flower Terrace. The Zhonghua gate remained in Chinese hands and the Rain Flower Terrace still stood high over the Chinese defenders. The Japanese army once again had to leave thousands of their comrades' bodies in the graveyard that Nanjing had become.

"Fantastic news. Every soldier in the 88th division is a hero!" The division commander Sun Yuanliang took immense pride in the achievement.

On the afternoon of 12 December, the Japanese army first broke through the Zhonghua gate and had thought that taking the Rain Flower Terrace would be simple. They never expected the unswerving resistance of the Chinese defenders in the 88th division between the Rain Flower Terrace and the Zhonghua gate, which caused the deaths of more than 400 Japanese soldiers. However, the situation the 88th division had found themselves in wasn't grounds for optimism. Commander Zhu Chi of the 262nd brigade and Commander Gao Zhihao of the 362nd brigade sacrificed themselves for China in addition to more than 2,000 Chinese officers and soldiers.

During this defensive battle for Purple Mountain and the Rain Flower Terrace, other heroes fought against the Japanese army, including the reinforcing regimental officers who later got wounded, including Colonel Zhang Lingfu of the 305th regiment of the 74th division and Division Commander Wang Yaowu of the 51st division. The 305th regiment led by Zhang Lingfu suffered the most serious losses. The regiment lost thousands of officers and soldiers, and almost all of the soldiers below the rank of company commander were killed, while Zhang Lingfu was seriously injured and forced to leave the front by Wang Yaowu. Zhang had famously come to the front with his subordinates carrying his coffin behind him.

On 12 December, the Battle of Nanjing raged just outside each of the city's gates and the battlefield by the Guanghua gate was no different. The fighting had left it covered by blood.

The Guanghua gate was an important position in Nanjing's defences. Nanjing had eight breathtaking city gates and was firmly defended by the city's moat, which was 35 metres wide and five metres deep. When Major Nakagawa, the aide-de-camp for Ito's army, secretly conducted a scouting mission to the Zhonghua gate with light armoured vehicles, he was surprised by the defences and wondered how the Japanese would ever take Nanjing. The Chinese defenders at the Guanghua gate were locked into a fierce battle at that point; the roads leading to the city gate were protected by anti-tank trenches and five barricades, with five thick barbed wire fences on both sides of the roads to halt any advances to the moat. The western part of the gate and city wall had 28 openings for heavy machine guns to fire through, and the defenders here were the vanguard of the Nationalist army, including the guards regiment. To breach Nanjing, the Japanese would inevitably have to take the well-defended Guanghua gate.

Nevertheless, the Japanese army was determined. It was the dawn of 9 December when the Japanese army attacked the Guanghua gate. The elite 9th division launched the first ferocious attack against the Chinese defenders at Hongmao Mountain outside the city gates with the help of vast numbers of tanks. One camp from the 2nd regiment of the teaching corps was defending there, but nearly half of its soldiers were lost and they had to withdraw to the Guanghua gate. Just after dawn, Japan dispatched aeroplanes to bomb the Guanghua gate. With bombs raining down from the sky, the Chinese defenders had nowhere to hide and more than 100 soldiers were killed or wounded. Seeing that the city gate was being razed to the ground and realising the seriousness of the situation, Commander Tang Shengzhi dispatched the 2nd guards regiment to immediately reinforce the troops fighting at the Guanghua gate.

Taking their weapons with them, the 2nd guards regiment went straight to the Guanghua gate in several vehicles.

As soon as the platoon leader of the reinforcements, Xiang Yuanhong, arrived at the city gate, a man near the city walls, an officer with a face blackened by the battle, cried out with excitement: "You're here! What are our orders?!"

Xiang finally realised that he was now the leader of these soldiers and in a puzzled tone he said: "I'm not sure. We're confused about the status of the enemy and we need your help."

"No problem. Thank God you came." The officer pointed to outside the city gate, wiping away tears at the same time: "Our enemies are about 100 metres from here. Don't raise your head to look. Some of my soldiers have been killed doing that."

At the same time, Xiang heard an aeroplane swooping overhead. "Get down!" As soon as these words left his mouth, several bombs were dropped on the city gate behind them.

"These Japanese have gone too far! They've already killed my two brothers and I have no more soldiers left! I'll fight them to the death!" A platoon leader with a Sichuanese accent threw himself on Xiang and then picked up a submachine gun and opened fire outside the city gate.

The sound of gunfire led to a volley of shells and machine gun fire from the Japanese army.

"Don't shoot!" Xiang stopped him as quickly as he could and said: "Our enemies outnumber us, we need to preserve our ammunition."

How could they find out more about the current status of the Japanese army? The gunner next to Xiang said: "I have an idea." After saying that, he took out a small mirror from his pocket and tied two rifles together with the mirror tied to the end. After this, he carefully moved towards a gap in the wall, with his back to it, and used the mirror to investigate the conditions outside the city. He found that the Japanese were moving towards the city gate in secret under the cover of nine tanks.

"They're trying to take the little mill over there and attack the city gates by surprise!" Xiang looked in front of where the Japanese army was approaching and saw that there was a wooden mill about 30 metres away from the Guanghua gate tower. The roof of the mill was higher than the city wall and if the Japanese army took it, the situation would indeed be incredibly perilous.

"We need to destroy the mill first; if we don't, we'll lose the city gate and all be killed!" Xiang sweated with anxiety.

The defending soldiers shouted: "How could we do that?"

Xiang responded: "We'll organise a suicide squad to burn down the mill before they can take it. Is there anybody who wants to go? If the task is completed, the member of the squad will be promoted to platoon leader."

"I'll go!"

"Me too! The promotion doesn't matter. I'd die to hold the city gate!" A dozen soldiers quickly shouted that they were willing to go.

Xiang was extremely moved: "We can't go there with too many people. You boys should go there along the city wall in a line with straw and matches. Then hang down the burning straw with ropes."

They went into action. The first soldier only managed to drop the straw down about a metre before he was discovered by the enemy and shot. The same happened to the second soldier.

A third soldier said: "My turn. We should move to somewhere else and change tactics." The soldier was remarkably resourceful: he changed the place where they were hanging down the straw from and suddenly jumped down when the straw hung down at about halfway.

"Cover him!" Xiang immediately ordered his soldiers to open fire at the Japanese army.

A flame shot up around the mill while the two sides were locked in fierce fighting. The defenders at the Guanghua gate cheered again and again.

The Japanese army couldn't tolerate the loss. Seeing that their frontal attack had been blocked, they changed tactics. Under the cover of a pervasive mist of gunpowder, a Japanese squad dressed in civilian clothing charged towards the Guanghua gate along the city moat, attempting to fight hand to hand with the Chinese soldiers defending the position and break through the city gate.

"The Guanghua gate is at stake. Is there anything we can do to repel the Japanese army?" Gui Yongqing asked Colonel Xie Chengrui for advice over the phone.

Defending the Guanghua gate was the responsibility of the 2nd guards regiment with Xie Chengrui acting as colonel. "Nothing can be done. Our soldiers have been either wounded or killed over the past several days without any convincing victories. Maybe it's time to use our trump card," Xie Chengrui said gnashing his teeth.

"What trump card?"

"Ask the corps to provide us with several carloads of petrol. I'll carry the petrol to the city walls myself."

Gui Yongqing went quiet at the other end of the phone. After a short moment, he said: "Okay. I'll ask the chief of staff to send you the petrol."

As soon as the petrol was sent, Xie Chengrui, leading two dozen soldiers with petrol cans, hurried to the Guanghua gate. While it was still night, they poured petrol along the city gate one can after another.

The Japanese army never thought that the Chinese defenders would ever do anything like this and were concentrating on launching their so-called "final assault" under cover of darkness on the gate.

A flame shot up suddenly at the Guanghua gate and it grew into a wall of fire, shooting like lightning towards the enemy positions.

The Japanese army could be seen panicking in the flames and they soon turned into balls of fire, either burning alive or collapsing.

The Japanese army outside the gate fled in panic.

Suddenly, the Guanghua gate, motionless over the last several days, opened, and Xie Chengrui led the defending soldiers to furiously open fire on the enemy with a dozen machine guns.

It was an utterly devastating counterattack and the Guanghua gate henceforth became a symbol of valiant resistance against the Japanese army.

The Guanghua gate had been blocked off and China's defending soldiers defended their positions with a mad bravery, while the Japanese army attacked with an equally insane ferocity.

The members of a Japanese suicide squad tied white headbands around their heads with the characters for "victory" written on them. They rushed towards the city walls with no concern for their lives under the covering fire of a tank, light machine guns in one hand and broadswords in the other.

"Hand grenades! Use grenades against the tanks!" Seeing the Japanese army's berserk rampage nearly arriving at the city gates, the leader of the Chinese defenders quickly planned a barrage of hand grenades and finally stopped the enemy tanks at the city gate. At that moment, a dozen of the Japanese soldiers had already reached the city gate.

"Stop them! Kill them! Quickly!" Seeing this, the Chinese soldiers hung over the city wall they knew so well and annihilated the enemy forces far more effectively than they had expected.

"Sir, I think we deserve a promotion, just look at this!" Several battalion commanders under Deng Longguang and a dozen soldiers carried baskets containing Japanese weapons and war trophies.

Commander Tang Shengzhi agreed that they deserved a reward after hearing the news, but before he could do so, news broke that the Guanghua gate had been breached by the Japanese army.

The Chinese army believed that the fighting at the Guanghua gate, which had lasted for more than three days, was the most horrifying part of the Battle of Nanjing after the Second Sino-Japanese War. The rapidly fluctuating battle between China and Japan was far more ferocious than anyone could ever have described and led to the death of a great deal of soldiers. Colonel Xie Chengrui was among them. The colonel had been sick before the battle and was then burned during the fighting while defending the city gate. Late at night on 12 December, several hours after the Guanghua gate had been breached, Colonel Xie Chengrui withdrew towards the riverside. At that point, soldiers preparing to escape across the river passed by the Yijiang gate and trampled Xie Chengrui to death due to the panicked conditions.

"That's Colonel Xie Chengrui! Stop!" Liu Yongcheng, an officer in the guards regiment who'd fled along with Xie Chengrui, knelt down and wept for him when he saw that Xie was being trampled to death by a crowd of soldiers. But it was in vain. This was just one tragedy that took place in the final hours of 12 December.

Appalling tragedies were taking place both inside and outside Nanjing on 12 December 1937. Nanjing was taking its last gasps for breath before being enslaved by the Japanese.

The Zhonghua gate was the position most coveted by the Japanese troops. The Zhonghua gate. Nanjing. The Chinese government. These were all interlinked in the minds of the Chinese as were they in the minds of the Japanese. Therefore, Iwane Matsui ordered the Zhonghua gate to be taken as the final push in the assault on Nanjing. Both the strategic and symbolic importance of taking the Zhonghua gate made it an essential target.

Japan dispatched the 6th division to attack the Zhonghua gate, in addition to several fighter squadrons, two tanks and several regiments of infantrymen and sappers.

China's defending soldiers consisted of many large forces, including the division led by Wang Yaowu. The city wall at the Zhonghua gate seemed to be even stronger than at the Guanghua gate and the defending forces made it seem impregnable. Machine guns could be seen positioned every 50 metres on the city wall and more than 30 mortars were deployed between each and every machine gun. Outside the city walls, residential buildings had been razed to the ground before the Japanese army had even arrived as an essential defensive strategy. As a result, the soldiers could see for more than 200 metres when they stood on the city wall, able to see every move made by the enemy. This was a clever move by the Chinese defenders. Nonetheless, the Japanese army knew about the high levels of vigilance at the gate and planned an offensive strategy to mitigate it.

On the dawn of 12 December, artillery guns on the land and aeroplanes in the sky began to bombard the position, launching a fierce and shattering attack on the Zhonghua gate. After the bombardment, the gate was covered with roaring flames and clouds of gunpowder smoke, engulfing the entire position.

After 10 minutes or so, the Japanese army tried to assess the situation but were incredibly disappointed: the Zhonghua gate and the city walls still stood strong with no signs of collapsing or being breached.

The Japanese commander was speechless. After a while, he suddenly shouted his orders and several 75-ton tanks rapidly advanced towards the gate to try to smash it open like a battering ram. However, the gate remained firmly closed.

The Japanese commander was stunned again. Several sappers equipped with explosives advanced this time. Covered by heavy artillery fire, they advanced close to the bottom of the wall with huge amounts of explosives.

Bang!

After the smoke from the gunpowder cleared, the grand wall was seen still standing proudly, save some chunks of plaster and bricks. It was as if a swarm of tiny insects had tried to bite an elephant. The Japanese army was completely stunned and was getting desperate. They gave up on their advanced weaponry and ordered teams of soldiers equipped with shining bayonets to storm the walls.

The *bushido* spirit was their last weapon and the Japanese army believed that it was also their most powerful, just what they'd need to defeat their enemies. However, this time when fighting against the Chinese troops at the Zhonghua gate, the *bushido* spirit failed to win the day.

The commander of the 153rd brigade, Li Tianxia, and the regimental commander of the 306th regiment, Qiu Weida, in turn ordered officers and soldiers to defend against the attacking Japanese soldiers at the bottom of the wall, using guns and hand to hand combat, for more than 10 Japanese charges.

The battle was intense. Chinese and Japanese troops fought fiercely. Fallen soldiers began to pile up in the battlefield.

"Retreat! Commander Tang has ordered us to retreat in a telegram!"

The injured regimental commander Qiu Weida couldn't believe it. The brigade commander Li Tianxia couldn't believe it either. But it was true. When dusk had nearly descended upon Nanjing, a staff officer had been sent to deliver Commander Tang's orders. All of the troops defending the Zhonghua gate, including the 153rd brigade, were to retreat to the edge of the Yangtze River and prepare to cross. Qiu Weida cried bitterly, unwilling to give up the gate.

However, the orders to retreat were true. On 12 December, the Nanjing headquarters issued the following orders:

1. The troops under the command of the headquarters are hereby ordered to head to areas near Huizhou.
2. Troops directly under the command of the headquarters and the 36th division should cross the river to assemble and await orders tonight (on the evening of 12 December).
3. The orders for each unit are specified in another table.

The orders are on the right.
A table specifying the orders of each unit crossing the river is attached.

— Signed, Nanjing Defence Commander Tang Shengzhi

According to the memoirs of Tang Shengzhi and other KMT leaders, at noon on 11 December, Tang received a call from Gu Zhutong. Gu delivered Chiang Kai-shek's order demanding the defending troops to retreat from Nanjing, asking Tang Shengzhi to cross the river to retreat to the Jinpu road while ordering the defending troops to break out of the encirclement.

"If we retreat now, the soldiers at the front might not follow the orders." Tang Shengzhi was conflicted.

Gu Zhutong said: "The committee has issued its orders. Don't hesitate. Hurry to Pukou and I will tell Hu Zongnan to wait for you there."

Tang Shengzhi shook his head: "It's not right. If I retreat, how could our troops go through with their orders? I won't go!"

"You should leave a staff officer to explain the matter to them," Gu Zhutong said.

Tang Shengzhi didn't leave that night. He thought about it all night. He thought that it'd be unfair to all of the defending soldiers, who'd be left fighting a bloody battle on their own if he went.

At 5am on 12 December, Tang Shengzhi gathered his officers in the headquarters, calling army commanders and division commanders to his office. He informed them of Chiang Kai-shek's orders and handed out the previously prepared order to retreat to every leader of the defending forces. Finally, he took out a piece of paper and demanded that the commanders sign their names under the words "agree to retreat".

"He did this so he didn't have to take responsibility. He didn't discuss it with us at all and forced us to sign our names on the paper," a division commander present at the time later recalled the incident and was still angry with Tang Shengzhi.

After Tang retreated from Nanjing on 12 December, he arrived in Wuhan a few days later and submitted a Nanjing battle report to Chiang Kai-shek, saying: "It was all my fault. Please give me the punishment I deserve." Chiang Kai-shek said nothing. Later, Tang claimed that he was ill and went back to his hometown in Hunan.

When Tang gave his orders, Deng Longguang and Ye Zhao's auxiliary troops from Guangdong retreated as planned, as did Song Xilian's troops, who retreated to Pukou. Among the rest of the troops, a few Chinese defending soldiers retreated as per their orders, but most of them didn't know that the headquarters had given the orders to retreat. Some troops were fighting fiercely against the Japanese so there was no way that they could have received the orders. Chiang Kai-shek's communications and signals troops had packed up and left the city after noon that day.

The soldiers on the front were in a lamentable condition. What fate awaited these unfortunate souls on the last night and day of Nanjing's freedom? Some may have thought it, but most didn't realise that all that awaited them was death.

12 December 1937. Snow was falling from the skies in Nanjing. Meanwhile, the ground burned and blood boiled in the flames.

2

THE FIRST DAY OF THE MASSACRE

The horrors of December 12 had passed. It was now 13 December and new horrors awaited the city. For the Chinese defending soldiers and citizens of Nanjing, 13 December was doomsday, a humiliating and hopeless doomsday. It was also a day worth remembering for thousands of years and every man, woman and child who strives for peace would do well to remember 13 December 1937.

For people from Nanjing, 13 December 1937 is synonymous with death. Today, after more than 70 years, 13 December is a public memorial day for all Chinese people. However, on 13 December 1937, the tragedies unfolding inside and outside of Nanjing preluded the horrors of the Nanjing Massacre.

Memories of the Defending Troops

For the defending Chinese soldiers garrisoned in Nanjing, the fall of the city on 13 December had been unexpected, of course, apart from for those 100,000 plus garrisoned soldiers and the top commander Tang Shengzhi who'd been evacuated by boat the night before.

It isn't just the Japanese who face the blame for the ensuing massacre, but the level of Chiang Kai-shek and Tang Shengzhi's culpability has also been a subject of debate in China. The Chinese communists have their own opinions on Chiang Kai-shek's role in the tragedy. In general, as previously mentioned, in the words of Mao Zedong: "After 1936, relatively serious efforts were made in the anti-Japanese battles and it was Chiang's responsibility for doing so." As for the senior commander of the defending troops, most people initially thought that Tang Shengzhi was useless. When Nanjing was under threat, at first, no one dared to stand up for the city and lead its defence. Then, Tang, a sickly man, made an impassioned speech and became the commander-in-chief of the city's garrison. Chiang Kai-shek didn't say anything in Wuhan when he later heard Tang's report on the defence of Nanjing. Why?

Tang Shengzhi was the top commander of more than 100,000 defensive troops. Their actions and sacrifices when the Japanese attacked Nanjing should be written into history. With this in mind, the following extract is from the memoirs of Tang Shengzhi's associate, Tan Daoping, who was advising the headquarters section chief. It contains detailed descriptions of the episode:

> At four o'clock that afternoon, under the urgent circumstances, Tang Shengzhi called Luo Zhuoying, Liu Xing, Zhou Lan, She Nianci and commanders above the rank of division commander to his official residence for a meeting. This was the last meeting in the defensive Battle of Nanjing. Tang Shengzhi at first declared that: "Nanjing is in crisis. Some soldiers have now stormed the city. Are you confident of our success in its defence?"
>
> They looked at each other and the atmosphere of the room went from cold to a biting chill. Then, he read out Chiang Kai-shek's message: "If the city can't be defended for long, you should seize the opportunity to retreat and make plans for the future." The orders were to retreat from the gates, break out of the encirclement and then advance to a rallying point. The commanders present were all speechless with an unspeakable silence that made everyone uneasy. They were in a state of profound grief and indignation.
>
> Tang Shengzhi said again: "The battle doesn't end today, but it continues tomorrow. The battle doesn't end with the defence of Nanjing, but it extends outside of the city. Please remember the humiliation we suffer today and swear to take revenge for today's hostilities. Each commander should explain this to their units. If the troops can't be led and are outside of our control, then cross the river with me."
>
> After the plan to break out of the encirclement was issued, it quickly grew dark. Looking out of the window of the commander's office, we could see that Purple Mountain had been heavily burned in the distance. Fires were burning near the Rain Flower Terrace, the Zhonghua gate and the Tongji gate. Nanjing was in chaos.
>
> A fierce fight broke out in the streets in the northeast of the city that night. Li Zhongxin and I were still collecting documents in Tang's residence. When we hurried out, the guardsmen were pouring petrol on the house. We learned that when Tang Shengzhi had got into the car, he gave the guardsmen 500 yuan and 20 bottles of petrol and told them to burn down the house. We left Tang's residence and hurried to the railway ministry office. There was no one there, save some soldiers who were walking around. When we went into the cellar, we saw several one-yuan bills scattered on the floor. A corpse lay there. After Li Zhongxin and I burned the remaining documents, we hurried out of the building.
>
> We wanted to get out of the city through the Yijiang gate. However, when

we walked to the gate, we came across a small road with barbed wire on both sides. Soldiers from the 36th division were carrying rifles and forbidding people from moving in and out, pointing their guns at some of them. Officers and soldiers from the 87th division, the 88th division and others who would later retreat were arguing with the civilians amidst the sound of crying and shouting. The sound of guns could be heard everywhere. Flames blazed on Purple Mountain as an endless stream of refugees flowed behind carrying the young and the old. We had to stop in front of the fortifications. I suddenly realised that this regiment from the 36th division must have come to the city following orders to prepare for combat in the streets. I then went up to a soldier and said: "Where's your commander? I have important orders for him!"

"Who are you?" he asked.

"Section chief of the ministry of officers' garrison. I have papers here."

After he checked our papers, Li Zhongxin and I were allowed to pass through the barbed wire. When we arrived at the Yijiang gate, we saw a company commander from the 36th division. I then told him their new orders.

After we safely left the gate, we could see that the docks along the river were in utter chaos. The sound of gunfire continued to ring out. There were hundreds of thousands of people, but there were only two or three ferries. The Yangtze River had become the boundary between life and death. As soon as a boat came to shore, a couple of people jumped over to it and fell into the river. No one paid any attention to them. Several hundred hands tightly gripped the edge of the boat. People onboard shouted angrily at those on the shore who wouldn't let them move, some of them firing into the air. A sailor politely pleaded with them and tried his hardest to pilot the boat. Some were still holding tightly onto the edge of the boat and flew out to the river with it as it pulled away. Some of them fell into the river and were carried off to the east by the current. It was now chaos, caused by the stupidity of war and insidious warmongers. When the boat had made its way into the middle of the river, gunfire could be heard in Pukou across the river. They forbade boats from the south from coming close to the shore, so the boat had to stay in the middle of the river. Tang Shengzhi had previously given an order to the commander of the 1st army, Hu Zongnan, that the people in Nanjing shouldn't be allowed to cross the river privately. Although the 1st army had been informed of this retreat over the radio, Hu Zongnan was stationed in Chuzhou at the time. The orders hadn't spread to his soldiers on the northern shore, leading to a tragic misunderstanding.

Some Japanese troops had crossed the river into Jiangpu County by then, but Li Zhongxin and I didn't know that was the source of the intensive gunfire across the river. We crawled over to the coal harbour while the sound of gunfire continued before we finally got to the navy's docks. There was a boat moored there as well as the Jiangning Fortress intelligence headquarters. After we got on the boat, we saw that there were 300 or 400 people on board. They were officers and soldiers from the ministry of officers, but Tang Shengzhi, Luo Zhuoying and She Nianci were nowhere to be seen. Many proposed immediately setting off from the dock, but I tried hard to stop them and we continued to wait for Tang Shengzhi's arrival. After an hour, Tang Shengzhi accompanied by an adjutant from the garrison headquarters arrived. Luo Zhuoying and Liu Xing later arrived too, but She Nianci and Liao Ken still hadn't. Tang Shengzhi demanded that we wait for another hour. After that, he was afraid of delaying the plan to cross the river, so he ordered the boat to set off.

This ship has an interesting story behind it. When the battle began, to prevent defending officers and soldiers from crossing the river without permission, Tang Shengzhi ordered for all the ships to be under the 36th division's watch. No ship was allowed to leave. Anyone who disobeyed the order would be punished. On 7 December, the Jiangyin defensive command shipped some people and military supplies to Wulong Mountain outside Jiangning Fortress, and the ship was left outside of the blockade line. Now, the chief of staff, Zhou Lan, insisted on collecting the ship for immediate use, so the commander of Jiangning, Shao Baichang, was ordered to take it from the harbour by raft and moor at the coal harbour. The defending officers were relying on this ship to escape.

They arrived in Pukou at 10pm. They went north along the railway and tried to go to Chuzhou. However, they were ambushed in Huaqi camp. According to the report, Japanese troops from Jiangpu were going to attack us so they changed direction to go to Yangzhou and approached Gu Zhutong's troops. Tang Shengzhi had difficulty walking as he hadn't yet recovered from his illness. His followers tried to think of different ways to help, but they only found a handcart which had cow dung on it. Tang Shengzhi refused to use it. As a result, his bodyguards continued to support him. After walking a few miles, Tang Shengzhi couldn't walk any longer and asked his adjutant if there was a car they could use. He replied: "There's still that handcart." Tang Shengzhi sighed: "I've led troops for 20 years and have fought in more than 100 battles, but I've never been as uncomfortable as this." Having no choice, he got in and they carried on. He frequently stopped the handcart and asked his followers with a pained and sullen voice: "Have all the officers crossed the river? Have Chief of Staff Yu and Section Chief Liao arrived yet?"

Shortly into the journey from Pukou to Yangzhou, we saw a burning wooden bridge. Approximately 400 or 500 people in our group quickly crossed the burning bridge. We looked back at Nanjing and flames lit up the sky. Purple Mountain blazed like the sun. Aeroplanes soared in the skies above Nanjing, Pukou and Wulong Mountain. The sound of guns, cannons and bombs still roared.

Tang Shengzhi, the senior commander charged with the defence of the city, had left. He had surely left with a heavy heart. However, the only thing that made him truly uncomfortable was that he would now be Chiang Kai-shek and the government's scapegoat. He had lost the capital, Nanjing, which had been his responsibility, and he had escaped, a failure and an embarrassment.

Historical materials and the memoirs of senior leaders in the Kuomintang reveal that Chiang Kai-shek only gave orders to Tang Shengzhi and a few key members of staff around him to retreat. The other members of staff and soldiers had been given vague orders to break out of the encirclement. Although Tang Shengzhi's strategists developed a plan, no one implemented the poorly drafted strategy. Tragically, many troops who were fiercely fighting against the Japanese army at the front didn't receive the orders. Not until several hours after their supreme commander had already left via the Yangtze River did they begin to realise that they had orders to retreat. It was too late. The Japanese army's bayonets were now pointed at their necks and they couldn't get out even if they'd wanted to. How could these soldiers defending the gates pull back with no concern for the sacrifices made by their fallen brothers in arms?

They couldn't, nor could any soldier. Nanjing had fallen. The Zhonghua gate had been taken by the Japanese army at 12.30am on 13 December and key defensive positions like Purple Mountain, the Raining Flower Terrace and the engineering schools were occupied one after another. The Japanese army then immediately launched a violent attack on the city. After several hours of fierce fighting at the Zhonghua gate, the Japanese flag was erected by the proud Japanese army. The Japanese had now declared the occupation of Nanjing. The aggressive Japanese army instantly stormed the city like a flood. Some defending soldiers fought in desperate street skirmishes against the Japanese army. Meanwhile, some of the troops who'd heard Tang Shengzhi's orders to retreat became enormously confused. Some soldiers didn't understand why they had to retreat from the battle, but they too fell into the panicked rush of soldiers fleeing towards Xiaguan just outside the city. All of Nanjing stood in horror and desperation. In addition to the 10,000 or 20,000 people who had been killed over the past several days, 120,000 Chinese soldiers were now retreating. Several people were leading these retreating soldiers in an attempt to get them them to withdraw in an orderly fashion.

However, the calm stream of retreating soldiers was soon met by a tsunami of panicked people and they were immediately scattered in the crowd. Commanders couldn't find their soldiers. Soldiers couldn't find their commanders. Artillerymen abandoned their artillery and disguised themselves as cooks. Machine gunners picked up walking sticks. The infantry took off their military uniforms and put on civilian clothing. The commanders now resembled drowned rats and nobody took any notice of them. It was believed that anyone ahead of the others would survive, but in fact the people in front were in more danger than those behind. The Yijiang gate to the Yangtze River ferry crossing at Xiaguan was closed without any reason. A lieutenant commander stood on the city walls, holding a pistol, and shouted to the sea of officers and soldiers: "Stop retreating! Go back!"

"Damn it! We're following Commander Tang's orders! Let us pass!"

"We'll shoot if you don't let us pass!"

The fleeing troops were in chaos. There were officers, soldiers and civilians with guns, bags and suitcases. Seeing that they were being blockaded by their own people, they began to grow angry. Some of the officers even shot into the sky.

"I'm a colonel regimental commander. You're just a lieutenant colonel. Get out of the way!"

This annoyed the lieutenant colonel. He waved his hands and told his gunner: "Shoot anyone who approaches!"

"Damn! How dare you shoot your own people? Just let us go!"

Some of the fleeing troops within the city opened fire while others rushed towards the Yijiang gate waving their sticks.

Machine guns and rifles shot at the city gate. Flames then shot into crowded stream of unprepared people. The unarmed retreating soldiers collapsed. People in the front collapsed. People behind not only didn't retreat, but they continued to violently rush towards the gate.

"The division commander has ordered that we have to guard the gate. No officers or soldiers are allowed to escape from here! Fight! Drive them back to the city!" The lieutenant colonel had gone insane, as had the soldiers fighting their own comrades. The fleeing soldiers who rushed towards the Yijiang gate didn't know why they were being killed by their own soldiers.

Zhang Yonglong, an elite soldier, had retreated with his camp commander and his troops. The scenes of the retreat shocked him:

> The troops of Song Xilian's 36th division hadn't received the order to retreat, so the officers and soldiers guarding the Yijiang gate didn't open it. Soldiers rushed towards the gate, attempting to force it open and gain a chance of

survival. However, the defending officers and soldiers wouldn't let them pass. Eventually, both sides opened fire. They first fired into the air and then shot each other. The defending soldiers on the city wall shot with their machine guns from their superior positions. People who'd been shot fell down on the ground, but people behind them swarmed ahead and had to step on their corpses. The corpses of the recently killed were soft. You could easily slip if you weren't careful. If someone in front fell over, they'd be trampled on and killed by people behind them. The people who fell became fresh corpses, one after another. Such a waste. No one stopped shouting, but no one could stop it from happening.

The threat of death spread among the more than 100 retreating defending troops. They were now frightened.

More and more people were trying to retreat through the Yijiang gate. Some of the soldiers who were rushing out of the city gate thought they were being clever and took wooden doors and wall partitions and put them on the corpses. Hundreds of thousands of fleeing people jumped on the planks and wooden doors and continued to rush ahead. The corpses under the planks resembled ghosts with undistinguishable features. People ran ahead desperately, wiping off the blood on their faces. People behind thought that they would die if they didn't advance quickly. They knocked down people in front and these people later died. Piles of corpses were left badly mutilated, and their blood splashed onto the people rushing from behind.

It's estimated that at least several hundred people were shot by Song's defending troops or injured by the stampede.

This incident also wasted a large amount of time when the Chinese troops were supposed to be breaking through the encirclement. These fleeing soldiers had abandoned their weapons and orders and were at the mercy of the Japanese troops.

As more and more Chinese soldiers fell down in waves, torrents of blood flowed into the Yangtze.

Fortunately, most of the Chinese soldiers managed to escape to the banks of the Yangtze in the Xiaguan district as not all of the Japanese troops had arrived in the city, and relatively few were aware of the escapees. However, what awaited these soldiers was much more miserable than the Yijiang gate incident. What happened next was the bloodiest event in the Nanjing Massacre. More than 100,000 Chinese prisoners were killed.

Survivors - veterans of the Nationalist forces - have left many precious memoirs about what the Japanese troops did to the Chinese people captured by the Yangtze River.

Tian Xingxiang, the platoon leader of the Nationalist ground force of the 613rd regiment of the 103rd division, was transferred from Luobu in Hubei Province to Jiangyin in Jiangsu Province at the end of August 1937. He, along with his regiment, was first assigned to block off the Japanese forces in Changshu before being evacuated to Zhenjiang, and then finally fighting in the decisive battle at the Guanghua gate. With a total of 7,000 soldiers, the 103rd division entered Nanjing. The division commander had said to officers like Tian Xingxiang: "As General Tang says, Nanjing is our capital, a city of international importance. We have a dozen divisions and special forces here, amounting to a total of over 100,000 soldiers. I've already made up my mind to fight for our capital with you all. It will be a perfect chance for us to fight against the enemy for our country." The division commander's words inspired the soldiers, now prepared to risk their lives for China.

Tian Xingxiang recalls: "We relieved the garrison and followed the conventional method, with the main force placing troops on garrison duty at the first-tier area around the city wall. However, it turned out to be the main target of the Japanese troops and was attacked by rounds of artillery, tanks, planes and infantry, which led to serious casualties. We then changed our strategy, withdrawing the main force so that the companies and battalions would take turns to fight. But the enemy attacks became more and more violent, destroying the city wall and city gate, filling it with holes. Our army had to intercept and attack the enemy while also trying to fill in the holes, which caused many serious casualties. People in the companies and battalions were killed in under 20 minutes, their corpses littering the ground. The Japanese also suffered heavy losses."

As he remembered, at dusk on 12 December, Japanese tanks and infantry rushed in from different directions. The division received an urgent update over the phone, saying that general headquarters was out of contact. At the exact same time, a power failure struck the power plant, leading to all of the electric lights in the city being cut off. But the city looked just as bright as it did in the daytime as heavy fires roared in areas like Purple Mountain. Leaderless troops collapsed in disorder, gesturing to head over to the Xiaguan district through the Yijiang gate to escape to the other side of the Yangtze. Tian recalls: "We had to go back to Xinjiekou, and the nearby Zhongshan Road was tightly packed with military vehicles, refugees and all kinds of luggage. The pursuing enemy tanks and infantry got nearer and nearer and the dead and wounded lay everywhere. Battalions, companies, and even regiments were completely dispersed, as refugees and soldiers alike were gesturing towards the Xiaguan district. When I approached the Yijiang gate, tens of thousands of people were blocked off because the 36th division under

Song Xilian hadn't received the order to leave. They blocked the gaps in the three main gates with solid sandbags, more than two metres high, so the desperate soldiers shot at the defending troops on the city wall. Blood flowed like a river."

He continues: "Just then, I happened to see a dozen comrades from Guizhou, including the lieutenant director Wang Jingyuan from the division headquarters and the squadron leader adviser Cen Yuanbiao. Blocked in front and pursued from the rear, Lieutenant Yang Jiyu suggested climbing onto the city walls to escape. Following his advice, we hurried to a draper to get pieces of silk to tie on the battlements and climbed up and outside. It was midnight when we finally got to the Xiaguan district. We hadn't expected to see the tens of thousands of soldiers and civilians crowded there. They were all there for the same reason: to take a boat to the other side of the Yangtze. But there weren't any boats. Consequently, people who wanted to survive used various objects to help them float to the other side, like wooden poles, chairs, tables, bedsteads, doors and so on. They sat on these objects and attempted to row over to Pukou. Unfortunately, it was December and the water in the river was frozen, so countless people drowned in the water. Seeing the tough situation, Director Wang suggested that we leave Xiaguan district as soon as possible and look for boats in Swallow Rock. So, we headed there and found a small fishing boat with a fisherman. We thought we had found a way out, so we pulled the boat out into the river. However, it began to sink as soon as we got in".

As the highest ranking officer there, Wang said: "Don't worry. Let me take the boat to Bagua Island on the other side and ask a lieutenant to pick you up with a ship." Several of them, including Tian, then had to get out of the boat.

As the boat rowed out to the middle of the river, some soldiers had now gathered on Tian's side of the river. Someone shouted at Wang to bring the boat back. They then started to shoot at it when he didn't respond.

Tian and his comrades realised that it would be impossible to cross the river, so they ran downstream with several others to the reed fields.

"By noon on 13 December, soldiers, horses and refugees had spread all over the reed field. Just then, a Japanese warship approached in the river and their aeroplanes circled above. They savagely bombed the reeds, lighting the area up within a second. Deserters and civilians were immediately burnt to death and those who jumped into the river either drowned or were shot by the enemy." At this point, Tian and his comrades had broken up, leaving him and just one other trying to escape together. The two hid at the foot of a hill, suffering from hunger, coldness and desperation. They had to hide and wait for dawn. As expected, columns of Japanese forces holding their national flag turned up to search for Chinese soldiers. Dozens of metres away from where Tian and his comrade lay hidden, nearly 100 Chinese soldiers who had recently arrived in the area were all shot by the Japanese forces. Tian and his comrade had to play dead to avoid being caught.

"We can't wait here," said Tian. Getting a boat to cross to the other side was the most pressing task. It was much better to drown than be shot by the Japanese. Unable to find any boats, they decided to use a wooden basket used by local women to gather water caltrops. Two enamel bowls left by the soldiers were also adapted for use as paddles.

"It was dusk when we started to row out into the river, which made us shiver. No more than half an hour later, a gust of wind blew, throwing us into the river and I suddenly lost consciousness." Tian continued: "When I woke up, it was already noon the following day. Seeing the sun shining above me, I suddenly found that along with the wooden basket, I had been kept afloat by reeds. I was incredibly happy but too tired to cry out." He was even luckier as later on he was rescued by an old traveller on the river.

Not until one year later did Tian get to find out what happened to his division when he fled Nanjing: the division commander He Zhizhong had barely escaped with his life to Wuhan from the Xiaguan district and the assistant division commander Dai Zhiqi saved himself by dressing up as a fisherman. Out of all the soldiers of the 103rd division, only around 1,000 survived. The other 6,000 were all killed by the Japanese. More than 400 officers were captured and killed by the enemy, and only Cai Guoxiang, a lieutenant colonel who had been shot seven times, survived the massacre.

The troops from Guizhou, who had miraculously survived, built the Anti-Japanese Martyrs Monument near the Sanqiao district in Guiyang to commemorate their comrades who died in Nanjing. The names of the senior officials who died were carved on the monument, but unfortunately, it was destroyed after the establishment of the People's Republic of China as they were KMT Nationalists.

The massacre on the 13th in Xiaguan is remembered by a few survivors, some of whom were KMT Nationalists who left for Taiwan after the end of the Chinese Civil War. The crimes committed by the Japanese troops in the massacre remained fresh in their memory and many memoirs were written on the incident. I was fortunate enough to be able to find some of these materials when I visited Taiwan and many articles on this topic were published in the *Taiwan Shin Sheng Daily News* in the 1950s and 1960s. The following is an extract from someone named "Veteran", taken from the *Taiwan Shin Sheng Daily News*, on 29 April 1964:

On the morning of 12 December, with the Japanese armies having already stormed the city, our defending troops were fighting against them, fighting in dramatic street skirmishes. Nevertheless, as Japanese tank units were in the city, it was certain that our side would lose if we tried to fight them.

When the Japanese troops followed our fleeing soldiers and citizens through the Yijiang gate and the Xiaguan district on North Zhongshan Road, our soldiers even fought with one another, leading to countless deaths and injuries.

The people who wanted to escape from Xinjiekou to the Xiaguan district formed a stream several miles long. When they arrived at the city walls, the gates were forced half open by the crowds. Those who were eager to get out of the city competed with each other to rush to the Xiaguan district, making the crowd ripple like a tide against a shore. Due to the vigorous competition, the people in the front couldn't get out of the gate, and at the same time, those in the rear of the group competed with each other to push to the front, causing tragic chaos. Among the soldiers who were in the rear of the crowd, some even shot at those in front or drove into them. Those standing at the front either died or collapsed. The chances were that if someone fell down, they wouldn't stand up again even though they were alive. This was because the crowd behind them would step on them without hesitation. Several hundred people were trampled on. Being at the back of the group, I saw a mass of corpses at the city wall which were piled up to the height of an average man. It was later proven that more than 5,000 people died here. Seeing that it was hard to get out of the city, I turned back to the Shuixi gate to find another way out.

We then arrived at the riverside. What we saw there cannot be described by simple words like "chaos" or "terror". Every one of us wanted to flee to Pukou by ship, but there weren't enough ships along the riverbank for all the people there. Several large cargo transport ships left to never return and a couple of small ships filled with crowds of refugees once they approached the riverbank. The ships had hardly left the wharf when they sank due to carrying too many people. Others, seeing that the ships had left without them, shot at those on the ships until they sank into the river. Some people even hired wooden boats in an attempt to row to the other side, but they sank too due to being overloaded or shot in the frenzied gunfire, meaning that no one could reach the other side. Someone even made a raft out of a board to get away from the danger, but they ended up being tossed into the river because of the crashing waves. Heads and dead bodies bobbed all along the river while the air was filled with desperate screams for help.

I lowered myself down the city walls with a rope to get out of the city through the Shuixi gate. Once I arrived at the riverside, I saw a boat not far away from me instantly sink into the river due to being overloaded. By the sinking boat, a pretty and fashionable girl carrying a small leather suitcase in her left hand and a board in her right fell into the water. She screamed out that if anyone rescued her, she'd give them all of her jewellery, 2,000 yuan in cash and would even marry them. But everyone was too busy focusing on their own survival to even consider helping someone else.

While hundreds of thousands of soldiers and citizens in Xiaguan struggled to cross the Yangtze, they were submitted to violent explosions and gunfire from above. Within an instant, 1,000 victims lay dead in pools of blood. Before people even realised what was happening, columns of cavalry and tanks suddenly appeared and rushed towards the riverbanks from both the Yijiang gate and the streams that fed into the Yangtze River. After a series of explosions, half of the crowd had been killed and thousands more dead bodies floated on the river.

Realising that this was a life or death moment, I decided to hide in a nearby slum. I was luckily able to buy a ragged cloth with five yuan just after I left the riverside. I hurriedly took off my uniform and dressed like a pauper. I then found an old woman crying and begging. I carried her on my back along with her basket and walked downstream slowly with a sweet potato in my mouth, chewing it slowly. I suddenly heard the sound of iron boots behind me and I noticed that there were more than 20 Japanese soldiers approaching me. I carried on walking, deciding not to turn back. A brute of a soldier roughed me up, saying words that I couldn't understand. I stayed calm, very calm. I pretended to be disabled by just saying "yah, yah" and acting as if my left arm was crippled. Thinking that I was just a lame beggar, the soldier pushed me to the ground as they roared past. A long time later, I gave two yuan to the old woman, put her down and decided to find a new way to survive.

Due to the lack of transportation, there was no way of escaping immediately. Although I had kept myself away from the cruel Japanese soldiers for the time being, how could I survive in the long run? Finally, in the afternoon, I decided to register in the refugee camp at Gulou Hospital, which had been built by a foreign church, intending to hide there for several days. I hadn't expected to find 5,000, maybe 6,000, people already there, but what else could I do to survive? Nothing but stay there. It was said that countless refugee camps had been established and every single one of them was full of refugees.

That night, a group of Japanese soldiers arrived at the camp while we were sleeping. We knew exactly why they were here: to search for young women while also checking if there were any Chinese soldiers present. We stood in lines in front of the Gulou Hospital entrance. Then any woman they deemed attractive was picked out and pulled into their vehicle. At the same time, young men who had shaved heads or had signs of having worn a helmet were forced into their vehicles. As an artilleryman who looked incredibly unkempt after having suffered so much, and dressed in such ragged clothes, I luckily escaped arrest. Just when those who hadn't been selected thought that they'd averted disaster, someone suddenly shouted for the soldiers to stand to attention. Everyone who responded to the command was pulled into the Japanese vehicles. Although I had been trained in the army and did normally stand to attention when I heard the order, I didn't do so this time as part of my disguise and I knew the true reason they gave the command, so I pretended to have no reaction to it at all. I escaped arrest again but one of my comrades was caught this way.

One week later, on 21 December, the veteran secretly travelled to the other side of the Yangtze as soon as the water transports returned to normal. He then arrived in Changsha by train and returned to his division.

Tang Guangpu, who lived in Liuhe in Jiangsu Province after the Chinese Civil War, was another one of the few veterans who survived the Nanjing Massacre. As an officer's assistant in the 3rd battalion of the central military academy teaching corps prior to the Nanjing Massacre, he witnessed the disaster on 13 December. He revealed the following:

I was just a teenager in 1937, an officer's assistant in the 3rd battalion of the teaching corps, defending the Huangpu River in Shanghai. As Chiang Kai-shek had announced that all the troops were to withdraw, I, along with the teaching corps, retreated one step after another from the Huangpu River and finally escaped to Nanjing. No more than one month after we reached Nanjing, the Japanese troops approached the city. The teaching corps was then appointed to be the defending force, with its headquarters in the basement of the Bank of Communications sponsored by the Nationalist Party, and I was made a guard.

Almost as soon as we'd arrived in the bank's basement, the Japanese troops attacked the Zhonghua gate. When the news came that the Japanese troops had stormed Taiping Road, the leaders of the teaching corps quickly ran away without hesitation. So, I, along with six other comrades, rushed over to Xiaguan. One of them, named Tang Hecheng, from Yancheng, Jiangsu Province, had always been a good friend of mine, and we ran away together.

We followed the crowds rushing to the Yijiang gate. On the way, we saw waves upon waves of retreating soldiers from the Nationalist Party and when we finally arrived, the Yijiang gate was blocked off by a countless amount of people. Those who had been pushed over by the crowd were unable to stand up again. Therefore, we decided to tie our arms together so that if any of us fell down, the others could pull him back up. By doing so, we managed to eventually pass through the Yijiang gate.

All the streets and roads brimmed with fleeing soldiers while the masses were at a loss as to where to go. We aimlessly followed the fleeing public. Suddenly, a man who seemed to be a senior official rushed into the crowd on a horse and shouted with a microphone: "Brothers! Anyone who wants to survive should follow me!" When they saw an official take command, the frantic soldiers gradually began to calm down. Then, the official made a gunner walk in the front, carving a way out to the Shangxin River. The infantry followed behind him. When the soldiers reached the river, the bridge over it turned out to be too narrow for the crowd to cross. Tang and I didn't manage to cross and the other guys from our group had been separated from us. Not knowing what to do, we decided to run to Longtan and Zhenjiang along with the others who'd failed to make it onto the bridge.

We ran into a reed field and hid. When we approached a bridge, we found that the Japanese troops had now taken the area near the city wall, with several machine guns set up ready to shoot those who wanted to cross the bridge. Many people who attempted to get across the bridge were killed and their bodies covered the bridge. Seeing that the enemy was taking a break, we rushed across the bridge and ran to Swallow Rock. When we finally arrived, there no one was to be seen. We found a board and lifted it with all our strength to the riverbank. We then put it in the river and tried to use it to help us swim over to the other side. However, no matter how much we tried, the board did nothing but flow down the riverbank. Unable to cross the river, we had to go back to Swallow Rock.

It was dark then and the sound of gunfire slowly approached. Using all our energy, we ran onto the mountain and hid ourselves in caves, afraid to even make the smallest of noises. It wasn't until dusk that we were found by the Japanese troops. We were sent to an open field with our arms tied together and standing back to back. The field was filled with people like us and many more were arriving. Everyone who had been arrested was then imprisoned in a temporary Nationalist Party teaching corps camp, which was originally used for field training. The camp was divided into seven or eight long prisons made of bamboo and the captives then filed into them in a line. With nothing to eat, we'd been locked up for three days before we were finally given a little bit of water. The Japanese troops shot anyone they wanted. We were starving and on the verge of death but on the fifth day we made a decision. Seeing that the enemy wanted to starve us to death, some brave prisoners believed that it'd be better for us to risk our lives resisting than starving to death, so they conspired to use a flare as a signal for everyone to rush out of the prisons together. That night, one of the bamboo prisons was set alight while a flare suddenly shot up followed by all of the captives rushing out of the prisons. There was a deep and wide moat filled with water behind the prisons where everyone jumped in to try to swim away. Unfortunately, there was a wall on the other side of the moat. When they got to the wall, the stunned crowd was shot in the back by the frenzied Japanese troops, and soon after, the water in the moat turned red as blood floated to the surface. We were then sent back to the camp and because of the building that had been burned down and space limitations, we had to stand close to each other, which made it hard to breathe.

On the sixth day, the Japanese troops forced us into the yard before sunrise, tying our arms together. It wasn't until 2pm that they'd finished tying us up. Then, they forced us with their bayonets to go to Tiger Mountain in a line. Although we were too hungry to walk any more, the Japanese soldiers walked around the line and stabbed anyone who walked even a little bit slowly. By the time we walked around three miles it was dark, so we were forced into an open field near the riverbank. Without any food for a total of six days on top of an exhausting march, everyone in the line sat down weak and limp as soon as we stopped, unable to get up again. All of a sudden, countless people appeared in the field.

Although we were exhausted and weak, a sense that the Japanese troops were going to kill us spread among the people. So, we tried to break the ropes that tied our arms together in an attempt to escape. Before we managed to do so, searchlights turned on all around us, making the night as bright as day. We felt faint. Then, guns from two ships on the river and three on the high ground opened fire on the crowd, marking the beginning of the massacre.

Once the first gun was fired, Tang and I jumped down on the ground. We heard many people shouting "down with Japanese imperialism!" or "long live the Republic of China!" and after wave upon wave of gunfire and shouting, many people collapsed. Several bodies fell on top of me, with their blood staining my clothes. I held my breath, afraid to even move a muscle. Twenty minutes later, when the sound of gunfire stopped, I touched Tang gently and asked him softly: "Are you okay?" He answered: "Yes, and you?" Before I could answer him, the sound of gunfire returned, frightening me while I hid motionless among the corpses. After the new wave of shooting stopped, I found out that Tang wasn't moving anymore, which filled me with dread. I shook him hard but got no response. When I touched his head, I felt that he'd been shot in the head, blood flowing out. I was petrified and had to hide myself among the corpses.

A long time later, when the sounds had stopped for a while, I felt that I had to get away as quickly as possible. So, I tried to stretch my head above the corpses, slowly and softly, only to find that the piles of corpses blocked my view. Thinking that it'd be easy to get out if I crawled forwards, I decided to go through the corpses and slowly get away. When I approached the pile of dead bodies, I was too frightened to move for a while.

The searchlights had been turned off for a long time and the dark night covered the cruel scene of the massacre. The flow of the river sounded like miserable crying. A long time later, I heard the Japanese troops preparing to leave followed by the sound of ships leaving. So, with my heart in my throat, I scrambled downstream for a few miles. I crawled over to a cave, finding many dead bodies of my fallen comrades lying there. Despite this, I scrambled into the cave to take shelter from the wind.

I waited from sunrise to noon in a daze. When I saw a boat approaching, I was so scared that I felt like I was going to have a heart attack. The boat then pulled into shore and it was two Chinese people, an old man and a young guy. It turned out that they wanted to take the boat to Bagua Island to stay away from the Japanese troops and get some straw for their cows, taking advantage of the enemy patrol ships not being there. I ran out of the cave instantly and rushed over to the boat, pleading with the old man to save me. Seeing the blood all over my body, the old man hid me in their ship with the straw, taking me to Bagua Island.

13 December was an extremely brutal day for the soldiers defending Nanjing. It also marked the day of the highest number of deaths and most barbaric murders in the entire massacre, with retreating Chinese soldiers who'd managed to leave Nanjing but had failed to get across the Yangtze being the main targets.

When the Chinese soldiers received the orders to withdraw, they had risked their lives to rush to the Yangtze to get away from the unfolding disaster. However, what they neglected in the panic was that crossing the Yangtze was no small feat for hundreds of thousands of soldiers. After they arrived in Xiaguan, they found out that there weren't any boats for crossing the river at all. Nearly all the boats and ships had been shot and sunk by the Japanese troops with their naval guns, so the soldiers had to cross the river using any other methods available. One survivor recounts: "They took coffins out of a local house, making them into canoes, but no one had expected the shocking amount of soldiers trying to cross to survive. One coffin had to hold a dozen or even several dozens of people. Those inside the canoe rowed out to the centre of the river in a mass and they eventually capsized, sinking deep into the water. The coffins became the caskets of countless soldiers, but those who had been submerged in the water didn't stay in the coffin long. Most of them were later eaten by fish and a few survivors were caught by Japanese naval vessels. These poor soldiers were then set on fire, dying covered with wounds."

Yan Xinyi, a sergeant, was recognised for his courage and loyalty in the teaching corps as he killed many Japanese soldiers each time he led charges against the enemy. Guo Qi, his battalion commander, particularly liked the brave soldier. On 13 December, Yan Xinyi lost touch with the retreating troops at the Yijiang gate. Using his fearlessness and strong will to survive, he rushed forwards among the crowds to Xiaguan. Getting to the river, he tried to look for a floating object to use to get to the other side of the Yangtze. Standing on the riverbank and looking around, he was somewhat frightened by the sheer amount of people there. He was at a loss about what to do when suddenly someone shouted: "The Japanese devils are coming!" Suddenly, the riverbank descended into chaos. Some jumped into the river. Others hid in the reeds. Most aimlessly ran around on the bank.

Yan Xinyi tried to tiptoe to check where the Japanese were coming from, but before he could do so, Japanese artillery and machine gun bullets started to fall around him.

Tens of thousands of people fell in the hail of bullets. Many were still running to escape as others wailed. Yan realised the extent of the chaos and fled in panic. But his legs were trembling and weak, unable to get a good footing. Looking down, he was stepping on the casualties hit by the machine guns and artillery shells. Yan heard people screaming below his feet and felt others pulling at his legs. He looked down but quickly looked away again, the sight too appalling to see. He had to get out of here.

Yan felt ashamed as he'd seen faces he knew in the stampede but he couldn't stop, otherwise he'd become a victim too. He had to survive himself. Yan desperately tried to find his own way out amidst the sea of officers and men. Suddenly, he heard: "Attention!"

It was strange. Who could be here shouting orders? Yan was frightened and when he looked back, there was a Japanese officer shouting instructions in Chinese and waving a sword on a mound.

Yan Xinyi didn't react. He then saw many Chinese soldiers suddenly stop running. One stopped, a dozen followed suit, then more people stopped. Yan stopped too when he saw that those who didn't were shot.

"Attention!" The Japanese officer shouted again.

Yan took advantage of the situation to calculate the number of Chinese soldiers. There were about 2,000 or 3,000 soldiers who had managed to survive. The officer suddenly shouted: "Turn back!"

"Turn back? That's towards the Yangtze!" But Yan just instinctively followed everyone who turned back. He saw the ferocious torrents of the Yangtze.

"March forward!" The officer ordered.

Yan Xinyi hesitated for a while as he watched the majority of people following the order and walking into the biting cold river. Among those splashing into the river, some were struggling, some swam back, while others continued to swim forwards. Whether they swam forwards or backwards, they were then shot by machine guns and bobbed motionless in the river. The waters of the Yangtze were dyed red.

In just 10 minutes, thousands of his comrades had been killed. He wanted to cry but had no strength, and just as he hesitated, Japanese bullets flew at those who didn't advance into the river.

He had an idea. Perhaps pretending to be dead would save his life. But the bullets were quicker than him and suddenly he felt something hit the back of his head. He immediately fell down. He must have been hit. With just a trace of consciousness left, he threw himself onto a pile of corpses.

Yan Xinyi felt as if he was on his way to hell. He noticed that something odd was flowing from his head towards his mouth. "It's blood! Is it my own?" Yan Xinyi thought to himself, terrified.

He touched his head lightly with his left hand. It was sticky, but nothing serious. The blood by his mouth wasn't his. The others couldn't move. He assumed that they must be dead, or like him, more dead than alive.

"Shoot them all! Finish them off!"

Yan heard a sound by his ear and thought that it must be the Japanese because they couldn't speak Chinese well. Keeping his eyes closed and pretending to be dead was his only chance of survival. He closed his eyes quickly as if he were dead. Yan knew the Japanese were checking the bodies for survivors and that those pretending to be dead would be shot again.

The Japanese soldiers stopped next to him and it was muffled for half a second. Yan had his heart in his mouth as the Japanese examined his "corpse". Suddenly, he was struck in the waist; a Japanese soldier had kicked him. Now his mind was aware that his body was being rolled down by the heavy kick with his face in the ground. After another half second, something was stacked on his body. He guessed that it was two of the nearby bodies.

Yan found it hard to breathe, but he would much rather this than the alternative. It was likely he'd escape from the Japanese. He'd made it. The

Japanese moved away from the pile of bodies after stabbing them and Yan several times with bayonets.

No one knows how much time went by afterwards, even Yan doesn't remember. He was semiconscious and appeared to have passed out. When he woke up again he heard: "Oh my God."

Who was it? Yan held his breath. It couldn't be the Japanese. He opened his eyes: an old man.

"You're not dead?" The old man's eyes met Yan's. This time Yan opened his eyes wide and asked: "Uncle, are the devils gone?"

"Gone, they're all gone!" The old man nodded, then leaned over and asked: "Where are you hurt?"

"I think my head…" Yan said feebly.

"You're lucky you didn't die! Stand up!" The old man helped him up.

Looking around, Yan Xinyi was completely overwhelmed. How could all of them be dead? He broke down in nausea; his intestines seemed to have been pulled at with a hook and his throat was full of some sort of disgusting liquid.

Anyone would have been upset by what he saw. Next to Yan was a mountain of bloodied steaming corpses; some with white brain matter strewn everywhere, some with their heads attached to their bodies by a thin layer of skin, some naked. The bodies were covered with so much blood and mud that it was hard to tell who was who.

"Uncle, what are you doing here? Aren't you afraid?" Yan asked while looking around to see if there were any Japanese forces.

The old man gave a long sigh and said: "I'm old. I'm not afraid of anything. After seeing so many people dead, I thought that there must be someone alive. It's only you…"

"Thank you for coming!" Yan felt as if he had a thousand words to say but didn't know where to start. "Let's go, it's not safe here."

"Is there anywhere safe in Nanjing?" Yan stood up shaking and took a look at the mountains of bodies and the bloodied river. He burst into tears.

"Don't let yourself be heard! Let's go!" The old man covered Yan's mouth with his hand and swiftly pulled him away from the waterfront. This was the morning after 13 December 1937.

The number of Chinese soldiers killed on 13 December has been a topic debated for decades by many Japanese right wingers, with some even saying that the Chinese fabricated the massacre. With that in mind, let's take a look at what the Japanese soldiers who participated in the massacre have said about their experiences.

Memories of the Japanese Troops

The Japanese military has a very clear and detailed record of the rape of Nanjing. From General Matsui, who commanded the entire offensive campaign, and Division Commander Lieutenant Kesago Nakajima, to the ordinary soldiers who stormed Nanjing on the 13th, they have left behind a good understanding of the horrors that unfolded.

To the Japanese, the day was simply "a joyful and grandiose celebration". In Tokyo, millions of people got ready to participate in victory parades. This was the emperor's will: "To celebrate the victory of the Japanese nation for the initial occupation and domination of another country that has existed for thousands of years."

Before presenting the reader with information from the first day of the massacre when the Japanese soldiers entered the city, I have included an article here entitled *I Have Witnessed the "Nanjing Tragedy"* in vol. 61 of the *Nanjing Massacre Historical Collection* written by the *Asahi Shimbun's* Jiro Suzuki, a war correspondent from Tokyo. He wrote:

> We have abused defenceless captives.
>
> Be it the Japanese military or China at the time, everyone thought that if Nanjing fell, the national government would surrender and the war would be over. Therefore, the morale of the Nanjing occupiers was very high. Besides being proud of their victory, which reduced how much they cared, the Japanese also practiced the so-called three alls policy (burn, kill, steal), so in just Nanjing alone, up to 300,000 people were massacred.
>
> The next day, i.e. on the 13th, dozens of people, including the painter Nakagawa, follow-up reporters and photographers from Osaka's *Mainichi Shimbun* and the *Tokyo Shimbun* moved into the silenced city along with the frontline headquarters. The government at the time once again returned to the Zhongshan gate.
>
> That was the first time I saw the tragic massacre. On the walls, 25 metres wide, the captives were lined in a row and stabbed with bayonets one after another. Many Japanese soldiers were wielding bayonets, stabbing the captives in the chest and waist. Blood spattered in the air and the scene was horrifying. Seeing this, I just stood there for a long time.
>
> There was a strange phenomenon I do not understand and can never forget: the facial expressions and attitude of the victims. In this brutal scene, the people who were to be killed gave a cold smile and some even waited their turn to be killed. On the battlefield, this group of people, unafraid of death, had fought in hand-to-hand combat with the Japanese soldiers.

I was stunned and left the scene. On the way back, I sneaked into the Lizhi society courtyard again. There was a tree I hadn't noticed before where a dozen prisoners had been tied to it with wire. Everyone's faces were as pale as paper and they were all shirtless. Some sat there, some stood, and others just stared at me blankly.

Then, several Japanese soldiers arrived and started yelling, two or three of them were carrying axes. I knew they were our soldiers. They didn't even glace up at me even though I was there. One of them stood in front of the tree, and shouted: "These guys also wanted to attack our companions!" He stuck the defenceless captives with an axe. After a sharp slicing sound, blood began to spray everywhere. Other people watched the struggling body, but did nothing and allowed the violence to happen. This was simply an appalling tragedy... Some of the captives were soldiers in military uniform and others were civilians.

After seeing this horror, I knew I had no way of preventing it so I had to leave.

But the imprisoned soldiers and civilians couldn't escape the Japanese atrocities. Their fate was death.

It's worth looking at how the Japanese officers and soldiers committed these inhumane crimes and their feelings after the occupation of Nanjing.

Ryo Takashima, who had enlisted just two months before the rape of Nanjing, wrote about what happened on 13 December in Nanjing and the scene on the 14th:

The gunfire stopped before dawn. It seemed that the enemy, who had clung on to the defence of the city for three days, had retreated. The 6th squadron marched to the highlands.

At dawn, when the gunfire had stopped, Nanjing clearly emerged from the fiery smoke that had enveloped it the day before. When its long walls could be clearly seen, all of our eyes filled with tears.

The vanguard forces excitedly hoisted the Japanese flag on the watchtower. One of them wrote on the gate: "Occupied by Noda at 9am on 13 December."

Several hundred unarmed prisoners knelt in the trenches. They were skinny and ignored the army.

The troops set out for operations again. The first team caught over 200 enemy stragglers. They had no idea about the fall of Nanjing and had fled here. I asked Oshima, the aide, how to deal with the prisoners. Oshima said: "Whether it's 200 or 500, just take them somewhere and kill them all!" So, the captives were taken to an empty area and the heavy machine gun team, assisted by the first team, killed them beside the Yangtze.

The prisoners were taken out one by one, all naked and having trouble breathing, shouting: "Please, we just want water, water." "You bastards," I swore. They went to drink muddy water with their hands. Then, the prisoners were lined up into four teams with their hands raised up. We took 50 people to the river.

We put grenades by their feet so there was little risk involved. If we hadn't, as there was just a small team, with Kondoh and I being junior officers, things would have got out of control if they began to riot. We took the prisoners out from the truck and the warehouse, totalling 1,200 people, and got them to sit facing the river. After receiving their orders, our soldiers, hiding behind the trenches, fired their heavy machine guns together. The prisoners fell down like dominoes and bloody chunks flew everywhere. The dozens of people jumping into the river were shot dead by the light machine guns on the jetty and their blood turned the river red.

What a cruel scene. If these people moved, they were shot again. Our warships were on the Yangtze and the sailors onboard saw everything.

We began to conduct raids between the station and the town. Outside the city, almost everything had been burned to ash. Before the war, it must have been very busy, but now not a soul was left. While resting outside the Yijiang gate, we noticed that the city gate by the lookout tower had been blocked by planks and sandbags. Several ropes were hanging from the wall with clothing scattered on the ground. The likely explanation was that the refugees had tried to escape by using these ropes and nets while carrying their belongings. The soldiers caught several fish floating on the river and enjoyed the fruits of taking the city.

We entered the Yijiang gate carrying the flag. On the gate, we wrote: "On 13 December, the Sichuan troops were defeated". We stepped over the charred corpses and went up the city gate tower. I didn't know why the tower had been burned. Half burned corpses were scattered in the streets with clothes, bayonets, ammunition and abandoned antiaircraft guns all over the place. We fell over the fallen telephone poles and the spiderwebs of wires. Our transports did a good job of carrying away the captured antiaircraft guns. Words had been written on the grass like loyalty, filial piety, faith, peace and love, not to mention big anti-Japanese slogans and cartoons. The official buildings that had originally belonged to the ministry of railways became the corps headquarters where the defensive sailors had been positioned.

There was a spacious residence among the majestic buildings flying the British flag and a plaque reading "Official Residence of the British Ambassador to China". Is this the residence of the British ambassador who'd always acted so strangely every time we fought? We started to raid the city. All the streets, apart from the government streets, were just like rural raids. The warehouse and the barracks of the 88th division had nothing left, I just put a telephone in my bag. We could see grenades all over the place.

There were several groups of captives with their hands tied behind their backs. You could hear a rumbling sound and the burning of fire everywhere. After entering Nanjing, many soldiers had an expression of joy and relief on their faces.

A lance corporal described his memories of the 13th:

Nanjing came into view! Never did I expect to see the place we were attacking. When hoisting the Japanese flag, we couldn't help but shout a resounding "banzai".

The Nanjing city wall extended to the right so we could see the streets of Nanjing. But our vision was obscured by the rays of the sun. Cries of *banzai* sounded over and over again. Dozens of Japanese flags were erected on the wall.

It had been more than 90 days since Mizutani had been enlisted in the Japanese 9th division. He had almost died many times during the Battle of Shanghai. Following the Japanese victory, he came to Nanjing and scaled the wall. Now images of the emperor, his parents and his siblings flashed into his mind and he uncontrollably wept.

Mizutani recalls that moment at 7.20am on the 13th. Standing on the wall with a gun in his hand, he shouted *banzai* in a hoarse voice:

I took out the Japanese flag my elder brother gave me and tied it to my gun, repeatedly shouting: "Banzai!". Everyone was moved to tears. This was the Nanjing city wall we had been waiting for so long to take and a handful of us were overwhelmed by the excitement. We were filled with desire and happiness. It was a good day to be Japanese!

Masuda, a new recruit in the 16th division recalled 13 December like this:

The 12th year of Showa [1937], 13 December, the day of the fall of Nanjing, will always be a brilliant day in our history. Needless to say, Nanjing was the KMT headquarters and China's headquarters for the fight against the Japanese due to its special geographical location. The city faced the Yangtze on one side and the three other sides were surrounded by mountains. With such advantageous terrain, it was easy to defend while extremely difficult to attack. With such advantages, the Chiang regime wanted a final showdown with the Japanese. Unfortunately, Chiang's shield was too weak to stop the IJA when faced with our justice. Chiang Kai-shek's army was vulnerable and we defeated it in three days. We hung our Japanese flag on the gates and the IJA flooded into the city.

The Zhongshan gate was first occupied by the Osaka squadron, one of Ono's famous units, at 1pm. Ono commanded the soldiers, holding the remains of those killed in action. The whole unit valiantly drove into the city and the officers of the middle squadron had no chance to rest. Then, under the command of Lieutenant Tanaka, the Japanese began to attack the remaining soldiers. We entered the Nanjing Public Hospital five or six metres away from the Zhongshan gate. The hospital was a magnificent four-storey building made out of reinforced concrete. It was used to treat the wounded from Shanghai, Changshu and Wuxi.

No soldier was allowed to walk alone and we had to operate collectively. What remained were bloodstained hospital uniforms, hats and blankets and other broken items. Although this was just a shelter for the hateful Chinese army, it made us angry. The cabinet, desk, medicine cabinets, appliances and a box-type clock had all been shattered. Photographs of different kinds of specimens had been pierced by bayonets.

After withdrawal, on the way to the Zhongshan North Road, we saw weapons, ammunition, clothing, horses, vehicles and the like dropped by retreating soldiers all over the place. Row upon row of businesses had been looted by the Chinese army. We could see nothing on the street, not even a dog.

That night we decided to sleep indoors, which we had been unable to do for a long time. We didn't initially intend on looting, but in the past few days, we had had almost nothing to eat or drink and had continuously fought at night. We looted, but just for today to celebrate the fall of Nanjing. Was this not the reason why so many of our comrades had died so gloriously?

The 13th division corporal's adviser recalled the 13th:

We got up at 3am and at 4am, we took to the road towards the fortified hills around Nanjing to launch an attack. On the way, enemy prisoners were gathered everywhere. It was said that there were about 13,000 of them, with a wide range in ages from 12 year old children to people in their fifties. Two women were also included. The enemy kept surrendering and the total number of prisoners captured reached about 100,000. At 5pm, we saw the Nanjing city wall and our forces established their positions outside.

Nakamura, a Japanese sailor, described the day as "a sin" in the *Asahi Shimbun Numazu* newspaper on 10 July, 1991 like this:

13 December, sunny with no wind, the Yangtze like a mirror flowed slowly. Our fleet collaborated with the army and went upstream towards Nanjing. At 3pm, we rushed onto the Xiaguan trestle bridge and arrived on the shore. Before doing so, we had captured seven Chinese people in the middle of the night. We killed them on the deck and kicked them into the Yangtze. The most brutal scene I had ever witnessed began from that point.

We didn't go ashore for a long time so we watched the battle off the shore. One side of Nanjing faced the Xiaguan gate along the Yangtze and the rest was surrounded by walls (10 metres high and 4.5 metres wide). Many areas had strong gates and our army controlled all of them from the outside so people in the city couldn't get out. We were very surprised to see that Nanjing had become a ghost city. No people, no vehicles and no horses, not even any cats or dogs. All we could see was endless mountains of dead bodies. The road, the square and the embankment were all filled with corpses. Soldiers, businessmen and farmers of all ages were dead. Because of the cold weather, the dried blood had turned black while the blood underneath the corpses remained a bright crimson.

The navy rarely went ashore and it was difficult for them to meet women. Maybe that was why some of the heartless ones poked at the breasts of the female corpses with sticks or lifted up their clothes to take a look at them.

The next morning, we went to the river shoal near the trestle bridge. There were piles of corpses there too that hadn't decayed yet. Traces of blood still remained on the sandy soil. There were no cuts on the corpses, and it seemed as if they'd all been shot dead.

All I am describing is what I saw with my own eyes. The question is who caused it? How many victims were there? 300,000? 100,000? 10,000? I don't know the answer. I don't believe anyone could ever get reliable facts under such chaos. But there must have been thousands upon thousands of people.

We didn't hear any gunshots from the next day. Some Chinese children were playing happily near the naval vessels. They wore Japanese flag armbands, maybe their mothers made those armbands for them. I liked those children.

I still have copies of the letters of thanks from our senior officers for our laudable performance in combat, photos of our vessels firing artillery, photos of how we dealt with prisoners of war and photos of children playing near our vessels.

The First Day of the Massacre | 151

A Japanese soldier in the 6th division, Yoshio Akahoshi, recalled when he went to the front on the 13th:

> The enemy had positioned a machine gun every 50 metres on the city wall by the Zhonghua gate and there were approximately 30 mortars in between those machine guns.
>
> In an extremely violent offensive, we marched to 200 metres or so away from the city wall and then stormed a destroyed large human settlement. It was barren.
>
> Before the dawn of the 12th, at about 5am, we started a coordinated attack on the city wall by the Zhonghua gate. The field guns fired together at the gate, while bombers began to attack in a series of waves. However, the gate was still tightly closed, and the 20 metre tall city wall still stood firm, showing no signs of collapsing. Then we tried to use the 75-ton light tanks to ram the gate but failed. At the same time, the engineer corps about 50 metres away from the gate put explosives on the city walls and tried to blow it up, but they also failed. A mass of mortars and machine gun fire shot at us relentlessly from the solid city wall while our army fired field guns non-stop from the rear. We fought back with light tanks on the road. The fierce battle lasted for an entire day.
>
> We couldn't advance anymore, so we stayed in houses 200 metres away from the Zhonghua gate and spent the night on standby.
>
> The next day, on 13 December, we launched the general offensive on the Zhonghua gate. Field guns opened fire on and near the Zhonghua gate, which had once been considered indestructible. Soon after, the strong wall became contorted so our soldiers could climb up.
>
> After the bombers retaliated against the mortars and machine guns on the gate and the wall in a series of attacks, three suicide squads with light machine guns and rifles rushed forwards and hooked a rope ladder to the deformed wall. They climbed up the wall under our protective fire as the enemy continued to attack. As the heavy gunfire continued, about 40 infantrymen carried on scaling the walls but the enemy's attack persisted.
>
> After some time, the Japanese flag was hung high above the Zhonghua gate. It was 10.30 in the morning of 13 December.
>
> All of us then raised our hands and cheered: "Banzai! Banzai!" I felt moved and couldn't help thinking that I was lucky to be here. "We captured Nanjing first" became our slogan.
>
> Two or three hours after the suicide squads had scaled the city wall, the Zhonghua gate finally opened.
>
> Under the orders of the unit leader, we all advanced and entered the city. The entire city was filled with sandbags 10 metres high and four metres wide.

Citizens' residences had been ruthlessly destroyed or were ablaze. There were distinct signs of bombs and artillery fire; the stench of gunpowder lingered in the air.

A deep crimson covered everything, with mutilated corpses scattered everywhere, some without their heads or with their internal organs spilling out. We could barely bring ourselves to look.

Except for the Red Cross refugee zones in the city, we couldn't see anyone who looked like guerrillas or remnants of the defeated army.

Now Nanjing was in the hands of the Japanese.

We mopped up the city time and time again, but we hardly ever met any resistance. That evening, we still took measures to act as a deterrent in a corner of the city.

The next day, we set out for the banks of the Yangtze running through Nanjing. We looked out at the Yangtze River below from the fort gun fixtures and could see many stick-like objects floating in the river.

We went down Lion Mountain and on the way to the Yangtze, we saw the corpses of Chinese soldiers lying on the ground; some decapitated, some were just torsos, signalling the horror of the attack.

The banks of the Yangtze were the same as any other wharf where ships came and went. But when we stood there looking at the Yangtze, we couldn't believe our eyes.

Countless corpses were floating for about a mile in the river, maybe more. When we looked around, we could see nothing but corpses, both on the riverbank and in the river. These were the corpses of civilians rather than soldiers. Adults and children, men and women, all drifted slowly along the river like lost rafts. Looking away from it upstream, there were more mountains of corpses. Bodies as far as the eye could see.

There were at least 50,000 people floating in the water, and almost all of them were civilians. The Yangtze had become a river of corpses.

All I heard about it was as follows. The day before, up to tens of thousands of Chinese soldiers and refugees retreating from Nanjing had crowded into ferries that could only carry about 50 people at Xiaguan Port in the Yangtze River basin, which was only eight kilometres away from here, wanting to cross to the other side of the river.

At the time when the fighting in Nanjing was at its peak, the navy advanced up the Yangtze with artillery and machine guns, aiming to ambush the retreating army and ferries carrying refugees. When the ferries arrived at the other side of the river, all the guns and artillery opened fire. Shells and bullets rained down like a storm accompanied by a deafening roar. The ferries were shot directly and blown apart. All the ferries sank into the water.

When I heard about all of this, I couldn't help thinking: "Why did these irrelevant and innocent people have to suffer?" Then I thought that maybe this was the truth of what happened at the Nanjing Massacre.

One Japanese sailor, Sho Mitsui, witnessed and participated in the massacre on the 13th:

> I was 18 that year. I joined the Japanese navy and I was the youngest new recruit on the vessel. Our vessel was one of the most cutting-edge destroyers in the Japanese navy, the *Umikaze* - or Sea Wind - and it belonged to the 24th destroyer fleet. The fleet was made up of four vessels called the *Umikaze*, *Yamakaze*, *Suzukaze* and the *Kawakaze*. All four vessels fought in the upstream battle.
>
> On 13 December 1937, the news of Nanjing's fall spread to the ship. That morning, we all felt a little nervous at first. We berthed near Pukou on the other side of Nanjing, awaiting orders and continuing artillery action against the port gun fixtures on the banks of the river in Nanjing. As the Japanese naval guns were very accurate and powerful, it didn't take long for the enemy positions to be destroyed.
>
> Afterwards, the artillery action ended along with all other attacks. We saw several rafts floating in the river, full of dead Chinese people. The mounds of corpses were one and a half metres to two metres high, and were neatly stacked like a cube that had been designed. We all felt that it was very strange and were afraid that it was disguising something dangerous. So about 20 of us all desperately shot at the potential hazard on the rafts.
>
> All of us opened fire in a frenzy, but there was no response. Four rafts just floated by. Then we realised that the rafts were actually just the corpses of Chinese people.

Suzuki Tanaka (alias) was a Japanese veteran who served in the Second Sino-Japanese War. He was a heavy machine gunner in the 66th grand fleet. After the war, he became involved in publishing with the anti-war publications board in the youth arm of the Japanese Soka Gakkai Buddhist sect. He described that day in detail in a book published in August 1983:

> Simply because of the aforementioned reason, when the troops were going to be transferred, it was commonplace for the captives to be killed. We locked four or five captives in a cabin and surrounded it with a squad made up of 30 soldiers. The soldiers shot at the cabin until there was no sound, which gave us a weird unearthly feeling. Shouts calling for help would be heard at first.

The shooting continued until the sound finally disappeared. We thought of nothing but kept shooting. However, shooting at unarmed civilians was never pleasant. When it was all finished, as we had to hurry to pursue the main force that had set out beforehand, we had no time to dispose of the captives in the cabin. If we set the cabin on fire, the smoke would be a target for the Chinese troops. We hadn't made sure that the captives had died and someone had apparently escaped from the cabin after we left. Gunfire was heard everywhere before Japanese soldiers left a village.

Every time we heard gunshots, we'd say: "Well done!"

This once happened on a small bridge in August Showa 12 [1937]. Some infantrymen said that they wanted to test their guns on the captives. The soldiers used rifles and acted like they were in a 4,000 metre firing range. The rifles were able to punch through a three centimetre iron plate. I remember it was sunny that day. The soldiers discussed testing their rifles with interest:

"How about I take a shot at them?"

"Go on!"

Maybe it just began on a sudden impulse. There were about 13 or 14 captives and the struggling prisoners were strapped to wood. We then stood by and watched how many captives they could shoot. Some of the captives gave up resisting and lost their spirit, while others yelled and struggled for help. Some of the Japanese soldiers stood, some kneeled and others lay down to shoot. When they opened fire, bullets hit the captives' bodies, one, two, three, falling like dominoes in the dust.

The captives shot by the bullets groaned, bent their heads, and died right away. The captives were shot down one by one. I can still remember their groans and cries when the bullets pierced their bodies. Even so, our soldiers still fired away, taking turns to do so. The soldiers were asked about how it felt.

"It feels like hitting tofu."

"It feels good."

Other soldiers then said that they wanted to try.

Several more soldiers then started shooting. Other soldiers stood nearby and happily watched with interest. When all the participants had finished shooting, they dug a hole in the ground and buried the corpses. Japanese soldiers may have had some sort of psychological collectivism in battle. There was a worry that they wouldn't survive to see the next day. Those wretched memories are never pleasurable when I recall them now.

Something else happened in September in the same year in a rural homestead. After breakfast, I left for the squadron two kilometres away from our battalion to discuss the battle positions for the machine guns. I ran on the village footpath hoping to quickly complete my task. There was a small ditch used for irrigation between farms. A peasant family home was on the other side of the ditch. Their garden had tall trees in it, used for hanging clothes. I saw something strange hanging between two trees. I stared at it and saw that it was three Chinese soldiers. They had been pierced through the ears by a thick iron wire and seemed dead. I don't know the full story, but I guess that it takes a dozen soldiers to lift three people. The soldiers might have strung the victims up the night before. When they strung three living people up by their ears, they must have been met with a desperate struggle and painful cries. That's what I speculated at least. I now believe that the Japanese soldiers who did this might have been acting with a collectivist mentality. I left immediately to complete my unfinished task. Someone may have later brought them down and buried them under the squadron's orders. If the battalion chief had heard about it by chance, it would presumably have caused a great deal of concern. I heard some soldiers saying that it had gone too far.

Massacring prisoners like this can only be partly explained by these reasons. Another cause was the Marco Polo Bridge Incident. When word got out in Japan about common Japanese nationals in Beijing being slaughtered by Chinese soldiers, young soldiers swore in outrage to kill them. They used these stories to justify their actions now.

They committed these atrocities out of curiosity, indignation and a collectivist mentality. Although it was against military regulations for high-ranking officers to leave such breaches in military conduct unchecked, they still refused to discipline the soldiers appropriately. They usually ignored it and pretended that they hadn't seen anything. This may have been because if the leaders actually came forward and stopped the soldiers from treating the captives so appallingly, they might have become targeted themselves.

I'll talk a little more about the field hospital. After the battle finished, we went back to where we'd fought earlier to dispose of the corpses of our brothers in arms, tend to the wounded, and send the severely wounded soldiers to the field hospital. Though it was called a field hospital, it was just a place covered with straw in the burnt remains of peasant mud huts. Limited facilities meant that all the injured could do was lie down in the hut, which could hardly be described as a hospital. No one knew when medical treatment could be provided. When it was our turn to treat the injured soldiers, all we could do was clean septic and infected wounds with bamboo splints. Even so, the soldiers would still be ineffably happy. When someone died, we would dig a hole and put dozens of the deceased into it. We then set them on fire and burnt their bodies. The high flames and smoke would often incur a Chinese attack. At that point, the wounded soldiers who could still move and the military surgeon's bodyguards would be the only ones able to fight them. In the ship's hospital on the way back to Japan, many people died. Sometimes we woke up in the morning, finding that our brothers in arms had died beside us. When I was finally taken in by a Japanese hospital, there were just a few of my comrades left alive.

Masaharu Iwasaki was a private first class in the Japanese independent military engineer regiment assigned to Shanghai. He later died in a battle in Anhui Province against the Chinese army on 9 June 1938. This Japanese private first class had written a letter to his girlfriend, Fumiko Yamaguchi, in Japan after the attack on Nanjing. He described the situation when they entered Nanjing, particularly the day of the 13th:

We read the newspaper on 14 December in Nanjing. At home, people are flying flags and marching in parades. It must be very lively. When you get together to celebrate the festival, do you think of us in Nanjing? We're dressed in shabby military uniforms. We haven't slept for many nights because of the cold. All we eat is rice grown in Nanjing. We can't get Japanese rice; otherwise we wouldn't eat Nanjing rice. Because our troops have advanced too quickly, the supply units haven't caught up with us. During the three days from the 10th to the 13th, we have only had rice as dry as dust and pickles to eat. We can't get used to the food in China. It's torture for us. On 12 December, we were ordered to attack Nanjing, which is a difficult city for people at home to imagine. The city wall is about 12 metres tall. It's said that the perimeter is two kilometres. Once we got the order, we rushed to the military engineer school about two kilometres in front of us. As expected, the school is truly spectacular as a well-known Chinese person is in office as its principal. On the night of the 12th, the military engineer school was completely under our control. At that point, there was only one wounded on our side. People in the school abandoned dozens of their weapons and ran away. We captured 77 defeated soldiers and executed them by firing squad. They are truly worthy as regular armed forces, some soldiers died courageously, some stood in a dignified and impressive way with a smile on their faces as our guns aimed at them. If men like them account for even one tenth of the Chinese population, it will be very difficult for us Japanese to fight them.

From what I've heard about the Sino-Japanese War in 1894, China didn't seem to be as strong back then as it is now. However, it looks like the Chinese troops aren't always invincible. The Chinese people are very tenacious. When we rushed towards them, they didn't flee. When we attacked Nanjing, our artillery fired intensively at the city wall. After such a violent attack, the six metre wide 10 metre tall city wall was gradually destroyed. If we stopped bombing and shooting for 20 or 30 minutes, they'd instantly block off the gaps in the wall with sandbags. Before dawn on 13 December, we went around Nanjing and captured vessels and vehicles on the riverbanks of the Yangtze behind Nanjing, as well as 15 cars, three tanks and two motorcycles that were nearby. The navy's forces then arrived at the shores of the Yangtze and kept firing. On land, bullets fired continuously into the city. What a grand sight! The engineer corps occupied Xiaguan station at daybreak. We engineers shot about 800 defeated enemies ourselves on the banks of the Yangtze. We didn't even realise that we were killing people and left the Chinese drifting in the river.

We spent the whole morning today patrolling the vicinity so we had a rest this afternoon. After we killed the Chinese soldiers on the land, we stacked their corpses in a pile, poured oil on them and set fire to them. The corpses were stacked up in layers of two or three bodies in an area as large as the playground in Aikawa Primary School.

The ceremony celebrating the entry into Nanjing was held today. I didn't attend (only one officer and 12 soldiers attended the celebration ceremony). For the ceremony, we gathered together all of the 2,000 Chinese people left in the city last night and killed them all before dawn. On the Yangtze Riverbanks alone there were about 5,000 corpses sprawled everywhere. A fish in the river that looked like a dolphin pecked at the corpses in the river, moving them back and forth.

From the stories left by the Japanese officers and soldiers themselves, we can clearly see that, amidst the cheers and excitement of the Japanese soldiers after their invasion of Nanjing and the complex mixed feelings of happiness and sin when they wantonly slaughtered Chinese civilians, this is all irrefutable evidence of the horrors committed by the Japanese army in Nanjing.

The most convincing evidence of the Japanese atrocities on 13 December 1937 is the memoirs of the Japanese generals themselves. This is an extract taken from the diary of Lieutenant General Kesago Nakajima, the commander of the Japanese army's 16th division:

13 December, sunny.

In the morning, the scout team [the troops consisted of all the core soldiers led by high-ranking officers higher than second lieutenant, with the aim of scouting out the condition of the enemy's military and the surrounding terrain] in the 30th wing of the infantry corps entered through the Zhongshan gate. However, they didn't find any trace of the enemy. We were then informed of the occupation of Nanjing.

The 33rd infantry wing came down from the main peak and occupied the watchtower at 8am. All the other units later approached the city wall step by step. We ordered the artillery troops to take precautions and also ordered infantry and engineer troops to prepare for a flexible coordinated battle, which turned out to be a completely secure plan for gradually and completely mopping up the entire city.

On top of that, yesterday the Sasaki detachment encountered enemies that had retreated from Nanjing and had defeated the soldiers retreating from Zhenjiang. These soldiers blocked our advance so we had to leave quite a few troops in the rear to cover our advance.

As we may have risked losing the opportunity to seize Xiaguan, I ordered the 33rd infantry wing to rapidly march to the Taiping gate and then ordered the central force to immediately pursue the brigade to the northeast of Xuanwu Lake. We had already sent out a battalion the day before.

I also issued an order to the 2nd field gun squadron and the 1st light howitzer squadron to come back and follow the Sasaki detachment.

The cavalry regiment arrived at the Qilin gate at about 1pm and they were commanded to follow the Sasaki detachment at once.

During the day, the defeated Chinese army appeared on the road in the woods near the Xianhe gate and assaulted our rear units. In response, I ordered troops to prepare a squadron to mop up the invaders. At the same time, I ordered the Katagiri troops to mop up the area southwest and south of Purple Mountain.

After midday, the spearhead of the 20th infantry wing entered the city and began the mopping-up operations. I initially intended to intercept the 9th brigade and enter Nanjing first. But I failed to do so, making me feel extremely ashamed. As a result, I gave up on my original intention of entering Nanjing through the Zhongshan gate. To direct the battle in Xiaguan, I decided to move our operational focus over there.

I sent Lieutenant Colonel Nakazawa [the chief of staff in the 16th division] to Major General Kusaba to ascertain the military situation near the Zhongshan gate and asked him to take the next step. However, I believe that we are likely to encounter other defeated enemies near the road east of Purple Mountain. As it might be safer near Fugui Mountain, we had better move there. So, I decided to set off after lieutenant colonel Nakazawa's arrival. At 3pm, according to Nakazawa's report, the Taiping gate had already been occupied by our troops. Kusaba had also agreed to transfer our troops to Fugui Mountain. I then decided to relocate to the combat headquarters in the western hills right away.

We marched here to direct the battle today and found that the communication facilities had all been prepared.

During the battle near the watchtower, we captured a lieutenant commander who was the instructor of the military engineer school to get information about the location of mines. After interrogating him, he claimed that he didn't know exactly where all the mines were. He was instantly killed by our infantrymen.

As mentioned above, we stayed in the western hills post office to deal with mopping up issues until 6pm. Troops were then provided accommodation in the post office.

It was reported that the Sasaki detachment had occupied Xiaguan at 3.30pm.

Bombers attacked Nanjing at around midday.

Last night, when the 33rd infantry wing occupied the first peak, the commander gave a speech commending them for their achievements and awarded them with a barrel of sake, three bottles of whiskey and fruit. These awards were distributed to the 33rd infantry wing and the artillery troops who'd helped.

Nakajima's war diary features clear descriptions of their "disposal" of Chinese prisoners who had been left guarding Nanjing. All these stories are facts that cannot be erased. As for what really happened, only the people behind the atrocities can know the full details. Sasaki's forces, who were mentioned by Nakajima, were actually executioners. Major General Sasaki, the general officer of the 30th brigade, 16th division, was one of the major war criminals involved in the rape of Nanjing.

What's hard for many Chinese people to comprehend is that both Sasaki and the main culprit behind the massacre, the senior general Iwane Matsui, were China hands who'd had a friendly but complex relationship with the revolution that had founded the Republic of China. As previously mentioned, Iwane Matsui wasn't just Chiang Kai-shek's "respected teacher", but also a proactive supporter of Sun Yat-sen's revolution.

When he was young, Sasaki had been a hot blooded youngster who showed a great deal of enthusiasm and support for China's revolution. He had gone to China after his graduation from military school and had previously been a military consultant for Sun Yat-sen in Guangzhou during the Xinhai Revolution. At that point, he was the only foreign military expert who had easy access to Sun's base camp with a pass card. It was also at this point that he met Chiang Kai-shek, who was the chief of staff. According to Sasaki himself, Sun Yat-sen asked him to visit a Japanese-style tailor shop in Shamian in Guangzhou to specially design the Chinese tunic suit for members of the Kuomintang.

Iwane Matsui was a very thin and small old man. He was 59 when he had commanded the Battle of Shanghai and the attack on Nanjing. Many of the younger and fitter Japanese military men called him a "little old man" in private. This "little old man", with the blood of the Chinese people on his hands, was a pretentious "scholar" who liked trying to show off his literary talent. He used to write Chinese poems to commemorate almost every one of his "decisive" triumphs. For example, after the victory at Lake Tai during the assault on Nanjing, he wrote two Chinese poems. One of them was called *After the Battle at Hudong*:

The enemies we are battling are becoming weaker and weaker;
Our banners and flags shine in the skies above Hudong.
Do not talk about the foolish ways of the common folk;
It would be a shame for us Japanese not to conquer Nanjing.
Another poem was titled In Response to a Friend:
The Hudong battle is near its end;
Our emperor's strategy is bright with hope but it has not won his reward.
I stand high and see there are enemies in the northwest;
When can our emperor rule Asia?

Sasaki wasn't as thin as Matsui. He had a face like a slab of meat and the demeanour of a typical soldier. He also enjoyed trying to show off his meagre literary talent and not only wrote a diary but poems and verses too, which were quite clever. It's a pity that Japanese people today often criticise him, a so-called "collaborator", for his detailed but emotional narration and description of the true history of the Nanjing Massacre. Below is an excerpt of his writing demonstrating his feelings and the situation on 13 December 1937:

On the night of 12 December, I could hear the roar of artillery after midnight. Nanjing was soon to be occupied. If the reserves found enemy soldiers in the highlands to the west, they would be trapped. On top of that, only one squadron was stationed there due to a lack of troops. Still, they appeared relatively calm. They kept in contact with the division headquarters the entire night to receive orders and intelligence. The pursuit was launched at almost 6pm. Now, the sound of gunfire bursts in my ears as vast quantities of bullets are fired at the city wall.

At 8pm, I approached the sound of nearby gunfire. All the messengers, transportation forces and stewards were shooting.

"What's wrong?!" I asked as I ran out of my quarters.

"Although we've defeated them, a lot of enemies are coming down from Purple Mountain."

"Retreating forces?"

"They suddenly attacked us from the front while we were conducting reconnaissance. They came down, group after group of them. There's about 500 or 600 people in each group."

"Have you disarmed them?"

"How could we ever have time to disarm them? We just have to kill them all."

An endless stream of Chinese soldiers kept rushing down Purple Mountain and they were all we could see. They were all soldiers from the teaching corps stationed on the mountain. They were trying to cut their way out through the gap in our troops and counter-attack to break through.

Because the enemies may have wanted to escape and pass off as civilians instead of being trapped in the house they'd holed up in, the enemies who had arrived in small groups all threw their weapons away or left them in the house that they'd set alight. They were very thorough and professional. The troops were Chiang Kai-shek's personal soldiers after all, as well as the bravest and strongest ones. They fought valiantly to the end.

There were skirmishes taking place in many different areas. Soon after, according to the reports of different forces, our troops on the front had taken the enemy's positions and forced them to retreat. From midnight to 10am, light armoured vehicles took Xiaguan and shot at the defeated enemies that had gathered by the riverbank trying to jump into the river. It's estimated that it took about 15,000 bullets. Meanwhile, the 38th infantry wing occupied five city gates in the north, which reduced the amount of enemy escape routes. The commander of the 38th wing and a battalion of the 33rd wing followed the armoured vehicles and then approached the Yijiang gate. They fought with the enemy there, who had no chance of escape.

A reserve infantry squadron affiliated with the high command attacked from the left, front and rear and fought with the enemy several times. Signalmen, transporters and even messengers took part in the battle and defeated the enemy. After that, they pursued and attacked the enemy's forces. The field artillery had difficulty advancing due to the conditions of the road and it was attacked during the night. A squadron and the engineer corps, which was responsible for defence, joined the battle and fought for as many as four hours. There were originally two defensive squadrons in the rear. However, they also joined the battle and fought the enemies who'd broken through any gaps and were looking to counter-attack. We eventually defeated them. The cavalry stationed nearby in the rear were also suddenly attacked by the enemy in the dark. The enemy rushed into the field and we lost about 200 people and 60 horses. It was chaos. Then the cavalry asked for artillery support without considering their defensive capabilities. Our troops had a battle line that ran for miles and were fiercely fighting enemies from both sides.

At 10am, several artillery shells were fired from the rear, near our positions in the west highlands. They made sure to cover us but there was confusion and our troops were trapped in the chaos. Soon after, another 30 shells were fired. The mountaintop was suddenly covered with thick smoke and it was clear that something terrible had happened. An artilleryman had lost his mind and attacked his own troops. Fortunately, only a small area had been blown up.

As I previously mentioned, at about 10am, our light armoured vehicles occupied Xiaguan and completely blocked the path to retreat. Our infantry then also took all the city gates in the north and locked them. The enemies could escape from the city no longer.

Afterwards, some of the forces from the 6th division came from the south and gathered at the riverbank while the 11th naval fleet went up the river and fired at the enemy's boats, reaching Xiaguan at 2pm. The Kunisaki detachment reached Pukou on the opposite bank at 4pm. Other forces attacked the city walls and entered Nanjing. They then began mopping up. This battle had them surrounded and had turned into a complete annihilation.

Today, in my area of command, over 10,000 enemies have been killed. On top of this, prisoners have been killed by our mechanised soldiers and many more have been captured by different divisions. My troops alone have more than 20,000.

At 2pm, the mopping up ended and security was won. The troops then assembled and advanced to the Heping gate.

After that, many enemies surrendered, numbering in the thousands. Excited soldiers paid no attention to their commanders and killed everyone they captured. Thinking of the hardships and sacrifices we've suffered over these 10 days, even I wanted to say: "Just kill them all!"

At present, no rice can be found. Although there may be reserves in Nanjing, our forces will not transport food for the prisoners.

We climbed onto the Hepin gate and shouted *banzai*. It's sunny today. Japanese flags waved everywhere on the walls of Nanjing. I burst into tears when I saw them.

Sasaki was incredibly excited that day and couldn't sleep that night because he had also fought in Nanjing a decade earlier. It was as if the revolution with Sun Yat-sen and Chiang Kai-shek had been only yesterday. He couldn't resist writing a poem called *Attacking Nanjing*:

The moat of Nanjing is endless;
Battle lasts for 77 days.
Cross, cross, cross the moat forever.
Conditions I cannot recall.
Under the grass are all the corpses;
Bodies immersed in the water;
Such a long history of 4,000 years.
The Yangtze River never stops flowing;
Cavalry advances along the bank;
The Purple Mountain stands by the sky,
And the Ming Xiaoling mausoleum sits at its feet.
Who would not sigh for a nation's rise and fall?
Night has just gone and the dawn is coming.
Glorious sunshine will cover the whole city.
Our flags fly high on the wall.
The remote eastern sea;
Is the place where the sun rises.
Sounds of banzai echo above the clouds.

After writing this, Sasaki still felt overwhelmed with emotion, so he continued to write:

I'm certain that there was no one more moved than myself when standing on the walls of Nanjing. This isn't just because I lived here for two and a half years and know it well, nor is it because the city has undergone profound changes; it's now an astonishing modern city instead of the large sprawl of hare and pheasant filled farmland I knew when I left eight years ago. When I was in my twenties, Meiji 44 [1911], I had a good rapport with the Kuomintang with the aim of resolving the Manchuria issue. However, they adopted a policy of coexistence with and support of the Chinese Communist Party. Chiang Kai-shek in particular sold out to the American government, which made me frustrated. I left this place in anger as I had deep worries about the nation's future. All my experiences in Meiji 44 are clear now.

Treacherous people should be punished by God.

The soul of Sun Yat-sen that forever rests by Purple Mountain will weep because of Chiang Kai-shek's short sightedness. The modern city has been destroyed in but a few days. The fires still roar while thick smoke soars up to the sky.

I now truly understand the scale of the country's ruin.

Still unable to sleep from his excitement, Sasaki kept writing in his diary:

I led two units and took to mopping up both inside and outside the city. The troops had discovered all the remaining defeated soldiers, but they had thrown away or hidden their weapons. We took between 500 and 1,000 captives. They didn't look afraid, just exhausted. Perhaps they haven't eaten anything.

Up until the night of 11 December, there were electric lights and running water in Qilin village just outside of the city. According to our intelligence, the general commander of Nanjing, Tang Shengzhi, crossed the Yangtze with many officials along with their family members, escaping downstream.

There's a controversy regarding whether Colonel Hashimoto's artillery bombarded a foreign ship. It may have been a British ship that was carrying crowds of soldiers and citizens, but no one knows exactly what it was carrying.

Nanjing University took in hundreds of young women, and the former department of foreign affairs took in many wounded soldiers. They claim that they are under the protection of extraterritoriality and are receiving treatment.

No one is more miserable than these abandoned Chinese soldiers after their chief commander fled. It's unclear whether they had a strong will to fight or if they had to struggle with all of their effort as they had no other choice.

Although they are wounded or defeated, some soldiers still lurk in the villages or the mountains to act as snipers. We immediately kill these stubborn and disobedient people, and gunshots can be heard all day.

The moat outside the Taiping gate is filled with corpses.

Empty houses have been robbed. Military equipment is scattered on the ground. Hand grenades and bullets have been left everywhere. Many landmines have been buried in many significant positions. It's very dangerous here.

Many large fortifications had been set up in the main streets for street fighting and air defence. Engines have been destroyed and burnt out cars have been abandoned. Abandoned clothes and belongings are strewn everywhere. Our aerial attack has totally destroyed their governmental buildings, military academy and other military facilities, as well as the airport outside of the city.

Houses have been burnt down and some fires continue to rage. We cannot see any citizens, just homeless dogs.

Central Xiaguan has been reduced to ash. Hundreds of cars have been abandoned along the streets and hundreds of corpses float in the river.

It's been 10 years since 1927 when the national revolutionary army entered Nanjing after the February revolution. The population surged from 300,000 to 800,000. A proud modern city was established by successfully exploiting the farmers. However, all these are just memories. Anyone who sees the city's current pitiful state would surely be filled with complex emotions.

This extract indisputably and thoroughly once again proves the truth of the Nanjing Massacre. If anyone still has any doubts about the massacre, they should read the following interviews with Japanese people themselves.

Memories of the Frontline

Some may claim that the testimonies of the victims may not be entirely true, so is there any more damning evidence than the diaries written by the Japanese soldiers themselves? At least hundreds of thousands of people witnessed and participated in the massacre, many of whom have shown no remorse for their crimes. However, others do feel ashamed and haven't wanted to talk about the incident since leaving China. Some have confessed to their crimes due to an overwhelming sense of guilt, thus giving them some form of relief. These latter confessions are respectable and go a long way to winning the forgiveness of the people of China.

I shall introduce a Japanese lady here named Tamaki Matsuoka. Matsuoka was born in 1947 after the Second World War and became a teacher. After 1987, she began to study the history of the Japanese invasion of China. The crimes committed in Nanjing deeply moved her, while she also heard Japanese right wing representatives like Shintaro Ishihara constantly saying that the Nanjing Massacre was made up by China. Driven by a sense of justice, Matsuoka then felt an increasing responsibility to tell the Japanese people the truth of the nation's history. She then established a Nanjing Massacre hotline with colleagues from the national assembly for the 60th anniversary of the Nanjing Massacre from 10 to 12 October 1997. To her surprise, the hotline was very effective. Hundreds of veterans called the hotline and asked to reveal their experiences in the war. Matsuoka then began the five-year long and arduous task of interviewing Japanese veterans, which won her the praise of Zhu Chengshan, the curator of the Nanjing Massacre Memorial Hall: "She's brave and has never given up, her work is painstakingly done and truly remarkable."

"The veterans are all more than 80 years old now," Matsuoka says. "They're nearly at the end of their lives. If we cannot find the truth of what really happened now, then the truth will be buried forever in the darkness of history. There will never be a second chance to research, interview and get evidence about atrocities committed by the Japanese soldiers during the

Nanjing Massacre." Her work had only just begun. However, it was a difficult task indeed, being accused of treason by Japan's right wing elements. "The research has begun, however, even though veterans have been found, things have still been problematic. This is because some of them never talked about Nanjing. Some even said that they'd never seen a single dead body. Others said that their unit hadn't done anything in the war. There was no way other than interviewing them over and over again or trying everything to get them to finish the conversation." She never gave up and just kept on going. She said that during the repeated interviews, the testimonies relating to the Nanjing Massacre increased and more veterans appeared to assist with interviews. All of this gave them courage in the project and led to a firm belief in the need to collect more testimonies. They then raised the frequency of interviews and travelled around Japan to conduct them.

Over the five years, Matsuoka and her colleagues visited more than 200 soldiers. They were determined to find out whether the interviewees had killed unarmed citizens in China and whether the interviewees had raped Chinese women. When the veterans and their relatives attempted to deny the atrocities, Matsuoka would make a scene until they eventually told the truth. Matsuoka then organised the materials acquired through the confessions of 102 soldiers based on interviews with more than 200 soldiers. The materials were compiled into a book that was later published.

In 2002, the Chinese version of *Torn Memories of Nanking: Testimonies of Chinese Survivors and Japanese War Veterans of the Nanking Massacre* by Matsuoka Tamaki was published by the Shanghai Lexicographical Publishing House. Zhu Chengshan wrote the preface for the book.

Zhu opened a special area dedicated to Matsuoka on the exhibition walls of the Nanjing Massacre Memorial Hall to introduce her achievements and her book, speaking extremely highly of her.

I was lucky enough to get my hands on this precious material. The following extract features a Japanese soldier recalling what he had seen and experienced on 13 December 1937.

Yasushi Furukawa (veteran gunner in the 33rd group in the 16th division of the Japanese army):

We didn't know the location or the exact name of the place, but I was sure we went to Xiaguan. I can still remember Xiaguan now. To get there, we looked at the map as we marched. We passed the Xuanwu Lake, turned west and entered Xiaguan.

We lost many soldiers in just three days during the fighting at Purple

Mountain. When going down the mountain, we'd greet our comrades and friends by saying: "Hi, still alive?"

We assembled together in Nanjing after we went down the mountain. The following two or three days were quite quiet, and nothing really happened. We then accepted the mission to handle the defeated Chinese soldiers. We carried heavy machine guns to go to the rail yard by the Yangtze River. The freight cars were arranged in a row and were full of Chinese soldiers. We opened the doors of the cars. Although it was winter, the Chinese soldiers were all very hot and couldn't even breathe because the cars were so crowded. Most of the soldiers had taken off their clothes and were naked. We asked the naked, weak soldiers to get out of the cars and get on the rafts on the Yangtze. We shot them with the heavy machine guns.

Each raft could hold 20 to 30 people. We stood at one side of the river and used the heavy machine guns to shoot the Chinese soldiers on the rafts coming towards us in the current. Some Chinese jumped into the river and others just floated downstream. They would be shot with great accuracy if the distance was relatively short. If the Chinese were hit, they'd fall into the river in agony. I didn't know who made the rafts. The order was conveyed to our group and I was asked by my squadron commander to follow it.

Each military unit consisted of a squadron of gunners. Each squadron consisted of four groups. Each group carried two heavy machine guns. I was the team leader of our group, so I took the two guns to carry out the orders.

I did missions like this two or three times. Every time, I pulled the Chinese soldiers out of the freight cars and got them onto the rafts to let them drift into the river. I ordered our team to shoot at them several times. There were several different types of rafts. Some of them were made of iron drums with logs on them while others were made of wood. There were soldiers tasked with making the rafts, probably sapper teams. This lasted less than two weeks, but I can still remember it clearly. Other groups didn't tie up the soldiers either. They put the weak ones on the rafts directly and shot them.

We couldn't figure out whether the people who were being shot on the rafts were soldiers or ordinary people because some were naked, some were in Japanese military uniform and others were wearing civilian clothes to hide their identities. We didn't know whether there were any farmers among them, so we just killed them all.

Mines had also apparently been buried outside the city walls. They gathered together Chinese soldiers there and hundreds of them died when the mines exploded. When Nanjing fell, our mission was to deal with the defeated Chinese soldiers. We spent quite a long time killing them all. We also heard that other groups were doing similar execution missions, which was likely what's known as the Nanjing Massacre. It's true that we did these cruel things.

I saw other kinds of executions besides guns and mines. Most of the new or reserve military officers became commanders after becoming sub-lieutenants. They always gave orders to do "test kills". We then caught Chinese people under the pretext of them being defeated soldiers and cut off their heads. The new commanders always cut off the heads in front of the Japanese soldiers. The best way of doing it was to leave a thin layer of skin at the back of the neck when cutting off Chinese people's heads. I saw people being beheaded in front of me. This also happened before Nanjing fell and many people were caught in the villages and killed in this way. Their heads were cut off by the commanders.

We did many despicable things to the Chinese people. When I recall all this, I remember things that happened at the time and their effect on my dreams. I often dreamed that I was being chased by Chinese soldiers in the war and this horrible dream lasted until several years ago. I always woke up from the nightmare in a cold sweat. Sometimes, my wife would wake me up to see if I was okay. The nightmare scares me to this day.

Shunsuke Okawa (veteran gunner in the 1st gun team of the 33rd group in the 16th division of the Japanese army):

We shot the fleeing Chinese soldiers on the Yangtze. The river was wide and there were many people there. We shot them from behind. I was a gunner at the time and I shot them because I was covering the soldiers crossing the Yangtze. However, the Chinese people never fought back. We chased and shot them, but no one collected the dead bodies. People who'd been killed in the war lay everywhere...

Hiroji Sawada (veteran chemical soldier in the 33rd group of the 16th division of the Japanese army):

On 13 December, when we were driving the Chinese soldiers from Purple Mountain to the foothills, we saw dead bodies that had been flattened by tanks. After walking across the dead bodies, our team raced down to the bottom of the mountain. Before we entered Xiaguan, we saw dead bodies everywhere on the road. Nanjing had been attacked and occupied by the team that had advanced there first. The infantry was incredibly fast and they rushed to the gates of Nanjing. Japanese soldiers followed behind with tanks and artillery but they mistakenly identified them as the enemy. Many of these soldiers were shot by friendly forces.

We followed behind them and entered Nanjing through the Yijiang gate with its high walls and mopped up all the defeated soldiers in the city. Our team didn't do this, but almost all the other teams that did the mopping-up operations caught everyone who looked like a man. They'd say: "This one seems suspicious, he might be a Chinese soldier." They'd then arrest him. This repeated hundreds of times a day.

There was a row of storage space in the docks in Xiaguan, which was filled with captive Chinese men. We couldn't count how many people we put there. There were hundreds of men in each unit. After the mopping-up, we heard that they were going to kill them so we all went to the dock to watch the executions.

There was a detachment from the 9th squadron waiting at the entrance of the storage space with 10 soldiers and two light machine guns, whose muzzles were aimed at the storage space to ensure that everything went smoothly. Another two light machine guns were used to kill the Chinese. They dragged them out of the storage space and ordered five defeated soldiers to stand in a group and run from the dock to the trestle. The Japanese soldiers then shot them in the back. Sometimes they ordered the Chinese men to face the dock and run. This repeated several times until all of them were killed. The Chinese men were wearing civilian clothes. Some were in work uniforms. We didn't care about whether they were soldiers or not. We just asked them to run and killed them. We all thought that the killing was horrible. The men we shot all fell into the Yangtze so we didn't need to get rid of them. All the corpses fell into the river and disappeared.

When doing the mopping-up operations, we received an order that we had to examine every single house one by one. If we found that there were enemies who'd gone into buildings that belonged to foreign countries, we could enter and check. The places to be checked were divided by regiment. All the regiments were involved in mopping up Nanjing. We accepted the order and examined every house one by one. We didn't know who our enemies were, so we just took all the men who may have been soldiers. We could go anywhere in Nanjing. We began our mission by where we'd entered Nanjing through the Yijiang gate.

There were dead bodies all around the Yijiang gate. The Japanese attack had been so quick that the Chinese didn't have any chance of escape. The dead were in regular army uniforms and civilian clothing. It wasn't just around the city gates that were covered with dead bodies, but inside Nanjing too. All the squadrons were involved in the mopping-up so there were some places in Nanjing that had more than one squadron assigned to them. One time we went to a house and there was no noise at all. We thought it was empty until we found that everyone inside the house was dead. Some people saw that we'd entered their house and wanted to run away. We just shot them from behind. People were killed in all kinds of ways. It was truly horrible. We killed all the suspicious men and took the men who'd tried to escape to the first killings on the dock. I think the Nanjing Massacre refers to what happened on the dock. We got the men to run on the dock and we shot them from behind until they were all dead. The dock was huge and each storage unit could hold hundreds of people. There were many storage units so the number of people killed was shocking. I heard that they weren't able to shoot everyone so they just set fire to the storage units and burned them to death. If we'd shot everyone then it would've taken hours to finish.

The current on the surface of the Yangtze was slow, while it was very rapid as it got deeper. As a result, none of the Chinese soldiers who fell into the river could have survived. I heard that some squadrons poured petrol on the dead bodies and burned them on the riverbanks. There were too many people to be killed because we'd brought all of the Chinese men in the city here. I think there were thousands of them. We couldn't kill them with just our squadron alone, so the others did it too. The Nanjing Massacre probably refers to the killings next to the Yangtze. Lots of civilians were killed. Some people had nothing to do with the soldiers, but, they were still killed. Even the postmen were killed. Few people knew about this in Japan. I don't know what they were thinking or why citizens were killed.

Shige Okazaki (veteran private first class of the 38rd group in the 16th division of the Japanese army):

The 33rd group was the spearhead. The 33rd group and 38th group exchanged tasks at 12pm that night. We could see the Heping gate, which was two miles away. The orders were for three detachments to take the Heping gate. The mountain artillery and other guns behind us opened fire and someone shouted: "Come on!" However, the soldiers from the other two detachments shouted back: "We'll die if we run to the front. We should stay here for a while!" As a result, only one of the three detachments rushed to the frontline. I packed 500 rounds for my gun and ran for 50 metres. Bullets fired down from the city gate. Although we fired back in all directions, we were still being targeted by the Chinese soldiers. We lost many comrades. The Heping gate was the first target we took in Nanjing and the first soldier who set foot on the Heping gate was from our detachment. We waved the Japanese flag and ran into Nanjing. The Chinese soldiers didn't know that we'd already taken the gate. Approximately 1,000 Chinese soldiers ran into Nanjing from outside of the city. They were lined into four rows with military flags on their arms. We arrested them, took them to a truck and brought them to Xiaguan. We told them to stand in four rows and then opened fire with our artillery. We killed them all.

I beheaded five men in Nanjing. It was like swatting flies. The key thing to remember was to keep the last bit of skin on their necks intact so that their heads didn't fall off. We told them to sit down with their legs crossed and their arms crossed in front of their chests. This meant that they fell forwards when their heads were cut off. They all fell towards Purple Mountain, which means that they all fell towards Japan's imperial palace. We also tied the Chinese to poles left over after a big fire and got our soldiers to stab them to death. The fighting in the Dabie Mountains had been intense. Three soldiers had probably been wounded for each soldier killed. The entire 2nd team from the 38th group had been wiped out and 1,000 people had died. Horses had just been thought of as weapons and soldiers were expendable. It was total misery. So, when we killed the Chinese, it didn't bother us any more than killing a bird. I thought that the war would be over after taking Nanjing.

Yoshitaro Tokuda (veteran private first class from the 1st team of the 33rd group in the 16th division of the Japanese army):

We entered Nanjing's Taiping gate at about 8am on 13 December. All their soldiers had received orders to stand down. I remembered that my detachment leader had asked us to kill all the men in the city. After entering Nanjing, we were reminded that we couldn't enter anywhere that belonged to other countries. If we didn't pay special attention to this, it'd likely lead to an international incident. We only arrested men as we only received orders to arrest men. We took all the men and asked them: "You were soldiers before, right?" By asking such a casual question, we caught them. Many arrests were made around the Taiping gate and they were terrified. We then arrested more than 3,000 people including men, women, the elderly and children. Outside the Taiping gate, some soldiers on the right of the gate placed poles in the ground and used wire to surround the place. We took the Chinese there and buried mines underground. We wrote "mine" on a piece of white paper to make sure the Japanese soldiers stayed away. The mines exploded once we pulled the detonator. The dead bodies resembled a mountain range. There were so many people to be killed that guns were simply not efficient, so we used mines instead. Then we went up the walls and poured petrol on the mountains of dead bodies to burn them. It was difficult to burn them because there were too many dead bodies lying on top of each other. People on the top were mostly dead, but the people at the bottom were mostly alive.

The leader of the detachment commanded the recruits to stab them to check if the bodies were still alive, and then to kill them if not. I stepped on corpses to search for survivors. If I found someone alive, I just said: "This man is still alive." Then the other soldiers stabbed him to death. Bayonets were plunged into their throats. Blood sprayed out and their faces immediately turned white with a scream. The Chinese didn't die easily. Soldiers from other squadrons were also there, as well as the leader. Our squadron was mainly in charge of the stabbing. The entire squadron did this. Other squadrons were in charge of dealing with the dead bodies, so the dead bodies were left there for the time being. Dead bodies were tied up with electrical wire and sent to Xiaguan. If we calculated the acreage of the mountains of dead bodies like farmland, it was about 815 acres.

When I went to contact the commander at the rear of my squadron, there were five or six captives with uniforms and guns. I told them to lay down their weapons. Naturally they refused to do so because guns were their only means of survival. They escaped for Xiaguan. I let them go because I thought they'd eventually be killed in the Yangtze. There were plenty of soldiers who surrendered. We didn't contact our group and arrested them ourselves to be brought to the places where the landmines were buried. There were some Chinese soldiers who'd changed into civilian clothing and hid in the refugee camps. However, they were still discovered and taken away. They were pathetic. This may have happened at the other gates as well, but we just captured and killed people by the Taiping gate. We did so many cruel things. Recently, I've heard that the names of the victims have been carved onto the walls of Nanjing. I'd like to go but I'm very scared to do so. I thought that it wouldn't be true even if I went there, so I gave up on the idea.

I heard that people in Xiaguan were killed with machine guns, although I never saw it. There were so many Chinese people to be killed that guns weren't efficient, so they were killed with land mines by the Taiping gate.

Uichiro Shimomura (veteran artillery gunner of the 33rd group in the 16th division of the Japanese army):

There were more dead bodies around the Taiping gate than anywhere else in Nanjing. There was a ditch in front of the Taiping gate filled with corpses. In the morning, some "dead bodies" were still twitching. It showed just how intense the fighting had been at the Taiping gate.

We dug ditches and buried the dead so that our vehicles could pass through. Places where vehicles wouldn't be passing through were just left exposed so we could see corpses everywhere. The corpses were buried on the ridge of the grassless mountain with their feet exposed. All the dead bodies were apparently Chinese because all the Japanese bodies had been dug out and cremated.

The ditch was two and a half to three metres wide and three metres deep. The length was unknown. We didn't know how many ditches we'd dug.

No one knew how many people were buried there. We were so tired. I heard that the 6th squadron had killed many people in a short period of time.

We saw the walls of Nanjing when we passed through the Taiping gate. There were ditches nearby. There were no other squadrons, just us. I didn't know whether the arrested Chinese had been killed there because I hadn't seen what had happened. It was probably true. Some of the bodies were still twitching.

I originally considered paraphrasing what these Japanese veterans had said in the third person. I then found that no matter how good my writing was, the original confessions were always more powerful. We not only learn about what happened on 13 December 1937 from these records, but we can also feel their joy, thoughtlessness and numbness from when they killed the people of Nanjing. Nothing could be more horrible than this feeling. This is war.

There's no need to use the veterans' memories as Japanese testimony to the massacre in this book, but they are instrumental in showing just how brutal the Japanese soldiers were. The true scale of the horrors is perpetually remembered by the city itself.

Memories of the City

Among the huge piles of historical materials, no exact number can be found regarding how many Chinese prisoners of war were killed by the Japanese in the first day they took Nanjing. However, in Nanjing today, I've found dozens of monuments dedicated to the victims of the massacre. Most of these monuments were built in the 1980s by the Nanjing municipal government according to the number of victims and locations of the massacre. Others were donated by individuals at the end of the Second Sino-Japanese War. These monuments mark where the people of Nanjing were once killed by the Japanese. Today, these monuments, like an immortal memory, stand strong in the city and are remarkable and sobering reminders of the horrors of the massacre. The inscriptions on some of these monuments are as follows:

The Swallow Rock Memorial beside the Yangtze River

This monument is in Swallow Rock Park next to the Yangtze River.

In December 1937, the people of Nanjing began to flee when the Japanese invaded the city. Among these people were 30,000 unarmed soldiers and 20,000 civilians. They were swarming towards the area by the Yangtze known as Swallow Rock in an attempt to cross the river and go north. However, the river had unexpectedly been blocked by Japanese warships and people were stopped from leaving. The Japanese army then surrounded these people and shot them, killing 50,000 in total. The riverbank was covered with bodies and the river turned red with blood. Such a huge amount of death and monumental misery is rarely seen. It was a tragedy that remains painful. This monument has been built to remind us of the tragedy. The dead shall be at peace in their graves while the living shall learn from it, strive to be strong, rejuvenate the nation and maintain world peace.

The Eastern Nanjing Memorial

This monument lies east of the Nanjing Institute of Physical Education in eastern Nanjing.

In December 1937, the Japanese invaders brutally massacred our compatriots in Nanjing. The fields in the east of this city were covered with bodies and the farms were dotted with skeletons. The uncollected bodies were left there to rot. It wasn't until April the next year that they were first cleared by charities like the Benevolent Association (Chong Shan Tang). From Zhongshan to Maqun, 33,000 bodies in total were collected and buried in the fields nearby. Several months later, even more bodies were found scattered in the countryside, occasionally alerting others to their presence with their smell. In December 1938, the government at the time asked the public health bureau to collect the bodies. Three thousand more were collected from places like Maqun, Maoshan, Maan, and Linggu Temple, and were buried together east of Linggu Temple. In January 1939, the Tombstone for the Wondering Souls Monument was built. While the inscription remains, the original monument is gone. It has been rebuilt in memoriam and continues to tell this tragic episode of Nanjing's history to anyone who wishes to hear it.

The Shangyuanmen Memorial

This memorial is in Shangyuanmen next to the Yangtze River.

On 13 December 1937, after the Japanese army occupied Nanjing, 57,000 unarmed soldiers and civilians crowded by the banks of the Yangtze in an attempt to cross the river. They were captured by the Japanese army and were all imprisoned in four or five villages at the foot of the Mufu mountains. After being tortured for several days, some of them froze or starved to death. On the night of the 18th, the rest were tied together and sent to Shangyuanmen where they were shot. The few who survived were later stabbed. The bodies were then burnt and the remains were thrown into the river. It was a dreadful sight and the land turned red with blood wherever the Japanese and their bayonets went. The innocent victims were even abused after being killed. Our hearts ache whenever we think of this tragedy. This monument was built to remember this great sadness and to never forget to strive to be strong.

Pude Temple Compatriot Victims Memorial
This memorial has been erected in the Youth League on Rain Flower Terrace Road in the south of Nanjing.

In December 1937, the massacre committed in Nanjing by the invading Japanese army shocked the entire world. Purple Mountain and the Qinhuai River were dyed red with blood as more than 300,000 of our innocent countrymen were murdered. Pude Temple is one of the burial sites of their remains, where 9,721 bodies were buried one after another by the Red Cross of Nanjing. The high number of bodies buried here has given it the name "the pit of 10,000 corpses". Dates and burials are listed as follows:

In 1937:
    22 December, 280 buried
    28 December, 6,468 buried
In 1938:
    30 January, 486 buried
    23 February, 106 buried
    25 March, 799 buried
    14 April 1,177 buried
    26 May, 216 buried
    30 June, 26 buried
    31 July, 35 buried
    31 August, 18 buried
    30 September, 48 buried
    30 October, 62 buried

On the 40th anniversary of the Chinese people's victory in the anti-Japanese war, this inscription has been engraved to remember the deceased and encourage future generations: "Remember this miserable history and aspire to rejuvenate China".

Jiangdong Gate Compatriot Victims Memorial
This tombstone can be found in the Nanjing Massacre Memorial Hall.

On 16 December 1937, Japanese troops imprisoned tens of thousands of unarmed Chinese soldiers and civilians in the former military prison compound and brought them to the Jiangdong gate in the evening. Under the light of burning civilian buildings, the Japanese violently opened fire on the crowd with heavy and light machine guns. The victims cried out in agony and fell down in a pool of blood one by one. The place was strewn with dead bodies, damming the river. The scene was appalling as they were left exposed to the elements, battered by the wind and the rain. Months later, the bodies slowly started to decay as the weather became warmer. Charities in Nanjing later began to bury the tens of thousands of bodies in two graves nearby, which were named the "pits of 10,000 corpses". The erection of this tombstone is to pay respect to the deceased and encourage future generations to love their country, strive for progress, oppose wars of aggression and to protect world peace.

Only a few words have been inscribed on these memorials but they serve as graves for the many victims. The content is shocking and describes some of the most terrible scenes in human history.

It is of utmost importance that these words are read around the world so that the criminals behind the massacre never forget to atone and repent for their sins.

3

NANJING IS SUFFOCATED

While the Japanese were certainly frenzied on the first day they entered Nanjing, after 14 December, when the ancient capital fell under the heel of the Japanese troops, the brazen madness of the Japanese conquerors reached to its zenith. Over the following week, the Japanese soldiers became beasts that bullied, slaughtered and enslaved the Chinese as they pleased.

"The Japanese soldiers charged at me with their guns in hand, so I put my hands up and got out of the car. After they ascertained that I wasn't a soldier, I climbed over the broken city gates and passed through the streets strewn with the dead bodies of Chinese soldiers. I saw that the Japanese had played a joke by placing the heads they'd chopped off on the city walls with a biscuit in the mouth of one and a Chinese pipe in the mouth of another." Charles Yates McDaniel of the *Associated Press* was one of the few western journalists the Japanese allowed to enter Nanjing after 13 December. He recorded what he saw and heard in a report he delivered to the *Chicago Daily News*:

> On 14 December, the Japanese soldiers sacked the entire city. Along the road to the North gate, which was littered with the bodies of men and horses, I saw a Japanese vehicle drive into the city, with its tires struggling to get a grip on the road of bloodied bodies.
>
> On 15 December, a slave belonging to the ambassador's escort went to visit his mother but only found her corpse in a ditch. Another staff member's brother had also died. This afternoon, I saw some soldiers who I'd once helped to disarm being dragged out of a house and shot dead before being kicked into a ditch. At night, about 500 civilians and unarmed soldiers were tied up and escorted by Japanese soldiers armed with swords. None of them returned alive.
>
> On 16 December, on my way to the river, I saw yet more dead bodies in the streets and chanced upon a line of Chinese people whose hands were bound. One of them suddenly ran up to me and knelt down in front of me, begging me to save him, but I could do nothing. The dead Chinese are all I can think of, the image of them lingering in my mind.

McDaniel only stayed in Nanjing for a few days before leaving because he couldn't bear the "hell on earth". He told his American colleagues that he "would suffocate" if he stayed even just one day longer.

The journalist Archibald Steele, who accompanied McDaniel to Nanjing, left a day earlier. He wrote a report titled *A Witness's Description of Four Days of Hell in the Fallen City*, which he sent to the *Chicago Daily News* on 15 December:

> (Nanjing, 15 Dec) Four days of hell is the most accurate description of the occupation of Nanjing.
>
> I have just left on the *USS Oahu* along with the first batch of foreigners to leave Nanjing after the siege. Upon leaving the city, the final scene we saw was a group of 300 Chinese people standing in front of the city walls near the river and being executed one by one, with their bodies piling up as high as a man's knee. It's a symbolic portrait of the madness in Nanjing.
>
> The fall of Nanjing has been an unimaginably panic-stricken and chaotic process, with the deaths of tens of thousands of Chinese people following Japan's occupation. Many innocent civilians have been murdered in cold blood. Japan glibly proclaims its intension of friendly relations with China, yet its atrocities during the Nanjing Massacre deprive them of any opportunity to win over the Chinese.
>
> After Chinese morale was demolished and blind panic swept through the populace, Nanjing almost seemed to let out a deep sigh of relief when the Japanese troops entered the city as they thought that the Japanese couldn't be any worse. This naiveite didn't last long.
>
> In fact, the Japanese troops could have taken the rest of Nanjing without a single bullet being fired if they'd spared the lives of the defeated Chinese soldiers trapped in the city. However, they instead chose to systematically slaughter them.
>
> They slaughtered men as if they were livestock. It's difficult to estimate how many were trapped and killed; the number may be between 5,000 and 20,000.
>
> As the land route had already been cut off, the Chinese army rushed to the river through the Yijiang gate, which quickly became crowded. One now has to drive over the bodies, which pile up as high as five feet, before crossing the city gates. Hundreds of Japanese trucks and artillery have been driving over the bodies.
>
> Streets all over the city are strewn with the corpses of innocent civilians and the abandoned equipment and uniforms of the Chinese army. Many soldiers just jumped into the river because they couldn't find a ship. Most drowned to death.

Knowledge of the historical truth of the Nanjing Massacre is largely attributed to McDaniel and Steele as they travelled around Nanjing to investigate at the risk of their lives. However, the Japanese authorities then realised that their crimes were too blatant and shocking so they decided to clear the city of foreign journalists. The killings were mostly covered up over the next few days. However, decades later, we have a wider range of sources to use to obtain information. This has allowed the crimes of the Japanese over the following weeks of the occupation to gradually come to light instead of fade away with the passage of time.

Kill Every Male in Sight

On 13 December, the first day the Japanese troops entered the city, they killed the Chinese soldiers who'd failed to cross the river in Xiaguan. This violence only continued, killing Chinese prisoners in the most savage of ways on 14 and 15 December. There were two main reasons for the bloodthirsty slaughter. First was out of fear of Chinese resistance and second was because they enjoyed killing. With this mix of fear and perverted pleasure, tragedies continued to unfold as every able-bodied adult was targeted.

On 14 December, a Japanese military unit came down from Purple Mountain before capturing a Chinese major and forcing him to lead the way to the city through the Taiping gate. At this point, they chanced upon a Chinese unit and immediately surrounded them. Through the help of a translator, the Japanese told them that their commander had already fled and given the order to surrender. The Chinese did as they were told and when they were asked which division they belonged to, they said that they'd retreated from Zhenjiang, thinking that Nanjing was still safe. The Japanese burst into laughter, seeing these Chinese soldiers as sitting ducks. But it wasn't long before the Japanese became concerned. There were now more than 1,000 captives while they barely had 100 soldiers. The Japanese initially tied up their prisoners with ropes and led them to the edge of the city walls, but they couldn't handle them all as there were too many of them. Even if they could, how would they feed them all? When they asked their superiors what to do, the Japanese senior officials refused to provide them with food for the prisoners. This wasn't much of a big deal for them as the prisoners would die after several days without food. But the Japanese soldiers didn't want to be deprived of rape, robbery and looting because they had to guard these Chinese soldiers, so they asked their superiors how to deal with them again. This time the answer was: "Get rid of them there."

The Japanese, laughing and joking, took the Chinese captives to a corner and lined them up before opening fire.

More than 1,000 people were killed within 10 minutes. The captain of the unit then walked through the streets of Nanjing with a blood-soaked bayonet and the Japanese flag on his shoulders.

On the same day, a machine gun unit from the 38th regiment of the Japanese army came down Purple Mountain, walking down a railway track. The soldiers were anxious, fearing that there might be remaining Chinese soldiers lying in ambush, so they hastily got down and set up their machine guns. Their instincts turned out to be correct as a brigade of Chinese soldiers soon appeared, running towards them along the railway from the Yaohua gate. As they were waving a white flag, the Japanese didn't fire at them.

"What should we do with these 10,000 soldiers?" the Japanese captain asked his superior. He told him to bring the captives into the city.

The Japanese troops thought that it was impossible to escort so many prisoners with so few soldiers of their own. They then asked for reinforcements, who arrived later, and were required to take the captives into the city overnight.

Escorting 10,000 captives with just 200 soldiers was still problematic. As night fell, the Japanese acted aggressively and in control while they were actually terrified.

When they entered the city, the captives were stuffed into trucks already parked in an open space, allegedly to be disposed elsewhere in batches. The captives clearly had no idea about this.

The 10,000 prisoners were then brought to the banks of the Yangtze and slaughtered. The Japanese had many ways of killing captives. Some just shot them with machine guns and some used other measures. Masao Asakura, a Japanese veteran, recalls: "There was a slope, so they just pushed the truck down it and it rolled down by itself. When people shouted to throw them into the river, we'd push the truck loaded with prisoners into the Yangtze."

More Chinese captives were taken into the city. Some of them were brought to the riverbanks in trucks and dealt with directly, while others were brought to the deserted warehouses near the riverside and lied to that it was to help them get settled. There were so numerous prisoners that the Japanese worried that they'd unite and resist. A far crueller fate awaited the prisoners. Toshio Oda, a Japanese veteran from the 3rd unit of the 33rd regiment in the Japanese army, explains:

> The warehouses were filled with captives. Several days later, we were told to set fire to the warehouses. The people inside all burned to death. Those were

our orders but we felt sorry for them. The warehouses in Nanjing were made of bricks or corrugated iron so thick smoke poured out of the windows. When there were no more warehouses, the Chinese were told to stand in four very long lines. There were so many of them. We formed several lines, with each of us holding a heavy or light machine gun. When we received our orders, we opened fire. It was mad. The entire regiment did the same thing.

Captain Eishiro Kondoh of the 8th squadron from the 19th regiment of the Japanese artillery recorded his involvement in an operation near the riverside on 16 December in his journal:

A shelter for 20,000 captives was burned tonight. I'd swapped shifts with the squadron watchmen. It was eventually decided that a third of the captives, that's about 7,000 of them, were to be gunned down along the Yangtze. We'd been ordered to keep watch until everyone was killed and those who lay dying, twitching and kicking, had been stabbed with bayonets.

The moon was hanging high in the sky. The dying prisoners groaned under the bright moonlight. Such miserable scenes can only be found in war. I returned at about 9.30pm. It was an experience I shall never forget.

The Japanese slaughtered more than 17,000 prisoners who'd surrendered while descending from the Mufu mountains over three days from 16 to 18 December, using the same cruel techniques.

To confirm the atrocities, I found an onsite record from the period. This example comes from Nobutada Kurosu, who was in the same squadron as Eishiro Kondoh. He recorded in his journal on the 16th:

At 1pm, 20 of my artillerymen were sent to wipe out the remaining enemies in the Mufu mountains. A few days ago, some of the arrested Chinese soldiers - there were about 5,000 of them - were taken to the banks of the Yangtze and shot there, followed by impulsive bayonet executions. I slaughtered about 30 of those hideous Chinese soldiers.

You had to pluck up all your courage and use all your strength to kill after climbing over the dead bodies, which piled up like a hill. The Chinese soldiers - old and young - were groaning with agony. We killed all of them and tried to behead them. The massive operation was unprecedented. I was so exhausted after coming back at 8pm. Both of my hands ached.

These records expose the scale of the savage atrocities committed when Chinese prisoners were executed.

The Japanese soldier Meguro Fujii kept a brief yet detailed account of the executions, writing about the crimes the Japanese forces committed and the number of Chinese captives slaughtered:

On the 16th: Yamada's army shot dead about 7,000 POWs at 4pm. Dead bodies piled up like a mountain on the banks of the Yangtze. It was appalling.

On the 17th: We were asked to perform a task at 5pm, shooting about 13,000 of the enemy's forces. Yamada's army killed nearly 20,000 enemies in two days. The armies' other captives seem to have been eliminated.

On the 18th: It was windy and it began to snow at 3am. The mountaintops were covered in snow when we got up in the morning. It was the first snow. The troops gathered inside and outside of the city amounted to about 10 divisions. After taking a break, we shot about 15,000 remaining enemies at 5pm.

On the 19th: We got up at 6am when we should have been resting. We were asked to dump the bodies of tens of thousands of enemy forces that had been killed yesterday into the Yangtze. We worked until 1pm.

This was an appalling atrocity; killing had just become part of a daily routine for the Japanese, who considered the Chinese to be no better than beasts.

The pain the captives must have suffered is beyond imagination. When the Chinese soldiers surrendered after their defeat in the Mufu mountains and other places, they assumed that the Japanese would follow international law. However, the Japanese blithely ignored international laws and basic humanitarianism. When the captives were brought to the riverside and locked into warehouses, they had no idea about their impending doom. Some even begged the Japanese soldiers for food by slipping them notes. From the content of their messages, we have a clear picture of the misery that the prisoners endured and the atrocities committed against them by the Japanese. The Japanese lieutenant Miro Amano preserved this note from the Chinese captives, which he sent to his relatives back in Japan:

Great Japanese officials,

We hope that you can help us get settled as we have left our forces and have surrendered to you. We have been here for three days without any news from you. We've been starving for four days and the food you give us is too little to sustain us. At this life-and-death moment, we anticipate your salvation and will devote ourselves to your service in future to repay your grace. We are willing to do anything you want just for a bowl of congee or rice.

— Sincerely, Ad hoc representative of the surrendered army

Tricked into going to the riverside with an empty stomach, the Chinese soldiers had to face the only fate that awaited them: death. This is all that the, at least, tens of thousands of Chinese soldiers who'd laid down their arms could expect. It is truly tragic.

At this point, the Japanese thought that in addition to the Chinese troops who'd fled to Xiaguan on the night of the 13th and the morning of the 14th, about 20,000 soldiers were hiding in Nanjing itself. Therefore, almost every man under the age of 50 was deemed to be a Chinese soldier and they were arrested regardless of what they were wearing or their occupation. The Japanese dealt with these captives as they pleased.

Goro Matsuda and other machine gunners from the 33rd unit of the 16th regiment participated in a mopping-up operation on 14 December and arrested 25 Chinese people in an alley. However, these junior Japanese soldiers didn't know what to do with the captives. After consulting their superiors, they were allowed to do as they pleased with them.

The captain then ordered the captives to stand in a line and for the Japanese soldiers, bayonets in hand, to stand in front of one captive each. Matsuda recalled: "I took out my bayonet and stabbed a captive who was wearing a padded jacket, which blocked it. It became stuck instead. I knew that it wouldn't work this way, so I pulled the trigger of my rifle and the man immediately dropped dead with a bang. We only captured defeated soldiers after entering the city, so many young men changed clothes to disguise themselves. At that point, it was the captains who were asked to await orders, so we ordinary soldiers had no idea about their plans. Our captain just told us to find captives. So how did we distinguish the plain-clothed soldiers? We captured all the young men." Matsuda vividly remembers what he did in Nanjing. Decades later he still remembers: "When we killed people in the city, we killed them right on the spot."

On that day, his detachment captured more than 250 Chinese people. They were all killed on the spot.

The following relates to a Japanese sailor who'd been recently recruited and hadn't been allowed to disembark until the 17th. He was in high spirits after landing, saying: "A dozen soldiers from each ship disembarked on the Sun Yat-sen wharf and formed a marine corps of fewer than 100 people to head towards the city along the Zhongshan North Road. Clothes were scattered everywhere along the road as if someone had thrown them."

After a while, they finally managed to enter the city through the gaps in the Yijiang gate that had been tightly stuffed with bundles of straw. Upon entering the city, the new recruit was numb with shock at what his brothers in arms had done:

> We walked around and saw dead bodies piled up like mountains in two squares. They'd been a tennis court and a children's park at one time. Some of the bodies were tied up with their hands behind their backs; some had been stabbed to death and some had been shot. What shocked me most was that many of the bodies were naked that winter day. It was obvious that a variety of killing methods had been used. Bodies were scattered all around and mountains of corpses were piled up everywhere. I even saw two pallid headless bodies lying down in pools of blood. Their necks had shrunk into their bodies. It was a horrible sight for an 18 year old new recruit. I will never forget the dead silence in the north of Nanjing. There was no sign of life. No birds were to be seen, let alone any Chinese survivors.

What this new Japanese recruit later saw was indelibly imprinted in his memory for all eternity:

> I think it was 18 December. I was standing guard at the bridge when I heard a machine gun. I ran to the dock and saw people being shot one by one, screaming and shouting. This happened every single day after the Japanese army took Nanjing. I instinctively knew that those being killed were Chinese, but I didn't know why.
>
> Every day, when I was standing guard from morning to night, I could see Chinese people being taken there in trucks. I couldn't tell whether they were POWs or civilians. I can only say that they'd been driven to Hezhong from Zhongshan dock and were then killed with machine guns on the slopes of the riverbank. The scene could be witnessed clearly from several hundred metres away, but with my telescope, I could see every detail of the slaughter. The killing often lasted for just 10 seconds and then the screaming and shouting stopped. Some of the prisoners managed to jump into the river, but when they floated up again they'd inevitably be killed. These killings happened all the time. I wondered why they were being taken there and why they didn't try to escape if they knew what was going to happen. No matter how hard I thought, there seemed to be just one answer. I thought that they may have been told to go there to do some work.

I could sometimes hear screaming from the other side of the river. All I saw was murder and fire. The next day, I could see dead bodies through my telescope burnt like scorched charcoal lying on the ground. As the water level of the Yangtze reduced every day, piles of bodies would emerge in the mud left by the river. Several Chinese people were forced to clear away the bodies. Some bodies were thrown back into the river and some were buried in big pits. I kept thinking about what happened to them afterwards. They were probably all killed.

The Japanese recruit stressed that the Zhongshan dock massacre took place after 17 December, further saying: "But the shooting hadn't stopped by the time I went back on 28 December. We took turns to stand guard and I saw Chinese people being killed every day. Many other soldiers shouted while they watched."

After taking Nanjing, killing Chinese people was just a game for the Japanese army, their soldiers wearing expressions of indifference and excitement.

The frenzied massacre was hell for young Chinese men, especially for officers and soldiers who had no place to go. If the Japanese soldiers caught them, there was no doubt that they'd be killed.

At the Jiangdong gate, which had once been a prison built by the KMT, about 50 Chinese soldiers held white flags and walked out on the street with no weapons. They then encountered a team of Japanese soldiers. Thinking that they might have a chance of survival, they begged: "We're your prisoners now. We'll do whatever you wish."

However, these Chinese soldiers were taken to a vegetable field near the prison, guns pointed at their backs. They were told to line up in front of the Japanese soldiers, who then took out their swords and killed them.

"I only remember the savage face of the Japanese soldier swinging his sword at me. I had no idea what happened next," said Liu Shinghai, the only survivor out of the 50 Chinese soldiers. He found himself buried along with two bodies after he woke up: "All the others were dead, I still have a 10 centimetre scar on my neck."

After that, Chinese soldiers wouldn't walk on the street in groups as they'd immediately be killed by the Japanese army if they were seen.

A group of Chinese city guards, following their captain's orders, tried to flee to a nearby rubbish dump to hide. In order to slip by the Japanese soldiers, they pretended to be farmers transporting manure. However, when they were stopped by a group of Japanese soldiers, they were told to put on a shoulder pole and line up together. The Japanese soldiers then beheaded them without hesitation. Blood gushed out of their necks while the Japanese soldiers laughed and called it "a smelly fountain of blood".

A Chinese civilian was also stopped at around the same time. Two Japanese soldiers saw calluses on the man's hands and took off his belt and wound it around his neck. They then started to play tug of war. When the Chinese man was strangled to death, the two Japanese soldiers cut off his head and kicked it around like a football.

Blood spilled all over the street and the soldiers laughed loudly.

The Japanese soldiers had a way of telling whether a Chinese man was a soldier or not, which was by looking at his hands. Anyone with calluses on their hands would be killed in any way they wanted as they believed that calluses were a sign of holding a gun. Terrified Chinese people were slaughtered in the streets. They weren't left alone even after they died. The Japanese soldiers stabbed them again and again wherever they pleased.

The Chinese officers and soldiers with no place to hide had to pretend to be civilians as they walked on the streets. The Japanese then came up with a new way to trick them: they'd call them to attention. As the Chinese soldiers were accustomed to the order, they'd stop abruptly and stand to attention without thinking. The Japanese soldiers found this highly amusing and either immediately shot them or tortured them until their blood and brains inevitably spilled out into the streets. Many Chinese soldiers died as a result of this trick.

One Chinese officer, recognising the unusual accent giving the order to stand to attention, pretended to be a cripple. "You're a soldier!" a Japanese soldier shouted, cutting the man's left leg off. He ordered: "Stand to attention!" When the man failed to stand up, the Japanese soldier raised his sword again and cut off the man's right leg. After giving the same order a third time, he swung the sword at the man's head.

Some Chinese men were stripped in the cold winter weather and killed. One day, two Chinese men who were machine gunners in the army had just walked out of a small alley when they were ambushed by several Japanese soldiers. "Show me your hands!" the soldiers ordered. The two Chinese men said that they were shopkeepers and they showed their hands, which had no sign of calluses. However, the Japanese wouldn't believe them; they ordered the Chinese men to take off their clothes and turn around. It was snowing that day, the first snow of the year in Nanjing. The two men were shivering. "You're soldiers!" the Japanese shouted, pointing their swords at their shoulders. "No, we're not! We're shopkeepers, shopkeepers!" they replied in terror. "You have calluses on your shoulders; you're clearly gun carriers in the army!" said the Japanese soldiers. They then started to slash at the men's calluses with their swords. Blood spilled down from their shoulders, dripping down their chests and finally to their feet. Their swords then moved to their genitals. The Japanese soldiers swung their swords and the two men's bloodied penises fell to the ground. There was no time for them to feel the agony of the assault as their heads soon fell to the ground too. One body, three parts: head, body and penis. Many Chinese men were slaughtered by Japanese soldiers in this way.

Mataichi Ika, a private first class in the 2nd squadron of the regiment, was having a meal with several other Japanese soldiers in a civilian's house. Some of the Japanese wanted spring onions but couldn't find any, so they captured several Chinese men on the street and ordered them to find spring onions for them. When it got dark, at about 5pm, Mataichi was ordered to bring the Chinese men back to their unit. "There were already 161 other Chinese men in the unit when we got there. Watching us with great fear, they had no idea what was coming," he recalled.

Afterwards, the Chinese men were brought to a stronghold near the Linggu Temple and locked in a small house near a pond. "Then the slaughter began," said Mataichi. "A group of five people killed them with their longswords and some of them screamed hysterically. This was the fate of the defeated Chinese soldiers." Mataichi participated in the slaughter and recalled: "Their hands and heads were bound with iron wire. They were beaten with clubs. Some of them bravely sang songs, some jumped into the water and some climbed on the roof. We then set fire to the house with petrol. When we saw three human fireballs rushing out, we stabbed them."

The entire place instantly became a living hell. To cover up the brutal act, Mataichi and his comrades burned all the bodies and the house.

This, however, was not all the people of Nanjing had to endure. The survivor Fu Liqin, living in Yuhua county, saw a dozen Chinese civilians being arrested after being accused of being Chinese soldiers. They were ordered to stand in a line. Instead of shooting them with machine guns, a Japanese soldier shot one man in the head and the bullet then passed through a second man's head. They were ecstatic when they found that they could use just one bullet to kill two or three Chinese prisoners.

Fu said: "There was a man who survived it and lived long after liberation. It's a miracle anyone could survive that."

Slaughter in the Air-Raid Shelters

Before the Japanese army took Nanjing, the defending troops and the national government built more than 5,000 air-raid shelters to get away from the Japanese bombs. Some were for military use and others were just for taking shelter from the bombs. There were also additional tunnels built by civilians underneath their houses and gardens, the biggest of which could hold hundreds of people while the smaller ones could hold a small family.

When the Japanese army first found the underground shelters, they thought that they were vaults belonging to Chiang Kai-shek and were used to store money. Some were locked with reinforced concrete doors and were deep and hard to find. Others were equipped with military facilities. Afraid of what they suspected lay hidden, the Japanese army just bombed or buried these shelters when they came across them.

A voice came out of the entrance of a shelter after the Japanese soldiers bombed it: "There are people down here!" Two bloodied men crawled out and stretched out their arms, begging for mercy.

"Go to hell!" shouted the Japanese soldiers. They stepped back and shot them with their machine guns and rifles.

When the situation became calmer, several Japanese soldiers entered the shelter and saw dozens of bodies inside; they were all Chinese, some of them had been soldiers and some had been civilians. Japanese soldiers arrested more than 100 Chinese soldiers in a national government shelter. They ordered them to stand together and shot them with a tank machine gun. In under three minutes, all of them lay dead in their own blood. That wasn't enough for one of the tank crewmen who then took out his gun and shot the bodies repeatedly until he ran out of ammunition. Body parts flew into the air, which was part of a game the Japanese soldiers called the "watermelon smashing game". They found it incredibly amusing.

Afterwards, the Japanese army decided not to search every shelter they came across and instead bombed or buried them, regardless of how many people were inside.

There was a great deal of small shelters that had been built by civilians, but the Japanese soldiers didn't trust them at all and had a way of handling the problem. There was a public bath near the Fuzimiao Temple where several wounded soldiers, five children and many other civilians had taken shelter. When the Japanese army found them, they shot at them from the entrance and set fire to the shelter. No one survived.

Li Xiuhua, a survivor of the Nanjing Massacre, lived in Xigan Alley in the west of the city. When she was 11 years old, her entire family hid in an underground shelter near her house while the Japanese soldiers searched the house. Not noticing the adults, the Japanese soldiers started to give sweets to the children to get them to tell them where their families were. As the children were too afraid to say anything, the Japanese soldiers continued the search and finally found a shelter. They then threatened to set fire to it. Li Xiuhua's brother, a 19 year old who'd just got married two days earlier, came out of the shelter first. When the Japanese soldier saw him, he thought he was a Chinese soldier and hacked him to death with a sword. The second one to come out was Li's cousin, also 19, and he was stabbed to death. The third to emerge was Li's uncle and he was killed in the same way. After killing the three men, the Japanese weren't done with them. "They burned them," Li recalled several decades later.

Less than an hour after the Japanese soldiers left, another unit arrived. This time they raped Li's sister-in-law. An older woman, more than 50 years old, thought that the Japanese soldiers would let her go, but instead she was also raped and killed. Her naked body was left in the street for all to see.

Wei Yankun's family lived in 18th Alley, Changbai Street. After the Japanese army entered the city, his father took his mother to hide in an underground air-raid shelter underneath an unfinished building near Chengxian Street, but there were more than 30 people already hiding there. A civilian heard something and looked outside from the shelter's entrance. The Japanese soldiers saw him and he was immediately shot. The Japanese soldiers then forced those inside to walk out one by one at gunpoint. While this was happening, Wei Yansheng, who was a little boy at the time, slipped into a chimney near the wall and escaped. A moment later, he heard gunshots outside the chimney. As he slowly crawled out of the chimney when it got dark, he saw the bodies of his parents and more than 30 other civilians lying on the ground.

To deal with these civilian shelters, the Japanese soldiers adopted a three-fold strategy, that is, to kill every man they found, rape every young woman they saw and finally throw them into shelters, which they would then burn.

This was just one of the methods used to kill Chinese people in the Nanjing Massacre. No one knows for sure how many people were killed in these shelters.

Slaughter in Civilian Homes

These were the most common atrocities committed by the Japanese army in the first week after they took Nanjing. A family of four and a family of nine lived in a courtyard on Neixing Street by the Zhonghua gate. In the second family, seven year old Xia Shuqing and her three year old sister were the only survivors. That day, a group of Japanese soldiers broke into Xia's courtyard. They first beheaded all the men in the two families and raped all of Xia's female relatives before killing them.

Xia's sister cried loudly, which annoyed a Japanese soldier who became irate and kicked her. Xia tried to use her arms to protect her sister but the angry Japanese soldier screamed at her and stabbed her in the back. When he realised she was still alive, the soldier stabbed her again, this time in her left arm.

When Xia woke up at night, she was surprised to find that she was still alive. However, with the exception of her three year old sister, her entire family had been killed by the Japanese soldiers.

Qin lived in Baita Alley, Shiba Street, in the north of the city. He owned three houses that he'd inherited from his parents and their parents before them. When the Japanese army entered the city, Qin was reluctant to leave his property. He, his wife and his children were hiding in the house when several Japanese soldiers broke in. Although he was frightened, Qin smiled at the Japanese soldiers. As Qin didn't look like a Chinese soldier, the Japanese soldiers, wearing angry expressions, asked: "Who are you?" "I'm a businessman, this is my shop where I sell tofu, and this is my tenant, the postmaster here," said Qin. The Japanese soldier asked: "Are there any Chinese soldiers in your house?" "No, we're civilians," Qin answered, to which the soldier replied: "Are there any girls here?"

"No..." Qin answered with a faint voice, thinking about his wife and children hiding in the house, along with his tenant's wife.

Annoyed, the Japanese soldiers dragged Qin and the postmaster, Xu, into the alley and hit them with the butts of their rifles. The two men fell to the ground. However, the Japanese soldiers didn't want to leave empty handed. They broke into Qin's house once again and soon found the two men's wives. The soldiers shouted with laughter: "There are women here!"

Several Japanese soldiers soon rushed in, stripped off their clothes and raped the two women, including Xu's elderly wife, taking turns in front of Qin's four children.

When Qin and Xu came to in the street, they heard crying and screaming inside so they rushed back into the house. Seeing his wife being abused by the Japanese soldiers, Qin tried desperately to fight them. But before he could do anything, the soldiers stabbed him to death with their bayonets.

The Japanese soldiers swaggered off and went away without punishment. Having been violated by the Japanese soldiers at such an old age, Mrs Xu no longer had the will to live and decided to drown herself in a lake. "What are you doing? I haven't died yet, you can't die!" Xu, nearly 60 years old, stopped his wife with a sigh of relief.

Mrs Qin, left naked, had been raped by the Japanese soldiers in front of her children. She felt humiliated and wanted to die. Later, she tearfully took her four children, the oldest of whom was just 11 years old, and jumped into a nearby lake. While they were fortunate enough to be rescued by passers-by, the youngest child drowned to death.

Unwilling to leave, Li Fuyi and his son stayed in their home in 22 Yudai Lane while others fled to the countryside following the Japanese invasion.

One day, the Japanese soldiers knocked at the door and shouted at them to open up. Li was petrified and couldn't bring himself to do it. The soldiers were furious and fired several shots. Li had to make it clear that he was going to open the door. "Baka!" the Japanese soldier shouted and kicked him in the chest before he could fully open the door. Despite falling to the ground and posing no threat at all, Li was dragged to one corner of Yudai Lane and continuously stabbed with bayonets along the way until he died.

Staying inside the house, Li Xuecai, Li Fuyi's son, now trembled with fear. The Japanese soldiers weren't going to let him go and after killing Li Fuyi. They went back to Li's home, straight into the living room and stabbed Li Xuecai repeatedly in the chest.

Li Xuecai screamed in agony. He tried to drag his bloodied body in an attempt to escape into the back garden. The Japanese soldiers caught him and forced him into the corner of a wall, shooting his throat and head several times. His brains were left strewn on the wall and although the houses had stood strong for a very long time, the invading thieves ruined them with their swords and guns.

In Xinjiekou in central Nanjing there was a grand courtyard where Mr Yang lived, a typical intellectual born into a rich family. Mr Yang's ancestors had apparently been officials during the Ming and Qing dynasties, which meant that the old courtyard was of a very good quality and built to a high standard. After the Nationalist government had been established, they had wanted to expropriate the house as a military institution but they'd failed to do so. When the Japanese arrived, Yang's entire family fled to seek refuge, apart from Mr Yang who'd say: "They're just Japanese. I don't fear them at all. I don't owe them anything."

As a result, only two servants were left to attend to Mr Yang. The Japanese entered the city and they began their indiscriminate orgy of looting and violence. Mr Yang's compound was inevitably targeted.

The Japanese soldiers banged at his door with the butts of their rifles. The door stayed closed.

The sound continued as loud as thunder.

"Mr Yang, someone's knocking at the door. Shall we open it?" the servant asked. "Open it! It's our custom to open the door for people!" Mr Yang said, smoking a hookah and squinting at the servant. The servant quickly opened the door. Five or six Japanese soldiers, staring at the servant, rushed over to her and stabbed her to death. "Gentl..." the servant never got the chance to finish saying "gentlemen" and died as blood spilled out of her body. The Japanese soldiers rushed into the vestibule, then into the middle of the house and finally into the back garden where Mr Yang was sat. "Who are you? Why didn't you open the door?" the Japanese soldiers poked at Mr Yang's nose with a bayonet, forcing the hookah out of his hand with another bayonet. Mr Yang raised his brow and said coldly: "I, a Chinese man and a citizen of Nanjing, stayed at home and did nothing wrong! I can smoke, can't I?" The Japanese soldiers were appalled because Mr Yang had answered in Japanese. "You... are you an ally?" The Japanese soldiers, now scared, waited for an answer. Mr Yang smiled contemptuously, and said: "I'm not your friend. My grandpa was a translation secretary when China negotiated with Japan on the follow-up treaties after the Sino-Japanese war of 1894-1895."

"Well, good!" the Japanese soldiers jeered as they looked at one another.

"Are you hiding any Chinese soldiers?" they asked.

Mr Yang shook his head and said: "Our family has never cared for politics."

"Then why did you delay opening the door?" asked the Japanese soldiers.

"What did you say?" Mr Yang pricked up his ears and acted as if he hadn't heard anything.

"Why didn't you open the door quickly?" the Japanese soldiers responded angrily. Mr Yang had actually understood what they'd said and he smiled lightly, replying: "I'm deaf, it's hard for me to hear you."

The Japanese soldiers thought that this old Japanese speaking man was trying to trick them, so, without any explanation, they stabbed him in the chest several times with their bayonets.

"You damned Japs!" Mr Yang spat at the Japanese. The soldiers took out their bloodied bayonets and struck the stubborn man again.

"Devil!" Mr Yang fell down, cursing the soldiers in Japanese again. Mr Yang was killed by the Japanese and his centuries old ancestral home was burned to smouldering ashes.

After the Rain Flower Terrace was occupied, on around 14 December, the Japanese approached a temple in Wanshou just by the Zhonghua gate. Hong Liang, a monk, asked his master Fan Gen whether they needed to hide somewhere. He told him that there was no need to worry as the Japanese were also Buddhists.

Fan Gen told all the monks to recite sutras in the hall and burn incense. All the monks knelt on futons and paid homage to the charity of the Buddha. A unit of Japanese soldiers armed with guns and knives surrounded the monks. One of the officers walked into the hall, patting a monk on the shoulder, indicating that he wanted him to go to the yard and kneel down.

After the monk knelt down in the courtyard, he continued to chant: "Amitabha." The Japanese then shot the monk.

A second monk was called out, kneeling on the ground and chanting scripture. He was also shot. The monks were told to come out one by one to be killed.

Seventeen monks were shot in cold blood, left lying in their blood-stained robes. When the Japanese soldiers found a man who wasn't acting like a monk, they ordered him to chant to prove that he was a monk.

This man was Wu, a local who sold fried dough sticks known as *youtiao*. The Japanese soldiers had arrived so quickly that Wu hadn't found anywhere to hide. Panicking, he came to the temple master. Fan believed in the Chinese proverb that it was better to save a man's life than to build a seven-storey pagoda, so he provided Wu with shelter and also gave him a robe to disguise himself as a monk. After the Japanese realised that he couldn't chant, he was beheaded on the spot with a knife. However, the neck wasn't totally severed and was still attached by the trachea. With his head drooping down, he bled out profusely. The old man rolled on the ground in agony. Two more Japanese soldiers approached him and stabbed him twice to finish the job. He died instantly.

The Japanese soldiers suddenly found themselves attracted to a monk called Long Hui, who had white and soft skin. Long Hui was more than 40 years old and wasn't Han Chinese. He didn't have any facial hair so the Japanese soldiers thought that he was a woman. Excited, they stripped off his clothing only to find that he was a man. After realising their mistake, the soldiers became enraged. They grabbed the naked monk, lifted him up and then dropped him on a large stone. The monk's brains were dashed and he died immediately.

This temple in Wanshou had enjoyed peace for hundreds of years but it was destroyed in an instant, only leaving behind the 13 or 14 year old Hong Liang and Miao Xiang, who was even younger than him.

The terrified Hong Liang had nowhere to hide and had to flee to Puzhao Temple, an ancient temple a millennium old where many other people also hid, including many elderly people and women. On about the 15th or 16th, the Japanese entered the Buddhist shrine and seized a 60 year old lady. They wanted to rape her and after finding a group of young women hiding behind a Buddhist statue, they raped all of them too, including an 11 year old girl. These heinous Japanese soldiers continued their atrocities and tormented their prisoners by forcing the monks and women to have sex. A monk, who held his hands together in prayer as he chanted, was ridiculed by the soldiers. They said that he was useless and impotent, so they cut off his penis with a bayonet. The poor monk writhed on the ground in agonising pain before he finally died.

Such atrocities didn't faze the cruel Japanese soldiers one bit. There was a 70 year old Chinese priest from the temple in Wanshou by the Nanjing Xiaoxin bridge. He saw that the savage Japanese soldiers were committing unspeakable atrocities and wantonly murdering civilians, so he ordered the nuns to stack firewood in the hall. He sat on top of it alone with his legs crossed. When the Japanese soldiers stormed the building, the priest set himself on fire and burned along with the temple. This stunned the Japanese soldiers and they fired into the sky to show their respect.

Xu Fujiang's house was located by the river and he was worried about his house being stormed by the Japanese.

The next day, the Japanese soldiers entered the city and Xu found a canoe with his family members to use to hide somewhere in the Shuixi gate area up along the Huimin estuary. However, halfway on the journey, the canoe began to leak so he quickly took his entire family to the embankment and set up two temporary shelters on the marshland dozens of metres apart. Xu shared one with his second and third daughters and his wife shared another one with their four young sons. That night, his youngest son, only a few months old, cried loudly because he was hungry. This attracted the attention of the Japanese soldiers. The Japanese then discovered Xu's wife's shelter with a flashlight.

When the Japanese soldiers saw Xu's wife, their perversion was unleashed. Xu's wife clung on to her son tightly and the Japanese soldiers fired twice, one shot at his wife and one at his child. They died where they lay.

Xu and his two daughters could do nothing but weep. They didn't come out of their shelters until the Japanese soldiers left at midnight. Xu placed the bodies of his wife and his youngest son in a wooden box and put it on the embankment to be laid to rest in the morning. A group of Japanese soldiers unexpectedly passed by that morning and took him away. Xu's daughters never saw their father again and had no idea whether he was alive or not.

Xu's second daughter, just 13 years old, bore the responsibility for looking after her siblings. Before nightfall on the third day of hiding, the girl tried to find something to eat, but the second she appeared on the bank she was found by the Japanese soldiers.

"You, pretty girl!" the Japanese soldiers said when they saw her. They terrified her and she desperately ran towards Heyun School. However, she was incredibly weak and was caught. The Japanese soldiers tried to rape her but she resisted violently and even slapped a Japanese soldier in the face. Outraged, they split her head in two with a sword.

Now the Xu family only had four children left alive and the 11 year old girl became the guardian of her three younger brothers. She was eventually taken away as a child bride. She later hanged herself because of the abuse. The three surviving sons were also taken away and changed their surnames. The tragedy of the Xu family represents the fate of hundreds of families in Nanjing under Japanese occupation.

The Massacre Before the City Was Stormed

For the Japanese invaders, the occupation of Nanjing was a high profile event as it was the first time that Japan had occupied another nation's capital. To celebrate the occasion, following orders on the 13th, they began the processes of "military action", "city rectification" and the "elimination of the remaining enemy force".

The original planned date for official Japanese entry into the city was set for the 15th but it was delayed to the 17th because Matsui, the general commander, was apparently in poor health and was bedridden for several days. They also added that: "Order in the city is not yet stable."

The Japanese soldiers killed the most people from 13 to 17 December. In military language, the term "mopping-up" was used and it clearly implies annihilation. "Rectification" was a term commonly used in the news, but in actuality, everyone understood this to be synonymous with "massacre".

I made a surprising discovery when trying to clarify the events of this period: the historical records left by the Japanese about the incident.

As the Chinese civilians and soldiers in the city were fighting for their lives, they were less likely to calmly write in detail about what was happening around them outside of their struggle to save their own lives. Therefore, only the Japanese soldiers kept clear diaries about what they did on a daily basis, allowing for the truth of the Nanjing Massacre to be revealed through the eyes of the perpetrators.

For example, on 7 December, before entering Nanjing, Matsui explicitly ordered that: "Each division and regiment should raid the city as support troops." After entering Nanjing on the 13th, all units were issued with more specific mopping-up orders. On 14 December, Sasaki's 30th brigade issued a mopping-up order that featured 10 articles, including commands that: "Today, on 14 December, the brigade should completely annihilate the northern part of the city and outside of the city"; "Unless explicit orders have been given to the contrary, all divisions are not to take any prisoners" and: "Independent light armoured vehicles should be used" (*Historical Collection of the Nanjing Massacre*, vol. 11, p. 49). It is clear that mopping-up is a euphemism for massacring Chinese civilians and unarmed soldiers guarding the city. The order to take no prisoners clearly tells the Chinese people left in Nanjing that even if they surrender, the Japanese will still kill them.

Other squadrons further elaborated on the meaning behind these mopping-up orders. I read a detailed military report from the 38th infantry 12th regiment, which details the regiment's assignments, its specific tasks and the final result at the end of the day. It ends with the date 14 December Showa 12 (1937) with the signature of a commanding officer named Nakagawa. Three tables are attached to this report, two of which list the consumption of forces and bullets. A total of 3,085 rifle, machine gun and pistol rounds were used. A shocking sentence is written under "Remarks" in the third table: "The 11th squadron was ordered to be stationed near the Yao gate. At 8.30am or so on the 14th, thousands of enemies waving white flags arrived. In the afternoon, 7,200 unarmed prisoners were escorted to Nanjing."

On the 14th, these 7,200 prisoners were taken into custody in Nanjing and quickly shot dead after being escorted to the riverbank. This is evidenced from another Japanese soldier's diary, which clearly describes the event.

I also read how mountain artillery and tanks were deployed in a detailed battle report by the 7th infantry regiment, including the top secret order number 105 which reads: "We should deploy about two-thirds of the troops." It continued: "A tank squadron (coordinating with the two engineering teams) should be responsible for raids on roads that have special markings." On 15, 16 and 17 December, the mopping-up order was issued. In other words, essentially two-thirds of the Japanese troops were involved in the mopping-up operations inside and outside the city, slaughtering anyone they suspected of military involvement.

How many unarmed Chinese soldiers and civilians were massacred by the Japanese during the mopping-up operations remains unclear as few survived.

However, Japanese military intelligence reports and soldiers' diaries can help to reveal the truth.

The Kunisaki company was one of the elite forces in the 10th army and was an especially vicious unit that harboured many murderers. There is a part in their military intelligence report from 14 December where they write: "We've discovered a great deal about the surviving soldiers on the riverbanks so we ordered a garrison to wipe out the island with the help of an independent mountain artillery regiment. The assault team arrived on the island with about 2,350 unarmed captives." In other words, on that day alone, they killed 2,350 prisoners and don't deny that these prisoners had surrendered. The Japanese soldiers themselves wrote about such events many times.

The Kunisaki company's military intelligence report on the 15th said: "There are many enemies that still remain on Jiangxin Island so we sent a third battalion to raid the island." However, the report does not specify the number of Chinese soldiers and civilians who were mopped-up and it just mentions how control of the enemy troops was designated: (a) close to Jiangfu, mainly the 58th and 78th divisions and parts of the 18th, 80th, 85th, 88th, 138th and 178th divisions controlled a total of about 3,000 people; (b) near Pukou, mainly the 78th and 88th divisions and parts of the 10th, 18th, 73rd, 80th, 85th, 117th, 178th and 181st divisions controlled a total of 5,000 people. The Japanese had caught 8,000 people in these two areas who were killed on the spot.

These tragic and bloody scenes have been described earlier in this chapter but most of the mopping-up that has been described so far took place along the Yangtze and inside the city. However, most of the operations took place in the outskirts of Nanjing.

Here is what a Japanese soldier who participated in the suburban village raids recalled:

> On one occasion, we suspected that guerrillas were hiding in a village so we set fire to it and killed all the villagers. Another time, we suspected on nothing more than a hunch that there were enemies in a village so we destroyed it and killed all the residents, leaving no survivors.
>
> This was really an unexpected tragedy because the Japanese soldiers had no real reason to commit such an atrocity.
>
> The first time I fell into the sins of the Japanese soldiers was burning the houses in a neighbouring village called Jurong on the way to assaulting Nanjing. At that time, the force to which I belonged was a group of reserve soldiers and we followed the frontline troops.
>
> As we got closer to Nanjing, the Chinese forces began to resist even more stubbornly. Not far from Jurong, the situation had turned to stalemate so the

troops temporarily stayed in the area. In this brief stay, Noro and five other members of his unit went somewhere to look for food.

At that point, there were still many defeated enemy forces lurking nearby so it was dangerous for soldiers to leave the roads. The battle was full of uncertainty and we could be told to advance at any time.

I suddenly felt uneasy. If they came back safe and sound, all was well, but if not, things would be terrible. Unfortunately, a general attack was about to be launched and our troop had also received the order to advance.

I couldn't keep anything secret at the time, so I tremblingly reported what had happened to the commander. Although he was very angry, they couldn't do anything since it had already happened.

In situations like this, some captains might order their troops to depart saying that it's in everyone's best interests, but considerate lieutenants would immediately send out search parties after them and then later convene to discuss the mission with them. The temporary search party that was formed was composed of six members from Noro's unit and other members from the Niwa unit; all of them were experienced and Miyake was in charge.

With just two detachments, these soldiers dared to go into dangerous and difficult to navigate areas full of enemy guerrillas. They passed through two or three small villages and found nothing suspicious. After about eight kilometres, a village surrounded by walls came into view and was home to about 50 or 60 families.

"This place is very suspicious," the squad leader ordered the soldiers to halt in front of the village. He then went personally with three soldiers to investigate. About 30 minutes later, they captured three men who looked like local residents. The leader of the squad wanted to interrogate them. As expected, they called over Mizoguchi, a translator, to question the prisoners.

"Have you seen Japanese soldiers in the vicinity? Be honest. Tell me where they've gone. How they are now? If you hide anything, you'll be killed."

One of them was too scared to speak when he saw the soldiers take out a sword. The squadron leader thought he was simply refusing to talk and yelled: "You bastard! How dare you not cooperate! I'll kill you." He held his bayonet high in the air, ready to strike.

I honestly didn't think he was going to do anything, so when the sharp blade struck him, I was shocked.

His head was cut off in one fell swoop and it rolled into the grass with blood gushing out of the wound, staining the nearby plants. The other two were terrified and revealed everything they knew. They said that all the residents living in the village were ordinary people but recently there had been dozens of Chinese guerrillas sneaking in and out. During the day, a few

Japanese soldiers had suddenly appeared and gunshots were later heard. They hadn't heard anything else since then and were unaware of the Japanese soldiers' location.

Hearing this, we all believed that Noro and his accomplices were dead. Consequently, the next step was to confirm what the villagers had said and then prepare to collect the Japanese bodies. However, with fewer than 30 soldiers, challenging the villagers head on was too dangerous.

It was therefore decided that we were to wait until nightfall and when all the villagers would be sleeping, we would set fire to the village. As the residents fled in panic, they would all be wiped out in a single stroke. The leader was a battlefield veteran who had a lot of combat experience and had a gift for battle strategies.

Late, after midnight, believing that the villagers were sleeping, we scaled the walls and set fire to everything we could. The fire quickly spread and flames were everywhere, covering almost the entire village. The civilians who were awoken by the fire hurried out of their homes to flee.

We then decided to launch a sudden and violent attack, killing them one after another. In just a few minutes, everyone was dead and the corpses were strewn everywhere. There were some guerrilla fighters among them but they didn't resist us. Perhaps because the raid had been launched while they slept, they were so terrified that they mistook the two small teams as an entire squadron, losing the will to fight.

At the end of the battle, while checking the corpses in the light of the fire, we found that they were almost all ordinary civilians. There were mothers clutching babies, young children about 10 years old and elderly men and women.

When the Japanese army attacked the outskirts of Nanjing, they mostly killed innocent civilians. They would normally sweep the outskirts with surprise attacks so the villagers would be unable to protect themselves. They couldn't hide like the people in the city because all they had were a few straw sheds. As a result, when the Japanese army entered the villages, most of them stayed at home waiting to be killed.

I've read a few materials included in the *Nanjing Massacre Survivors' Oral Dictation*, written in 2005 by Zhu Chengshan et al. It was created following a survey conducted by a group of university students over their holidays, and most of the reports were from Nanjing Massacre survivors on the outskirts of the city. I have included a few reports here for readers to analyse.

Tao Changman (85 years old, lived in East Village in Yongning)

The Japanese army tied up eight people on stools with a footbath placed next to us. They were stabbed to death and the blood spilled into the basin. The basin was full of blood, as much as you'd expect to see after slaughtering a pig. The Japanese army also tied up four people who were caught in the village and tied large pillars to their backs. They pushed them down the mountain and they died as a result. In the village, an old man called Tao Longhe, more than 50 years old, was shot and killed by a Japanese soldier. Another man called Ye Weirong, who suffered from mental illness, was also shot by a Japanese soldier. Another man called Yu Xiujin, more than 50 years old at the time, had his house set alight by the Japanese soldiers. They wouldn't let him leave. He burned to death inside.

Fang Youjun (84 years old, lived in East Village in Yongning)

We had more than 10 thatched cottages where our entire family, more than 10 people, lived, including my uncle, aunt and many siblings. When the Japanese soldiers entered the village, we had to run to the river for shelter, so our house and everything inside was destroyed in a fire. At the time, I was 17 years old, the eldest of four. One of my brothers, Longhai, was killed by the Japanese soldiers. He was 11. They also shot my mother. There was a man called Liu Zhijun in my village, and he was too frightened to run away when he saw the Japanese. The Japanese shot him right in front of me.

Zou Wanbo (80 years old, lived in the village of Houchong in Yongning)

The Japanese soldiers shot chickens and dogs all over the place and took them away. They ordered the children to help them catch chickens. If they failed to catch any, the Japanese soldiers would beat them. I saw the entire village of Wangjialou burned to the ground. A man called Xiao Hejia, who was 40 years old, was stabbed to death in the river with a bayonet. There was also a man, Chen Dejiao's father, whose name I've forgotten. Because he was an intellectual, the Japanese soldiers tied him up, poured petrol over him and set him alight.

Ding Chengying (76 years old, lived in the village of Gaoli in Yongning)

In the winter, Japanese soldiers suddenly stormed the village and set it on fire. On that day, there was a family hosting a wedding feast and the Japanese soldiers blocked the door to the building, branding them as enemies, and set up their machine guns to kill 13 people, including Li Bangguo's father Li Chang'an, and his second brother Li Bangyou.

Zhang Jialin (lived in the village of Hebei in Yongning)

I was about six or seven years old when the Japanese soldiers entered the village that year. I only remember that the Japanese soldiers killed everyone they saw, it must have been more than 100 people. At that time, the Japanese soldiers had occupied the entire railway, so if adults wanted to cross the railway line, they'd assume they were enemies and order their dogs to rip them apart. I saw a resident of Nanjing fleeing in the wrong direction. He was killed by a Japanese soldier with a bayonet.

Yongning was a small town and wasn't included in the mopping-up area the Japanese were targeting. Nevertheless, during the initial period after the Japanese occupation of Nanjing, they conducted many mopping-up operations in the town, killing thousands of civilians.

The Japanese soldiers used extremely cruel methods in their mopping-up operations. Many of the diaries and memoirs of the Japanese soldiers leave detailed descriptions and records. There was a Japanese veteran called Tadokoro Kozo, who was the lance corporal of the heavy machine gun forces in the ll4th division in the 10th army. He wrote:

> I mopped-up the remaining enemy forces in the town and tied the prisoners to a tree. The officers were teaching us how to shoot and kill. They then killed them. Officers and sergeants cut off the heads of the prisoners who were squatting in pits. I was just a common soldier at that time so I was only allowed to use a bayonet. Executions like this lasted for 10 days inside and outside of the city.
>
> Our army was stationed in Xiaguan at the time. We used iron wire that had been taken from barbed wire to tie people together in groups of 10. We then set fire to them with kerosene and referred to them as bundles of straw. It didn't bother us any more than killing pigs. After doing this, it just seemed normal to kill people. To make the prisoners afraid, we used many methods like cutting off their ears, cutting off their noses or stabbing them in their mouths. The list goes on and on. If we used knives to stab just below the eye, their eyes would immediately sag down like goo, not too dissimilar to fish. Since arriving here, we've had very little to do for a very long time. If we couldn't do things like this, how would we have any fun?
>
> — (FROM *NANJING MASSACRE AND SANKO SAKUSEN* BY KOHEI MORIYAMA, SICHUAN EDUCATION PRESS, 1984)

Words like 'brutal' and 'inhuman' completely fail to describe the scale of the Japanese army's cruelty.

On the afternoon of the 15th, in the village of Dingjie in Pancheng County, Shi Jiayou's father had just left home when he was stopped by Japanese soldiers. They used four bayonets on the end of their guns to stab his father in the throat, both sides of his chest and his heart. He died on the spot. Liu Qingying from the village of Hongmei said that her son Han Xiaobin and her neighbour Mr Zhang's two sons were well-built. The Japanese soldiers assumed that they had to be soldiers and killed them. The two brothers were beheaded just in front of their house. Han Xiaobin was stabbed nine times and killed, stabbing him four times in the stomach, once in the arm and in several other places. Another villager, Xu Jinfeng, said that the Japanese soldiers set fire to her house and dragged her husband to the river, stabbing him in the heart with their bayonets and shooting his head so it burst. The Japanese soldiers then left howling with laughter.

While the city's suburbs suffered heavily, the Japanese soldiers committed even more atrocities in the city centre.

Hou Zhanqing, who lived on Beiting Lane, survived the massacre. During the tragedy, four Japanese soldiers set him on fire for the sheer hell of it. He was covered with blisters and then thrown out of the way to die. If the Japanese soldiers hadn't seen several young Chinese men walking down the street and coming to help, Hou Zhanqing said that: "I would have been burned to death like a suckling pig." Wang Ershun of Wangfu Lane wasn't as lucky. He was arrested by the Japanese, who stripped him and broke his leg. They then unleashed a pack of dogs to rip him to shreds. As Wang Ershun was now crippled, although he tried his best to escape the dogs, they seemed to have been starving and frantically gnashed at him. Soon, Wang Ershun was too weak to escape and begged the Japanese commander to let him go. However, he didn't stop the dogs, instead unsheathing his sword to cut off his other leg. Wang completely lost the will to resist and was bitten to death by the dogs, his intestines and entrails ripped out. Disgusting scenes like this made the Japanese soldiers burst into fits of laughter.

Until now, I haven't been able to write about the notorious contest between two Japanese soldiers to kill 100 people using a sword, which was reported on by a Japanese war reporter. This event has not been recognised as a fact by many Japanese people in recent decades.

The earliest report on the contest wasn't broadcast to the people of China, but was released by the Japanese media. On the way to attack Nanjing on 6 December 1937, when the Japanese army arrived in Jurong, a suburb of Nanjing, two Japanese war correspondents called Asami and Suzuki sent an article to the *Tokyo Nichi Nichi Shimbun* entitled *The Behead 100 People*

Competition Is Close - Brave Mukai and Noda are at 89 and 78. The content is as follows:

> Two young high-ranking officers have participated in the "contest to kill 100 people using a sword" on the way to Nanjing. They were two second lieutenants from the Katagiri division, Toshiaki Mukai and Tsuyoshi Noda, who had fought on the front when they attacked Jurong. The record before they entered the city was Mukai having killed 89 people, while Noda had killed 78 people, making it difficult to decide who will win.

Six days later, on the 12th, the Japanese war correspondents Asami and Suzuki published another article from Purple Mountain in Nanjing. On the next day, 13 December 1937, when the Japanese occupied Nanjing, this report was also published in an important column in the *Tokyo Nichi Nichi Shimbun*. The full text was as follows:

Incredible Record in the Contest to Behead 100 People: Mukai 106, Noda 105, Both 2nd Lieutenants Go into Extra Innings
 Special correspondents Kazuo Asami and Jiro Suzuki report on 12 December from Purple Mountain

Before occupying Nanjing, Toshiaki Mukai and Tsuyoshi Noda, the two heroic 2nd lieutenants from the Katagiri division, participated in the "contest to kill 100 people using a sword". When they attacked Purple Mountain on the 10th, they set two incredible records: 106 and 105. At noon on the 10th, the two second lieutenants met, holding katanas. Noda: "Hey, I killed 105 people. How about you?" Mukai: "I killed 106!" The two 2nd lieutenants laughed. They had ultimately failed to discover who had been the first to kill 100 people with a sword. "It seems that this time ends in a draw, how about we begin another contest, with the aim being 150 kills?" They agreed. The contest to kill 150 people using a sword began on the 11th. At noon on the 11th, Mukai was busy mopping-up the defeated army in Purple Mountain, which overlooks the Sun Yat-sen Mausoleum. He revealed details about the contest that had ended in a draw. He said: "Both of us have killed more than 100 people without breaking a sweat. It's really enjoyable. My sword's edge has warped because I cut a person's head in half while he was wearing a helmet. I promise I will donate this sword to the newspaper office at the end of the war. At 3am on the 11th, our forces choked out the defeated enemy on Purple Mountain with remarkable tactics. I was exhausted too, standing motionless while holding the sword in a hail of bullets. Ah, it's like destiny! And thanks to this sword, I haven't been shot." As bullets continued to fly, he showed the journalist the katana that had killed 106 people.

Next to the report, *Tokyo Nichi Nichi Shimbun* also published a photo of Mukai holding a sword. There's no doubt of the veracity of the report. But why there weren't there any follow up reports on the contest to kill 150 people? The two reports on the contest had caused outrage in the west. In order to protect the image of the Japanese army and the country's reputation, reporting on such contests was banned.

This prohibition didn't mean that there wasn't a contest to kill 150 people though. From Mukai's rhetoric in the latter report, the Japanese soldiers' aggressive personalities and the objective fact that the Japanese army massacred Chinese people after the occupation of Nanjing, there is one thing I can be sure of: these two Japanese butchers frantically slaughtered countless Chinese people. As to whether they killed 150 people or 200 people, we can't say for sure. But it would be naïve to think that these two Japanese 2nd lieutenants didn't do anything after they entered the city. More than 300,000 Chinese people were slaughtered by the Japanese troops in the Nanjing Massacre. This number relates to the number of Chinese people killed during the Japanese occupation of Nanjing, while Mukai and Noda's contest had been from 10 December, two days before the Nanjing Massacre. The next few weeks were a utopia for bloodthirsty Japanese soldiers, free to murder, rape and loot. Would these two monsters who vowed to kill 150 people in a contest suddenly stop killing? Even if Mukai and Noda stopped killing, would Yamamoto and Matsui? Yamamoto and Matsui didn't just slaughter 100 people, or even 150 people; they are responsible for the deaths of 300,000 people during the Nanjing Massacre. Thinking otherwise would be delusional.

A key issue in recent decades has been that in order to cover up their heinous crimes, some Japanese have even denied the fact that these two notorious executioners killed 106 people and 105 people respectively before 10 December. Some have said that the reports were false and some have claimed that even the best katanas couldn't kill that many people, while others have maintained that even if they killed 10 people a day, they couldn't have reached the 100 people record.

The shamelessness of some Japanese people is staggering. Although we don't know whether Mukai killed hundreds of people using the katana or if it was warped after a few days of use due to cutting off so many heads, it's said that the katana was famous in Japan and the emperor even recognised the feat. But one thing is irrefutable: many wartime stories were written by war correspondents and if they were not reported how they liked, then the Japanese military would never allow it to be published. Another point to consider is that is there really any difference between killing 100 Chinese people with one katana and killing them with 10 different ones?

Mukai and Noda killed Chinese people. That is an irrefutable fact. Those who try to hide or deny the truth as time passes are shameless.

The crimes of one nation against another should be thoroughly punished and condemned, and if an offending country tries to deny what happened, then they risk alienating themselves from the world.

Justice will eventually triumph over evil. Facts are impartial and objective. In early December 1947, Mukai and Noda were prosecuted by the Nanjing War Crimes Tribunal established to try the Japanese war criminals after the Second World War:

> Toshiaki Mukai and Noda were in the 16th division of the Japanese troops serving separately as the sub-lieutenant captain and the aide-de-camp. Gunkichi Tanaka was from Hisao Tani's troops attached to the 6th division and served as the company commander. He planned the massacre to vent their anger because they had encountered strong resistance when they attacked Nanjing in December in the 26th year of the Republic of China. Tanaka killed more than 300 prisoners and noncombatants in the southwest suburbs of the capital area with a sword. Toshiaki Mukai and Tsuyoshi Noda carried out killings in the foothills of Purple Mountain and they competed against each other for entertainment to see who could kill the most people. They used their weapons to kill anyone, both the young and the elderly. Tsuyoshi Noda killed 105 people while Toshiaki Mukai killed 106, so the latter won. After the Japanese surrender, Noda and others were seized in Tokyo GHQ and sent to Beijing by our delegation to be prosecuted by the court.

After a month of court reviews and establishing the facts, these two war criminals were sentenced to death on 27 January 1948. The court notice was as follows:

Death penalty notice for Toshiaki Mukai and other war criminals
27 January 1948

During the fighting, Toshiaki Mukai, Tsuyoshi Noda and Gunkichi Tanaka (namely accomplices in the Nanjing Massacre) jointly and continuously massacred prisoners and noncombatants. With the evidence found conclusive, this court sentences each of these defendants to death and this shall be reported to the chief of staff of the department of defence. Under the orders of Chiang Kai-shek, the president of the government, on 26 January (37), section 0005 shall check this and it will be implemented. Then at noon on the 28th, the court will prosecute Toshiaki Mukai, Tsuyoshi Noda and Gunkichi Tanaka, who will each be positively identified and escorted to the Rain Flower Terrace for execution. The report is as follows.

Guilty:

Toshiaki Mukai, war criminal, male, 36 years old, Yamaguchi Prefecture native, artillery captain.

Tsuyoshi Noda, war criminal, male, 35 years old, Kagoshima Prefecture native, aide-de-camp of the 16th division brigade.

Tanaka Gunkichi, war criminal, male, 43 years old, Tokyo native, commander of the 45th regiment.

27 January on the 37th year of the republic
   Tribunal chairman: Shi
   Prosecutor: Lee

On 28 January 1948, these two notorious war criminals were put to death on the Rain Flower Terrace by Chinese executioners. Hearing this, the people of Nanjing cheered.

History does not allow amnesty for such monsters nor the monsters who seek to downplay or deny their crimes.

When I finished the previous chapters, I made a surprising discovery when reading *Japanese Militarism Education - Contest to Kill 100 People Using a Sword and Documents from the Consulate in Nanjing*. The *Tokyo Nichi Nichi Shimbun* had in fact published another article titled *Sword* dedicated to the deadly competitor Mukai in the Han River on 19 May 1939. The report details the Japanese occupation of the eastern part of the Han River. The following is an excerpt:

> The war correspondent met with the "courageous" lieutenant, Mukai, in a small village known as Temple Village. Mukai was a young and fearless lieutenant who was known for the promise he made with his comrade Noda to kill 100 people in the Battle of Nanjing two years ago, beheading 107 people. After the battle, he shaved his long beard and made another promise with Noda to behead 500 people. He went to Xuzhou, the Dabie Mountains, Hankou and Zhongxiang and killed 305 enemy soldiers. But Noda was killed in Hainan [author's note: *in fact, he wasn't dead but was executed as a war criminal after the*

war]. Now he [author's note: *Mukai*] was struggling alone to achieve the target of beheading 500 people.

The lieutenant actually wanted to kill 1,000 people. "Is your sword sharp?" a reporter asked him. The reserved lieutenant replied: "Very sharp except for the tip, which is a little bent, but I trust it and it doesn't matter. Since the war, I've been sick but I've never been wounded at the front, which is incredible. Perhaps the body is born to do this and it can thrive during a long war."

— HISTORICAL DOCUMENTS OF THE NANJING MASSACRE, VOL. 66, P. 34

This is the warmonger that the Japanese tried to cover up. This report had not been discovered at the time of the Nanjing trials as otherwise they would have been sentenced for even more crimes. Another excuse could have been that because the indictment was limited to the Nanjing Massacre, it may not have included the heinous crimes they committed in China later on. I then felt angry because of the Japanese jingoists, both then and now, who have tried to deny Japanese crimes in China to save face. This is also the reason why even in the face of such clear and conclusive evidence about the Nanjing Massacre that some Japanese have a completely different view of what happened.

At the time, the killing contest was actually widespread in Japan. Mukai and Noda weren't the only soldiers killing people like this because using a katana to kill one's enemies in battle was a Japanese military tradition. However, the famous Japanese katanas actually originated from Chinese swords. On 28 February 1939 when the Japanese army was storming China, the *Tokyo Daily News* also published an article written by Iwasaki. Titled *Analysis of the Katana*, it reads:

The name *nihonto* [editor's note: Japanese sword or katana] was used 800 years ago, imported from *Shina* [author's note: China]. The Japanese started to use them in the late Sengoku Period. In this violent period, the Japanese heavily relied on the *nihonto*, which almost became a religion for the Japanese. No matter how advanced modern weaponry gets, in the end, the sword is absolutely indispensable. Swords have also been very important in inspiring soldiers.

At the outset of the Japanese invasion, the katana became an important weapon, especially in fighting against the poorly equipped Chinese army. Japanese soldiers found them to be very useful when beheading the Chinese. A Japanese warrant officer told a Japanese war correspondent in Hankou: "In Shanghai, Nanjing, Xuzhou and Hankou, I beheaded about 75 enemies. When setting out for the battlefield, I brought two swords. The first was a new katana that broke in the Mufu mountains after only killing eight people. The second one was also a new tool named after the famous swordsman Miyamoto Musashi. This eight inch blade was defective. In my experience, the longer the handle of a blade, the easier it is to wield. Going by what I've learned from *kendo*, pushing out makes it more difficult to focus on your movement, so I think it's better to hold it in."

In the same article, the reporter also interviewed another soldier called Sakai who talked about his experience killing Chinese people with his sword: "In a year and a half, I killed about 100 people using a sword. It's an ancestral broadsword and it's only three inches at the tip. The ancient sword is hard to damage and it doesn't go rusty after you kill three people." The article then mentions another soldier: "Sawatari was a brave man who ran into combat in Nanjing to reach the enemy positions and kill 15 people in one go" (*Fukushima People*, 17 April 1938).

Other notable extracts on the topic include: "It was the first time he had taken out his sword. When he reached the enemy, he bravely stabbed seven people..." (*Fukushima People*, 2 March 1938) and: "In the attack on the fortress, the captain and lieutenant reached the enemy and beheaded 26 people" (*Tokyo Daily*, 27 January 1938).

After the Nanjing Massacre, reports like this appeared in Japanese newspapers propagandising their victories in the war and celebrating the katana's notable role in the killings.

While boasting about the power of their katanas, which had been a Chinese invention, the Japanese never questioned whether they should be killing so many innocent Chinese people. Instead, they used their swords to slaughter Chinese civilians and unarmed soldiers for the sake of fun and glory. A monstrous notion indeed.

The people whose lives were taken by the Japanese swords will never forgive them, but what makes it even more heinous is that Japanese jingoists and murderers try to deny culpability.

Let's consider the massacre committed by the Japanese army after they entered Nanjing.

In fact, massacres like this happened again and again during the occupation of Nanjing, not just in the few weeks after the Japanese army entered the city. This was directly related to the tacitly approving and complicit supreme commanders in the Japanese high command in Tokyo and on the front. At the end of Timperley's *What War Means: the Japanese Terror in China*, being the first journalist to expose the Japanese army's atrocities in Nanjing in the 1930s, he discusses this matter:

Did the many atrocities of the Japanese in China stem from the deviancy of their soldiers celebrating their victory? To what extent did it reflect the planned terror implemented by the Japanese authorities? Some readers may be wondering such questions too. The facts tell us that it was the latter. The army's atrocities took place soon after they occupied the city at a time when the tired army was about to end their military actions because of the occupation, although it seems impossible to tell the difference. The atrocities of the Japanese army in Nanjing lasted for three months after the city was occupied and it didn't end by the time I left China in early April 1938.

As Timperley said, the atrocities committed by the Japanese army were either under no one's express control or the Japanese authorities knew about their atrocities and turned a blind eye to them.

The Japanese army and high command had been trying to bury what happened in Nanjing, telling their citizens a positive story of the occupation. Killing people was termed to be inspiring the spirit and national morale in a heroic fight against the enemy. There were just 10 overseas correspondents still in Nanjing at the time and they were only able to stay for just 15 or 16 days to witness the most savage atrocities as they were later driven out of Nanjing. Even so, sporadic reports were delivered by the evacuated overseas correspondents, which shocked the world with their horrifying descriptions: "Nanjing today is housing a terrorised population who, under foreign domination, live in fear of death, torture and robbery. The graveyard of tens of thousands of Chinese soldiers may also be the graveyard of all Chinese hopes of resisting Japanese conquest" (*The New York Times*, 18 December 1937).

An article in the *Chicago Daily News* on 4 February 1938 wrote:

On 14 December, I saw the Japanese soldiers plunder Nanjing. A Japanese soldier used a bayonet to threaten citizens and blackmailed 3,000 yuan from them in total in the safety zone. Walking along the streets filled with dead bodies of both people and horses on the way to the North gate, I saw the first Japanese vehicles entering the city, their wheels struggling to get a grip on the dead bodies. I finally arrived at the river, boarded the Japanese vessel and heard the news that the *USS Panay* transport ship had been sunk.

[Author's note: *there were various warships from the UK, the US and other nations in the Yangtze. The USS Panay was an American vessel. On 12 December, while transporting Americans and expatriates of other nationalities, as well as Chinese refugees, it was sunk in the Yangtze by the Japanese and many people were injured or killed. A diplomatic war between the western world and Japan soon broke out.*]

The Japanese troops carefully combed the city for Chinese soldiers and "plainclothes soldiers". Hundreds of people were discovered in a refugee camp and murdered. The dying people were sent to a nearby slaughter house in groups of two or three and shot with rifles and machine guns. A tank was once sent to execute hundreds of prisoners.

I saw a massacre. A group of hundreds of dying people covered by a Japanese flag was in the street with several Japanese soldiers guarding them. Small groups of them were being driven to a clearing and murdered with their guns. A Japanese soldier stood on the increasing piles of dead bodies and shot any survivors.

For the Japanese troops, this is war. But for me, this is murder.

This is murder and the Japanese troops responsible were doing so in a sober and rational state of mind. What makes this more appalling is that the slaughter had an aim and had been planned.

However, while murder is always horrible, rape makes it worse.

4

RAPE:
SCREAMS ON MOCHOU LAKE

The abuse of women seems to be a constant factor in war and rapes are unfortunately routine. This is one of the many reasons that people hate wars. The scale of the atrocities committed by Japanese soldiers against Chinese women during the rape of Nanjing is extremely rare in history due to the appallingly high number of victims and the brutality of the atrocities.

I had been wrestling with the idea of skipping this chapter because of the disgusting and inhumane content it contains, but the scale of the Japanese crimes is so great that I am left with no other choice than to document it.

On 16 March 1938, the *South China Morning Post* wrote an article on the rapes committed by the Japanese troops in Nanjing: "From the third day after Nanjing fell, there were 1,000 rapes a day. A large number of women were killed after being raped repeatedly. The victims were aged from 10 to 70 years old."

In fact, Japanese troops had raped Chinese women since they had first invaded China. Rapes just became more frequent on their advance towards Nanjing following the Battle of Shanghai. After the Japanese troops entered Nanjing, they saw themselves as the city's masters and rape to them was, according to a Japanese veteran: "As essential as eating and enjoying the spoils of war."

In China's 1947 military tribunal's declaration regarding the Japanese war criminals, there's a paragraph that reads:

After the Japanese troops captured cities, they raped women everywhere to satisfy their debased urges. According to statistics from the International Committee, between 16 and 17 December in the 26th year of the republic (1937), more than 1,000 women were raped in deranged and abhorrent ways, the likes of which history has never seen. Take Mrs Tao Tang for example. The Japanese army disembowelled her and burned her body on 23 December in 5 Dong Ren Hou Li by the Zhonghua gate. In addition to her, Mrs Xiao Yu, who was eight months pregnant, a 16 year old girl named Huang Zhuying, the young girl Chen Er and a 63 year old woman were also raped near the

Zhonghua gate. Meanwhile, in an alley by the Zhonghua gate, a country girl called Ding Xiao was stabbed to death by Japanese bayonets in her abdomen as she couldn't stand the Japanese army's brutality and had screamed for help while being gang-raped by 13 Japanese soldiers. From 13 to 17 December, the Japanese army not only raped many young girls in front of the Zhonghua gate but forced passing monks who had declared a life of celibacy to join in. If they refused, they were castrated and killed. Three other young girls died after drowning themselves in the river because of the humiliation they suffered after being raped by Japanese soldiers outside the Zhonghua gate. Every woman in Nanjing lived in fear as people rushed to the safety zone set up by the International Committee to seek refuge. But the Japanese troops still raped women, disregarding the international presence. Every night, Japanese soldiers climbed over walls into homes searching for women to rape, young and old. Although many foreigners protested to the Japanese authorities on behalf of the international community, the Japanese general Hisao Tani and other generals turned a blind eye to it, letting the Japanese rape as they had before.

Crimes like these demonstrate the unprecedented mutilation of Chinese women by Japanese soldiers. Mr Ma Zhendu, a researcher from the Second Historical Archives of China as well as a famous Nanjing Massacre expert, pointed out in the paper *The Japanese Army's Atrocities on the People of Conquered Countries and Their Reasons* that:

The Japanese army's sexual assault on the people in conquered countries featured an extraordinarily rare and unprecedented level of cruelty. Their brutality and damage surpassed even those of the German fascist soldiers. Wherever the Japanese troops went, so too did a wave of sexual assaults. In late 1937 and early 1938, more than 300,000 people were slaughtered by the Japanese troops in the Nanjing Massacre. The Japanese army's sexual assaults and crimes peaked with a total of tens of thousands of women being raped and massacred in Nanjing. On 4 November 1948, the International Military Tribunal of the Far East judged that: 'Approximately 20,000 cases of rape occurred within the city during the first month of the occupation.' But actually this statistic is far lower than what actually happened. Some studies reveal that: 'Most women, both young and old were raped in the city.' About two thirds of the women of Nanjing had been raped by early May 1938. With this in mind, 80,000 is a conservative estimate of the rape victims in Nanjing. On top of that, according to the records of one Japanese soldier, Kozo Tadokoro: 'There is no soldier who did not rape and most of the women were killed afterwards... to avoid trouble.' There was mass genocide after the battle for Nanjing and frenzied gang-rapes and murders constantly happened everywhere, with no consideration for the victim, a level of cruelty rare in the history of humanity.

Ma Zhendu and other experts believe that the weaponisation of sexual assault by the Japanese can be seen as one of the greatest crimes in history, with gang-rape being their preferred method. One soldier said: "We hadn't touched any women since we'd landed, so we gang-raped women violently. 'Rape and torture people to death' has become our motto."

The actions of the Japanese soldiers were brutal and inhuman. They took Chinese women away and then repeatedly and brutally raped them. Some Chinese women were gang-raped more than 40 times. In addition to raping them, the Japanese soldiers used all sorts of bizarre methods to kill the Chinese women. They would find anything they could and stuff it into the victim's genitals, including wine bottles, crabsticks, bricks and even lit candles. They'd take perverted pictures of women lying naked, raped and abused. They raped pregnant women, young girls, old women and nuns. They forced them to be comfort women and set up comfort stations. They forced incest between mothers and sons, fathers and daughters and fathers-in-law and daughters-in-law. They even forced women to give them oral sex until they suffocated. The acts of the Japanese soldiers were brutal and beyond any sane person's imagination.

Ma Zhendu adds that the Japanese army's sexual assaults were never isolated incidents done by individuals; instead they were organised collective acts carried out by the entire Japanese army. During the Second World War, wherever the Japanese troops went, so did sexual assault. Japanese officers at all levels, ranging from expeditionary army commanders to junior captains, all openly talked about the attacks and even indulged in them themselves, making sexual assault in the Japanese army very common. He explains: "Among the Japanese frontline troops, it was sometimes the Japanese officers instead of the soldiers who took the lead in doing these evil things. Some powerful commanders and captains would take women with them before and even during battle since they were easily captured. It was said that those officers slept with these women every night." The regimental commander of the 30th brigade in the 16th division, Sasaki, who was also the commander of the watchmen regiment, inhumanly raped young girls every day. This was proven by Bates, an American professor at Jinling College, who said that: "After they came into the city, Japanese troops searched every street, every alley and the safety zone [set up by the International Committee for Nanjing] for women, with many Japanese officers among them." George Rosen, the German foreign secretary in Nanjing, described the Japanese soldiers as "beasts" when he saw their actions. He wrote in a report to the German foreign ministry: "The big fire started by the Japanese troops lasted for a month after they captured the city, combined with humiliations and rapes of the young and old. Their disgraceful actions in Nanjing deserve a memorial. This was not done by individuals but the entire Japanese army, which means that this brutality and criminal act is the responsibility of the entire Japanese army."

The significant reasons that the Japanese soldiers are so hated by the people of China are that they invaded their land, killed innocent Chinese civilians, looted Chinese property, and violently killed and molested Chinese women and girls after they'd been raped and gang-raped. It's no mystery then why they're known as "devils".

Unwatchable Scenes

After the Japanese troops entered Nanjing, the brutal rape, gang-rape and arbitrary killing of Chinese women was everywhere, with many appalling scenes in the city. Several of these uncountable instances are described below:

Location: Dong Yang Street

In the summer of 2002, Xu Guangfa revealed the following to a group of university students who were researching the Nanjing Massacre.

At dawn, on the streets of the city, armed Japanese soldiers chased after frightened people while terrified citizens locked the doors to their houses and yards. But, it was useless. The heavily armed Japanese soldiers could go wherever they wanted.

A group of Japanese soldiers blocked an alley and killed three men with their guns. Two tattered women, their faces black with soot, who'd been with them ran away screaming. But they were stopped by the Japanese soldiers after just a couple of metres.

The two women were stripped naked, their bodies exposed by the Japanese soldiers as quickly as if they'd been plucking a chicken.

A frenzied Japanese soldier tossed his gun to the side, unbuttoned his trousers, grabbed the girl to the side of the street and raped her. The other soldiers kept watch.

The two women were gang-raped by eight Japanese soldiers and were finally killed with two gunshots, one to the chest and one to the head.

At this point, a baby's cry could be heard from another house. The

Japanese soldiers laughed excitedly and the two soldiers nearest the house kicked down the door.

The baby's crying stopped abruptly, followed by a woman's scream. Loud crashes could be heard from the room.

"You monsters!" another woman shouted hoarsely.

The Japanese soldiers left with a look of satisfaction on their faces.

The rest of the soldiers then went in. They then promptly carried a naked old woman out of the room.

With her hands thumping the ground the old woman cried: "You killed my grandson and my daughter-in-law! You bastards!"

A Japanese soldier seemed annoyed, so he hit her in the mouth with the butt of his gun. One of the soldiers took out a rope to bind her breasts, tied two stones to the ends of the rope and ordered the old woman to crawl on the ground and said: "You! Crawl forwards!"

She struggled and the Japanese soldiers laughed.

Suddenly the old woman's genitals were stabbed with a bayonet. More bayonets soon followed.

A five year old boy in a house near the street witnessed the crime: "The old woman was murdered so brutally."

Location: *Caoqiao Mosque*

On the first day of the Japanese troops' occupation, Nanjing was in chaos. A 15 year old Hui girl called Ma Fang [this is an alias], living in Caoqiao Mosque, went to buy food for her parents as usual in the morning. Just as she was stepping out of her home, she saw a group of Japanese soldiers stabbing a Chinese man; several bayonets were stabbing him from five different directions. Suddenly blood streamed out from his head and back.

The girl let out a loud scream and ran home with her hands on her head.

"Dad, the Japanese soldiers killed a man!" Ma Fang said to her father after she rushed into the room and hid in the back.

Her father understood the situation and called his family to hide as he locked the door. It was at that point that the Japanese troops knocked on the door.

"Open the door! Quickly!" the Japanese troops shouted outside.

Ma Fang's father had no choice but to open the door.

"Are there any pretty young girls here?" the Japanese soldiers shouted, pointing a bayonet at Ma Fang's father as the soldiers walked towards the back room.

Ma Fang's father was appalled as he had never imagined people could act like this and answered: "No, there are not!"

This served as a warning for Ma Fang, who was in the back room, and she started to run towards the river and quickly jumped into a bomb shelter.

"Pretty girl, over there!" a Japanese soldier saw her and a group of soldiers howled and ran towards the bomb shelter Ma Fang was hiding in.

"Come out pretty girl, come out!" The Japanese soldiers looked in, picked up a brick and threw it into the hole.

Ma Fang cried when she walked out.

Two heavily bearded Japanese soldiers caught Ma Fang from two sides and walked towards the nearby mosque.

After entering a room, they pointed several bayonets at Ma Fang's breasts and forced her to take off her clothes.

Ma Fang cried and took off her clothes.

"Take off your pants!" the Japanese soldiers ordered.

A Japanese soldier couldn't wait for Ma Fang to finish taking off her pants and raped her immediately.

While the shivering young girl didn't know what was happening, another Japanese soldier took over. After being raped by the five soldiers for about half an hour, Ma Fang, a virgin, was covered in blood, her body left black and blue.

"Xiaofang! Xiaofang!" Suddenly, Ma Fang's mother's desperate cries were heard from outside the door.

Ma Fang shouted out suddenly: "Mum! Help me!"

The Japanese soldiers ecstatically turned around and saw Ma Fang's mother in front of them.

"What are you doing?! I'm here for my daughter. You..." Ma Fang's mother was thrown to the ground mid-sentence by two Japanese soldiers, with one soldier covering her head and another soldier stripping off her clothes. A Japanese soldier raped her, followed by the second one and the third one and more.

"You monsters!" Ma Fang's father heard what was happening and used a club to hit the Japanese soldier who was raping his wife. Another Japanese soldier kicked him hard. Ma Fang's father fell over and wanted to stand up, but they shot him in the shoulder.

"Mum! Dad!" Seeing the Japanese soldiers leaving, Ma Fang stood up with her pants in her hands, looked at her naked mother and bleeding father, and collapsed to the ground.

. . .

Location: *Wang Fu Yuan*

Qiang and his family of nine were temporarily living in a residential building.

On the morning of the 13th, Qiang's father said to his wife and children: "We need to go, I've heard that the Japanese have entered the city, we need to find a bomb shelter to hide in!"

"Keep up with me!" Qiang's mother held her two year old son and her eldest daughter, pushing along her other children at the same time. After the family walked for a while, they came across a group of Japanese soldiers.

"Pretty girl!" Japanese soldiers surrounded Qiang and his family.

"Are you Chinese soldiers?" asked two Japanese soldiers in the front, stopping Qiang's father. They knocked him over and he fell on his knees.

"We're not. You can see that we're a big family," Qiang's father argued angrily. They then stabbed him in the chest and back with bayonets.

Qiang's mother watched and screamed, then her two year old son fell down on the ground.

"Pretty girl here!" A Japanese soldier yelled and pointed a bayonet at Qiang's mother's chest. Another Japanese soldier used a bayonet to strike Qiang's little brother, who'd fallen to the ground, in the rear. He then threw him to the side. There was no sound at all.

"My little brother!" shouted 10 year old Qiang when he saw what happened, then he pushed the Japanese soldiers' bayonets and rushed over to his brother. Qiang wanted to hold him, but a Japanese soldier kicked him to the ground.

Then, Qiang's four other little brothers started crying. The mother was worrying about her children being abused by the Japanese soldiers, so she rushed to protect them. The Japanese soldiers got angry, so they pointed their bayonets at her. Qiang and his brothers suddenly became brave. They all sprang on the Japanese soldiers, biting them and screaming. They grasped at the bayonets to protect their mother.

Somewhat taken aback, the Japanese soldiers forcibly pulled their bayonets away from the children, and then slashed at the five children in the head and chest as if they were cutting open watermelons.

All the children were covered with blood.

Qiang's mother screamed hysterically.

Qiang broke down as well.

However, the Japanese soldiers became more enthusiastic, laughing: "Pretty girl, let's have some fun!"

The Japanese soldiers gang-raped Qiang's mother and his sister on a stone next to the bloodied ground.

After an unknown amount of time, Qiang suddenly bolted up from the ground, having escaped death. "Mum, mum!" Qiang looked around for his family. Finally, he found them. First, he saw his sister lying on her side with five stab wounds, but she was still alive.

His mother was lying still, with a pool of blood under the lower half of her body. When little Qiang showed his crying little brother to his mother, she untied the buttons in front of her breasts, and took out her nipple and put it in her little boy's mouth. It was at this point that Qiang saw his mother's head slant to one side, never to move again.

Qiang cried his eyes out. But then he realised it was no use crying and that he had to check whether his other family members were alive.

He saw his father kneeling down with hands on the ground.

Qiang thought that his father was still alive, so he pushed him, only to find that he fell down. He turned his father over and saw that he was bleeding from the wounds in his chest and back.

Now, out of a family of 10, only Qiang, his elder sister and their two year old brother were still alive.

The 10 year old Qiang took his brother to a nearby room and then dragged his sister in later.

As soon as Qiang walked in, he heard a woman sobbing in the next room.

Qiang went to investigate and found a beaten women sitting on the ground weeping. It was quite obvious that she was another victim of the Japanese.

She said: "My husband was an opera actor, he was killed by the Japanese too. You guys look so terrible, shall we go to my house?" The woman was pretty and had a little baby fat, so Qiang and his sister called her "Pangmama", meaning chubby mummy.

The warm-hearted Pangmama helped Qiang carry his sister and brother to her house. She gave them food and helped them recover. On the third day, three Japanese soldiers broke into her house and gang-raped his sister and Pangmama again.

Qiang's sister had been abused so badly that she couldn't move the lower half of her body for days while Pangmama's breasts had been bitten badly, leaving swelling and bruises.

One day, Pangmama heard that there was a refugee camp near the Jinling College that was able to protect women. So Qiang and Pangmama helped his sister to go there.

However, the shelter wasn't safe either. The Japanese soldiers broke in several times, raping his sister and Pangmama over and over again.

Once they returned from the refugee camp, Qiang couldn't find his little brother. His neighbour told him that his little brother had died in the cold weather, and his body had been taken away by others.

In just a few days, out of the 10 members of his family, only Qiang and his sister were alive. Unfortunately, his sister died from an infectious disease a while later. Qiang was left alone and became an orphan.

Young Qiang's full name was Chang Zhiqiang, born in December 1928. He previously lived in Yanziji Chemical Industry New Village.

Location: 17 Shenjiaxiang Courtyard

Several families lived in this courtyard. While richer families had fled to other cities or their relatives' houses, poorer families had no choice but to stay, resigning themselves to their fate.

One day, Japanese soldiers saw smoke pouring from a chimney inside the closed-door courtyard, and so they broke in.

"Any beautiful women here?" one Japanese soldier asked. Zhao Tingdong, who was the only child of his family and had just got married, lived in the courtyard along with his wife and mother. The 18 or 19 year old Zhao Tingdong, a strong young man, was found by the Japanese and arrested after being accused of being a Chinese soldier and killed on the street. After this, how could Zhao's weak wife and mother fight against the Japanese? The bride and mother were gang-raped by five Japanese soldiers.

Zhang Yulong's wife, who lived next to Zhao, hid under the bed. The Japanese used a bayonet to force her to come out and then raped her several times for about an hour. Afterwards, the wife was so ashamed that she tried to take her own life, but was stopped by her family.

Mrs Li, who made a living as a rubbish recycler, also fell victim to the Japanese. She wasn't just raped, but also dragged naked onto the street. She was forced to jump up and down. The Japanese broke her legs, leaving her dead on the street. The Japanese didn't stop there and inserted a glass beer bottle she had picked up into her vagina and left her body lying on the street.

Several days later, Shi Xiulan flew back home and saw Li's body still on the street.

Location: Chunhua

The Japanese were routinely looking for attractive women at the time, acting like they were unstoppable. Suddenly they saw a woman and her daughter walking on the street. It was snowing, so the woman and the girl were holding an umbrella.

The Japanese soldiers were like hungry wolves seeing meat, so they ripped off their clothes and were about to rape them. Frenzied as they were, they were still fearful, and also afraid of their horses escaping, so they tied their ankles and horses' legs together with ropes before they raped the women.

The mother was naked and being raped. She felt so ashamed when she saw pedestrians nearby, she opened her umbrella without thinking. The black umbrella suddenly opened, scaring the horses. One horse neighed and ran away, dragging its Japanese owner more than 100 metres away.

"I'm going to kill you!" the bloodied Japanese soldier was furious and took out his bayonet, rushing over to the mother and her daughter. The two women knew there was nowhere to escape, so they jumped into the river next to them. The soldier shot into the river. The two of them died.

This group of Japanese soldiers was outraged by this incident. They then called for more soldiers to take revenge on two nearby villages. More than 30 men were arrested and brought to the back of Chunhua Elementary School. Some women, most of whom were the wives or daughters of the men, were brought there and raped in front of them. The men were all killed and very few of the women managed to escape.

Location: Jiangxin Island

Surrounded by the Yangtze River, this area was one of the major locations where the Japanese army slaughtered Chinese prisoners of war and raped Chinese women.

Jiangxin Island is enveloped by the Yangtze, with pools of water everywhere and reed fields all over the island. Many of the farmers here also owned boats, making it a perfect place to hide out. This is what concerned the Japanese, so they scoured and attacked the island, raping countless women in the process.

One day, a group of Japanese soldiers arrived on the island by power boat. They found four women who'd fled the city hiding in Li Yongnian's granary and pulled them out one by one and raped them.

Among them, a girl, the daughter of the resident Wang Yongmin, heavily resisted. A Japanese soldier wanted to kill her with a bayonet. The girl was smart, however, and waved her hands saying: "Let's do it by the water, no one will see us that way."

The soldier ecstatically agreed and followed the girl to a pool of water. The girl pointed at a small boat on the bank of the pool and suggested: "Let's have sex on the water."

The soldier was very excited and did what the girl said again. She skilfully rowed the boat into the pool of water, and when they were dozens of metres away from the bank, she suddenly capsized the boat and covered the soldier with it until he died.

The next day, the Japanese retaliated in Jiangxin Island with an attack on both the land and water. At first, hundreds of villagers like Wang Huaming and Wang Yuede from Yuhua village were killed, along with some refugees in the area. Their bodies were later thrown into toilets.

Next, men from Nanshang Village were brought to a crop field and were forced to have sex with women from their village. Their heads were cut off if they refused.

A number of women from Xixia Village hid in haystacks. The Japanese army stabbed and set fire to the haystack to get them out. The women were then dragged onto the floor and gang-raped. The women were also forced to lick the Japanese soldiers' genitals after being raped. If anyone refused, they would be decapitated.

A businessman's family fled to the island from the city and hid in a boat covered with reeds. After being found by the Japanese, they rowed into the river to escape. However, there was no way they could outpace a Japanese power boat. The boat was then pulled next to the power boat and they shot a man and young boy. The women were raped onboard more than 10 times before they were thrown into the river and shot dead. The family of five's blood surrounded the boat.

Location: *Tangshan town*

This was a hilly area so when the Japanese arrived, the people would either run to the hills or dig a hole near their house to hide.

The Japanese weren't stupid. They brought dogs with them to scour the hills while crowds of women fled. One grandma was struggling to get away. A Japanese soldier found her and slyly tricked her in Chinese: "Don't be scared, we're the Chinese army, please tell them to come down!"

The grandma didn't realise and thought that the people who were speaking Chinese had good intentions. She shouted and told the women hiding on the hill to come out. About five women then came down the hill.

"All women! Delicious!" the Japanese soldiers laughed and revealed who they really were, brutally raping the women one by one, even the grandma who was more than 70 years old.

Later, when three Japanese soldiers rode to the village of Mengtang on horseback, they burned the entire place to the ground. They stood on the hill near a back alley and shot everyone they saw. The Mao family hid in a shelter but a mischievous child poked his head out of it. Unfortunately, he was seen. The Japanese opened fire and seven of them died as a result. A newly-married bride in the family was pulled out by the Japanese soldiers.

"Take off your clothes!" ordered a Japanese soldier. "I can't... I'm pregnant... please don't..." the weeping bride begged.

The soldier didn't care and took off her clothes straight away, raping her in front of the entrance to the shelter. When another Japanese soldier was about to rape her, she saw red and bit the man, which made him angry. He stabbed her stomach with a bayonet. Her baby was also cut out.

The bride died, as did her baby. Even after this, the Japanese still carried on, aroused by dead women.

They later went to the sides of a pool of water west of the village of Huangmeiqiao. They dragged a man out of Pang's house and asked him to help them find "beautiful women". His wife was hiding in the shelter next to them.

The man shook his head. A Japanese soldier immediately cut his throat.

The hiding woman didn't know what had happened outside, so she poked her head out and was found by the Japanese as a result. She was dragged out and gang-raped in front of her dying husband. Later they were thrown into the water and shot dead.

Many more miserable incidents like this happened, but I don't have the heart to describe any more of them. There were even more disgusting rapes that took place, but they are best left unwritten and unread. Because of all these horrible tragedies, I couldn't get the incidents out of my mind and suffered from nightmares every night.

Guo Qi, a KMT veteran who was the Zizhong battalion commander responsible for defending the way into Nanjing, witnessed the horrible crimes of the Japanese while he hid in the city for three months after getting separated from his unit. After being saved, he wrote a lengthy book called *The Bloody and Crying Capital*. He later appeared as a witness to testify against the Japanese crimes at the military court trial of the Japanese war criminals. The following extracts from his book reveal how the Japanese raped Chinese women:

The Deaths of the Unshakable Girls at the Shuixi Gate

As the Nanjing Massacre was unleashed, tragic stories took place one after another. An old man, a respectable intellectual, had two daughters, and one of them got married. After Nanjing fell, his son-in-law had been unable to escape and became a slave. Since then, he lost contact with this family. The old man and his daughters worried about him a great deal and didn't know what to do. One day, three Japanese soldiers broke into their house as the younger daughter was walking through the living room. The Japanese soldier who came in first became aroused, with his eyes wandering and his mouth watering as soon as he saw her. He then quickly turned his head to tell his comrades that he'd found a beautiful woman.

As the younger girl expected something bad to happen, she became terrified and hurriedly ran upstairs. Meanwhile, the old man knelt down, begging them to leave his daughter alone. However, the three Japanese soldiers who had broken in were so aggressive and aroused that they didn't consider stopping. They pushed the man to the ground, muttering in Japanese, and ran straight upstairs.

On the first floor, the elder daughter saw the three lecherous soldiers rushing upstairs and knew that there was no way out. All she wanted to do was to save her unmarried sister, so she stepped forwards with tears in her eyes. However, while one Japanese soldier pushed her to the ground, the other two went chasing after her sister all over the first floor. As the landing was full of Japanese soldiers, the younger girl was quickly caught as well.

The old man wept on the ground. He saw how his elder daughter was trying to save his younger daughter. With the elder sister crying and the younger sister pleading with the Japanese, there was chaos upstairs. How could the old man, or any parent for that matter, bear this situation? However, he was too old to fight against the bloodthirsty Japanese troops. They'd already pushed him to the ground, so even if he managed to get upstairs, what could he ever do to fight them off? Agonised by his racing thoughts amidst the screams of his daughters, the heartbroken old man struggled to crawl towards the door to his home because he simply couldn't bear to see or hear his daughters suffer.

As soon as he reached the door, he heard the sound of footsteps. It was the Japanese soldier who'd first raped his daughter. After handing the girl over to his comrade, he pulled on his trousers while walking downstairs. Although Chinese women ranging from 10 to 80 couldn't avoid the nightmare of being raped by the Japanese during the Nanjing Massacre, the heinous soldiers would still feel ashamed and afraid while raping women in the open. They worried about the retaliation of Chinese men, so they usually searched for women in a group, and once they found them, they unashamedly gang-raped them in turns with one of them keeping watch.

The soldier who went upstairs and came down first was supposed to go out to guard and keep watch for his comrades, but he saw the old man struggling to crawl to the door. He thought that the old man was going to try to find help and the Japanese soldiers neither had the time or energy to keep an eye on him. So, the soldier approached the old man and shot him in the forehead without any hesitation. He then stabbed him in the chest.

The two girls upstairs heard the sudden gunshot and their father's scream while they were being tortured by the Japanese. With a deep and burning hatred in their hearts, being raped and tormented while their father was being murdered, they could stand it no more. The two girls used all of their strength and energy to fight off the soldiers by punching, hitting, kicking and biting them. The aggressive and lecherous soldiers went mad, so one grabbed his bayonet and stabbed the two naked girls without thinking. The two girls died.

After the humiliated girls had been slaughtered, the Japanese soldiers put on their clothes and escaped in a hurry. Meanwhile, the old man was still alive despite having been shot and stabbed. The bloodied old man tried his best to move towards the stairs, wanting to see if his daughters were okay. However, he was too weak and fell when he was halfway up the stairs. It wasn't until the Japanese soldiers' vehicle left that the neighbours dared to check on the family. With the help of his neighbours, the old man sat down and told them what had just happened. Then, the kind neighbours went upstairs and put clothes on the two brave and wounded girls who lay dead. The neighbours wept as they told him that his beautiful daughters were dead. The old man wailed: "Oh God! What kind of a world is this?" He had lost too much blood and later passed away.

12 Year Old Rape Victim

Mr Zhou and his wife lived with us along with their 12 year old daughter, the apple of their eyes, at the Italian embassy in China. We became friends and as they say, "a friend in need is a friend indeed". But, Mr Zhou's mother lived in the countryside, just outside of the Zhonghua gate. As a loyal son, Mr Zhou always had his mother, who lived alone, in his heart. So, one day, he called on six good friends to set up a team to go to the countryside with him, planning to cross the blockade established by the Japanese army at the Zhonghua gate. Mr Zhou intended to go to the countryside to visit his mother while his friends would take this chance to run away from Nanjing, which had suffered so much from the massacre.

On the day he left, after the team of seven was created, he came to me to work on some plans. As Nanjing was full of danger, I wasn't in any position to stop Mr Zhou and his team, so I asked him: "What about your wife? Will she go with you as well?"

Mr Zhou answered me with a forced smile: "I worry that she'll be in danger on the journey so she won't be coming with us, I'll only bring my little girl with me."

I immediately replied: "As far as I'm concerned, your daughter should stay as well."

But Mr Zhou wouldn't listen, responding: "My daughter is just a little girl, don't worry! I'll disguise her as a boy."

Even her own father wasn't taking the matter seriously, so I decided I should stop worrying, otherwise I'd just be anxious and cause a scene. At about 8 or 9 o'clock in the morning, as planned, we helped to disguise the seven team members, including Mr Zhou, Mr Dong and five others, as workers by getting them to wear old and shabby clothes. They looked just like poor hard labourers. As Mr Zhou planned, his 12 year old daughter put on boy's clothes and she looked just like a little boy.

I was worried that all the money that Mr Zhou was taking with him would be discovered by the Japanese soldiers, so I came up with a unique idea. He would roll the bills together in deep-fried dough known as *youtiao*. That way he would be able to evade the Japanese soldiers.

Before they hit the road, we carefully checked over the eight team members again. Good friends of ours who were staying in the same room were all satisfied with their disguises, believing that there was nothing that would expose their real identities as the seven men really just looked like coolies, while Mr Zhou's little girl behaved and looked just like a boy.

Finally, we went with Mrs Zhou, who pretended to be calm while she was incredibly anxious inside, to see off the team as they left down the road. They gradually disappeared out of sight. We prayed we wouldn't receive any news from them, as no news meant they were safe.

However, to our surprise, within two hours, a shocked Mr Dong returned with tears in his eyes. As soon as I saw him, I had a bad feeling deep down, so I asked what had happened.

Mr Dong was in tears. He sat down and bitterly seethed: "Damn! Those Japs are monsters! They're sons of bitches! No, they don't even deserve to be called monsters!"

He terrified Mrs Zhou, who kept asking: "Mr Dong, where's my husband? Where's my daughter? How are they? Have they come back with you as well?"

Mr Dong looked into her eyes with tears streaming down his face. After a while, he answered with a forced smile: "M... Mrs Zhou, please don't worry, they're fine now, an... and they're out of the city."

But Mrs Zhou stared at Mr Dong's face, looking as if she didn't believe him. She was still scared and worried. She didn't give up and kept asking about her husband and daughter over and over again. But Mr Dong hesitated and didn't say a word. It was distressing to watch Mrs Zhou continuously asking while Mr Dong said nothing. After a while, he didn't know what to do and firmly said that the reason he had complained just now was because he had been beaten by the Japanese soldiers and had come back full of anger. At the same time, we comforted Mrs Zhou, which eliminated any doubts she had about her husband and daughter's safety. Later, and not until Mr Dong saw Mrs Zhou walk back into her room, he revealed in a stifled whisper what had really happened. I couldn't believe that such a tragedy could be real.

After the eight people reached the Zhonghua gate without any trouble, the Japanese soldiers deployed there ordered everyone to go outside of the town to wait in a line and they would check everyone individually. Mr Dong and his comrades knew that they couldn't get out of it, so they had no choice but to wait in line as required. The procedure to leave the city was incredibly strict as everyone had to be searched, which was a ruse commonly used by the Japanese. They patted down the civilians all over their bodies as they passed through. When it came to Mr Dong's turn, he and the other seven members of the group took out their refugee cards. The Japanese just glanced at them and then told them to put their cards away before searching each of their pockets. The good thing was that they'd expected this and had prepared a small amount of money to be placed in their pockets. So, as soon as the greedy Japanese soldiers found and seized the money they had on them, they let them go.

There was no way that the soldiers could have known that most of their bank notes had been rolled in *youtiao* instead.

When all of the eight people in the group safely passed through the checkpoint, they felt that they'd been incredibly lucky. They walked over to the Jinling warehouse outside of the city walls with a sigh of relief. Suddenly, an armed Japanese soldier chased after them, shouting at them in awkward Chinese: "Stop! Stop!"

They stopped, confused about what was happening. None of them could have guessed what this soldier wanted. To their surprise, when they stood still, the Japanese soldier took large strides towards them and silently dragged off the little girl to a room nearby.

The seven men panicked, especially her father Mr Zhou, who was angry and afraid. His face turned a bright red, desperately wanting to chase after them as the soldier pushed the crying little girl into the room, locking the door with a bang. Although they all knew of the extent of the Japanese rapes in the city, they thought that there was no way that they'd be interested in a 12 year old girl who'd barely reached puberty. Suddenly, two gunshots were heard from the room and the little girl stopped crying. Meanwhile, the other men tried their best to stop the tormented Mr Zhou, preventing him from being killed by the other Japanese soldiers around them. Later, there was a horrifying scream from the room. Everyone, including Mr Zhou, heard it clearly. How could the Japanese even consider tormenting a 12 year old girl like this? At that point, fires of rage burned in everyone's bellies. Mr Zhou was so angry that he wept profusely. They were sitting ducks surrounded by armed Japanese soldiers, so no one dared risk their lives to save the suffering little girl.

They waited in anguish for just a few minutes, but it felt like many days and nights. When Mr Dong thought of the little girl's tragic experience and his inability to do anything, he cursed himself for his cowardice. With tears in his eyes, Mr Dong couldn't bear to watch the extremely distressing scene of the father being reunited with his daughter. He turned around to go back to the city filled with rage, giving up on the opportunity to leave the city and escape the danger.

In hindsight, Mr Dong realised that when they'd been inspected and searched by the gatekeepers, the perverted Japanese soldier had discovered that the little girl was actually in disguise. Japanese soldiers knew that the women and girls were scared of them, and no woman in the city dared to go out in public, even older ladies in their fifties or sixties. Some women ran away, some hid, and some put on men's clothing to disguise themselves from the Japanese. As a result, the Japanese soldiers used extremely cruel and immoral methods to prevent women from disguising themselves as men. Whenever they checked civilians, after having taken everything they had, they'd also grab their crotches to check their gender. The women of Nanjing suffered a great deal.

Just a few days after the tragedy that befell the Zhou family, to my surprise, I witnessed another tragic event from the upstairs of the Italian consulate where I lived. There was a perfect western style building close to the Italian consulate, which had tall and solid walls surrounding it. Looking out from the window of the room where I lived, I had a wide and clear view of the situation there. The owner of the house had already gone away and disappeared without a trace. Since Nanjing fell, there had been about 40 or 50 refugees who'd moved into the building. Among them, there were about 20 middle aged women who had already had lots of children so they assumed that they wouldn't be targeted by the Japanese soldiers. When the Japanese soldiers came to loot the building for the first time, the women and their children didn't even try hiding.

On that day, dozens of Japanese soldiers entered the building. The badges on their lapels were black or yellow, but I couldn't make out the designation of their military unit, and there were no officers leading them. They knocked loudly on the door. One refugee took a long time to open the door, so the soldiers grabbed him and started to beat and kick him. The poor soul was being beaten within an inch of his life until the Japanese soldiers caught a glimpse of the women in the living room. They let go the nearly dead man straight away. Some of the soldiers shouted cruelly while some laughed. They drove all the men there into the living room and then dragged the elderly women over to them. They then brazenly took off the women's clothes right in the living room, and assaulted them right in front of the children. Three on one, five on one. They came and went and then returned again. The vicious scene replayed again and again. The assaulted women screamed and cried loudly at first, but before long, they only had the strength to beg for mercy. The children had never seen anything as terrible before, and they cried in fear. Some Japanese soldiers even patted the children on their heads while they were raping their mothers, shamelessly saying to them: "There, there. Don't be afraid."

Outside of the living room in the courtyard, the husbands of the assaulted women had all been beaten senselessly, filled with shame. Some of them leaned against the wall and wailed forlornly; some buried their heads in their hands and stood transfixed to the ground, while the elderly could do no nothing but shake their heads and give a deep sigh. There were also some men who kept their hands behind their backs and paced up and down the courtyard, looking restless and resentful. Sometimes they scratched their ears and cheeks out of embarrassment, or stamped their feet and sighed in anguish. Seeing what was happening in the living room and the courtyard, I felt an intense pain in my chest and was filled with anger. I couldn't help tightly clenching my hands. I could only close my eyes.

I'd assumed that this collective gang-rape would be over quickly, and I never could have imagined that even more nightmares awaited them. After one batch of soldiers had satisfied their sexual desires and done up their belts, they hurried out of the door and went out into the street. They came across another group of Japanese soldiers, so more of them arrived. The Japanese soldiers then summoned more of their gangs. When one batch was still assaulting the women, the next batch arrived and rushed into action after they were finished. They came one after another without a break. The poor women in the living room were already too faint and weak to cry out for help.

After the Japanese soldiers captured Nanjing, they raped, looted, burned and killed. They used every measure of extreme violence imaginable; as a result, Nanjing had become a ghost-town and a centre of terror. No man dared to say that he would survive to see tomorrow, and no woman dared to say that she would remain unviolated. It was said that the Japanese soldiers were just following the vicious methods used by the warlords when they took land and cities during their reign. After unscrupulously plundering the city for three days, they would then put down their swords to reassure the people. Therefore, people only needed to survive the first three days, and they would then be safe and sound. But that wasn't the case this time. Three days later, a week later, and a month later, their atrocities still continued. Even after three months, the Japanese soldiers continued looting, rioting and raping everywhere. The citizens who lingered onto a feeble existence in Nanjing lived with a bitter sense of shame. They could only pray to be delivered from oppression and persecution.

But how could the Chinese women under Japanese occupation escape and keep their dignity intact?

This distressing and haunting description by Mr Guo shows the pain experienced by the people of Nanjing.

The Japanese Crimes in Their Own Words: Nothing But Carnal Torture

The Japanese military and government set very rigorous rules on their troops during Japan's invasion of China, especially for things like slaughtering innocent Chinese people. That is to say that soldiers were strictly prohibited from revealing what they had done, including their wanton slaughter and looting in China, not to mention writing articles on the subject. After the Japanese surrendered, Japan carried out an exceedingly rigorous review and investigation of all the officers and men back home. All written records, including diaries and notes kept in the battlefield, were banned from being brought back to Japan. Once someone who had gone against the order was found out, they would be punished severely. As a result, it became rather difficult to get any first hand materials about this historical event from Japan itself. Even so, many still strived to obtain some fragmentary materials like diaries and other records kept by the Japanese soldiers at the time. There has been a point, however, when some Japanese veterans have reflected on the conflict, hating war with an increasing zeal as they get older, with some still reflecting on it in shame today. Some of these veterans began writing memoirs, the content of which became a more realistic reflection of the Japanese soldiers' atrocities in China, particularly in the Nanjing Massacre. Several other pacifist anti-war activists, like Tamaki Matsuoka, even took things into their own hands and visited Japanese veterans to investigate and uncover the atrocities they'd committed in China. As a result of these works, I have been able to get some of the materials written by the Japanese veterans themselves, which factually reflect upon the gang-rapes committed by Japanese soldiers in China.

If a man is involved in the gang-rape of a woman, he will be severely punished in any country in the world and it is seen as an atrocious crime. As such, hardly any men who have taken part in such atrocities will tell the truth about it. It's clear that not only were gang-rapes common in the Japanese army, but the level of harm inflicted upon Chinese women by the Japanese troops, especially during their occupation of Nanjing, was exceedingly hideous and despicable. The Japanese officers and soldiers who have admitted to the atrocities state that nearly everyone was culpable in the assaults. Gang-rape was as normal as eating; it was a casual necessity that just had to be done.

No matter if they were busy or not, Japanese soldiers would look for women to attack. The purpose of imposing grain levies or levying other taxes was to look for women to satisfy their sexual desires. They looked for women at both day and night, soldiers and officers alike. When Nanjing fell, it was the rapes that the Japanese soldiers most looked forward to.

In a letter written by Mills, a foreign missionary, to his wife, he described the miserable situation inflicted upon the citizens of Nanjing by the Japanese army:

> In this battle, the worst thing for the citizens of Nanjing hasn't been the burnt buildings and destroyed hometowns. Although these have been heart-wrenching too, the most unbearable thing has been that many men will never come back and many women will lead tormented lives, both physically and mentally, due to the rapes. I cannot say whose fate is better: the men being taken away and killed or the women surviving in terror and living under the burden of memories of rape.
>
> — *Historical Materials of the Nanjing Massacre*, vol. 70, p. 770

"Things like raping women wouldn't be recorded in diaries," said the descendant of a Japanese veteran. Even so, I still found references to the rapes in several diaries belonging to Japanese veterans. The following is from Tanaka's diary, a veteran who served in the 33th wing of the 16th division of the Japanese invading army:

20 January
Our comrades-in-arms in the squad finally brought us a woman. She wept out: "I have a baby at home, I beg you, please let me go!" Though we didn't

have much sympathy for parents, we felt sorry for her, so someone did a good deed and let her go.

22 January

Another girl has been brought here. Uproarious noise lasted for an entire night and kept us from sleeping.

23 January

This morning, I shouted: "It's too noisy, let them go!" They went too far this time and it was very irritating.

The following is original material from personal statements provided by Japanese veterans who were involved in raping women during the Nanjing Massacre when they were investigated and interviewed in the 1990s:

Akiyama:

If they wanted to get food, they needed to have sex with us in exchange.

We found girls in the refugee zone as well. We looked for girls everywhere. At first, we broke into houses searching for them. Once we found a woman, we raped her instantly.

Ten to 15 days after we captured Nanjing, I went to the refugee zone. When I arrived, I just said to them: "Have sex with me, then I'll give you some leftovers." I remember that I was there holding a pot in my hand, so I said that they could make a deal with me. When you met a woman, you just needed to say "food, food, sex" or "sex, exchange". A woman would then ask you to give food to her, so the deal was done. Many people had already fled, so it was empty in most of the houses. I just said: "Let's go." Then we did it. In that period, the military situation was much more stable than at the very beginning.

Kita:

Once we found a woman, we'd rape her on the spot. We did house to house searches when we mopped-up the city. Whenever and wherever we found girls, they'd be raped on the spot. Usually those girls would hide under the bed or behind the curtains. When they were discovered, they didn't resist. I didn't know whether the reason for their reaction was fear or something else. As there was no discipline from the commanders, we could do anything we liked. There were no limits. Those Chinese women's faces were all painted with ink or something. I can hardly remember how many women I've raped. The only thing that I really remember was when I caught a mother and her daughter who were fleeing together. The mother said that her daughter was too young, so she begged us to do it to her alone. I called her an idiot and pushed the mother away. Then we raped the two of them with two or three other soldiers. When I raped them, I felt that it might not have been the right thing to do, and I also asked myself that if Japan was being invaded and occupied, what would I do if my daughter or my wife was being raped. However, at that point, I didn't even know if I was going to see tomorrow, so while I was still alive, I did what I wanted to do. This had nothing to do with the emperor's orders. This was just what was done. I have experienced rape in Nanjing and it happened everywhere. There were a lot of empty houses in the city, so I could rape women on the bed in these empty houses. In normal times, I'd also bring rice with me in order to exchange it with mothers for their daughters. Also, some women ran away from the refugee zone and came to see us to exchange themselves for rice. The rice we used for the exchanges were from our grain rations; we gave them about enough to fill a sock each time. When things like this happened on the outskirts of Nanjing, if the Kenpeitai *gendarmerie* caught us, we'd get into trouble, so we killed the women. I only entered Nanjing during the mopping-up, but I did kill people.

Considering these things, I think we were at fault in the Nanjing Massacre. I think I have done evil things.

Nishikido:

Rape was the main thing we were interested in during raids. It happened everywhere we went. It was inevitable. I've seen my comrades holding women by their shoulders and raping them, and even old women were caught. After the rape was over, the women were killed. It was incredibly cruel.

Two days after the occupation of Nanjing, when we went looting in Xiaguan, we took rice and food from houses and also raped women. We opened a suitcase in a house and found a young woman hiding inside. Because her feet had been bound, she couldn't run quickly and we easily caught her. We then stripped off her clothes and raped her on the spot. Because she had only been wearing a pair of trousers and wasn't even wearing any underwear, we raped her with ease. Right after we finished raping her, although she begged us not to, we aimed a gun at her chest and killed her. There was a tacit agreement among us. If the Kenpeitai *gendarmerie* were to turn up and realise what we'd done, it would be regarded as a crime, so we had to kill all of the women we raped. We all knew this, so it's what we did.

It took a long time for public security to improve. The *gendarmerie* ordered all soldiers in the force to line up in a row. Then the women who had been raped were brought over and were ordered to point out who had done it to them. Being handled differently from usual, this wasn't really considered a crime and the soldiers who'd raped women only received a slap on the wrist while the *gendarmerie* officers said: "Don't do it again." There was no punishment or anything else; we just got scolded. So we committed acts of great evil as we pleased and nine soldiers in 10 had raped a Chinese woman, but what's worse, they were even proud of it and often boasted about it.

Most of the troops brought more than 30 women with their unit called "comfort women"; almost all of them were from Korea. Our forces also set up comfort stations. They weren't located in the squadron, but in the wing of the Noda forces. We also set up comfort stations near the Guanghua gate in Nanjing.

We also knew a lot about where women in the city hid. Women, old and young alike, were all raped. To avoid getting into trouble for raping women, we killed them after we were done. Both before and after we went into Nanjing, it was said that you could rape as many women as you liked with no punishment at all. Someone boasted: "After raping a 70 year old woman, my waist became more flexible." There were many women left behind in the city, almost all of them hiding in shelters. Even the establishment of comfort stations didn't help to reduce the rapes. The women in the comfort stations were all Koreans and they were divided into two categories: officer use and general use. Comfort women cost about one or two yen. The general wage of most soldiers was about eight yen. Because I was a corporal, I got paid about 15 yen. Our detachment behaved relatively benevolently in comparison to some of the other more reckless forces. Nearly every soldier committed rape. If they went into the city, they could rape women with ease.

We also went to the refugee resettlement area that only took in women, it may have been the Jinling College. We stood in the house, gesturing towards the women and arbitrarily selecting them, and then we raped the women we'd chosen on the spot. One man in the same force as me, I don't remember his name, had been hit on the head by the defeated Chinese soldiers while he was raping a woman. Since then, whenever someone was raping a woman, there'd be another soldier keeping watch. We did this both during the day and at night. We usually set off in detachments and went out looking for women about a dozen times. It was like this with almost every detachment.

Soldiers would say to each other "help me out and keep watch over here" and "keep an eye out in that direction". They weren't bothered if there was someone else next to them. You'd hear: "Have you finished? It's my turn now." This was just the way it was.

Soldiers threatened to kill women while they dragged them out. The women were afraid of being killed so they immediately agreed to do whatever we said. Although their faces had been painted with the ash from the bottom of pans, you could easily tell they were women. We virtually did nothing else but catch women, and although we felt scared sometimes, they were all we cared about.

Even when I was really hungry, if I saw a woman, I'd immediately feel ready to go.

I was 25 years old when I set sail from Kobe port on a vessel called the *Tonegawa*, which was loaded with about 1,000 soldiers on their way to Nanjing. When we arrived, I took part in the fighting in the Dabie Mountains and at the battle at Hankou. The soldiers around me had all previously been involved in the Nanjing offensive. I heard about the way the 9th division had murdered people, which was to force Chinese people to run on a bridge and then to shoot and kill them from behind.

In China, following our leader's orders, in order to toughen up soldiers like me who had recently arrived from Japan, we were ordered to stab bound Chinese prisoners with bayonets. A Chinese man groaned and let out a cry. The first time I raped a woman was during the Battle of Anlu. While we were suppressing the Chinese people, I participated in arson and looting. I have committed every kind of sin, and I learned all of them from the soldiers who had arrived earlier. I broke into civilian homes and if I saw something valuable, no matter what it was, I would take it. When we were in China, we just looted wherever we went. We did whatever we liked and stole anything we wanted.

We all started looting after we took off our collar badges [different troops had different coloured collar badges]. Even if we were hungry, we'd be full of energy whenever we saw a woman. We immediately chased after and caught women we saw. Everyone in the army did it, so we did too. When the women we'd caught resisted too much, we beat them to death. Generally, we wouldn't let young women leave easily. Those who dared to resist would be beaten, while those who accepted their fate obediently might survive. We usually killed those who desperately resisted.

If one of our comrades was killed, we would be infuriated. We took vengeance on the Chinese people and did cruel things to them. I have no idea how many people we killed. I remember killing a woman with a pistol. We burst into a house and forced the parents to hand over their daughter. They refused to do as we said, so we then shot them to death. The frightened daughter came out to see what had happened. We caught her and raped her. There were six of us there at the time. In the end, the girl appeared to be dead. I didn't feel any pity for her. I thought that Chiang Kai-shek was to blame. When we stole from and raped Chinese people, we always thought that it was Chiang Kai-shek's fault. I always thought that Japan was the country of the gods, so we could do anything we liked. At the time, I always thought about how I was taking the opportunity to do things that others could never do.

During the Greater East Asia War, I had sex with Dutch women in Sumatra, not in a comfort station, but in an asylum for captives. It was with a woman who'd been taken in there. I did the same evil things I did in China. Because the women were all hungry there, I used food to get them to have sex with me. When Japan was defeated and the soldiers were ready to go back home, 20 or 30 women in the asylum were taken so that the authorities could investigate the truth and find out who had done the terrible things to them. Because I shaved my beard, I was able to slip through unpunished. That was truly terrible.

In China, when we entered a village, if we met any resistance, we set it on fire. This was revenge. I remember about 10 or 20 Chinese people being killed like this, the others I struggle to recall. Only one person was shot. The rest were almost all stabbed with bayonets. The dead were almost all men, but there were two or three women too. These men had been killed because they hadn't given us women. It was difficult to stab someone to death with a bayonet. Stabbing them once wouldn't kill them, and sometimes even twice wasn't enough. An hour or so later, we could still see bloody foam bubbling out of their mouths. At this point, I said: "You must hate Chiang Kai-shek and this is all his fault." I didn't think twice about murder. I wasn't the only one to do this; we all did it. We were all very young, so it was normal that we craved women and sex. Our biggest desire was to get a drink of water from home and to hold a Japanese woman. Chinese women gave off a different smell to Japanese women. Taiwanese women had a special Taiwanese smell and Korean women had a special Korean smell. It was probably because of their diets. I've raped more than 10 Chinese women, maybe even 30 or so. I can't remember it clearly. This was what the frontline troops were like. They were relentless. Using the excuse of controlling order, we aimed to catch women. Because we often attacked by surprise, it was too late for the women to run away so we could catch them easily. Our main goal was to take women, so we didn't touch the elderly or children. I only raped young women.

Tadokoro:

The women who were caught were taken to a garrison and the detachment would keep them there.

Until 15 December, it was still an offensive war. I served as a guard from 16 December to 11 January the next year in the area around Nanjing. Comfort stations began to be set up in the outskirts of Nanjing. The station was a small cottage made from straw. It was so narrow that it could only contain a bed.

There were 15 or 16 girls in the comfort station, and they were all from Korea. The soldiers all stood outside waiting in a line. Because I was a junior officer, I went there after the soldiers had all left the station. The price was one and a half to two yen; it was paid for with military currency. We didn't have any Japanese currency with us. When we were training in the detachment, we'd catch women and take them to the garrison, and they were kept by the detachment. After a week or two, we let them go and caught another batch of women to replace them. There were many women in temples. Because temples were usually large, nearby girls would go there to take refuge. All we had to do to get girls was go there. There were also women in civilian homes. If we looted the first floor of a house, we'd find girls hiding there. Girls would hide in piles of straw on the first floor. Their parents would send them food every day.

The detachment was stationed in residential buildings. We brought about three girls with us, and provided them with room and board. We swapped them for other girls if we got bored with them. At first, the girls couldn't stop crying. However, after we took them to the detachment and gave them food, they'd be all right. When we were marching towards Nanjing, we found women and raped them. We just put our backpacks on the ground and raped them on the spot. There were young women among them, as well as old women aged about 50 years old. They were all rural women. Their parents didn't hide them; they usually stayed in storage attics or in temples. When we were marching, I was usually in a bad mood and had low morale. In total, I've raped at least 50 women. Now I recall it, I know that what I've done is inhumane. At the time, I didn't know whether I was going to live or die so I turned into a real beast. High ranking officers wouldn't pay attention to us because they did it themselves too. The gendarmes didn't investigate us. When I was in China I never saw the *gendarmerie*, not even once. As for killing the women after we'd raped them, we never did anything like that and we never heard of anyone else doing it either. I didn't know if it really happened. However, in Shanghai and Nanjing, I often saw dead women. In northern China, I also saw similar sights, and the corpses of the women were always naked. When we attacked Nanjing and Xuzhou, because we were all busy fighting, there was no time for us to rape anyone. At that point, the most important thing was to get something to eat. We desperately searched for rice and eggs every day. Because I was too busy taking care of the captain, I didn't steal food that often.

Miki:

When we were guarding Prince Yasuhiko Asaka's headquarters, our troops specifically went out to look for girls. Because the headquarters were in Jurong, not far from Nanjing, our squad acted in unison with the squadron leader and performed guard duty day and night. Jurong was dozens of kilometres away from Nanjing; I couldn't hear the sound of artillery. Although we were actually staying back in the rear, the newspaper reported: "Announcement: Prince Yasuhiko Asaka Visits the Frontline". Squadron leader Amano was the lieutenant commander. He didn't follow the orders of the wing commander Noda. When he was guarding Prince Yasuhiko Asaka's headquarters, he even slept with a woman overnight. Back then, Amano told us soldiers: "Robbery, rape, arson, murder, you can do whatever you want."

In Jurong, when the other people in our unit were out at night looking for girls, I thought to myself "I can't do something this stupid", so I didn't go out. Suddenly, guns were angrily raised and I fell down in shock. Hearing the sound, Amano shouted: "You're such a dog!" He came over to me. Because I didn't want to go with them to look for girls, he was very angry with me. I remember thinking that if he kept shouting at me, I was going to kill him. But suddenly, someone said from the outside: "There, there's a girl." On hearing the news, Amano was in a good mood once again and wasn't angry any more. He said: "What? A girl! I'm coming." His spirits were suddenly raised once again. If the girl who was brought over was struggling, Amano said to the other soldiers "this suspicious girl needs to be investigated" or something to that effect, and then took the girl away in private. Amano ordered us to catch different women for him every day. The women being caught and brought here were of different ages, some were young and some were already mothers. We let them go after sleeping with them.

After we entered Nanjing, he sent the entire detachment to catch girls. Before the 16th division left Nanjing, all the soldiers in the detachment were forbidden from going out and were all under investigation. Amano was finally sent before a military tribunal for his actions. When we left Nanjing, Amano disappeared. According a friend stationed in a neighbouring village, Amano had been summoned to stand trial in Tokyo after he returned to Japan. But because he denied everything, he eventually got away without punishment.

Drawing Lots to Gang-rape Girls

In Nanjing, we raped girls because we had nothing to do all day. The fact that the soldiers in the forces were casually catching and raping women was no secret to the officers. But they said nothing about it, which is tantamount to tacit approval. Because we were all male, it was torture for us to be away from women for a year or two. We couldn't stand it any longer. If you're a man, then this is just the way it is. If you're a man, it's normal to have sexual desire. Whenever we broke into the people's houses, we always found women hidden everywhere. Some were hidden at home and some were hidden in the rice paddies. Almost all of the women painted their faces dark with grey ash collected from the bottom of pots. Chinese women were always dirty because they never washed. But in big cities like Nanjing, many of the girls were very clean and pretty. We just needed to say: "Let's take a look at you." This really meant we wanted them to show us their genitals and we used Chinese to do so. Almost all of the women would obediently roll up their clothes and show us their bodies.

All of the girls fled to where they hung the International Red Cross flag. There were no girls on the street, so we searched for girls on the outskirts of Nanjing during our mopping-up operations. When we caught the girls, we raped them in the villages dotted around Nanjing.

Groups made up of several people looked for girls together and whenever they caught one, they'd push the girl to the ground and draw lots to determine the order to rape her. The first to rape them had to clean the ash on the girl's face before he sexually abused her. Five or six people took turns and the girls later foamed at the mouth because the soldiers were so passionate with their strong and healthy libidos. The girls trembled all over out of fear of being killed. Another lady wearing nice Chinese clothes, she looked like the wife of a KMT senior official, took off her clothes without any resistance when we told her to show us her genitals. We raped her without any opposition. Maybe she was scared of being killed. When it was finished, we thanked her and shook her hands to say goodbye. As these soldiers were young, not knowing if they were going to live to see tomorrow, they were desperate to sleep with women. Of course, it was always fun to be with a lady. The people at the top took care of the soldiers' needs and brought them Koreans and comfort women.

I've heard that after the soldiers finished that some would kill the girl to conceal the truth. I also heard that some Chinese men and women were ordered to have sex while the Japanese watched and teased them.

When girls aged 19 or 20 were taken, their parents came too, kowtowing and begging us not to rape their daughters. But it was all in vain because the soldiers were so desperate to have sex and no one cared about them. Five soldiers or so forced down a girl who was a virgin. She fainted and started foaming at the mouth. Her parents just begged us to stop, but nothing could stop us. I did this. It was a tragedy. All the Japanese soldiers did things like this, whether they admit it or not. If there were 10 people in a squad, then 10 people did it. The longer the war went on, the more you wanted a woman.

Active duty soldiers didn't have much experience in that way so they behaved fairly well. However, the enlisted soldiers did the opposite as they were all married and missed sleeping with women. In fact, because of this, they were tricked into fighting for the emperor.

Ota:

We caught a guy who made a living making tofu and we got him to look for "beauties".

Generally, the girls had to listen to all of us because if they resisted, they died. If you encountered someone who had the strength to rebel, they were thought of as belonging to a women's detachment so they'd also be killed. There were also some who wouldn't be killed on the spot, instead, they'd be told to carry their belongings to be brought elsewhere to be raped. Even if the captain found out about this, he'd just lightly say "Don't be evil, friends." They'd laugh, and because the captain was a man, he knew what his men were doing. We replied: "Yes sir." We then let almost all of the girls go home after we were finished.

Chinese people served us by doing the cooking. When our detachment caught a man and two women, we got them to cook and do the laundry. The man we caught made a living making tofu. He was terrified and his body trembled. He desperately begged us to spare his life and showed that he was educated by writing "spare my life" on a piece of paper. We felt that this man may be useful, so we gave him an armband with "public" written on it and let him stay in the unit to do errands.

The man knew exactly where to go to steal pork, chicken, blankets, clothes and so on. Because he was a businessman, he knew everything that was happening on the streets. Wearing the Japanese armband, he easily stole watches, meat and more. We were the envy of other detachments. He also brought us a tofu pot to cook for us.

We then got him to go to a silk shop, stealing clothes and quilts for us. The man also called several of his associates, selling the goods he'd stolen from the shop. Despite brazenly stealing valuable goods from the Chinese, he seemed in quite good spirits. Although the people who owned the store were very poor, we still got the benefits.

We wrote "beauties" on a piece of paper and gave it to him, gesturing for him to go and bring some girls back. Before leaving, the man immediately said: "Good, very good." In general, when referring to girls, "good" meant fine and "very good" meant beautiful. He went to the refugee area and soon brought over two beautiful girls, both of whom were students wearing skirts. They gave each of them a room and got them do the laundry during the day, while at night, of course, they weren't allowed to go back and had to stay here for us to play with. As we were young, it was inevitable for us to have sex. There were dozens of units there, so two girls were enough. They were just put in our unit and we didn't allow them to go out. Japanese soldiers were everywhere outside and they knew that if they failed to escape that they'd be killed, so they wouldn't try. I also went along with the man to the silk shop to carry silk and shiny clothes for the girls to wear, trying to make them happy. Other troops were jealous of us and also took girls, locking them up. When we took girls in Nanjing, they painted their faces with soot to look old. But we still found the young ones and as they were our enemies' women, we decided to rape them.

When hearing words like "death", "open" and "show your breasts", women knew what was going to happen. When we took away girls, their parents or grandparents would beg for their lives. We'd stab their relatives to death or set them on fire. We then went back. I heard that if you didn't obey orders, you would be sent to a military tribunal. When we entered Nanjing, the people there were very poor.

Our team was equipped with light machine guns, so we were involved in localised operations, firing our guns under the cover of the infantry. We would be punished if we didn't fire. We had to kill the enemy first or they'd kill us; we had to kill to survive. As long as you had the courage to kill someone, you could be awarded and get a gold medal. If you died, you had no chance of getting one. So, we tried to kill as many enemies as possible. On the 13th, along the Yangtze River, when the rifle team began to open fire, the light machine guns fired instantly too. After that, someone would shout: "The next batch is here, get the people lined up and killed." I felt I was taking revenge for my fallen comrades, I was so worked up that I even killed women and children. I thought Nanjing was the capital of the enemy and we'd worked very hard, and many of my comrades had died in battle. It was time for them to taste hardship. Because of our dead brothers-in-arms, it was inevitable that we'd hate the Chinese with a burning hatred.

The Nanjing Massacre happened, there's no doubt about it. Those who deny that it happened just arrived later, and they'd only seen the conflict from Tokyo. Our soldiers had actually seen it.

Now China and Korea have raised the issue of compensation and it's indeed true that too many poor people died in the war and Japan made them suffer brutally. We should be blamed. The Nanjing Massacre happened and we killed thousands of Chinese people along the Yangtze River.

Sawada:
Women were the primary objective when looting. Wherever the troops went, from the second they first burst into Nanjing, they completely sacked the

city. This included rape, seizing goods and materials, murder and more. All the troops were guilty of this.

Rape was very popular. We began looting after the campaign ended. Some of our soldiers killed Chinese people and threw them into the river, and some were thrown into wells. There were a couple of people who were sent to take women, but they were killed. While women didn't usually appear at the frontline, they could be seen everywhere during our raids. Due to the battle ending, they had returned home. Women often hid in dirt. Sometimes when we lifted the lid on water barrels, we'd see a woman hiding inside. Our soldiers often found them in these sorts of places and raped them. During the Nanjing offensive, whenever we came across a haystack we'd set fire to it, which forced a bunch of women to run out. The battle had turned into total war, so everything looked as you could imagine. Unlike two or three day battles, we had plenty of time and everything else, so we could do whatever we wanted. The troops stationed in the area immediately went to a nearby village and raided it. The primary goal in raids was women. We were all men, about 20 years old, so you can imagine what went on.

Comfort stations were considered necessary facilities for soldiers. As soon as the troops were stationed, comfort women were brought over. If they weren't brought over, the locals would bear the brunt of our frustrations. I think they brought them in out of fear of bad things happening. Comfort stations were established within 10 to 15 days after the troops had settled in the area. They were set up in booming places like Nanjing. I don't know if there were any in Xiaguan. Although our unit didn't do anything like that in the city, I think there were such places close to the Osaka unit. Despite that, I didn't know much about this myself. Troops generally built these sorts of places. Comfort stations were everywhere, and you could hardly tell which units had established them. Among the comfort women, there were Koreans and Japanese. Once the security improved, Japanese women were sent to the troops in a stream. People from the army would go to the comfort stations almost every day. We didn't have a comfort station in our squadron. I was convinced that the comfort women had been brought in by the units in charge of comfort stations. I had no idea where they had got those women.

Kawanaka:

Two or three people were sent to take girls while a group of people went to take food.

When the fighting began, each person carried the 10 days of rations they had been assigned. In addition to rice, we also had nonessential food, so it was no easy task to travel with it. I had a horse to help, which made it actually rather easy. During the battle in Nanjing, detachments were sent to loot food. We sometimes caught chicken and pigs, and we survived by seizing local goods.

There was some rice in Nanjing, but most was unhusked rice. We still had to take it to eat. After capturing the city, the distribution system among the troops improved. During this period, we survived by looting pork and chicken and eating food delivered by the army. For goods, we went in groups, while for girls, only two to three people would go. Although these people knew where they were hiding, they occasionally got ambushed. Even some who'd had impressive military achievements died in these sorts of incidents. To stop them from dying in vain, we would attack the defeated soldiers when we saw them. When we began to collect goods and materials, I had an opportunity when I saw more than 20 women hiding in a haystack by a house. However, I did nothing and left.

Each wing of the armed forces set up comfort stations. Without formal establishments like comfort stations, we'd go and take women and do bad things to them, so comfort stations were necessary. We didn't stay there long, so I don't know much about Nanjing. However, I went there before going to Tianjin. Because we were all young, there was a fleeting feeling that you just couldn't control. Of course, everyone's situation was somewhat different. On the front line, we ate and slept together as no one knew if we would see tomorrow. Whether they were new recruits or soldiers who'd been in military service for two years, everyone joined the raiding parties.

Shiyama:

Most of the soldiers who raped women were married. We went from Shanghai to Nanjing by boat along the Yangtze. We got into Nanjing over the hills. We pulled the horses off the boat on the quay and rode to the city. We then went there on a big steamboat. When I got there, I didn't see any dead bodies and Nanjing had already fallen for a long time.

In Nanjing, we were responsible for guard duty outside the city's military academy. Outside of the city, we later arranged defences for the aircraft. I worked as an aircraft guard, climbing up to the hill where the military academy was located.

As no one lived in the city, keeping watch felt unnerving. I'd heard that there were still some enemies so there was a fear of being killed. At the morning meeting, the 9th division had issued an order making the refugee sector off limits.

Some people still went there to take women. Maybe because the soldiers who were married found it harder to curb their desires so they raped women.

These sorts of soldiers could be found in the cavalry. They grabbed women and raped them at home. I even saw this happen in the middle of the road when someone in our squadron attacked a woman. The division had orders not to rape anyone. I'd heard rumours that the *gendarmerie* had also entered the city, but this ultimately didn't appear to be true. Women were killed after being raped. I heard that such incidents had also happened in our division, and I also heard stories being proudly told, with one saying that he'd been spotted by the Chinese when raping a Chinese woman in the middle of the road.

Because we were new recruits, we didn't go to the refugee zone, but we still took meat and other food. I was warned of ambushes and told not to go alone. Since we had to eat, we went to a farmer's house to take chickens, corn and rice, which were the army's provisions before the main supplies arrived. The unit captain often said: "Women are not to be flirted with." Women were everywhere and hid in civilian homes. One time, we entered a home that was occupied and the women had painted their faces with ash. Because of the ash, they looked like elderly ladies, but we could tell who the young ones were. Once, four or five people went to a village to take goods. The women were scared and stood still because the enemy had come. We gang-raped the women in the house.

Oyama:

I was a new recruit, responsible for looking for women. I also raped them. We were doing things out in the rear. After the frontline had moved on, we searched for hidden people. As a result, there were lots of women wearing dirty clothes, trying to make themselves look ugly on purpose. I saw some girls being killed by soldiers once they were found. I often saw naked female bodies. I remember one in the shape of the Chinese character for "big" [大] with something like a bamboo spear thrust into her genitals. When I saw things like this, I knew we were doing some very bad things indeed.

After we were stationed there, I also looked for comfort women and raped them on the spot. Some in the army said it would be very dangerous for us once others found out, even if it had just been a trivial crime. As a result, soldiers would kill girls after raping them. I heard that some troops killed them under the pretext that they were politically opposed to the Japanese forces. If a woman was suspected of hiding weapons, or looked suspicious, their house would be burned down. From Shanghai to Nanjing, we were behind the frontline, so all we saw along the road were the ashes of burnt villages.

In Nanjing, we were stationed in detachments for about a month. Nanjing was the capital of China, quite a prosperous city with silk, quilts and everything else. After the homeowners fled, they left some of their belongings behind. We collected everything we could eat. We took turns in the unit to take women or get food. We also went looting in rural areas. Although some people lived there, nobody ever showed any resistance. Even the men were afraid of Japanese soldiers, kneeling down and begging for mercy. I was a new recruit, so it was my job to find girls. I'd be scolded if I didn't so that was that. Orders from seniors could never be disobeyed, so I tried to look for girls. In houses and in other buildings, they hid behind brick walls. They also hid in bamboo or hay fields. They never hid in a room in the house, but behind brick walls. If you brought back two women, one had to be given to the squadron leader. The other one would be gang-raped by 10 people taking it in turns, the head of the unit going first. We were new recruits so we didn't have a say. After they were gang-raped, the girls would be killed.

I fought in the war and was detained in Siberia. The Japanese don't feel comfortable with the war. Japan's military did whatever they wanted and went too far. We had to work in places like Siberia. People who committed crimes got the same punishments.

We should not wage any wars.

Morita:
The girls were dragged into the squadron's private comfort station. When the massacre happened, I was in the 3rd brigade headquarters. I'd spent a month marching towards the Guanghua gate in Nanjing. Skirmishes were fought along the way. The fighting wasn't interesting and the enemies just ran away. It was the middle of December when we arrived in Nanjing. However, because we had advanced on the Guanghua gate so quickly, the supplies had been unable to keep up and were delayed. Rice was all we had after two or three days, but we never thought that the food still wouldn't come after seven to ten days later. Under these circumstances, we had to ask the soldiers to loot. When we went into farmers' houses, they were abandoned. However, we did manage to find girls. The residents were very honest and didn't resist.

We also took the girls. The farming girls climbed onto roofs. We could tell whether there were girls in a family by looking at their furniture. Whenever we went to collect food, we were looking for girls too. Because of the language problem, we didn't encounter any strong resistance. The girls trembled. Each unit acted alone on these missions. Some units brought over girls and secretly set up comfort stations. A brigade would basically have about 10 girls, all of whom were managed under their rules. I had no idea where they came from, but I knew that there were lots of Korean girls. In Chunhua, we caught girls when we were looting and didn't have any comfort stations. We raped them when we caught them.

Kodera:
A squadron leader went strolling around the streets, and because the boss acted like this, we could do whatever we wanted. I like women. Soldiers brought over the woman they'd caught and said: "Let's play." Even if she didn't want to, we just raped her somewhere in private. Veterans like us committed a lot of crimes, but there were also soldiers who never did because they were incredibly religious. The soldiers came from all walks of life.

It's hard not to feel sick when reading the descriptions by the Japanese veterans above. However, this is the ugly and brutal truth of the Japanese invaders' behaviour.

A Unique Report on the Atrocities

In addition to China, archives in the US and the UK and universities in other countries hold a large amount of valuable historical information about the Nanjing Massacre, most of which was documented by news reporters, missionaries and expatriate businessmen who stayed in the city. Most of them were China's international allies in the security zone and they protected millions of Chinese refugees by staying in the city and risking their own lives. I extracted and compiled records from the *Japanese Atrocities Report*, which describes the rape and murder of women committed by the Japanese as witnessed by China's international allies.

The historical archives report is based on entries written in a very straight forward manner, using reports made up of several people's collections of protests against the Japanese. Therefore, some of the entries are not in chronological order. The report in full includes incidences of murder, arson, rape and gang-rape. It includes more than 400 cases related to rape. Due to space limitations, I have chosen just a few entries to give you an understanding of the Japanese atrocities, which are below. Note that the missing numbers generally refer to cases where Japanese soldiers robbed Chinese people:

No. 4: On the evening of 15 December, seven Japanese soldiers broke into the library of the University of Nanjing, abducted seven women and raped three of them on the spot.

No. 5: On the evening of 14 December, Japanese soldiers broke into the houses of Chinese civilians, assaulted the women and sometimes abducted them, which led to a severe panic. Yesterday, hundreds of women were transferred to the school of arts and science. Meiqiao and two others had to stay overnight in the university to protect the 3,000 women and young girls.

No. 10: At midday on 14 December, some Japanese soldiers broke into a house on Jianyin Lane, abducted four girls, raped them and released them two hours later.

No. 12: On the evening of 14 December, 11 Japanese soldiers broke into a house on Jianyin Lane and took turns raping four women.

No. 15: On 15 December, some Japanese soldiers broke into a house on Hankou Road, raped a young married woman and abducted three women. Two men, the husbands of two of the three women, were tragically shot.

No. 18: On the evening of 15 December, a large number of Japanese soldiers broke into a dormitory in the University of Nanjing and raped 30 women on the spot. Some of them were raped by six Japanese soldiers, who were taking turns.

No. 20: On the evening of 16 December, seven Japanese soldiers leapt in through the window and terrorised the refugees. The university staff did not give them money, goods or girls so they stabbed the members of staff and raped two women on the spot.

No. 22: On the evening of 16 December, Japanese soldiers brutally attacked the policemen near the university and ordered them to supply them with girls.

No. 28: At 4pm on 16 December, the Japanese soldiers broke into a house at 11 Mogan Road and raped women there.

No. 33: On 17 December, the Japanese soldiers broke into 5 Luojia Road, raped four women there and stole a bike, bedding and other goods. We rushed over there and the Japanese soldiers scurried away like frightened rats.

No. 37: On 17 December, on Xiaotaoyuan Road behind my house, Japanese soldiers raped a woman and stabbed her. If she can be treated, she may be saved. Her mother was also hit on the head.

No. 39: On 17 December, a string of reports came in about rapes committed by Japanese soldiers right in front of the University of Nanjing and near Mr Tianxiang's residence on Ertiao Lane.

No. 40: On 17 December, on Mianlang Road, just opposite Luojia Road, Japanese soldiers dragged a young girl into a room and raped her.

No. 41: On 17 December, near the judicial court, Japanese soldiers assaulted a young girl and then stabbed her in the stomach.

No. 42: On 17 December, Japanese soldiers dragged away a woman in her forties and raped her.

No. 43: On 17 December, many Japanese soldiers raped two girls near Jiansanyuan Road.

No. 44: On the evening of 15 December, in Santiao Lane, a gang of Japanese soldiers broke into civilian homes and raped several women.

No. 45: On 17 December, Japanese soldiers dragged many women into a primary school by Wutai mountain, raped them overnight and didn't release them until the following morning.

No. 46: On 17 December, in the Wu family's garden, three men were killed and two women were taken.

No. 47: At 8am on 16 December, two Japanese officers and two Japanese soldiers broke into Ganheyan Lane and kicked out the men. The nearby women tried to run away but the women inside who could not escape were gang-raped. A Japanese soldier left his shirt behind in the room.

No. 50: At around 11am on 17 December, Yao Qingcai, who lived at 1 Shanxi Road, came to report that the Japanese soldiers had broken into his house and taken his son, Yao Xiucai (the deputy director of the metropolitan police branch), and his 19 year old granddaughter.

No. 52: On 17 December, two Japanese soldiers broke into the house at 9 Mogan Road where they took away Wang Bosheng's son, daughter-in-law and aunt.

No. 53: At 3pm on 17 December, Japanese soldiers raped three girls in the refugees' house at 10 Dafang Lane. One of the women was shot and seriously wounded.

No. 55: At dusk on 18 December, 450 horrified women fled to our office for shelter. Many of the women had been raped.

No. 57: 16 December, Japanese soldiers took seven girls aged 16 to 21 to the military academy and released five of them. As reported on 18 December, each of them had been raped six or seven times every day. On 17 December, Japanese soldiers scaled the walls, broke into a room, abducted two girls and released them 30 minutes later.

No. 58: 17 December, Rabe reported that about 15 Japanese soldiers had broken into his house. Some scaled the walls, unsheathed their bayonets, and intimidated and robbed money and documents from his servant Han Xianglin. He issued a list of the lost documents and sent it to Squadron Leader Nagai. Squadron Leader Nagai kindly wrote a notice and pasted it to Rabe's door to prohibit Japanese soldiers from arbitrarily intruding. Rabe was a German and four Nazi Party banners flew on his roof. However, the notice had no effect. When Rabe returned at 6pm, two Japanese soldiers had broken in and one of them was undressing to rape a girl. Rabe told them to get out and they scaled the wall and escaped. The Japanese soldiers stole a car from Rabe's house and left a note reading: "Thanks for your valuable gift! Sato from Japan." Rabe asked for an official receipt but was refused. The car was worth about 300 yuan.

No. 59: 18 December, Squadron Leader Nagai paid a visit to Rabe's residence, the chairman of the International Committee, at 10 Xiaotaoyuan Road. Four Japanese soldiers then broke into the house opposite Rabe's and one of them started to rape a woman. Hearing the call for help, Nagai rushed over there, slapped the soldier's face and told him to get out. The other three escaped when they saw him coming in.

No. 60: At 10.30am on 19 December, Mr Hitz reported that he found two Japanese soldiers who were trying to rape some women in an air-raid shelter near Ninghai Road. There were about 20 women in the shelter. When he heard the women's cry for help, he immediately rushed into the shelter and drove away the Japanese soldiers.

No. 61: At about 10am on 19 December, I (Dr Smythe) went for a meeting regarding the developments. After we discussed the disaster, we went to Jinling College to see how the refugees had spent the previous night. When we arrived there, we found that three girls had been raped by Japanese soldiers the previous night. One of them had been gang-raped by three Japanese soldiers in a house next to the school gate. When we approached the gate, the Japanese soldiers were still there. At that time, Ms Wu Baolan came over to the school gate, closely followed by three Japanese soldiers and a military officer on a horse. We immediately stopped the Japanese soldiers and asked Ms Wu to get into our car. The Japanese officer on the horse angrily blocked our car in an attempt to stop our advance. But the horse was afraid of our car, so we left the gate, took Ms Wu to the Japanese embassy and asked them where Ms Wu would be safe. Eventually, she went to help in Gulou Hospital.

On 18 December, a Japanese soldier seized some kerosene from a child on Ninghai Road and the boy was lashed severely; a pig was stolen at 6 Pingcang Alley; five Japanese soldiers stole a multitude of horses; several girls were assaulted at 12 Jardine Road. A 17 year old girl was gang-raped by seven Japanese soldiers in a teahouse and died on the 18th; three Japanese soldiers raped four girls from 6pm to 10pm last night; several Japanese soldiers raped a girl at 5 Mogan Road; the Japanese soldiers took three girls last night from Jinling College and released them this morning, all looking incredibly gaunt. A girl died after being raped by three Japanese soldiers. Imprisonment and rape happened repeatedly in the vicinity of the Yinyang camp.

Also on 18 December, 504 refugees were taken in at 83 and 85 Guangdong Road. Groups of Japanese soldiers went looting repeatedly from the 13th to the 17th. They used trucks to take young girls at night and just released them the following morning. More than 30 women were raped and women and children cried all night. Words can never describe such misery.

On 19 December, Japanese soldiers broke into the house of the district health director six or seven times, situated on 59 Beiping Road. Two days earlier, two girls had been raped and one nearly died as a result. The following day, the Japanese soldiers took another girl, looting all of their belongings from the refugee asylum.

At 2.30pm on 20 December while a gentleman was preparing to collect two girls from the classroom for school work, a mechanic hurriedly arrived reporting that the girls had been found by the Japanese soldiers and were about to be raped. We immediately went to 13 Pingcang Alley and saw three Japanese soldiers raping two naked women. We stopped them right away and the two Japanese soldiers fled hurriedly with another one looking for the janitor to check his hands, back and feet because they suspected he was a soldier. The two women who had been raped quickly dressed and ran into the gentleman's car to go to Jinling College.

On the night of 17 December, a search team led by a Japanese officer forced all the staff at the shelter in Jinling College to gather at the gate. About an hour later, the officer tore the files he had found during a search to pieces. Meanwhile, Japanese soldiers broke into the shelter and took 11 women.

At 7.30pm on 19 December, two Japanese soldiers raped a 17 year old girl who was nine months pregnant. At 9pm, the pregnant girl started to feel waves of pain and she gave birth at midnight. At 2am, the mother was sent to hospital for insanity, but the baby was born healthy.

At 3pm on 20 December, three Japanese officers broke into the Hankou Road Primary School refugee shelter office. The staff tried to communicate with them via an interpreter, but they were ignored and asked to leave. After that, the officers raped two women.

On 20 December, Japanese soldiers broke into Ting's house, who was a member of the International Committee, which they shared with Pastor Meche. Shilov was put in charge of electricity recovery, while Ziyal was responsible for repairing cars for the Japanese. The Japanese soldiers raped several women in front of Meche's Chinese friends, most of whom were from Christian families in Xiaguan. They were horrified when they saw the scale of the brutality.

On the afternoon of 21 December, about 100 women living in the neighbourhood flocked to our office to hide last night. However, all of them were raped.

At 3 o'clock on 23 December, two Japanese soldiers broke into the shelters at the elementary school on Hankou Road. They searched the property and raped a female member of staff, Miss Huang. We immediately reported this to the special military police. By the time the military police arrived at the shelter, the Japanese soldiers had already escaped. They took Miss Huang's testimony as a witness. At dusk, several Japanese soldiers came and gang-raped Mrs Wang's daughter. At about 7 o'clock, another three Japanese soldiers came and raped two girls, one of whom was only 13 years old.

At about 10.30am on 2 January, a Japanese soldier broke into Liu Peishen's house at 5 Liujiangxiang Lane, which was home to seven people. The Japanese soldiers repeatedly assaulted Liu's wife as she tried to get away. Liu Peishen punched a Japanese soldier out of anger. The Japanese soldiers ran away filled with hate. At 4pm, the Japanese soldiers returned with guns. Their neighbours knelt down and begged in vain. Liu Peishen was then shot dead in the kitchen.

According to the report on 3 January, six women had been taken by the Japanese soldiers several days earlier at 6 Qianyinxiang Lane to nominally wash the officers' clothes. One of them went to Gulou Hospital on 30 December. According to her report, the Japanese soldiers took them to somewhere in town, which seemed like a hospital for wounded soldiers. The women washed clothes during the day and were raped at night. The older ones were raped 10 to 20 times every night. The younger and more beautiful ones were raped up to 40 times every night. On 2 January, two Japanese soldiers kidnapped a woman from a deserted school and stabbed her in 10 places, stabbing her neck four times, her arm once, her face once and her back four times. The Japanese soldiers thought that this was enough to kill her and left her there. Later, someone found her and sent her to hospital. She might recover, but her neck may never work properly again.

On 8 January, four Japanese soldiers broke into Yuan's house and raped three women (21 years old, 25 years old and 29 years old respectively). If they got bored, the Japanese shot them dead.

On the afternoon of 25 January, a woman came to Gulou Hospital. According to her report, she had lived with her husband in a straw shed near the Bible teachers training school in the refugee camp. On 13 December, the Japanese soldiers took her husband away and took her somewhere in the south of the town, raping her seven to 10 times every day. They only let her rest at night. She'd been infected with three kinds of sexually transmitted diseases: syphilis, gonorrhoea and chancres. Five days ago, she was released and went back to the refugee camp.

On 29 January, a young married woman (22 years old) went from the refugee camp to her home at 3 San Pailou Street and was raped by the Japanese soldiers twice. Several days earlier, her husband was stabbed and wounded by the Japanese soldiers when he went back home.

On 30 January, a 16 year old girl from Yao Caizhen went to Gulou Hospital to visit friends. When she got close to Gulou, she was dragged into the square by two Japanese soldiers and raped.

On 28 January, three Japanese soldiers broke into Song's house on 1

Dashamao Lane. They robbed all their clothes and raped a young girl. The next day, the Japanese soldiers came back and wanted a young girl from the house. They said that that they didn't have one so the Japanese soldiers burned the house down.

On 31 January, in the lane next to a seafood shop on Caixia Street, a woman who was more than 60 years old and a girl aged 20 years old were raped by Japanese soldiers. They were then stabbed in the vulva with bayonets and died in agony.

On 7 February it was reported that Japanese soldiers had shot and killed three men and a woman behind a booth at about 5 o'clock on 6 February. Before noon today, the neighbours of the deceased came to our office to verify the incident. At 4.30pm, a girl came to report that the dead woman was her mother and begged for our help. Her mother had left the shelter several days earlier, taking all the cash to go and live elsewhere. She had hoped that she could take the money from her mother's corpse.

On 5 February, three Japanese soldiers broke into a house belonging to an old woman with the surname Zheng in San Pailou Street. One soldier guarded the door and the other two took turns raping her. This old woman was more than 60 years old. After that, a Japanese soldier forced the old woman to lick the filth off his penis. They stabbed her grandson twice because he was crying so much.

The report above shows the scale of the crimes committed by the Japanese. But reading the victims' personal descriptions of rape, gang-rape and murder shows the individual horrors suffered as a result of the these cruel and violent atrocities.

The Victims' Personal Descriptions

Rape is always a traumatic event that we avoid discussing, especially so with the use of relentless rape and gang-rape as a weapon. This was the case with the victims of the Nanjing Massacre. After a couple of years, it was still not discussed. However, in order to understand the scale of the crimes committed by the Japanese in the Nanjing Massacre, in the 1940s, 1980s, 1990s and early in this century, the Chinese government and people have interviewed many of the rape and gang-rape victims to ascertain how many incidents of rape occurred when the Japanese occupied the city. Thousands of oral materials from the Chinese women who were raped or gang-raped have been preserved and collected by the Nanjing government, the Nanjing Massacre

Memorial Hall, the Second Historical Archives of China and Nanjing University. These materials are incredibly valuable as they prove the crimes committed by the Japanese army. Even more commendable is the fact that these victims overcame their shame and bravely revealed the Japanese soldiers' atrocities to the world. I have selected several victims' oral accounts below. Here, I would like to express my most sincere respect to them. When I read these accounts, I can't help but cry and join them in their anger.

> My name is Zheng Guiying. I was 16 years old when the Nanjing Massacre began and I lived on Dengfu mountain, near the Rain Flower Terrace. There were three people in my family who lived there: my uncle, my husband and I. Another uncle and my aunt had been separated from us.
>
> When the Japanese army entered the town, we ran away from them to Shazhouyu, a suburb of Nanjing. A couple of people, including me, took shelter in a simple large shed that was in a dry depression in the ground. One day, a group of Japanese soldiers arrived. They shouted across the river and wanted us to row our boats to collect them. After we picked them up, the Japanese soldiers sat on a stool and laughed. I didn't know why they'd come. At first, I wasn't really afraid. When a Japanese soldier grabbed a girl and took her into a room and raped her, I did start to feel afraid. The Japanese soldiers took katanas with them and had guns in their hands. A Japanese soldier shot into the air, which terrified us. After that, we fled from Shazhouyu to the mountains. The girl who had been raped by the Japanese soldier cried while she ran on the road. She looked so forlorn. The Japanese soldiers later went to another small valley. Eight of the nine people in the valley were shot dead. Why? When the Japanese soldiers entered the valley, the girls in the valley had all escaped. When the Japanese soldiers couldn't find any girls, they began to kill people. The person who'd survived told us to get away quickly, which scared us, so we ran to the mountain.
>
> We hid there for almost the entire winter. We didn't come back until the next year [1938]. A couple of houses in the valley had been burned down and more than 20 people were living in half of a shabby room that hadn't fallen in. I was a short 16 year old girl. I wore ragged leggings with ash on my face. One day, a car filled with Japanese soldiers arrived and stopped on the road side. A group of Japanese soldiers approached us with katanas. They were all young, a little older than 20. A Japanese soldier tried to catch me. A young friend in the valley called Xiaoerzi said to the Japanese soldier that: "She's only 10 years old! She's just a child!" At that point, several girls hid under the bed. The Japanese soldiers saw that there were people under the bed and went to catch them. I seized the opportunity to run away. Those girls weren't as lucky as me.

One afternoon, I was walking on the muddy road and ran across a Japanese soldier. He grabbed me, but I couldn't do anything apart from say to him: "I'm scared sir!" He dragged me to an empty house and I knew exactly what he was going do to me. I had to do as he wanted and nobody could save me. I was so scared and we went back towards my home. I arrived at the rundown house. There were some women hiding there and my grandmother was among them. She begged for mercy for me from the Japanese soldier, who then slapped her twice. The Japanese soldier then fired his gun once and left.

Later, another group of Japanese soldiers arrived. They dragged a girl into a room and raped her. The people outside the room were all scared and didn't dare try to save her. An old woman begged a Japanese soldier to let the girl go because the girl was her granddaughter. The Japanese soldier then angrily hit the old woman. They went away after they'd raped the girl. We hid in the mountain. Unfortunately, we were once again found by the Japanese soldiers. We were too scared to risk our lives by running away and all we could do was wet ourselves. The girl who'd just been raped was taken and raped again by the Japanese soldiers. A Japanese soldier wanted me to walk away, but the girl wanted me to come with her. I was too scared and I ran away. I trod on victims' bloody corpses in a ditch and climbed over two mountains to escape.

The Japanese soldiers killed many people; one was called Li and another was called Pang. I don't remember the others. They were all killed. The Japanese soldiers tied many people up with rope and shot them with machine guns. Some women were killed after they were raped. An old woman was pushed into the river after a Japanese soldier raped her in the snow. She struggled back to the bank and the Japanese soldiers laughed and pushed her into the river again. The mother of one of my aunts hid in an air-raid shelter. The Japanese soldiers used smoke so she couldn't breathe. They dragged her in and out three times and tortured her over and over again.

There were two or three mass graves somewhere near Pude Temple by the Rain Flower Terrace. The graves were the size of a house. I saw the Red Cross burying many civilians with my own eyes, with children among them.

— Zheng Guiying: Female, born on 9 November 1921 In December 1937, she was 16 years old. She lived on Dengfu motuntain, near the Rain Flower Terrace.

My name is Tang Runzhen and I'm 75 years old. I lived at 2 Nantai Lane. There were six people in my family, my elder brother, my little brother, my sister, my parents and me. My father made a living knitting cloth with a soft nap.

My elder brother's name was Tang Zhengnian and he would be 75 years old. He was a bricklayer. After the Japanese soldiers entered the town, he was at the entrance to Nantai Lane. He was caught and stabbed to death. After it happened, I scrambled to the pavilion and hid there until the Japanese soldiers went away. Our families were all afraid of the Japanese army and didn't dare bury my brother. Later, the Red Cross moved his corpse away and buried it.

Another three of my neighbours were stabbed to death like my brother. One of them was surnamed Ming. His mother had been assaulted by the Japanese army in the countryside. Another one had made a living by pulling a rickshaw. She was about 40 years old. I don't remember the others.

Other people in our courtyard were killed by Japanese soldiers. One wrote his name and address on the wall of the courtyard in his own blood: Yanliao Lane. Dying people begged others to deliver messages to their families.

One day, we ran there to find the dead man's family. We finally found the relatives of the victim, who lived at 11 Yanliao Lane. They came and carted him off. It turned out that he'd ran into the courtyard as soon as he saw the Japanese soldiers coming. However, he was stabbed repeatedly by the Japanese soldiers, and wrote his name and address with his blood on the wall before he died. Some characters were not clear, but the words Yanliao Lane could be read.

In the refugee camp along the Gan River, I saw Japanese soldiers take two sisters away. They were about 16 or 17 years old and were both raped. The elder sister was killed and the little sister was released soon after. She's still alive and lives in Nantai Lane.

I also know that there was a Japanese comfort station in Tieguan Lane. It was a two storey small villa. The prostitutes there were all Japanese.

On the night my brother was killed, our families escaped to the refugee camp along the Gan River and lived in a staircase. We lived off of congee. The Japanese soldiers sometimes climbed over the wall to find Chinese girls. I once saw a woman get caught; she's still alive now.

— TANG RUNZHEN: FEMALE, BORN ON **31 MARCH 1925**, HAN CHINESE, HOMETOWN IN JIANGDU *SHE WAS 12 YEARS OLD IN DECEMBER 1937 AND LIVED AT 2 NANTAI LANE.*

I was 13 years old when the Japanese arrived in Nanjing and lived at 8 Fuxin Bridge. There were seven people in my family: my grandmother, grandfather, my mother, my brothers and me. Before the Japanese soldiers entered the city, our parents took us to Taowu, Jiangning County. Our grandmother was more than 60 years old and was left to look after our house. The Japanese soldiers came and demanded young women. She said that there weren't any there. The

Japanese soldiers then kicked her and punched her in her mouth. She later ran to the refugee zone. She told us what happened when we came from Jiangning to Nanjing.

There were many dead people in front of our house. There was a granny who was more than 60 years old, called Chen. Her son was a cobbler. She'd been raped by the Japanese. A bottle had been forced into her genitals. Her corpse was later left by the side of the river. There was a man everyone called Xiasantuzi who was about 40 to 50 years old. When he was guarding his house, the Japanese asked him for young women. They didn't find any, so they stabbed him to death.

A Japanese soldier also raped a woman called Huang and asked a man named Zhu Qi to have sex with her. Zhu kowtowed and didn't want to do it. The Japanese soldier stabbed him and his blood went everywhere. He was lucky not to die.

— DING BOXIANG: MALE, BORN 12 OCTOBER, 1924, HAN CHINESE, NATIVE OF NANJING *HE WAS 13 YEARS OLD IN DECEMBER 1937 AND LIVED AT 8 FUXIN BRIDGE.*

My name is Wang Huazhi. Before the Japanese occupied Nanjing in 1937, I lived at 48 Hou Village near the Cangbo gate in Nanjing. There were eight people in my family: my mother Mrs Wang (née Cao, aged 48), my brother Wang Hualin (aged 24), my aunt Mrs Wang (née Cao, aged 18), my sister Wang Huazhen, my three cousins and me.

On 13 December 1937, when the Japanese occupied Nanjing, we escaped to Maoshan Temple in Jiangning County. Under the tree in front of the temple, I saw three monks who'd been stabbed to death by the Japanese army. Their blood was still warm.

On the seventh day of the first lunar month, 1938, my brother Wang Hualin and our helper Liang Donglai (23 years old that year, from Banqiao, Nanjing) with two other people from our village took food from the Cangbo gate to Longtan, passing the Qilin gate. Three of them were killed by Japanese soldiers. Another had been injured, breaking his leg. My brother and the helper Liang Donglai were both killed.

My brother was stabbed seven times by the Japanese. Before he died, he crawled for more than two miles in the snow towards the Cangbo gate, enduring the pain. When he arrived at the Wanying valley, he bled to death. His fingers had been worn down and the knees on his cotton-padded trousers had worn away. His path was stained with blood.

I saw my brother's miserable burial. The news that my brother and two others had been killed was told to us by the only survivor, who'd crawled all the way back.

In April 1938, my aunt was raped by Japanese soldiers. My aunt was incredibly depressed about her husband's death and her humiliation. She developed mental problems as a result. She later gave birth to a girl, who was conceived after she was raped by Japanese soldiers. The child died when she was two years old. My aunt passed away in 1988.

My cousin Wang Huaying was also raped by Japanese soldiers. She was 15 years old at the time and died in 1984.

— **WANG HUAZHI: MALE, BORN ON 25 OCTOBER, 1926, HAN CHINESE, NATIVE OF NANJING** *HE WAS 11 YEARS OLD IN DECEMBER 1937 AND LIVED AT 48 HOU VILLAGE NEAR THE CANGBO GATE.*

Our family made a living by growing vegetables by the Caochang gate. I'm an only child. When the battle began in Nanjing, we were driven to the town by the central army. My adopted father, Zhao Yongxing, was more than 50 years old. He also made a living by growing vegetables and lived at 6 Sitiao Lane by the Drum Tower. Our family moved to live with them.

From the ninth lunar month, I began making flags at the Jinling College, which recruited many young girls, 200 to 300 in total. There were 10 people in a class. The flags we made were hung around the refugee zone.

The Japanese entered the town in December. They killed people everywhere and captured women. At the time, my mother and I hid at 300 Jinling College. My mother sometimes went to see what was going on in 6 Sitiao Lane. Eight days after the Japanese entered the city, several soldiers arrived at 6 Sitiao Lane. They searched for belongings at first. My father Wang Shihe was 50 years old at the time. The Japanese didn't find any money on him and knocked him down on the ground, stabbing him twice. My father clutched his wounds and escaped to number 5, next door, enduring the pain. The next day, he was sent to Gulou Hospital for treatment. His lungs were severely damaged. He died after several months.

The people who lived opposite my adopted father had the surname Shao. The Shao couple didn't want to leave the pharmacy they'd set up by the Shuixi gate and never left Nanjing. Their youngest son, who was more than 20 years old, had asked his parents not to leave and so they stayed. Their son was stabbed 12 times by the Japanese. He screamed all night and died the next day. His mother cried herself to death. Miss Shao, who was Mr Shao's sister, disobeyed and slapped a Japanese soldier while she was being raped. Her breasts and privates were then cruelly cut off by the Japanese.

The Japanese would always drag women to 6 Sitiao Lane and rape them. Mrs Shao (née Zhang) was more than 50 years old and was raped by the Japanese many times.

There were many corpses near Gulou and Shanghai Road. It was ordinary civilians and women who were killed. There were also many corpses left by the side of Shanxi Road.

My father once went out and bought something. On his way back passing through Gulou, he saw the Japanese peel off a person's scalp and pour alcohol on it. They skinned people and forced my father to watch. My father was scared to death and had no appetite when he got back home. The Japanese soldiers were so cruel.

— WANG XIULAN: FEMALE, BORN ON 11 AUGUST 1914 SHE WAS 23 YEARS OLD IN DECEMBER 1937 AND LIVED BY THE CAOCHANG GATE IN NANJING.

In 1937, I lived at 2 Banshan Garden near the Zhongshan gate. Whenever the Japanese army launched an air raid on Nanjing, we always hid in the air-raid shelters. My brother was sent to my aunt's home in the countryside. Later, the Japanese planes bombed the city more severely and the Zhangshan gate area became crowded. My mother took my neighbours and we went to seek refuge in the refugee zone.

I remember we went there at night. We arrived at Doucai bridge when it was daybreak. We took some rice and two chickens with us. There were many refugees in Wutaishan and Huaqiao Road and we had nowhere to live. We had to pick some shabby blankets to set up shelter. We later found some rugged reed mats to use. So many people lived in the shelter and it was tough living there. There was no toilet so we had to relieve ourselves outside. We didn't feel awkward about doing it back then.

Three days later, the Japanese soldiers arrived in town. Traitors put up Japanese flags outside to welcome the Japanese army. The Japanese soldiers often came to Doucai bridge to find young women. One day, they found an old man and forced him to take them to find women. They wanted a woman who was more than 30 years old. The old man begged a woman: "Please! Save my life!"

The woman had no choice but to follow the Japanese soldiers. When she later returned, she couldn't speak and just cried. I saw a woman crying while walking, her hand on her rear. Her trousers had been ripped by a bayonet.

The gold ring my mother wore was also stolen by the Japanese soldiers. At first, she didn't know that the Japanese soldiers wanted the ring. She saw them pull out a knife and she gave them the ring straight away, scared to death. One day, a girl from my neighbourhood and I went to Xinjiekou. We saw a man get caught in front of the military police station in Xinjiekou. They took his clothes off, only wearing shorts. The Japanese soldiers gestured with a knife on his body. We were so scared when we saw this that we immediately went back home.

My aunt lived in Dongliu. My uncle was killed after the Japanese soldiers went to Nanjing. My aunt and my cousin once went to the bathroom. When they saw the Japanese soldiers, they quickly turned around and ran away. They were then stabbed to death. My cousin's name was Xi Xiaoniu. He was about 12 or 13 years old at the time. My aunt's name was Mrs Xi (née Zhu). She was more than 50 years old. My mother told me about what happened.

Three rooms in my house were burned down. Many houses near the Zhongshan gate to Xinjiekou were burned down. When we went back to the Zhongshan gate, it was still in chaos. There was an old woman there who was more than 60 years old. While she had been sleeping at home, she was raped by Japanese soldiers. She nearly cried herself to death, and my mother and her neighbours helped her recover from the trauma.

We lived in the mountains and didn't have any water to drink. One time when my brother and I went down the mountain to get some water, there was something wrong with the faucet and it couldn't be shut off. A Japanese soldier came over and thought that we'd broken it. He punched my brother twice and kicked our bucket over. We cried and ran back home.

— ZHU XIUYING: FEMALE, BORN ON 16 JUNE 1925, HAN CHINESE, NATIVE OF NANJING *SHE LIVED AT 2 BANSHAN GARDEN NEAR THE ZHONGSHAN GATE.*

I'm 79 years old. I lived in Tiger Bridge, Ximen in 1937. Our house was small and it was a rental. My father was in the KMT. My mother was known as Mrs Zhang (née Yan, she passed away this year). My mother, my little brother - Zhang Jinpu, he lives in Taipei now - who was seven years younger than me, and I stayed at home. My mother made a living as a seamstress.

Before the Japanese soldiers entered the town, my mother carried my brother to seek refuge in the Jinling College with me. Miss Hua was tall and treated the refugees well. She was very kind and gave us rice and vegetables. The Japanese soldiers sometimes climbed over the wall into the refugee area and looked for "pretty women". She didn't allow it and tried hard to resist. She kept dogs to bite them and even shot at the soldiers. We went home when it was close to the Spring Festival.

The Japanese soldiers killed many people. On our way home, we came across a group of Japanese soldiers when we walked to Zhongshan Road. We saw a pregnant woman's stomach split open by the Japanese soldiers. They played with the foetus with their guns. I was scared and hid behind my mother; I couldn't watch. My brother was so scared he started crying. My mother covered his mouth and didn't let him make a sound. We were young, so the Japanese soldiers didn't touch us. When we got back home, we closed the door and didn't dare leave. The sound of the Japanese soldiers' leather boots terrified us.

— Zhang Huiru: Female, born on 7 November, 1923, Han Chinese, native of Nanjing She was 14 years old in December 1937 and lived in Tiger Bridge, Ximen.

My name is Mrs Wen née Sun and I'm 82 years old. I lived in Xiaguan originally. I got married in the 11th lunar month in 1936. My husband was surnamed Guo originally, but he changed it to Wen after we got married because he was my family's favourite son-in-law.

In December 1937, on the day the Japanese army entered the city, many defeated Kuomintang soldiers tried to cross the river to escape. Some even took our doors from us. When it was nearly dark, our families went to seek refuge in the Hutchinson International. On the way there, we saw Japanese warships firing at the soldiers crossing the river.

There were many people taking refuge there. One day, about six or seven Japanese soldiers with guns and katanas arrived. They took about five or six girls from the crowd of people taking refuge. I was there in the crowd. I remember one of the girls. Her nickname was Xiaoqiaozi. A Japanese soldier dragged me into an empty room. I remember that he was fat with a beard. As soon as he entered the room, he forced me to take off my trousers. I'd die if I didn't obey his order. I had no choice but to be raped. After that, the Japanese soldier told me to go away and let me go.

In order to escape the harassment of the Japanese soldiers, several women, including myself, were transferred to the basement of an egg-breaking plant at night. Among them were some girls who were refugees fleeing Suzhou. I hid there for more than half a month. My family members secretly sent me food. After I'd stayed there for a year, I went back home. My husband knew that I had been raped by the Japanese soldiers and supported me. He passed away several years ago. At home, I couldn't bring myself to tell my children. I'm afraid of being looked down on if I tell other people.

My cousin was in his teens. He was caught by the Japanese soldiers and never came back. I saw the Japanese soldiers kill many people. We had a neighbour, Granny Shen, who was 80 years old. She thought that because she was old that she'd be safe staying at home. She was eventually killed and disembowelled. A man who made a living making tea, not wanting to lose his property, didn't leave and was killed at home.

> — Mrs Wen née Sun (alias): Female, born on 7 October 1919, Han Chinese, native of Nanjing She was 18 years old in December 1937 and lived in Xiaguan, Nanjing.

I'm 74 years old now. I lived with my grandmother, my parents and two brothers on Jianye Road in 1937. Prior to the Japanese invasion of Nanjing, my father helped others to produce cloth and later sold alcohol as we were poor at the time. Quite a few rich men fled while we had to stay in Nanjing. We couldn't afford the fare and we had a large family to feed.

When the Japanese army entered the city, we went to hide in a dye mill run by my grandma's sister-in-law in an area where many of my neighbours were also hiding. The Japanese soldiers killed many people in the room next to ours. We heard their constant groaning and they later died. I was so young at the time. The adults were hiding in the room while I was outside shouting: "Mummy! Mummy! Where are you?" I was terrified when a Japanese soldier suddenly stood behind me. A grey-haired old lady then pleaded with him to spare my life, claiming that I was her granddaughter. The Japanese later left and I was hiding in a shelter in the hall, shivering all over. The Japanese soldier had been looking for girls in the area and the old lady bribed him with eggs. Later, another Japanese soldier arrived, rambling incomprehensibly. Many people were hiding upstairs while some were in the dye vat, so the old lady said things directed to us refugees like "I'll take this soldier to find some girls", while taking the Japanese soldier to the backyard, giving us an opportunity to escape. However, my grandma's brother was taken away and never came back. His surname was Wang. He was a tall man in his seventies at the time. When night fell, we all came out to discuss our next move, agreeing on fleeing to the refugee zone as we couldn't stay here any longer. So, we glued things that had been dyed red to a sheet of white paper and made a Japanese flag to wave. My two aunts rubbed their faces with coal and ripped their clothes. They also wore their torn clothes inside out and put cotton rags on their heads, trying to look like beggars. We stepped on dead bodies along the way to the refugee zone and came across more bodies in Daqiao.

My mother didn't come with us as she had freckles on her face, so she wasn't considered pretty and the Japanese weren't likely to assault or rape her.

My father worked in congee production in the refugee zone. A lot of people were in the refugee zone. Young women went to live in the Jinling College and it was incredibly busy, even in the corridors. I slept on a concrete floor and lived off congee. My aunt was in the college at the time. She had a baby girl still in a cradle and I helped babysit her in exchange for some food. One day, a Japanese soldier came and saw the baby, then he said something incomprehensibly, perhaps looking for the baby's mother. I couldn't understand him, so he just raped me. I was just nine years old at the time.

— Ma Yuxiu (alias): Female, born on 6 November 1928, Han Chinese, a native of Nanjing *She was nine years old in December 1937 and lived on Jianye Road in Nanjing.*

My name is Peng Shanrong and I'm now 83 years old. I was born in 1918 but my ID card states 1920 as I was afraid of being forced into service during the Japanese occupation of Nanjing and so I lied about my true age. My father once had a shop called Pengrongji Scaffolding in Youfu West Street. He passed away when I was 14 and two years later my mother was gone too. I lived with my brothers and sisters at 50 Hongwu Road. My brother Peng Shanzhi and I were both electricians. My brother-in-law was called Chen Wenju, who was a bailiff that delivered official letters. I was engaged to a primary school teacher called Xie in 1937. Within one month of our engagement, the Japanese army bombarded Nanjing, reducing it to total chaos. We had to postpone our wedding.

As the Japanese kept dropping bombs, we had to move to the Fuzimiao Temple. Many had already fled there, so they were surprised by our actions. We stayed there for a night and then moved to the refugee zone on the third day, staying in Xingye near a theatre. A colleague of my brother-in-law had fled Nanjing, leaving his wife - who was barely 30 - and his teenage daughter with us. To be on the safe side, my sister and sister-in-law went to live in the Jinling Women's College, where they'd be protected by Ms Hua. The wife of my brother-in-law's colleague didn't go and instead she dusted her face with ash. The Japanese army seized the city a matter of days later.

The Japanese looted and set fire to a lot of places including the majestic theatre and the ministry of communications building while we were hiding inside holding our breath. One day, a Japanese soldier came up to us looking for some girls. We told him that there weren't any girls here but the wife of my brother-in-law's colleague happened to come out. The Japanese soldier immediately saw her and forced us out of the room. He then locked the door and raped her. She was absolutely devastated and despite our best efforts to comfort her, nothing worked. Days later, she left to seek refuge elsewhere with her daughter.

My brother was taken away by the Japanese about a week later. One day, my brother-in-law went to the college to take food to my sisters, leaving me with my four nieces and nephews at home. The Japanese soldiers returned with translators looking for girls but they couldn't find any. They then went upstairs and threw the doors open, rummaging through everything before coming down interrogating me about my job. I told them that I was an electrician. They examined my hands and head and asked me to roll up my trousers before stabbing my leg with a bayonet. Blood streamed down my leg. It wasn't until they left that my neighbour, Yang, came up to me with several cigarettes and applied the ash to my wound. I still have the scar.

My brother was taken to Gourong by the Japanese and didn't come back until several weeks later. Just a few days later, I was also taken away by the Japanese along with 22 others. We were asked to take wheelbarrows filled with goods to Tangshan. It was dark by the time we arrived. The Japanese asked me to cook for them, but I'd never cooked before, so the rice wasn't cooked properly and they almost beat me to death for it. My back still hurts when the pressure changes and my hearing is also poor as a result. One night, we all escaped without the Japanese noticing. We continued nonstop along ridges and alleys for dozens of miles, instead of following the main roads, until the day dawned when we arrived at Lake Hejia. We didn't leave until we found an elderly couple who helped us to find an empty house filled with hay. Dead bodies were buried under the hay and we just lay on top of them, with our heads in our hands. We hit the road again when it got dark. We were caught by the Japanese at the Qilin gate who forced us to carry goods again. We followed them into the city and delivered the goods to the examinations syndicate in Jiming Temple. Two of us tried to escape but were beaten to death on the spot. Another one was also later beaten to death.

One of our neighbours, a woman in her thirties, was raped by the Japanese in Xingye.

There was no food in the city. One day, I went to find something to eat with others outside the Shuixi gate, but we were caught by Japanese soldiers who forced us to look for girls with them. They found a woman hiding beside a coffin and four soldiers gang-raped her while forcing us to watch.

We came across Japanese soldiers looking for girls again to the east of the gate while picking vegetables. A woman was found hiding in her home and four Japanese soldiers entered the room to gang-rape her while we were ordered to stay outside.

— Peng Shanrong: Male, born 20 August 1918, Han Chinese,

NATIVE OF NANJING *He was 19 years old in December 1937 and lived at 50 Hongwu Road in Nanjing.*

I was born in the year of the monkey and am now 82 years old. I was living in Shengzhou Road in 1937. My father ran a grocery store and my mother was a housewife. I also had a sister who was married at the time. My brother was forced into service by the KMT and he didn't come back until the 1950s. I had two younger brothers, 15 years old and 10 years old respectively. I'm the third child in the family and I was 17 back then.

Several people living next to us in number 183 were killed when Nanjing was bombed by the Japanese. Prior to the Japanese invasion of the city, my sister fled to the countryside with her husband's family while the rest of us hid in the refugee zone. My younger brother, Wang Daosheng, was so tall that the Japanese mistook him for a Chinese soldier and captured him. My mother didn't dare plead for his life and begged an old lady to get him. Everyone who was arrested for being a Chinese soldier was taken away by the Japanese.

While we were looking for shelter in the refugee zone, my younger brother was seriously beaten by the Japanese with rifle butts. It took a long time for him to recover, though he never truly did. He died in the 1970s due to haematemesis.

I went to the Jinling College before New Year's day in 1937. Dead bodies were lying all over the place so we didn't dare go out to find food.

One afternoon after the Spring Festival, I went out to find something to eat with two girls and we soon ran across two drunken Japanese soldiers. One of the girls, who was a little older than me, ran away while being chased by a Japanese soldier and the other girl hid in a store with me. The girl hid under the counter and refused to come out, so one of the Japanese soldiers killed her. I was hiding at the back of the store. The Japanese then raped me. I was too scared to resist.

I married late because of the effect this nightmare had on me. At the age of 26, I was introduced to someone by my mother and sister and married outside of Nanjing. My husband worked as an accountant in a mine. Together, we've travelled the length and breadth of the country and have gone through many hardships. Now we are settled in Liupanshui, Guizhou Province. I still hold a grudge against my sister.

My husband has been aware of my experience while my seven children are all still kept in the dark. I have been keeping this painful experience secret the whole time. I'm a Nanjing native and I miss the city very much. My husband passed away in the 1970s and I moved his ashes to Nanjing. I also plan to be buried in the city and my youngest daughter got married in Nanjing too.

I'm here in Nanjing to visit my husband's grave and I still hate the Japanese with a passion. I was going to go back to Guizhou today, but I decided to postpone it after much thought and came to the Nanjing Massacre Memorial Hall to tell my horrible story.

— WANG WEIQING (ALIAS): FEMALE, BORN ON 17 FEBRUARY 1920. HER ANCESTRAL HOME WAS NANJING SHE WAS 17 YEARS OLD IN DECEMBER 1937 AND LIVED ON SHENGZHOU ROAD IN NANJING.

In 1937, when the Japanese army entered Nanjing, my house was burnt down along with the rest of Mixing Street. My cousin Xu Dajun's house in Xinfuhe was also reduced to ash and he actually died in a fire started by the Japanese troops. My paternal cousins, Shi Chaoyi and Shi Chaonian, were killed by the Japs and my sister-in-law was maimed after being gang-raped. Their grain shop on a small hilltop outside the Guanghua gate and all the furniture inside were all burnt down.

Nanjing was eventually besieged and the Japanese soldiers broke into the city, killing and plundering as they went. They slaughtered every man they saw and raped every woman they could. The flames lit up the sky. The Japanese burst into my aunt's house in Nima Alley where the Shi brothers were hiding and my two sisters-in-law were dragged out from a haystack and gang-raped by the monsters. The scene was grim. The Japanese also found my two brothers. They were in their twenties; Shi Chaoyi had just had a baby girl while Shi Chaonian had just got married. They dragged them out of the house to the bomb shelter and killed them. My two sisters-in-law were then raped again, making their swollen genitals unbearably painful. The elderly in the neighbourhood recommended treating them using a traditional method. It wasn't until the pus, blood, and dirt was removed from their wounds that they were spared death. This never really came to light because the victims were ashamed of it. But my two sisters-in-law have been infertile for the rest of their lives since they remarried. In the past few decades, they have passed away and the baby Shi Huiru, who was born before the war broke out, also eventually died young. The Shi brothers have no descendants.

— XU DACHANG: MALE, BORN IN 1923, HAN CHINESE. HIS ANCESTRAL HOME WAS IN NANJING HE WAS 15 YEARS OLD IN DECEMBER 1937 AND LIVED IN MIXING STREET OUTSIDE THE TONGJI GATE

My name is Wan Xiuying. I was 10 years old and lived by Erban bridge, Xiaguan, in 1937 along with my father Wan Xuehua, my mother Mrs Wan (née

Yu), my brother Wan Laigang and my sister Wan Fengying. Before the Japanese invasion and having to flee to Xijiadian, we did business in Jiangpu. My brother and I later returned to Nanjing.

Many were killed in Xiaguan during the Nanjing Massacre. My brother Wan Laigang was seven years older than me and we were hiding in a shelter at the time. He was out looking for food before being captured and taken to the John D Hutchison & Co. Ltd food processing plant where a lot of people were imprisoned, many of whom were executed by firing squad. I saw the Japanese dump the dead bodies into the Yangtze River, which washed up on the shore when the tide turned.

At Erban bridge, I saw three Japanese soldiers gang-rape a 19 year old girl before stabbing her genitals with a bayonet while her mother watched and screamed nearby.

I cut my hair and put dirt on my face to avoid the Japanese. One morning, my brother and I went to catch prawns. On our way to the riverside, we ran into some Japanese soldiers who tried to drag my brother away. One Japanese soldier, wearing boots, kicked and injured me as I pulled my brother's sleeve, refusing to let him go. They then chopped off my brother's arm in one fell swoop and he then bled to death.

My father worked in a teahouse when my parents returned to Nanjing. We ate prawns from the river and bean curd dregs to survive. One day, my mother went to gather wood in Sanchahe and on her way back near Guiliancheng, she was killed in an explosion as shrapnel stabbed her in her right armpit. We saw a lot of dead bodies in Chaizhou when we were looking for my mother.

My sister Wan Fengying was hiding in the shelter day and night after the deaths of my mother and brother. Being slim and tall, my 13 year old sister was an easy target for the Japanese. Since I was thin and small, I was responsible for begging for food every day. It was biting cold outside, sometimes my feet became raw with the cold and I had to crawl on my knees. Tears well up in my eyes whenever I think of this. The nightmarish experience was so unbearable. I'll never forget what the Japanese did to us.

— WAN XIUYING: FEMALE, BORN ON 18 MARCH 1928, HAN CHINESE. HER ANCESTRAL HOME WAS IN BAOYING *SHE WAS NINE YEARS OLD IN DECEMBER 1937 AND LIVED BY ERBAN BRIDGE IN XIAGUAN.*

My name is Zhang Xiuying and I'm 86 now. My husband is Li Chuntian and we come from Cao County in Shandong Province. I was 23 when the Japanese occupied Nanjing. My whole family fled for safety and we went to Wuyu Street in She County on the outskirts of Nanjing. The village was home to more than 300 people and we were helped out by a rich family.

When the Japanese came, the rich ran away while the poor, like us, were left behind. The Japanese didn't cause much trouble on the first day. The next day, they took away 40 or 50 women and forced us to take off our cotton-padded clothes. They forced us to run in a field and threatened to shoot us if we failed to do so while they laughed and cheered nearby. I had two children, the oldest was a three year old boy and the younger child was a baby girl. I was holding my son in my arms when a Japanese soldier told me to follow him or else he'd kill me. Granny Tao persuaded me to go with him, saying: "Just go with him, otherwise he'll kill you."

I had to leave my son and go with him. He took me to a house in Taojiahang and raped me while I screamed and cried. When I returned, the Japs had already burnt down my house. I screamed: "Granny Tao! Help! The baby is still in the house!" The house was reduced to ashes, along with our belongings and my daughter.

I fled to a temple with my three year old son, yet was caught by another Japanese soldier who almost beat me to death. I couldn't understand what he was saying, but he found a bed and wanted to rape me. I was on my period at the time, so he was annoyed, beating me severely and hitting me with his gun and shouting. Then he stabbed me with a knife. I defended myself with my left hand, leaving an inch long cut on my finger and even exposing the bone. My finger is still bent and I still have the scar. I cried my eyes out and an old woman said: "Just get out of here quickly! The Japanese cavalry are coming again!" It was snowing and I was starving. I then hid in a cellar and caught a cold, unable to eat a thing for months. Later, someone showed me a traditional cure, applying rice straw ash to my navel, and I gradually recovered.

I later found my husband, who'd been caught by the Japanese and worked carrying coal to the old estuary at the wharf by the river. One day, I was delivering food to wharf number nine. I came across a Japanese guard who wanted to check my police certificate when I was passing wharf number four. He cornered me for more than an hour and wouldn't let go of me. He said: "You're my wife and I'm your husband. You must sleep with me!" He continued and said that the emperor was "great and marvellous". I ignored him and he pushed me into the water. I cried and screamed. He had to let me go because he was on duty at the time. After that, I didn't dare go to the wharf.

It was scary as the riverside was filled with dead bodies. The coolies captured by the Japs were stuffed into straw bags and drowned in the river if they didn't need them anymore. The wolfhounds they raised were ferocious and they terrified the Chinese. The gangplank placed at the dockside was extremely narrow. If you fell into the water you'd die as no one would be able to help or avenge you.

I was 23 years old back then with a shaved head and a dusty face. It was unbearable! My suffering was beyond description. The Japanese were killing people everywhere. Three people from one family were killed in Taojiaxing. I saw the second and third eldest children in the family hiding behind a ridge. They were seen by the Japanese and shot dead when they raised their heads. Their brother also died. My daughter was burnt to death by the Japs. She would be 63 years old now if she'd survived.

A woman with four children was on a ship. Her husband, a sailor, fled elsewhere and never returned. She was left on her own and gang-raped by some Japanese soldiers. I heard that there was a young man who was forced to rape an old lady by the Japanese. He refused to do so and was shot dead. I also saw people slaughtered by the Japs along the Yangtze. Many people were taking dead bodies there.

After liberation, I acted as the director of the neighbourhood committee. In 1958, I was head of the Wanlihong carpentry factory. I've revealed my experiences before when comparing the past miseries to my present happiness. I'm a witness to the Nanjing Massacre.

— ZHANG XIUYING: FEMALE, BORN ON 16 APRIL 1914. HER ANCESTRAL HOME WAS IN CAO COUNTY, SHANDONG PROVINCE *SHE WAS 23 YEARS OLD IN DECEMBER 1937 AND LIVED IN WUYU STREET, SHE COUNTY.*

My name is Li Sufen. My family was living with my uncle's family in Chuanban Alley in Xinqiao in the north of the city. Altogether, there were nearly 20 people in the family in 1937. When the Japanese invaded Nanjing, we were terrified as they committed all sorts of crimes. My adopted mother sought shelter in the Jinling College with my younger sister while we girls were hiding in our house's basement. But several days later, the Japanese soldiers began to set fire to houses and the fire spread all the way from Xinqiao to our house, leaving nowhere for us to hide. So, we fled to the Jinling College to look for my adopted mother at night. It wasn't until we found her that I found out that my sister had been raped by the Japanese. She was only 10 years old. What kind of monster could have done that? My poor sister died a few days later due to the physical trauma.

My parents were worried about things at home, so they ran back one night. But unfortunately, they ran into the Japanese and my mother was raped while my father was traumatised. He died of a cerebral haemorrhage several days later. My mother went mad and passed away before long. My aunt was interrogated about whether she'd seen any Chinese soldiers and was later killed by the Japanese because she couldn't give them any information.

I will never forget it. I was orphaned by the Japanese and I want them to pay for it.

— LI SUFEN: FEMALE, BORN ON 12 MARCH 1923, HAN CHINESE. HER ANCESTRAL HOME WAS NANJING SHE WAS 14 YEARS OLD IN DECEMBER 1937 AND LIVED IN CHUANBAN ALLEY IN XINQIAO IN THE NORTH OF THE CITY.

My name is Yang Mingzhen and I lived in Dongwensi Alley in Nanjing along with my father Yang Guangyuan, a 53 year old artisan who made things out of bamboo strips, and my mother, Mrs Yang, née Song, a 51 year old housewife. I was six years old back in 1937. Now I live in 6 West Village in Luolang in Nanjing.

The Japanese entered the city on 13 December 1937. They came to our house several times on the first day they occupied Nanjing. My mother initially welcomed a Japanese soldier but he kicked her to the ground. Two Japanese came in after the first one looking for matches and cigarettes. They punched and kicked us for not doing what they wanted until my father sent them away with some tobacco. Two more Japanese soldiers came and took away our smoked meat. At noon, about five or six Japanese soldiers barged into our courtyard armed with guns and bayonets. They first shot the doorkeeper, Pu Gouzi, who was in his fifties. He died that night due to excessive blood loss. Then they shot and killed the landlady Mrs Zhu, with the bullet hitting her in her stomach. My father was also shot in the left arm by the Japanese while he was in the central room and the bullet stayed lodged in his arm. In the evening, the Japanese came again, looting my mother's jewellery, our money and our quilts.

On the morning of 14 December, we were getting ready to seek shelter in the refugee zone before daybreak. However, some Japanese soldiers blocked our way when we got to the Dazhong bridge and aimed at us with their guns, forcing us to go back to Dongwensi Alley. At about 3pm, a Japanese soldier with a full beard on horseback, armed with a gun and a sword, rode into our courtyard. He grabbed me and immediately started to unbutton my padded gown and take off my trousers. I was terrified as I screamed and cried. The soldier sliced my forehead open with his sword and I still have the scar. My father saw this and grabbed me back from the soldier, who punched him twice and kicked him down. He also stabbed my father's neck three times. My father was seriously injured and passed away before long. His body was buried in the middle of nowhere by the Red Cross.

On the third day of the Japanese occupation on 15 December, my mother and I were hiding at home. To avoid the Japanese rapists, she covered her face with ash and wore a rag around her head. At about 1pm, two Japanese soldiers barged in armed with guns and bayonets. One of them ripped open my mother's clothes with a bayonet and took off her trousers before brutally raping her. He forced his finger into her genitals and then inserted the barrel of his gun. My mother was in agony and begged for mercy, but the soldier wouldn't let her go. The other soldier forcefully unbuttoned my padded gown and raped me.

Later, my mother was hysterical and just wept. She passed away before long. With both my parents gone, I was orphaned with no one to depend on. First, I begged for food; then I did some small business selling sesame seed cakes and deep-fried dough sticks to earn a living. The impact of the Japanese sexual assault on me was devastating, not only leaving me incontinent, but also psychologically traumatised.

The daughter-in-law of one of my father's colleagues was a child bride. She was very young when she was raped by the Japanese, who inserted a gun into her privates, thrusting until she died on the spot. She was murdered on Jiankang Road. The Japanese raped any woman they saw. A 12 year old girl was also raped and killed by two Japanese soldiers.

— YANG MINGZHEN: FEMALE, BORN ON 9 FEBRUARY 1931, HAN CHINESE. HER ANCESTRAL HOME WAS NANJING *SHE WAS SIX YEARS OLD IN DECEMBER 1937 AND LIVED IN DONGWENSI ALLEY IN NANJING.*

My name is Li Xiuhua and I'm 74 now. I lived in the main alley in Xigan Lane along with my mother, siblings, sister-in-law and brother-in-law while my father worked elsewhere.

On 13 December, my elder sister was killed in a Japanese bombing raid and my elder brother, Li Wanmin, also died that afternoon. The Japanese dragged him out of the cellar, claiming that he was a Chinese solider. They cut his throat with a sword and killed him. He was only 19. I had a 21 year old cousin called Zhou Wanqiang who worked at the grain supply centre at that time. He was smart and strong. The Japanese stubbornly insisted that he was a Chinese soldier and killed him. Another cousin of mine was also taken away and murdered by the Japs. My brother-in-law was caught by the Japanese before he escaped half a month later. On the same day, my great aunt's family also fell victim to the Japanese. Her second son, daughter, eldest daughter-in-law and my younger great aunt were all killed by the Japanese bombs.

My 17 year old sister-in-law fled with us to Qili hill by the Shazhou dyke. One time when she was hiding in a haystack, two Japanese soldiers forced her out with their bayonets and raped her. Three days later, another Japanese soldier broke in and raped her. She then fled to the Dasheng pass and is still alive.

I saw two Japanese soldiers raping an old lady, as well as a teenage girl from the Fang family. The young girl was stabbed to death after being raped and was left on the side of the road completely naked. Although locals covered her corpse with clothes at night, the Japanese threw them away the next day, leaving her dead body exposed until half a month later when her family finally buried her. Masses of people died in the Yinqiao district, some of whom were Chinese soldiers and some were just civilians.

— Li Xiuhua: Female, born on 13 May 1926, Han Chinese. Her ancestral home was Nanjing. *She was 11 years old in December 1937 and lived in Xigan Lane.*

It would take days to relate all of the crimes the Japanese committed against the women of Nanjing, which include heinous acts that would drive one mad by reading them. This is the real reason why Chinese people call these brutal Japanese invaders "guizi" and "yaonie", meaning "devils" and "evildoers".

Among the piles of archives about the women who were raped and slaughtered by the Japanese, I noticed the number 37 being mentioned in the files of two women: one who was raped 37 times in a day; the other was stabbed 37 times for resisting rape.

These two incidents that occurred in that cold Nanjing winter of 1937 show the shocking fate of many Chinese women. However, the crimes this chapter has explored are just a tiny part of the tragedy of the Nanjing Massacre.

JOHN RABE AND THE INTERNATIONAL SAFETY ZONE

John Rabe, the son of a German captain, was a key individual in the Nanjing Massacre. He died of a stroke on 5 January 1950 when he was just 67 years old.

His Views on the Nazis

This book will introduce Mr Rabe in anti-chronological order, starting with his life from the end of the Second World War.

In 1945, when the Soviet Red Army occupied the Nazi capital Berlin, where Hitler was bunkered down, they rigorously punished and cleansed all the Nazis in the city. During this period, it was reported that John Rabe was a Nazi. So, Mr Rabe, who was working as a common clerk in Siemens at the time, was arrested by the Red Army.

The Red Army conducted interrogations to uncover all of the crimes committed by the Nazis and to eliminate any remaining Nazi supporters. However, Mr Rabe received a far better fate than many. He was acquitted and released as the Red Army claimed that he, as a German citizen, had made a special contribution to the antifascist struggle by protecting tens of thousands of civilians in Nanjing from being brutally slaughtered by the Japanese fascists.

After being released, Mr Rabe was given a very good job opportunity, which was rare for Germans in 1945. Berlin lay in ruins under the occupation of the Soviet Red Army and its allies; you would struggle to find even just one house left in a good condition. Siemens, a company that manufactured weapons for the Nazis, was unsurprisingly among the list of targets to be cleansed and persecuted by the Red Army and its allies. However, in order to allow the Germans to recover, the centuries-old Siemens corporation was kept open so that some of the workers and citizens who weren't linked to the Nazis could stay in work. Mr Rabe may have been the only Nazi to recover his job, and Siemens kept his position open for him with great enthusiasm.

Siemens was located in the northwest of Berlin, an area under British military control following the Second World War. The difficult task of reconstructing Germany lay ahead, but the Soviet Red Army and its allies struggled to find Germans they trusted to put into important positions, so Rabe, being one of the few Germans they deemed trustworthy, was employed as the chief translator for the British. However, during the reconstruction process, the Germans continued to be tormented by a tough question: who posed a hazard to future German peace? As the Germans had completely given up on their military goals and dreams of conquest, all the supporters of Nazism and Hitler were to be purged and punished, and government departments and important enterprises weren't allowed to hire workers who had ties to the Nazis, especially not crucial posts. Although there was much debate on the matter of Rabe's employment, he was eventually fired.

Out of respect and consideration for Rabe, Siemens stated that he had retired in advance and could still do some odd jobs for the company. According to messages from people who knew Rabe, without any source of income, it was as tough for Rabe's family now as it had been for the two million or more refugees he had helped in Nanjing, living in hunger and cold. Although China tried to help its hero, it had a negligible impact. Rabe remained depressed and unwell in his later years.

Due to the intense stress and pressure he was under, Rabe died suddenly following a stroke. Even so, he was considered to have passed away relatively decently compared to many other Germans, which placed a great strain on the country.

Rabe had returned to the Siemens headquarters in Berlin on 5 April 1938. For more than a decade after he returned, he stayed in Berlin and went through great hardships for two reasons: one was that he was repeatedly persecuted by the Nazi regime for exposing the barbaric acts of the Japanese fascists in Nanjing; the other was that he was discriminated against by the new anti-Nazi German society for having been a member of the Nazi Party.

Rabe was a German whose beliefs and actions were one and the same. As he hadn't betrayed his country, even his nationalist ideals, and remained a loyal subject to Germany under the regime of the Nazi Party, he was inevitably attacked by the country's enemies and Germany itself. He later died from a stroke due to the intense levels of stress he was under.

When Rabe returned to Berlin, Germany, Japan and Italy formed the Axis Alliance. Apparently, the Nazi government had pressured Siemens to order Rabe to come back from Nanjing. He had witnessed all of the horrors of the Nanjing Massacre during the three month period before he left Nanjing, which was an experience he never forgot, having a profound impact on him.

As a result of this, he became a friend of China and a supporter of peace, remembered by the Chinese people forever.

Rabe was akin to a saint while he lived in Nanjing, known as "the living Buddha" among the Chinese population. However, he was still a German, and as such, wouldn't be forgiven for betraying his nation and ideology. As a man who was kind hearted, righteous and compassionate by nature, tens of thousands of Chinese have come to commemorate him by visiting his statue, which stands in front of the house on the Nanjing University campus where he once lived. As a German, his controversial political and ideological links, which were influenced by the social and political climate in Germany at the time rather than his own political and personal views, were the main reason for his misfortune in the years to come.

Although Rabe was indeed a member of the Nazi Party, history has proven that being a member of the party does not automatically make someone a bad person. Rabe joined as he somewhat supported the sorts of new policies that were being promoted by Hitler after his inauguration in the early 1930s. Being a strict and often even stubborn German, he always adhered to the belief of the importance of serving his country despite having been sent to work overseas for Siemens. However, without much of an understanding of German domestic politics and Hitler, he joined the *Nationalsozialistische Deutsche Arbeiterpartei*, NSDAP, better known as the Nazi Party, for a specific reason on 1 March 1934.

In 1934, Rabe, who'd been working in China for 20 years as the representative of Siemens in the country, founded a school in Nanjing for the children of Germans who worked in China, so as to respond to the German government's policy of establishing a good relationship with the Chinese government. In fact, the Nanjing Nationalist government led by Chiang Kai-shek had an extraordinary relationship with the German government at the time. As previously mentioned, Chiang Kai-shek's military consultants, even during the Nanjing Massacre, were mostly Germans, and the heavy and sophisticated weaponry used by the Chinese troops to combat the Japanese had mostly been bought from Germany. As Rabe, being the superintendent of a German school in China, could only apply for education funding from the German government if it was approved by the domestic authorities and ruling Nazi Party, he joined the Nazis.

The *Nationalsozialistische Deutsche Arbeiterpartei*, or National Socialist German Workers' Party, literally refers to a party that represents the interests of the working class, which didn't seem out of the ordinary for Rabe who'd worked overseas for a long time and now had little understanding of domestic affairs. This honest German was completely convinced of his subjective judgment after having watched many of Hitler's speeches, believing that the Nazi Party represented the interests of the working classes and that Hitler was a good man. Rabe joined the party and insisted he was a devoted member. However, it was proven by Kreisler, a French historian, in her study on Nazism in China, that people like Rabe didn't join the Nazis out of a genuine belief in and adoration of Hitler. She showed that the board of directors in each school run by the Germans contained a member of the Nazi Party who exercised executive power as a representative of the NSDAP, therefore: "Joining the Nazi Party was inevitable for German diplomats, journalists and representatives of national enterprises" (*List of Nazi Members in China*, Kreisler, 1998, p. 27).

Rabe valued his identity as a member of the Nazi Party. He wrote in his diary on 21 September 1937: "The most important reason, which may not be important to others, but is quite reasonable to me, for keeping me here is that I am a member of the Nazi Party who has a duty and was even appointed to be the associate director of the regional group." Rabe apparently valued his party membership, and he deeply valued the honour of being a Nazi.

Sadly, however, despite being a Nazi Party member, Rabe wasn't acquainted with his own party, and was even ignorant of Hitler's true intentions. As he only went back to Germany twice for short periods of time over the 30 years that he lived in China, he had no idea about domestic affairs, the Nazi Party and the real Hitler.

As he never renounced his membership of the Nazi Party, Rabe was devoted to a party that was entirely different to the one he thought it was. The only way for him to get information about domestic affairs and the Nazis was from trivial articles and news in English language newspapers delivered from Shanghai to Nanjing. The content was mostly crafted by the Nazi regime to deceive German citizens at an early stage, including Germans living overseas like Rabe. His diary clearly shows that he was ignorantly devoted to his party and Hitler:

Yes, we are the soldiers of the workers;
We are the government of the workers;
We are the friends of the workers;
We will not desert the workers in distress or the poor.

These lines from Rabe's diary show that he was as enthusiastic about social revolution as every other German. Rabe sincerely respected and valued his identity as a member of the Nazi Party. He saw it as a symbol of excellence for the working class, which prevented him from seeing the party's true nature. As a result, he was bewildered when he was subjected to continuous harassment after he exposed the Japanese crimes in China.

Before Rabe returned to Germany, he held a crucial press conference where the many Japanese crimes in Nanjing that he had seen or heard about were exposed to the world for the first time.

Rabe always believed that this was something that he had to do as a conscientious and responsible Nazi, and China was enormously grateful for his act. Rabe was not a complacent man. Rather, he was modest, humble, loyal and unpretentious. He states in his diary:

> Now I am sitting in Shanghai as comfortably as worms beneath the bark. What embarrasses me most is that everyone thinks that I'm a hero but I can't figure out why I am afforded this honour. Whenever someone compliments me, I'm reminded of an old story. A young man saves the life of his drowning friend. Later when his friend's father comes to thank him, he says, now lying in bed: "Saved his life? I didn't do anything." He then rolls over to sleep.
>
> — (RABE'S DIARY, JIANGSU EDUCATION PRESS, 1999, P. 699)

Rabe's friends described him as a modest man, content in being a businessman. One of his friends, the German Erwin Wickert, said: "He's helpful, humble, rational, and humorous, and his humour is fully expressed, especially in hard times, for he can always calmly come to an agreement with others. Although he has always been humble, sometimes vanity prevails, such as whenever he posed in front of Berlin's famous photographers wearing a tuxedo with his many medals."

It was because of Rabe's typical German character, being modest, loyal, benevolent, hardworking, enthusiastic and compassionate, that all of his friends complimented and trusted him. Wickert said: "He is more Chinese than German since he's lived in China for about 30 years. He's a legendary man who knows China well. He speaks excellent English and communicates with Chinese people using pidgin English instead of Chinese. Rabe understands Chinese thinking, and also appreciates and loves the people of China." All of these traits helped him in his protection of the people of China from the brutal Japanese invaders.

Rabe, who lived in China for a long time, actually knew very little about Germany, and he saw it in a very idealistic way. It was because of this idealism that in early 1938, Rabe decided to expose the crimes he'd seen committed by the Japanese in Nanjing, which would inevitably cause a rift between Rabe and Hitler.

Rabe thought that he'd be respected for his benevolence and heroic deeds in China, but he was wrong. However, everything went well for a short time after Rabe returned to Germany in 1938, when Hitler was still hiding his plans and remained on friendly terms with China. One factor that needs highlighting is that Germany officially allied itself with two other fascist countries, Italy and Japan, two years later in 1940. Before this, Hitler had deceived innocent Germans like Rabe, and even sophisticated politicians like Joseph Stalin and Franklin Roosevelt.

Rabe still trusted Hitler, even after what he had seen in Nanjing, which proved that he wasn't objective or impartial in regard to his views on the Nazis.

After travelling for nearly a month, Rabe, along with his wife, returned to Berlin on 15 April 1938.

At the time, Rabe was recognised as a hero by the entire world, except for Japan. The international community was shocked by the reports in the newspapers, and the crimes committed by the Japanese, which he had exposed in several public lectures in Shanghai and Hong Kong. Supporters of peace around the world spoke highly of his heroic deeds. When he left China, the Chinese government awarded him with a jade medal with blue, white and red ribbons, and the German ministry of foreign affairs also awarded him with the German Red Cross.

After he returned to Germany, Rabe frequently lectured on what he had seen in the international safety zone during the Nanjing Massacre, which aroused interest from the German government, and even the German army. On 25 May, Rabe was invited to report to the department of defence, where he received a great response. What most interested the German army were the photos that Rabe had brought with him. They had been taken by John Magee and depicted the Japanese troops' barbaric acts. Rabe was unaware that the German army regarded the fascist forces in Japan as their role models.

Before long, Rabe received a message from the district Nazi group director, forbidding him from reporting on the subject any longer.

"Why?" Rabe was confused.

"The content of your report is a threat to our relationship with Japan," he was told.

Rabe was dumbstruck.

"You should let the *führer* know about your experience in Nanjing and show him all those files. It's your responsibility as a Nazi," someone suggested.

Rabe agreed and he considered it his mission to report on what was happening in China to Hitler. He then prepared and sent the manuscript of his lecture to Hitler on 8 June 1938, enclosed with a letter:

Distinguished *führer*,

Most of my friends in China do not believe that any comprehensive reports on the situation in Nanjing have been presented to you yet.

I have enclosed here the manuscript of my report, not for publicity, but to fulfil a promise to my Chinese friends, that is, to report to you the suffering of the people of Nanjing.

My mission would be considered accomplished if you could let me know that this manuscript has been received.

I have been informed that reports and photos regarding the massacre in Nanjing are no longer allowed to be made public. I will follow the rule, and adhere to German policies and the government.

I pledge to follow you and to remain loyal to you,

— JOHN RABE

Nevertheless, things didn't turn out as he'd hoped. While Rabe was looking forward to hearing back from Hitler, the Gestapo came to his house and arrested him.

Two Gestapo officers searched his house and took away six of his diaries, along with the pictures and videos taken by John Magee.

Rabe was interrogated for several hours in the police office.

"Am I a criminal?" Rabe asked angrily.

The Gestapo glowered at him, and asked: "If you promise that you will keep silent, follow the discipline and responsibilities required of a Nazi Party member, and not produce any more reports or books, you will be released immediately. Can you ensure that this will happen?"

Rabe nodded after a short silence.

He was then released. Four months later, his diaries were given back to him, while Magee's pictures and videos remained confiscated. It wasn't until the end of the Second World War that these valuable documents were found, and they serve as convincing evidence of the Japanese crimes. Since then, he lived in fear and under the watch of the Nazis, his own party, until Berlin was freed, meaning that the Chinese people in Nanjing and the international safety zone would never see him again.

Rabe never left Germany, which kept him at a distance for the rest of his life.

A Kind Man to Act as President

Although as a German, Rabe had no national ties to the war between China and Japan, he still became involved. It was due to his involvement, and that of his colleagues, that tens of thousands of Chinese people's lives were saved, which astonished the world as this was no small feat for a humanitarian, let alone a Nazi.

Rabe never expected to play a role of any kind, especially not as the chairman of the International Committee for the Nanjing Safety Zone. When the Japanese and Chinese armies were fighting in Shanghai, he and other Germans were preparing to evacuate from China. However, as Rabe was in charge of Siemens in Nanjing, he had a great deal of work to do, and because of the chaotic situation in the city, the company had yet to decide whether they were going to pull out of China or not. What most concerned Siemens in a Japanese held Nanjing was whether or not their business and property in Nanjing and other Chinese cities could still continue to operate safely and whether they could still do business in China during the war. This was Siemens's priority and there were several businessmen like Rabe devoted to their duties.

The Germans have a reputation for being among the most dedicated and the best problem solvers in the world. Rabe is no exception to this stereotype.

Rabe was born in Hamburg in 1882; his father passed away when he was young. Rabe became an apprentice after he left secondary school and later worked for a British company in Mozambique where he learned to speak English fluently. In 1908, he moved to China, where he lived for the next 30 years. He met his wife in Beijing and his two children were both born in China. Rabe became an agent for Siemens in the third year after he came to China. During the First World War, China declared war on Germany following international pressure. However, Rabe still chose to stay. "He strategically convinced Chinese officials that it would benefit both China and Siemens if he could remain in charge of the branch office of his company in China. It wasn't easy for him to make it in China," said one of his friends.

However, two years into the First World War, due to pressure from the British, Rabe and other Germans were expelled from China. But Rabe was a very smart man and found a way to return to China just one year later, contributing a great deal to Siemens in their expansion in the Chinese market.

In 1931, he worked as a managing director for the Siemens Nanjing office. The Siemens Nanjing branch specialised in telephone services and the establishment of several power plants. As an effective player in the company, Rabe was recognised by Siemens for his achievements in expanding the business. But if it hadn't been for what happened later, Rabe would have just remained an outstanding international representative for Siemens and his name wouldn't have become known all over the world.

The Japanese invasion of China and its capital changed Rabe. His best features were on show in the Nanjing Massacre, proving himself to be a talented businessman, a great coordinator and an excellent and positive leader.

That's why I am writing about Rabe today. It makes sense for John Rabe to be seen in the same light as Oskar Schindler, a man who saved thousands of Jews.

As a foreigner in China and a Nazi official who opposed the Japanese army, Rabe saved thousands of residents of Nanjing who were in dire need. He had no idea that he risked being impeached by his fellow countrymen for his actions. "Rabe didn't realise at all that what he was doing was against Germany's interests, and it was pretty dangerous," said one of his German friends.

Rabe's humanitarian efforts were made a few years before Schindler's. Rabe not only saved countless Chinese people's lives, but his complete documentation of the Japanese crimes during the Nanjing Massacre are valuable historical records. "With so much going on at the time, it was hard to believe that Rabe could still get around to writing a diary," said his German colleague in praise.

"A moral man of integrity, patience, compassion and enthusiasm." That's how his friends described him, all using similar words. Chinese people generally believe that a character isn't made in one day, it depends on how one behaves over the course of one's life. Rabe's efforts to protect innocent Chinese civilians were related to his sense of justice, which had been shaped earlier in his life. Erwin Wickert, one of his good friends, once said: "Germany was under the rule of Wilhelm II when Rabe left the country in 1908. In 1919, he went back to Germany for a short period of time, when the German Empire came to an end and ushered in the republican era, but there was still social unrest. In Hamburg, when he saw a civilian being beaten up by a gangster, he helped them out of sense of justice, but as a result, he was beaten as well." In Berlin, when Siemens employees took to the streets to strike, he saw machine guns being brought out on the streets. Since then, he decided to start writing a diary, which became a habit over time.

Looked down upon for using a diary as a method to monitor injustice and violence, Rabe became a sort of vigilante, taking action against the wrongs of the age.

It's worth noting that German businessmen received wide acclaim among the locals of Nanjing due to their advanced technology, dedication and integrity. The local government, military and residents all liked the Germans, which was made clear to the Germans themselves.

However, in the late 1930s, events in China were disturbed by another country: Japan.

Back then, the Rabes were in Nanjing, the capital of China. In the summer of 1937, Nanjing was too hot to bear, living up to its reputation as one of China's so-called three furnace cities, so Rabe's wife went to the Beidaihe district at the end of June. By then, it was already a popular tourist resort for rich and foreign businessmen. Following the Marco Polo Bridge Incident, Rabe and other people believed that "the small incident that happened in northern China will be settled by local mediation" (*The Diaries of John Rabe*, p.4). As a result, Rabe soon took time off work, taking a steamship to Qinhuangdao for a holiday with his wife.

"My dear crow, you're finally here!" His wife hugged him. She kissed Rabe while rubbing his nose with her finger and said: "Look! You've lost weight because you've been working so hard!"

"But now I can unwind with you for a little while," Rabe replied with a big kiss.

In German, "rabe" is the word for "crow", so Rabe was always called "crow" by his wife and friends.

The beautiful blue bay was tranquil and superbly romantic, far removed from the intense fighting with Japan in the northern areas like Beijing and Tianjin and in Shanghai to the south. However, the people here were still nervous and worried about the war.

Surrounded by these worries, Rabe became increasingly anxious. On 28 August, Rabe said goodbye to his wife at night and set out for Nanjing, boarding a train heading south. Fifteen hours later, he arrived in Tianjin.

At that time, the city of Tianjin had been taken by the Japanese army, and people were fleeing all around the city. Standing among the refugees, Rabe began to see how terrible the situation in China was following the Japanese invasion: "As soon as the train stopped, you could see desperate beggars spread along the train windows."

On 7 September, when he went back to his job as a managing director, letters had piled up like a mountain, including letters from the German embassy in China, some of his friends and even an air defence warning from the Nanjing government's air defence committee.

"Mr Rabe, we've got to go, you need leave this hell as well! Otherwise we'll be bombed by the Japanese too!" His colleagues in the company were all packing, getting ready to go back to Germany or escape elsewhere. They told Rabe that the day before yesterday, Japanese soldiers had dropped bombs in the area, with one of them falling just a little more than 100 metres away from the company. His colleagues panicked as they told him that several Chinese people had been killed.

While they were talking, the air-raid siren went off. Rabe's colleagues, who had already suffered from the Japanese airstrikes, knew what was coming, so when they heard the alarm, they dragged Rabe with them and ran to a basement in the company's courtyard.

A second before Rabe hid in the basement, he saw a Nazi flag, three metres long and six metres wide. The swastika could be seen easily.

"Is that flag useful?" he asked his colleagues.

"It is," another colleague answered with pride, "the Americans and the British envy us because only the Germans have a good relationship with the Japanese. Other countries can't escape their bombs."

Rabe beamed when he saw the swastika, realising that if Japan were to one day invade Nanjing, the flag would be a useful shield.

The basement was incredibly crowded and filled with water as 30 people packed into a tight space. It didn't seem fitting for the Germans to suffer. During the several hours spent hiding in the basement, he remembered seeing how the structures had been carefully built while he was in Beidaihai. He felt like the basement wasn't adequate and should instead be prepared for the war. He was a very cautious man.

On his first night back in Nanjing, Rabe couldn't sleep. As his German colleagues in the company were all preparing to go back to Germany or somewhere safer like Hankou, he couldn't help but worry about what would happen to the property of the company and other foreign firms. Was he just going to leave it all behind? He couldn't, not with his reputation as a Hamburg businessman with integrity, not to mention the great number of Chinese staff there who had come from northeast China, their homes already occupied by the Japanese. "If you stay, we'll stay by your side in Nanjing!" said his Chinese employees, which greatly moved him. He chose to stay, even if the others left. There was no way he could just give up and flee the city.

"I'm also a member of the Nazi Party!" This was another incredibly important reason for him to stay.

"What should we members of the National Socialist Workers Party do? We should never give up on any workers and poor people in need!" In Rabe's mind, the Nazi Party was the party that represented the workers and the poor, people just like those in need in Nanjing.

"The host country I've been living in for more than 30 years is now facing enormous problems. The wealthy have fled while the poor have no choice but to stay. The poor don't know where to go with no money. Aren't we supposed to help them? Can't we at least save a few? What would we do if they were our own compatriots?" Rabe responded angrily when someone from the German embassy came to urge him to evacuate. They replied: "If you don't leave today, it will be hard for us to guarantee your future safety." Rabe still refused.

"Fine, do as you wish sir," said the embassy representative reluctantly.

The next morning, after seeing off some of his colleagues as they returned to their home countries or fled elsewhere, Rabe asked his Chinese employee Han Xianglin and others to go down to the basement to fix the drainage system and reinforce the structure for the rest of the morning and until the afternoon: "Han, please tell a few of our colleagues to come here. We need to repair the basement again. We also need to prepare some food and collect as much medicine as possible. We should go to my house to fetch some medicine." Rabe was acting like a director. Later on, he went with some of his colleagues to take all the medicine he had in his home, including a bandage that could be soaked in vinegar to protect against gas attacks.

One of the Chinese workers who'd been with Rabe the whole day looked at the sky and asked: "Why aren't the Japs bombing today?"

Rabe was equally puzzled. He then turned on the radio and found out why: it was raining in Shanghai. "They won't be coming today," he said.

"How do you know?" they asked.

"Because it's raining in Shanghai, they can't fly in the rain."

Everyone understood. The Chinese workers liked Rabe and believed that he knew everything: "You're so much smarter than everyone else, and you're such a good problem solver! You're so kind too!"

"But I'm short sighted!" he joked. He then pointed to his abdomen and said jokingly: "My pancreas doesn't work either, I've got diabetes!" He had misheard and didn't really understand what they'd meant when they said he was kind in Chinese.

"Mr Rabe, you're not only kind but you've got a great sense of humour," Han Xianglin continued to compliment him, but he'd confused Rabe even further.

"My dear Han, is that a compliment?"

Han laughed. One day, when they were passing by the Fuzimiao Temple,

Han explained to Rabe: "When I said you're not only kind but also have a great sense of humour, it means that I think you're just as great as our famous ancestor Confucius!"

Rabe blushed and said with a smattering of embarrassment: "I'm nothing like Confucius! I'll keep learning from his moral example though."

On 22 September, Rabe saw the incredible power of Japan's bombing campaign in Nanjing for the first time and saw how the city's residents had been mentally scarred. That day, Japanese aircraft had bombed the city from 10.30am all the way to about 2.30pm. Rabe felt the ground shake during the lengthy attack. Twenty-eight people, including Rabe and his guests Klein and Schroder, were taking shelter in the crowded cellar. With the exception of those three, the Chinese people in the shelter stayed silent, too scared to say anything or make a noise.

"This is terrible! No matter who started the war, this is inexcusable!" Rabe was furious. As a person who was aware of the horrors of the First World War, he knew that Japan was dropping an enormous number of bombs on Nanjing. After the second all clear in the afternoon, Rabe decided to go downtown to see how bad the damage had been and to check on the condition of German property in the city.

Looking out of the car, Rabe saw that central Nanjing was ablaze, so he decided to head towards it. The KMT headquarters was on fire. The administration and broadcast buildings of the KMT's central radio station were also on fire.

It was clear that Japan's airstrikes had targeted departments of vital importance to the KMT government. However, what really concerned Rabe was that some of the Japanese bombs also seemed to have been dropped at random, with one of them landing just under 200 metres away from the house of his fellow countryman Dr Schroder. When Rabe reached the crater left by the bomb, he found that it was six metres wide and three to four metres deep. It would have killed Schroder and his family if they hadn't have already left for Hankou. Seeing the broken windows of his friend's house, Rabe thought that it made sense for foreign embassies to require their citizens to leave Nanjing as quickly as possible.

After leaving Schroder's house, Rabe saw several bomb craters near the German embassy as he walked down the bustling Zhongshan Road. Conditions here were relatively okay as no one had been injured or killed. However, the scene on the way to Jiaotong School was much worse. A group of people had gathered, some of them were crying while others were shouting. Rabe approached them and suddenly saw the ruins of what had been houses. Next to the ruins was a giant crater where some people were digging. People seemed to be buried there.

Rabe saw a few coffins around the pit; these were victims of the bombings.

Women in the crowd of people screamed and wept, cursing the "Japanese devils".

"It was horrifying. One bomb killed eight residents near the KMT headquarters. One person's head was blown off and found far away," Rabe had heard. He still understood some Chinese although he couldn't really speak it.

The bombing raid on the 22nd showed Rabe how cruel the war was, adding to his compassion for the residents of Nanjing. He seemed to regard himself as one of them, believing that the Japanese shouldn't have bombed the city and its innocent civilians.

In addition to attacking the KMT government, Japan's bombing of Nanjing was also meant to serve as a warning to the British and Americans who supported the Chinese in the fighting against them. However, they failed in this, and instead, it outraged the British, American and French embassies in China. Their respective ambassadors reached an agreement: they wouldn't evacuate from the city any longer and chose to stay in Nanjing. Rabe was thrilled to hear that the German ambassador had also decided to stay in Nanjing for the time being.

"It's excellent. We haven't had any bread to eat since Mr Scheer left, but apart from that, we've been unfazed by the Japanese bombs," Rabe said to one of his friends. Another thing that made him happy that day was receiving an order worth £1,500 from the KMT resource committee. He had been recognised by Siemens's Shanghai headquarters for doing such a good job despite the awful conditions in the city, writing him a letter showing great concern for his safety.

Rabe wrote in his diary, expressing his worries: "The letter has told me that I'm authorised to take any steps that I feel would protect me, including fleeing the city. I'm incredibly grateful for this and it makes me feel extremely happy. But how should I deal with war insurance if I choose to stay?"

The Japanese bombing of China outraged the entire western world. From letters and telegrams from his friends in Shanghai, Rabe found out the next day about how western governments and the world media had denounced Japan for their disregard of civilians and international law, and for attacking the rights and interests of local civilians and foreign embassies in China.

The following is a telegram from the Associated Press on 22 September:

Twenty Americans, including seven women, were put at risk in a storm of Japanese bullets, bombs and shells as they attacked China.

Although the UK and the US have both made their opposition to the bombing of civilians and private property clear - later joined by France and Germany in talks with the Japanese - the densest population centres in downtown Nanjing have been bombarded, home to the consulates and embassies of the US, Italy, Germany and the Netherlands, as well as most Americans living in the city.

Each of the 30 plus areas in the capital city have at least suffered from one Japanese bomb. China's two major railway lines, namely the Tianjin to Pudong and Beijing to Shanghai lines, were also hit. American, British, French and Italian warships anchored in the nearby Yangtze have also been hit.

The American government has lodged its strongest possible objection to the Japanese bombardment of Nanjing, which is now the second formal strong opposition in just a few days. In addition to this, after the Japanese bombed Nanjing on 22 September, on behalf of the government, the United States department of state not only a lodged serious and immediate objection against Japan, but also sent its ambassador to submit a letter of protest from the American government to the Japanese ministry of foreign affairs.

The following is a report from the *New York Daily Mirror* on 23 September:

Protest from Secretary of State Hull: Bombing Nanjing is a Threat
22 September - INS Washington

Today, the US has launched a strong objection against Japan for the second time, warning against the use of continuous "inappropriate" airstrikes conducted by the Japanese on the vulnerable residents of Nanjing.

This objection was a quick response to the Japanese military's cruel and destructive bombing of Nanjing yesterday.

The US strongly reminds Japan of the following points:

1. *The US "opposes" the danger threatening Americans and noncombatants and advises Americans in Nanjing to evacuate.*

2. *It is "not right to bomb ordinary residential areas, breaking laws and humanitarian principles".*

3. *As the city of Nanjing has been subjected to this bombardment, Japan's so-called guarantee that people's lives and property would not be damaged is deceptive.*

4. *Japan is accountable for any American casualties and damage to American property caused by its military actions in the Nanjing area.*

The announcement states that Japan should cease its bombing campaign.

Following the "strong objection", the US government states: "We hope that Japan will stop bombing Nanjing and the surrounding areas as a result."

As is standard diplomatic practice, the written protest requires a formal response from the Japanese.

The American announcement was given by Secretary of State Hull. The following is an extract:

The American government maintains that regardless of what has happened, it is illegal to launch a comprehensive bombardment of a general area with a large population that is engaged in peaceful activities. This is against the law and humanitarianism.

Japan constantly promises that: "In the process of launching targeted attacks, close attention will be paid to people's lives and the property of countries that enjoy friendly relations with Japan." However, in the American government's experience, regardless of the circumstances, Japan does not work to protect people's lives or property in areas affected by war.

As American ambassadors are doing vital work in important American institutions in Nanjing, where the Chinese government is located, the American government strongly opposes the situation where it is forced to choose between surrendering institutions like the US embassy and being exposed to huge danger.

As a result, the US government reserves the right to protect itself and American citizens during the Japanese military's attacks in the Nanjing area. We hope that Japan will stop bombing Nanjing and the surrounding area.

Through the western media, Rabe was able to discover more about what had really happened during Japan's bombing raids. The following is an example of this and is a report from the *New York Post* on the bombing attacks on 22 September:

Despite protests from both the UK and the US, Japanese authorities in Shanghai still claim that Japan has not given up on its intention of decimating Nanjing, which is at the centre of China's fight against Japan. The airstrikes continued as Japan released the announcement.

More than a million people in Nanjing rushed into shelters and other protective facilities as the Japanese planes attacked, while others chose to hide in the hills. The panicked civilians were fleeing in all directions as bombs exploded in the city's streets.

Before the Japanese planes arrived, 13 fighters made in the US were flown by young Chinese pilots heading northwest, ready to fight against their enemies.

However, 30 to 40 Japanese planes suddenly and unexpectedly appeared from the southwest at an altitude of 10,000 feet. The Japanese planes immediately dived and dropped a huge number of bombs; bombs fell like raindrops in the south of the city where the central government is located.

The Chinese antiaircraft guns in the hills next to the ancient city walls promptly opened fire, lighting up the sky in a hurricane of steel. The Chinese fighters dived violently into the Japanese squadron. Soon, four fighters crashed down in flames.

At almost the same time, a comparable number of Japanese planes dived from the northwest and bombed the famous Nanjing residential area of Gulou.

The author of the article presents readers with an intense bombing scene, while another western newspaper reporter observed and criticised another phenomenon. An article entitled *Americans Insulted by the Angry Citizens of Nanjing* appeared in the 22 September edition of the *New York Daily News*. It stated on 22 September, a Sunday, from Nanjing via Shanghai (AP): "Today, there still remain a small number of Americans in the capital who live under the threat of airstrikes. When they were retreating to the embassy, the angry citizens of Nanjing, who were nervously waiting for the arrival of the Japanese planes, repeatedly insulted them."

After the heavy bombing, the American ambassador and other embassy staff fled to the *USS Luzon* gunboat, moored on the Yangtze. However, Rabe had his own opinion of the international attitudes at the time. He wrote in his diary on 24 September: "There were low clouds with rain today and we were happy to be able to walk outside." He was referring to the fact that the enemy wouldn't bomb Nanjing on rainy days. He continued: "All of the newspapers have published stories about the protests of European countries and the US against the Japanese air raids on the civilians of Nanjing in violation of international law. The Japanese have calmly responded to this and said that they had just bombed buildings or military targets and they had no intention of harming the citizens of Nanjing or the nationals of friendly European countries. But this isn't what happened! So far, most of the bombs haven't been dropped on military targets, in fact the truth most resembles the opposite. A huge number of bombs have been dropped on civilians instead of military targets. There have also been surveys showing that the poorest civilians have been the most severely affected and the trains and warehouses packed with refugees have suffered the most violent bombings. The Japanese are lying. They kill innocent people."

That night, Rabe angrily denounced the Japanese crimes when attending a forum at the German embassy, but he was opposed to promptly leaving Nanjing as had been advised by some of the ambassadors.

Ambassador Trautmann patiently tried to persuade Rabe to go. He whispered to Rabe: "The German government has chartered a British ship from Jardine Matheson, the *Coulter*. It's 1,000 Mexican pesos a day, so the price is fair. It will carry everyone who's ready to leave Nanjing by river to Hankou, where it's safe." Rabe shook his head.

"You're too fond of China, Mr Rabe!" Ambassador Trautmann said. He continued: "Well, you must at least have some items you need to send home."

"I do indeed. Many company items need to leave Nanjing so the Japanese don't bomb them."

"A businessman! A real German businessman!" Ambassador Trautmann said to Rabe with a mix of sarcasm and admiration.

Rabe laughed: "I'm a real Hamburg businessman!"

The Japanese ignored the solemn protests of the Americans, British and other countries. They carried on bombing as usual, but with an increasing intensity.

On 25 September at 9.00am, the air-raid siren went off four times in a row. Rabe and his colleagues had to stay in the shelter for almost a day, which made him very uncomfortable and angry. At about 4.00pm, he took Han Xianglin to Xiaguan to see the ship at the waterfront that had been prepared by the German embassy. On their way, the siren sounded again. Rabe couldn't stand it.

The Xiaguan power plant was the Japanese planes' main bombing target. Eight bombs were dropped there, killing a woman and a child who were by the entrance. The mother and child were of course blown up before they had time to escape to the shelter. Rabe witnessed the event and felt an incomparable sense of sadness.

Rabe saw that several bombs had blown up the concrete slabs that made up the roof of the power plant and the top of the distribution equipment. A bomb had seemed to have just hit the distribution room, so all of the equipment had been blown to pieces. The factory's office had been reduced to ruins, leaving just two reinforced concrete columns, bent over like frail old men. The Siemens staff were excellent engineers and extremely good at fixing unusual problems, but Rabe found that the power plant had been almost completely destroyed with glass shards littered across the entire floor several centimetres thick. An extremely powerful shock wave caused by an explosion was certainly responsible for the damage.

The Xiaguan power plant was Nanjing's main source of power, so Chiang Kai-shek made fixing the Japanese damage to the plant a high priority. Rabe, the supplier of the Siemens motors to the plant, was responsible for restoring its power generation capabilities.

"Since the loss of electricity, it's almost like the city has returned to medieval times," said Rabe to Han Xianglin on the way back with a sigh.

"Hey, the streetlights are on!" Han suddenly pointed at the city's streets with excitement.

Rabe felt that there was something odd going on. They asked someone and found out that they had got electricity from the Pukou power plant.

"It looks like Chiang Kai-shek was prepared for the bombs," said Rabe, realising that the Chinese government had spared no effort in defending against the Japanese bombs. Nanjing was the capital of China after all.

"Quickly, Mr Rabe, you need to get up now!" At midnight, Han and others suddenly awoke Rabe. After putting on his glasses amidst the chaos and confusion, he realised that there was a siren outside.

"It is 2.31am!" Rabe looked at his watch with extreme anger.

"No time to put on your tie!" Rabe's Chinese employees said to him as they grabbed him to go outside.

Rabe was in his pyjamas when they went to the shelter. Wearing such informal clothes, the German gentleman felt incredibly uneasy.

It rained very heavily the next day. One of his colleagues ran up to Rabe and happily told him that they'd get to sleep well today.

"Yes, we should certainly make the most of it!" Rabe strongly agreed. Rainy days were peaceful days as the Japanese planes wouldn't attack.

"I caught up on my sleep and it feels so good!" wrote Rabe cheerfully in his diary.

On sunny days everyone lived in fear, but on rainy days, people cheered. This unusual reaction to the weather was a direct result of the cruelty of the Japanese invaders.

Rabe was concerned about the interests of both Germany and Siemens, so he ran to Zhongshan Road where he was shocked once again. Not far from the offices of a German company, just opposite a traditional pharmacy and some international company offices, rows of Chinese houses had been levelled by Japanese bombs. The bomb shelter in front of the houses had been insufficient and more than 30 civilians had been violently incinerated.

Rabe cursed with anger.

Faced with the shameless crimes of the Japanese military, Rabe's love for China and his Chinese employees grew along with his contempt for the Japanese. That night, he was profoundly moved by the arrival of Chow and the Chinese engineers from Siemens in Shanghai. Under the orders of the national government's ministry of transport, Chow arrived in Nanjing in 26 hours. However, it usually took just a few hours by train from Shanghai to Nanjing. The war had made the two cities seem thousands of miles apart.

Rabe, as head of Siemens in Nanjing, was responsible for looking after his Shanghai colleagues. Rabe asked: "Chow, bombs are being dropped on Nanjing every single day, is your family worried about you?"

Chow smiled and said: "I told my wife that if anything happens to me, don't ask Siemens for anything, just go back home in the north and live off the land with the children. This business trip isn't just for Siemens, but for China."

After hearing this, Rabe was moved to tears and gave Chow a warm hug. The reason why Siemens's business in China had been able to expand wasn't just because of excellent managers like Rabe but also because of the hard work of the Chinese employees and their dedication to the company. Rabe expressed his great admiration to the sincerity and selflessness of patriots like Chow.

Fewer and fewer foreigners stayed in Nanjing. The ship rented by the German embassy set sail on 3 October, the German *Erntedankfest* harvest festival, carrying the first group of people away from Nanjing. The ambassador held *Erntedankfest* celebrations on the ship for all the Germans onboard from Nanjing. Rabe went there as he had an important mission: ask Chow to take away his 16 diaries to Hankou after the task.

"Give these things to Mr Hahn and ask him to keep hold of them," said Rabe pointing to four boxes.

Although the *Erntedankfest* celebrations were being held on a ship that was at risk of being bombed, they were still very enjoyable. Ambassador Trautmann gave a speech at the celebration and paid tribute to all the German women leaving Nanjing and men staying in Nanjing. Finally, with everyone drinking coffee, they sang the national anthem, saluted Germany and shouted "sieg heil" three times.

"The national anthem sounds like Beethoven's *Funeral March*," Rabe and a few friends whispered to each other. Nanjing was just behind them and the sound of Japanese bombs could be heard, adding to the sombre tone.

For the next few days, apart from one rainy day, Rabe stayed in the bomb shelter with his colleagues and employees, quiet and bored. This didn't suit the hardworking Rabe; he felt anxious but could do nothing to make things better. In addition to his diaries, Rabe was now writing a feature about staying in Nanjing for a friend, Mr De Man, who sponsored the *Far East News*. His article *Reports from the Ship*, written on *Erntedankfest*, had attracted the attention and praise of readers in Germany, so he was given a part time job for the newspaper and was hired as a guest writer. As Rabe was a very humble person, this actually made him somewhat depressed and he wrote to his friend who had regarded Rabe as a hero on account of his article.

This adoration made Rabe feel uneasy, so he wrote a letter explaining his reasons for staying in Nanjing:

Dear Mr De Man,

Thank you for your letter on 6 October. I am very grateful for being appointed as a guest writer for your newspaper and I am convinced that "Far Eastern News (guest) writer" will look very nice after my name on my business card, not to mention the fact that my British friends, who attach great importance to cards with many titles on them, will envy me. But Mr De Man, I am afraid that you are asking for trouble. You don't really know me that well and you might be underestimating your readers. It's claimed that this is an "extremely serious" matter but I don't much mind it. I just have this terrible talent to make people around me happy at inappropriate times with my so-called sense of humour. I would like to use communication between my family members as an example. My boy, 20 years old, is currently participating in a volunteer work scheme in Germany. He wrote to me: "My dear father, I wish you could hear what the radio has said about China (it's unbelievable!). However, the report in the newspaper is worse and I don't want to look at it. As ever, I am confident that you are looking after yourself. I give you my cordial greetings." I'm not going to say that the current situation isn't serious since it is very serious indeed. If someone does not see this, then they're a fool. The situation isn't just tough, but it will become more difficult. So how can we deal with this critical situation? I think we need to keep our sense of humour and say to fate: "I'm sorry, but I'm not going anywhere." If the sky falls in, then as we all know, all the sparrows will die; if a bomb falls and it happens to fall on a raven's head, then it will die to never caw again. But the Yangtze River will continue to flow and my daily prayer is still the same: "Dear God, please bless my family and my sense of humour and I'll take care of the rest."

Now you must want to know what we're going to do here, what our lives are like now and why we are willing to endure this bombing. Well, I personally came here by boat after a holiday in Beidaihe in early September, and the following reasons explain why I came here:

1. As a representative of a German firm and its interests.

2. There are many old things that I miss (although there's a lady in Berlin who keeps telling me to stop worrying about old things that only cost 50 pfennigs).

3. I have a clear conscience and wanted to be a responsible person, and didn't want to leave the Siemens employees and their families abandoned. I wanted to help them and they shouldn't be taken for granted.

For the first reason, I must point out that Siemens is grateful to its Chinese customers who still place orders and sign contracts with us, but the following conditions must be complied with:

Payment Terms:
   (1) 5% prepaid when signing the contract
   (2) 95% should be paid off within four weeks after the victory of the war. Delivery time: it should arrive at our door in Nanjing within two months. War risk insurance: not necessary, but if you are willing to insure it, that is fine. If it doesn't work, I sincerely apologise to the customer.

On the second point, I have to admit that the lady in Berlin is right.

For the third point, first of all, there needs to be a safe air-raid shelter, but we, obviously, don't have one. Although no safe shelters have been satisfactory, the number of shelters we have here are enough.

We all know that Rabe's establishment of an international safety zone saved tens of thousands of citizens of Nanjing. As a matter of fact, before the Japanese invasion of the city, Rabe made another important contribution to the safety of its citizens, which was the Rabe style bomb-proof dugout. In August 1937, the Japanese stirred up trouble in Shanghai, which led to fighting for three months in the Battle of Shanghai. During this time, Japanese planes began to attack Nanjing and other targets. This resulted in many innocent lives being lost in the bombing raids. During the Nanjing Massacre, 300,000 Chinese people were killed. However, this number doesn't include the amount of people in Nanjing killed by the Japanese prior to 13 December. Air-raid shelters seemed to be the only facilities that civilians could use to protect themselves and survive during these attacks. But many of the civil defence facilities were so poorly built that many people were simply crushed to death when attacked by the bombs. This was a result of a lack of sufficient construction knowledge. However, Rabe was a German engineer, and the Germans were known for their prudence and superior technical abilities. After Rabe became aware of the problem, he created a method to help people build durable dugouts. The Rabe style dugout first spread among his colleagues, the embassy staff and foreign missionaries, and it was later even adopted by some of Nanjing's defensive military and administrative departments. This prevented many people from being killed or injured as a result of unsafe shelters, and as such, Rabe deserves credit.

Rabe told his friends about the method through a letter. They then spread the information further by publishing the letter in newspapers:

How can someone build a bomb shelter? If they have a lot of money, they can commission a Chinese designer to work in a dugout field and do all the work themselves. Naturally, when I did this first, the designer knew nothing about it before this programme, but I paid him; an architect should receive between 500 RMB and 3,000 RMB for this. As a result, based on the payment, the designer was able to acquire wood, planks, sandbags, rails, clay, cement, pipes, and other things that I had no knowledge of. I personally made arrangements for these things. I later hired 10 coolies and asked them to dig a rectangular pit and not to stop until they felt water at their feet. The pit was 1.5 metres deep when they hit water. After that, we placed some bricks and round logs at the bottom of the pit and then covered the floor with slabs. A hole needed to be left so we could get water. You must have heard of how to lower the ground water level. It's very simple. What we did was just use a bucket or an empty food can to lower it every day. We also erected a few pillars around the wall to support the crossbar above and then put square planks on top of them. We covered it with a lot of dirt, mud and sand, and then built a mound on top of it about 1.5 metres high. We then put my wife's flowerpot on top to disguise it because the Japanese planes wouldn't be able to recognise what was hidden below. What made it more hidden to the Japanese was digging the pit underneath a tree so that its roots would grow on top of it. We covered the walls with clean straw mattresses and built two doors, one for letting people in and out, and the other for goods. Sandbag barricades were later put outside the doors to protect against blast damage from any bombs.

People came to my dugout to get a seat! Why? I didn't know! It had a reputation for being rather strong. After I built the shelter, I estimated that up to 12 people could take shelter inside. But after it had been built, I found that I'd forgotten something as 30 people were taking shelter inside like sardines. Where had all these people come from? Very simple! Each handyman had a family, including a wife, children, parents and grandparents. If someone didn't have a child, they'd adopt one to take in. This was a thriving enterprise. On top of this, I had to take in a neighbour who was a shoemaker along with his family. Before the war, he'd charged 20% extra for a service he gave me, which made me very angry. Then I found out that he was a relative of my servant, so what could I do? In the end, I let them all come in and treated them generously. I put an office chair in the shelter for myself, while the others were squatting on short stools. I had to enter the dugout whenever there was heavy bombing. The women and children felt at ease when they saw me sitting with them. I realised that the decision to come back from Beidaihe as soon as possible had been a good one.

If I ever wrote that I wasn't afraid, then I was lying. During bombing raids, the dugout would begin to shake violently and I couldn't help but think: "Oh well, time to say goodbye!" I have a home medical kit, portable lights, shovels, pickaxes and mortise chisels in the dugout, but, to be frank, if all of us had been buried alive in this rat hole, then they wouldn't offer me much of a sense of security. Honestly, I was frightened. However, in order to get over the fear, we'd tell some happy stories or jokes to make people laugh, which would considerably reduce the fear caused by the bombs. To be honest, as long as the bombs didn't land on us directly, we gradually got used to it. Whenever a wave of bombs came to an end, the children would quickly run out. All this was understandable, but anything could happen in a matter of seconds.

Bombing raids at night were a two-sided coin. After the first warning siren sounded, the power was turned off. I didn't need to wear a tie, but I needed to at least put on a pair of trousers and boots in a few minutes. Then, after I'd got everyone into the shelter, I could sit quietly in the dark. I often felt my way back to my living room, quietly looking for a comfortable chair where I'd soon fall asleep. This is what I did as a child whenever there was a thunderstorm. I often did this during the bombing raids. But after the danger had passed, we'd naturally leave. In addition to paying wages, things need to be done to keep up discipline.

I will now write a little about the city and its warning sirens.

If someone had been familiar with Nanjing before the war, and had seen the constantly busy downtown traffic, especially at noon, and were told that 800,000 people had died out of a population of about a million citizens, I doubt they'd feel surprised when seeing the deathly silence and nearly empty streets of Nanjing during the air raids. All the red tiled roofs were painted black, and even all of the red residential brick buildings had been painted black. Every 50 to 100 metres there was a bomb shelter for pedestrians to hide in; some were just holes in the dirt, just big enough for a person to crawl into.

All the cinemas, most of the hotels, most of the shops and the pharmacies were closed. Some artisans still quietly worked behind ajar doors and shutters.

Gaps could be seen between rows of houses, areas the equivalent of about six to 12 houses. This destruction was caused by the bombing. After these disasters, a relatively large number of people died, but the sites were cleaned up so people would never notice what had happened and forget the tragedy that had taken place there.

Buses, also painted black, still travelled on the roads. Buses were packed with passengers at rush hour when government officials from different central departments were on duty because they went to work as usual, even on Sundays. It would have been hard to find any fault with order on the streets as soldiers, policemen and workers did their jobs as required. Only half an hour went by before holes on the main macadam pavement of the Zhongshan Road caused by two bombs were filled, repairing the road. Traffic carried on as usual while the road was being repaired.

No foreigner was disturbed, although not many foreigners were still there as there were only about 12 German females and 60 German males. On the contrary, they were treated kindly as locals looked on in surprise after they insisted on staying.

"Thank God! We're still alive!"

This is what Rabe and the citizens of Nanjing said every day while the Chinese troops fought in ever fiercer battles with the Japanese in Shanghai.

However, Nanjing was no longer a safe haven and the city descended into chaos after the air raids. On 19 October, even Rabe began to lose his mind.

It was barely 2am when the first siren sounded and the bombs dropped, shaking the entire house before Rabe could put on his boots.

"Why are you still in bed?" Rabe saw his friend still lying down, motionless like a rock.

The siren sounded again.

"Hey! The siren's gone off again!" Generally, the second siren meant that a more intense bombing raid was on its way. Rabe became angry and impatient as his friend lay motionless on his back.

"Yes, all right! I hear you! I hear you!" his friend finally replied, getting up in a carefree way.

That night, Rabe used a torch produced by Siemens in the shelter. What he saw in the crowded air-raid shelter immediately annoyed Rabe. He saw that a fat man from the ocean shipping company was taking up more room than he needed, giving less room to the women and children around him.

Rabe approached him and said: "I hope you can make room for the others. It's crowded enough here as it is, and you can't take up three seats that belong to women and children." But Rabe slipped before he could finish and fell into a ditch in the shelter, soaking his arms.

Rabe came out of the shelter the next morning and wrote a notice in German, Chinese and English straight away:

To my guests and members of foreign companies,

Anyone who takes refuge in my air-raid shelter should abide by the following rules:

Women and children - regardless of who they are - should take the safest places, meaning the places in the middle of the shelter.

Men should only occupy spaces on the sides or they can just stand.

Anyone who breaks the above rules will be excluded from using the shelter in the future.

— John Rabe

The notice was put up at the entrance to the shelter. "The *laowai* is so thoughtful!" said the locals, cracking a smile whenever they saw Rabe's notice. Only the fat man was unhappy.

The Japanese air raids were a real nuisance. The all clear sounded at 4am, but the siren sounded again half an hour later. Rabe dressed and got up before the second all clear was sounded minutes later. It turned out that it had been a false alarm as a Chinese fighter plane was patrolling in the sky.

Everybody grumbled, but who was to blame? Rabe comforted them.

However, Rabe was seething silently. He could hear antiaircraft fire as he lay down, with troops on the ground firing violently at the sky. "This is mad. They better be careful not to shoot down their own planes!" Rabe thought to himself.

"A bomb wouldn't kill me anyway, I just need to sleep," Rabe thought as he pulled his quilt over his head and tried to fall asleep. But he couldn't get to sleep. Morning had broken. What should he do? Take a shower? Rabe went to the bathroom.

The siren sounded again at 8.55am. Rabe stood at the entrance to the shelter and cursed the Japanese planes: "Nothing will ever get done if it carries on like this! The Japanese are so disrespectful!"

The all clear sounded at 9.55am. Hostile planes didn't appear however as it was said that they'd flown past Nanjing to the north.

The siren sounded again at 12.15pm. "Just ignore it! It could be a false alarm again," Rabe told himself. Many people paid no attention to it, even Rabe, who was normally cautious, had become less vigilant, wondering if there was still enough time to get to the shelter when the siren sounded again.

Suddenly they heard a roaring sound. It was a real air-raid this time and people shouted: "Quickly! Get into the shelter!"

Fierce fighting broke out in the skies above Nanjing from the moment they hurried and scrambled into the shelter. Someone poked their head out of the entrance and saw that several planes, the Japanese and Chinese air forces, were fighting in the skies while antiaircraft guns fired their rounds like thunderbolts piercing the sky.

The Japanese fighters attacked the north and south of the city, with the power plant Rabe had worked on taking damage. Places that had suffered the most were the railway administration in Pukou and the nearby coal yard. Nine people were killed and dozens were injured.

The bombing continued the next day with the death toll mounting. However, people in Nanjing seemed to have become used to it as long as the attacks weren't too excessive. Air raids were just a part of daily life.

Rabe was able to read newspapers from Germany, the UK and the US sent via Shanghai. Reports in the newspapers claimed that people in Nanjing had now become used to Japanese air raids. "They should report it more seriously! How about they spend a day here and experience it for themselves!" Rabe was rather upset by the reports. However, he nodded in agreement with a forced smile when his friend asked if he himself was used to climbing in and out of the shelter.

"What could you do if you didn't get used to it?" Rabe wondered.

It was Sunday 24 October. Rabe thought that his Chinese friend Han Xianglin was normally right about everything, except for asserting that the Japanese wouldn't bomb on Sundays. Rabe thought this was nonsense. On this clear blue Sunday, bombs rained down on the north and south of the city, more intensively than ever.

"The Japanese are attacking today with 700 bombs!" Han told Rabe.

"700 bombs?" Rabe and Han were in a German butcher's run by a Chinese man when the air-raid began that afternoon. Rabe had found nine bottles of beer and bought them all, hoarding them away as if they were priceless treasure. That night, Rabe drank the beers with his German friend who was visiting.

The next day on 25 October, Rabe was in high spirits as it was his 28th wedding anniversary. His wife in Beijing had entrusted Han to give him four pots of chrysanthemums. She also wrote two poems for him, which greatly moved Rabe.

One of the poems read as follows:

The hazy predictions have become clear;
Destiny is never an accident;
The trail of life is like that of a planet;
Only the wise prevailing in the universe,
Can determine unity or separation.

This is indeed true, even the wisest can't foresee their destiny or those of their family members, especially so in war. Rabe was in awe of his wife's talent while feeling depressed about being caught up in the war.

The power plant in Nanjing was an important project run by Siemens in

China and his friend Ribe was in charge of the business. Japan's constant bombing had made maintenance work on the factory a top priority. As the director of Siemens's Nanjing office, Rabe was responsible for the normal operation of the plant. To his relief, the turbines were functioning normally and so was the old boiler. "The boiler was made six years ago. You see, our German products surpass those of the Americans." Rabe couldn't understand why some Chinese always thought so highly of everything made by the Americans and he proved to them with hard facts that the best products were made by the Germans.

The day after his wedding anniversary, Rabe went to the power plant with Ribe, who'd done an outstanding job in its maintenance. Ribe was supposed to leave but a telegraph sent by Siemens's headquarters in China asked him to stay in the country to continue working for a while longer. "My friend, you're going to stay here with me and experience the Japanese bombs together," said Rabe. The two become close friends.

On their way to the plant, Rabe and his friend received information that the Japanese had taken Taicang, meaning that the outer defensive line of the Chinese capital had been fractured once again. However, there was also some good news. The Japanese had lost 10,000 troops in Shanghai. It seemed that Chiang's troops were fighting well.

But Rabe was quickly saddened again by news about Nanjing he heard from his friend. More than 200 people had been killed and 400 had been injured in the past 60 air raids, while there were even more refugees running for their lives.

"Look! Mr Rabe, your company has sent a large package of Christmas gifts to you again!" said Han, picking up a large package from a car and giving it to Rabe.

Rabe saw that the package contained 100 copies of brand new German calendars sent by a company from Hamburg. The calendar could also be used as a notebook and as a gift to send to clients, so it was well received by Rabe and his colleagues. However, a sadness overcame Rabe when he saw the Hamburg winter wonderland imprinted on the exquisite postcards.

Christmas was coming up. Back in Germany, people were starting to get ready for Christmas, but in Nanjing, which was under fire now, Rabe had forgotten all about it. Tears welled up in Rabe's eyes as memories raced through his mind. Han comforted him.

Rabe collected himself. That night, he sat in the air-raid shelter thinking about his hometown and his wife and children. All sorts of feelings raced through his mind and he thought of one of his wife's poems:

I assure you again and again,
Please be sensible;
But squatting in front of the shelter,
Is far from being sensible!
First, the bombs drop from the planes,
Dropping from above;
Shrapnel drops from the sky,
Injuring whoever is in its way;
If you don't take shelter in time before an explosion,
You wonder,
Is there still enough time?
But I only want to take a peek;
Be quick and hurry,
Get into your shelter!
Common sense commands you!

He had gone in and out of the shelter hundreds of times now. Rabe was busy working every day, collecting money, pressing for payment and helping the Chinese to repair their equipment. He eventually fell ill, seriously ill.

The doctor prescribed him many drugs, three times more than usual. He wanted his wife to deliver some medicine to him but he was hesitant to send her a telegraph because his wife would surely come to Nanjing regardless of the Japanese air raids. Rabe blamed himself for not asking her, thinking: "But Ambassador Trautmann's wife in in Nanjing, if she could make it, why can't my wife?"

However, he knew he couldn't put his wife in danger.

Rabe picked up his aspirin and quickly took several pills before drinking them down with a whole glass of water. He wrote in his diary: "Whenever a Hamburger and a Berliner meet, they'll argue. Each boasts of a silver tongue and considers themselves eloquent. I will naturally support the Hamburger as although they tend to exaggerate a lot, Berliners lie a lot, which is even worse. For instance, a Berliner may say: 'Fools are beyond remedy, even with aspirin.' This isn't true. Aspirin works great for me, I feel a lot better today!"

Rabe was grateful for the drug and he soon recovered somewhat. The siren sounded again before Rabe could finish his diary and he was pulled up from bed by Han Xianglin before rushing with him to the air-raid shelter.

"Mr Rabe, I heard from the top that citizens are preparing food for three days' rations," Han said to Rabe.

"Why?" Rabe was confused.

"When you were sick in bed, the Japanese planes didn't come."

"Because of the rainy weather! It's not the Japanese being merciful," Rabe replied.

"Yes, but after rainy days, the Japanese always bomb Nanjing on a far larger scale with a fiercer intensity and for far longer than usual," Han reminded him.

Preparing three days' rations of food meant hiding in a dark shelter for three days. Rabe shook his head and sighed deeply. He continued his diary: "Modern warfare is hell on earth. We're going through a disaster in China. It may appear insignificant when compared with the threat of a new war in Europe, but hopefully destiny will spare us from suffering."

Bombs exploded outside the shelter. Rabe and the citizens of Nanjing weren't spared from suffering as the misery inflicted on them by the Japanese continued to get worse, with even greater suffering lying ahead.

After rainy days, people in Nanjing thought that the bombs going off overhead exploded like firecrackers set off during festivals. To Rabe's surprise, the Chinese air defence fighters had disappeared. What had happened?

"Chiang has lost in Shanghai, Nanjing is at risk!" Han had realised the situation before Rabe.

Rabe had participated in the First World War and wars in Africa, and knew that Nanjing was in great danger. The severity of the ever changing situation could be seen through several warning signs: his Chinese staff had been conscripted into the army. Most of them were aged between 30 and 35. They often trained for several hours in the morning and were then dragged to the front to fight with the Japanese in the afternoon, making for a grim existence.

"Chiang seems unable to hold on any longer," Rabe said in private with his German friends still in Nanjing. What were the foreigners left in Nanjing to do? This question was the one that most concerned Rabe and his friends.

It was raining nonstop. Rabe hated rainy days because the rainwater would seep into the shelter, which was unbearable for a German gentleman, especially for staff who worked in major companies like Siemens. For people like Rabe, everything related to engineering or machinery had to be perfect. But for the people of Nanjing, rain was a blessing as the Japanese planes wouldn't attack.

The Japanese planes didn't attack on 12 November, which Rabe attributed to the rain, as did the other citizens of Nanjing. Actually, the Japanese had no intention of attacking Nanjing that day as they were busy celebrating their victory in Shanghai. By using a characteristic blend of oppression and violence, they had replaced the Chinese flag, throwing it into the Huangpu River, with the Japanese flag.

"Raise the flag! Today you need to raise the Chinese national flag!" A handyman called Cai relayed an order from Chinese high command early in the morning.

Rabe refused assertively: "Why? I'm a German and I will not lower my national flag for the Chinese flag!"

"This isn't my decision. It's the government's orders," said Cai, feeling irritated.

"Nobody is going to lower the German flag here, no matter who orders it!" replied Rabe in anger. "It's what our company has always done and is part of our trade agreement with your country. No one is going to damage it arbitrarily!"

Another handyman, Zhang, grabbed Rabe and explained: "It's not like that. Cai made a mistake. Today is the anniversary of Sun Yat-sen's birthday and the government asked us to fly the flag at half-mast in honour of him."

Rabe was getting irritated now: "Who exactly should I listen to?"

"Listen to me. He's made a mistake," Zhang said to Rabe as he smiled.

Rabe finally realised what they meant and said: "Run up the German flag with your flag and fly them at half-mast."

Rabe didn't leave until he saw the two workers raise the flags, wondering why the Chinese man hadn't been able to relay the message.

The fall of Shanghai didn't just inflict a great amount of suffering on the Chinese, but also on foreigners like Rabe. He found out from the transport company in Shanghai that Ribe, who'd left Nanjing the day before yesterday, had been attacked but not killed by Japanese planes while the cargo he had been carrying had been destroyed. "Make a list for me! I shall demand double compensation from the Japanese once the war is over!" Rabe was so furious as he gesticulated that his glasses fell off his face several times. Everything he'd entrusted to Ribe had been lost.

Life was getting harder in Nanjing. Government officials were in turmoil as everybody was busy packing and moving. Key departments were left almost abandoned while the other departments and authorities were scrambling for every means of transportation available. Wealthy citizens did everything they could to flee to their friends and relatives, or move to Hong Kong, Hankou, or even further afield. The poor were left behind to expect a dim future with a glazed over look in their eyes.

Foreigners like Rabe were few and far between. The embassy of every country was coordinating the evacuation of its nationals with dozens of foreign ships anchored in the Yangtze ready to set sail at any time. Only one

German ship had been left by the embassy for the last of their evacuees from Nanjing. The ship was only equipped with 50 sleeping berths, so everyone had to cram into it like sardines.

"Mr Rabe, please help me however you can. My wife and I want to go to Hankou by ship. I beg you to negotiate with the ship owner. We're more than willing to double our fares." Wang, an engineer from the military communication school, came to Rabe as they were business acquaintances.

"Bear with me. Let me speak with the ambassador first." Rabe was a kind man and would help others as much as he could, but this time he came back dejected.

"The ambassador has refused. He says the ship is just reserved for Germans," said Rabe, humiliated as he reported back to Wang. "But the ambassador has agreed to let your wife board the ship as she's Austrian. But not you, Mr Wang," he added.

Wang asked his wife: "What do you think?"

"No! I can't do it without you!" His wife shook her head, trying to hold back her tears.

Seeing his friends leave sadly, Rabe clenched his fists and bit his lip, thinking: "The Japanese will pay for this."

It was raining on 17 November. The people of Nanjing loved the weather, but in Rabe's words: "We don't need bombs now. It's already a mess here."

Whether it was night or day, the streets of Nanjing were incredibly crowded. There were cars, carriages and bikes; anything that could be rolled was being used. Hordes of big lorries and tanks could even be seen going down the street. They were all doing the same thing: loading belongings and withdrawing from Nanjing. Rabe helped one of these removal units. He was prepared to carry out his role at Siemens until the last moment, but his colleagues and friends wanted to leave. Many of Rabe's belongings were being moved to safety so he was one of the many people busying themselves with packing and transporting their belongings. Rabe also hadn't expected so many of his friends, who'd heard that he was staying in Nanjing, to ask him to look after their houses and belongings.

"My radio is very expensive, but it's too heavy to take with me. Mr Rabe, please take care of it no matter what happens," said Ambassador Trautmann's wife. She was polite and spoke in a gentle voice, asking Rabe to forgive her for "disturbing" him time and time again.

"I'll do what I can," said Rabe, who sent her away with a smile. He blamed himself for doing too much, just like many Chinese people there who took too much on at their own cost.

The Xiaguan docks were in absolute chaos. It reminded Rabe of his time in Africa. His own six cases were put in his friend's cabin, and they fitted well. When he wanted to close the cabin, he met with an acquaintance, Mr Segal. He wanted to load a trolley of cases onto the ship but couldn't find any space.

Rabe spread out his hands, as if to say: "What can I do to help?"

"Half of these cases are your old friend's, Litz. You've got to help him," said Segal.

Hearing that it was his old friend's things, he frowned and waved for him to follow. They put two of Litz's five cases into the shipping space Rabe had bought.

There was a sudden racket on the dock as a man shouted: "Out of the way!" Rabe popped his head out, seeing that somebody was carrying a long object, frantically rushing along the bank to the dock. One docker fell into the water and another swore.

The man was clearly disrespecting the other people there. Rabe couldn't stand it. He rushed over and told the man: "You can't do that. You have to obey orders when getting on this ship."

Unexpectedly, the man raised his voice and said to Rabe: "Don't get involved! You have no say here! I'm carrying the rug of the German ambassador. He has to get on the ship first".

"Even the ambassador doesn't have the right to treat people like this!" Rabe was angry now. He covered the man's mouth with his hand while shouting loudly to get him to stop.

The man carrying the rug was frightened by Rabe. His face turned bright red and he said nothing for a long time.

"You can go on first, but you can't just bring up the ambassador to bully others, do you understand?" whispered Rabe into the man's ear. The man nodded.

It was raining torrentially. Rainwater and mud covered both the dock and deck of the ship, soaking people's clothes and shoes. The situation was chaotic for everyone there. Rabe then unexpectedly saw the engineer Wang and his wife again.

It was Wang's Austrian wife who found Rabe. She said: "Mr Rabe, he couldn't bear staying in the luggage compartment. There was nothing to eat. He wants to change to get on the train to Hankou."

Rabe shook the rain from his head and stared at Mrs Wang: "If that's the case, you can go back. It's not too late to get on the train".

Mrs Wang started sobbing again and said: "I don't want to get on the train. This is a German ship. The Japanese won't bomb it. Taking the train is too dangerous."

Rabe was annoyed now, but he stopped himself from getting angry. He then lowered his voice and asked: "What are you going to do?"

"We don't know," she wept.

Rabe started to feel sorry for the woman. He opened his arms and hugged her, saying: "I think it's for the best that you get on this ship."

"Okay, we'll take your advice." The woman then stopped crying and went back to the luggage compartment to find her husband. "I'll come find you if I ever run into trouble, Mr Rabe," said the woman.

Rabe watched as she walked off and couldn't help but shake his head. He wrote in his diary that day: "Rabe, you're too kind. You deserve all of this."

There were more and more signs indicating that a Japanese attack on Nanjing was imminent. Chiang Kai-shek's resolution to defend the capital was wavering. Questions raced through the minds of the residents of Nanjing, Chinese and foreigners alike. How long could Nanjing hold out? What would happen if the Japanese army were to attack Nanjing? As the Chinese government began to pull out of the city, every foreign embassy began to move to Hankou along with Chiang Kai-shek's governmental institutions. They also tried to maintain friendly relations with the Japanese, wanting to protect their assets and rights in the event of a Japanese occupation of Nanjing. After seeing the strained political ties that some major powers, like the US and UK, had with Japan, most countries' embassies believed that their assets and rights in Nanjing wouldn't be guaranteed, so they decided to withdraw from the city. As its capital, Nanjing was arguably the most famous city in China. Since the opium wars, the western powers had held a great deal of influence in the city, especially international churches. The missionaries and priests had deeper ties to the city than the foreign embassies. Schools, hospitals and missions established by churches were spread throughout the city and the surrounding countryside. After the introduction of western science and technology, companies involved in the field, like Siemens, had branch offices and agencies in Nanjing. All of these institutions and the staff who worked for them made up the foreign presence in the city. Their stances regarding the situation, however, were different, as were their attitudes regarding staying in the city. The institutions and staff that stayed all had different reasons for doing so. One group that should be noted is the Christian missions, who didn't want to risk their efforts in China by leaving the poor at the mercy of the Japanese. They hoped that they would be able to help with their kindness. A second group of people that stayed were doctors and teachers, both of whom played an invaluable role in the city's wellbeing. Another group of people who stayed in the city were businessmen like Rabe.

"As we're staying, we should propose our requests to the Japanese army together and try to guarantee the dignity and rights we deserve," some suggested. Other foreign missionaries, teachers and businessmen all agreed.

The people who left Nanjing were wise, but the people who stayed were heroes. The foreigners that stayed in the city began planning how they would be able to make things better for Nanjing and how to keep the peace as the war raged on.

Some of the Americans who stayed in Nanjing proposed following the example of Father Robert Jacquinot de Besange, a French Jesuit who'd set up a neutral zone in Shanghai. During the Battle of Shanghai, the Shanghai neutral zone not only helped to protect the interests of the foreigners who lived in Shanghai, but it also helped to protect thousands upon thousands of civilians. As a result, the foreigners in Nanjing thought about establishing their own safety zone. Rabe didn't write about the process behind the proposal of the International Committee for the Nanjing Safety Zone in his diary. However, I found a translation of the state department's file from that year in the historical archives. This valuable historical source describes the proposal in detail.

Proposal for the provisional establishment of a safety zone in Nanjing
17 November 1937

At 5.30pm, Mr W P Mills, Dr M S Bates and Dr Lewis Smythe (the latter two are professors at the Jinling College) made an agreement and went to Peck's house.

Mr Mills and the others explained the situation to Peck.

(I) The proposal to establish a temporary safety zone was made to help people take refuge if fighting breaks out near Nanjing or within the city. The safety zone is also known as the refugee zone or the noncombat zone. (II) A range of places were searched before settling on a location. The western part of the city was deemed appropriate. (III) When Colonel Robert from the embassy was asked for his opinion, he said that the Chinese military authorities would agree to not use the western part of the city for military use as this would not weaken their strategic deployment. He said that they believed that if any fighting broke out, it would take place in the east or south of the city. (IV) In regard to this plan, Dr Hang Liwu made a statement to the minister of education, Wang Shijie. Minister Wang not only approved it, but also took the initiative to discuss it with the chief inspector of military training, Mr Tang Shengzhi, who was now the commander of the garrison in the capital. General Tang didn't state his opinion on it, but he agreed to discuss the plan with Chiang Kai-shek, who wasn't in Nanjing at that time.

The attendees then asked that if the plan was implemented, would the embassy inform the Japanese authorities? Mr Parker said that they had come to the conclusion today and that they would answer the letter from the Jinling College president Minnie Vautrin. He would personally be prepared to accept the task and deliver the message to the Japanese.

Mr Parker then made a statement, which is paraphrased below.

If somebody found out that it had been an American's idea to establish a noncombat zone, then the person who came up with the plan would without a doubt be open to criticism from others. Therefore, he believed that the people who'd proposed and supported this plan should adopt an approach where there could be no misunderstandings about their intentions so that they couldn't be blamed for its failure. This meant that the Chinese authorities would take the initiative in implementing this plan.

Mr Parker further said that the American embassy wanted to know about the decision before it made it clear to the Japanese authorities that the noncombat zones had been based on information received by China. The attendees approved of this opinion.

Mr Mills proposed that, as Mr Parker had said, it was a good idea to try to discuss the matter with Dr Sun Ke if he met him in the embassy that night. One of the attendees would then discuss the safety zones with Mr Parker tomorrow. Then, the meeting was over.

That night, the ambassador had supper with Mr Parker and Dr Sun Ke. General Zhang Qun and the mayor of Nanjing, Ma Chaojun, sat with them. During the meal, the ambassador said that they should introduce the previously mentioned plan. The idea was made to look like it had come from ordinary civilians who didn't have any official business. It was then discussed. If asked about it, they were to say that they were ready to tell the Japanese authorities about the plan when it was all organised.

The mayor didn't voice any opinion about the proposal. However, he seemed to consider it during the entire supper. When he was asked about it, he said that he planned to stay in Nanjing. When talking with him about it, it seemed unlikely that he would stay.

At Ambassador Johnson's request, Mr Parker made it clear to the Chinese what had happened during the meeting with Mills, Bates and Smythe that afternoon.

General Zhang Qun was at the supper and was one of the core people involved in the national government during the period. He suggested that it was too early to discuss the issue of the safety zone. However, this hid a more sinister meaning, which was that the Japanese army were approaching Nanjing. It may have just been to relieve the tense atmosphere at the supper.

— (NANJING MASSACRE, VOL. 12, P. 84-86)

We can see from this proposal that several American professors had the idea for the safety zone. After asking for the advice of the American embassy in China, they told the plan to senior leaders in the Chinese government and got approval. They then put the plan on the agenda.

On 18 November, the day after Smythe and Bates had spoken with the officials who had the power to do something, like Zhang Qun, they got together to discuss other important issues, like who should be head of the organisation.

"Mr Rabe from Siemens would be a good choice," said Smythe, thinking of the German he'd met before.

"It has to be him. And he's a member of the Nazi Party. The Japanese would treat him with special respect."

"We met him. He's a kind and industrious person from Hamburg. I believe he'd do a good job."

Some of the Americans and missionaries were delighted by the choice of Rabe. "The Japanese have crossed the Nanjing outer defensive line set up by the Chinese army. We can't hesitate in establishing the neutral zone. We have to ask Rabe to come and discuss the matter tonight," suggested Smythe.

The next day, on 19 November, a dinner was held at Smythe's home and everyone had a good time. Almost all of the Americans working in Gulou Hospital and the Jinling College came. Rabe came too.

On behalf of the Americans, Bates proposed to Rabe that an international safety committee be set up before the Japanese army occupied Nanjing. Meanwhile, they talked about what they needed to do to establish a neutral zone like the one established by Father de Besange in Shanghai. They also told Rabe about what they had to do and invited him to take up the post as the president of the international committee.

Rabe enthusiastically listened to his friends' presentation and asked with a look of surprise: "You are all outstanding individuals. Why did you choose me to be the president?"

"We think that you're the perfect choice at present. On top of your skill and kindness, your nationality and identity as a member of the NSDAP is something we don't have," John Magee the missionary said. He continued: "Of course, as this is a voluntary and difficult position, we would be in your debt if you're willing to take it."

"Yes, we all think so," said Bates as the others turned to look at him with appreciation.

Rabe looked at the expressions on the faces of the Americans and realised that they were being sincere. He prudently said: "I would do as you wish if you think my nationality and identity will be useful with the Japanese."

"On behalf of all the Americans and other foreigners staying in Nanjing, here's to President Rabe."

"To President Rabe!"

That night was the first time that Rabe got to know many Americans, including John Magee. They were all his "subordinates", and members of the international committee.

On his way back to the office, Rabe told Han Xianglin about what had happened. Han immediately said: "On behalf of all the citizens of Nanjing, I am so grateful. We'll support you no matter what."

"I can't imagine what Nanjing would be like under Japanese occupation. I don't even know if I'm competent enough to undertake this position. Han, you're Chinese. You have to help me to fulfil this task. My honour as a German and as a member of the Nazi Party is at stake," said Rabe as he stared at Han Xianglin, a man he trusted a great deal.

"Trust me, Mr Rabe. If you want me to do something, I won't hesitate, not even for a second," said Han. Han had said to Rabe before that he'd stay in Nanjing with no regrets if Rabe stayed in Nanjing. Hearing Han's promise to him, Rabe was moved and gave him a big hug.

"Han decided to share both his happiness and sadness with me. He is an honest man," wrote Rabe in his diary.

Rabe was an ambitious man and was ready to do something to make a difference. Negative news constantly streamed in from Shanghai, which made him worried, saying that he was concerned about "the honour of Germany being destroyed". Rabe was now determined to help. When he reported the plans to Ambassador Trautmann, he approved. The ambassador told Rabe that three people were to stay in the embassy, including Dr Rosen.

"Rosen doesn't want to stay in Nanjing. How could someone like him do a good job?" asked Rabe, who was no fan of Rosen. He thought that Rosen was scared of death. He hoped that the ambassador would order Rosen to withdraw, but he didn't do so.

Han Xianglin advised him: "You need to have a good relationship with the people at the embassy. They might end up lodging a complaint against you."

"I'm not afraid of people secretly complaining about me. People like us who stay in Nanjing are heroes. We are about to face the Japanese bayonets. Rosen is too timid. How could he ever be our comrade in arms? I don't know how the ambassador can even consider it," said Rabe angrily.

On the morning of 22 November, the embassy called Rabe to ask him to come to a meeting at the embassy. Dr Rosen was the one who made the call.

"I need to have a special car permit, or it'll be too difficult," proposed Rabe. Rabe's negativity was obvious, but this was understandable given the situation in Nanjing, where Chiang Kai-shek's government had declared martial law during the nights several days earlier. As a German representative and the president of the future International Committee, it made sense for Rabe to propose this requirement. However, Dr Rosen didn't agree. He thought that Rabe was beginning to put on airs now he had been assigned the position of president.

"There's no argument to be had here. It's like the screws in every machine at Siemens. Everything needs to work and be in the right place. As a German representative and the president of the International Committee, I need to have a special car permit," demanded Rabe when he met Rosen at the embassy, taking off his gloves while doing so.

"Well, I'll discuss this with the Chinese government," replied Rosen, shaking his head.

"I know that you're afraid of death, but asking the Chinese for a special permit poses no danger to you," Rabe rebutted, less than pleased.

At 5pm, the International Committee was officially established, creating a neutral zone for the civilians of Nanjing. Rabe was elected as its president.

Rabe's inaugural speech was rather short, leaving the people present somewhat disappointed as they had expected to hear a rousing German speech: "I appreciate everyone's trust in me. I shall endeavour to lead this organisation well and hope that each member effectively fulfils their respective roles." He explained: "In times of crisis, we need just the essential words and action. Action is more important than words." Everybody laughed.

Rabe was a very careful man. Under his leadership, the International Committee immediately drafted a statement about their plans to send to the Japanese authorities. This statement was to be sent to the American consul general over the American embassy's radio. It would then be relayed to the Japanese ambassador in China.

President Rabe began considering the complicated diplomatic process: "We shouldn't publish our statement until the Japanese ambassador receives it. It involves diplomacy and our organisation isn't sided with the Chinese or the Japanese. We should consider neutrality to avoid any problems."

All the committee members present agreed.

The International Committee's first document was released. It was published in English and Chinese and targeted at the Chinese and Japanese governments. The main content of the statement is paraphrased below.

Fighting was likely to break out in or near Nanjing. The International

Committee, consisting of Danish, German, British and American nationals, strongly suggested that the Chinese and Japanese governments agree to establish a safety zone for any refugees.

The International Committee was responsible for getting a guarantee from the Chinese government, who stated that they would remove all the planned military facilities in the safety zone, including military traffic guidance institutions. Armed people were not allowed in the safety zone, except for civil police who carried guns. No soldiers or military groups were allowed in the safety zone, regardless of the property they had there or their rank. The International Committee would strive to gain recognition and implementation of the guarantee.

The safety zone was to be located in the west of the city. The Japanese air force would not target it when launching air strikes.

The suggested safety zone was as follows:

East: Zhongshan Road would be used as a boundary, going from Xinjiekou to the Shanxi Road intersection

South: Passing from the intersection at Hanzhong Road and Shanghai Road to Xinjiekou.

The International Committee would mark these borders with white flags or other clear signs to identify them. The committee suggested that the area should be established as a safe zone from the day they received the agreement of both governments.

The International Committee strongly hoped that the Japanese government would respect the safety area and guarantee its safety from a humanitarian perspective. Applying precautionary measures for civilians would show that both of the liable governments were responsible and honourable. They required the response of the Japanese government as soon as possible so that they could continue essential negotiations with the Chinese government to protect the refugees.

The International Committee hoped for the idea to be taken into serious consideration by the respective governments.

The 15 members of the International Committee then signed their names in the following order: J M Hansen, G Schultze-Pantin, P H Munro-Faure, John Magee, P R Shields, Iver Mackay, John H D Rabe, J V Picketing, Miner Searle Bates, Eduard Sperling, Rev W Plumer Mills, C S Trimmer, J Lean, Charles Riggs, Lewis S C Smythe. After the Japanese occupation of Nanjing, eight of them stayed in the city: John H D Rabe, John Magee, Miner Searle Bates, Eduard Sperling, Rev W Plumer Mills, C S Trimmer, Charles Riggs and Lewis S C Smythe. They held important positions, such as college professors, doctors, crewmen and businessmen, like Rabe. Their respective embassies didn't support their refusal to leave Nanjing. This decision took a great deal of courage and sacrifice. So why did people like Rabe choose to do this? Many people asked that question during the Japanese occupation of the city. Mr Bates, one of the people who'd proposed an international safety zone and a professor at Nanjing University, once explained himself in a letter to a friend:

> ...we've been forced to do so by this cruel war.
>
> What's happened over the last one and a half years has made it hard for any philosophical person to believe in generosity and virtuous faith. I can't see any sign of God in this overwhelming wave of cruelty and greed. The value of human beings, people's lives and Jesus's message here couldn't be any smaller. Fighting for people's lives in defence of truth and humanity, unarmed and in great danger, knowing that one may be killed by some unforeseen power, has been a true inspiration. Their lives and sacrifices are eternal. This feeling is truly new, bravely fighting for everything with the guidance of the bright light created by God. Life is valuable even though it ends right now. The value of sacrificing oneself so that others may live is priceless. We have now had some success, including an emergency programme to follow in case of a battle and the hope of defusing the situation. However, a person's lifelong career can be utterly destroyed by a vengeful military policeman or a narrow-minded person following orders.
>
> "Peace on earth and good will to men." Is the peace we are facing a merciful peace? Every soul will inevitably face severe conditions and must accept their role. I believe this role cannot be contorted or changed. "Be not overcome by evil" is a strong call that speaks directly to the human heart. Overcoming evil with good requires good to be more powerful than people can usually see. This is undoubtedly the correct course of action.

Love can be found everywhere, even in hopeless places where one would never normally expect it.

On 23 November, Rabe received two special gifts from his wife when he awoke: a telegram from his wife wishing him a happy 55th birthday and a beautiful scarf.

He smiled to himself. He was in the tub, naked, holding the telegram and scarf. The radio near the tub was playing a Chinese song called *Wish You a Long and Healthy Life*.

He closed his eyes and relaxed in the hot water. "Cleanliness is next to godliness," he thought to himself, laughing. Mr Lorenz, a German captain and young consultant for the Chinese army, called him before 5am, hoping that Rabe would be able to help him board the German ship in the Yangtze because he had just arrived in Nanjing from the front line. "I'm afraid the boat left last night," said Rabe, feeling somewhat sorry for the young captain. The doorbell rang as soon as he hung up the phone. It was Mr Huldeman, the editor of the *Far East News*. Rabe was annoyed and closed the door. He lay in the tub and enjoyed his birthday alone.

Rabe was somewhat surprised. He wanted his servants to make him a birthday cake with candles to share with his Chinese friends and German colleagues. The chef was sick and the handyman, Cai, claimed that he didn't know how to make a cake out of candles.

Rabe thought this was incredibly funny and laughed loudly alone in the tub.

Han Xianglin came when he heard Rabe's unusual laughter. He gently opened the door and said: "Sir, you're in a great mood today!"

"Of course! Today is my birthday!" Rabe started to stop laughing.

"Really? We should celebrate it. I'll get the servant to make you birthday noodles," said Han excitedly.

The phone rang again.

"It's Smythe, he insists that he needs to speak to you," said Han.

"Hello, what? Those damn Americans! How can they do that?! Alright, I'll call and apologise. An apology is essential," said Rabe before hanging up, with the jubilant atmosphere gone.

"What's happened?" asked Han.

"Smythe said that Reuters accidentally leaked our plan to establish a safety zone. This is just the beginning. The Japanese will see this as us ignoring them by not informing them of the plans. We have to do something." He put on his clothes and got ready to write a letter of apology.

Han then told Rabe: "Mr Rabe, today is your birthday. It's too late for me to get you a gift. But a friend of mine is giving you a truck with 100 tanks of petrol and 200 bags of flour to help set up the safety zone."

"This is the best birthday gift I could have asked for. Thank you, Han," Rabe said, hugging him excitedly. Thinking about how Han's entire family had stayed in Nanjing with him and had given him such a big present, his eyes filled with tears.

"I'm not a man who's easily moved. But, today I'm incredibly touched. Thank you. God bless your whole family," said Rabe.

Han was moved too: "Thank you. I really mean it. Rabe, so many people know that you're going to build a safety zone. Once the news gets out, the people of Nanjing will truly thank you."

"Well, we should look after the people together." Rabe then acted presidentially and said: "When is the truck going to arrive here? I have to see this incredible gift."

"I'll take care of it all," promised Han.

Rabe's excitement was infectious. He paced the room back and forth, murmuring to himself happily.

It was 5pm, just before dinner, and General Zhang Qun, the Chinese diplomatic leader who held the real power in Nanjing, was holding a dinner party at his home. The meeting was being held by the Chinese government. Many notable people attended the party: Tang Shengzhi, who'd taken up the position as the KMT garrison commander-in-chief just a few days earlier; Wang Gupan, the Nanjing police commissioner and Ma Chaojun, the mayor of Nanjing. The other 50 guests were foreigners who'd stayed in Nanjing, mostly from the US, the UK and Germany. Tang Shengzhi made a speech at the gathering. What most interested Rabe was the Chinese plan regarding the current political situation, as well as the preparations for the Japanese invasion. The opinion of the Chinese government on the establishment of the safety zone was evident in the speech.

"President Chiang's resolution can be clearly seen at the Battle of Shanghai. We released a statement on the 12th about the issue of protecting Nanjing. Like all the soldiers who defend Nanjing defiantly, President Chiang is resolute and steadfast. We will fight to the death." Tang then continued: "As we gather here today, I want to say that our resolution and will shall not be shaken. This dinner party is a good place for us to communicate with each other about the changes in the situation and any other important information. Minister Zhang, I recommend that you hold a dinner party every day."

"I completely agree. General Zhang is too kind!" Rabe responded while giving a big applause.

The foreign guests and Rabe supported the proposal. Sat around a round table, the dinner party provided an opportunity for the Chinese leaders and Nanjing government officials to communicate fluently during the crisis. Rabe told the Chinese officials that Beijing had done this during the First World War.

It was late when Rabe returned home. He saw four gorgeous Christmas trees in his living room and laughed. They must have been from his wife.

"Dora, I love you!" he said as he kissed the picture of his wife on the bedside table again and again.

After such an eventful autumn, Rabe had had enough. He received information that Reuters's inadvertent mistake had been misunderstood by the public. The safety zone was being discussed by a non-governmental organisation, but the public saw it as a project being implemented by the

American embassy in China. The Japanese government strongly protested as a result. They replied that as the American embassy had been moved from Nanjing to Hankou, there was no reason for them to propose the establishment of the safety zone.

The Americans didn't want to make enemies of the Japanese during this sensitive period. The International Committee wanted to avoid worsening things as much as possible, so they sent a telegram to Rosen, a member of staff at the German embassy. Rabe didn't like him at all, but Rosen accepted the mission and sent the following telegram to the US department of state through the German consulate general. American delegates were then dispatched to Japan to explain everything. The content of the telegram is below:

> This is from Rabe, a representative of Siemens Germany, and other foreign members from the UK, the US, Denmark and Germany, all from the International Committee. As few areas of the city have escaped damage from the air raids, we propose the establishment of a safety zone for citizens to protect them from possible fighting between China and Japan in Nanjing. The American embassy has delivered this to the Japanese embassy in Shanghai and the Japanese government. The new safety zone would provide protection for noncombatants only under special circumstances. We also hope that the areas which have been destroyed will be safe in the future.
>
> Considering that the president of the organisation is a German, we hope that this humanitarian suggestion is supported with enthusiasm.

Creating a strategy to win the battle didn't interest Rabe. What interested him was his responsibility as president. What could he do when Japan took Nanjing? Were his colleagues and he able to protect the property of the civilians of Nanjing and any foreigners from the war? To his anguish, the Japanese didn't fulfil their promise to not bomb Nanjing. Rabe's bomb shelter had been filled with rainwater. "This is unacceptable!" he shouted. Rabe's people went to remove the water with bowls and ladles. There was another matter that greatly irritated Rabe. The driver of the truck that had been a present to Rabe drove it away out of fear of being killed by the Japanese planes during the fighting. The truck that was filled with petrol and flour was detained by the 88th garrison division.

"This is unacceptable! I have to get the supplies. Just look at the hundreds of thousands of people who've been wounded; they're on the verge of death! It's our duty to save them!" Rabe was furious and asked Han to do everything he could to get the supplies back. With the help of a KMT official called Hang Liwu, he eventually managed to do so.

"Hang the German flag in the car so it doesn't get seized by the Chinese army," suggested Rabe, one of the many ideas he proposed, but it wasn't enough to mitigate the ever increasing chaos in Nanjing. The mayor, Ma Chaojun, ordered all citizens to evacuate from the centre of the city as quickly as possible.

However, the people of the city had not been notified that the Japanese army was approaching. The citizens had no idea that the Japanese army had managed to advance all the way to Nanjing without any problems.

Mayor Ma called Rabe: "Mr Rabe, I'd like to invite you to a party at Mr Zhang's house tonight."

"Okay, I'll be there," Rabe replied.

Mayor Ma told Rabe that Chiang had approved the proposal for the creation of a safety zone. But there was no response from the Japanese. Rabe returned home, annoyed, suffering from insomnia. As the chairman of the International Committee and a member of the Nazi Party, he felt incredibly ashamed and embarrassed by the prospect of failing to accomplish his mission. But what else could he do? The Japanese were incredibly stubborn, never listening to anyone.

Rabe suddenly had an idea: "I can ask for help from the *führer*! Japan will surely listen to him." He wasted no time in writing a letter to Hitler via the Shanghai general consul:

To the *führer*,

As the group leader and chairman of the International Committee in Nanjing, I request your excellency to persuade the Japanese government to approve the establishment of a safety zone in Nanjing as 200,000 innocent people will be in danger in the coming battle.

Heil Hitler,

— Rabe, Representative of Siemens in Nanjing

Would Hitler pay any attention to this letter? Rabe believed he would. Something else worried Rabe: this important telegram, which concerned hundreds of thousands of lives, could be detained by the consul general as the cable charge was extremely high. With this in mind, Rabe wrote another telegram to the German consul general in Shanghai:

Dear Consul General,

I hope you are able to support my action in persuading the *führer* in establishing a safety zone in Nanjing, otherwise there shall surely be a bloody massacre.

I will pay the cable fee if necessary. You can charge it in advance from my account at Siemens (Shanghai, China).

— Rabe

Rabe was an incredibly thoughtful and honourable man. He selflessly devoted himself to the citizens of Nanjing. This is why Chinese people hold him in such high esteem.

He attended the British Council's dinner party at 69 Peking Road, invited by the mayor. There was no news and the dinner party was being held as a farewell party for Holt, a British general. It was a good opportunity for Rabe to deliver the two telegrams to Acheson, a member of staff at the American embassy.

The news on the radio made Rabe more and more anxious: Jiangning, the vital fortress that protected Nanjing, was about to fall.

"If this is true, then the end is soon upon us," Rabe said to Han. They looked at each other in silence.

"God bless Nanjing. God bless us," Rabe waved his hands over himself in the shape of the cross.

The next day was 26 November, a bright and sunny day. A Chinese man came to Rabe's home and insisted on seeing him.

"What can I do for you?" Rabe asked in Chinese. He got by in Chinese and understood simple sentences for communication purposes.

The man said: "A relative of mine runs the Capital Hotel. Can we hang the German flag in our restaurant?"

"What for?" Rabe asked cautiously.

"Well, the people of Nanjing are afraid of being killed by Japanese bombs. We know that they won't drop bombs on Germans, so…" explained the man with a smile.

When Rabe heard this, his face went bright red: "Definitely not! There's absolutely no way!"

"Why?" The man was confused. Why was this foreigner, who had a reputation for being a good man, so furious? Even if he didn't want to help, there was no need to be angry.

"It's the principle!" Rabe angrily reasoned.

"Principle? How is this anything to do with principle? We just want to use your flag for a bit," said the man before he left in confusion.

"It's the principle of Germany! I could never tolerate anything like this!" seethed Rabe, feeling that he and the dignity of his nation had been insulted.

But he soon calmed down after considering the myriad and often contradictory rumours spreading all over Nanjing. People sometimes said that Chiang Kai-shek had fled Nanjing with his wife, or that Japanese spies had infiltrated key camps of the Chinese army. Other times, people said that Hitler had helped China to reach a compromise with the Japanese. In the midst of all the news spreading around the city, good news and bad, only one thing was certain: the Japanese planes continued to bomb Nanjing every day. Bombs were dropped on residential areas and buildings. The Japanese gunfire was drawing nearer and nearer.

"Sir, there's a telegram here from Shanghai, it's been sent by the consulate general," reported Han to Rabe. Han asked him: "Is this the response from your leader?"

A wave of disappointment washed over Rabe's face as he stared at the telegram. He said: "It isn't from the *führer*. It's my company. They want me to leave Nanjing as soon as possible."

"What? Siemens wants you to leave Nanjing? Do you... do you want to go?" Han Xianglin asked with a pang of anxiety in his voice.

Rabe looked at him and said: "Take it easy, I'm not going anywhere!"

Han was relieved but couldn't help worrying again: "What are you going to do?"

"I have a plan." Rabe then sat in front of his desk and began to write a message.

To Siemens Shanghai,

I have received your telegram and want to express my sincere gratitude to you. I have decided to stay in Nanjing and take charge of the International Committee to set up the neutral zone to protect the safety of 200,000 people.

— Rabe

The message was short but it contained an extremely important message.

Who else would bear the international responsibility for the 200,000 civilians at risk in the city? Rabe was an honest and determined man. He was prudent and unswayed by others when making decisions, and it came down to his determined personality. He believed that he was making the right choice and no other course of action lay open to him as the Japanese army approached Nanjing.

There was another short meeting that night at the dinner party. The head of the Nanjing police department, Wang Gupan, reported new information updates like usual, but it left Rabe with the feeling that the Chinese were holding back some rather unpleasant information. However, it wasn't all bad news that night as Rosen, a man Rabe didn't like all that much, did a great thing for him. Rosen was a German diplomatic officer who had once been reluctant to stay in Nanjing, which was why Rabe hadn't liked him, thinking that he was a coward. Rabe saw this sort of behaviour as a disgrace to Germany. However, Rosen had a thoughtful gift for Rabe.

"You really want the house?" Rosen asked Rabe in a serious tone.

"Of course," replied Rabe eagerly.

"Okay, I'll do what I can." Rosen agreed to try to get it for him.

The following day, Rosen brought Rabe the good news that he'd got him his dream house.

Rabe was extremely grateful. He could never have guessed that a person he'd disliked so much would ever do something so nice for him. Zhang Qun's house had been offered to Rosen, but he asked for it to be offered to Rabe. He was incredibly touched. What moved Rabe even more was that Rosen quietly gave a good word for him to the British consul general. With this recommendation, Rabe would be able to board the British Jardine Matheson ship in Nanjing whenever he wanted. The ship was one of the few foreign emergency ships left docked in Xiaguan, which could take him upstream to Hankou.

Rabe had been mistaken; Rosen wasn't just a good person but he also came from an enviable family. As Rabe got closer with Rosen, he discovered that his grandfather had been a friend of Beethoven, and Rosen still kept the letters that Beethoven had written to him. The Rosen family had been in the diplomatic service for more than 100 years. Rosen's father had once worked as a government minister. However, Rosen hadn't been so fortunate and was just a secretary. This was because Jews were despised by the German government in the Nazi era and experienced severe discrimination, so as Rosen had a Jewish grandmother, it harmed his career.

After learning more about Rosen, Rabe's negative impression of him transformed into complete understanding.

That day was 27 November. Tang Shengzhi had shown up at the dinner party again that evening. As the commander of the Nanjing garrison, he still seemed like a very powerful man, and made a "frank and important speech" where he mentioned the following:

- His determination to defend Nanjing to the last man.
- Nanjing would soon become a battlefield.
- Foreigners were therefore in danger and were advised to leave Nanjing. He would do everything he could to ensure the safety of those who stayed and the property of the foreigners.
- In a few days, his garrison would shut all the gates. If necessary, he would also try to take foreigners out of the city, either through the gates or over the walls, but there still were potentially dangerous conditions outside of Nanjing.
- Nanjing would be defended by well-trained troops. Special measures had been taken to resolve the issue of illegal armed militias in an area of about 50 kilometres around the city.
- The troops deployed around Nanjing came from many provinces so that riots would be unlikely in the city.

In a later private conversation, Tang said that if the Japanese successfully captured Wuhu, then the Chinese army deployed in Nanjing would be under siege, and the only course of action left to the Chinese army was to break through their lines.

Rabe and the other foreigners felt that Tang had been so blunt that it was difficult to take. How long would Nanjing actually hold out for? Tang seemed unsure. While on the one hand, Tang's determination to defend Nanjing seemed resolute, on the other hand, he seemed pessimistic in private conversations. Rabe and the other foreigners knew that the superficial confidence demonstrated by Tang Shengzhi, who was in charge of 150,000 troops, didn't really matter.

The fate of Nanjing was now in the hands of the Japanese, even though the Japanese army was still more than 100 miles from Purple Mountain. But for the well-equipped Japanese army, this distance would only take three to five days to cover. This was what really concerned Rabe.

The International Committee meeting was held once again at Smythe's house. Everybody was discussing the issue of Japan not responding to their proposal of establishing a neutral zone, leading to a heated debate on how they should proceed given the increasingly urgent state of affairs.

Rabe believed that without a Japanese guarantee to respect it, even if the

International Committee were to establish a neutral zone, it was akin to herding together a group of sheep to make it easier for the wolves to catch them. They would no longer be the protectors of the people, but the organisation responsible for leading Nanjing to disaster.

"What President Rabe's saying here isn't out of the question," agreed Mills. "The Japanese are a pack of ravenous wolves, and as soon as they invade the city, if they don't recognise the neutral zone or argue that the zone was created without their consent or any other reason, the more refugees we have there, the greater the crime they will commit. This is unacceptable. We should try to ask the Chinese leaders to consider giving up Nanjing peacefully so that the Japanese don't have any excuse for committing genocide after their attack. The way the war is going, if the Chinese army stay in Nanjing it'd be absurd!"

The Chinese director general Hang Liwu from the newly elected International Committee disagreed with Mill's proposal. He said: "We've fought the Japanese well so far, if we let Chiang down and leave empty-handed by surrendering the capital, then even if Chiang Kai-shek agrees, it would be unacceptable to the Chinese people."

"You mean we have to wait for a response from the Japanese?" Fitch, another recently elected director general, asked Hang.

Hang nodded and said: "I see no other way, we have to wait patiently for a positive response from the Japanese, otherwise the president's predictions may come true. All our efforts would be for nought."

"Ridiculous! We've put our lives at risk but they still might end up hating us?! What can we do?" said an impatient attendee.

The meeting was heated. Everyone appeared to be swayed by their emotions.

"Doctor, what do you think?" Rabe knew that Smythe was famous for his intellect so he asked for his opinion.

Smythe stood up and took a cigarette from Shi Peilin, who'd come with Rabe. He took a drag and said: "Everyone's opinions make sense. But it was us who put forward a motion to establish a neutral zone. No one gave us any authority and we adhere to God's will, using our beliefs to do what we can to reduce the suffering of the citizens of China and Nanjing. This action is noble indeed. If there are any mistakes, we know that we are following God's will and that we have a mission. This is to say that any mistake is not ours to bear. Secondly, we can see that the Japanese are certainly uncomfortable because we are obviously not doing as they wish; as conquerors, they wish to reap their rewards of crime and slaughter. The Japanese think that once they occupy Nanjing, they can do as they wish with the city. However, we have established a neutral zone, and by doing so, we have obviously limited their right to do this. The Japanese are inevitably going to feel a certain hatred towards us. Now the problem is that we are imposing these limitations, but we want to get their guarantee to respect the safety zone. Do you think they'll ever agree? Not likely. I don't think things are going as well as we imagined, but it's really not that bad. I advise that we wait and see what happens but do whatever we can do establish a neutral zone."

"I completely agree Dr Smythe." Rabe was very excited and waved his hands in the air: "We will do whatever we can, come what may."

The course of action was still unclear, but each member of the International Committee, especially President Rabe, had more confidence in the organisation. He believed that with people like Dr Smythe, a devoted and highly intelligent Christian, and people like German businessmen who had a strong sense of purpose, the safety zone would help the people of Nanjing, and at least let the civilians who faced calamity find refuge from the despair.

Back at his new home on 1 Xiaofenqiao, Guangzhou Road, Rabe got Shi Peilin to hang a large German flag at the gate of General Zhang's great building that had been emptied for Rabe. "Such a beautiful place, at least we can host more refugees here. We need to protect it and make sure it isn't destroyed by the Japanese bombers," he said. Rabe thought that now was time for action, as Dr Smythe had said. If they weren't as prepared as possible for the worst now and didn't establish a civilian safety zone, then in a few days, things would be even worse.

"Director, are you staying in Nanjing?" Rabe had quietly asked the police director Wang Guqing earlier that day. Wang Guqing replied: "I'll stay here as long as I can." Once Rabe heard this, he immediately knew that Wang was planning to leave the city.

What most concerned Rabe was how many people were actually still left in the city.

It was said that there were still more than 200,000 people in the city, but the truth is that no one knew for sure. Wang told Rabe: "Many people have left and quite a few are now seeking refuge with their family and friends. But refugees from the places that the Japanese have already taken have poured into Nanjing. The people thought that as Nanjing is the capital it'd be safe. This will be hell in a few days."

Rabe was shocked by what the chief of police had said.

What would these people do when faced with such danger? Rabe found that he was panicking and was finding it hard to breathe, overwhelmed by the pressure.

How many were still in Nanjing? No one seemed to know. How much space needed to be prepared for the safety zone? With the assumption that there were still 200,000 people, how much food would they need a day? What if there were still 300,000 or 500,000 people in the city?

Rabe's head throbbed with pain whenever he thought about it. The issue of how many people were still in Nanjing prior to the massacre remains a problem that has affected the credibility and accuracy surrounding the estimated death toll of 300,000 victims. The debate between China and Japan has been going on for decades. In all honesty, the historical materials that I have used offer many different figures. But there's an official Chinese source that deserves attention. This is further explained below.

The Nanjing government archives of the Republic of China recorded that Nanjing's urban and rural population was approximately 1,015,450 in June 1937. Before the fall of Nanjing, the population radically changed, partly due to emigration along with the national government and partly because the rich left Nanjing. According to the Nanjing municipal government's letter to the Nationalists' military commission's rear services on 23 November 1937: "The current population of this city is greater than 500,000." Relevant information can also be acquired from Japan. On 27 October 1937, Okamoto, a consul general in Shanghai, sent confidential letter 2144 to Foreign Minister Hirota: "Civil servants and military dependents in Nanjing have shelter, and the population has decreased sharply. According to the police investigation, the current population is more than 530,000. Most are civil servants, people whose property cannot be transferred and local business people who need to stay in Nanjing." This letter was the result of a survey of Nanjing by secret agents who were sent by the general consul in Shanghai. After the fall of Nanjing, in March to April 1938, International Committee member Dr Smythe conducted a survey that revealed: "In 1937, the population of Nanjing was just a little more than 1,000,000 until August and September when the population decreased sharply. However, at the beginning of November the population rose to 500,000." This data shows that the population of Nanjing before it fell was about 500,000. With the addition of the Chinese soldiers who failed to withdraw from Nanjing and the refugees who'd fled there from Shanghai and Suzhou, the total population of Nanjing would be greater than 600,000 (historical data sets on the Nanjing Massacre and *John Rabe's Diary*, p. 115, Jiangsu Education Press, 1999 edition).

People like the American citizen Dr Smythe, who were highly educated and versed in the ways of the Christian church, were proficient in the Chinese language and had worked in China for a long time. As a result, they were extremely careful in their work. Therefore, I believe that their painstaking research led them to accurate and credible conclusions. With this in mind, I think that the population estimate of 600,000 people prior to the Nanjing Massacre is close to the actual figure.

"Sir, you don't look very well at all these days, how's your blood sugar? You need to have your insulin injections," said Han Xianglin, who paid great attention to Rabe's health. Meanwhile, Rabe was concerned about the safety of Han's family: "You need to move your family here. I worry about them. All of Nanjing may be in danger in a few days, and it'll only be slightly safer here." Rabe had an obligation to tell Han about the seriousness of the situation.

"Thank you, sir. I'll see to it. I dread to think what would happen if you weren't here," Han said with tears in his eyes.

"We help each other out," Rabe said as he patted Han on the shoulder to comfort him.

In truth, they needed each other. A servant came in and told Rabe that the insulin he needed was ready, and he had enough for a month.

"You need to take this much?!" asked Han, surprised to see so much insulin.

Rabe said: "This is preparation for the war. Just think about how busy I'll be as president in the coming months. If I don't prepare now, if any health problems arise, what use would I be to the thousands of civilians in the safety zone?"

Han said emotionally: "If the Chinese officials were like you, the Japanese could never take Nanjing."

There was then a deafeningly loud bang outside.

Rabe soon learned from foreign sources that 30 Chinese trucks had been attacked and blown up shortly after they'd left the city. More than 40 people had been killed.

A terrible tragedy. However, events like these weren't big news in the city as all of Nanjing was in chaos with people trying to flee.

On 30 November 1937, the International Committee was officially established with Rabe serving as its president. The American, British and Chinese media published the news. Rabe received both good and bad news that day. Some said that the police chief, Wang Guxin, had resigned, while others said that he'd been arrested. This was because Wang Guxin wasn't a soldier himself and was terrified of the task that lay ahead. The other news was more welcome. Smythe told Rabe that there were 60,000 bags of rice in the city and 34,000 bags in the Xiaguan district.

"It's been getting colder, and I'm sure that the refugees will need straw mats and other goods to survive in the cold," said Rabe. He believed that supplying all of this wasn't solely his duty, and felt that Mayor Ma should be considering these issues as well.

"He's the mayor; I'm a foreigner, a businessman!" complained Rabe in front of Han and other Chinese colleagues.

"I think you'll be the mayor soon," Han said, half joking.

"Me? Mayor? What a silly notion!" Rabe laughed in disbelief.

Rabe Becomes the Mayor of Nanjing

With the mayor leaving the city, Rabe became Nanjing's de facto mayor, as forecasted by Han Xianglin.

On 1 December, the panic-stricken city was like a little boat battered by the wind and waves; none of the people in the city had a plan, including Chiang Kai-shek and his wife Soong Mei-ling. Only the two dozen foreigners who were determined to stay in Nanjing as members of the International Committee seemed relatively calm.

While the entire city was in chaos, Rabe and the other members of the International Committee were arranging materials and goods for the preparation of the safety zone.

At 9.30am, Rabe rushed to Ping Chang Lane for the International Committee meeting along with his assistant Kroeger and Shi Peilin. Following Rabe's proposals, the committee assigned the roles to members as follows:

President: Rabe
   Secretary General: Dr Smythe
   Director General: Fitch
   Deputy Director General: Hang Liwu
   Finance Supervisor: Kroeger
   Chinese Secretariat Director: Tang Zhongmo

  Five Subcommittees:
   General: Shi Peilin

  Food Commission Director: Han Xianglin
   Deputy Directors: Includes Thorne, Sun Yaosan,
   Cai Zhaosong and Zhu Jing

  Housing Commission Director: Wang Ting

Deputy Directors: Includes Riggs, Zhu Shuchang and Wang Mingde

Health Committee Director: Shen Yushu
  Deputy Director: Dr Trimmer

Director of the Transportation Committee: Hirsch Begg
  Deputy Director: Harz

"Mr Rabe, really? I'll be no good as an officer!" asked Han Xianglin, who was very surprised and touched to be appointed food committee director.

"Of course you will! I believe you are more than capable of handling all the grain collection. You're the most suitable candidate out of everyone," Rabe said as he patted Han on the shoulder. He continued: "You've already performed these duties well, didn't you just get several trucks of food?"

"I... I will try my best," said Han humbly. He was proud of finally being an official and was determined to get a lot more food for Rabe.

"You'll do fantastically. What do refugees worry most about? Two things: eating and surviving! Now this is a great responsibility, so I want to give it to people I trust, like you," Rabe said.

"So I'm the official food committee director?" asked Han excitedly, unable to believe his ears.

"Of course! I appointed you to the position personally. Why ever wouldn't we?" replied Rabe as his eyes widened.

Han had never been so excited. He hummed a happy tune as he went to tell his friends and family his news.

The mayor of Nanjing, Mr Ma, also attended Rabe's meeting and brought them good news: the government would deliver 30,000 bags of rice and 10,000 bags of flour to the future safety zone.

"This is incredible!" Rabe and the members of the committee came over to the mayor to shake his hand and show their gratitude.

The mayor replied: "I'd like to say thank you on behalf of all the citizens for your selflessness and sacrifice, and for guiding a way out of the chaos for thousands of people."

Rabe was very busy that day. After the meeting, he asked Han Xianglin to send 12 barrels of petrol to Gulou Hospital and then took a water tank back to his yard. A third air-raid shelter in Rabe's yard had also just been built; the top of the sheller was a solid iron plate, while the entrance was made out of rather strong brick.

Rabe arrived at Tang Shengzhi's headquarters that afternoon and collected the first 20,000 yuan donation of the total 100,000 yuan that Chiang Kai-shek had promised the International Committee.

"When can we expect the rest of the donation?" Rabe wisely asked the Chinese representative Dr Hang Liwu. Hang shrugged and said: "Maybe tomorrow... maybe never."

"Is that so?" Rabe paused for a long time and thought that the money may be for future refugees' food. Still, something was better than nothing.

5 Ninghai Road was now the headquarters of the International Committee, so Fitch, Kroeger, Smythe and other members went in to inspect the organisation's president's new office. "Mr Rabe, you should change your name to John Rabe Rockefeller!" Dr Smythe joked to Rabe after seeing his luxurious office.

Rabe smiled. Rockefeller was an American oil magnate who'd become the world's richest man at the beginning of the 20th century. Smythe had called Rabe Rockefeller because he now also had an incredible house. Chinese style two storey buildings like his were highly sought after at the time in Nanjing. Considering the large lawn covering the front garden, it was a good place to use as a shelter for refugees. It had a good ambience with a lot of space. It was also perfect for taking shelter from the Japanese bombs and for use as Rabe's headquarters.

At 6pm that evening, Rabe and the members of the committee held another meeting at the British Council. Unlike the previous times, this time they invited many media representatives. On behalf of the members of the International Committee, Rabe announced officially that a safety zone had been created in Nanjing. The Chinese and foreign journalists were incredibly interested in Rabe and the committee, and the many questions left Rabe feeling a little overwhelmed.

"What is Japan's stance on the safety zone?"

"They haven't stated their policy," replied Rabe.

"This means that Japan may not actually recognise it. If so, will the safety zone assist the Japanese troops in slaughtering Chinese people?"

"No one can anticipate how the war will progress; however, the safety zone is supported by international humanitarianism. Any country that violates humanitarianism will be judged by the international community," answered Rabe.

"The Japanese soldiers have already proven that their troops don't care about international condemnation. They've also been dreaming about taking China's capital for a long time. What would you do to protect citizens if the Japanese troops occupy Nanjing and slaughter them in the safety zone?"

"We have no guns, no bullets. But we have a sense of justice. I believe that justice is stronger than bullets," Rabe replied, peacefully yet firmly.

"It's been said that you've written to Hitler to ask for support. Have you received a reply?"

"Not yet. But I believe that he won't let me down!" said Rabe proudly.

"Really?"

"Yes, I believe so."

The crowd roared with laughter.

With his face red with embarrassment, Rabe stood up and said: "I promise that as a member of the Nazi Party that the *führer* will understand and support the establishment of the international safety zone."

Laughter broke out again.

Rabe later found out that he'd been wrong. Saying one thing and doing another, Hitler hadn't just cheated the Germans, but many other countries. Germany had entered into an alliance with Japan and Italy, becoming the largest power among them. Rabe, who'd always been proud of his identity as a Nazi and a German, deeply regretted his membership of the party as time passed.

However, at that point, Rabe was still expecting Hitler to at least persuade Japan to respond to the International Committee.

After the press conference, the committee convened again in the Capital Hotel, with the focus still on how to proceed without a response from the Japanese. They couldn't reach an agreement so Rabe had to make a decision.

"I believe that our initial proposal has been just. One reason that Dr Smythe recommended me for president is that Hitler stands behind me. I am still convinced that he will not let me down!" wrote Rabe in his diary. He obviously trusted Hitler a great deal at the time.

"Thank goodness! We're saved!" said Rosen. He'd told Rabe that the message to Hitler had just been submitted by Raman, the Nazi director in China. Rabe almost cheered when he heard the news.

The conference ended at around 8pm, after which Ma Chaojun, the mayor of Nanjing, came to the Capital Hotel with a group of people to dine with the members of the committee. He had an important announcement to make: "My dear President Rabe and friends, I've come here to say goodbye to you. As you are aware, it will not be long before the Japanese troops enter Nanjing. We will evacuate the city soon. Once we leave, there will be no one in the city to govern the hundreds of thousands of citizens here, and they will only be able to depend on you. I implore you to please help them!" He then drank three glasses of wine and shook hands with every member present. He shook hands with Rabe for a long time and said: "Mr Rabe, I've effectively not been in control of the city for several days now. From now on, I officially hand over the title of mayor to you my dear Mr Rabe."

"No! No! No! You're still the mayor!" said Rabe in surprise.

When he returned home, Han Xianglin, still excited from being appointed to an important post, said: "I knew it! You're the mayor now!"

With a serious look on his face, Rabe said: "I'm just the president of the committee. How could I ever be a mayor, let alone the mayor of Nanjing?!"

Rabe was still anxious about Japan's stance on the safety zone. The next day, on 2 December, the French Jesuit Robert Jacquinot de Besange transmitted a telegram from the Japanese authorities in Shanghai:

> For the attention of the International Committee for the Nanjing Safety Zone:
>
> The Japanese government has acknowledged receipt of your application for establishing a safety zone, but we are sorry to report that it has been rejected.
>
> The Japanese authorities will not bear any responsibility for the improper handling of Chinese civilians and possessions by Chinese troops. However, as long as the safety zone doesn't conflict with any necessary Japanese military action, the Japanese government will endeavour to respect the zone.
>
> — GAUSS, OFFICER AT THE AMERICAN EMBASSY

Rabe held the telegraph, reading it over and over again, as he sat at his desk without saying a word.

Han asked anxiously: "Sir, do they recognise the safety zone or not?"

"It's clear they don't!" said another servant.

"But the last sentence says that they'll aim to respect the safety zone as long as it doesn't affect their military activities."

"Diplomatic parlance is rather complicated."

Eduard Sperling came over and said: "I just heard over the British radio station that our plans have been rejected."

"They think so?" asked Rabe. Sperling nodded.

Rabe got out of his chair and said while he paced back and forth: "I don't think this is an absolute rejection because from a diplomatic angle, Japan's reply still gives us some leeway - a prerequisite for our plan - as long as we don't conflict with their military activities, they may allow the establishment of the safety zone. So, Japan's reply is favourable on closer inspection."

"You really think so?" asked Han Xianglin, whose face beamed with excitement.

Rabe nodded approvingly.

The servants cheered.

"Mr Sperling, we need to ask the American embassy to send our reply and goodwill to the Japanese authorities," said Rabe.

"You mean..."

"Send a telegram to the American embassy in my name announcing our plans after receiving their reply." Rabe sat at his desk, took out his pen and drafted:

> We warmly request you to convey the following message from the International Committee for the Nanjing Safety Zone to Robert Jacquinot de Besange.
>
> We sincerely thank you for your help. The committee agrees with and is grateful for the Japanese government's attitude whereby Japan will respect the international safety zone as long as it doesn't affect Japan's military activities. Furthermore, the Chinese authorities fully agree to implement our previous suggestion. Therefore, the committee will continue to work on the safety zone. We hereby inform you that refugees have started to move into the safety zone, and we will formally inform the Chinese and Japanese governments of the opening of the safety zone at an appropriate time after undergoing any necessary examinations.
>
> The committee sincerely requests you to contact the Japanese authorities once again in the friendliest way and to notify them that if the Japanese authorities respond to the committee positively, it would greatly relieve the anxieties of the citizens stuck in the conflict. We sincerely look forward to the prompt reply from the Japanese government.
>
> — SIGNED: JOHN RABE, PRESIDENT OF THE INTERNATIONAL COMMITTEE

Rabe held a press conference that night to publicise the Japanese telegram along with his reply requesting Japan to respect their application for a safety zone. The press release quoted a part of Rabe's speech, which says: "To save thousands of citizens whose only source of asylum is the safety zone, the committee must immediately start working on preparations. We hope that Japan responds to this humanitarian suggestion as soon as possible."

Rabe, who was now in charge of Nanjing, had to resolve many issues in a variety of fields. At the press conference held on 2 December, Rosen told Rabe that Trautmann, the German ambassador in China, had suddenly returned to Nanjing with his wife.

"They've come to support me?" asked Rabe in shock.

"No. They've come to help the Chinese authorities reach a deal with Japan," explained Rosen.

"Sir, please make sure you go to the Fuchang Hotel tonight. Dr Hang Liwu is leaving!" reported Han as he hurried up to Rabe.

"How can he leave?! He's the director of the housing committee! What are we to do without him?" asked Rabe worriedly.

"He's apparently leaving because Chiang Kai-shek has personally assigned him a special mission," explained Han. An insider later reported to Rabe that Hang had been dispatched to escort shipments of treasure from the Ming Palace.

When Rabe met Hang that night, Hang whispered to him: "14,000 cases of treasure have been left by our ancestors. This assignment is essential."

"It's a shame we have to lose you. There's no one out there better suited to your role," said Rabe in a depressed tone.

"When our country is being threatened like this, none of us have a choice," sighed Hang.

"The requirement put forward by Japan is that the safety zone shouldn't interfere with their military activities, so Chinese military activities and soldiers are prohibited in the safety zone. Commander Tang, whether the safety zone is a sanctuary for the citizens of Nanjing depends entirely on this single condition. Please issue a special order to your soldiers to not interfere for the sake of hundreds of thousands of people," Rabe later asked Tang Shengzhi in a solemn voice.

Tang stayed silent for a while and finally said: "Mr Rabe, we respect your suggestions. I will order the troops to cease all military activities in the safety zone, including building defences."

"Thank you Commander Tang!"

However, Rabe soon discovered that Tang's orders hadn't been followed, or had never even been issued in the first place. The day after Rabe met with Commander Tang, members of the International Committee reported to Rabe that soldiers in Nanjing were still building defences in the safety zone, and were even rebuilding military radio stations in some areas.

"This is unacceptable. If this continues, I have no choice but to resign!" Rabe told the Chinese authorities.

Rabe sighed with relief after the Chinese authorities promised that they'd cease operations in the area. However, Rabe knew that now not even Chiang Kai-shek could control the soldiers and civilians in Nanjing. With this in mind, Rabe calmed down, thanks to Han Xianglin always providing him with a Chinese perspective. He was always very grateful to Han for doing so.

Work on the safety zone couldn't be halted and stalled as this would make the impending disaster even worse. As a result, Rabe decided to make all the citizens aware of the safety zone and its function as quickly as possible. He made an announcement to the press and police titled *Temporary Orders for Settling Citizens and Dispensing Food in the Safety Zone*, which said:

1. The safety zone has not been prepared to shelter vast numbers of citizens because there is no need for doing so considering the current state of the war.
2. In order to limit the number of refugees in the safety zone to a minimum at this urgent moment, the committee suggests each family discusses residency arrangements with their friends and family in advance. The right to settle refugees in this zone is reserved by the committee.
3. A special committee in charge of settling refugees is currently able to check houses that refugees can settle in. The committee can help refugees who cannot find a residence through personal relationships. However, it will not do so until the conditions of the war make it urgently necessary. If that moment comes, we will formally announce the safety zone's operational launch.
4. Only private houses are available for personal arrangements. Public buildings and schools are not included.
5. As space in the safety zone is limited, only bedding, clothes and food can be brought into the zone. Furniture or other possessions are not permitted.

This was the International Committee's first announcement and it also specified when the safety zone would be opened, which was: "After all Chinese soldiers and military facilities have been withdrawn." Rabe said this for two reasons: one was to urge Commander Tang to be as stern as possible in the retreat; the other was to show compliance with the demands of the Japanese authorities.

"The Germans are so shrewd!" said Tang Shengzhi when he read the news the next day. He then issued a strict order: troops that had been left to guard the city were to withdraw from the safety zone, and any military facilities or military operations in the area would cease.

St Paul's Church rang its bells on 5 December, the first Sunday of the month. Preacher Forster was preparing the service as usual: "I shall pray for all of you today. The Lord is your keeper and stands beside you night and day from now and forever." The soft and somewhat gloomy sound resounded around the city. Although fewer people had come to the church than usual, there were still more than Forster had thought, and most of them were women. When the service was over, Forster went to John Magee the missionary's home. While he was on his way there, three shells hurtled over his head, followed by antiaircraft guns opening fire nearby. Forster immediately escorted the women that had come out of the church with him over to the air-raid shelters at the end of the road. When he got to Magee's home, they intensely discussed with a few others how to persuade the Chinese authorities to surrender the city.

"Although there's no way of preventing the Japanese invaders from entering the city, opening the door to them is still regarded as stupid. Why do we provoke them and risk them slaughtering civilians?" asked Magee.

"I'm afraid that Chiang Kai-shek would never agree to surrender. He's been criticised by the Communist Party for not resisting the Japanese for years. He's now doing everything he can to get some sort of victory, and all elite troops have been dispatched to Shanghai," said Forster.

"And what's happened?" asked Magee. "China cannot best Japan. Chiang did all he could to defend Shanghai, but he still lost. What could he do with Nanjing? China is incapable of defending itself so it's better to just open the gates now."

Forster laughed and said: "We're just clergymen. How could we influence Chiang? All we can do is to pray for the citizens of Nanjing."

Magee and Forster prayed for peace in front of a statue of Jesus.

There was another loud bang.

Things were rather different for Rabe as he was closer to Japanese targets with bombs being dropped near his office. Sometimes, due to the explosions being so powerful, he asked his servants to move his desk away from the windows. There was a radio on his desk, which had become his closest friend, and he used it to receive all the important news stories from the Shanghai radio stations.

He heard on the radio that some Japanese troops had already arrived just 13 kilometres away from Nanjing. "If this is true, the Japanese will break into the city in just two or three days, not two weeks like Commander Tang said," hypothesised Rabe.

"Could it be that soon?" asked Han anxiously when he heard what Rabe had said. "The safety zone isn't ready yet, and the citizens don't really understand what's going on with it. Shall we make an announcement or something to the public?"

"Good idea. Some members of the committee are still trying to persuade the Chinese authorities to open the gates to the Japanese," said Rabe.

Han stayed silent for a while and asked: "They mean surrender?"

Rabe glanced at Han and said: "Not defending is also a military strategy. It's not necessarily a surrender."

Han insisted: "I don't think there's much difference between not defending and surrendering. Opening the gates without any resistance is the same as surrendering. I'm afraid it'd be hard for the Chinese troops and citizens to accept it. It's tragic."

Rabe shook his head and muttered: "The Chinese are so obsessed with saving face, even when it just means more people are going to die."

"Mr Rabe, our intelligence indicates that there are still quite a lot of soldiers in the safety zone. This is a very dangerous situation," said Dr Rosen as he hastily approached Rabe.

"Last night Commander Tang clearly promised me that he'd issue an order to get the Chinese troops to withdraw from the zone and stop all military operations there," said Rabe in an irritated tone.

Rosen replied: "Commander Tang did issue that order. But the soldiers are worried that once the Japanese break into the city, all of them will be killed. So, the soldiers are now sneaking into the safety zone in every way imaginable."

Rabe anxiously rubbed his hands together and said: "This is extremely dangerous! We have to put a stop to it now!" He promptly told Han to arrange for a group of staff to guard every entrance to the safety zone in the next few days and to prevent soldiers, even those dressed in civilian clothing, from entering.

Early in the morning of 6 December, the air-raid sirens sounded and wouldn't stop. News from Wuhu confirmed that two ships, the *Takvo* and *Da Tong* from foreign firms in Yihe and Taigu respectively, had been hit by Japanese planes while docking, killing hundreds of Chinese people. The captain of a British ship that was docking in the area was also injured in the air-raid.

The situation in Nanjing was becoming more urgent. The Japanese had bombed Pukou Railway Station, immediately killing 20 people.

Rabe then went to visit Colonel Huang, who'd been left to guard Nanjing, to discuss stopping soldiers from entering the safety zone.

Colonel Huang objected to the idea of establishing a safety zone and said: "The safety zone demoralises the soldiers."

Huang explained: "It's quite obvious that we lost the last battle. Now it's time for us to defend Nanjing. We need to do whatever we can in this battle to stop them from taking our land. But because you've established the safety zone, many citizens have taken refuge there, as well as some soldiers. So, who'll be there to fight when the Japanese invaders take the city?! I am completely and utterly opposed to the safety zone."

Colonel Huang appeared to be angry, turning his back on Rabe and storming away.

Rabe thought Colonel Huang's argument was absurd. He needed to make Huang understand the objective and significance of the safety zone: "Colonel, the citizens going into the safety zone are those left behind in Nanjing. The reason they're staying is because they don't have enough money to escape with their family and their possessions. They are the city's poorest, should they pay the price for the mistakes of the military?"

"When did I say that the poor should take the blame for our mistakes?" barked Huang angrily. "I'm sorry, my Chinese is rather rusty," Rabe apologised hastily. He explained: "My dear Colonel Huang, my question is: why isn't it okay to give orders to the wealthy citizens of Nanjing who've fled with their money, while it's okay to ask the city's poorest to sacrifice themselves?"

After a moment of silence Huang said: "The establishment of the safety zone should be at the last moment possible. After the Japanese break into the city, there'll be fighting in the streets. It would be better to build a safety zone while this is going on."

Rabe objected: "I don't think that's very realistic. If you don't prepare in advance and the Japanese army storms Nanjing faster than expected, the Chinese army may have to pull back before there's any chance to fight in the streets. I'm afraid that it'd be too late to establish the safety zone we need at this point." Colonel Huang remained as stubborn as ever: "No! It can't be established until the last moment, otherwise it will damage the morale of our army. I won't allow it. It'd damage the dignity of the image of China and the Chinese army's combat effectiveness." The exchange with Colonel Huang had left Rabe frustrated. When Rabe returned from the meeting, he felt a painful sorrow and stooped over his desk silently for several minutes contemplating his next move. Rabe then thought of the Japanese. The only course of action that lay open to him was asking the Japanese for authorisation to build the safety zone. If the Japanese agreed, Rabe's committee could get to work straight away. Japan had declared its stance regarding the zone, so they needed to seize the opportunity and put forward the committee's proposal. Rabe immediately started to draft another telegram to the Japanese authorities:

6 December 1937

For the attention of the Japanese authorities:

1. The International Committee has received the response from the Japanese authorities and its content has been noted. The Chinese authorities are currently reducing the number of military installations in the region and withdrawing military personnel from the area. The committee has started using a flag to mark the boundaries of the safety zone. The flag is made up of a red cross in a red circle against a backdrop of white (the red circle symbolises the safety zone). The flag will be flown at the boundaries of the safety zone or on the roofs of buildings.

2. Considering the gradual withdrawal of the remaining Chinese military personnel and the safety of tens of thousands of refugees pouring into the area, the committee would like the area to not be a bombing target and not be attacked before or after its establishment. The International Committee will do all it can to complete its work as quickly as possible.

3. The International Committee understands that the Japanese authorities have made a commitment in their reply and we are grateful for it. Japan has made the following commitment: the Japanese army has no intention of attacking locations where Chinese armies, military facilities or deployments are not present.

4. The International Committee hereby informs the Japanese authorities that 15 to 20 foreign volunteers are managing the safety zone. The fact that foreign nationals are staying in the city shows their belief in the honesty and credibility of China and Japan in regard to their stance towards the safety zone. In addition to this, the committee shall also be responsible for all relevant safety regulations implemented in the zone.

— SIGNED: JOHN RABE, PRESIDENT OF THE INTERNATIONAL COMMITTEE

When he finished writing the message to the Japanese, Rabe thought about it for a while: this wasn't enough. To make sure the safety zone operated effectively, Rabe needed the cooperation of Tang Shengzhi, who was still in control of Nanjing. Tang had also expressed his support for the safety zone several days earlier. The problem lay with his subordinates and military officials like Huang. He had to secure the support of Tang Shengzhi. Rabe then began drafting a telegram to him:

My dear General Tang,

Following a discussion yesterday between a friend of yours and the president of the committee, the committee would like to extend its heartfelt thanks to you for your approval and support of the committee's work in helping refugees and civilians in Nanjing. The committee is particularly grateful for these guarantees regarding the safety zone:

1. *Not establishing new military facilities, trenches or other shelters in the safety zone, and not leaving artillery in the zone.*

2. *All military personnel being forbidden from entering the safety zone after its borders have been clearly marked.*

3. *All those who belong to the military or other departments having to gradually withdraw from the zone.*

So that our proposals for the safety zone can be effectively implemented, the committee will immediately put these guarantees into effect with all Chinese military personnel following your orders. The committee has consulted Mr Fang, the police chief subject to your orders, with the military being notified to briefly describe the nature and role of the safety zone so that they understand why they are forbidden from entry.

The committee has shown great concern regarding your statement, namely that its specific implementation will face great difficulties. In this regard, the committee notes that accepting large numbers of refugees entails certain difficulties. These refugees seek protection, but if there are any military facilities or personnel present, such protection cannot be guaranteed.

The committee does not deny the validity of your argument that it would be hard to withdraw armed military personnel in a short period of time. However, the committee would like to take the liberty to point out the increasing difficulty in communications that would make it difficult to ensure that the Japanese authorities have been informed about the formal establishment of the safety zone if all the military facilities are just removed at the last minute. During such an event, the Japanese would bomb the area while accusing the Chinese military of being responsible because of its presence.

To this end, the committee hopes that you can ask the army to withdraw all troops from the safety zone as soon as possible. The committee has issued a statement expressing its full confidence in the commitments you have made.

Finally, the committee would like to express its gratitude in this regard for your support and concern regarding the interests of the civilians. It also looks forward to receiving your friendly cooperation and recommendations for the safety zone, which affects so many Chinese people.

Yours sincerely,

— John Rabe

Rabe sent the two letters and wondered if the Japanese would pay attention to a member of the Nazi Party member. He worried that General Tang would be too busy with the preparations to withdraw to think about the safety zone.

Rabe comforted himself in the knowledge that there was nothing he could do now. One morning seven days later, a large number of Chinese planes flew overhead and proved that Rabe's decision to stay had been of utmost importance. Chiang Kai-shek said goodbye to his capital, and Colonel Huang, who'd argued with Rabe until the last minute, also went with him.

Now just three types of people were left in Nanjing: the poor; unarmed but idealistic foreign missionaries, businessmen, professors and doctors; and garrisoned soldiers who had no experience of warfare and were ready to evacuate at any time.

The soldiers defending the city had two tasks. They closed the majority of the gates and set fire to houses outside of the city, afraid that they'd give the Japanese an advantage if they fell into their hands. The entire city was engulfed in flames and clouds of smoke as the people whose houses had been destroyed poured into the city and took shelter in camps, with some inside Rabe's safety zone. "These people aren't the poorest in the city. They can use their money to stay with their relatives. The truly poor still haven't arrived," Rabe said to Han, who shared his opinion. They talked to refugees in the area to discover their concerns.

"Is food a big problem?" Rabe asked Han, being the director of the food committee. Food was the top priority.

"The zone must be open to school students," said Rabe, who believed that university, secondary and primary school students should be protected first.

"What kind of food should we provide them?" Han looked on glumly as he saw children filed into rows entering the security area.

"Congee, of course, congee! Where would we get the money to get anything else?" said Rabe as he turned and stared at Han. He felt that Han should have come up with the solution. Rabe continued: "It would be okay if everyone gets a bowl of congee to eat."

A key issue was that although several truckloads of rice were to be sent to the safety zone, only half got through in most cases. Soldiers and other unknown groups of people intercepted and robbed them, but this was nothing new. "Today we received 2,117 sacks of rice, less than half of the agreed amount," fumed Han to Rabe. Rabe replied pragmatically: "Don't complain, it's useless. High command promised me 100,000 *fabi* but we've only received 40,000 *fabi*. The rest will never come, but who can I blame?"

Areas were marked out in the safety zone with a notice posted on bulletin boards:

To the citizens of Nanjing,

Not too long ago, during the Battle of Shanghai, an international committee proposed the establishment of a refugee zone in the south of the city to the Chinese and Japanese authorities. This area was agreed upon by both sides. Chinese authorities promised that the Chinese army would not enter the specified area. As there was no Chinese military presence in this area, the Japanese also agreed that they wouldn't attack. This agreement was observed by both sides. Although horrors took place outside of the area, the refugee zone was set aside and used to save tens of thousands of lives.

Now the International Committee in Nanjing has made the same proposal for a refugee zone with the following boundaries: the eastern boundary spans Xinjiekou in the northern section of Zhongshan Road to the Shanxi Road square; the northern boundary is from the Shanxi Road square to Xikang Road, which is the southwestern boundary of the new residence; the western boundary is from Xikang Road towards the south to Hankou Road, which is the southwestern boundary of the newly built residence, and then it goes in a line southeast towards the junction between Shanghai Road and Hankou Road; the southern boundary is surrounded by Hanzhong Road and Shanghai Road. This area's borders are marked with flags, which have a red cross, a red circle surrounding the red cross and three words: "the refugee zone".

To make these areas safe for civilians, the garrison commander has promised that all soldiers and military equipment within the area will be evacuated as soon as possible and that the military cannot enter any sections of the area. Japan has stated: "It would be difficult to assume responsibility for the safety of the area." However, it has also stated: "Naturally, we do not intend to bomb areas that do not hold any military equipment, fortifications, soldiers or anything for military use." Considering the promises of both sides, we hope that we can provide real security for civilians within the designated area. However, during times of war, people's safety cannot be guaranteed. We cannot ensure the total safety of everyone who enters the safety zone. We believe that if both sides comply with their commitments, this place will be much safer. Welcome to the safety zone.

— INTERNATIONAL COMMITTEE FOR THE NANJING SAFETY ZONE, 8 DECEMBER 1937

To make sure that citizens entered the zone in an orderly fashion, Rabe asked Smythe to publish detailed information regarding accommodation and food in the newspaper as follows:

1. Accommodation:

(1) Residents are advised to reach agreements on private accommodation in the safety zone. The required rents should be as low as possible; lower than during peacetime.

(2) Public buildings and schools are reserved for those who cannot afford to sign a private accommodation lease in this district. Schools are only open in case of emergency.

(3) For those who are staying in public buildings and schools, family members can be placed together, but bedrooms will be segregated by gender. The accommodation is free in bedroom areas and each person will be provided with no more than 1.5 square metres due to the vast scale of the resettlement of refugees.

(4) If these facilities are insufficient for resettling all the refugees, the homeless shall be accommodated in vacant houses or houses that are only being partially used by the owner if the committee sees fit.

2. Food:

(1) Reserves of rice and flour have been designated to the committee and are to be sold through merchants chartered by the committee.

(2) Meals (congee) for the poor will be provided at a low cost by congee stations controlled by the Red Cross. The congee stations are located near Wutaishan, Nanjing University and the Shanxi Road crossroads.

Rabe was inundated with work. There'd been reports for a while that cars loaded with rice had been unable to enter the city and Rabe was later told that safety zone flags had been taken by soldiers in several places.

When Rabe heard the reports, he was furious and rushed over to where the flags had been removed.

"Look, the mayor of Nanjing is coming!" someone whispered when they saw Rabe.

This secretly shocked Rabe as he still wasn't used to the idea of being mayor. He suddenly remembered that two years ago, Ambassador Trautmann had jokingly called him the mayor of Nanjing at a dinner party in Beidaihe. Now he really was the mayor of the city.

"I remember being somewhat irritated by the ambassador's joke but now it's almost come true. Of course, under normal circumstances, a European is unlikely to ever be the mayor of a Chinese city, but now things are different. Mayor Ma, who had been cooperating with us, left yesterday so the committee has had to get involved in issues like municipal management and refugees in Nanjing. I'm rather like an executive mayor. Rabe, you're getting carried away now!" Rabe wrote in his diary on 8 December.

"I'm the senior leader in this area. Your commander personally promised the establishment of a safety zone, which China clearly agreed to on 22 November. Now, you've re-entered the public's safety zone and picked up flags without permission. This is treason! I urge you to immediately correct the error!" Rabe shouted as he stood angrily in front of the Chinese soldiers who'd been removing the flags.

"Who are you? How dare you prevent our military operations?" said several lower ranking soldiers, unconvinced by this meddling foreigner.

The soldiers' leader seemed to know Rabe. He came over to Rabe and said: "Don't be angry. We're just following orders. If you object, we'll withdraw."

"Of course I object! I have a map of the safety zone here!" Rabe took out the previous day's newspaper, which had published a map of the safety zone with pieces titled *Announcement to the Citizens of Nanjing* and *Safety Zone Map*.

The soldiers looked at each other. "Come on. Let's go," they said, whistling as they walked away arrogantly.

Rabe stood there gobsmacked.

"You really look like a mayor today sir!" Han Xianglin smiled next to him.

Rabe was happy to hear this. He straightened himself and asked Han, squinting his eyes: "You think so?"

"Yes! Just look at you giving orders! The army didn't dare disobey you."

Rabe then left with Han and several others to investigate other areas of the safety zone.

The Japanese carried out their air raids unchecked as the Chinese military appeared to have abandoned any aerial resistance. Perhaps they simply didn't have any fighters left. On 9 December, Japanese planes dropped a large number of bombs in the south of the city, making it hard for rice shipments to enter. When one truck was allowed to pass through the gates, a Japanese bomb immediately landed on the city gate, killing more than 40 people on the spot.

At 2pm, Rabe, Bates, Sperling and several others were accompanied by a Chinese colonel as they patrolled the safety zone. They stood on a hill as they looked out at the billowing clouds of smoke that rose up to the skies from burning houses, enveloping the city's suburbs.

"There's an antiaircraft position over there!" shouted Sperling suddenly.

He had a good eye and was pointing to a place within the southwestern boundary of the safety zone.

"Why is there an antiaircraft position in the safety zone?" Rabe angrily asked the colonel, seeing rows of antiaircraft guns firing as he cleaned his glasses.

Before the colonel could answer, three Japanese fighters roared overhead.

Rabe quickly dropped down to the ground and shouted at the others to do the same.

The antiaircraft guns in the safety zone suddenly and violently opened fire at the Japanese planes. Rabe and the others looked up at the sky. They had failed to hit the target. "They're lucky they missed, otherwise the Japanese planes would kill us all," Rabe said solemnly.

"Colonel, if you don't withdraw troops from the safety zone, I'll tell the *führer* that General Tang has been lying to us. Our safety zone cannot continue to operate like this!" Rabe was angry at the colonel as he got up from the ground before dusting himself off.

The colonel seethed resentfully: "I can't do anything. It's been done now. Who can stop the Japanese army? You should ask General Tang about it directly. He's already ordered the troops to withdraw from Nanjing. We'd be better off throwing eggs at the Japanese!" Rabe didn't say anything for a long time and just stared at the colonel.

"Let's see what Tang thinks about a truce," said Rabe finally, having calmed down somewhat.

"Would the general change his mind?" Sperling and several others had doubts about Rabe's plans.

"As long as there's even a chance of hope, we have to try." Rabe was determined.

When Rabe proposed a truce to Tang, the general unexpectedly expressed consent with understanding: "All right, I have no objections to it as long as you can convince the president."

"It looks like he's given up all hope of defending the city. Now the truce depends on Chiang's decision," said Rabe excitedly. Rabe seemed to hold the fate of Nanjing in his hands as he rushed off to the American gunboat, the *USS Panay*, to meet Mr Acheson from the American embassy.

"Mr Acheson, on behalf of the International Committee, I'd like your ambassador in Hankou to propose a truce with immediate effect to Chiang Kai-shek and the Japanese authorities," Rabe said to Archeson, unable to contain the excitement in his voice.

"Excellent news. The US will be incredibly pleased if you can make this happen."

Rabe sent two similar telegrams to the American embassy in Hankou and asked the embassy to forward it to both China and Japan:

> If the Japanese authorities give up the military offensive in Nanjing, the International Committee and the safety zone it has established in Nanjing will recommend the Chinese authorities to take no further military action in the spirit of humanitarianism. To achieve this end, the committee recommends that all armed forces near Nanjing cease fire for three days and in these three days, the Japanese will not advance while the Chinese troops withdraw from the city. Taking the large number of endangered civilians into consideration, the committee requests immediate action on this proposal.
>
> *Yours sincerely,*
>
> — RABE, PRESIDENT OF THE INTERNATIONAL COMMITTEE

Rabe was excited yet nervous, feeling the effects of working on a deal that would affect thousands upon thousands of people. He was excited about being able to help thousands of people in a foreign country as a humble businessman, but he was also nervous about his authority being questioned if Chiang Kai-shek and the Japanese authorities ignored his telegram. Rabe's heart beat with interchanging waves of purpose and vanity.

After the *USS Panay* docked, there was no way Rabe could pass through Xiaguan, which was in flames, and he went another way through town instead. After a press conference finished at about 7pm, Rabe heard that the Japanese army had fought their way to the Guanghua gate. There was no denying the development as fires illuminated the Nancheng and Guanghua gates.

The street lights in town had all gone out. Injured soldiers were being carried away from the frontline and troops could be seen retreating all around in the night. They all aimlessly wandered the streets. A lot of people swarmed into the safety zone, soldiers who'd taken off their military uniforms among them. This made Rabe incredibly anxious.

He sombrely said to Han: "When the Japanese army enters the city, the entire safety zone will be at risk if they see those soldiers. We have to do something. No soldiers are allowed in, not even unarmed soldiers in civilian clothing."

Han Xianglin thought this was impossible. He said: "How could we ever verify all of their identities? Just look at them, they're so tragic to look at."

Rabe raised his voice: "Having sympathy for them means more civilians dying. Our mission is to protect as many civilians as possible. Do you understand?"

Han accepted Rabe's viewpoint, but were things really that simple? Rabe reviewed and approved another announcement before it was published in the news on the evening of 9 December:

Safety Measures in the Safety Zone:

No place is guaranteed to be safe in war. Even in the foreign enclave in Shanghai, more than 1,000 people were killed as a result of bullets, antiaircraft ammunition and bombs dropped by Japanese and Chinese aeroplanes.

We should remember that the Japanese never guaranteed not to attack the safety zone.

The Japanese only guaranteed that they wouldn't attack the safety zone if there were no Chinese military personnel or facilities in the area.

We urgently call on residents to go into air-raid shelters or basements during air strikes. Houses with tiled roofs can also help people take shelter from artillery fire.

Even if only the sound of gunfire is heard in the city, people should still go into air-raid shelters or basements, or take cover near walls.

During air strikes, artillery strikes and gunfire exchanges, people should take shelter in craters or near walls if they are on the street and unable to find a safe place quickly.

If battles take place within the city or in surrounding areas, people should not form a crowd and should scatter themselves as much as possible.

Casualties can be sent to Gulou Hospital. Please dial 31624 if you need an ambulance.

Please dial the following numbers in the event of a fire:
Dafang Lane fire station: 31058
Gulou fire station: 31093

— INTERNATIONAL COMMITTEE FOR THE NANJING SAFETY ZONE

At the gate of the ministry of transport building, several hundred civilians holding bedding and food desperately tried to make their way through so that they could go to hospital, but they were stopped by men acting as police at the safety zone.

"What's wrong?" Rabe asked the guards as he passed by. They told Rabe that they'd found weapons and bombs in the rooms there.

"Find somewhere else for the refugees," advised Rabe.

On the night of 9 December, all the citizens of Nanjing and its suburbs were awoken by the earth-shaking sound of gunfire and bombs. The International Committee members had one word in their minds as refugees and men in plain clothing flooded into the safety zone: "Wait". They were waiting for what they'd dreaded for so long. The Japanese army was about to enter the city.

Wounded people made up the majority of the city. Disabled people were everywhere. Doctors became godlike figures that were needed more than ever. The central army's surgeon, Dr Jin, reported to Rabe that eight military hospitals and more than 80 surgeons under his supervision were able to offer their services to the safety zone.

Rabe was tremendously moved and hugged Jin, saying: "The more the merrier. Doctors will be the most welcome of all in the next few days. I'm sure of it."

Magee reported to Rabe that he'd requested to set up an International Red Cross branch in Nanjing. "That's a good suggestion. If your request is approved, you can recruit in public. What worries me most now is saving the sick and wounded," said Rabe, supporting Magee's actions.

"We will support every single suggestion and activity as long as it helps provide a service to this city's refugees." Although Rabe was a cautious man, he had an open mind. He acted very much like an activist mayor, which made Han greatly admire him.

"The soldiers in Xiaguan want to burn our food. What should we do?" Han reported to Rabe.

"This is madness. I'll never accept it." Rabe thought that the Chinese army was insane. They were attempting to stop the Japanese army from entering the city by burning everything they could.

Rabe received more bad news: "The artillery position in Wutaishan has been firing at the Japanese army. If it carries on, the Japanese army will attack the safety zone with 10 times as many bombs."

Rabe couldn't stand the foolishness. He asked Han to follow him to find the Chinese defence headquarters to furiously complain: "If you insist on playing with your compatriots' lives, then I can't do anything about it." While dramatic, what Rabe said was true. If the army continued to fight against the Japanese army in the safety zone, it was natural to expect the Japanese artillery to retaliate even more ferociously; the Japanese didn't care who died.

What Rabe focused on most was whether there had been any response from Chiang Kai-shek and the Japanese army to his suggestion for a truce. Rabe learned from Ambassador Johnson in Hankou that the telegram had been delivered to Chiang Kai-shek and that Ambassador Johnson and the

American embassy had supported the suggestion. From an informal message from the ambassador, Rabe found out that Chiang Kai-shek was angry at Tang Shengzhi for approving the truce and had disagreed with it. This meant that Chiang Kai-shek didn't approve Rabe's suggestion.

Rabe was distraught. He sent another telegram to Chiang Kai-shek and made the American embassy in Hankou transfer it:

For the attention of Generalissimo Chiang Kai-shek,

The International Committee sincerely pleads you to convey this message to Chiang Kai-shek. The garrison commander General Tang Shengzhi welcomes the suggestion for a truce from a humanitarian perspective. General Tang is tasked under orders to protect Nanjing, so the decision to withdraw the Chinese army should be made by the top commander. Hundreds of thousands of civilians in Nanjing have been left destitute and homeless as a result of military action. Two-hundred thousand lives are in danger. At this urgent moment, the International Committee urges you to seriously consider our suggestion. We hope that you can approve it quickly.

— Signed: Rabe, *President*

Rabe divided his diary into sections: morning, afternoon and evening. He introduced the events of 10 December:

We felt the ground shaking in Nanjing on 10 December. It was so abnormally depressing in Nanjing that people found it hard to breathe. The general commander of the Japanese army, Iwane Matsui, issued the terms of surrender to the soldiers defending the city and gave Tang Shengzhi one day to respond. However, the Chinese soldiers under Tang's command didn't respond to Matsui within the specified timeframe. The Japanese army therefore thought that the Chinese army didn't want to surrender. The decisive battle for Nanjing began, which was fiercer than ever.

Rabe described the situation in Nanjing after midnight that day in his diary:

The sound of gunfire broke out at 2.30am, the sound of machine guns among them. Bombs whistled and flew over our roofs. I got Mr Han and the other servants to enter the air-raid shelter. I wore a helmet, showing that my head was my most valued belonging and that it was important for it to remain in pristine condition. There was fire in the southeast. Fires illuminated the surrounding area brightly for several hours. All the windows crackled and burst. The buildings quivered at regular intervals of several seconds during the attack. The artillery positions in Wutaishan were bombarded and counterattacked. My house was within the targeted area. There were also artillery attacks in the south and west. After I got a little more used to the piercing sound of the explosions, I got back into bed. I couldn't actually sleep, but I did have a little nap.

None of the city's residents were able to sleep soundly as the Japanese attacked. The next morning, Rabe got up cautiously without making a sound. He was somewhat afraid of opening his windows and door, scared that Japanese soldiers would be outside pointing guns at him and shouting.

Things, however, were calm for now. There were no Japanese soldiers outside his door. But the water and power had been cut off. When he looked out at the street, Rabe saw the citizens of Nanjing appearing to swarm out on the streets. When he looked more closely, he realised that they were refugees who'd transferred to the safety zone to escape the gunfire.

Rabe didn't know whether to be delighted or depressed. Several days earlier, Rabe and others in the committee had been busy posting announcements and positioning flags to identify the location of the safety zone. The citizens now appeared to know exactly where it was.

Having seen the vast military power of the Japanese, Rabe suddenly seemed to lack some of the confidence that he'd had before. When he saw masses of soldiers in the crowds swarming into the safety zone, he felt his heart in his throat. Rabe had repeatedly claimed in telegrams and to the news that there were no soldiers in his safety zone.

Rabe was worried because he knew that the Japanese army had been waiting to use this as an excuse, and would attack saying that the safety zone was being used to harbour Chinese soldiers.

Rabe collapsed into his chair, feeling quite unwell.

"Han, quickly see to the people in the safety zone. Make sure to make the soldiers drop their guns and any other weapons. We need to gather them all together…" Rabe then suddenly lost his voice. He called for Han again in a hoarse voice.

"What do you want the weapons for? Are you going to fight the Japanese?" Han was curious and didn't understand the orders.

This worried Rabe even more. He stamped his feet and said to Han: "You fool! Do you want the Japanese to kill us?"

Han suddenly understood and repeatedly nodded his head: "You mean that we're going to hand over the weapons we've confiscated after the Japanese arrive. Okay, no problem, I'll see to it as soon as possible."

There was a sudden loud bang.

The first wave of Japanese bombs finally hit the safety zone. Sperling reported the situation at Fuchang Restaurant, an area he was responsible for, to Rabe: 21 people had died on the spot and 12 people had been severely wounded.

"My arms were hit by fragments of glass and have been bleeding a lot," said Sperling. He also reported the outcome of the attack on a middle school in the safety zone: 13 students had died and more than 20 people had been injured.

"I'll check the safety zone at once," said Rabe, knowing that he could only expect more casualties. He immediately went to find John Magee. They both got into a car and went near the Shanxi Road plaza. They saw many soldiers there digging trenches. They asked the soldiers why they hadn't followed General Tang's orders to cease all military operations in the safety zone. The soldiers ignored them. On Zhongshan Road, there were more soldiers carrying sandbags and building roadblocks following their commander's orders. Many trees had been cut down, placed in the middle of the road and connected with a wire mesh. Rabe negotiated with the commander present. He was polite, but he firmly rejected Rabe's pleas to stop all military operations saying: "The Japanese army is going to attack the city. We have to do everything we can to resist."

Rabe didn't say anything. He thought to himself that if there was even a slither of hope of resistance, then he'd be willing to stand by them as a veteran of the First World War. However, he refused to resign himself to delusions.

At night, a press conference was held, similar to the previous ones. Unfortunately, apart from members of the International Committee, including Rabe, and a few journalists from several news agencies, no one else attended.

The journalists didn't gain any valuable military intelligence from Rabe. Smythe reported to the journalists present that the members of the International Committee had caught a thief in the safety zone. Without anything else to do, the journalists became interested and asked Rabe how the committee dealt with thieves.

Rabe and the other members didn't actually know what to do. The International Committee had a plan for all the refugees, but hadn't planned anything for crimes committed inside the safety zone.

"We don't have any legal institutions. All the courts in Nanjing have closed. What option do we have?" Several astute foreigners then discussed the matter together and joked that after a deliberation by the temporary "jury" formed by the International Committee, the thief was to be sentenced to death.

The journalists couldn't believe their ears and laughed.

Rabe then announced that given the lack of prisons and any other detainment facilities at the present time, the penalty had been reduced to 24 hours of detention.

The journalists burst out in laughter again.

Rabe laughed with them. The thief was actually promptly released because there was nowhere to detain him.

On 12 December, Rabe felt powerless. He occasionally stopped and questioned men who looked like soldiers at the western entrance to the safety zone, hoping that they'd drop their weapons. It would be even better if they didn't go into the safety zone at all. He sometimes ran over to the eastern entrance to help the vulnerable - women, the elderly, the weak, the ill and the wounded - into the safety zone. Even if he had 10 arms and legs, he wouldn't have been able to help the flood of refugees. There was nothing he could do.

No one knew what to do on the streets. People who'd been running frantically stopped suddenly; neither the civilians nor the soldiers knew what to do. No one knew whether they were going to live or die.

It was a terrible scene and Rabe felt scared for the first time. What terrified Rabe more than anything was panicked chaos.

Rabe didn't know what to do. He went back to his room and packed medicine and toiletries into his leather bag. He felt that he'd soon be caught by the Japanese and shipped off to some hellish prison. He felt like he was a marionette with no control over his fate. "Everyone has become puppets," he wrote in his diary.

At 8pm, the final act of the tragic opera began. Fierce gunfire shook the ground. The gates of Nanijng seemed to be at breaking point.

The following is an extract from Rabe's diary prior to the Nanjing Massacre. More than 200 people were in his garden, bidding farewell in the firelight to the last few days of a Nanjing unoccupied by Japanese soldiers:

> The sky in the south of the city glowed red with fire. The refugees in the garden have been crammed into the air-raid shelter, which is full to the brim. People have been banging loudly on the two gates into the garden. Women and children have begged us to let them in. Several bald men climbed over the back wall of the German school and tried to enter the garden for protection. I couldn't bear the lamentable begging. I asked them to open the two gates and

let them all in. There was no room in the air-raid shelter. I found places for them in between buildings. Most of the people brought their own bedding and lay down in the open air. Some cunning people placed their bedding under German flags that had been hung horizontally. The German flags had been prepared to prevent the Japanese planes from bombing the area. This place was seen as a bulletproof zone.

Bombs and bullets roared and the sound became more intense as it drew closer. The entire Nanjing skyline became an ocean of fire, with deafening noises all around. I wore an iron helmet and got my Chinese assistants and the kind Mr Han to wear them too because we didn't go into the air-raid shelter. There was no room in there. I ran all over the place like a dog, making my way back and forth through the crowd, getting angry with some and helping others along the way. After a while, everyone followed my orders. When it was close to midnight, there was a horrible sound in front of my garden.

My friend Christie had arrived, the safety zone's minister of finance. "Oh, my god! What are you doing here?" I said to him with a mix of excitement and anxiety. "I came to see you," he said calmly. He continued: "Someone was just selling an unused bus for just 20 yuan. Do you want it?" I went a bit mad, saying: "Now isn't the time, Christie!" "If it's okay with you, I'm going to take him into my office and sort it out," said Christie before he went away. I looked as he walked away. All sorts of feelings ran through my mind, but mainly pride at the people in the International Committee who had made such massive achievements so effortlessly.

In the north of the city, the beautiful ministry of transport building was engulfed in flames. I ached everywhere. I hadn't slept for 48 hours. My guests all slept. Thirty people were in my office. Three people were outside the coal cellar. Eight women and children slept in the servants' toilets. More than 100 more people were placed in the air-raid shelter, in the garden and on the cobbled road.

What the people of Nanjing faced the next day was one of the cruellest events in human history. While the Japanese marched into the city, the Nanjing Massacre soon followed.

The Safety Zone Is Put to the Sword

Early in the morning of 13 December, Rabe was awoken by a loud *ratatat*. He then heard the loud noise again and again.

Rabe quickly put on his clothes before rushing downstairs. He ran out onto the ground floor and into the yard and asked: "Have they killed anybody?" The small hallway and yard were filled with people, far more than the 200 people who'd taken shelter there last night.

"There could be more than 300 people here!" a servant told him. Rabe ordered his servant: "We need to count them to get an accurate number."

Vast numbers of bombs were raining down from the sky. Many nearby houses were ablaze to the sound of children crying and adults shouting. Civilians swarmed over to Rabe's yard one after another.

"Tell them that the safety zone isn't far from here. My place can't hold many people. They have to find somewhere safer," ordered Rabe, worried that his gate would be forced open by the flood of refugees.

An elderly couple with nowhere to run had brought seven or eight people with them, seeming to be their children or grandchildren. They knelt down before Rabe to beg him to let them enter. He relented: "Okay, come in, but only you. The others need to get to the safety zone. You can be there in 10 minutes. Not all of the Japanese forces are in the city yet. You have to find somewhere safe. Go! Quickly now!" Standing by the gate, Rabe persuaded hundreds of the refugees who passed by to go, although he knew his attempts at persuasion weren't often so effective.

"This situation has been unexpected. I need to go to the committee headquarters to consult them," said Rabe. He ordered his servants once again: "Don't open the gate, no matter what. If the Japanese soldiers come, you need to hold this flag." He pointed at the Nazi flag in the yard, which had become a sort of protective amulet.

On 13 December, John Magee, the president of the Nanjing branch of the International Red Cross and a Yale graduate, announced that: "The Japanese army is entering the city. The high numbers of wounded people is the most pressing issue at the moment. The Red Cross can't stand by idly, so its establishment in the area has been formally announced." He then stated that the coming days were the most urgent period for the city's refugees. They were surrounded by urgent emergencies and urged every member of the council to do everything in their power to help.

Rabe was chosen as a member of the newly established council. Magee told Rabe that when the civilians he'd sent away to find safety passed a printing centre by a theatre, a Japanese bomb landed on the street right in front of them. At least 11 people died on the spot. Magee continued: "Later on, when we passed by the Jinling College, a house on Huaqiao Road was hit by a Japanese bomb. At least 20 people were killed. Seven or eight people were thrown into the air by the power of the bomb and killed. A poor elderly couple almost cried themselves to death. Their 33 year old son's face had been caved in by the explosion and he just lay there, dead."

"This is what I've been worrying about most," said Rabe with a sombre expression on his face. "Come on, let's go to the security zone," he called on his assistant and drove to the area.

Bullets whistled past them on the street with the occasional bomb flying overhead as cars flying the Red Cross and German flags made their way through trying to avoid the explosions. The wounded lay chaotically sprawled across the ground waiting for treatment at the military hospital by the entrance to the ministry of foreign affairs building.

A group of Japanese soldiers later pointed guns at the cars to get them to stop. A Japanese soldier who spoke some German reluctantly allowed the car through when he found out who Rabe was. The soldier told him that their officers were about to enter the city. "Now take the short cut to get past them!" Rabe told his aides as they cut through a pathway, pretending to salute the Japanese soldiers.

Rabe saw Chinese soldiers from three detachments. He quickly jumped out of his car and told them to lay down their arms immediately. Rabe shouted: "If you don't drop your weapons, you'll be killed by the Japanese! Drop them now!"

"Why should we? No! We want to fight the Japanese devils!" The soldiers disagreed with him, despite Rabe being perfectly reasonable.

Rabe explained: "You have to disarm otherwise all of you will be killed!"

"Isn't your safety zone safe? Let us in there!" begged the soldiers as they surrounded Rabe with fear in their eyes.

Rabe looked at the poor Chinese soldiers and loudly said: "The safety zone doesn't provide shelter for the army. I'm just responsible for the civilians' safety."

As soon as Rabe finished talking, the soldiers immediately dropped their weapons, while others took off their uniforms and threw them away. They continued to beg Rabe to let them into the safety zone. "Well, make your way to the ministry of foreign affairs building and the supreme court," said Rabe.

"Why should we go there?" asked the soldiers, unaware that these two places had become safety zones. When Rabe mentioned the supreme court, they became tense and didn't go until Rabe explained the situation.

Rabe met more than 400 Chinese soldiers by the entrance to the ministry of railways building. He persuaded them to lay down their arms in the same way, but one officer refused as he thought that these "rancid foreign ideas" damaged the reputation of the Chinese military. He then picked up a carbine rifle and rode away on horseback, screaming: "We shall never surrender!"

Rabe felt powerless as there was nothing he could do. He continued to the others: "If you want to come to the safety zone, you have to disarm. Otherwise, I won't allow you in!" After a few minutes, most of the soldiers did what Rabe had asked and dropped their guns before fleeing to the safety zone.

"I later found out that by doing so, I had killed them," Rabe once wrote. He could never have imagined that persuading the Chinese soldiers to disarm would lead to their easy arrest and execution by the Japanese soldiers. He wrote about this tragic realisation several days after the major incidents of the Nanjing Massacre.

"We had no choice! If fighting breaks out near the safety zone then the Chinese soldiers who've surrendered will undoubtedly withdraw into it, despite it being demilitarised. Even if it isn't destroyed, it will be under heavy fire by the Japanese. All we can do is hope that these soldiers face no further danger and are treated as prisoners of war," Rabe explained in his diary.

Rabe quietly ordered an aide to disarm the officer riding the horse. The officer didn't obey and had to be subdued. Rabe spoke to the sceptical officer: "I hope you understand that we cannot sacrifice hundreds of your soldiers' lives simply because of your defiance. This is to protect you too!"

"Damn you! You're protecting me?" answered the officer angrily.

Rabe couldn't provide any guarantees to the officer as there would be severe consequences if the Japanese found out. "If you want to enter the safety zone, then my word is law," said Rabe in spite of this, clearly expressing himself.

The officer stopped being so stubborn and rapidly withdrew towards the safety zone with his soldiers. Refugees flooded into various safety zones, not hundreds, not thousands but tens of thousands.

The huge crowd contained tens of thousands of Chinese soldiers, which placed Rabe in a difficult position. If Rabe refused them entry, he was effectively sending them to their graves; the Japanese soldiers would not treat them well. If the Chinese soldiers were allowed to come into the zone, the Japanese would have grounds to invade and destroy the safety zone.

"You have to send more people. It's just Mr Sperling guarding the gate!" said Rabe to the members of the committee as he looked at Sperling handling weapons and vigilantly scouring the safety zone.

"It's impossible, Mr Rabe," said Han. He gave Rabe a suggestion: "We should immediately put up notices throughout the safety zone, telling the people who want to come in to follow the rules."

"Okay, get to it now," said Rabe, immediately ordering his secretary and aides to act. This notice became the first document signed by Rabe after the Japanese army entered Nanjing:

Important notice to refugees in the shelters:

1. Everyone is urgently advised to stay off the street as much as possible.
2. In the most dangerous cases, hide in a house or anywhere you will not be spotted easily.
3. Please note that the refugee areas are set up specifically for refugees. We regretfully cannot provide protection to Chinese soldiers as it goes beyond our abilities.
4. If the Japanese come to check or inspect the refugee area, they should be allowed entry without any resistance.

Rabe, who was later given the nickname "the good man of Nanjing", warned citizens to stay off the streets when the Japanese entered the city unless there was an emergency. However, these civilians had no awareness of how to behave in a war.

As could be expected, this was not the case. One day, Sun Zhongfang, who lived at 18 Bamboo Alley on Pingxi Street, took to the streets out of curiosity with several female friends after hearing that the Japanese had entered the city. Someone suddenly shouted: "The devils are on our doorstep!" They looked up and saw a group of armed Japanese soldiers standing on a tower, aiming their rifles all around. Gunfire immediately broke out. Sun Zhongfang was lucky to escape and ran home. Persuaded by her mother, the 18 year old picked up her son Xiao Gouzi, who was younger than two years old, and followed her brother with the defeated army to Anhui. However, she got separated from her brother and son. She remarried to Huang Shiqing, a KMT soldier, to survive. Sun's first husband, a policeman in Nanjing, couldn't escape the clutches of the Japanese and her mother was brutally raped by the Japanese soldiers, dying soon after. After the war, Sun went to rural Guangxi with her husband and stayed there for 50 years. After her second husband died, Sun married a local villager called He Chengcai, who passed away in 1990. Although Sun was more than 80 years old at that point, she hadn't had any children with her two husbands because she missed her special Xiao Gouzi. In the summer of 2000, Sun Zhongfang went back to Nanjing to look for her lost son. This news drew a great deal of attention in Nanjing and Shanghai. The staff at the Shanghai public security bureau found a man called Sun Jiacai, who they believed was likely to be her son when they checked the domestic archives. After he'd been identified, she'd finally found her long lost Xiao Gouzi. Xiao Gouzai was now a 66 year old retired worker. On 19 July that year, the mother and son were finally reunited after 63 years apart. "Xiao Gouzi, I've finally found you!" said the 89 year old woman as she touched her wrinkled son, struck by a wide range of emotions.

However, those who didn't flee Nanjing weren't as lucky as Sun Zhongfang and her son.

In a long alley in the Qinhuai district, Zhou Xianglian, who lived at number 3 with eight or nine other family members, stayed with her grandmother at their old house as she couldn't bring herself to part with it. After the Japanese entered the city, her grandfather and father guarded the door. Zhou Xianglian's 39 year old father knew that the whole family had to be protected. On the morning of 13 December, he was immediately shot dead by Japanese soldiers when he went out to Wuqiao, just outside the south gate as fires raged in the streets. Her mother fainted as soon as she heard the news and her grandfather was determined to find his son's body. He never came back home either. Serval Japanese soldiers holding guns broke into the house. When they saw Zhou Xianglian's mother, they shot her without any explanation, stripped off their clothes and raped her in front of her family.

"There are some beauties in here!" shouted a Japanese soldier. The soldiers raped the 17 year old girl and her 13 year old sister repeatedly for many hours.

At a dugout in a house in Xinjiekou, in the centre of Nanjing, a child no older than six was unaware of the danger as he stood at the entrance of the dugout without any adult supervision. Japanese soldiers on the streets waved to the child, seeming to say something that was hard to understand. Bang. The child was shot dead when he tried to stand back. Hearing his mother's cries, several Japanese soldiers armed with machine guns threw grenades and frantically opened fire. The shelter collapsed in a matter of seconds and no one survived.

Rabe wrote in his diary: "A group of Japanese soldiers went to the Gulou Hospital's gates, having spotted some Chinese men in military uniform hiding in the alley. They quickly blocked it off at both ends. I then heard intense gunfire as blood covered the ground of the small alley."

Rabe had been unable to stop the Japanese soldiers' atrocities. At almost every 200 metres they went in the car, Rabe saw bloody atrocities and the dead bodies of Chinese soldiers and civilians lying in the streets. He described the day in his diary: "I checked the bodies and found that most had been shot in the back. It seemed that these people had been running away when they were hit and killed from behind." Rabe saw many houses and public buildings on the side of the road in flames, and he heard terrible cries.

When he tried to rescue the people inside, Japanese soldiers stopped him with their bayonets and rifle butts.

Rabe could only really afford to be concerned about German property. The Kissling bakery seemed to have been ransacked by the Japanese soldiers before he'd arrived, while the Heim Per hotel had also been plundered.

Rabe thought that they should remind the Japanese army of the location of the safety zone, which they would not be allowed to attack. He set out holding a German flag and wearing the Red Cross on his sleeve. He was suggested to hold a Japanese flag by someone who said that the Japanese soldiers didn't attack people who held their flag.

"The German flag is more than enough!" shouted Rabe. Needless to say, he didn't follow their advice. He'd seen the people who'd flown Japanese flags at the city's gates being brandished as traitors. Many Japanese soldiers marched into Nanjing through the city's gates. Rabe wore a formal suit and tie while holding a map he'd made. He approached a Japanese official to tell him the location of the safety zone.

"You're German, right? We like you!" said the Japanese official. He smelled of blood and sweat and gave a thumbs up to Rabe. Rabe was unclear whether the gesture was genuine or not. Rabe didn't care about the gesture and only concerned himself with making the safety zone's boundaries clear to save large amounts of lives.

"I've asked my employees to place a number of small flags around the zone, so please don't come in when your soldiers see them," said Rabe to all the soldiers who went past. Was anyone listening? Rabe didn't know, but he still had to try.

Leaving the city gate, Rabe got into a taxi and rushed to the safety zone. On the way, they saw a group of about 200 Chinese workers being detained by Japanese soldiers.

"Mr Rabe, can you save them? The Japanese soldiers are going to kill them!" said the driver. Rabe immediately jumped out of the car and tried to ask the Japanese soldiers to release the workers. A Japanese soldier looked Rabe up and down for a moment, and then said something rudely as he poked him in the stomach with the butt of his rifle. Rabe protested to the Japanese soldier about his rudeness.

The Japanese soldiers carried on with an insulting smile. Rabe looked at the workers' poor faces and slumped his shoulders. He drew the sign of the cross, praying for their safety. Rabe began to leave, but didn't get far before he heard the sudden burst of gunfire and screams. Although his vision was blocked by a wall, he knew that the workers had been shot dead.

13 December was an important day for Siemens as it was the birthday of

its founder, Ernst Siemens. Rabe would normally drink a toast to his health, but Rabe was now more concerned with the devilish soldiers making their way into the city.

Rabe helplessly watched in the ministry of justice building as 400 or 500 Chinese soldiers lay down with their arms tied up before being shot dead. "They're beasts! This is a brutal massacre! A massacre!"

Before returning to his home, Rabe felt incredibly angry. Just 50 metres away from his garden, a Chinese soldier had been killed, strung over a bamboo pole and burned. The smell of scorched flesh and the charcoaled body made Rabe feel sick.

Rabe furiously cursed the Japanese for nearly half an hour after he returned home. If Smythe hadn't come to report on the problems facing the safety zone, Rabe would likely have spent the whole night doing so.

"I'm not saying that I don't know anything about the arts, but I have to admit that I rarely spend time reading poems or anything like that. I feel that it doesn't match my career as a businessman. But as time goes on, I've begun to read more artistic books to remedy my shortcomings in the field. I often look around in fear of being discovered. But I don't know who'd tell anyone. Many women seem to use poetry, turning a blind eye to our mistakes, especially mine. Anyway, I unconsciously put a poem into my diary, with the edge of the paper note poking out. I'm now fascinated with this poem," wrote Rabe. Gunfire continued outside and women and children could be heard crying in the yard. Rabe's colleagues constantly sent him copies of bloody reports.

He sat at his desk, holding a piece of paper in his hand and reading silently:

With every heartbeat, there's the will to win;
The advent of each ray of daylight shows the endless struggle of life.
Death does not frighten us as from every silence the will of life sprouts.
We hate hypocrisy and giving up halfway.
We truly love liberty and light.
This is our life: with every heartbeat, there's the will to win;
The advent of each ray of daylight shows perseverance in endless struggles,
With the heritage of our ancestors and the earth,
And life, the people and the country's good fortune.

This poem, entitled *Life*, had been written by his wife. Tears welled up in Rabe's eyes as he began to read. He felt that he now had a better understanding of the meaning and value of life.

But what about the Chinese lives being cut short by Japanese soldiers in Nanjing? Rabe felt pained by the matter.

He wanted to stage a protest. Seeing the brutal crimes committed by the Japanese soldiers, he wanted to show the world what had happened in Nanjing. Smythe rushed over to tell Rabe that there were too many people coming from the railway and police headquarters so they could no longer take in any Chinese soldiers retreating from the frontline. Smythe continued: "More troubling still is that they're still armed and haven't taken off their uniforms. The Japanese soldiers insist that these Chinese soldiers are causing a lot of problems and have to be pulled back from the safety zone! But everyone knows that once they're taken away, they'll all be killed." Smythe asked Rabe for advice.

"Let's go and see Fukuda. As a counsellor in the Japanese embassy, he's the only one who'll speak with us," said Rabe. They found Fukuda, who told them that: "I believe that our troops will do what's right."

Rabe felt proud of himself when he left the Japanese embassy. However, a few hours later, Rabe received a message that more than 1,300 Chinese soldiers in the ministry of railways and police station had been forcibly taken away and shot dead. "Are Richard and Kroger monitoring their operations?" Rabe asked Smythe after hearing the news. They were afraid that the Japanese soldiers would break their promise, so they sent two members of the Red Cross to keep an eye on the situation. Smythe replied: "Richard said that the Japanese soldiers immediately removed them after we left." Rabe couldn't stand it. He told Smythe to ask all the members of the committee to write down all the crimes they'd heard or seen committed by the Japanese. Rabe explained: "By doing this, they cannot deny it. We can force them to correct their ways and to stop committing crimes."

"The Japanese believe that there are at least 20,000 Chinese soldiers in the city, some of them are still resisting, while others are hiding in the shadows attacking the Japanese. They're mixed in with the civilian population and are a big threat to the Japanese, so they're killing every soldier in sight," reported Smythe, having heard this news from the directors of areas of the safety zones. After a moment of silence, Rabe told Smythe: "In any case, we have to have a dialogue with the Japanese. If a soldier lays down their arms, they shouldn't be executed. This has been observed since the Hague conventions before the First World War. How can Japan just do what they want? As the mayor of Nanjing, I have to formally protest, or the city will be reduced to a slaughterhouse." It was too late to prevent Nanjing from being drenched in blood. On 14 December, in the outskirts of the city, tens of thousands of Chinese soldiers were killed next to the Yangtze, dying the river red with blood. Bodies were piled up like mountains, making the scene scarring and unforgettable. The same could be seen inside the city. Walking down the street, Smythe saw 50 Chinese men bound and stabbed by the Japanese soldiers. Survivors were shot in the head.

"No! I cannot tolerate such barbaric atrocities," shouted Rabe, who was extremely angry. He stooped over his desk and quickly began writing to the Japanese embassy counsellor:

The International Committee for the Nanjing Safety Zone was deeply shocked by the slaughter of Chinese soldiers who'd laid down their weapons. From the outset, the committee spared no effort in making the safety zone out of bounds for the Chinese military. The work in this area went well until the afternoon of Monday 13 December. That afternoon, hundreds of Chinese soldiers approached and entered the safety zone, asking us for help. The committee explicitly told them that we could not provide any protection. But we also explained to them that if they laid down their arms and gave up all resistance to the Japanese, that they could expect leniency from the Japanese. That night, as a result of panic and confusion, coupled with some of the soldiers removing their uniforms, the committee was unable to distinguish them from civilians. The committee believed that these Chinese soldiers, once verified, would be seen under the eyes of international law as prisoners of war, while also hoping to prevent any disasters involving Chinese civilians.

Rabe continued writing that the Japanese should give prisoners of war leniency in accordance with relevant laws, regulations and humanitarian principles. He believed that the prisoners of war should be worked as labourers and fed and kept happy until they could return to their peaceful lives.

Rabe must have seemed very naïve. "I can't believe these Germans and Americans expect to stop us simply by establishing these committees," Harada, the chief of general staff of one of the Japanese military divisions at the time sneered to Fukuda after he saw Rabe's signature on the letter.

"Most of them are missionaries who voluntarily rescue and help refugees," stammered Fukuda.

"Then why don't we arrange a meeting with them this afternoon?" suggested Harada.

"Yes, sir. I'll contact them."

At midday on 15 December, Rabe, Smythe and Sperling met a senior officer from the Japanese army for the first time on behalf of the International Committee in the Bank of Communications.

Before the three representatives could ask any questions, Fukuda warned them: "The general will only respond to your letter. No further questions."

Rabe cursed under his breath.

The general gave his response: "The emperor of Japan protects all civilians. However, we are now in the middle of a war, which means that we have to adopt some unconventional measures. Therefore, I must reiterate the following. Firstly, we will search for any remaining Chinese soldiers in the city. Secondly, we will set up sentries at the entry points of your so-called safety zone. Thirdly, you shall help us mobilise civilians to return to their homes as soon as possible. Fourthly, you shall hand over all Chinese soldiers to us and have faith in our humanity. Fifthly, guards hired by your group can patrol the safety zone but they must listen to our orders, which means they must help our soldiers and not hinder their operations. Sixthly, you have 10,000 packs of rice stored for the refugees, but our soldiers need rice too. If we need rice, you must hand it over to us. Seventhly, you shall help us restore electricity and water provisions. Eighthly, you shall soon provide us with labourers."

"They're treating us like their captives. They've never seen us as the leaders or organisers of the safety zone," Rabe whispered to Smythe in English.

"Any questions, my honourable German comrade?" asked Fukuda. To Rabe's amazement, Fukuda also spoke English.

"You win this time, sir, and to the victor the spoils. But I have to protect all the Germans and civilians in Nanjing during wartime and the *führer* has approved my mission. Therefore, I sincerely hope that your distinguished general could offer us his help and support," Rabe responded in German with a Hamburg accent. Fukuda translated the answer for Harada.

Harada nodded, and his facial expression showed that he respected both Rabe and Hitler. He asked: "Could you please show me around the safety zone this afternoon, sir?"

Rabe exchanged glances with Smythe and thought that this may be a good opportunity. He agreed.

However, he never got the opportunity to do so. In the afternoon, Rabe hastily drove over to the safety zone when he heard that some Japanese soldiers wanted to take away a group of unarmed Chinese soldiers, knowing the miserable fate that awaited them. He shouted to the Japanese soldiers: "I am a member of the Nazi Party in Germany. Everything I have done here has been reported to the *führer*. On both my reputation as a member of the Nazi Party and as a German, I can guarantee that all Chinese soldiers in this area have been disarmed. They will never have any military conflicts with you. You should set them free. If you insist on taking these men away, then take me along with them!" Rabe positioned his rotund body in front of the Japanese, obstructing and surprising them.

Several Japanese soldiers angrily took out their bayonets, trying to scare him away. But Rabe was unfazed, standing there motionless with his dignity intact.

Finally, a Japanese officer came to Rabe's rescue and apologised.

Other members of the committee were still waiting for Rabe in the headquarters. They claimed to have something important to report. Rabe got the officer to deal with the angry Japanese soldiers and didn't leave until he saw them move away.

"Bad news, sir. Approximately 100 Japanese soldiers have just taken away more than 1,000 Chinese prisoners," one member later reported as he gasped for breath.

"Get back to the safety zone!" Rabe said to Smythe and Mills, angrily cursing the dishonest Japanese soldiers. When they arrived, the Japanese had already taken the prisoners away and wouldn't set them free no matter how much Rabe tried.

More than 1,300 Chinese prisoners were taken away in front of Rabe's eyes. Filled with rage, he wanted to beat the Japanese monsters, but was stopped by Smythe.

"How can you Americans be so cowardly? Just look at these beasts!" protested Rabe.

Smythe was too ashamed to reply. He said: "You might not have heard the news yet that the Japanese have bombed two of our ships. Two people have died."

Rabe was astonished.

"I just received news that the Japanese have bombed the *USS Panay*. An Italian reporter and the ship's captain died. Mr Paxton, our ambassador, was badly wounded and Captain Hughes has lost a leg," continued Smythe.

Rabe patted him on his shoulder: "God have mercy on us."

"Let's go and see Mr Fukuda. He's the only Japanese person we can trust." Rabe went to the Japanese embassy again with Smythe. Fukuda agreed to negotiate with the army on their behalf.

"If you insist on doing this to the Chinese, I will never provide you with any labourers," said Rabe, hoping that the army would consider the consequences of its actions. However, the soldiers didn't care about that. Their top priority was to arrest all the Chinese soldiers in Nanjing. Although they'd occupied the city, they were afraid of resistance, especially street fighting and guerrilla warfare. They heard that many Chinese soldiers had taken refuge in the safety zone. It wasn't at all surprising that the place had become their white whale.

Since 14 December, the Japanese army had continued to dispatch forces to the safety zone. All men aged 15 to 50 had to show their ID. Japanese soldiers examined their hands, shoulders and hair to see if they'd been holding or carrying guns, or had worn a helmet. They shot anyone who had even the slightest marking on their hands, shoulders or hair. Wearing a normal hat would also leave a mark on one's hair, so many men began to shave their hair. However, the next day, the Japanese soldiers specifically seized bald men. Many innocent civilians were cruelly killed.

However, there were incidents that were even more brutal.

On 15 December, six cleaners were cleaning the streets near the Gulou district and encountered a group of Japanese soldiers. The soldiers took the poor workers away and stabbed them to death next to a wall just because they were all men.

On 16 December, Wu Changde, a man who worked in the International Committee headquarters, was taken away as he was believed to be a Chinese soldier. He had been a policeman in Nanjing. Wu was taken to a clearing across from a theatre and forced to stand there for several hours. More than 1,000 Chinese men ended up being sent there. They were then all taken to the Hanxi gate and divided into many different groups to be executed with machine guns. Wu was in the final group to be shot and it was dark by the time his group went to the execution grounds. Wu was very lucky to survive being shot, struck with a pickaxe and burned together with the other corpses. After the soldiers left, Wu escaped successfully. Ten days later, he went back to the International Committee headquarters by pretending to be a beggar. Only then did Rabe get a clear picture of the extent of the cruelty of the Japanese army.

Rabe thought it was essential to document all of the Japanese crimes. He made Smythe arrange materials to formulate a report on the crimes of the Japanese soldiers in the Nanjing Safety Zone, and lodged a furious protest to the Japanese army through Fukuda:

> What the Japanese soldiers did yesterday has increased the panic among the refugees; many of them are now too afraid to even go out to get their rice rations. We now have to send rice to shelters, which has added to the difficulties of providing food to the public. We cannot find any carriers to help us transport rice and coal to the congee station. In order to provide enough food to all the Chinese refugees, some of our members have had to drive trucks

to the safety zone because many of our personal cars were taken away by the Japanese army yesterday.

He continued to suggest several urgent measures to prevent damage to the safety zone:

1. All searches should be formally supervised by a commander as most crimes have been committed by groups of soldiers loitering without any commanding officer.
2. At night, and daytime if possible, the entrance to the safety zone should be guarded by a sentry (we raised this suggestion to your distinguished captain yesterday), to prevent miscreant soldiers from entering the zone.
3. Vehicle passes should be issued immediately and we will stick the passes onto the windshields of our vehicles to avoid being seized by your men. Even during the harshest fighting, the Chinese military headquarters still gave us passes. Although some cars were seized, we soon got them back a day after submitting a written appeal. In addition to this, back then the Chinese army was undergoing a very difficult period, but in spite of this it still gave us three trucks to transport rice. Now, the Japanese army controls the entire city and the battle has come to an end, and you definitely have much better equipment. Therefore, we firmly believe that your men should protect and care for the civilians of Nanjing in a better way.

Remembering his first meeting with Harada, Rabe was all the more furious. He added: "Your senior commander arrived in Nanjing yesterday. We'd expected a better and more orderly city, but we didn't want to throw around any accusations. But last night was even worse. Therefore, we have to believe that these awful things are going on with your knowledge."

Rabe felt sick at the level of cruelty of the Japanese army, but what else could he do? For him, the worst part of his past 50 years had been dealing with the insidious Japanese.

His wife's poem came to mind again:

We truly love liberty and light.
This is our life: with every heartbeat, there's the will to win;
The advent of each ray of daylight shows perseverance in endless struggle.

He found this poem incredibly enlightening. Life is the will to win and persevere in an endless struggle. In the face of the criminal Japanese army, one could only have confidence in victory through persevering in struggle.

Rabe strived for dignity, as did all Germans. But in Nanjing, the Germans in the city lost all their dignity in the face of the sins of the Japanese army. Japanese soldiers could enter Rabe's house whenever they pleased, taking whatever they wanted. People were afraid of going out. For the benefit of the International Committee, he often asked his servant to leave his door open. However, this led to another problem: women and children outside the door would flood in. He was unable stop them as they knelt down and kowtowed. How could he turn them down? Rabe had to compromise. But how could he accommodate all of them? There were already more than 600 people cramped into the small yard. There were issues with food and sanitation. A dozen women and children were cramped into the small washroom and people lay one next to another on the lawn. Some lay on the bench, others sat by the door. In spite of all of this, they still suffered at the hands of the Japanese soldiers.

At night, Rabe heard a banging downstairs. Someone was kicking at the door. Rabe stopped his work and asked: "Who's there?"

"It's the Japanese soldiers. They want to come in," said the servant nervously.

A beam of light suddenly shone directly on the faces outside as Rabe turned on his flashlight. The soldiers quickly ran away.

Rabe told the servants to open the door and run after the soldiers. Running past a small alley, he saw bloodied decomposing corpses everywhere. The servants ran back in fear when they saw what had happened. Rabe wasn't afraid of dead bodies, but he found the stench far too revolting. He went back to the yard. All the women and children were staring at him with panic in their eyes.

Another two incidents made him even more outraged. One was that the consul general in the Japanese embassy regarded the International Committee as "legally groundless". The other was the murder of 50 policemen in the safety zone, suspected of being soldiers. Rabe saw these as severe provocations of the International Committee, and he couldn't simply do nothing and not retaliate.

"Every action that tries to belittle or neglect the International Committee hides the aim of the wanton slaughter of the Chinese. We shall never compromise!" thought Rabe, who disagreed with the Japanese army on every level and was determined to reveal the military conspiracy. Therefore, on 17 December, he stated his position to the Japanese embassy once again:

We have never sought any political power or cooperation with your government. We are hereby forced to remind you that as of 1 December 1937, Mayor Ma of Nanjing handed over almost all administrative power to the International Committee, including the administration over the police, public institutions, and the disposition of property, food, and civic hygiene. On the morning of 13 December 1937, when your distinguished army occupied the city, we continued to hold the right to manage the city. The International Committee was the only institution that was still running at that time. Naturally, our power was limited in the safety zone and we did not have sovereignty.

Your government stationed in Shanghai has promised us that you would not wantonly attack the safety zone if there weren't any military institutions or organisations here. Since we were the only managerial institution at the time, we tried to contact your leader when your army occupied Nanjing. On the afternoon of 13 December, we met a captain from your army and we explained to him that we had marked the boundaries of the safety zone on the map. In addition to this, we respectfully marked the three Red Cross hospitals and informed him of the numbers of unarmed Chinese soldiers. The cooperative spirit and poise the captain demonstrated made me feel that you understood us.

At night and on the following morning, we drafted a letter and translated it into Japanese. Mr Rabe, Dr Smythe and Father Forster tried to find some senior officers so as to submit the letter to the Japanese government. Fukuda, the counsellor in the Japanese embassy, was able to do that. We contacted five officers in your army and they all told us that we should contact the chief commander who was to arrive the next day.

On 15 December, the next day, Mr Fukuda Tokuyasu and Mr Sekiguchi visited the International Committee. Mr Sekiguchi gave us a letter of salutation from the captain of a naval vessel. We then gave our letter to Mr Fukuda and promised Mr Sekiguchi that we were willing to offer assistance to restore electricity provisions. That afternoon, we were honoured to meet your chief commander in the Bank of Communications. He gave us an oral response to our letter.

However, since then, our trucks have been sequestrated if there aren't any Europeans inside. The next morning, when the ambulances from the Red Cross hospitals started to collect corpses in the safety zone, they were either taken away or sequestrated. Yesterday, 14 workers from the Red Cross hospital were even taken away. Our policemen have also been threatened as 50 of them were arrested by your men and killed. You also took away a further 45 voluntary policemen. Voluntary policemen were established by our committee on the afternoon of 13 December because of security personnel shortages. They did not wear uniforms, nor did they carry any weapons. They only wore badges similar to those of European boy scouts. They also took responsibility for some minor tasks including cleaning, keeping public order and offering to help in any emergencies.

On 14 December, four of our fire engines were sequestrated for transportation purposes.

We have tried to remind your embassy and army that the people have endowed us with managerial power over the city for everyone's benefit. However, if the Japanese government, or any other institution, establishes any sort of managerial branch, we would be happy to hand over power. Unfortunately, your soldiers have continued to hinder our work and have damaged our system to protect civilians. Since the morning of 14 December, they have interfered with our necessary activities. More specifically, on 13 December, when your army occupied the city, we rallied all civilians in the safety zone. The safety zone only suffered from minor bombing, and the Chinese army didn't rob the safety zone when retreating. We effectively and peacefully took over the safety zone for the benefit of your army. We tried to restore transportation as soon as order in the city was restored. But on 14 December, the Japanese soldiers started to rob, rape, and slaughter civilians in the zone, which shocked all the Chinese and us 27 Europeans.

The letter mentioned the slaughter of voluntary policemen, which has not been discussed much in other pieces on the Nanjing Massacre. However, it is an important part of the crimes committed by the Japanese army in the city.

When the Japanese army approached Nanjing after the establishment of the safety zone, Ma Chaojun, the mayor of Nanjing at the time, responded to Rabe's appeal and dispatched 450 policemen to safeguard the safety zone. Wu Jianpeng, the director of police station six in Nanjing, had assumed the position as head of the guard. However, later on, the number of refugees flooding into the zone surged, leading to a shortage of policemen. Therefore, the day after the Japanese army occupied the city, the International Committee organised a voluntary police force by choosing refugees, similar in status to the boy scouts, with no uniforms or weapons. They only wore a special badge showing that they were with the International Committee. Rabe had promised the delegates of the Japanese embassy and army that these voluntary police would only carry batons. However, in the searches that were to follow, almost all of the volunteer policemen were killed under suspicion of being Chinese soldiers. In the war criminal trials in November 1945, Chen Yongqing, a policeman in Nanjing at the time, testified that: "The Miyuki division took more than 2,000 soldiers and policemen from the refugee settlement in Nanjing and took them to the Hanzhong gate, where they shot them. They then burned all the victims with petrol." Zhong Ke, a vice platoon leader from the 87th division of the Chinese army also testified to that effect: "Suddenly more than 100 enemies arrived. They arrested us and thousands of refugees. On the way to the Hanzhong gate, an additional 400 or more plain clothed policemen joined us. The enemies were laughing manically. When we nearly approached the gate, one of the enemies signalled us to stop and then tied our hands with hemp rope as thick as my arm. People were taken out of the gate in batches. Roughly 10 minutes later, we heard the sound of machine guns." According to an investigation prior to the Tokyo trials, the Japanese army had slaughtered more than 2,000 policemen, mostly policemen and voluntary policemen guarding the safety zone.

Rabe protested many times about the cruelty of the Japanese soldiers, hoping that the Japanese army would send more guards and patrols to the city to keep order. The Japanese pretended to listen to Rabe's protests, but their soldiers carried on recklessly committing crimes. Rabe protested again to the Japanese in writing:

> From 8pm to 9pm last night, five members of the International Committee patrolled the safety zone and we couldn't find a single sentry inside or outside the area. Faced with the threat of your army and our policemen being slaughtered, our own guards have disappeared from the streets. We only saw a couple of your soldiers loitering in the area, robbing and raping. This means that you never actually considered what we raised in our letter. For example, item number two stated that at night, and daytime if possible, the entrances to the safety zone should be guarded by a sentry to prevent miscreant soldiers from entering the area.
>
> If the riots and destruction of the past three days cannot be stopped, the difficulty of our relief work will be made even worse. We organised the safety zone by encouraging every family to arrange their accommodation through individual personal consultations as much as possible to reduce the burden felt by our organisation due to the current situation. If the current situation fails to improve, most of the residents will starve in a matter of days. All the families have run out of food reserves and heating supplies, not to mention the fact that their money, clothes and personal property have been robbed by your soldiers. People are afraid of walking on the streets and don't dare to open their stores for business, so business and other activities have to be done on a small scale. Our supplies have also been ground to a halt. Since the morning of 14 December, the transportation trucks have essentially been paralysed. Before

your army came into the city, we mainly focused on carrying grain reserves to the safety zone. We will have to distribute food after a period of time as we only asked residents to take food reserves to support them for a week. In order to prevent food shortages in some shelters, the European members of our committee have to transport food and grain to shelters using their private cars after nightfall.

Thinking about the arrogant attitude and actions of the Japanese consuls and generals who'd ignored the existence of the International Committee once again, Rabe found it hard to calm down. He continued to protest:

If normal food supplies cannot be reinstated soon, then people will starve. Another factor that pains the Chinese people is the endless harassment by your army. Some families have complained to us that their houses have been broken into and robbed, and women have been raped as many as five times in one night. These people flee their houses the next morning to try and find a safe place. Is that so out of the question? Your soldiers have taken advantage of the situation to kill people, which is absolutely unacceptable.

Rabe gave an example of one such incident:

Yesterday afternoon, three officials from your army headquarters came to my home to request help in restoring telephone communications. But at the same time, a number of telephone workers were being driven out of their homes in the safety zone. They had all been wearing the committee's armbands, and we don't know where they've gone. If this kind of terrorism continues to take place, we will not be able to provide you with the necessary workers to help restore provisions which are of great importance to the livelihood of the people. If the actions of your soldiers in the city do not improve immediately, then we cannot guarantee the safety of more than 20,000 Chinese civilians and they will be at risk of starvation!

Rabe wrote the last sentence furiously. He believed that if he didn't point out the serious consequences to the Japanese, then they would continue the massacre.

His stubborn attitude and persistence deserve China's respect and should serve as a lesson. Rabe thought that his serious statements and protests weren't enough to remind the Japanese of the need to stop the atrocities, and so the next day, he asked another member of the International Committee to draft a more detailed letter to the Japanese ambassador:

To the Japanese embassy in Nanjing,

Due to the continuous looting, violence and rape committed by your soldiers, the entire city has been enveloped in an atmosphere of fear and misery. Seventeen thousand people, the majority of whom were women and children, fled to our buildings for protection. At present, an increasing number of people have been pouring into the safety zone because the situation outside is far worse than in here. I will list below the atrocities that have occurred in our buildings over the past 24 hours, none of which are considered to be the most serious atrocities.

University affiliated high school next to the river:
A frightened child was stabbed to death with a bayonet; another was stabbed and severely wounded and will likely die soon. Eight women were raped. Several of our employees were trying to help these poor people and provide them with food, but our employees were beaten by the Japanese soldiers for no reason. Many Chinese people were unable to sleep for three days, and they suffered serious physical and mental trauma, often becoming hysterical. If one day this cocktail of fear and despair leads to a resistance against your soldiers' rapes, there will be a devastating massacre, for which your authorities will be entirely responsible.

The American flag was torn down by your soldiers in a humiliating way.

Silkworm factory, Gold and Silver Street:
Two women were raped.

Tools warehouse, 11 Hu Jia Garden:
Two women were raped.

11 Hankou Road:
Two women were raped where our committee members live.

23 Hankou Road:
One lady was raped where the American members of our committee live.

A small peach garden at the Agricultural Department:
The department has suffered from constant malicious harassment by Japanese soldiers, so all women have fled from this place. When I went there to look around this morning, six Japanese soldiers stood in front of me. Although I asked them some questions very politely, and asked if they were having any

problems, one of the soldiers pointed his gun at me with his finger on the trigger.

The above incidents don't mention the issues faced by the poor people who've been harassed by wandering Japanese soldiers for up to 10 times in a day and as many as six times at night. The Japanese soldiers wander the streets either to find a woman or to loot, both of which demonstrate the necessity to immediately implement effective control.

Some of your representatives have claimed that police sentries have been placed at the entrances to all of these buildings, as well as other places where there were large numbers of refugees, but we have been unable to find even a single sentry. As Japanese soldiers are everywhere, the use of just a few sentries will do nothing unless you restore discipline and order in your army.

If your soldiers' behaviour does not improve, then the Akiyama brigade command, set up in the former residence of He Yingqin, will be a great threat to the people living nearby. If your generals are concerned about such matters, then this place could even become an area where you can provide protection to people.

Not just in the safety zone, but also throughout the entire city, residents' food, money and property has been looted by Japanese soldiers. As a result, these people have been driven into a desperate situation. On top of this, many people's clothing and bedding has been stolen by Japanese soldiers, so there are many people suffering from diseases because of the cold. What are your plans to resolve these problems?

Every street in the city is full of the public's tears. They say that no one and nothing is safe in the presence of the Japanese soldiers. I presume that this is not your government's intention. The residents of Nanjing hope that the Japanese can give them better treatment.

Should you have a chance, I suggest that you visit some of these areas with me. It's one terrorist incident after another in your occupied city, which has brought tragedy to Nanjing.

While I was writing this letter, I was interrupted by seven Japanese soldiers who came here for an inspection, and I had to deal with them. The so-called inspection is nothing but a check to see if there are women for them to drag out and rape during the night.

I sleep in this building at night, and I will continue to stay here overnight, hoping to be of some benefit to the helpless women and children, giving them whatever modest help I can.

My friends - the Europeans and Americans - and I have been threatened by your soldiers many times during the process of our humanitarian work. If we are killed or hurt by your drunk or undisciplined soldiers while doing our humanitarian work, then there is no question about who is to be held accountable.

I have tried again and again to write this letter with the spirit of friendship and understanding, but I cannot hide the despair and grief we have suffered since your army's occupation of this city.

Only with your prompt and just action can the current situation be controlled.

Signed,
M S Bates, *Chairman of the Relief Committee at the University of Nanjing*

After the letter was sent, Rabe knew that this wasn't the end and that they needed to continue to struggle against the Japanese army if they wanted to get the Japanese army to stop the atrocities.

At 5pm on 18 December, as representatives of Germany and the US, Rabe and Smythe decided to go to meet with the arrogant Japanese consul general Okazaki.

"Today we come here as representatives of German and American expatriates. I hope that Mr Okazaki is fully aware that Smythe is a famous professor in the US and that I'm a member of the Nazi Party in Germany, which is Germany's highest honour. We have come here to reflect and express our opinions," started Rabe who wore a slim suit with an easily recognisable swastika. When he saw Okazaki, he submitted the long letter and the previously prepared report on the atrocities committed by the Japanese army in Nanjing.

This made Okazaki feel somewhat uneasy. He, as a representative of the Japanese government, was not afraid of the German and American in front of him, but of the Nazis their leader Adolf Hitler. As a result, Okazaki changed his tone somewhat, and even made Rabe feel that the Japanese soldiers would no longer arbitrarily take men from the safety zone to shoot them as they had done a few days earlier.

Under John Rabe, European and American professors, businessmen, doctors and missionaries had used their own bodies as a shield against the powerful Japanese army. They selflessly and fearlessly followed the most basic and primitive human sense of justice in their negotiations with the Japanese, even protesting directly to their faces. At the same time, they made the atrocities the Japanese army committed in Nanjing public through their secret channels, which greatly irritated the Japanese government. After General Matsui led his troops into the city on 17 December, he seemed to have implemented policies to improve order and protect his reputation. For instance, they no longer entered the safety zone to take and shoot men suspected of being Chinese soldiers, which was an important contribution Rabe had made to stop the Japanese from killing Chinese people on a massive scale.

This outcome had not been easy to get. Now, every time Rabe went to work, he couldn't avoid the sight of the charred bodies of Chinese soldiers hanging from bamboo frames. His heart then filled with an immense sadness, and he even silently wept for the suffering Chinese soldiers and defenceless civilians.

Tears flowed like rain this winter.

Save the Women

Rabe's hands were violently trembling now, which was unusual for him. He'd fought in the First World War, and his hard days in Africa had provided him with a strong psychological endurance to face reality, no matter how cruel it was. However, he couldn't calm down when he held a letter to the International Committee written by the refugees living at 83 and 85 Guangzhou Road:

To the International Committee for the Nanjing Safety Zone,

We, the 540 refugees who are signing this letter, have been placed in 83 and 85 Guangzhou Road, where it is very crowded.

On the 13th and the 17th of this month, our houses were raided and robbed many times by the Japanese soldiers in groups of three and four. Today, the Japanese soldiers returned and continued with their robbery. All of our money, jewellery, watches and clothes have been taken. Every night, young women are taken away from our house. The Japanese put them in a truck and don't send them back until the next morning. So far, more than 30 women and young girls have been raped. Women and children's cries can be heard everywhere day and night. The situation here is indescribable. Please help.

Yours,

— The refugees, *18 December 1937*

Signed on behalf of 540 refugees housed in the overcrowded buildings on 83 and 85 Guangzhou Road

The content of this letter from the refugees wasn't what horrified Rabe. The issue was that the people had suffered so much and normally wouldn't express themselves. They didn't often appeal to others even in the face of inhuman suffering and death. It seemed that everything was just tolerated. Too much blood, tears and suffering had made the citizens numb. However, in this numbness, when people couldn't find a solution, they turned to Rabe for help. They screamed until they lost their voices begging for help. Rabe couldn't think of anything more miserable.

Rabe, who was usually an austere man, read the letter and burst into tears. He blamed himself for having failed to protect his subjects, especially the women and children, as the mayor of Nanjing. He couldn't forgive himself.

Few people had ever seen Rabe cry. That day, Han found Rabe crying at his desk, his shoulders trembling and his eyes red.

"Those damned Japanese! I'll tell the whole world about their crimes!" Rabe cursed the Japanese again and again.

A few days earlier, Rabe had anxiously tried to protect and save the lives of thousands of Chinese men as the Japanese soldiers suspected almost every single man in Nanjing of being a Chinese soldier. Now, however, although he'd recently done some good by protecting the men, he couldn't have predicted the terrible mass rape and murder of the city's women by the Japanese soldiers.

He couldn't let this go and had to do something to help. A report about the safety zone from the members of the International Committee shocked Rabe even further:

Ms Zhu, a 47 year old widow whose husband died nine years ago, lived in a very remote road near the south gate with her mother and daughter. On the morning of 13 December, Japanese soldiers broke into her home and took all of the money and property that her husband had left her. On the 14th and 15th, Japanese soldiers went to her home 10 to 20 times each day and Ms Zhu was raped more than 20 times. Her mother and daughter also suffered the same fate. On 15 December, when the south of the city was set alight, Ms Zhu led her elderly mother and her daughter to escape to the north with their bedrolls. Unfortunately her mother got separated from them not far from her house. Ms Zhu and her daughter walked along the street, but were repeatedly raped by the Japanese soldiers. The mother and daughter were so scared that they jumped into a well by the side of the road. Fortunately, the well was very shallow, so they could hide there in safety for a day. A passing vendor eventually saved them. On 16 December, the mother and daughter arrived at the safety zone and survived. However, the safety zone was not safe. That night, three Japanese soldiers raped Ms Zhu and one man forced her to swallow the filth on his genitals.

"Revolting! This is the most revolting thing I've ever read! Mr Rabe, you don't need to look at all of the specific cases. I have a detailed record of all of them here." Smythe held a thick stack of materials, which contained a compilation of all of the atrocities committed by the Japanese soldiers as reported by every member of the committee. Smythe continued: "Since 14 December, at least 1,000 women have been raped and gang-raped by the Japanese soldiers every day, and this figure doesn't include the many women who've gone missing."

"The same thing happened in the house next to me last night. There were more than 20 women hiding there, and several Japanese soldiers broke into the house and took several of the women away and raped them. When the soldiers were raping them, someone came to report it to us. Hartz then rushed to the house immediately and got rid of them. Smythe, what do you think we should do?" said Rabe as he took off his glasses to clean them. He then looked at the ingenious Smythe once again: "Do you have any new proposals? We have to stop these brutal acts immediately."

"New proposals? The Japanese won't listen to Americans. They have contempt for everyone apart from you Mr Rabe, a distinguished German," replied Smythe as he shrugged his shoulders, unable to come up with a solution.

"Mr Fukuda is a Japanese ally who can pass on a message for us. We have to send another protest to him and hope that he passes it on to the commander of the Japanese army. The most crucial thing now is to get the commander to send their gendarmes to protect the eight regions where the women are concentrated," said Rabe.

Smythe thought for a moment and said: "This is the only way, but as far as I know, the Japanese army has only stationed 18 gendarmes in the entire city. These 18 gendarmes are responsible for thousands of their comrades."

Rabe shook his head: "It's obvious that the commanders aren't intervening with the soldiers' raping, killing, burning and looting. I'll go with you to their embassy tomorrow."

But the next day, on the morning of the 19th, Rabe was unable to go with Smythe because of a dangerous situation that had developed in his garden the night before. Six Japanese soldiers had scaled the fence like common thieves and jumped into the garden. They then tried to open the gate from the inside to let in more soldiers.

"The Japanese are here!"

"Help!" Suddenly, the garden was filled with screams.

The Japanese soldiers angrily punched and kicked anyone who was shouting or crying. Faced with this critical situation, Rabe stormed in front of the Japanese soldiers. He burst out with a flashlight and then pointed it at the face of one of the soldiers.

The soldier angrily pulled out a pistol and pointed it at Rabe: "Who are you? The imperial army wants women. Get out of here!"

Rabe shouted in English: "How dare you! I'm a German! Have a good look at this sign!" He showed his Nazi armband to the Japanese soldier. He shouted angrily: "This is my yard and the *führer* authorises me protect it. If you don't want any trouble, then leave now!"

That Japanese soldier froze when he saw the swastika. He then put away his pistol and waved his hand to his five other comrades who'd jumped into the yard with him, walking over to the gate.

"No, you have to leave here from where you entered!" Rabe rushed forwards quickly to stop the Japanese soldiers and pointed to the wall, telling them to climb out.

This scene delighted all of the Chinese refugees and members of the International Committee present. Six Japanese soldiers scrambled over the wall like drowned rats, with Rabe's torch acting like a spotlight.

"Hahaha! Mr Rabe, only you could get Japanese soldiers to crawl away! You're fantastic! Long live Germany!" Han and all the other Chinese people who were taking refuge there knelt down to kowtow to Rabe as they cheered.

Even American and British members of the International Committee gave Rabe a thumbs up. Rabe, who rarely smiled, felt proud of himself as he stood beneath a plane tree. He pointed to the wall, which was taller than any person, and said: "If we added another metre, the Japanese soldiers wouldn't be able to scramble away so easily, even if they could get in!"

Rabe's words were greeted with waves of uproarious laughter all over the yard. This incident, which happened that day in Rabe's garden, became a popular story and was recorded in Rabe's diary and in the valuable historical materials left by many members of the International Committee.

However, there was no forgetting that Nanjing was still under the control of the Japanese. Would the Japanese soldiers, who'd committed so many crimes, forgive the foreign mayor who'd humiliated them?

"Mr Rabe, you can't leave here today. The Japanese are not easily bullied, and they hold grudges. They will look for any opportunity to retaliate. There are more than 200 women here now, and all of their lives depend on you!" pleaded Han after listening to the concerns of the refugees.

"But I'm the president of the International Committee, and I'm responsible for the 200,000 people in the safety zone. I was supposed to meet with the Japanese embassy staff today. What should I do?" Rabe rubbed his hands together, a symptom of his anxiety.

"Mr Rabe, you can't leave. If you leave, the Japanese will jump in and kill us all!" Rabe appeared hesitant, but he was surrounded by pleading women and children, kneeling and crying on the ground in front of him.

Rabe couldn't stand it. He looked up at the sky and sighed. He then threw his hands and said: "Well, today I'll stay at home and protect you then."

"You're a good man!"

"Mr Rabe is a good man!" From then on, the citizens of Nanjing began to call Rabe the "good man", and this nickname spread.

Meanwhile in the Japanese embassy, four members of the International Committee, including Smythe, Bates, Wilson and Fitch, were submitting the two previously prepared "letters of opinion" to Fukuda and the other Japanese diplomats. They didn't dare call them "letters of protest" in front of the Japanese. However, they were indeed full of complaints.

One of the letters was a letter of protest from Wilson who wrote the letter as a doctor. He protested about an incident that had taken place on the night of the 18th at his hospital:

> Please allow me to highlight an incident that occurred in the university hospital on the night of 18 December. There were more than 180 patients present, in addition to hospital medical staff and employees. The hospital has previously had the privilege of providing medical care to the staff of the Japanese embassy.
>
> At nearly 8pm, three Japanese soldiers broke into the hospital from one of the back doors and brazenly stormed the hospital. Ms Heinz, a 65 year old nurse, accompanied these intruders. Although she repeatedly stated that her watch was her private property, they still took it from her. In addition to this, six pocket watches and three pens were stolen. Two of the three soldiers left the hospital and we did not know where the other one went.
>
> At 9.15pm, the hospital was informed that the other Japanese soldier had forcibly broken into the nurses' dormitory. I then checked the room and found six nurses and the Japanese soldier. By the time I arrived, three nurses had been raped. All the hospital's medical staff were shocked.
>
> We originally thought that the hospital would be protected from such events, so there has been no rush to request special protection from you. Faced

with the current situation, we have to make such a request. Please position a sentry at the entrance to the hospital or take other measures to prevent such atrocities from happening again.

Wilson, who graduated from the Harvard medical school with a doctoral degree, was permitted to work at Nanjing's Jinling College hospital in 1936. He was the only surgeon left in Nanjing and witnessed the massacre after the fall of the city. As a doctor, he had been busy performing medical work for wounded Chinese patients since September or October 1937. Wilson saw the injuries that had been inflicted by the Japanese in cold blood on many civilians and soldiers who had laid down their arms following the city's occupation, with many having died. The written protest he submitted to the Japanese embassy that day had only been a short document that Rabe had asked for with little notice to make sure that they had adequate reports. However, a letter from Wilson to his family on the night of 18 December recorded the atrocities committed by the Japanese in detail from 13 to 18 December. He wrote to his family:

> Today is the sixth day of living in a modern version of Dante's *Divine Comedy*, filled with blood and obscenity as many have been slaughtered and tens of thousands of women have been raped. It seems that nothing can stop these monsters' lust for cruelty. I initially smiled at the Japanese out of fear of irritating them, but gradually I grew more indifferent as it's clear that smiles don't work.
>
> I returned after dinner only to discover that three Japanese soldiers had already rummaged through my residence. Ms Heinz, a 67 year old American nurse, led them to the back door and one of them disappeared inside the house. He must have hidden somewhere nearby. I gestured to the Japanese soldiers outside, specifically telling them that this was an American hospital. How could they do this? The two soldiers then agreed to lead the others away after stealing pens and watches, including one that belonged to Ms Heinz.
>
> I feel I should tell you about something else that happened recently. Last night, the house of a Chinese teacher at the Jinling College was destroyed and two of his relatives were raped by the Japanese. Two girls, 16 years old or so, living in the refugee camp were raped to death. About 8,000 refugees were hiding in the middle school affiliated with the Jinling College and the Japanese scaled the walls 10 times to rob food and clothes and rape women until they were satisfied. They also stabbed a boy to death with a bayonet. In the morning, it took me half an hour to stitch up an eight year old boy who'd been

stabbed five times. One had pierced his stomach, exposing part of his peritoneum. I think he may survive.

I saw the third Japanese soldier walking out of my home earlier. He was on the fourth floor of the nurses' dormitory where 15 nurses were living. This darkest chapter in their lives has scarred them. I have no idea how many girls he had assaulted but he stopped when I arrived. He wanted to take one or two watches and their cameras away with him, but I asked him to return the cameras. To my surprise, he did as I asked. I then accompanied him to the front door and sent him off rather emotionally, which, unfortunately, he did not appreciate. The soldier smiled with a frightful grin and I felt grateful that he didn't shoot me.

Today I treated a man with three bullet wounds. He was the only survivor out of a group of 80 people, which also included an 11 year old boy. They were brought from two houses in the safety zone to a slope west of Xikang Road, where they were later killed. He came to when the Japanese left and found that the rest were all dead. He wasn't seriously injured though. Only a few of the victims had been former soldiers.

There was a girl who I think was born mentally handicapped. She had grabbed a Japanese soldier who'd tried to snatch her quilt, but he slashed her in the neck.

Another 17 year old girl with a horrible scar on her neck was the only survivor in her family. She used to an employee in the Jardine engineering corporation in Nanjing.

After inspecting 150 of my patients, I left the hospital for home. A full moon was rising from behind the Purple Mountain on this balmy night, the beauty of which was beyond description. But the city under this moon was seeing its darkest days since the downfall of the Taiping Heavenly Kingdom as 90 per cent of its citizens had left and nowhere was safe from the Japanese. The safety zone was packed with nearly 200,000 frightened citizens.

These refugees face starvation and fuel shortages for the coming winter. This was not the pleasant winter we had expected.

In December 1937, Nanjing experienced a biting cold winter. The first week after the Japanese occupation in particular was a living hell. No wonder Wilson compared the suffering of the citizens of Nanjing to Dante's *Divine Comedy*.

Smythe presented an even more damning written protest to the Japanese diplomats as it was a report on 54 offences committed by the Japanese in the safety zone. Prior to this, he and Rabe had already submitted 16 cases to them. Collecting pieces of evidence like this proved useful for westerners against their enemies in the Second World War and ever since then.

Faced with bloody cases of rape, gang-rape and murderous adultery, arrogant Japanese officials, who prided themselves on their logic over others, shook their heads in resignation when faced with Smythe and Rabe's evidence.

"We shall tell the military to improve their discipline," assured Fukuda.

"Mr Rabe has to protect the 300 women and children hiding in his courtyard so he can't leave them at risk. I apologise for his absence. Mr Rabe also hopes that you can satisfy Mr Wilson's request by setting up sentries at the entrance to his hospital and the 18 safety zones we listed and provided yesterday. This means that we'll have at least 19 safe areas to protect a quarter to a third of the city's civilians from the soldiers' rampant pillaging and looting," argued Smythe.

The Japanese made an oral commitment. However, Rabe later discovered that they did not keep their promise as there were only a dozen Japanese military policemen in Nanjing, including the 19 safety areas and the hospital. In addition to this, these military policemen didn't perform their duties properly and so the Japanese soldiers became even more frenzied, raping girls and killing innocent civilians.

On their way back from the Japanese embassy to Jinling College, Smythe and his colleagues saw that an American woman was being taken away. Smythe's colleagues had been investigating an incident where three female students had been taken away the night before. One of the female students had been raped at the entrance to the college.

"How dare they assault American women!" Smythe and his colleague, Fitch, were enraged and wanted to help.

"What are you doing here?" Smythe jumped out of the car and rushed towards the Japanese, shouting at them and blocking their way.

The Japanese were obviously annoyed, pointing their bayonets at Smythe and Fitch.

"We demand that you let her get in our car," said Smythe. "She's an American!"

The Japanese resolutely refused.

"Alright. We'll settle this issue at your embassy." Smythe's threat worked.

Fitch seized the opportunity and took the American woman into the car as she trembled with fear. But the Japanese wouldn't let them go without a fight and tried to block their car. However, they stopped when the engine roared, letting Smythe successfully rescue the American.

"This is outrageous! They need to pay for this!" Smythe wanted the

Japanese embassy to have a clear idea of the horrifying actions of its soldiers, so he and Fitch drove to the embassy once again to protest to Ambassador Tanaka.

Ambassador Tanaka frowned and muttered: "We are indeed responsible for the safety of your countrymen." Smythe asked: "Ambassador Tanaka, where do you think the American girl would be safe?"

Tanaka hesitated and looked rather embarrassed. He finally blurted out: "You'd better sort out this problem yourselves."

"Is there any nation more arrogant than Japan?!" Smythe complained all the way back from the embassy, surrounded by looting and pillaging. Foreign witnesses showed that the Japanese invading army and the government that had conspired with them had treated the Chinese like cattle as the Japanese soldiers descended into a rampage.

Having found a place in the hospital affiliated with the Jinling College for the American woman who'd been assaulted, Smythe and his colleagues went to report to Rabe at his home. On their way there, their car was constantly stopped by Chinese civilians who either complained to them about the Japanese atrocities or desperately asked for help. They didn't manage to meet Rabe until the evening even though it was just 10 minutes away.

At this moment, news that would further outrage the members of the International Committee came from Wilson's hospital: a 19 year old woman who was six and a half months pregnant had been stabbed due to resisting the Japanese soldiers' sexual assault. She had 18 wounds on her face and several more on her legs with a deep gash in her abdomen. The girl was at death's door and had lost her baby.

Rabe and Smythe were horrified and hurried to the hospital as soon as they heard the news. Wilson was doing everything he could to save the girl. "Not now, it's too horrible in there," said Wilson as he persuaded them out of visiting the girl. He said that he'd treated thousands of injured people since August, but the girl had had the most wounds of all. "This would shock even the devil himself," muttered the doctor.

The girl was called Li Xiuying and she'd miraculously survived with the help of Rabe and Wilson. She later became an important witness to the Nanjing Massacre. She used to travel to Japan along with Zhu Chengshan, the curator of the Nanjing Massacre Memorial Hall, and discussed her experiences with the Japanese authorities regarding the atrocities their soldiers had once committed.

On 8 September 1999, Li Xiuying, who was 80 years old, was interviewed by a Dr Hallot, a German academic conducting research on Rabe, in the

Nanjing Massacre Memorial Hall. She revealed her rape at the hands of the Japanese and the help she'd received from Rabe:

> I was born on 24 February 1919. I had to look after my younger brother at the age of 13 when my mother died. I married in 1937 and my husband worked as a typist in Shanghai. I planned to go back to Nanjing when the Battle of Shanghai broke out. At the time, the Nanjing Yangtze River bridge hadn't yet been built, so I had to cross the river by boat, which was quite hazardous. The boatmen were unwilling to take me because I was six months pregnant, which be an extra worry for them. They didn't agree to take me until I begged them relentlessly.
>
> After the Japanese occupied Nanjing, some foreigners established a safety zone, which covered a large area. We all thought it was safe to go there and that the Japanese wouldn't bother us. However, the Japanese soldiers held up their guns at the boundary of the safety zone and shot or raped anyone they saw, which caused panic among the citizens. The Japanese were downright evil and they'd fire at people if they were far away and stab them if they were near. This happened in the safety zone. They went mad and dragged women away the second they saw them.
>
> The safety zone we lived in back then was a school run by the foreigners. It's in the neighbourhood of the stadium now. We lived in what used to be a basement in the school. There were even desks inside. We settled down there after taking out the desks.
>
> The Japanese entered the city on 13 December and they came to our basement on the 18th. They captured some young men in the afternoon that day. Several elderly people set up camp above and cooked for us every day. We ate in the early morning and at night when the Japanese wouldn't see us. Just two meals a day. We women hid behind the elderly and children when we heard the sound of the Japanese.
>
> On the morning of 19 December, the elderly gave meals to us down in the basement and then blocked the door with chairs and desks. But soon after breakfast, we heard the footsteps of Japanese soldiers, which made us quite nervous. They came looking for young women, which was bad news for me as I was pregnant and unable to run away. So, I knocked my head against the wall, passing out on the spot. An elderly person brought me back to my senses when the Japanese left with other young women, but I was still lying in bed sleeping. It was a low bed. We didn't have any watches or clocks at that point and the room was empty and dark. In winter, the days were short. Light could only filter in through the small window to our basement. The Japanese came again that night, so some elderly people woke me up, telling me to get up as I

couldn't sleep there anymore. But I'd injured myself after knocking my head against the wall, so I didn't want to get up. I lay there preparing for death, knowing there was no way out. Then two Japanese soldiers came in and they both dragged a young woman out of the room. As I was lying in bed, the other refugees told the Japanese that I was sick. One of them saw my wound and left, but another wasn't convinced as he lunged at me and tried to take off my clothes. I knew I couldn't get away, so I took out his sword while he wasn't paying attention and stood up to him with my back against the wall. He was scared as he didn't expect a woman to have the guts to do this. He threw himself at me, grabbing my hands tightly. But he was shorter than me, so I pulled his collar and bit him on his arm. He was screaming in agony. Immediately, the two other Japanese soldiers loosened their grip on the other women and rushed towards us with bayonets. They stabbed my legs but I would have rather died than let go of the Japanese soldier's collar. The two Japs stabbed me frantically and then stabbed my face as blood immediately streamed down, blurring my vision. This was followed by a pang of pain in my stomach and I fell into a coma.

This happened more than six decades ago. You can see the scar on my face. The outer layers of my skin have been stitched up, but not the inner layers.

It was dark and everything was a blur. The Japanese ran away thinking that I was dead. My father returned when they left to get food and clothes as we lived close to Wutaishan at the time. He panicked the second he entered the room. Someone told him that I fought against the Japanese and had been killed. Everyone thought I was dead because I was covered with blood. My father thought so too as he touched me and couldn't feel me breathing. Two elderly people carried me out of the room on a door, planning to bury me. However, I was spitting up blood as it was cold outside. People saw this and shouted that I was still alive before rushing me over to Gulou Hospital. The hospital was run by Americans and a foreign surgeon came to stitch up the wounds on my face when I arrived there. I later found out that it was Dr Wilson who saved my life.

The baby was dead when they got it out. A missionary named John Magee took several pictures of me when he heard that there was a woman who'd survived even though she'd been stabbed 37 times and had lost her baby.

There were no places available in the hospital as casualties were admitted every day. They were going to release me when I got better. But where could I go? It was Mr Magee and Mr Rabe who later helped me find somewhere in the safety zone.

Rabe was in charge of the safety zone and everybody knew that he was a good German. Many Chinese people lived in Rabe's house and in the area, and they turned to Rabe whenever the Japanese tried to cause any trouble. Back then, we had no idea whether Rabe was a Nazi or not. His identity didn't really concern us as he was a good person anyway. The citizens of Nanjing will always remember Rabe and be grateful for him. That's the Chinese way; we repay even the smallest favour. Not many could stand up to the Japanese at that time, so you can't imagine how many Chinese people would have died without Rabe.

"The Good Man Rabe" has been a well-known phrase in Nanjing in the decades following the massacre. It is actually used to praise both Rabe and all the friendly foreigners who stayed behind and helped rescue Chinese refugees in Nanjing under Rabe's leadership.

What Rabe had to deal with in the face of the ferocious and manic Japanese soldiers was far more difficult than we can ever imagine. It wasn't just a matter of Rabe and his colleagues staying alive, but also their responsibility for the safety of more than 200,000 refugees in the safety zones across the city. What about those scattered outside of the safety zones? Christian doctrine and a sense of humanity obligated them to protect the vulnerable, the disabled and the weak. They didn't fear death.

Rabe knew that he needed perseverance more than anything else in his struggle with the Japanese.

To save them from Japanese sexual assaults, Rabe decided to transfer as many of the women scattered throughout the safety zone as possible to the Jinling College. At least the Japanese may somewhat restrain themselves when tens of thousands of these women were under his personal protection.

This was easier said than done. First Rabe had to do this in secret because if the Japanese found out their intention, they would think that Rabe wanted to stop them from taking girls, which would cause a lot of problems. However, Riggers, a member of the International Committee, ran across a group of Japanese soldiers searching for girls in 28 Hankou Road when he was transferring women to the college. One was killed and four were wounded in the struggle. Smythe came across four Japanese soldiers raping women when he was on a mission to 19 Hankou Road, so he and other foreigners shouted at them, getting them to leave angrily. Smythe then quickly took the women somewhere safer.

Even Rabe, who made detailed notes about every incident, couldn't figure out exactly how many women had been raped or murdered by the Japanese when they took Nanjing. Smythe's report on the rapes included more than 400 cases, which was just the tip of the iceberg. How many cases had escaped their attention? Smythe calculated that the real number was several times larger as these 400 cases had just been witnessed by members of the

International Committee. A journalist from *The Manchester Guardian* said that "at least 20,000" women had been raped. This was just a rough calculation. In addition to this, even more women were raped and murdered after Rabe left Nanjing in February 1938. However, had it not been for Rabe and his colleagues, who went to great lengths to stop these atrocities and went to the Japanese embassy to protest against their brutality, even going to their commander-in-chief Iwane Matsui, the number of women that would have been raped or murdered would have been several times larger than the estimate stated by *The Manchester Guardian*.

The debt of gratitude owed by the people of Nanjing to foreigners like Rabe can only be compared to the endless Yangtze River. The next chapter shall discuss the contributions made by another towering figure in humanitarianism in Nanjing. However, we shall get to that later.

First we shall review more significant contributions made by Rabe and the other foreigners.

The Foreign Buddha

There's no doubt that Rabe's reason for setting up a safety zone wasn't just to protect women and children, but any refugees harassed by the Japanese soldiers.

This was by no means a simple task.

Some 20 foreigners, more than 200,000 refugees and tens of thousands of brutal Japanese soldiers. What could Rabe do?

On Christmas Eve 1937, the Japanese troops in Nanjing struck again with a renewed brutality as they tried to burn down the ancient city.

Flames rose up to the heavens all over the city, lighting it up during both the day and the night. The refugees couldn't figure out the cause of the fire since the Japanese soldiers had stopped bombing the city. They then realised that the fires had been deliberately started by the Japanese.

But why? People were at a loss until someone finally unveiled the truth. It turned out that some foreign journalists had managed to report the atrocities committed by the Japanese to the outside world. They were therefore under a great deal of international pressure and tried to cover up all their crimes by setting fire to the evidence. They tried to burn everything that revealed the extent of their crimes.

"At 2.30 am, I was awoken by the sound of walls and roofs splintering as they gave way. The fire had spread to Zhongshan Road. It was very dangerous at that point as the fire was spreading to the final row of houses between my home and Zhongshan Road," wrote Rabe in his diary on 22 December. His words reveal the horror of the scene.

To protect the American embassy and American property in Nanjing, 14 Americans, including Smythe, Wilson and Magee, jointly telegraphed an urgent message to the American consul general in Shanghai, informing them that American diplomatic representatives were urgently needed in Nanjing to cope with the crisis.

This revealed the extreme panic and concern felt by these Americans as the Japanese had tried to kidnap ambassadors in public, tear up the American flag, burn American property and even loot and burn their churches. The Japanese soldiers committed all kinds of atrocities, and even burned the German embassy and German property. This was horrifying enough on its own, let alone combined with the brutality suffered by the Americans who crossed the Japanese.

Meanwhile, the American Northern Presbyterian missionary Wilson Mills created a report that recorded 13 brutal Japanese intrusions in a short period of time in their mission in Shuangtang, southwest of Nanjing:

5.10am: two Japanese soldiers intruded.

11.25am: two more Japanese soldiers intruded.

2.00pm: three Japanese soldiers intruded and took away a female refugee from the church hall.

3.25pm: two Japanese soldiers intruded and took a man to work for them.

3.30pm: two Japanese soldiers intruded and tore down the notice on the door.

4.00pm: four Japanese soldiers intruded and took bribes from the refugees in the camps as they also looked for women. An hour later, they grabbed a married woman called Pan, took two cents from a male refugee called Liu and also stole the armbands and badges that belonged to a refugee called Guan.

9.00am the next day: a Japanese soldier intruded.

2.00pm: three Japanese soldiers intruded.

3.00pm: a Japanese soldier intruded.

3.10pm: two Japanese soldiers intruded and kidnapped a married woman called Chen.

3.12pm: two Japanese soldiers intruded and took another girl called Chen.

5.00pm: three Japanese soldiers intruded and took away two married women called Qin and Fan.

6.00pm: three Japanese soldiers intruded and took away a married woman called Pan.

Bates, an American professor at the University of Nanjing, wrote 13 letters of protest to the Japanese embassy about their troops violently entering the university campus and the homes of American expatriates following the Japanese occupation of Nanjing. Among these is a letter of protest from 15 December:

> In the recently built library, we are responsible for more than 1,500 civilians. Among these civilians, four women have been recently raped, two have been abducted, raped and released; a further three women have been seized and have still not come back; another woman was abducted but released thanks to the intervention of the gendarmes near the embassy. These acts of the Japanese soldiers have brought tremendous pain and fear to all their family members, their neighbours and people living in this city. This afternoon, more than 100 similar cases that took place in other places within the safety zone beyond my jurisdiction were reported to me. The reason why I have mentioned these cases is to show that the looting and rape taking place near Nanjing University is only one example of the soldiers causing great suffering for the people.

The American embassy's premises didn't escape Japanese harassment. In December, Japanese soldiers broke into the building and took away three cars, five bikes and money belonging to the embassy staff. Japanese soldiers even pushed bayonets against the neck of the embassy's secretary, forcing him to open the door as they attempted to rape Chinese women in the courtyard. They ripped and trod on the American flag several times. The most unacceptable incident was when Allison, the American diplomat, protested, he was slapped by the Japanese.

Rabe somewhat ridiculed his American friends with a mix of pride and sympathy: "The Americans are in a very uncomfortable position indeed. So far, whenever I've shown my Nazi armband and the German flag on the house and car, it works. But these Japanese don't take Americans seriously."

On 20 December, Dr Trimmer and Dr McCallum were almost killed when they were shot and wounded in separate incidents involving disputes with the Japanese in Gulou Hospital. It caused mass panic among the members of the International Committee.

"Mr Rabe, be honest, how long can we control this situation?" asked Smythe sincerely. He added that if a Chinese man killed a Japanese soldier who'd raped his wife or daughter in the safety area, then the situation would get even more out of control. If this happened, would they be able to stop the Japanese soldiers from committing further massacres?

The question made the members of the International Committee, including Rabe, fall silent. If that were to happen, would the safety zone be safe? Would all their efforts be for naught? They didn't dare say anything as Rabe and his men had personally seen Chinese men killing Japanese soldiers for raping their wives and daughters. They had once rushed over to help a mother and her daughter who'd been raped by Japanese soldiers and found that two Japanese soldiers had been killed by the father. This was terrible news. The members of International Committee knew that this would cause trouble so they threw the bodies of the dead Japanese soldiers into a back room and persuaded the man to run for his life as soon as possible. With no one in sight, they set a fire to the house with the two Japanese soldiers inside.

Rabe said nothing about the matter when the Japanese asked about it: "We have no idea what happened and haven't even heard anything about this." They luckily escaped unharmed.

However, this didn't mean that the situation wasn't likely to get worse in future. Rabe had to be incredibly clever in his mission to protect the refugees, but it had started to lead to tremendous danger.

In the cold winter of December 1937, *Silent Night* could be heard from St Paul's Church, sung with a mix of holiness and sadness. When the Japanese entered the city, the pain could be felt in the song, grieving the loss of love, mercy, peace and justice. But there was also sacrifice, a core value in the Christian belief system.

I don't wish to preach Christianity, but in the face of war and death, many foreign Christians like Rabe stayed in Nanjing and made a sacrifice for the refugees of a foreign land because of their strong belief in love.

It is impossible to discuss St Paul's Church without mentioning Ernest H Forster. Forster was born in Pennsylvania in 1895 and graduated from Princeton University as a missionary before arriving in China in the 1920s to teach at Mahan School in Yangzhou. In 1936, Forster married Clarissa, the daughter of the prominent lawyer Irving Townsend. The married couple arrived to work in the church one month before the fall of Nanjing. St. Paul's Church was actually founded by the American missionary Gill and it had been very impressive before the war.

With construction starting in 1912 on Curtain Bridge Street, later renamed the South Pacific Road, the church was completed two years later. The new church was designed and supervised by Liu Zhaochang, the architect of the University of Nanjing and it cost $12,000 at the time. The simple and elegant Gothic church, which wouldn't look out of place in an English village, became a scenic highlight of Nanjing and an important place for Christians in carrying out their activities. After the philanthropic and pious Christian missionary came to Nanjing, Forster lived across from the China Hotel. The

Japanese bombed Nanjing in early December 1937 and the China Hotel was destroyed, which left two large holes in the Forster family's door. On 14 December, St Paul's Church was bombed by the Japanese and badly damaged. With the establishment of the safety zone, Forster joined the International Committee. He followed Rabe's instructions and remained devoted to his position, going to great efforts to prevent the intrusions of Japanese soldiers. However, there was no way these unarmed missionaries could resist the invasion. Still, Forster always made every effort to deal with the Japanese. His bravery intimidated the Japanese soldiers, but whenever he went away, they would secretly break into the mission and rape women in public.

Lu, a 40 year old evangelist, was quiet, gentle and kind, so when he saw the Japanese brutality it severely pained him. All he said every day was: "The devil has come, the devil has come." Forster tried to comfort him, but it was in vain. Soon, Lu threw himself into the river and drowned. Forster rallied all his followers to look for him and a few days later, his body was found in the water. With great grief, Forster bought a coffin and buried Lu as a Christian.

Since then, Forster spent almost 24 hours a day by the gate to the refugee shelter to prevent the Japanese from breaking in, giving hundreds of women, children and other refugees security and peace.

After consulting a range of historical sources, I found that Mr Allison - the ambassador sent by the American government to go through all the materials regarding Japanese damage to US embassy property and the security of its citizens - submitted several reports to the US department of state. One of the reports recorded the extent of the Japanese harassment in detail: "From yesterday afternoon until this morning, 15 cases relating to Japanese intrusion into American buildings and houses have been reported to the embassy. The Japanese have not only looted these properties, but have also forcefully taken away 10 Chinese women living there. The latest and most notorious incident happened this morning when Japanese soldiers drove two trucks into the courtyard of the United Christian Missionary Society and carried away a piano and other property, destroying a section of the wall."

I also found a record of a Nanjing Massacre survivor called Su Guobao who had told his story to a lady called Marianne Stenvig Andersen, one of the Danish hero Bernhard Arp Sindberg's nieces. She had come to Nanjing with Queen Margrethe II of Denmark on 27 April 2014 to present a bouquet of roses to the Nanjing Massacre Memorial Hall. The Dane was frequently described in Rabe's diary and he sheltered some 20,000 refugees during the Nanjing Massacre.

Su was only 10 years old when the Japanese soldiers invaded his village.

To avoid the Japanese atrocities, he fled with his family of four to Sindberg's factory south of the Yangtze. Sindberg saw the poor little boy and gave him one silver dollar as well as 18 kilograms of rice. Holding the silver dollar in both hands, Su knelt down in gratitude. Su told Sindberg's niece: "This silver dollar helped us live well for quite a while. Many, many men were killed back then, and to protect me and help me make a living, Mr Sindberg arranged a position for me in the factory and also promised that he'd send me to school after the war. He was really a good man."

Few people knew the story of Mr Sindberg until the arrival of a delegation led by Zhu Chengshan, the curator of the Nanjing Massacre Memorial Hall, in Denmark to hold an exhibition about the Nanjing Massacre. The curator inadvertently found out that the gallery was located in Aarhus, which was Sindberg's hometown, and felt excited about the coincidence. He published a story that he was looking for Sindberg in a local newspaper. As a result, Sindberg's niece saw it and called the Chinese embassy. From her, we found out that he had passed away 19 years earlier. The story of her uncle had deeply touched her and she planted special yellow roses to commemorate him.

"In Danish culture, yellow represents courage. Yellow roses are very difficult to cultivate, just like my uncle: brave, unique and not easily replicated," Marianne explained. In spring 2006, Sindberg's niece and six relatives from the US and Lebanon planted yellow roses in the Peace Plaza, and the next year they took those roses to the Nanjing Massacre Memorial Hall, where they opened the Sindberg Rose Garden.

"Justice will never be forgotten," said Marianne.

The people of Nanjing naturally haven't forgotten Sindberg, the "Greatest Dane". From 1937 to 1938, Sindberg had been employed by the Danish company FLSmidth, and was responsible for dealing with importing equipment for a factory that would produce 200,000 tons of cement a year. More important than the fact that its equipment was imported from Denmark, China's military and all circles of society, including wealthy citizens, were busy constructing military fortifications such as air-raid shelters, which made cement increasingly in demand. In turn, this promoted the growth of the factory. Sindberg and another engineer, Gunther, arrived in Nanjing on 5 December 1937. As soon as they arrived, they took up the responsibility of protecting the cement equipment that was under fire by the Japanese military.

The cement factory was located near Qixia Mountain. As the plant was run by a Danish company, Sindberg suggested a strategy: they would use small German flags to surround an area of up to 1,350 square metres to prevent being attacked by Japanese planes. At the time, quite a lot of Chinese soldiers and refugees fled into the area after China's military waged its final battle against Japan by Qixia Mountain. In order to ensure that it was safe, Sindberg applied to Rabe to make the plant a special security zone outside of the city under the leadership of the International Committee. They adopted the same method to manage the plant and closely cooperated with Rabe, accepting 15,000 refugees in total. This lasted until March 1938, when the Japanese army forced Sindberg to leave Nanjing to strengthen their so-called "well-regulated rule". The security zone outside the city was subsequently disbanded. To extend their thanks to Sindberg, cement workers and refugees specially prepared a silk banner that had the Chinese word for "courageous" on it as a gift, with 11 Chinese people writing their names on it.

Sindberg died in 1984. However, at the 1938 International Labour Conference, he revealed the truth about the Nanjing Massacre to the world and workers' representatives by playing a video of the Japanese atrocities that had been filmed by John Magee. The Chinese felt grateful for his actions during the massacre and noted on his passport: "a friend of China".

I noticed that Rabe frequently praised Sindberg in his diary, especially when the city was suffering from a severe food shortage, and Sindberg sent him a large quantity of congee, for which Rabe was incredibly grateful.

After the waves of robbery and rape on the days around 20 December, a new wave of crimes was being committed: arson. Sindberg often went into the city during this period. He spoke with Rabe about management issues, but also tried to resolve the food shortage and submitted evidence to Rabe and his colleagues regarding the Japanese crimes, including setting dead bodies and buildings on fire.

On 21 December, Rabe and 21 other foreigners in Nanjing from Germany, the US, the UK, Austria and the USSR mounted a protest against the Japanese embassy and proposed the following three suggestions using information provided by Sindberg about the situation in the city:

> Firstly, acts of arson should be halted in all areas of Nanjing to protect the rest of the city that has not been destroyed. Secondly, for the entire week, the Japanese troops have caused the citizens a great deal of trauma. They have to stop their destructive operations immediately. Thirdly, looting and arson have brought the city's commercial life to a standstill and all civilians have crowded into refugee shelters as a result. Based on this and considering the fact that the food reserve is only enough to feed 200,000 residents in the safety zone for one week, we are here to urgently appeal for immediate action to be taken to restore security, order and normal living conditions, and for additional food and fuel

reserves. The current situation will surely soon lead to famine, so we have no other request than for basic living conditions to be provided: shelter, safety and food.

Rabe took the protest directly to the Japanese supreme commander Iwane Matsui. "If you stand by and do nothing to stop this wave of arson then the city will be completely reduced to ash," Rabe said to Matsui and Ambassador Tanaka. "No, no! Nanjing won't be destroyed. We're here with the great Imperial Japanese Army, and just like you, they need to live and eat in security." Tanaka looked at Matsui and tried to belittle Rabe's assertions with a strange little smile. In contrast to the portly Rabe, the thin old man Matsui seemed very polite and patted Rabe on his shoulder, saying: "I understand you're from Germany. I really respect Germany, and I have one thing that needs your help."

Rabe was surprised and asked: "What can I do for you, general?" Matsui was extremely blunt and said: "You see, my army has been staying in the city for almost a week and our garrison has been established, but the citizens of Nanjing are all staying in your safety zone, which doesn't comply with metropolitan regulations. So, we would like people to be able to leave the safety zone and go back to their homes, return to work and live like normal people."

Rabe listened warily, wondering what Matsui was up to. Was this a trick? "Rest assured, Mr Rabe," said Matsui, seeming to know exactly what he was thinking. He continued: "We'll issue identity cards to all citizens so we can ensure their legal status. With legal status, they will be provided with security. Isn't that right sir?" What kind of trick was this? Rabe stared at the biggest monster in the Japanese army with wide eyes and responded with silence.

"Hahaha! Today's talk with Mr Rabe has been very meaningful indeed. Japan and Germany are great friends! We will always be friends!" Matsui stretched out his hands and embraced Rabe tightly with his shrivelled arms. He smiled and said: "Look after yourself!" He then asked the guards to escort Rabe away. Rabe left his "friend" and returned to his house, finding that his "friends" had broken into his home. Even his private office had been turned upside down. Rabe was so angry that his face turned a hot red. He found that his safe, which contained 23,000 yuan, had marks left by Japanese bayonets, but fortunately the locks had been too strong for them.

The city was still engulfed in fire. Rabe asked people to protect his yard. He'd always thought that there were just 200 or 300 refugees there, but the real number, as Han Xianglin had reported, was 603, including women, children and elderly people.

"I shall not allow my yard to be disturbed by the Japanese!" When he was ready to once again leave for the safety areas to help put out fires, six Japanese soldiers started to climb over the wall. Rabe stood boldly in front of the Japanese soldiers, thumping his Nazi armband with one hand and pointing to the wall with another, commanding his "friends" to go away.

The Japanese soldiers reluctantly left, obviously very angry, but they had to follow his orders. Once the intruders had left, Rabe lifted his head and proudly said: "My 'friends' are gone, so you can stay here in safety. I have to go and stop this madness." Rabe took a car and drove to a new arson site as quickly as possible.

That night, Rabe felt exhausted. He went back to his desk and gently pushed open the window, writing in his diary about seeing the refugees helplessly lying in the rain: "This terror is endless, and a positive outcome is unimaginable. Refugees cuddle each other in the rain as they silently stare at the beautiful and terrible flames. If the flames spread to us, there will be no way out for these poor people. I am their last hope."

Rabe was under extreme pressure. He was thinking about his meeting with Matsui earlier that day and wondered what trick the Japanese military would play on the poor refugees tomorrow. Nobody knew.

The next day was 22 December 1937.

That day, the Japanese posted a series of notices with poorly written Chinese characters all over the city, particularly in Rabe's safety zone, which read as follows:

Proclamation

As of 24 December, the commander-in-chief will issue ID cards to all refugees and civilians, which will be the solely acceptable certificate of both the right to reside and work in the city.

This requires all civilians to go to the Japanese army registration office to receive their card. ID cards must be received by the individual to whom the card relates and cannot be accepted by anyone else. The elderly, children and wounded must be accompanied by family members and shall go to the registration office. This requirement must be followed.

If anyone is found without an ID card, they shall lose the right to live in the city. This provision is extremely important. Notice is hereby given.

— 22 December, Showa 12, Japanese army garrison commander in Nanjing

People were terrified by the ominous proclamation. However, the most alarming part was the impact of this policy on the Chinese soldiers who'd surrendered and were now hiding in the safety zone. People screamed: "We're bound to die this time! We can't go to the registration office because they'll kill us." Rabe was saddened by the concerns of the desperate refugees. If they followed the notice as requested, more innocent people would be mistakenly identified as Chinese soldiers and any former members of the Chinese military would be executed. However, if they didn't register, Japan would use it as a pretext to disband the safety zone and the consequences would be disastrous.

The International Committee called a meeting at their headquarters and continued to discuss the matter for more than two hours. The ever resourceful Smythe was clueless as to how they could avoid disaster. No one spoke and a silence hung in the air.

Han Xianglin hesitantly raised his hand. Rabe encouraged him. Han said: "It would clearly cause a lot of problems if people don't go to register, but a lot of people will die if they do. We can only imagine how many people will suffer as a result. But I think there's at least one way we can help reduce the danger."

"Come on, Mr Han, what have you got?" Smythe asked impatiently. Han explained: "There are lots of elderly people and children in the safety zone, but most of these people have lost their parents or children in the war so they hate the Japanese soldiers. Meanwhile, we also have a large number of women and men who've laid down their arms in the safety zone, most of whom are single. This being the case, we can just get people to pose as families; the elderly and children can create 'families' with the widows and single men and then they can go to the registration office."

Smythe threw open his arms and warmly embraced Han, giving him a big kiss and saying: "Han, you're brilliant! What an amazing idea!! What do you think, president? I think it could work!"

Rabe considered it for a while and nodded his head: "I think Han's plan would work. But we should still keep our eyes on the Japanese, they're incredibly deceitful."

Han Xianglin explained: "If we do this soon, then a lot of people will be saved from the Japanese bayonets."

"Get started as soon as possible!" Rabe pointed to his head and said: "This is a secret mission, everyone, use your brain!"

In the west, 22 and 23 December are typically spent preparing for Christmas. That year, Rabe and 20 other foreigners in Nanjing used a pretext of preparing Christmas gifts and worked with Chinese workers like Han

Xianglin as they scoured every corner of the safety zone, bringing people who'd lost family members together to form makeshift families.

Early in the morning of 24 December, dozens of Chinese men wearing armbands with the rising sun emblem had already gathered at Shangxi Road square. They were temporary security staff who'd been appointed by the Japanese army the previous day. Fully armed Japanese soldiers surrounded them.

They then gave their orders to the crowd: "Everyone, the great Takao has ordered that from now on, every citizen older than 16 years old has to get a residency permit to walk freely in this city. It's like the previous citizens permit, but now the Japanese army is going to be sending them out. Before that, we have one task to complete: everyone's identity needs to be checked. You have to come with your entire family to be checked. If anyone tries to make a fool of us, they will be killed. Now, come and get your permits."

"Line up! Everybody, line up!"

"Listen everybody!" shouted the people wearing the rising sun armbands. "If you're with the central army, please stand to one side. As you have no family here you cannot wander around freely. If you can stand aside, Takao will take good care of you. You can stay here to work if you like, or you can go home. The Japanese will cover the travel expenses."

A man excitedly jumped out of the line and another man looked around suspiciously.

"You! Are you a soldier? Come out!" A Japanese soldier pulled suspicious looking men away from women and the elderly.

More and more people were being pulled aside, four of whom were lined in a row and forced to get into a truck. A Japanese soldier said: "Don't be afraid, Takao will give you good jobs and you'll be fed white rice." After he finished speaking, the Japanese all began to laugh, making the civilians feel sick.

Men were being taken away one truck after another.

"Go! Register! Register!" The Japanese forced the refugees to move along in a line.

The sound of gunfire could be heard nearby.

Rabe was furious. He said to Han in a low voice: "Tell everyone to be wary of the Japanese."

"Got it!" Han and the security staff with Red Cross armbands pretended to maintain order, acting like nothing had happened. They carefully warned the single people: "Don't be fooled. Insist that you're married and that you're a family!"

"We're married. We're family," they repeated.

After the makeshift families and married couples received their residency permits, they expressed their sincere gratitude to Rabe, quietly and carefully.

The registration office quickly descended into chaos once again. "You! Wash your face!" A Japanese solider pulled aside a woman with a dirty face and forced her to clean it.

The woman was forced to obey as he menacingly pointed a bayonet at her. "Ah, you're such a beautiful woman, beautiful!" laughed the Japanese soldier seedily. "You! Come over here!" he ordered as he pushed her aside with his bayonet.

"Take off your clothes! Quickly!" shouted the soldier at another woman.

The woman had no choice but to do so. This Japanese soldier excitedly felt her breasts and ordered around more women: "Good! Good! Go over there, you'll be working for Takao."

These women formed a line that grew ever longer. All of them were then taken by more trucks to the Japanese military camps. After one or two days, and sometimes even seven or eight days, many of them were released. However, they had been horrifically raped at least 10 times, some even as many as 20 times. Some didn't even make it back and died in the military camps.

"Using the excuse of selling identity cards, the Japanese army killed hundreds of thousands of Chinese men and violently raped many Chinese women. In the end, only 160,000 people received their ID cards. This means that many thousands of people were killed by the Japanese army in the process," said one expert on the Nanjing Massacre.

How many people were actually killed by the Japanese army? A passage in Rabe's diary explains: "In other areas of the safety zone, the Japanese army divided citizens into groups of 100. They took them over to the register office. As far as I've heard, about 20,000 people were taken away by the Japanese. Some of them were sent to do forced labour while others were executed by firing squad."

However, Rabe and his colleagues saved many thousands of people during this incident. They saved lives both in the register offices and by giving secret advice. Many thousands of single Chinese soldiers were rescued by pretending to be married and to have families in Nanjing.

With the pretext of issuing ID cards, the Japanese intended to control hundreds of thousands of people in Nanjing. They also had a more insidious plan: to weaken the power of the safety zone, and finally succeed in dissolving it. Japanese senior officers even tried to explain their aims to Rabe through their diplomats. Rabe, with many other members of the International Committee, however, resolutely protested.

"The Japanese are shameless. They will never control us," said Magee as he showed a film he'd shot to the members of International Committee.

"We shouldn't give in to them," Smythe said to Rabe stubbornly.

"As a German, I represented the *führer* and have a responsibility to the Chinese people. The reason why I've stayed in Nanjing is for the safety of the refugees. My stance is absolutely clear: we will not allow the safety zone to be dissolved, unless a better way of protecting the refugees emerges," said Rabe, making his decision clear.

Christmas is an incredibly important event for Christians. However, Christmas in 1937 was an unhappy and miserable experience for people like Rabe who'd stayed in Nanjing. Despite this, Rabe still felt that it was his responsibility to show Jesus's message of mercy and kindness to the poor people who were living in a debauched hell. Early that morning, he finished off the Froebel star decorations he'd prepared the night before and packed them carefully. He sent them to his colleagues in the International Committee along with the calendar he'd received from Siemens. Rabe wanted to give Dr Wilson a calendar to show his gratitude for saving people's lives on the operating table. Rabe took the opportunity to look after several casualties with Dr Wilson. He saw Li Xiuying, who'd been stabbed 37 times, and her condition was constantly improving. However, not everyone was so lucky, which made Rabe extremely sad. A young fisherman was among these unfortunate souls. Along with another 70 people, he'd been taken by the Japanese from a silk factory building in the University of Nanjing. All of them were taken elsewhere to be executed. They then doused them with petrol and burned them. This young fisherman had somehow survived the ordeal. He'd escaped the fire and lived. However, he had very severe injuries and severe burns covered two thirds of his skin. He ran to the hospital alone, bloody and injured. Wilson did everything he could and gave him emergency treatment. After several hours of surgery, Wilson said that there was little hope for him. Rabe was later informed that this young man had been declared dead some time ago. Rabe even went to the morgue, where he saw more corpses of those who'd been tortured to death by Japanese guns and bayonets. There was a young boy, only seven years old, who had four wounds on his tiny body. The wound on his stomach was three or four inches long. Wilson told him that this boy had been moaning in agony several days earlier when he'd been sent to the hospital, but he later suddenly died.

The smell of blood filled the morgue. Wilson tried to take Rabe away. Rabe solemnly told Wilson: "I have to see all of this. I have to see it for myself, I have to see what the Japanese have done. I'll tell the entire world about the inhumanity of the Japanese. We can never stay silent about their crimes."

Wilson couldn't agree more. Wilson was a fellow Christian and also kept a diary. He felt that God had given him and Rabe the same divine mission.

When Rabe returned home, a feeling that was both familiar and unfamiliar caught him by surprise. His house had been beautifully decorated for Christmas.

"Merry Christmas, Mr Rabe," said an employee, Zhang, loudly along with all of the refugees. He was invited to light the Christmas candles.

"Thank you! Thank you everyone!" Rabe said excitedly. It was rare for him to be this excited.

Rabe described the event in his diary:

I don't understand why everyone suddenly likes me. This is so strange. As far as I'm aware, almost no one could stand me before. Is this just an illusion? My dear Dora, my dear children. I know that you are praying for me now. I can feel it. I love and miss you. In the last two weeks, I've gone through so much. I'm now so grateful for what I have. Thank you so much for everything, I will pray for you and keep you deep in my heart.

The misery I am going through makes me think of my faith in my childhood. Only God can help me get away from these monsters that find pleasure in murder, rape and theft. The protests of the International Committee are in vain. People agree that this needs to be corrected, but I still can't see any changes.

I will end this entry with a prayer. Dear God, please save the people from disaster and bless people like us who face disaster. I have never regretted staying here. I have saved many lives. Even so, I can't bear the sadness and pain.

Amen.

After writing this, Rabe moved his hand over his chest in the sign of the cross as he closed his eyes. Tears ran down his cheeks.

The next morning, Sperling and other members of the International Committee came to his house to see "the only Christmas tree in Nanjing". A clergyman brought a bottle of wine with him. He said that the wine had been found among the ruins of the city. "Only half of the bottle is left," Sperling said to Rabe, holding it.

Rabe proposed a toast: "To our families."

Sperling and Kroeger insisted that Rabe should go and celebrate Christmas with them and his other American friends. However, Rabe declined because he had a duty to protect the 600 refugees in his yard.

Rabe didn't leave the safety zone or his yard that day, clearly wearing a

Nazi armband. No one was able to persuade him to leave. He said that he had a responsibility to his "subjects". "I'm the mayor of Nanjing now," he said with a mix of pride and distress.

The Japanese wanted to get the refugees to capitulate by registering them and issuing ID cards.

This was an act that was so despicably evil that Rabe couldn't believe it. He was terrified of further incidents and more refugees being killed as he would be unable to protect them.

The Japanese army then went directly to his yard and told Rabe: "These people have to be registered."

"They're all refugees. You can register them, but they have to decide for themselves whether they want to go home. You can't take anyone from here," said Rabe, refusing to make any concessions.

He was prepared to protect everyone there, even if it cost him his life.

It was an extremely tense and serious situation, and even the children stopped crying.

A Japanese soldier pulled out a bayonet and pointed it at Rabe's chest.

"I've already told you no!" shouted Rabe stubbornly.

The soldier shook with anger.

A child suddenly started crying loudly, followed by even more children's cries and women's screams.

Rabe was furious. He stared at the Japanese soldier without moving.

"Okay, just do what Mr Rabe says," relented the soldier. They weren't afraid of the plump Hamburger, rather the swastika on his sleeve.

Han Xianglin and Zhang cheered along with the 600 refugees. They clustered around Rabe and knelt down in front of him. They thanked this "foreign buddha" again and again.

Rabe couldn't bring himself to smile. He saw a burned corpse that nobody had dared bury. He found out that more than 20 boys had been taken away by the Japanese army under the pretext of registering them.

He had to continue protesting to the Japanese.

After receiving so many letters of protest from Rabe, the senior officials and diplomats from the Japanese embassy were furious about the situation.

Ambassador Tanaka didn't want to waste any time putting forward suggestions and hoped that General Iwane Matsui would make a decision. Everyone looked at Matsui.

"Although I understand Chinese culture well, they don't trust me. They choose to stay in the safety zone with the westerners. They see the Japanese Empire as the devil, but the foreigners as buddhas. Considering this, I suggest that we select a Chinese man to manage the Municipal Committee to replace the International Committee. As a result, the safety zone and the International Committee wouldn't have a legal standing. This would solve the problem."

"Great! A brilliant idea!" Tanaka was the first to applaud him and the others soon followed.

A new conspiracy was being plotted in the Japanese embassy. Meanwhile, Rabe and his colleagues were preparing coal for the refugees to keep warm, as well as other daily necessities. Where could they get the coal from?

Smythe sent Rabe a list of possible suppliers.

"This is amazing," said Rabe cheerfully when he saw the list. This was an incredibly valuable resource. With this, thousands of refugees would survive the cold. Hesitating somewhat, he said: "Some of this should be sent to the congee station or the refugees won't have any food and many will starve."

"I've already assigned the congee station part of the coal," said Smythe, who was always prepared for emergencies.

"What worries me is transporting it. If the Japanese discover it, they'll definitely take it." Rabe wandered around the room to think.

"You could use your title as a member of the Nazi Party," suggested Smythe.

"That title isn't as powerful as you'd think, I don't have that kind of power." Rabe smiled bitterly.

"Only you can do something about the Japanese," lamented Smythe.

Rabe shook his head. "You Americans are so cunning. You nominated me as president and pushed me into this danger."

"But Rabe, you definitely deserve the title!" Everyone present was laughing. Rabe began to laugh with them and quoted a Chinese proverb: "You've dragged me onto a pirate ship."

Seeing as Rabe was now on this "pirate ship", he had to play dirty sometimes, both publicly and privately. Rabe tried to establish a relationship with Fukuda, who was relatively easy to talk to. Rabe asked him to negotiate with the Japanese government to send some of the coal to the congee station. Undoubtedly, at least half of it would be detained by the Japanese. They would find the name of the vehicle transporting the coal and take it for themselves. Therefore, Rabe wanted to split the transportation into several journeys.

The German was intelligent in this respect, but the Japanese weren't easily fooled. They insisted on transporting the coal themselves and forced Rabe to tell them the storage locations and to leave things to the Japanese. Rabe knew that he couldn't oppose it so he had to make an agreement with the Japanese. The Japanese could take some of the coal, but they had to provide enough coal to the congee station. If not, they wouldn't provide the Japanese with the labour they needed.

The Japanese somewhat admired Rabe's business acumen.

However, intimidation is common in business and there was no doubt that Rabe was at a disadvantage when negotiating with the Japanese.

On 1 January 1938, the Japanese invited Rabe to attend the ceremony of the establishment of the Nanjing Municipal Committee. They informed Rabe of the event the day before and forced the people to "celebrate".

Out of politeness and strategic positioning, Rabe went with Smythe and another member of the International Committee. The president, the vice president, and a consultant in the Municipal Committee had all been members of the Red Cross. Rabe was shocked. "Hanjian!" Rabe shouted, meaning "traitor" in Chinese.

Rabe finally understood that the so-called Municipal Committee was being established to replace his International Committee.

Rabe left quietly before the ceremony ended. He couldn't let this farce affect him. Early in the morning, Han told him that the refugees had arranged a grand ceremony to express their sincere thanks to Rabe on this special day, the first day of 1938.

They drove back to Ninghai Road. Rabe heard the sound of firecrackers from far away, which was unusual considering the situation. Where had they found them? Zhang told him that they'd stolen them from the Municipal Committee celebrations. "What's the point of using them to cerebrate there? This is more important!" Han excitedly said to Rabe.

"I was welcomed like a king. They showed me their respect with firecrackers and flowers. I was surrounded by more than 600 people. They made a New Year's celebration card for me, with red ink and a white envelope. Everyone bowed to me and they were all so happy that I thanked them and put the card in my pocket," described Rabe in his diary.

He would never forget this. Han Xianglin and the 600 refugees were divided into two lines and kowtowed to Rabe in unison.

Rabe burst out in tears suddenly. He had never received so much respect.

He loved the people of Nanjing and China. He swore once again that he'd do everything he could to save them.

Rabe went back to his office and took out the card. It read:

Herr Rabe,

Mit den besten wünschen für ein glückliches Neues Jahr. Hundert Millionen sind Dir nah!

Die Fluchtlinge Ihres Lagers
   1. 1. 1938

-

Mr Rabe,

Happy New Year, we hope that you earn hundreds of millions!

All the refugees at your place
   1. 1. 1938

What were the hundreds of millions referring to? Had he won the lottery? Rabe was excited and asked Han what it meant. He then realised that they were wishing him good luck and that he'd receive a big fortune. Rabe was thrilled.

Rabe expressed his sincere gratitude to the Chinese refugees in broken Chinese.

The New Year didn't bring any changes to Japanese held Nanjing. They still carried on with every one of their despicable actions: robbery, arson, rape and murder. The so-called Municipal Committee was a mere puppet and outraged the citizens.

On the contrary, Rabe's international safety zone was still very popular and most of the refugees had chosen to stay there because people felt no security at home, especially women. People had initially thought they would be able to get back to normal with their residency permits, but most women were brutally raped and gang-raped by the Japanese soldiers on their way home, while others were caught and sent to comfort stations as comfort women. These women went back to Rabe's safety zone with their family members.

The Japanese had thought that the establishment of the Municipal Committee would make the safety zone gradually disappear. However, the safety zone was still very popular and lively, symbolised by the celebrations with firecrackers by the Drum Tower in Gulou. The winding and laid back Shanghai Road became home to Nanjing's most prosperous flea market. It was even called a communist market by some. It was said to be a business centre, but the things they sold were the refugees' belongings - old clothes, teapots, teacups, nappies - they were all everyday items and very cheap.

"I'll take it for one yuan! Please have mercy on me, I only have a few coins."

"Okay, that's fine!"

People would then come to a deal. This is what we call a communist market: don't bargain, be nice to each other and help each other out.

Suddenly one morning, a few people wearing fur coats and black glasses with rising sun emblems on their arms walked towards the stalls, waving sticks around, taking everything down.

"What the hell are you doing?" asked the refugees angrily.

"Imperial orders. Safety zones have to be dissolved! You can't set up stalls here! Get out! Burn all these stalls!"

A group of men wearing the rising sun emblem started hitting people. The man in charge of them was Fang Hao. Some refugees knew that he used to be a lawyer. Now, he proudly told everyone who knew him that he was now an "official" and all he was doing was "following orders".

Fang saw that the refugees weren't obeying, and some even called him a traitor. He was outraged and raised his voice to command his minions to set fire to the stalls.

The Municipal Committee group wanted to set fire to the refugees' tents but they resisted. Then, people on the street picked up everything they could, including stools, teacups, shoes and even bricks, and threw them at the heads of the group of Japanese puppets.

They were defeated and fled. The refugees at the communist market burst into laughter.

"Mr Rabe, I don't want to offend you and your friends in the International Committee, but there's a development that you have to accept. The new Nanjing council is a temporary agency in charge of Nanjing and has the approval of the Imperial Japanese Army. Their duties are to manage the citizens and the city, so your safety zone and International Committee can no longer be permitted. All jurisdiction now lies with the council." The Japanese embassy had sent people to Rabe to deliver their commands. They made it clear that if nothing was done, they would send in their soldiers.

The Japanese leaders were finally showing their true nature.

What could they do? The fate of the International Committee faced an important test. Rabe and Wallace held an emergency committee meeting to discuss their strategy.

"Despicable! They've threatened to confiscate our money and supplies," Han said.

"And they still refuse to do anything about their brutal soldiers. These are the crimes that I photographed last night," Magee protested.

"We shall never give up our rights! Rescuing refugees is the mission that God has given us, no one can stop us," said Wallace.

"This is the final fight. The Japanese are trying to subject Nanjing to their cruel rule, and we are the only thing that prevents them from turning Nanjing into a living hell. We will not back down!"

"Never!"

The headquarters at 5 Ninghai Road once again became a stronghold against brutal Japanese rule in Nanjing. More than a dozen International Committee members then requested Rabe to give a speech.

Rabe pressed his hands together and gestured at the committee to get them to calm down. He then said: "The aim of the Japanese has been clear from the start. They don't want the citizens of Nanjing to be under the control of an organisation that isn't affiliated with them, so their ultimate goal is to get rid of us. Because they are the occupying army and in control of the city, it's to be expected that they'd come up with all of these so-called reasons to harass us. However, I believe that we established the International Committee and safety zone for just one reason: human kindness. God has given us a responsibility in Nanjing today to protect hundreds of thousands of refugees. No one can take this responsibility from us, least of all the Japanese army!"

"Exactly!"

"Well said!"

"We will not give up the our God given right!"

The International Committee came to an agreement. First, they would restate the functions and responsibilities of the committee to Japan. Second, they would create a detailed summary of the various issues facing safety management in the city. They would issue the two documents to Japan to affirm the legitimacy of the committee and its safety zones.

Rabe characteristically wrote to them: "Isn't the goal of your so-called Municipal Committee to manage hundreds of thousands of refugees? You accused the International Committee of being illegal, so we will tell you what we have been doing recently!"

They then released extracts of inspection reports. Examples of these can be read below:

Third military academy refugee shelter
Inspected by *Wang, Mills and Forster*
Director: *Zhao Yongkui*
Refugees: *about 3,200 people, divided into 27 groups, each group has a leader.*

A number of labourers from this group of people have been sent to work at the request of the Japanese soldiers. The shelter distributes 10 bags of rice on average every day. About a third of the refugees settle this on their own, while the remaining two thirds of the refugees are provided food and accommodation by the International Committee. The refugees have been satisfied with the International Committee's management.

Environmental protection agency refugee camp
Inspected by *Wang, Mills and Forster*
Director: *Chen Chengmei, with about 40 assistants*
The total number of refugees is about 8,000.

The shelter gets 10 bags of rice every day. The red congee ration cards have been sent to 492 households, 3,000 people in total. Approximately 1,500 people don't receive free congee, approximately 2,000 people are self-catering, while the rest of the people are provided food by the International Committee. Most of the refugees are satisfied with the work of the International Committee.

Hankou Road Primary School refugee shelter
Inspected by *Forster*
Director: *Zheng Dacheng*
The shelter has more than 1,400 people.

Four bags of rice are distributed every day. There is no difference in treatment between adults and children when dry food, not congee, is distributed. Although the shelter is very crowded, the refugees are satisfied with the management.

After the inspection report of the safety zone was completed, another report on the current state of the International Committee was also drafted by Rabe and Wallace. Its tone made it clear it was aimed at Japan and the Japanese puppet organisation, the Nanjing Municipal Committee.

1. We are a private group that aims to help civilians suffering as a result of the war.
    (i) Food and money are for us to control, and they are used for the above purpose. We use our relief funds to allow the committee to continue to exist, but we should continue to adapt to the current situation here.
    (ii) The administrative management work we perform is paid for separately with our legal fund. We do not pay the police; the administrative institutions pay for them alone. We provide the police with rice. The proposed conditions for them were the same as those for other refugee and voluntary assistants.

Only the salary of the three workers the municipality has sent us will be cancelled.

2. We initially cooperated with the Red Crescent and the Red Cross, and the Municipal Committee will continue to do so. We will be ready to cooperate with them for judging suggestions regarding the best services to use for the goals of the committee and the services that are most conducive to the goals of the committee.

3. We will not give out our funds. These funds have been entrusted to us for safekeeping. We guarantee them with our reputation and these funds should only be used when necessary.

4. We must be alert. Don't let people diminish our financial resources or our task. Don't expect us to allow ourselves to lose control of the money.

5. The Nanjing Municipal Committee always has our full support and recognition to restore order and normal business. However, our fund is to be used first to avoid severe food shortages and to help people in other ways.

This was an internal document that Rabe and Wallace had marked as secret. Although it just looks like an introduction to the International Committee's work, its tone is very firm. It makes clear that although the committee is a private organisation, its mission, the capital it has offered and the work it has done both during and before the Japanese occupation cannot be altered.

Apparently, after the two aforementioned materials were sent to the Japanese, they had a huge impact on the senior level of the Japanese forces and the Japanese puppet Municipal Committee members in particular. Both the Japanese army and its Chinese lackeys knew that it was impossible to stop people like Rabe, as the committee was devoted to hundreds of thousands of refugees. The management was so well organised that it looked like Nanjing would cope with the food shortages.

"Mr Tanaka, I think we should let them manage it. We have no idea how to get so much congee and rice for the poor to eat."

"Exactly. I can't imagine where we'd even begin!"

The members of the Municipal Committee were the first to back down. Then the Japanese diplomats, including Fukuda and others, opposed the immediate cancelation of the safety zones. "I think we can use Rabe. Besides, they sort out their own financial support. Why don't we just leave them to it and save us some trouble?" said Fukuda.

"Fukuda is right. We should at least observe the situation for a period of time and then decide what to do." The Japanese military finally relented.

At the same time as writing a formal letter to the Japanese authorities, Rabe also wrote to Fukuda, the Japanese embassy counsellor. Rabe thought that Fukuda was the most honest and conscientious man out of all the Japanese there. In their previous dealings, this Japanese official had always tried to help Rabe, and this relationship was important to him. Rabe won the understanding, compassion, and even support of Fukuda through a private friendship. He was a useful contact who went above and beyond to help in complex matters where other officials wouldn't. Faced with an emergency, Rabe naturally first thought of Fukuda, and wrote him this letter in private:

Dear Mr Fukuda,

Concerning our meeting yesterday, I would like to assure you that the International Committee is eager to see order and normality quickly restored to Nanjing. I can also assure you that, to this end, the committee would be pleased to see the local Municipal Committee bear all responsibilities as soon as possible, such as public security, fire control and public health. Rest assured that the International Committee absolutely does not want to continue to perform any kind of administrative obligations that are usually the remit of the local authorities, nor does it want to acquire these obligations.

Our committee is first and foremost a relief organisation. It was primarily established to protect civilians affected by the war. These people are suffering from ruthlessness and misery, inspiring everyone's sympathy and compassion. During the war, various committees have been set up in China, such as the Shanghai committee. General Matsui personally made a remittance of 1,000 yuan to the committee, which proves that such a committee has previously received the approval of the Japanese military.

As our committee's funding has been especially commissioned for this purpose, in my opinion, the International Committee has a special obligation to prove that it is trustworthy. I do not believe that this funding can be given out to any other organisation. Of course, we would like to cooperate with other aid organisations, such as the Red Crescent and the Red Cross, which we currently cooperate with. But we must keep complete control of our funds. I believe that if you consider our situation, you will see that our reasoning is sound.

In addition to this, I would also like to point out that considering the current problems and demands, our funds are limited. Assistance is what our committee does best and I personally hope that the municipal government suggests more appropriate plans to complement ours. Our committee, the Red Crescent and the Red Cross will do everything we can, but we want the Municipal Committee to do more than our committee or any other organisation.

Finally, I also want to take the liberty to point something out. There is no doubt that the simplest and most effective way to help is to restore order and discipline among the soldiers. Until the soldiers improve their discipline, the refugees cannot return home, shops cannot reopen, traffic is unlikely to recover, and the power supply, water supply and the telephone infrastructure cannot operate as normal. Everything depends on this most important factor.

If military discipline is restored, the issues with relief will become easier to resolve, and the restoration of residents' living conditions will become more feasible.

I sincerely hope that the Japanese military authorities restore the discipline of their soldiers as their first and most urgent task.

Best regards,
Your faithfully,

— JOHN RABE, PRESIDENT

As we've seen the Japanese already discuss how to deal with John Rabe and the safety zone, Rabe's letter to Fukuda may well have played a vital role in helping the citizens of Nanjing.

"You're a hero John Rabe, you and the 22 foreigners you lead in Nanjing are as brave as the first Christians in Rome!" said Dr Rosen from the German embassy as he brought Rabe praise from the ministry of foreign affairs. This was a great honour for Rabe and it made him extremely happy. Rosen, however, said: "The Christians in Rome were eaten by lions in the Colosseum. The lions here prefer to eat the Chinese because the Japanese think that old businessmen from Hamburg are too tough."

Rosen laughed.

Rabe was grateful for the praise, but he'd just done what he could to make sure that more than 200,000 refugees got a bowl of congee and a little warmth.

"Good man!"

"Buddha!"

In Nanjing, everyone who saw cars waving Nazi flags stared at the people inside with a mix of gratitude and love, and honoured everyone who wore glasses like Rabe.

Rabe felt incredibly honoured, so his responsibility became even more pressing. He felt the strain of the pressure taking its toll.

Seeing this, Han asked with concern: "How are you sir?"

Rabe shook his head as he gently pulled out a telegram from his pocket to show Han.

"They want us to leave Nanjing to go to Shanghai?" Han read the telegram aloud. It was a message from the Siemens headquarters in Shanghai, the content of which ordered Rabe to leave Nanjing as soon as possible and go to Hankou "for a holiday". Han thought that the message was strange, so he asked Rabe: "Why do they want us to leave Nanjing?"

Rabe said: "I'm also trying to think why. I've been in Nanjing for quite a long time, and even the *führer* knows about it. Now almost everyone around the world knows what I've done in Nanjing. I really don't know why they want me to leave Nanjing now."

This greatly disturbed Rabe. That evening, he sent a long telegram to Mayer, the manager of the Siemens headquarters in Shanghai:

Dear Mr Mayer,

You transferred a telegram via the German embassy and I received it today. I would like to confirm receipt here. By the time I received the message, it was too late. You wanted me to go to Hankou, but although the Germans had a ship in Nanjing, this ship has already left for Hankou. In addition to this, I think that under normal circumstances you wouldn't want me to abandon my Chinese staff here, such as Mr Han and my other assistants. They are my responsibility and I should take care of them. As you may recall, in response to your telegram, I serve as the president of the International Committee here, and the committee's task is to form a safety zone. It is the last refugee zone for 200,000 Chinese civilians. The Japanese have refused to fully recognise the safety zone with the reason that senior Chinese military personnel and their staff were (before they left Nanjing) stationed in the safety zone, contrary to our agreement, so the relief work has been difficult as a result. We really started suffering after the Japanese bombing and occupation of the city. It seems as if the Japanese military authorities have lost control as the army has continued looting the city for several weeks. Approximately 20,000 women and girls have been raped, and tens of thousands of innocent civilians (including 43 plant workers) have been killed. There has been inhumane mass murder as civilians are executed with machine guns. They have also relentlessly broken into the houses of foreign nationals, including 60 Germans' houses, looting approximately 40 of them and setting fire to four German buildings. About a third of the entire city has been torched by the Japanese. Arson happens constantly, even today. Every shop has been looted by the Japanese. People who've been shot dead can be seen all over the city, lying all over the streets. We feel like undertakers for the Japanese. About 50 metres away from my house on 13 December, we found the tied-up corpse of a Chinese soldier on a bamboo pole. This is only a few metres away from the Japanese army's checkpoints. Many Chinese people have been shot dead with their bodies floating in the nearby water. As many as 50 dead bodies were floating there.

The committee set up a congee station and rice and flour distribution points. So far, we are able to support 200,000 residents who have poured into the safety zone in Nanjing. But now, the Japanese have forced us to shut down the food outlets because the newly established city council wanted to take over the refugee relief work as doing so meant that the refugees would be able to leave the safety zone and return to their homes. As I have already mentioned above, every house outside the safety zone has been damaged, so people are unsure of where to go. There are still many Japanese soldiers in the streets plundering and rampaging, terrifying the refugees. Our committee is trying its best to make the Japanese military and the new Japanese municipal government understand the issue and to at least ensure that the refugees receive food. In addition to this, if the Japanese and the Municipal Committee take over our work, we wouldn't have any say in the matter, and we hope this happens soon! Once order is restored in the urban areas and the authorities allow me to leave Nanjing, I will go to Shanghai. So far, all applications to do so have been refused by the Japanese. Please allow me to stay in Nanjing until the Municipal Committee is dissolved as just a few Europeans determine the future fate of so many people. In my house and yard alone, more than 600 refugees live in dire poverty. Since the night of 12 December, they have fled to my place to get away from the humiliation and murder of the Japanese marauders. Most of them live in straw shelters in the yard, living on a fixed quantity of relief food every day. Our committee has managed 25 refugee camps and approximately 70,000 refugees. Out of these, 50,000 refugees rely on our relief for survival because they have nothing else. You can hardly imagine the situation here. Before occupying Nanjing, the Japanese bombed the city for several months, but it can never be equated with the misery caused by the Japanese army after taking Nanjing. We don't understand it. How can we live in peace now? Please don't make this letter public because it might have a disastrous impact on our committee.

Best regards to Germany.
    Yours faithfully,

— JOHN RABE

After he sent the telegram, Rabe devoted himself to his work in the safety zone with his heart and soul. He thought that his work in Nanjing hadn't just been successful and widespread, but also effective in terms of protecting Germany's interests. "If it hadn't been for us hanging German flags in Nanjing every day, German property and even the German embassy would have been in ruins," Rabe once said to Dr Rosen. Rosen and Ambassador Trautmann agreed with Rabe. At the time, Rabe, who had experience with business but no political experience, was unaware that thousands of miles away, Hitler was not the leader he had expected and imagined him to be, but a fascist extremist who only wanted to take over the world.

Hitler, who hid his true intentions for many years, was planning how to achieve his violent goals, even more terrifying than the Japanese occupation of Nanjing. In order to realise his ideal, Germany, Italy and Japan secretly colluded with each other following a plan that had been concocted by Hitler. The scandals about the Japanese army's conduct in Nanjing were exposed and they were severely condemned. While Hitler didn't want to interfere, Rabe struggled with the Japanese soldiers at every step. The Japanese reported this to Hitler through their embassy in Germany. Hitler decided to intervene.

Hitler didn't have to give his orders in person, the message the Nazi Party sent to Siemens was more than enough: "Siemens cannot act in a way that goes against the interests of our Japanese friends."

When Rabe thought the letter he'd sent had definitely worked, Siemens's headquarters in Shanghai received orders from Berlin that Siemens in Nanjing had closed, meaning that Rabe's legal reason for staying in Nanjing had been cancelled by his own company in Germany.

Rabe couldn't believe it. He was angry for a long time. However, he later calmed down. He was a businessman and a Siemens veteran after all, so he was obligated to follow the orders of his company. He had to obey. This was also a quality he prided himself on as a Hamburger businessman.

But this news had come so suddenly. If the company was closed, then what happened with everything else like the employees' salaries? If Siemens closed with such little notice, then it would damage the reputation of the company. For this reason, Rabe quickly sent a letter to Siemens in Shanghai and asked them to pay the employees another month's salary or a bonus as compensation.

Rabe's request was approved. Now the most arduous and miserable task left for Rabe to do was explaining it to the Chinese employees like Han

Xianglin, who'd helped him so much in protecting refugees. Rabe was tormented and out of ideas. He didn't think he had the courage to tell Han and his employees. "What if I go without saying anything? Or if I leave a letter? No, it wouldn't work. Even if I wanted to go, I need to sort out the safety zone and the International Committee first. It might be better if I write a letter." Rabe held his pen, his hands shaking:

My dear Mr Han,

All business operations have ceased due to the war, so we have to regretfully inform you that our commercial office in Nanjing has to close due to instructions from our headquarters.

As a result, your work with our company has regretfully come to an end. But we are prepared to employ you in future if conditions permit it. Please tell us your address in future so that we may contact you if anything arises.

Representative of Siemens (China) in Nanjing
  Your sincere friend,

— JOHN RABE *19 JANUARY 1938*

The Chinese employees of the Siemens Nanjing office were Tong Baiqing, Mao Ziliang, Zhang Fugen and Sun Longsheng. Rabe wrote them similar letters and informed them of the decision.

After writing the letters, it was nearly dawn. Rabe was still tormented. For a month after Nanjing fell to the Japanese army, Rabe had transformed from a puritanical businessman to a social activist and a refugee manager. He had been confronted with many political, military, cultural and social problems in the past weeks. He was surprised by how he'd changed, and now thought that there was something more important than business: saving lives. In the past month, many tragic incidents had occurred, but he felt proud.

His only regret was that despite such a good beginning to his work in the International Committee, so many things remained unsolved, like the urgent matter of the survival and nourishment of several hundred thousand refugees, stopping the Japanese army from burning, killing and pillaging in the city, and the corpses that covered Nanjing. Thinking about this, Rabe unconsciously looked at the charred corpse of the Chinese soldier that had been left not far from the wall to his garden. Seeing it, Rabe felt disgusted and hated the Japanese. They had no humanity.

Rabe closed the door quickly, clenching his fists. He knew that he had a great deal of things to do before he could leave Nanjing with a clear conscience.

The Last Days Before Leaving Nanjing

Rabe couldn't sleep that night. He couldn't stop worrying about the hundreds of thousands of refugees in the safety zone. They were the poorest people in the city and needed the most help. Many of them had been savagely beaten by the Japanese and injured as a result, or had lost the ability to live a normal life. These people wouldn't survive the winter if there was no one there to give them food or to arrange accommodation. As the occupying army, the Japanese were responsible for these refugees and had a duty to at least offer them basic living conditions. However, the Japanese army neglected their responsibilities and just took some of them away as forced labourers. Obviously, the Japanese army didn't care about whether they lived or died. They even deliberately intercepted or destroyed things that the committee had given the refugees, such as food needed to survive the winter. Although more than 200,000 people needed large amounts of food every day, little food was allowed into the safety zone.

At the time, Bates, a member of the International Committee, described the atmosphere in a letter to his wife:

> The prospect of adequate food supplies is bleak. The Japanese have refused to sell any food to us. They forbid us and others from buying and selling food in the safety zone. We could only ship in food by boat. After tough negotiations for a long time, we had a large sum of money and 2,300 bags of rice. We took out 100 bags every day and handed them out to the congee station and the people who needed them most for free. The Red Cross got rice from an intelligence agency and set up two congee stations. The Municipal Committee is regarded by the Japanese as the agency that distributes rice. However, in reality they received 500 bags of food in 10 days, and a total of 2,500 bags in five weeks. We transported the bags by truck for them. Between 1,500 and 2,000 bags were consumed. As for flour, we distributed and sold it quicker early on. Most vegetables cost 10 times as much as they did before. Several thousand people didn't touch anything other than congee. We wanted to import 1,000 pounds of cod liver oil as medical supplies by using a warship. In general, the Japanese army have been indifferent. No Japanese soldiers have paid attention to the problems of the ordinary people. Coal for the congee stations has been a problem. We usually acquire coal by luck without needing an official permit.

The food supply in the city has almost all been used up, but nobody has come. Each ministry of the Japanese army has been pillaging and looting. A large amount of coal, rice and wheat has been burned.

An even more loathsome fact is that the traitorous officials behind the newly established Municipal Committee wanted to use the opportunity to make money. They couldn't care less about the plight of the refugees.

"If nobody else cares about them, then we should," Rabe thought. He racked his mind thinking about what the refugees needed, regardless of how long he had left in Nanjing. He turned on his kerosene lamp and had the idea of writing a letter to the three most important contacts he could think of: Mr Allison from the American embassy, Mr Brown from the British embassy and his old friend Dr Rosen from the German embassy. These three diplomats would have a direct role to play in the safety of the people of Nanjing. Rabe began to write:

Dear sirs,

Each of you is aware of the need to resolve the food shortage problems that face 250,000 civilians in Nanjing. As Dr Smythe expressed in his letter to Mr Allison on 17 January, I have discussed three matters with the Japanese. They are:

The Municipal Committee should distribute rice, flour and coal through commercial avenues as soon as possible.

The International Committee has been approved to acquire 3,000 bags of rice and 9,000 bags of wheat for relief that we bought from the Shanghai Commercial Deposit Band. At present, the food is stored in Xiaguan, near the Sancha river and outside the Hanxi gate.

The International Committee has been approved to ship 600 tons of food from Shanghai to Nanjing.

Yesterday, when Dr Smythe asked for a response regarding these matters for the third time, Mr Fukui asked him to find Mr Tanaka. Mr Smythe and Mr Fitch then found Mr Tanaka, who told them that the Japanese army had confiscated the rice and wheat in the aforementioned warehouse. When they reminded him that it was private property rather than the property of the Chinese army, he thought that the Japanese army may be using this food to send to Chinese civilians. The two aforementioned gentlemen repeatedly requested the Japanese authorities to allow them to ship 3,000 bags of rice from Shanghai, but all their requests were refused. They were told that no ships could be used to carry the 3,000 bags of rice and other 600 tons of supplementary food. When Mr Smythe and Mr Fitch mentioned the Japanese ships, Mr Tanaka didn't respond.

They had to ask the Japanese what their plan was. Mr Tanaka responded that the Japanese army would undertake the responsibility of resolving the Chinese civilians' food shortage issues.

Mr Smythe and Mr Fitch explained to him that the Japanese army had only provided 2,200 bags of rice and 1,000 bags of flour to sell to Chinese civilians since 13 December. Mr Tanaka thought that the supply had been more than this, but there was no exact data at hand. The Japanese army had actually given the Municipal Committee 1,200 bags of rice on 10 January and 1,000 bags of rice and 1,000 bags of flour on 17 January. The second batch of food was to be sold in the south of the city. The International Committee helped to transport the food because the Japanese army didn't provide appropriate transportation vehicles.

When the talk was over, Mr Smythe told Mr Tanaka that he wanted to know something. He asked whether the requests to transport the rice bought in Xiaguan and ship food from Shanghai had been turned down by the Japanese authorities. The answer was yes!

Later, a telegram signed by Mr Fitch was sent to Mr Boynton from the Shanghai National Christianity Council (we kept in touch through letters on this matter). I look forward to seeing how Shanghai will respond.

My dear gentlemen, we don't know what actions you will take on this matter, but I will try to inform you of any further developments of this situation and pass on our suggestions to you. We don't think that it is right to reiterate our request because Mr Tanaka has claimed that the Japanese army will be responsible for resolving the food shortage. It may be best to informally ask the Japanese to tell you what they have done if you get the chance.

The only solution to the problem is to restore order, reorganise transportation and redistribute rice through commercial avenues. What the International Committee has only ever cared about has been urging the Japanese army to recognise the serious situation regarding the food shortage and take measures to remedy it as the refugees cannot afford to buy food.

It is necessary for the Japanese army to understand what it means to be responsible for the Chinese civilians' food. So far, they have only treated this issue as a trifling affair and occasionally bring 1,000 bags of rice to the Municipal Committee to sell.

The requirements of the citizens are as follows:

Two thousand piculs of rice (the equivalent of 600 bags) or flour. One picul is approximately 60 kilograms and can support 100 adults for a day, so 250,000 people need 2,500 piculs. The fixed quota for younger child should be reduced.

Forty to 50 tons of coal or other fuel are needed every day.

The Municipal Committee hasn't had sufficient transportation equipment to carry this amount of rice, flour and fuel. However, Japanese military trucks are everywhere in the city, so the Japanese army should be responsible for carrying them into the Municipal Committee's shops. When we discussed this with Ishida, he told us that he was prepared to accept responsibility for transportation. It's a pity that these agreements have been cancelled by the Japanese superior officials.

Apart from the supply of rice and flour, measures should be taken to make sure that a certain amount of other foodstuff is supplied in order to prevent a range of diseases. We also plan to transport food from Shanghai. The transportation should be undertaken by the Japanese army.

If the necessary food can be provided to the Municipal Committee, then there will likely be no difficulty in assigning tasks to the committee. Of course, for the citizens who go back to their homes, the Japanese army should guarantee their protection. The Japanese should also protect the distribution and sale of food and fuel.

Thank you for your interest in our cause.
    Yours sincerely,

— JOHN RABE, *PRESIDENT OF THE INTERNATIONAL COMMITTEE FOR THE NANJING SAFETY ZONE*

Rabe's intention was clear. He hoped that the diplomats would care more about the refugees in the safety zone and take over the jobs he couldn't finish. He had been motivated by the miserable fate of the people of Nanjing. Money was essential for the survival of the refugees in the safety zone. After Rabe finished writing letters to the three diplomats, he suddenly thought of Brown from the British embassy and how he could help with the financial problems. Rabe then wrote a short letter attached to the previous letter he'd written to Brown:

Dear Mr Brown,

As a man who has worked closely with Nanjing, you must be familiar with the establishment of the Nanjing Safety Zone and the related refugee assistance work. I wish to say something else in regard to this refugee assistance work. Most of the 250,000 refugees in Nanjing are homeless due to the fires that have spread in the surrounding area. In many families, the people responsible for feeding their families have been taken away or killed by the Japanese army. As a result, the people who've been left behind face extreme danger. There are hundreds of thousands of them. As you are aware, the civilians' financial means have been utterly destroyed. Many residents brought just a little food and money to the safety zone. Their savings have almost run out. They now have nothing at all.

The donations that support the committee are diminishing. We have 100,000 yuan in Nanjing and we may be able to get a further 57,000 yuan in Shanghai. This is far from enough to support 250,000 suffering people. What worries us most is that these people don't just need food, but also a place to live. We should also help them to begin a new life.

Giving some of these poor families a little financial help would be very beneficial. We have no choice but to rely on donations to help them.

Therefore, please allow me to propose a request: I would be incredibly grateful if you could help me receive funds from the mayor of London. We have received donations from the American committee, which is included in the 57,000 yuan mentioned above. We also hope the British committee helps in the spirit of charity.

We express our sincere thanks to you for your support.
With kindest regards,

— YOUR HONEST PRESIDENT, JOHN RABE

Rabe constantly worried and took great caution in all of his responsibilities. In addition to providing the refugees with food and accommodation, water and power were also necessary for their survival. To this end, Rabe led scores of workers to work in the waterworks and power station near the Yangtze, risking being killed by the Japanese army. Rabe had come to the power station many times before the war, but after a month of Japanese occupation, it was beyond all recognition. The 43 technicians there had been assumed to be military staff by the Japanese army and were all killed by the banks of the Yangtze. The factories and machinery were also destroyed. What made Rabe angry was that those who'd destroyed the power station, the Japanese army, were yelling at him to help repair it. Rabe didn't want to work for these lovers of destruction. Considering that the refugees and members of the International Committee also needed power, Rabe gritted his teeth and reluctantly agreed to do the job. He employed several professional engineers in person from the Siemens headquarters in Shanghai and helped to restore the power station.

On New Year's day, several Japanese soldiers stormed into a civilian's home. They saw a mother and daughter and wanted to find women to assault. They went after the two women. The mother ran over to Rabe, crying, knelt down in front of him and begged for help. Rabe immediately drove his car to a house near Hankou Road. Entering the house, he saw a naked Japanese soldier on top of a young girl. Rabe couldn't hit him or drag the soldier off. He could only scold him, sarcastically wishing him a happy new year in a language he understood. As expected, the soldier became embarrassed, pulling away from the girl and putting on his trousers before fleeing.

Rabe had to deal with situations like this every day. They were just a part of his routine. Han Xianglin admired Rabe for his constant dedication.

At the end of January 1938, a diplomat from the German embassy received news that from 4 February, the Japanese army would be preparing to formally remove all refugees from the safety zone. This was a big development. Rabe thought that he had to discuss it urgently with the members of the International Committee. On 29 January, Rabe called the members of the committee for a meeting and focused on requesting the diplomats of their respective countries to clarify two important issues. First was whether the Japanese were going to remove Chinese refugees from foreign missions and property. Second was whether the Japanese were going to allow people like Rabe to accept more refugees into the small safety zones in their personal residences.

Rabe analysed the situation: "We should try to protect as many refugees as possible in this crisis. Of course, it would be best if the Japanese continue to operate our original safety zones, but now, we need to prepare for the worst. The Japanese want to put a stop to the safety zones."

The members of the committee were all silent but angry.

Rabe continued: "Nanjing is now under the control of the Japanese, but we still have to try our best to save those poor children and their families. Even though the Chinese call the officials in the autonomous government traitors, it's them who control Nanjing now. We have to use them to protect the city."

"Those people are even more corrupt than the Japanese. How could they ever help?" asked Magee incredulously.

Rabe hypothesised: "Do you remember when Mayor Ma promised to donate 10,000 bags of rice and 10,000 bags of flour before the Japanese occupied Nanjing? After they took Nanjing, that food fell into the hands of the Japanese. We want the Municipal Committee to ask for food from the Japanese to help the refugees. The people in the committee want the opportunity to make a contribution after all."

Rabe's plan later proved to have some effect. Although the Japanese didn't use all the food to save the refugees, it was still effective and had somewhat irritated the Japanese army.

On 30 January, the night before Chinese New Year, at 4pm or so, Rabe drove his car to Pingcang Lane. When his car got to Hankou Road, about 50 Chinese people in front of him stopped his car.

"Mr Rabe, please save that girl!" begged the Chinese to Rabe as they gestured towards a house.

Hearing this, Rabe instantly knew that there were Japanese soldiers currently raping women. Rabe followed the Chinese to 4 Jiangjia Lane as quickly as possible.

"The Japanese soldiers are in there," somebody said.

Rabe pushed the door open and entered the house. It had been robbed and left bare by the Japanese soldiers. There was a coffin in a room with an open door. Walking into the next room over, filled with straw and sundries, Rabe saw a Japanese soldier raping a woman. Rabe got angry and grabbed the back of the collar of the Japanese soldier, dragging him away.

"You! What are you doing?" The Japanese soldier was livid.

"You're a thief and a monster. I cannot allow this to happen," Rabe shouted back angrily. Seeing Rabe and his nearby car emblazoned with the German flag, he pulled up his trousers and ran away.

The Chinese people all clapped and cheered.

"Everyone, get out of here quickly in case the Japanese come back," shouted Rabe as he waved at the Chinese people around him. After all the people there had gone, he got into his car and left.

The first day of the new Chinese lunar year is the most joyous occasion in the Chinese calendar. Refugees living in the yard on 5 Ninghai Road got up early and lined up in a neat row, bowing three times to their saviour Mr Rabe. The women there also presented him with a red silk cloth, three metres long and two metres wide. A long line of Chinese characters was written on it. Rabe didn't understand so someone translated it for him: "It means that you are Buddha incarnate for hundreds of thousands of Chinese people."

"Good lord! Whatever have I done to deserve such a thoughtful gift!" he exclaimed, his face a bright red from embarrassment. A former Chinese government official, who was also an academic, then told Rabe with a smile: "I'll translate this sentence into a poem that you'll understand."

The translation was as follows:

You are as kind-hearted as the Buddha;
You are chivalrous indeed.
You have saved millions of unfortunate people;

And help others in distress.
May heaven bless you.
We wish you eternal happiness.
May the gods protect you.
From the refugees in your refugee camp.

"Thank you, thank you so much! May God bless you too!" Rabe was greatly moved once again by his "subjects".

Rabe felt the mild warmth of the sun that day. He then looked into the distance and saw that the corpse of the Chinese soldier outside the walls had finally been removed and buried.

On 4 February, Rabe got up early because he had to be on guard that day. Rabe wrote in his diary: "Today I have to be on guard duty. I have to keep watch over my refugee camp, looking over the 600 refugees in the German school behind my house and 5,000 or so refugees in the high school in front of my house. If the Japanese soldiers break into my refugee camp, although I may not be able to stop them, at least I can be an eyewitness and tell the world about their crimes. I shall try my best to protect my own home. We'll see whether they dare insult the German flag in front of me." He then put on a particularly neat suit and made the swastika on his sleeve particularly conspicuous. This showed that he would not allow the Japanese to undermine his authority in the safety zone and bully the Chinese refugees he protected.

Rabe wrote in his diary that night: "4 February has passed; it was a day full of fear and worry. Luckily, everything was quiet and calm, which means that as long as the Japanese respect my authority, we will avoid trouble. We all feel very happy about this situation. Today is the last day of the Chinese New Year celebrations. Despite the poor weather and the rain, the Chinese people are still excited to let off firecrackers in the yard. These poor people are so easily satisfied. They're just happy to be alive."

"Mr Rabe, you have to do something to save the refugees in the temple on Qixia Mountain. They're in a terrible position. You have to see," said Rabe's Danish friend Sindberg. He asked Rabe to listen to his news as soon as he met him.

"Go ahead," said Rabe, knowing that something terrible had happened. Sindberg then remembered to take something out of his pocket. "This is an open letter from the monks to you and all the other committee members."

Rabe took the letter and began to read it. His hands trembled with anger. The content of the letter was as follows:

To all this matter concerns in the name of humanity,

Faced with these trying times, we wanted to give you a brief report regarding the situation in this area and the harassment experienced by this temple.

Since the fall of Nanjing, hundreds of people have fled to the temple every day to seek our protection and temporary accommodation. At the time of writing this letter, the temple has already accommodated some 20,400 people, mostly women and children. Almost all the men have been shot or taken by the Japanese soldiers to work as coolies. Below is a brief list of the crimes committed by the Japanese soldiers since 4 January this year:

4 January: A truck carrying Japanese soldiers approached the temple. They stole nine cattle and ordered the Chinese to slaughter the cattle for them so that they could take the beef away. At the same time, they set fire to many nearby houses for fun.

6 January: Many Japanese soldiers arrived from the river. They took a donkey away from the refugees and stole 18 bedrolls.

7 January: Japanese soldiers raped a woman and a girl who was just 14 years old. They also stole five bedrolls.

8 and 9 January: Japanese soldiers raped six women. They broke into the temple as usual and looked for the youngest girls. They then intimidated them into submission with bayonets.

11 January: Four women were raped. Drunken Japanese soldiers wreaked havoc in the temple. They shot at people indiscriminately, injuring people and damaging houses.

13 January: Many Japanese soldiers arrived again. They searched everything and took a lot of food. They raped a woman and her daughter, and then swaggered off.

15 January: Many Japanese soldiers swarmed in. They gathered all the young women together and then picked out 10 of them. They raped them in the temple hall. A drunk soldier later arrived. He stormed in and demanded alcohol to drink and asked for a woman to rape. Someone gave him baijiu, but they refused to give him a woman. He became furious and started firing his gun without aiming at anything. After killing two boys, he left. On his way back to the railway station, he broke into a house on the side of the road and killed a 70 year old woman. He took a donkey and then set fire to the house to burn it down.

16 January: They continued to loot and rape.

18 January: They stole three donkeys.

19 January: Japanese soldiers wreaked havoc in the temple, smashing windows and furniture, as well as taking seven donkeys.

Approximately 20 January: A new unit arrived. This unit replaced the sentry located near the Qixia Mountain Railway Station. The new army commander was a second lieutenant. He was very kind-hearted. Since he arrived, the situation has markedly improved. He has appointed a new sentry in the temple. The guards at the sentry have tried hard to stop soldiers from causing trouble, stealing and taking away women. As a result, we have been worried that once the kind second lieutenant leaves and is dispatched to somewhere else, these terrible incidents will happen once again. So, we implore you, regardless of who you are, to help us stop this inhuman villainy from ever happening again. Eighty per cent of the refugees resettled here have lost everything; their houses have been destroyed, livestock killed, and their money stolen. On top of this, many women have lost their husbands and their children have lost their fathers. Japanese soldiers have killed most of the young men. As for those who've survived, some are wounded and some are ill. They lie here without doctors and medicine. Nobody dares go out on the streets out of fear of being killed. But we only have a small amount of food left. Our farmers no longer have any cattle or rice seeds. How can we begin the ploughing and sowing we normally do in the spring?

All of us are begging for your help.

— THE REFUGEES AT QIXIA TEMPLE (20 SIGNATURES OMITTED) 25 JANUARY 1938

After finishing reading the letter, Rabe sighed and said: "To be frank, the situation in the city is no better than in Qixia Temple. Take a look at Smythe's recent report."

Rabe picked up several sheets of paper from the desk and showed them to Sindberg. This was further material for the report on the Japanese atrocities in Nanjing, containing more than 300 cases.

Sindberg read the following report:

On the afternoon of 2 February, Mr Zhu tried to return to his home on Jiankang Road with his friends. When they arrived at Tieguan Lane, five Japanese soldiers blocked their way. They had to obey the Japanese soldiers' orders to work for them late into the night. From then on, they no longer dared to try to go back home.

On 2 February, Mr Jiang was going to his home in Xinjiekou, which was located on a corner of the intersection on Yunnan Road and Zhongshan North Road. Five or six Japanese soldiers found him and forced him to carry tableware to the Yijiang hotel. After this incident, he was about to go home in the neighbourhood around the ministry of railways building when he saw more Japanese soldiers. They asked him to carry rice to a city gate. By the time he finally finished it was too late, so he had to give up on his plans to return home.

3 February: At 9.00am, an 18 year old man called Xiaoxi left the refugee camp to go back home. When he reached Sixiang bridge, because he didn't bow immediately to the Japanese soldiers, they stabbed him with a bayonet. This afternoon, he returned to us for medical treatment.

3 February: At 10.00am or so, seven or eight Japanese soldiers broke into the home of Mr and Mrs Jiang on Baixia Road. They had just returned home from the safety zone. The Japanese soldiers ordered Mr Jiang to leave and attempted to assault his wife. Mr Jiang pointed to the International Committee emblem on his sleeve. The Japanese soldiers then angrily left. Mr Jiang took his wife back to the safety zone that night. They said that their home was now a terrifying place, so they decided to remain in the refugee camp.

3 February: On Mrs Ma's way back home, she was caught by three Japanese soldiers in front of a house on Tongren Street. She was dragged inside a room and gang-raped. Mrs Ma later returned to the shelter she had left earlier.

The subsequent parts of the report were all about cases relating to the many women who'd tried to leave the safety zone to go back home, but were raped or gang-raped by Japanese soldiers at home or on their way back. Sindberg couldn't bear to read any more. He said to Rabe: "This is vile! If we give up the safety zone it would give the Japanese soldiers a free pass to massacre the people of Nanjing! We cannot let that happen."

Rabe patted his Danish friend on the shoulder and said: "We're trying to contact other countries' embassies in China to get their support. We're also trying to work with Japan and the newly established Municipal Committee to take over the responsibilities of the International Committee."

"Have you had any luck?" asked the normally level headed Sindberg angrily.

"I believe it will work," Rabe replied. He continued: "Please send my regards to the Buddhist monks at Qixia Mountain. We'll try our best to help them. The biggest question now is what can we do to strengthen our ability to help and the Municipal Committee's ability to help in the safety zone, especially with food provisions."

"I understand," said Sindberg with a glimmer of hope before leaving the urban area, which was filled with rubbish and ash. He told Rabe: "If it wasn't for the thousands of refugees, I'd never come to the city."

Rabe smiled bitterly: "But we have to constantly guard the city and its hills of rotting corpses. This is our duty, and 200,000 refugees depend on us for our constant help."

Rabe was right. Regardless of how miserable and dirty Nanjing was, and regardless of how toxic its poison gas ridden air was, Rabe couldn't leave. 4 February was the first day of the evacuation of refugees from the safety zone. Apart from the refugee areas in the homes of Rabe and a few Americans that the Japanese army had not broken up, almost everywhere else was destroyed without exception, forcing the refugees away. The refugees in the middle school affiliated with the University of Nanjing that Rabe had always been concerned with, as it was very close to his home, had also been forced to flee. On the 5th, Grimes, who had been in charge of the refugees at the school, sent a letter to Rabe asking for help.

Dear Mr Rabe,

I am writing this letter to inform you that more and more refugees have returned to our school for protection. They said that they could no longer stay at home because the Japanese continued to harass them and that they constantly asked for girls. If they refused, the Japanese soldiers would threaten to kill them. The situation has never been so dire. How can these refugees go back home given the circumstances? I beg you to help them. I cannot turn to anyone else for help. I hope that you can discuss the matter with the German, American and Japanese embassies. The refugees have come to me for help, but I am unable to help them. The Municipal Committee cannot stop the Japanese crimes. People have told us that if it weren't for the International Committee that no one would have protected them. Even the wives of the officials in the Municipal Committee have suffered from the inevitable Japanese rape. I simply cannot understand it. How could the Municipal Committee order the refugees to return to their homes in such terrible circumstances? They are fully aware that outside of the safety zone, no one can protect the refugees from Japanese harassment.

The plight of these refugees is almost indescribable. I pray to God that you stay in China and save us. If you and your friends cannot help, then who else can? I sincerely request you and your friends to think of ways to help these refugees.

My dear, dear Mr Rabe, you are our leader. I weep as I write this letter. May God be with you, and please pray for us.

Yours,

— DG Grimes

"Inform the board at once!" Rabe said to Smythe. That afternoon, at Rabe's request, the International Committee's board of directors convened once again for an emergency meeting. They focused on the situation following the Japanese expulsion of refugees from the safety zone, the resettlement of the refugees and other matters that had arisen.

"Ladies and gentlemen, we can now say that we are entering the most difficult period since the establishment of our committee. Regardless, our faith and resolution has only grown and we also still have good reasons to fulfil our duties to the safety zone. Despite the fact that the Japanese have never directly admitted it, the International Committee has always received widespread support for our work here. The problem we face is that the Municipal Committee requires the citizens to go back home, despite most of the refugees being terrified of doing so. Some have even returned to the safety zone because they are so scared of Japanese harassment. What does this mean? It shows that the majority of the refugees trust us rather than the Japanese and officials in the autonomous government. Is there any better reason to help them than that? As long as we remain strong, victory will finally be ours!" Rabe was a businessman by nature and rarely spoke so passionately. Smythe and his other American friends all spoke highly of him.

A strong will to fight was now incredibly important for the members of the committee. This group of westerners took the problems in their stride, saying to each other: "This too shall pass".

It was 6 February 1938. Rabe received a warm letter from one of his assistants in the safety zone, Tao Zhongliang, on behalf of all the refugees in his charge. The letter read:

Dear Mr Rabe,

War broke out in Shanghai and tragically spread to Nanjing, leading to the International Committee establishing the Nanjing Safety Zone. It's saved refugees from danger and has ensured their safety. This work means that the refugees all owe you an unforgettable debt of gratitude that they shall never be able to repay.

As your assistants, we are willing to do all we can to help. This is our sacred duty. We received your letter on the Chinese New Year, in which you praised our work and also enclosed 15 dollars for us to celebrate the Spring Festival. Although we all think that we do not deserve this gift, we will not refuse it so that we do not upset you. In light of your instructions, we have already distributed the money to our staff. We write this letter to express our heartfelt gratitude to you.

Yours sincerely,

— TAO ZHONGLIANG, ON BEHALF OF ALL STAFF AT THE JINLING COLLEGE REFUGEE CAMP

Since the Japanese had announced the order to expel all of the refugees in the safety zone, Rabe had been extremely stressed. Although most news he received was alarming, there was the occasional piece of good news. For instance, Rabe found out from Rosen that as a result of the many efforts of Rabe and other parties, Shanghai had delivered 100 tons of broad beans to Nanjing. For the refugees in Nanjing living on the edge of starvation and death, this was life-saving. For Rabe, the success proved that the reputation of the International Committee was deserved. As these foods had all been charitable donations, even the Japanese military couldn't destroy them. The international community were now monitoring the situation. How could Rabe not be happy?

However, at the same time, Rabe received a few pieces of bad news. One incident that upset him was when a Japanese soldier broke into a house where a woman lived with her two daughters. The soldier wanted to rape the daughters, but he was met with strong resistance. As a result, the Japanese soldier locked the three women in the house and set fire to it. The two daughters were burned alive, but the mother escaped with incredibly severe burns. Faced with these constant atrocities, Rabe couldn't help but feel discouraged.

However, the International Committee never stopped its efforts. Rabe continued to propose ways of resolving the crisis to the Japanese. On 10 February, on behalf of the committee, he wrote a letter listing several requirements to the Japanese on how to restore order and discipline, tackle the food shortages, manage staff in hospitals and so forth.

While the aforementioned letter was sent to the Japanese embassy, Rabe also received a copy of a newspaper from Shanghai that had reprinted an article published in Hamburg:

A German's Successful Work
Shanghai, 10 January

Many reports in Nanjing have unanimously praised Rabe, the representative of Siemens (China) in Nanjing, for his commendable and successful work. Since November, when the Chinese authorities completely withdrew from Nanjing, as president of the International Committee, he has performed the role of the mayor. With the support of several Germans and other foreigners, he has worked to keep social order and has cared for the public's welfare. According to a report from a representative in the Japanese embassy, Rabe's work has been crucial in the transitional period and it has also been very beneficial by cooperating with the occupying forces to benefit the residents and refugees. Chinese residents who have remained in Nanjing have gratefully praised Rabe for his hard work.

— QUOTED FROM THE GERMAN NEWSPAPER *THE HAMBURG INFORMATION*

Rabe was a man with a particularly strong sense of honour. He took a great interest in this news from his home country, which became a source of motivation that inspired him to stay in China and contribute so much to the Chinese refugees. He talked about the article to his friends many times after he'd read it.

It was getting closer and closer to the date when he would need to leave Nanjing. Rabe felt that, as president, there were two things he had to complete. One was auditing the financial situation during the period when he'd been in office as the president of the committee, while the other was making a schedule for the future of the committee. This once again reveals just how dedicated he was to his work.

The financial statements and future financial budget were soon sent to him. Rabe noticed that the financial statements reported by Nanjing University weren't clear, so he urgently requested detailed additional materials to supplement them. He complained: "The payment of doctors and employees has to be arranged. If there are any problems left, I would rather not go!"

Rabe was about to sign a document that he thought was the most important one, namely changing the name of the International Committee for the Nanjing Safety Zone to the Nanjing International Relief Committee.

On 18 February, at the last meeting of the International Committee, Rabe gave a farewell speech, and Smythe kept a careful record of the meeting: "We have chosen this name to better reflect the nature of our work as a purely private relief organisation and to better express the reason for our existence. Dr Smythe and I formally made the aforementioned request to change the name to the Japanese. I am not going to preside over this new institution, but

I hope that Smythe, Magee, Sperling, Mills and my other colleagues will act as the leaders of this new institution. Their past work experience has proven that they are more than up for the job." These precious materials were later collected by Yale University and became important historical archives for later research on the Nanjing Massacre. I had the honour of reading them and also talking with missionaries, Christians and doctors about the unforgettable tragedies at the time.

Due to news of Rabe's achievements while presiding over the safety zone in Nanjing all around the world, not to mention his influence in Nanjing itself, when news about his leaving came out, many refugees wrote to him to pay their respects. The letter below was signed by 24 refugees and can be considered a good example of these letters:

Dear Mr Rabe,

After the Japanese occupied the city, the Japanese soldiers started to take away a lot of Chinese people from 16 December 1937. It's said that they took these people to force them to work. The majority of these people were young, some were even adolescents, and our children were among them. They are alone. Many of them were born into merchant families, so they have never been trained as soldiers. Others are artisans or small traders, but they are all honest men. Now only their lonely and helpless parents and grandparents are left at home, as well as their dispossessed wives and children.

We have never enjoyed a wealthy life. As you set up the Nanjing Safety Zone, we hoped that we would be able to continue working and living in the area without any problems. But 64 days ago, our sons were suddenly taken from us by the Japanese. We have lost all contact with them. Come rain or sunshine, even in the severe winter, we, old and young, women and children, who don't have any form of income, are still waiting for them to come back. If this continues, our people, who have never joined the army, will die from hunger and the freezing weather. We have no idea where our sons are and how they are doing. The families of the missing children cry all night, with the elderly and weak growing sick with sorrow. This sorrow cannot be expressed in writing. Your committee once said that you were responsible for investigating where the detained and missing had gone. We wrote to you twice before, on 28 January and 1 February respectively. Since then, two weeks have passed and we have received no response. Our families, who are worried about our sons, husbands and loved ones, do not know who else we could turn to. But we know that you are a kind person. So, we ask for your help once again, hoping that you could show us how to bring these children and breadwinners back home and save our lives. Would you please tell us what you can do for us? Are our children still alive? Where are they now? Will they come back to the safety zone? When will they come back? Please tell us everything you know. We know that you're a warm-hearted and compassionate man. We will be grateful for your help for the rest of our lives.

Best wishes,
    Yours faithfully,

    — Mr You and Ms Zhu, Mr Zhu and Ms Tang, Mr Wang and Ms Su, Mr Xu and Ms Zhu, Mr Xu and Ms Pan, Mr Fei and Ms Yu and 18 other signatures, Nanjing 19 Feb 1938

As a dedicated man, Rabe always responded quickly to letters like this, showing that he was committed to helping others.

On 21 February, a grand reception was held at the International Committee for the Nanjing Safety Zone headquarters to see off Rabe. The reception began with a beautiful but rather sad sounding song to honour Rabe, *The Nanjing Refugee Chorus*, created by McCallum the priest. McCallum had a reputation for having a good sense of humour and it had some rather funny lines. When McCallum explained the meaning of the lyrics to the audience, the entire auditorium burst into laughter. Even the Japanese dignitaries couldn't stop laughing. In Rabe's eyes, McCallum was a genius because he had unexpectedly created a song that addressed such a serious and complex diplomatic issue in a humorous and carefree way. This cheered up the entire reception.

On behalf of the International Committee for the Nanjing Safety Zone, Smythe announced that in Rabe's absence, an interim committee meeting had convened. He read out a resolution that had been made specially for Rabe:

Dear Mr Rabe,

We're honoured to inform you of the following statement, which was decided on at the sixth joint conference between nine regional leaders in the Nanjing Safety Zone and 25 refugee directors on 15 February this year. We are incredibly grateful for what Mr John HD Rabe, the president of the International Committee for the Nanjing Safety Zone, has done for the organisation and regulation in this area and for his efforts in providing assistance and relief. Mr Rabe is well regarded for his actions, which have benefited the residents of Nanjing. His name will always be in our grateful hearts.

The Chinese branch of Siemens and the German embassy in China shall also be notified of the above statement, letting them know how grateful the residents of Nanjing are for what Mr Rabe has done for them in times of such great hardship.

The conference also resulted in the signatories wanting to request the Chinese branch of Siemens to, if possible, keep Mr Rabe's house and position in Nanjing.

Although the Nanjing Safety Zone no longer exists, the residents of this city still suffer greatly, which is why they need more relief. To this end, all nine regional leaders in the Nanjing Safety Zone and the 25 refugee directors request you to, if possible, continue your work here. We feel a profound sadness that we have to say goodbye to a man like you, who has stood by in the face of hardship.

As such, we sincerely hope that our request will be accepted by Siemens, allowing you to remain here for Nanjing's sake, and that you consider remaining here against your agreement with Siemens. If this cannot happen, we would like you to come back soon to renew our friendship once again, which has been highly valuable to us in the past few months.

Yours sincerely,

— ALL THE REGIONAL LEADERS IN THE NANJING SAFETY ZONE AND ALL THE REFUGEE DIRECTORS

This resolution was written by Dong Shenyu and signed by all members of the International Committee, all the regional leaders in the Nanjing Safety Zone and the refugee directors. It remains in the Second Historical Archives of China. The long list of different signatures was proof of Rabe's achievements and prestige as the president of the International Committee for the Nanjing Safety Zone. This was the highest honour Rabe received, although it was not an official honour.

On 23 February, accompanied by his trusted assistants Han Xianglin and Shi Peilin, Rabe boarded the British ship the *HMS Bee*, which was anchored in the Yangtze River. When he got on board, he was warmly welcomed by the staff of the British embassy and the ship's captain.

The ship gave out a long whistle as the choppy river slapped against the sides of the boat. Rabe occasionally waved to the people at the harbour seeing him off. He felt excited, but emotionally torn.

On board, Rabe read a recently published editorial note called *In Tribute to Mr Rabe* in a German newspaper in Shanghai. It read:

When the Japanese army rapidly advanced towards the Chinese capital of Nanjing at the end of November, the western community in Nanjing came up with the idea of establishing a safety zone to provide shelter to foreigners who'd remained there and the Chinese civilians during the battle.

To coordinate their efforts, the westerners formed a committee, called the International Committee for the Nanjing Safety Zone, which brought together civilians from different countries (three from Germany and others from the US, the UK, and more). Trusted by all of the committee members, Mr John Rabe, a representative of the Siemens Nanjing office, was appointed leader of the group.

When the battle broke out, the safety zone had been well established. Members of the International Committee for the Nanjing Safety Zone could easily have evacuated. However, Mr Rabe and his fellow members decided not to protect themselves from the war and chose to remain committed to their important mission until the last minute.

Thanks to their selfless actions, in times of hardship following the Chinese withdrawal from the city and the Japanese occupation, hundreds of thousands of people were protected from cold and hunger. The members did all they could to protect them from suffering.

The members of the International Committee for the Nanjing Safety Zone were willing to risk their own safety and lives to make a great humanitarian contribution to China.

In spite of the intense pressure, the leaders of the committee made a great many achievements. In times of hardship, Mr John Rabe proved himself to be a perfect man. Germans and Germany are all honoured because of his dedication to China.

Rabe happily guessed that this must have been the doing of Kroeger and his other friends who'd arrived at the Siemens office in Shanghai earlier.

However, Rabe preferred another letter of praise that he kept in his pocket, as this letter had been written by Trautmann, the German ambassador to China. Rabe believed it was official recognition of his work by the German authorities and government:

Dear Mr Rabe,

I would like to express my appreciation for your successful achievements and humanitarian dedication as the president of the International Committee for the Nanjing Safety Zone, which has been reorganised as the Nanjing International Relief Committee, risking your own life without payment from November 1937 to February 1938.

In addition to this, I would like to extend my sincere thanks to you for your courageous endeavours and efforts to protect German property in Nanjing. What you have done in Nanjing has brought honour to our country.

I am happy to inform you that in order to recognise your remarkable efforts in Nanjing, I have already asked the foreign ministry to suggest that the German Red Cross present a medal to you.

— Dr Trautmann

Once in Shanghai, Rabe first told the public outside of Nanjing about the Japanese crimes and violence during the massacre. Ever since then, his name has never been forgotten. He did the same when he returned to Germany. However, several years later, when the Germans and Japanese lost the Second World War, Rabe's fortunes changed. Despite being a hero, he was a member of the Nazi Party, which meant that he couldn't avoid investigation after the war.

At this critical moment, the Chinese communities and others who supported Rabe provided evidence that proved the contributions Rabe had made in Nanjing. This was to prevent people from assuming that he was just another Nazi. The following is the verdict signed by the chairman of the Allied Control Council:

Rabe is hereby not judged as a member of the Nazi Party.

Currently working as an interpreter and sometimes as an interim employee with Siemens, Mr Rabe had been in China for a long time before he joined the Nazi Party in 1934. This was as a result of him needing to gain support from the German government for the German school he'd established. In 1935, John Rabe served as the acting director of the party's local organisation in Nanjing. The testimony from the witnesses proves that this German, who was in China, had no idea about the evil purpose and criminal actions of the Nazi Party. The Nanjing Safety Zone was set up after the Japanese army broke the defensive line. Under the request of the Americans and the British, Mr Rabe led the organisation. As the leader of the International Committee for the Nanjing Safety Zone, he protected the area from Japanese bombs. In 1938, when he went back to Germany, he was invited as a special guest to take the British ship the *HMS Bee* to Shanghai. When he returned to Germany, he gave hundreds of presentations about the brutal Japanese crimes during the war, leading to his arrest by the Gestapo and being forbidden from giving any further presentations. During the war, he was responsible for taking care of expatriates at Siemens.

Both Alfred Hope and Albert A Bruce Hulme, who were in China with Mr Rabe and were not Nazi Party members, can justify the above statement. Especially so as back in 1934, the policies and imperialist purpose of the Nazi Party were not known in China at all.

As a result, given the proof of humanitarianism provided by the witnesses, most of the committee members vote that this proposal that Mr Rabe is not a Nazi is correct.

Rabe's special contributions to Nanjing had saved him.

In one summer day back in 2014, I went to visit the house Rabe had rented in Xiaofenqiao, 1 Guangzhou Road in Nanjing. I bowed three times in front of a statue of this great Chinese ally. I couldn't help but be overcome with emotion when I touched the face of the statue because all Chinese know that without Rabe and his safety zone, the casualties during the Nanjing Massacre would have been a lot higher than 300,000.

6

A FOREIGN LADY CLINGS TO THE ISLAND OF LIFE

It's about time that I introduce a Nanjing Massacre hero well-known among the people of China who served as the inspiration for director Zhang Yimou's film *The Flowers of War*.

Zhang Yimou's film is based on a novella by the Chinese-American writer Yan Geling, *13 Flowers of Nanjing*, which was inspired by the diary of Minnie Vautrin. Zhang told Yan about the diary and she then finished *13 Flowers of Nanjing*, which was the original manuscript of *The Flowers of War*.

One day in 1995, an Asian woman quietly sat in a library at Yale University, carefully reading a stack of documents while taking notes on a typewriter. That woman was Iris Chang, who was so moved by what she'd read that she couldn't help shedding a tear. What had made her so emotional? She'd found another important document after the diaries of John Rabe: Minnie Vautrin's diary.

Once Chang finished reading the documents, she lamented in her diary about the way she had been forgotten: "After I finished Minnie Vautrin's diary and letters, I felt rather angry and confused about why these files hadn't been edited and published. Why had people forgotten Minnie Vautrin over the past 50 years? And why was Minnie Vautrin not a source of inspiration to the entire world?" Chang's grandfather was a KMT general who'd fought against the Japanese invasion. Her grandfather told her about the Japanese crimes in Nanjing during her childhood, which left a big impression on her. Wanting to make a difference, Chang threw herself into making sure that the public knew the story of Minnie Vautrin. While she worked on collecting and searching for important files about those who'd played important parts in the history of the Nanjing Massacre, like Rabe, she was also committed to helping translate Vautrin's diary into Chinese. Finally, back in April 2000, the historian Hu Hualing finished the translation and the Chinese version of Vautrin's diary was published in October that year.

However, history has a tragic way of repeating itself. Minnie Vautrin, who had dedicated herself to saving tens of thousands of Chinese civilians during the Nanjing Massacre, was suffering from schizophrenia and severe depression at the end of 1940. She had to return to the US for treatment, but her condition wasn't well controlled. On 14 May 1941, she committed suicide by using the gas stove in her apartment. Coincidentally, 63 years later in 2004, Iris Chang, whose family had originally come from near Nanjing and was a great admirer of Minnie Vautrin, committed suicide as well by shooting herself in her car.

Both graduates from the University of Illinois, Minnie Vautrin and Iris Chang both played important roles in the history of the Nanjing Massacre and suffered from similar illnesses. Tragically, in the end both chose to commit suicide. It is heartbreaking that two women born years apart share such a similar destiny.

A Childless Woman But a Mother to Many

Minnie Vautrin was an American missionary in China and an important witness to the Nanjing Massacre. She never had any children of her own, but she saved tens of thousands of children in China. In recognition of her remarkable impact, she was given the title "goddess of mercy" by the Chinese.

Minnie Vautrin had a Chinese name: Hua Qun. She was born in the small town of Secor in Illinois in 1886. At 26, the beautiful, young and well-educated American woman went to the poor city of Hefei in China to teach and preach Christianity on her own, devoting herself to the task. Vautrin's commitment to China is touching, especially her work protecting tens of thousands of Chinese women and children during the Nanjing Massacre.

She did incredibly well during this time. From 1919 to May 1940, Minnie Vautrin served as a professor, the master of studies, master of education and the dean of the college of arts and science on two occasions at Jinling College. Minnie Vautrin was an outstanding educator and as a missionary, she fully deserves her nickname the goddess of mercy.

Like all other missionaries, Vautrin's initial and most fundamental mission when she first came to China was to spread her religion and to save her "poor and ignorant sisters". But the brutality of the Japanese army's crimes changed her mission, transforming her from a missionary into a woman who the people of Nanjing would remember for generations.

In the summer of 2014, I went to the former college of arts and science at Jinling College to visit the statue of Minnie Vautrin. In front of me stood a kind and friendly looking western lady and I immediately fully understood the extent of her bravery when standing up for the Chinese civilians during the Nanjing Massacre. I then began to realise why Iris Chang had wept when she read Vautrin's diary.

There's an argument to be made that during his stay in Nanjing, Rabe used evil to fight evil when he had no other choice; he routinely scared off the barbaric Japanese by pointing to the swastika on his arm. On the contrary, Vautrin used kindness to fight evil instead. Vautrin wasn't born with a silver spoon in her mouth. Her father was a blacksmith who couldn't afford to provide any luxuries for his family. When she was 12 years old, Vautrin started to do odd jobs for her neighbours like taking the cows out to pasture in the freezing winter weather. Throughout her school years, she earned her tuition fees by working part time. She had to study part time at university, so it took her four years to graduate. She then moved to China to do missionary work, leaving her with no choice but to break up with her fiancé. She never married.

Vautrin devoted her entire life to China, but what left an impression on the country more than anything were her actions in protecting tens of thousands of refugees in the years following Japan's occupation of Nanjing.

By the summer of 1937, Vautrin, who was one of the directors of the college at the time, had been working at Jinling College for 19 years. At the time, Wu Yi-fang, a famous Chinese teacher, was acting as the college dean. Vautrin had actually been planning to return to the US for a holiday in the sweltering summer when her life changed completely. As Nanjing's destiny changed, so too did the fate of this remarkable woman, now in her fifties.

Whether it was due to intuition or a better awareness of international politics as an American, when Japan attacked China, Vautrin's heart immediately sank as she saw through Japan's imperial ambitions. Vautrin promptly shared her interpretation of the Marco Polo Bridge Incident that had occurred in Beijing that year. She wrote in a letter to one of her friends in the US several days after the event: "We heard that on 7 July, after one Japanese soldier went missing, a situation developed hundreds of miles away to the south of Beijing. So how did the Japanese soldier go missing? Why did it happen? No one knows the answer, but ever since then, the war has expanded. We don't dare to imagine what will happen in the future." Vautrin also sharply noted at the time that: "Milne once said about the First World War that: 'Two people were shot and killed in Sarajevo in 1914. What Europe then did for revenge was kill millions more.' This doesn't factor in the personal losses, deaths from anger and disease, financial costs and the increase in hatred. China didn't want to get involved in the war and it wasn't ready for it. I suppose that the Japanese people didn't want it either, but Japan has failed to control its warmongers."

Vautrin was a great teacher and loved peace. When graduates left Jinling College year after year and started to play their roles in society, Vautrin was filled with joy. Her job allowed her to explore all of her interests, find happiness and be awarded with a real sense of achievement, even if her family never really understood. This didn't bother her much as she enjoyed it and felt that it enriched her life.

She was pleased with the graduates of the summer of 1937, as 42 young women left for the world of work with nearly two thirds of them going on to become teachers.

"Education for women is key to them getting better job opportunities," thought Vautrin to herself as she beamed with happiness. Over the course of her career at Jinling College over the past 19 years, she got closer and closer to realising her goals there. Following the Marco Polo Bridge Incident, when Japan stormed Shanghai in early August, Vautrin and her colleagues were still discussing that year's plans. They reached an agreement that the start of the school calendar, which was normally in early September, was to be postponed to 20 September as the KMT government's department of education had suggested that schools in Shanghai, Nanjing and other dangerous areas postpone the start of the new semester to that date. This was because the KMT government was concerned about the coming difficulties in the fight against Japan in Shanghai, or in other words, it had no confidence in victory. What was the significance of 20 September? Would the war have ended by then? Did the government expect victory or defeat? No one knew the answers.

The situation was getting worse. It was late July when Vautrin returned from a holiday in Qingdao. She noticed the current state of affairs changing. She wrote: "I came across five military convertibles en route carrying soldiers, horses and other equipment. These soldiers looked very unwell in the heat, some of whom were teenagers." Vautrin was able to tell a lot from few details, such as the frequent military transfers of the Chinese army and the presence of poor teenage soldiers hinting that there were shortages in troops.

Vautrin had her own problems to deal with so she returned to Nanjing early, mainly to check the new faculty housing. The new apartment was a project that Vautrin had taken great interest in and Wu Yi-fang, the dean, had worked very hard on it. As they had gone overbudget, Vautrin, who wanted to own a US-style apartment, was somewhat worried; she wanted her dream home in China. However, after the Japanese invasion, everything changed, including Vautrin's opinions about housing.

Vautrin wrote: "After the campus lights went off, the sound of advancing soldiers and horses and the clatter of firearms hitting each other continued for more than two hours on the road outside the campus. The war preparations went on and on. Is there anything that can stop the war? All hell breaks loose when the madness of war is unleashed. However, a considerable number of pacifists will always try to stop wars regardless of the country."

Vautrin was a pacifist, so she was understandably angry about the march to war. But it was the result of the Japanese forcing China to do so as the Japanese military machine rapidly advanced. Vautrin's accounts reveal the atmosphere in July and August after returning to Nanjing.

The authorities promptly issued a controversial order, but it was quickly accepted by the people: every roof, including the red pillars underneath, had to be painted black or grey. The authorities said that this was to prevent the buildings from being targeted by Japanese bombs. As almost everyone was scared to death, the plan was soon implemented. Even the Drum Tower of Nanjing was painted grey. Vautrin found this unacceptable but Jinling College was exempt because Wu Yi-fang, Vautrin and the other professors and school board members were firmly opposed to it.

The authorities criticised them: "Do you expect the Japanese to make any exceptions for your college?" Nonetheless, the authorities let them off.

The Battle of Shanghai began on 13 August and all communication between Shanghai and Nanjing was cut off, as was the traffic. Nanjing began to descend into panic.

In the following days, Vautrin, like everyone else in Nanjing, spent her time digging out bomb shelters and carrying on with her job like normal. On the 11th, the missionaries John and Anna came to visit Vautrin, discussing their work in her office for more than an hour. They could do nothing but worry.

Vautrin told them: "Personally, I now boycott Japanese goods. I'll also try my best to contact the Japanese to make their workers and farmers understand what their armies are doing in China."

The following days made Vautrin and her colleagues extremely anxious as the Japanese bombed them whenever the weather permitted. The terrible sound of the air-raid sirens and the dullness of the bomb shelters frustrated and worried the women. To make matters worse, tragic news kept coming. People were being blown to pieces in Shanghai, while houses were being destroyed and people were being killed and maimed in Nanjing.

The US embassy repeatedly told Vautrin again and again: "You have to leave! Everyone who doesn't have to stay has to leave."

Vautrin told the embassy: "I've already told you that I'm staying. If I leave, Dr Wu Yi-fang and my Chinese colleagues will be under tremendous pressure. I'm in charge of teaching and I won't leave, especially not now. This has been both my responsibility and my mission in China for decades."

"We fully understand. Whether you stay or leave is completely up to you and we respect your decision." The embassy's response made Vautrin happy.

With her decision made and the embassy on board, she did what everyone else in Nanjing did: get ready to face the Japanese. As it stood, the people of Nanjing were helpless.

Not only was the start of the new school term delayed, now the college itself was forced to relocate immediately. This was the government's order, leaving just a caretaker behind, while the staff, students and teachers had to move away from the city. From August, all of Nanjing tried to chaotically relocate; adults were frantic, children cried, soldiers were overworked, and criminals thrived. The dignified Chinese capital was in chaos. The busiest three individuals at Jinling College were the headteacher Wu Yi-fang, Cheng Ruifang the warden and Vautrin.

1 September, the normal start of the school year, seemed entirely unlike previous years in the college. That evening, Vautrin, Wu Yi-fang and another colleague were in a hilltop air-raid shelter discussing how to continue the school's work with no students. They discussed the current situation in China and what the two women said surprised Vautrin: "If our country is defeated by the Japanese, it's not because of our people's lack of courage, but because we've been betrayed!"

Who was this traitor? Chiang Kai-shek? This was unlikely. Wang Jingwei? Vautrin had no idea who they were referring to, but one thing was clear: every night, when Japanese planes attacked Nanjing, the orders for a blackout in public places, important institutions and military installations were constantly being broken. Several traitors actually pointed their lights in the air to guide the Japanese military through the darkness. Perhaps these were the traitors Wu hated so much?

They later received news that in order not to leave any valuable resources and wealth in the hands of the Japanese, the authorities would be implementing a scorched earth policy. This meant that China would rather ruin Nanjing and other cities than let the Japanese gain any benefits if they fell into their hands.

"This is insanity. Both China and Japan have gone mad." Vautrin looked at the ancient Chinese capital and the Qinhuai River without understanding why they would do this. The only comfort was that Wu Yi-fang was a liberal boss with an independent streak, so she never followed blackout orders or implemented the scorched earth policy. Wu thought that even with the Japanese wolves at the door, they had to "show the pride and beauty of the

Chinese people". Vautrin greatly admired Wu and regarded her as a symbol of the soul of Jinling College. Wu had been one of the first graduates of the school and later went to the US to study a PhD. She took over the post as president of the school after returning from the US and was a truly experienced and passionate teacher. Due to the presence of Wu Yi-fang at the college, it enjoyed a good reputation in Nanjing and Chiang Kai-shek's wife often visited with gifts.

The Shanghai campaign was extremely brutal and a great deal of sick and wounded from the frontline were transported to hospitals in the Nanjing area. Vautrin and Cheng Ruifang were ordered by the principal to hand out sentimental gifts to them.

The women took to the streets to find donors and mobilised the women of the city to sew clothes for the wounded and even write to their families. Vautrin felt that she was fully integrated into the Chinese way of life, forgetting her own identity as a westerner and as an American. The Chinese people treated her as if she was one of them. People initially called her "foreign lady", but they later used "Miss Hua" when they found out her Chinese name Hua Qun.

The war had made people oddly innovative. Vautrin saw this when she went to the American embassy one day. The diplomats there were busy setting up a giant American flag on the roof. A member of the embassy staff said: "This is to stop the Japanese planes from bombing us."

"So what are the people of Nanjing going to do?" replied Vautrin, who felt pained by the sight. The people of China couldn't hide behind a flag like they could. For this reason, she hated the Japanese even more, racking her brains as to why they would want to invade China and harm its innocent people.

Japanese planes had bombed Nanjing with appalling levels of destruction. One day, two police officers came to the school and questioned Vautrin, pointing to some nearby geese: "Whose geese are these?"

"Do they affect the war?" Vautrin asked the police with a puzzled look. "Miss Hua, you may not know that Japanese planes actually drop bombs on places where they hear the sound of geese, so the government asks you to kill them," the police responded. Vautrin, even more confused, argued: "They're for a biology experiment. Killing them is unfair! Besides, if the Japanese know that they're geese, they probably won't bomb us because they know it's a rural area."

The police didn't have a response and still insisted that it was an order that she had to follow.

"Do you have any dogs?" asked the police. Vautrin nodded and said:

"They're obedient and follow us when we go into the shelter. They never bark without us telling them to."

The police seemed to believe what Vautrin said and told her before leaving: "You have to get them under control."

Vautrin looked at the police as they walked away. She couldn't help but laugh and shake her head. It seemed that the war had driven everyone mad. Nanjing and all the people who lived here were more severely infected with this madness than most.

16 September was a particularly sad day for Vautrin. She left the bomb shelter at 8pm and found her dog Peter lying still on the floor, eyes filled with sorrow and pitifully staring at his master. He'd been bitten by a venomous snake.

Vautrin picked up the little dog and went straight to the infirmary to treat him, but it was too late and Peter stopped struggling and passed away several days later. Vautrin was incredibly sad and wrapped her little dog in a white cloth and buried him under a small tree in a ceremony with Cheng Ruifang and several other friends.

Vautrin silently prayed for him. She felt that this had been an indirect crime by the Japanese. After Peter's funeral, Vautrin once again busied herself with preparations for the coming school year. As far as most people knew, Shanghai had been badly damaged in the fighting so they weren't sure whether they could open the college. Vautrin felt extremely angry and said: "War is war and children are children. Although we cannot stop the war, we should do everything possible to make sure the innocent children can go to school."

On 18 September, Jinling College decided to open on 4 October, which greatly encouraged Vautrin. That day, Vautrin, Cheng Ruifang and other colleagues notified all students majoring in biology to go to classes in Wuchang as there were already six of their students who'd been able to go to school there. In her diary that day, Vautrin felt proud of herself for having stayed in Nanjing: "In my opinion, if possible, mothers should go somewhere safer with their children. But if we can stand this enormous pressure, we should stay here and do all we can to work with so many young members of the church. If we leave when they are most in need, we'll lose an excellent opportunity to provide a service. The day I've looked forward to my entire missionary career is coming. On that day, women shall be treated as equal to men with the same roles and shall not be asked to leave with the mothers."

The next day was the Mid-Autumn Festival. Vautrin was incredibly happy; it was raining, which meant that the Japanese wouldn't bomb the city. After the rain passed, the sky was bright and clear as people enjoyed a beautiful day in a way they hadn't been able to since the start of August. Vautrin went to visit her students' parents that day, going from house to house. The citizens of Nanjing were overwhelmed by a potent mix of desperation and depression as the war raged on, which made them all the more moved when the friendly western teacher popped by to visit them.

"Sit down, please, Miss Vautrin, have a mooncake!"

"Miss Vautrin, will my children be able to go to school this year?"

Vautrin was warmly welcomed as she enthusiastically told her students and their parents: "There's going to be a school party this afternoon to celebrate the start of school. Would you like to come?"

At 2.30pm, Vautrin and the other teachers arranged a special party at a neighbouring school. More than 30 children and 18 adults came to the party, during which Vautrin sang a popular song with the children, filling her heart with hope for the future.

A bomb suddenly exploded nearby. Vautrin's hatred of the Japanese increased more than she could have imagined in the face of their devastating attacks.

"What do you have against children who just want to go to school? What's wrong with you?" Vautrin cursed the bombers flying overhead.

Cheng Ruifang struggled to pull Vautrin into the shelter while she continued to curse the Japanese, her voice quivering as she shouted.

On 20 September, Paxton, a counsellor from the American embassy, came to visit Vautrin and read a statement issued by the Japanese commander in Shanghai: "In order to end the war as quickly as possible, we will destroy all of the military facilities, airports and communication centres in Nanjing." The Japanese were going to devastate Nanjing the following day.

"We have orders from the government and hope that you will agree to immediately evacuate Nanjing and go west to Wuhu," reported Paxton. "How can I abandon the children?" asked Vautrin, as to be expected. "Ms Vautrin, you should know that the Japanese aren't as kind as you missionaries. This statement is an ultimatum. If you stay, they don't care whether you're killed."

"So will they attack the children and the schools?"

"Yes! Bombs don't discriminate!"

"In that case, I have to stay here. The Japanese will pay if they dare to bomb our school and children."

Paxton couldn't persuade Vautrin to leave and left disappointed. "If you need help, you can write to me and the embassy," he said in a friendly tone as he turned back. Vautrin rushed after him and asked: "I heard that you were going to lower the embassy flag, is that true?" Paxton confirmed that it was.

A Foreign Lady Clings to the Island of Life | 441

Vautrin leaned against a stone wall wearing a worried expression as she watched Paxton leave. She discussed the matter with her colleague Catherine and sent a message to the embassy: "I believe there will be a tragedy on our hands if every embassy lowers its flag and withdraws its staff. This means that everything in Nanjing can be destroyed with impunity with no formal declaration of war. I hope the Japanese air force is stopped."

She attended several Chinese weddings that day. She initially didn't understand why so many girls were suddenly about to get married. After talking with her Chinese friends, she found out that all the parents believed that finding a husband for their daughters would protect them from being hurt after the Japanese invaded.

Vautrin felt distraught when she heard about incidents like this, but she wanted to know what she could do to save innocent lives. She felt helpless, but what she could do was keep Jinling College from being destroyed. She thought that it could be both a place for her to work and an ideal home for children. If any of the children's homes were destroyed, any hope of stability for the child would be destroyed with it. This is why Vautrin chose to stay behind in Nanjing. Catherine told her: "Now that everyone has to leave and no one is left at the embassy, maybe we should ask them for their flag." Vautrin excitedly exclaimed: "That's a great idea. I heard Mr Rabe has several German flags in his yard so the Japanese never bomb it."

"The Japanese are scared of the swastika," said Catherine. Vautrin confidently replied: "Well, our Star Spangled Banner will at least make them think twice. I'll call the embassy quickly now before they leave."

Vautrin called and asked for the large flag on the embassy's roof. They told her that they'd let her know soon. "There's a chance," Vautrin told Catherine. The phone rang and Vautrin rushed to pick it up: "Ms Vautrin, we're happy to tell you that the ambassador has agreed to your request." Vautrin ecstatically thanked the caller and hugged Catherine. They reported the news to Wu Yi-fang. She was also delighted and asked them to fetch it as quickly as possible. Vautrin and several other colleagues rushed off to bring the new nine foot long American flag back to the school, unfurling it on the middle of the campus lawn. Once unfurled, Vautrin was unimpressed: "It's too small. I don't know if the Japanese planes will be able to see it clearly." Cheng came to take a look and agreed, while Catherine was also unhappy with it. Vautrin pondered for a moment and came up with an idea: "We'll go and buy some cloth tomorrow and try to make a flag three times larger than this one." Cheng and Catherine agreed that this was a good idea.

The Japanese kept their promise and began to level the city. "Forty-one people were killed by Japanese bombs in the ministry of industry building today," Wu Yi-fang informed Vautrin and the other teachers with a heavy heart.

The moon peeped out of the clouds with the dim light of the night. Vautrin left the shelter and went back to the college. When she opened her window, she saw the American flag on the lawn and couldn't help but walk out.

Under the moonlight, Vautrin's mind was flooded with memories as she stood in front of her country's flag. She remembered her hometown in Illinois, her sick father and her younger brother complaining about her decision to leave. But Vautrin missed much more than her homeland. She told herself that if her country hadn't been so selfish and greedy for so long, this flag and the country it represented could have had the ability to bring the Japanese actions under control. But now, everyone had gone and the American embassy was closed. Where was the justice?

Vautrin was heartbroken and gradually lost faith in her country, which is why she was willing to stay in Nanjing for so long, even with the risk of dying. She drew a cross over her chest and prayed: "I'd rather stay in this warzone for these children who are such a comfort to my heart. Please God, believe and understand me, and please let my devout Christian father understand me too."

Running a School Amidst the Bombs

The first thing the citizens of Nanjing did after waking up every day was take a look at the weather. However, their perspective on what constituted good weather had been perverted. On 25 September, Vautrin wrote in her diary: "The beautiful glow of dawn shows that it'll be good weather today, which makes me incredibly sad. As I stare outside through the window, the brilliant rosy rays of the morning sun sneak into my room through a long willow branch outside my eastern window. All I can think about is what the day has in store for us, or rather how much pain, sorrow and destruction it has for us, and how many mutilated bodies it'll bring with the tragic airstrikes." The sky looked remarkably beautiful, but her school, her students and Vautrin would have to face the Japanese bombs.

On 26 September, Vautrin visited the central government's new location following the air raids with Wu Yi-fang, invited by Dr Wilson from Gulou Hospital.

"They've been planning this for a long time," said Wilson furiously as he pointed to a hole in a hospital courtyard nearly 10 metres wide and six metres deep. He continued: "This is less than 50 metres away from our air-raid shelter. Fifty metres from killing more than 100 doctors, nurses and workers, myself included!"

Vautrin looked at the dirt that had exploded all around the crater, with some even landing onto the roofs of neighbouring buildings. The west wall of the auditorium by the east side of the tennis court had collapsed following the explosion. She then saw that all the other buildings in the hospital had been riddled with bullets by strafing enemy planes. A number of houses had been burned down, among which were accommodation for the nurses and table tennis rooms. Wilson continued to seethe at the Japanese: "Obviously, this was a well-planned assault. They cut away at our hospital like highly skilled surgeons."

"Where will the wounded in the hospital go?" Vautrin apprehensively asked Wilson.

"The government has arranged for another military hospital."

"Then where will the general patients go?"

"They've been asked to go home to the best of their abilities."

Vautrin saw many of the patients heading for air-raid shelters with the help of their family members. An elderly patient obviously had no family members to help him and he tripped over when struggling to make his way to the shelters. Vautrin rushed over to pick him up and asked where his family had gone.

"They left Nanjing last month and went to live with their relatives in a different village. Are you Miss Hua? We all know you! You're a good person!" said the old man, recognising Vautrin, which was a welcome surprise.

"Aren't you afraid of the Japanese?" asked Vautrin in a concerned tone.

"No, no. I'm not afraid of the Japanese!" said old man bluntly. He continued: "The reason I told my family to leave Nanjing is that they'll get to kill more Japs when the Japanese come to the city! Otherwise, the Japanese will think that we Chinese are easily pushed around. I have to stay alive to see what the Japanese do in Nanjing when they reach the city."

Vautrin was deeply moved by the old man. She wrote in her diary: "The Japanese are making the Chinese people, as a nation, much more closely united than ever before and it would do them good to understand that! I've never seen such courage, confidence and determination among the Chinese before."

At nightfall, Vautrin walked on the street alone and was surprised to see that nobody else was out. When she approached the neighbourhood near the school, she happened to see houses that she'd never really noticed before all being rented out. Even empty housing units that were just used for storage were filled with people.

"We think we'll be safe next to your school."

"The Japanese wouldn't dare use force against children."

When Vautrin heard civilians moving to the area say things like this, she felt proud yet worried. Would the Japanese really spare the children like the civilians assumed?

Vautrin thought that this was extremely unlikely. The fact that Gulou Hospital had been bombed was evidence to her that they didn't let off the sick and the wounded, so why would they let off women and children? However, she didn't say anything as she didn't want to destroy the hopes of the poor masses renting and living near the school.

10 October was the National Day of the Republic of China. It rained in the morning as the heavens provided a natural protective umbrella for the city. Vautrin was busy preparing for prayers in the church the entire morning and she later led a group of children to the hospital to visit the patients. That afternoon, she walked out on the street and saw that the flag of the Republic of China, with its red background, blue canton and white sun, was flying above every household, not to mention government agencies.

At this moment, all of Vautrin's worries were at ease, happy to experience this and to have chosen to stay in Nanjing. However, the Japanese planes appeared once again the following day and so did Vautrin's concerns.

What Vautrin cared about most at this point was whether her students would be able to go to school for the last 10 days in October. She heard from a friend at Jinling College that a little more than 100 new students had enrolled, one tenth of the amount during previous years. Students had moved to places like Wuhan and Shanghai if they'd been able. Senior staff like Vautrin were mainly busying themselves with coordinating student registration at affiliated schools and other administrative tasks before starting the school year. Although there was less demand for teaching, Vautrin and Wu Yi-fang still dedicated themselves to the students' wellbeing.

30 October was an important anniversary for the college, celebrating its foundation. For the entire day, stepping in for Principal Wu, Vautrin was busy writing letters to every affiliated school and student. She sent the following message to every affiliated school on behalf of the college:

> I hope that every member of Jinling College selflessly rises up to the burdens caused by the dangers and disasters that face the country through unrelenting self-education so as to live up to the dreams held by the founders of the college.

— JINLING COLLEGE, *30 OCTOBER 1937*

Vautrin was rather happy that day because she received a telegraph from the Wuhan branch of the college. The message was as follows: "Although we're separated, we won't let ourselves feel upset. Instead we have faith in our beliefs and we will be together again soon. Long live Jinling College!"

Vautrin held the message, kissed it and didn't want to let it go.

"Miss Vautrin, we should celebrate the college's anniversary today! We should have a party at the college this evening," Wu Yi-fang said to Vautrin that afternoon as she elegantly approached Vautrin. She continued with a sweet smile: "Could you ask all the faculty and staff to come?"

Vautrin happily agreed and devoted herself to preparing for the celebration with Cheng Ruifang and her other colleagues.

That evening, the college assembly hall was abnormally lively. Moments like these had been all too rare at the college since the Japanese air raids. There were 36 people in total at the gathering, 18 men and 18 women. All of them were split up and sat at six different desks, while beautiful chrysanthemums made the hall look extraordinary.

There wasn't any singing and dancing because anyone who was frankly any good at singing or dancing had left. But people like Vautrin still felt inspired by the atmosphere, although it was a strange cocktail of hope and fear. In the latter half of the party, there were eight talks on the programme, which included the lectures *Jinling College and the Current Crisis* by Wu, *How to Cope in the Current Crisis* by Vautrin and one of the most interesting talks *Let's Never Forget to Laugh* by John Magee, a talented orator with a good sense of humour. Although his talk was about God, it reflected the problems with belief in contemporary China and Chinese women. He was of the opinion that while the Japanese troops were aggressively attacking Nanjing, Chinese women had to believe in China and, more importantly, in God. This was the reason, he said, for Jinling College's existence in the first place. Magee expressed his opinions by discussing the initial wish of the founders of the college, which was to build the first women's college in the Yangtze River basin.

From 1911 to the winter of 1912, eight American missionaries gathered in Shanghai and formulated a plan to build a college for women in the Yangtze River basin, sending out proposals to preachers in the region. In the summer of 1913, a school board was established after selecting three people from the area's different churches, including the American Presbyterian Mission, the American Baptist Churches USA and the Methodist Episcopal Churches. The representative from the American Presbyterian Mission, Matilda Thurston, was recommended to be president of the consolidated school for women in the Yangtze River basin. The following year, the managing board of directors officially passed a motion to rename the school the Jinling Women's College. In 1924, the college bought land and built houses on Ninghai Road, officially established nine departments, including English, history, sociology, mathematics, chemistry, biology, physical education and medicine, and also established its affiliated experimental middle school. Later on, it also added a Chinese department. In 1928, Matilda Thurston resigned from the position as president, and Dr Wu Yi-fang succeeded her. In 1930, the school was renamed Jinling College. The aim of the churches after establishing it was to train female teachers in China. There is no doubt of the college's Christian message and the devotion of its staff and students, following the influence of the churches that had founded it.

The constant kindness shown by the western preachers and Christians to the local people during the Nanjing Massacre was both enormously helpful and proof of the goodness of humanity. Vautrin was without a doubt among these kind souls.

On the last day of October, Vautrin walked to the Drum Tower and went to church. Afterwards, she went to the college hospital's shelter. She cried as dozens of Chinese members of the church sang hymns for God to save China. After that, she said to Cheng Ruifang: "I feel as if I were Chinese. I'm distraught at the sight of my suffering motherland. I want to do something for her, even if it's just protecting the children from the shells and debris."

Determined to help the children of Nanjing, Vautrin went to three schools that afternoon to sing to and teach the children scared by the bombs, giving them just a moment of peace and happiness. When she saw the children smile as they looked at her, Vautrin felt as if she was the happiest person in the world.

After she said goodbye to the children, she went back to the college and stood in front of a statue of the Virgin Mary. Vautrin felt as if she was still closely linked with the students in the college's affiliated schools hundreds of miles away from Nanjing, like those in Shanghai, Wuhan and Chengdu. She prayed in pure serenity: "Children, I could hear you reading, singing and smiling. I know that you're becoming incredible young women. I'll always keep you in my prayers here and may God bless you."

Vautrin looked out to the sky every day and wondered if the children could hear her prayers.

Her students in the Chengdu school sent her a letter:

Miss Hua Qun, 20 people are participating in the celebration for the anniversary of the school. This year, the theme of the celebration activities is plants. Mr Chapman and his wife and all the students in our school participated. We all drew a hand, in the middle there's a school badge from our school to show that we all miss you and everyone else.

Her students in the Wuhan branch sent a letter via airmail. There had been 66 students and teachers who'd participated in the celebrations held in St Hilda's church in the city, which were lively but somewhat solemn. The children had a message for Vautrin:

It rained but our celebration activities were happy and everyone had a lot of fun. The theme of our activities was birds and nests because we're like birds who've flown away but we want to return to our nest soon.

Her students in the Shanghai school also sent a letter:

Although we could hear the bombs of the Japanese planes and the Chinese troops firing back as we celebrated, Miss Ruth and Madam Niu still sang songs as beautifully as usual.

Vautrin wrote in her diary that evening: "I feel as if I've been spoiled for staying in Nanjing; we received letters from three affiliate schools on the same day. This has been the happiest day so far."

When she woke up the next day, Vautrin, like all residents of Nanjing, was concerned about the weather. One of the Chinese members of the church said: "It's strange how much things have changed. Now we say that bad weather is good and good weather is bad. We all now make sure to go to church on rainy Sundays."

When the weather was bad, the citizens of Nanjing went out for a stroll or off to market, but when the weather was good, they hid inside air-raid shelters. However, the feelings of fear and helplessness stayed with them come rain or sun.

On 18 November, Vautrin first heard that her friends were preparing a safety zone for refugees and that it had been approved by the government with the praise of the American embassy. Smythe was one of the key members of the organisation, serving as its secretary. When he told Vautrin about the safety zone, she was instantly filled with questions. Was it true that the Japanese were going to attack Nanjing soon? Was Nanjing going to be destroyed? Would the Chinese troops be forced to retreat instead of getting trapped in Nanjing? Would there be looting or worse? How long was the fighting going to last? What could they do?

The embassy hinted that they knew that the Japanese would be attacking soon: "The embassy has prepared warships for you and you should leave soon. With each day you stay in Nanjing, you're putting yourself at more and more risk."

Vautrin said as she had many times before: "I'll only leave in a coffin."

Paxton from the embassy courteously accepted her decision as ever. Vautrin felt that the American diplomat was a very polite man who respected the will of others.

With the situation becoming ever bleaker, Vautrin wrote in her diary on Sunday 21 November:

> We saw that the wounded had gathered in groups all over the railway station. I think there were 200 people or so, but I'm not sure. With no doctors or nurses, some of the wounded were in great pain. Due to inadequate bedding, straw bags were used as quilts. There were other volunteers like us over there. We tried our best to comfort them. A soldier, whose eyes and nose had been seriously injured, was moaning in agony but we could do nothing but try to comfort him and tell him that we'd take him to hospital soon. Another wounded soldier's legs and buttocks had been damaged by bombs and his wounds hadn't been treated by doctors for a couple of days. I will never forget the smell of rotten flesh. When I returned home, I washed my hands with soap and water, but my hands still smelled. I then used facial cream and perfume, but it was no use. I can still smell it today.
>
> I hope that everyone who thought that it was necessary to fight in July and August gets to see the pitiful situation of so many of these wounded soldiers. I have no doubt that they'd admit that the war is a crime when seeing the results. These soldiers were just ordinary young men and children. They seemed to lack the training and equipment needed to fight in a modern war.
>
> I will never forget one of the poor men. When I passed in front of his stretcher, he asked me not to send him to hospital that evening. He said he was too relaxed and had been staying in the train station for two days, but he was in some pain. When I helped him adjust his seat to make him comfortable, I noticed that his bedding was sodden. I tried to find a quilt but only found some straw bags, so I just used them instead. He said that the previous foreign doctors had treated him very well and had given him drugs every day. He added: "You see, when I was last there, I said to the doctor that if I were a little bit younger I would have wanted him to adopt me." He smiled when he said it. I wondered who would look after these wounded and poor people in the months to come. There was no way they could go west. Would they be abandoned and end up as opium victims?

The next day, Principal Wu proposed and backed an emergency committee to be established at Jinling College to deal with the growing refugee problem, which was only expected to get worse. The fact that the Japanese had decided to attack and occupy Nanjing was obvious by now, so this committee was established to remedy the crisis. Vautrin enthusiastically supported the proposal when Principal Wu asked for her opinion. The first emergency committee meeting was held at 3pm that day. The participants discussed and identified several issues that needed to be dealt with during four stages. The first was the initial stages of the Battle of Nanjing, followed by when the Chinese military retreated. This was followed by the possibility of opportunistic criminals taking advantage as the troops and police fled the city. The final stage was when the Japanese occupied Nanjing. The committee consisted of five people, among whom three were men and two were women, namely Cheng Ruifang and Vautrin.

Cheng Ruifang said to Vautrin: "There's another emergency committee and they have more than 30 members in total."

"Great! We can help each other out," said Vautrin ecstatically when she heard the good news.

The college had been preparing for issues that they might face once the Japanese troops entered the city. Their priority was figuring out how they were going to dispose of the valuable equipment and assets left in the college. Transferring them was the first choice, followed by hiding them. However, having to make such choices was exhausting for Vautrin and her colleagues, who felt they were on the edge of a nervous breakdown. There was one more thing of prime importance left for Vautrin: working out how many people the college could hold and how many refugees there'd be in Nanjing. Rabe's safety zone was estimated to be able to hold more than 200,000 refugees. They'd also coordinated a plan with the governmental organisations that hadn't been evacuated. According to the plan, Jinling College was to hold approximately 200 to 1,000 refugees. Although numbers ranging from 200 to 1,000 were mentioned, Vautrin and Wu Yi-fang thought that even the lower end was still pushing it.

The college thought this way because they felt that they didn't have enough staff. In November, fewer than 30 people were staying at the school and able to work. If one person looked after 10 people, then 200 would be the maximum number of refugees who could take shelter in the college.

Rabe told Vautrin: "Nobody can predict how many refugees there'll be at the college. It could be 500, 1,000 or even more."

Losing control was the key concern, so after the first session of the emergency committee meeting was over, Vautrin went around the school to investigate how many women and children would be staying in Nanjing. After the establishment of the safety zone, the division of roles was clear. Jinling College was to mainly accommodate refugees who were women and children. Therefore, Vautrin felt that it was necessary to investigate what the situation of refugees in the area near the college would be.

25 November 1937 was Thanksgiving, an important festival for Americans. Thanksgiving in 1937 was special for Vautrin in a way that no other Thanksgiving had been as she busied herself with decorating the college campus, showing her gratitude for all she had.

This was a very special project. Several women, including Wu Yi-fang, had proposed the idea of decorating Jinling College like an American style manor, turning it into an "island of life" to protect refugees from the Japanese troops who'd be forbidden from entering.

After considering the college's terrain, Vautrin and Cheng chose four noticeable highpoints and a thoroughfare in the college and placed flagpoles there to mark where refugees would not be allowed to go beyond. The first flagpole was placed on top of Xishan hill and the second one in between two houses for male teachers. The third one was placed at the corner of the gate house, while the fourth one was placed in between two houses for male teachers on Nanshan hill. Another flagpole was placed in the affiliated middle school.

Vautrin came up with the idea of flying American flags on the flagpoles. She wanted Wu Yi-fang to support her idea because of the fact that Jinling College was still closely linked to American Christian organisations doing missionary work in the area. Wu agreed: "I see nothing wrong with this. Jinling College was founded by American churches, so the Japanese would probably understand."

"We should find the two signs we used to have on top of the college gates," suggested Wu Yi-fang. She'd been one of the first graduates of the college and asked Vautrin and Cheng to do whatever they could to find two old signs from back then that had "American Women's College" written on them in Chinese and English.

Although Vautrin had been at the college for 19 years now, she found this difficult because this had happened before her time there.

"I remember that there were some old things in the attic," said Cheng.

Vautrin and Cheng then scoured through dusty boxes and trunks in the attic. They later found an old sign with "Jinling College" written on it, which had been used before registration with the Nationalist government. Unfortunately, they failed to find the one they wanted.

"We may as well use this one now." Vautrin thought that the sign they'd found may be of some use. However, as soon as they took the sign, they noticed that "American Women's College" was miraculously written on the reverse.

Cheng Ruifang, a woman who seldom talked, let alone laughed, burst out into laughter.

Vautrin was also delighted, although she noticed that the characters were covered by a layer of thick red oil paint. Nonetheless, the message was still clear.

Cheng came up with the idea of filling in the gaps in the characters obscured by the paint. Vautrin thought it was a great idea and ecstatically held the old sign, touching it with her face.

After finding out what had happened, Wu Yi-fang was relieved and remarked that the universe works in mysterious ways.

Principal Wu had to leave. She was a government official and had been persuaded by Chiang Kai-shek's wife to leave Nanjing straight away. It was an order from the government and all important organisations and Chinese nationals had to leave Nanjing. Vautrin was incredibly saddened by the news, but later thought that it was better for her to leave because all the affiliated schools and most of the college's students had left Nanjing too, so they needed their principal to be with them.

Now, Vautrin was the most senior member of staff out of everyone left at Jinling College.

"Our school now has five students, and is perhaps the only school still running in Nanjing. The students still want to go to school," said Vautrin proudly.

As long as Nanjing stood strong, Jinling College would stay open.

A Solitary Island of Life

On 28 November, thunderous noises echoed throughout Nanjing as flames lit up the sky. Stray dogs whined in grief and people trembled with fear. The last days of November 1937 were surely the last peaceful days in Nanjing as the Japanese surrounded the city.

Nanjing had turned into a lonely island and everyone was in a state of total panic. Those with power and wealth in the capital fled, leaving behind the poor and some foreign missionaries, their dedicated disciples and a few doctors and volunteers. The defending troops took up a large proportion of the city's population, but they weren't in control of the city. Vautrin glumly looked at the chaos and wrote about that day in her diary:

Depression now dominated Nanjing as some thought the Japanese would arrive in three days while others claimed it would be several weeks. Some of the gates were shut that day to prevent soldiers and police from defecting to the Japanese. In turn, the wounded were also prevented from entering the city.

I went to a meeting at the embassy at 10 o'clock, which was also attended by Thorne from the theological seminary, the young Christian Fitch, Bates from the University of Nanjing and Trimmet from Gulou Hospital. Mr Paxton talked about the possibility of looting and the danger it posed. He said that foreigners should leave Nanjing as quickly as possible and those who couldn't leave now should be prepared to evacuate and board the *USS Panay* when the embassy staff transferred there. If the gates were shut, two places had been singled out by the embassy as rendezvous points that could be reached by climbing over the wall with ropes. We were then required to state our decisions or the decisions of our institutions. Bates and I thought that it was our responsibility to stay, and they respected and accepted our opinion.

Today, fewer than 20 people went for mass at the Drum Tower church, but more than 90 people attended mass at our school, not for communion, but to make sure that they could get into the college before any emergencies. We promised that we'd go to great lengths to protect the women and children, but that we could only let them in when the situation got incredibly bad. We also told them that they were only allowed to bring in bedding and food, no cases.

I was on my way from Shanghai Road to Mingde Middle School at 2.30pm. My heart sank as I kept bumping into women and children looking for the safety zone as they had heard about it and wanted to find where it was. I had to stop and explain to them that the precise location of the safety zone hadn't been decided yet and the municipal government would notify them once it had been. They looked like lost sheep without a shepherd.

I walked along Zhongshan Road to attend mass. Although it was an important road, it was empty and desolate as shops on both sides of the road were closed. Only four kinds of vehicles were still on the road, namely, military trucks loaded with war equipment like antiaircraft guns, ambulances carrying military officers, mule carts and rickshaws carrying the poor and their belongings.

All the post offices were closed except for the one in Xiaguan. The location of the safety zone was yet to be decided. Journalists from Reuters recommended that if women and children were allowed to seek shelter at our school, we should inform the Japanese commander about it through the American embassy. Although I wasn't happy about being the sole woman at the earlier meeting, I could still feel the value of my contribution.

It was now December 1937. The cold was pressing in on Nanjing as it suffocated in the smoke of war. Early in the morning of 1 December, huge explosions were heard echoing around the city, which, needless to say, were caused by the Japanese bombs. Vautrin wrote about the atmosphere:

> As we were just about to go to the Drum Tower church, the siren sounded followed by the Japanese planes bombing the city soon after. Dr Wilson later told me that the air-raid had taken place near the west flowery gate built during the Qing Dynasty. He told me that a mother and her daughter had been killed in the explosion as I lamented that it was the poor who were being forced to go through all the suffering. When Wilson found the father, who was numb with grief, he was still holding his child, whose head had been half blown off. I felt sorry for the Chinese soldiers when I heard that 50 wounded soldiers had walked 20 miles to Nanjing. They told me that many of their wounded comrades had died along the way.

Vautrin was now tireless in her humanitarian work. In order to help the refugees settle in the college, she oversaw people as they cleared out as many rooms as possible in the dormitories, science building, humanities building and the central hall.

"Make sure that the refugees won't be sleeping on the floor. Put down a layer of straw or some wooden boards, otherwise the children may get frostbite," instructed Vautrin patiently.

Standing on the lawn, Vautrin held a flag and instructed her assistants on how to deal with the incoming refugees: "If you're bringing a refugee into the school, you should tell her where to settle down and warn her about the importance of personal hygiene. People from the same family should be kept together. Refugees can only be taken to a new building when one building is fully occupied."

Her team was poorly staffed. Apart from Cheng Ruifang and several workers, the rest were the children of faculty members who'd stayed at the school. Despite their young age, they were just as hardworking as the others.

Women and children clutching bedding and bags were now gathering in front of the gate, calling out Vautrin's name and begging for entry. They obviously knew her because they lived close to Jinling College.

She busied herself with welcoming the refugees while instructing her guides inside: "Bring them to the affiliated school because everything is ready there. Be quick and help them settle down, but bring them some water to drink first."

Not many refugees arrived the first day, but Vautrin was already exhausted. She had just found a suitable place for an 80 year old lady when a three year old child defecated in the corridor.

Vautrin returned to her dormitory late that night, completely exhausted. She looked into the mirror before going to bed, thinking to herself: "I feel 20 years older already."

On 9 December, the city was abuzz with rumours and the people were convinced that one thing was certain: the Japanese were coming.

"Why are there flames in the northwest? Are the Japanese bombing us again?" asked Vautrin as she saw billowing clouds of smoke rising from the northwest early in the morning, with flames rising up to the heavens.

Cheng told her that the Chinese army had started the fire following a scorched earth policy. They burned down buildings and houses on the outskirts of the city - close to the city walls - out of fear that the Japanese would use them to take cover when they attacked.

"Will it work?" asked Vautrin incredulously, thinking it was a foolish strategy.

Cheng replied: "We have no idea. But it means that a large number of refugees have lost their houses and are flowing into the city. We might have more refugees coming today."

As predicted, Vautrin and her team received more than 300 refugees that day, with some of them coming all the way from Wuxi, more than 100 miles away. The refugees told them that the Japanese were killing everyone along the way and they had to flee to the capital. Some refugees explained: "Nanjing is where Generalissimo Chiang is. We figure that it must be safer than our hometowns and we'd rather die together with the officials in the capital."

This was tragic. How were they supposed to know that Nanjing had become considerably more dangerous than their remote hometowns? The officials the poor had fled to had already turned tail and ran. Vautrin felt extremely sorry for them.

Vautrin attended a press conference every night. The conference was held as usual that night, but Vautrin noticed that no one from the Chinese authorities was present, except for two journalists and two low level officials. The rest of the attendees were all foreign missionaries like Bates and Smythe.

Just 10 minutes into the meeting, there was a deafening roar that shook the room.

"Bomb! There's a bomb! We have to get out of here!" someone cried out.

Rabe turned to his colleagues in the International Committee and said: "Perhaps there won't be a conference tomorrow."

Vautrin returned back home and found that a flowerpot had fallen off her windowsill. Refugees complained to her in tears about their tragic suffering when she went to visit them. A woman told her that she had come to Nanjing to run an errand, but her 12 year old daughter had been denied entry while she couldn't get back out of the city. She pled: "My daughter is at the Guanghua gate. She was almost beaten to death there. She's in danger! Have pity on me, please help me find her!" The woman sat on the ground, crying her heart out. Nobody could help her. Vautrin despaired when she realised that she didn't know what she could do.

A girl from Sanchahe was frantically looking for her mother. Vautrin asked her where her mother was. She said she couldn't remember, only that they'd been separated from each other at the school gate. Vautrin discussed the matter with Cheng, wondering if her mother was in the calligraphy school nearby. "Come with me, I'll take you there to look for her," said Vautrin. They hurried to the school with the girl and found her mother there. They cried on each other's shoulders as soon as they were reunited.

Vautrin was dismayed when she found out that the school had already received more than 1,500 refugees. She believed that more refugees would likely come into her school the following day. What could they do next? She and Principal Wu had originally only planned to shelter 1,000 refugees at the very most. Only two days had passed. Vautrin rushed back to the college wondering what tomorrow would bring.

The next day was 10 December. Nanjing had been surrounded by the Japanese. The ancient Chinese capital was now stuck in the middle of a brutal war as conditions got ever worse. All of the streets were empty, apart from a few homeless refugees who had either been shot dead or were frantically looking for shelter.

"Come in! Quickly!" shouted staff as refugees gathered in a large crowd at the front and back doors of the humanities college. Soon, the former teachers' dormitory was full and the refugees began to occupy the central hall. Some of the refugees stranded outside the gate carried bricks and started building their own shelter. A small house was built quickly and several straw mats covered the roof, without the help of any masons.

"Ms Hua, come and see my house. What do you think of it?" A man proudly showed his recently built home to Vautrin. She was amazed but wondered whether it was safe or not.

However, the limited space in the school was only available to women and children, so it was great to see people, especially the men, being able to build shelters for themselves. Vautrin decided she liked the idea after all.

Explosions were heard suddenly as Vautrin was about to go through the gate. She felt the earth shake and almost fell to the ground. She managed to keep herself upright by holding on to the wall beside her. She turned her head and looked around in shock. The bombs must have been dropped on the theological seminary hundreds of metres away from the humanities college. Dust and flames left by the bombs seemed to have left her school isolated from the outside world. She thought to herself ominously that the college would soon become a solitary island of life once again.

At the gate, the mother who'd lost her 12 year old daughter was searching desperately among the confused crowd of refugees. Vautrin wondered where they'd all come from.

On 10 December, Vautrin's assistant Cheng Ruifang, who was also in charge of sanitation in the fourth district of the safety zone, noted in her diary:

> Number 700 is fully occupied today. People are on their way to the safety zone or our college. No vehicles are running on the streets, leaving people of all ages and both genders carrying their own belongings in spite of the bombings. The scene is tragic. Newly built houses have been occupied by refugees, some of whom pay rent while some have just moved in with no agreement whatsoever. Several buildings, including the newly built library, have been occupied by the refugees in Jinling College. Makeshift shelters have also been pitched to accommodate more refugees, including men and women, while we only provide shelter for women and children. The family members of the refugees will deliver meals as cooking is not allowed, and we will provide food to those who can't feed themselves. Water is also provided so that people can wash their faces and drink three times a day. We have to provide and deliver water to more than 1,000 people twice a day, which is exhausting. We are now preparing to build a congee station across the street so that everybody can live off congee within a matter of days. However, it's easier to deal with food than sanitation. Some have fled without taking their close stools, so children defecate wherever they choose. We've prepared buckets for them to go in outside the courtyard. These ancient buildings are coloured with rags and handmade nappies hanging out of windows and off of tree trunks. People wash the stool buckets and nappies in the pond in number 100 while they wash clothes and dishes in the pond near the library.

What is a refugee zone? Two words can be used: dirty and chaotic. But nobody cares about that. Safety is the priority.

What concerned Vautrin more was that some of the female refugees had recently given birth. On the morning of 11 December, she heard two women crying as their babies had died; one had suffocated while the other had been sick for some time. Cheng told her that five or six other female refugees were about to give birth.

"Pay more attention to the women and the newborn babies," Vautrin instructed. She was horrified and felt as if she'd lost her own children despite never having been a mother. Her maternal instinct made her incredibly sensitive.

12 December was the last day before the fall of Nanjing, as well as the most chaotic before it fell. Absolutely everyone, from the chief commander of the defending troops to the cats and dogs in the streets, seemed to be at a loss at what to do next. General Tang Shengzhi was busy carrying out Chiang's orders to retreat early in the morning and he finally evacuated from Xiaguan with the help of his security guards, leaving tens of thousands of defending soldiers in total chaos.

Stray cats and dogs, confused and disoriented by the bombs and bullets, gazed at the panicked people as they fled.

Vautrin noted down what happened that day in her diary, which may be the most accurate description of the events:

Sunday 12 December

It is 8.30pm. Violent gunfire can be heard in the southwest of the city while I'm writing this. The window is shaking so I'm sitting away from it in case it shatters. There have been air raids all day, and some say that the Japanese have already entered the city. The veracity of these claims I cannot verify. A soldier told our gatekeeper that the Japanese had broken through the Guanghua gate several times but were eventually beaten back. We also heard that the 87th division is replacing the 88th division, but to my regret, no Chinese troops have marched past the safety zone today.

At tonight's press conference, word had it that the commander-in-chief, Tang Shengzhi, is unable to control his troops any longer. Many places have been robbed, but not the safety zone. Judging from the explosions, I'm afraid the ancient city walls may have been reduced to nothing. Now Japanese planes are free to come and go, dropping bombs without interference from Chinese antiaircraft or planes.

I think it's a shameful mistake to burn down all the buildings outside the city walls and some of the buildings inside them. Who suffers? The poor Chinese! Why not leave the city intact?

I went to the Drum Tower church this morning at 10.30. There were about 68 people in the church. A member from the church's emergency committee gave a great sermon. Many refugees have settled in the courtyard of the church.

Now the gunfire has stopped and I have no idea whether this means that the Japanese have taken the city.

Refugees keep flowing into the college campus and three buildings are already fully occupied. Now the arts building is beginning to take refugees. Unfortunately, the congee station managed by the Red Cross isn't open yet, so the days are rough for the refugees who didn't bring any food with them. The station may be open at 9am tomorrow as we have repeatedly urged them to open. But if the city falls into enemy hands tonight, there'll be absolute chaos.

Something interesting has happened during this crisis. A tailor called Guan living across the East Gate Street allowed members of the New Life Movement committee to deposit some things in one of his rooms before they evacuated from Nanjing. Now that the Japanese are coming, he's more and more worried. Today I called Mr Fitch and together we asked him to destroy any documents. We also assured him that we'd accept responsibility for the destruction. Along with his wife and other relatives, Guan carried piles of documents to burn in our incinerator. They sweated the entire afternoon, destroying all the materials in time. Judging from the gunfire, the Japanese have entered the city.

Lin, the ever-capable superintendent of the central hall, has lost his voice from shouting tonight, trying to get the refugees to keep the floor clean. He told the gatekeeper this afternoon that trying to keep the children from urinating in public was killing him. The gatekeeper asked: "Why don't you just tell them to stop?" Lin replied in a hoarse voice: "Of course I tell them! But as soon as I turn around, they do it again."

I was on my way to the English department when I saw that a strip of land covering one third of the top of Purple Mountain was on fire. I had no idea how the fire had started, but it meant that many pine trees were being destroyed.

Mr Chen and I made the rounds at the campus between 9pm and 10pm. A worker from the washhouse called Hu and his neighbours had all arrived as they were worried that retreating soldiers may come for young girls in their houses. Many in the city are sure to stay up tonight. I can see from the apartment that flames are still roaring in the south of the city and so is Xiaguan. I will have to sleep in my clothes tonight in case I need to get up quickly. I hope this dark chapter ends soon.

Many thoughts must have rushed through Vautrin's mind, who loved China and regarded it as her second home.

13 December was the first day of the Japanese occupation. Everybody in the city seemed to be numb with fear, not knowing what the Japanese troops would do to them or what they could do themselves. Could they flee? Where would be safe?

There was indeed a safety zone in the city, but how could a few dozen foreigners be able to stand up to tens of thousands of invaders? Still, the safety zone was safer than the people of Nanjing's homes. With this in mind, the former defending soldiers got out of their uniforms and fled with the civilians and their families to the safety zones, including Jinling College.

"This is an all-girls school. Men cannot enter!" Cheng Ruifang and the others were able to prevent men from entering at first, but it was impossible as time went on. Two soldiers who feared the Japanese more than the safety zone staff climbed over the walls before they had time to change their uniforms.

"If the Japanese come and find you here, we will all be in danger!" shouted some of the support staff as they grabbed the soldiers.

"Please! We have nowhere to hide! If we go on the streets, the Japanese will behead us! Please! We beg you," begged the two soldiers as they knelt on the ground.

"Let them in! Take off your uniforms quickly!" Vautrin passed by and gestured to her assistant to let them in.

The two soldiers immediately kowtowed.

Vautrin just shook her head. She couldn't even remember how many cases like this she'd had to deal with today. Everyone in Nanjing was running for their lives while Vautrin and her colleagues had to manage hundreds of problems at once.

She recorded that day:

Apparently, the Japanese entered the city through the Guanghua gate at 4am. The gate in the south was said to have been under heavy artillery fire all night. Still, I thought it was in the west of the city. There was also heavy fighting inside the city. I couldn't sleep that night. While I was half asleep, I could hear the Japanese chasing after the retreating Chinese soldiers and firing at them. All of us were sleeping in our clothes in case of any emergencies.

After 5am, I got up and went to the front gate of the school, where everything was very calm. But the gatekeeper said a large number of soldiers had passed through the front gate. Some had even begged citizens to give them clothes. That morning, we found many military uniforms in the campus. Our neighbours tried to come in, but we tried to convince them that if they went to the safety zone they'd be as safe as us, anywhere in the safety zone was safe for them.

In the morning, the congee station in front of our school finally opened. We gave out breakfast to each dormitory building in order of when the refugees had arrived at the school. This meal ended at 10.30am. We served another meal in the afternoon.

At 4pm, we were told that there were several Japanese soldiers on the western side of the hilltop. I went to examine the situation at the Nanshan apartment. There were indeed several Japanese soldiers standing on top of the western hill. Soon, another worker called me and said there was a Japanese soldier breaking into our grounds to get chicken and other food. I immediately rushed over and told him that the chickens were not for sale.

After fierce shelling and bombing, the city was unusually quiet. Three kinds of danger had finally passed: soldiers looting the city, planes bombing the city and artillery bombarding the city. But we still had the fourth danger to face; our fate was in the hands of the victorious Japanese army. That night, everyone was very anxious because they didn't know what was going to happen.

At 7.30pm, the unit that was responsible for reporting to us said that Japanese soldiers were looting the house that had rice reserves opposite the school gate. I tried to get in touch with the leader of this group of Japanese soldiers, but I had no luck. Their guards at the entrance looked like monsters; they were truly loathsome. Later, I met President Rabe to discuss the matter. He said they would solve the problem tomorrow. But all of us agreed that we had to be cautious in dealing with this issue.

There were no lights and no water in Nanjing that night. There were no telephones nor telegraphs, not to mention newspapers or radio. All of us had been separated from the world.

This was a lonely island of life.

On 14 December, Japanese soldiers in Nanjing arrested and killed people everywhere, mainly targeting the Chinese soldiers who hadn't fled the city, dropping their arms and hiding throughout Nanjing. Blood flowed like a stream on the streets as the Japanese "mopping-up" operations began, which were directed at Rabe's safety zone.

People staying in the safety zone at the time didn't know what was happening outside, and few knew that Japanese soldiers were rushing over to them with their bayonets in hand. Vautrin realised that they could only operate within their limited power.

The following is from Cheng Ruifang's diary:

Today, more and more people came because the Japanese soldiers had broken into their houses in broad daylight to steal money and rape women. Many people were stabbed to death on the street. The situation was similar in the safety zone, but places outside the safety zone were much worse. No one dared to go out; the victims who were stabbed to death were mostly young men. Today, the third floor of building number 500 was filled with civilians. At midday, seven soldiers jumped over the bamboo fence behind building number 300. But Miss Watson wasn't here, so we had to let it go. Master Wei sent a message to Gulou Hospital this morning, but he didn't come back tonight. Perhaps he was caught by the Japanese soldiers. There were many people being dragged away on the street, their present whereabouts and situation are unknown. There are now 4,000 to 5,000 people staying at Jinling College.

As Cheng mentions, by 14 December, Jinling College had already received 4,000 to 5,000 refugees. "We're too busy! Too overworked!" Cheng Ruifang said to Vautrin about the situation that day.

But this time Vautrin seemed to be more concerned with what was happening off-campus as the Japanese were slaughtering the Chinese soldiers who'd laid down their arms in Xiaguan.

She was only able to accurately verify the disaster after hearing more than one witness's account. She made the following entry about the incident:

It seems that the city walls were still being bombarded heavily by artillery before dawn. Perhaps they were trying to clear away the roadblocks hindering the Japanese troops' advance into the city. There are occasional gunshots. Maybe the Japanese soldiers are opening fire on the retreating Chinese soldiers or on the looters. I can still hear gunshots from Xiaguan. In my imagination, these bullets are being fired at Chinese soldiers who are sitting on a crowded sampan, desperately trying to go north on the river. Poor people. They have almost no chance of escaping the merciless bullets.

Vautrin had a clear idea of the massacre that was happening in Xiaguan and elsewhere, and it was by no means just her "imagination". As a pacifist missionary, when it came to a woman's role in war, Vautrin said:

In my opinion, everyone has their duty in war, so everyone who supports the war against Japan should volunteer to help. Women can work in the hospitals and provide clothing and comfort to wounded soldiers. A lot of work needs to be done to equip and maintain a force, and even a schoolgirl can play a significant role. In high school or college, schoolgirls can participate in the military or the Red Cross, or they can go to social services departments. When the war ends, women and young people are going to face even more onerous tasks and will need to take care of the widows and orphans of fallen soldiers, not to mention help the injured and disabled soldiers.

We missionaries always believe that war is a crime; it is a sin contrary to the spirit of God's creation. We can dedicate our own strength to innocent victims, to citizens whose homes have been burned or looted or to those who have been wounded by aircraft and artillery during the war, and we can help them recover.

Vautrin had love and compassion for others and hated seeing the senseless brutality committed by the Japanese soldiers against Chinese women.

There were many reports from elsewhere in the city that the Japanese soldiers were grabbing girls and raping them. When she found out, Vautrin angrily told Cheng that: "We will never allow the Japanese to do this here!"

When she was making her way back to the college from a meeting held in the safety zone headquarters, Vautrin found that the school gate was being guarded by Japanese soldiers. She walked up to the gate at once, ready to struggle against them if they tried to take away any female refugees.

"You shouldn't be here!" shouted a Japanese soldier holding a gun as he raised Vautrin's dress with his bayonet, motioning at her to leave. Vautrin was determined and said: "This is my school. I have an obligation to guard the gate."

The Japanese soldiers had no choice but to stand aside. But she could see from their eyes that they were planning another way to deal with her.

15 December saw even more refugees squeezing into the college campus. For more than 10 hours from morning to night, except for a break for dinner, Vautrin personally stood in the gateway to prevent accidents, watching the steady stream of refugees entering the campus. Several groups of Japanese soldiers came, but when they saw American women with Red Cross emblems on their sleeves, they had to walk away despondently.

The campus was incredibly overcrowded. Vautrin and Cheng initially estimated that at least 3,000 new refugees had arrived. Vautrin said: "Someone said that having a place on the grass would be enough for them, but I don't think we have enough room even for that."

The most distressing part of it was that innumerable refugees complained to her about the misfortunes they and their families had suffered. Japanese soldiers had killed their husbands or sons; their daughters or they had been raped or gang-raped by Japanese soldiers. Vautrin was outraged.

"Today is a nightmare, it's the darkest day I've ever experienced," said Fitch, Vautrin's friend, on 16 December. Vautrin agreed with him.

Vautrin's diary entry from 16 December is as follows:

At 10am, Jinling College was subjected to an official inspection as Japanese soldiers thoroughly searched for Chinese soldiers. More than 100 Japanese soldiers came to the campus and headed straight for the buildings to search them. They asked us to open all the doors. If we were unable to find the keys for a short while, the Japanese soldiers would become very impatient. One of them even took an axe with him to chop down the doors. When the search began, my heart sank. I knew that there were hundreds of cotton padded wounded soldiers' uniforms in the geography department office upstairs. These clothes had been made by women in the National Salvation Association. We had no time to deal with these clothes. We didn't want to burn them because we knew that plenty of poor people were in dire need of winter coats. I led the Japanese soldiers to a room that entered to the left side of the room. The Japanese wanted to enter the room from the next door, but I didn't have the key. Fortunately, there were more than 200 women and children there, which distracted the attention of the Japanese soldiers. After dark, we burned all the clothes. Mr Kurt also threw his gun into a pond.

The Japanese soldiers seized our workers twice. These Japanese troops said they were Chinese soldiers and tried to take them away. But I said: "They're not soldiers, they're coolies." They were able to escape the certainty of being shot or stabbed to death. They searched all the buildings where the refugees live. Four Japanese soldiers, one of whom was a junior officer, wanted something to drink. So, we took them to Ms Cheng's dormitory. At the time, we didn't know that six machine guns had been set up in the campus while even more Japanese soldiers stood guard outside, getting ready to open fire in case anyone tried to flee. Before the highest ranking officer left, I wrote a letter for him confirming that there were only women and children here, which could help us keep out the other small groups of Japanese soldiers outside the school gates for the rest of the day.

Shortly after midday, a small group of Japanese soldiers came through the side door of the former infirmary. If I hadn't been there, they might have taken Tang's brother away. Afterwards, they went up the road and demanded to go into the laundry room, but I arrived in time then as well. If the Japanese doubted anyone, their fate would be the same as the four Chinese men tied up behind the Japanese soldiers. The Japanese brought the four men to the western hill. I heard gunshots soon after.

Nanjing has seen every crime imaginable today. Yesterday, 30 students were taken away from the language school. Today, I heard dozens of stories of girls being taken away last night. One of the girls was only 12 years old. The Japanese also looted food, bedding and money. They robbed $55 from Mr Lee. I imagine that every family in the city has had their home broken into and repeatedly robbed. Tonight, a car containing eight to 10 women passed by the college. When the car drove by, the girls in the car shouted for help. The later gunshots on the street and hill made me realise the tragic fate of some of these people, and they probably weren't Chinese soldiers. I spent most of the day keeping watch at the front gate or being called away to deal with other issues, like Japanese soldiers entering the school one group after another.

Tonight, Master Chen, the caretaker of our Nanshan apartment, came over and said that there was a light in one of the houses. My heart sank and I thought that Japanese soldiers must have occupied it. I went to have a look and found that it was Bates and Riggs as they'd forgotten to turn the light off.

The administrator of the science building, Master Chen's son, was taken away this morning. Another man, a Chinese man called Wei, hasn't returned yet either. We wanted to do something but didn't know what we could do. The city is in chaos so I cannot leave the school.

Tonight, Nanjing has become a sad, broken and empty shell of its former self. The streets are empty, all the houses are dark, it's full of terror.

I don't know how many innocent, hardworking farmers and workers were killed today. We asked all women over the age of 40 to go home and stay with their husbands and sons, only allowing their daughters and daughters-in-law to stay here. We've had to take care of more than 4,000 women and children tonight. I don't know how long we'll be able to stand this kind of pressure. It is an unspeakable terror.

From a military point of view, the occupation of Nanjing might be considered a victory for the Japanese, but it's an abject moral failure for them. It is Japan's national disgrace. This will destroy the future of Japanese friendship and cooperation with China and they have lost the respect of the citizens of Nanjing forever.

If only someone with a conscience in Japan knew what is happening in Nanjing. God, please stop these bloodthirsty Japanese soldiers, comfort the heartbroken parents of the innocent victims of today's massacre and watch over the vulnerable young women and girls during the long nights. May peace soon be upon us.

Vautrin got up several times that long and cruel night and prayed for her beloved Nanjing and the thousands of women and children staying in her campus. Her hatred for the occupying army grew and grew.

17 December was a day of celebration for the Japanese occupying forces. Their supreme commander Matsui was going to arrive as tens of thousands of Japanese soldiers held a grand ceremony for his entry into the city at the Zhonghua gate. However, this day was the most humiliating day for the citizens of Nanjing.

Vautrin thought that it was a disgrace. To protect the refugees on the campus, she confronted the Japanese soldiers that day. They slapped her and repeatedly shouted verbal abuse.

She wrote a very long entry in her diary that day, but every word and sentence it contains serves as a direct and powerful testimony of the massacre and the crimes that the Japanese have tried to deny:

> I arrived at the school gate at 7.30am and sent a letter to Mr Thorne, who was with Cheng. The Red Cross congee station needed coal and rice supplies. A lot of tired and frightened women arrived complaining of a horrible night. Japanese soldiers had come to their houses to harass them and everyone from a 12 year old girl to a 60 year old woman had been raped. Their husbands were forced to leave the bedrooms, while pregnant women's stomachs were cut open with bayonets. If only the Japanese people who have a conscience knew of these crimes. I hope that people here have time to document every miserable thing that's happened to them, especially the experiences of these young women who've blackened their faces and cut off their hair. The gatekeeper said they'd started arriving at 6.30am.
>
> Throughout the morning, I had to run around the gate and the side door where the Japanese soldiers had appeared, as well as Nanshan and the dormitories. I went there twice at breakfast and lunch today too. Over the past few days, I haven't had a meal without being interrupted by workers turning to me for help saying things like: "Miss Vautrin, three Japanese soldiers have broken into the science building."
>
> I spent all afternoon at the school gate managing the traffic and preventing refugees' fathers, brothers and other people with food and daily necessities from entering the campus. Originally, there were more than 4,000 refugees on the campus, and now 4,000 more people have arrived. The issue of food has become very complicated so we have to be cautious when choosing who can come in.
>
> The continuous influx of people has made us struggle to keep up with all the problems, with one coming after another. Even if there was enough room, we don't have enough time or energy to manage all of them. We got in contact with the University of Nanjing and opened one of their dormitories. A foreigner would be sent to guard it all night. From 4pm to 6pm, I received two large batches of women and children. It was truly heartbreaking as frightened young girls, tired women and their children, carrying bedding and clothes, hobbled over towards us. I was very glad that I walked along with them because we came across several groups of Japanese soldiers searching house to house all the way back. These soldiers were carrying all sorts of things that they'd looted from the houses.

Fortunately, Mary Twinam was on campus at the time so I thought I was able to leave for a while. When I returned, she told me that at 5pm, two Japanese soldiers had come in and saw the large American flag flying in the centre of the lawn. They pulled it down from the flagpole and tried to remove it, but the flag was too heavy to be loaded onto a bike, so they threw the flag on a mound in front of the science building. Mary found them in the electrical room. When she confronted them about it, they blushed and said they didn't think they'd done anything wrong.

When we finished our dinner, a boy in the central hall ran over to us and told us that there were many Japanese soldiers walking towards the campus dormitories. I saw two soldiers pushing on the door of the central hall, insisting that it be opened. I said that I didn't have any keys. A Japanese soldier said: "There are Chinese soldiers here, they're Japan's enemy." I replied: "No, there are no soldiers here." Mr Lee standing beside me also said the same thing. They slapped me in the face and also hit Lee hard as they continued to try to open the door. I pointed to a side door and let them in. They looked around upstairs and downstairs, seeming to look for Chinese soldiers. When we left we saw that two other Japanese soldiers had tied up three of our workers. They said: "Chinese soldiers." I said: "No, they're not soldiers, they're just workers and gardeners." They really were workers and gardeners. The Japanese soldiers took them out front and I went along with them. When I got to the front door, I saw a large number of Chinese people being forced to kneel down along the side of the road, including Mr Chen, Mr Xia and some of our other employees. A Japanese sergeant and his men were there. Ms Cheng and Mary also soon arrived after being escorted there by the Japanese. They asked who was in charge of the school, and I said I was. So, they asked me to identify every one of the workers. Unfortunately, some of the newcomers had only been recently hired for help, and one of them looked like a soldier, so he was brutally dragged to the left side of the road and carefully examined. When I went to identify the workers, Mr Chen tried to say something to help me, but he was brutally beaten by the Japanese soldiers and was taken to the right side of the road, where they forced him to kneel down.

We prayed for God's help during the entire ordeal. Then a car arrived carrying Fitch, Smythe and Mills. Mills then stayed and spent the night with us. The Japanese soldiers forced them out of the car and to stand in a row after taking off their hats. They also frisked them to check whether they'd brought a gun with them. Fortunately, Fitch and the sergeant could both speak a little French, which helped with communication. At first, they insisted that all foreigners and Ms Cheng and Mary leave, but when I said that this wasn't the time to leave my home, they eventually changed their minds. They then let all the male foreigners drive away. The prisoners of the Japanese were either standing or kneeling. We then heard screams and cries and also saw someone come out of the side door. I guessed that it must have been Japanese soldiers taking away a large number of male workers. We later discovered the trick used by the Japanese soldiers: they would trap the people in charge of guarding the front door and get three or four soldiers to pretend to investigate and track down Chinese soldiers, while other soldiers would take women from the main building. When they were finished with their dirty trick, the Japanese soldiers took Mr Chen out of the front door and we didn't expect to see him again. When they left, we were still unsure whether the Japanese soldiers really had left and were afraid that they were still outside and ready to shoot anyone who dared move.

I will never forget the scene as people knelt down on the side of the street, while Mary, Ms Cheng and I stood there. The howling wind rustled dead leaves. The women being taken away screamed in terror. While we stood there in silence, we were told that two women in the eastern courtyard were being taken away. We asked the person who told us to hurry over there. We prayed for Mr Chen and the others who'd been arrested and hoped that they would be released. I'm sure that even those who never prayed did so that night.

Time seemed to stand still. We stood in fear and didn't dare move for a long time. When it got to 10.45pm, we eventually decided to leave. The gatekeeper Du looked out of the door cautiously. No one was there. Then he quietly crept to the side door and found that it seemed to be closed too. All of us stood up and left. Ms Cheng, Mary and I went to the southeastern dormitories, which were empty. Ms Cheng's daughter-in-law and all her grandchildren were gone. I was terrified, but Ms Cheng calmly said that the other refugees must have hidden somewhere. Everything in her room had been turned upside down. It must have been robbed. We then went to the central building, Ms Cheng's family, Miss Wang, Miss He and Wu were all there. Later, Mary and I went to the affiliated school. What surprised me was that Mr Chen and Miss Luo were quietly sitting in my living room. When Chen told us his story, I thought it was a miracle that he'd survived.

On that day, Cheng Ruifang saw with her own eyes how Vautrin had been slapped by the Japanese soldiers and how the Japanese soldiers had bullied Vautrin's assistant Mr Chen. Cheng Ruifang wrote: "Even Miss Vautrin, who was an American, cannot avoid such suffering... This pain of being a citizen of a conquered country was truly unbearable. If it hadn't been for the country's revival, I would have struggled to survive. I wanted to commit suicide."

These are the outraged words of one of the many Chinese women forced to suffer. At this point, Vautrin, the "goddess of mercy", was suffering with similar depressed thoughts in silence. She became even busier with arranging the resettlement of refugees and tackling the never ending and complex problems.

Vautrin complained about the situation to Rabe and other members of the International Committee: "Early in the morning, terrified women, young girls and children flooded into the college. We can let them in, but we don't have anywhere to accommodate them. We told them that there's only room for them to sleep on the grass. Unfortunately, it's getting much colder now and they have to endure even more pain." She'd hoped that the members of the committee would be able to help her. However, she was told that the University of Nanjing and other places had accepted many more people than Jinling College. "President Rabe's home, which isn't that large, is now sheltering more than 600 people!" someone whispered to Vautrin.

Vautrin stopped complaining. They could only do so much. All the committee members had to concentrate on their individual efforts to help as many people as they could. It was a tragic situation for the citizens of Nanjing at the hands of the brutal Japanese soldiers.

Vautrin's biggest challenge was challenging the criminal Japanese soldiers. They often burst into the school armed with guns to look for girls, furiously shouting at Vautrin: "You! Why don't you let us in?" On the evening of the 17th, when Vautrin was busy throwing out a Japanese soldier, several other Japanese soldiers abducted 11 young women from the school right under Cheng Ruifang's nose.

"How could this have happened?" asked Vautrin furiously when she heard about the incident. As expected, the next morning, only 10 of the 11 people came back. They all hung their heads in shame and were embarrassed to appear in public. One woman told Vautrin that they'd all been raped by Japanese soldiers for the entire night, and some women were even raped more than 20 times. Vautrin was so livid that she uncharacteristically swore.

The Japanese soldiers likely knew that Jinling College was where most women were seeking refuge so they did whatever they could to sneak in and take girls, which kept Vautrin incredibly busy. Including her, there were only three foreign women at the school and only they could stop the Japanese soldiers. One time, when Cheng Ruifang tried to stop a team of Japanese soldiers from dragging a woman away, they immediately jabbed at her chest with bayonets and said: "If you dare stand in our way we'll take you away too!"

"This is an American school! You can't do this!" shouted Vautrin. Only when she appeared would the Japanese soldiers stop.

Sometimes the Japanese soldiers would get angry when they saw Vautrin. One time, several Japanese soldiers aggressively prodded Vautrin with their bayonets, determined to take away the girls and loot they'd just stolen.

Vautrin stood there motionless with her dignity intact as she glared at the Japanese soldiers who'd tried to threaten her.

The Japanese soldiers shouted as they took out their swords, about to strike down on Vautrin's head. They wanted to scare her off but the Japanese backed down first.

Vautrin stood still and sighed. Unmoved, she shouted: "Well?!"

Another time, several Japanese soldiers broke in when Vautrin and her colleagues were too busy to notice them. They tried to rape two women but Vautrin promptly stopped them. She shouted at them in outrage and they slipped away with an embarrassed look on their faces.

"We cannot just let them do whatever they want any more!" On the 18th, Vautrin went to visit the Japanese embassy accompanied by her secretary. She submitted a report on the numerous crimes that Japanese soldiers had committed in the campus to the Japanese diplomat and asked the embassy to do something about the situation immediately.

Vautrin's sense of justice and fairness impressed Tanaka, a Japanese diplomat, and he commented: "The only reason why any Chinese have survived the massacre at all is simply because of the joint efforts of these few foreigners in Nanjing."

This is true. The Chinese people will never forget those who offered their assistance in a way that no Chinese citizen could at that tough time.

Women and girls seeking safety had poured into Jinling College, which had made the burden on Vautrin and her colleagues even heavier. In the eyes of the refugees, Jinling College wasn't just an asylum that could provide them with temporary shelter, but a shrine to their chastity and life.

These women and their families would kneel down on the ground to beg Vautrin and her colleagues for shelter. Vautrin felt as if someone had plunged a knife into her heart. With tears in her eyes, she supported these poor women and their children and guided them into the campus. However, being in the college didn't mean that they were invulnerable to Japanese assaults.

Vautrin's actions are testimony of a sisterly bond that traversed nations, united in the struggle of being a woman at the time and determined to help each other in crisis.

Vautrin wrote in her diary on 19 December:

It was another terrible night last night. Many people were kneeling down outside the college gates asking me to give them shelter. I let them in although I really don't know where they are going to sleep tonight.

At 8am, a Japanese man came to the college with an officer from the Japanese embassy. We didn't have enough rice for the increasing amount of refugees so I asked the officer to take me to the safety area, and he agreed. In the International Committee headquarters, I took a German car to visit Mr Thorne, who was responsible for rice distribution. He promised me that he'd send rice to the college at 9am. I then took the same car back to 5 Ninghai Road as the only way to stop private cars from being sequestrated was to take a foreigner with you. On my way back to the school, I came across many people who kept asking me to bring their daughters or sisters with me to Jinling College. Among them was a mother who told me that her daughter had been a student at Zhonghua Middle School. Yesterday, her house was robbed repeatedly and she was no longer able to protect her own daughter.

When I arrived back on campus, I spent the rest of the morning running across the college from one corner to another, driving out groups of Japanese soldiers. I went to the Nanshan building twice and then to the backyard of the campus. After that, I was urgently summoned to the teaching staff building as two Japanese soldiers had apparently sneaked upstairs. In room 538, I saw one soldier keeping lookout by the door while the other was raping a girl. When they saw me and the letter from the Japanese embassy, they ran away quickly. If only I had the strength to beat them to death. I thought to myself about how ashamed the women in their own country would feel if they knew what terrible things these men had done. I was then called to the dormitories in the northwestern corner of the campus and found two Japanese soldiers stealing food. They ran away as soon as they noticed me.

The Japanese army robbed, murdered and raped civilians every day after they took Nanjing. A week after the occupation, the Japanese soldiers started to become especially interested in finding girls. They would rape and kill them. Jinling College had become a key safety area and, as a result, a week after the occupation, many women still flooded in with their children. Vautrin and her colleagues had initially only planned to accept and settle 200 to 1,000 refugees, but now, there were more than 10,000. Every inch of the campus was covered by these homeless refugees, including the lawn and paths. Cheng Ruifang and her colleagues were responsible for preparing meals for the refugees. All they had to eat every day was congee and they still needed a dozen large pots to make it. But how could they make so much congee? And how could they get so many pots? The refugees were unaware of any orders or rules so some would rush in and get more than one bowl of congee every day when they heard the meal time announcement. This meant that many vulnerable refugees didn't even get one bowl of congee to eat. The campus broke down into chaos with people crying and others stealing from fellow refugees. Cheng shouted to them: "Stand in the queue! Only people in the queue get congee!" Only in this way could she calm down the refugees and make sure that everyone got something to eat.

Giving them just one meal might be possible, but how could they keep giving them meals for an entire day or 10 days? Vautrin had to go to the International Committee and consult Rabe but he said that more than 10 refugees in the committee headquarters couldn't even have one bowl of congee a day.

"Does that mean we need to fix this problem alone?" asked Vautrin in a very concerned voice.

"Maybe there's an alternative..." suggested Rabe with a shrug.

"What alternative?" asked Vautrin immediately.

"Go to the Japanese and ask them for help."

Vautrin stared at Rabe and asked in surprise: "The Japanese? That's like a lamb asking a wolf if it's hungry!"

"You're likely right," said Rabe with a pained look. He continued: "But according to international law, an occupying army has a responsibility to ensure that the basic needs of refugees and prisoners of war are met."

"The Japanese don't care about international law. We have to come up with a solution ourselves. We have to figure out a way of feeding more than 10,000 people, not to mention providing healthcare, sanitation, and a whole range of other factors." Vautrin now knew that the only people she could depend on were her colleagues and herself.

But this didn't even tackle the most pressing issue. The greatest worry for women in the college was the Japanese raiding parties who threatened them every day in search of girls. If you didn't obey them, they would surely kill you. That isn't to say that many obedient victims weren't killed by the Japanese military.

"Ms Hua! Quick! Quick! Some Japanese soldiers are trying to rape women near the Nanshan building!"

"Terrible news Ms Hua! Some Japanese soldiers have somehow broken into the teaching staff dormitories! They're raping women in the dorm room!"

"Ms Hua! You have to save the girls! The Japanese soldiers are attacking them again!"

Vautrin was busy every second of 20 December, rushing back and forth from the Nanshan building to the central hall shouting at the Japanese to get out. Whenever they saw Vautrin, they quickly stopped raping and robbing. While they were angry with her, they had no choice but to run away. It wasn't because they were afraid of her, but because her identity as an American meant that she could go to the Japanese embassy and reveal their shameless crimes. Therefore, lecherous Japanese soldiers lurked in the shadows outside Jinling College, waiting for Vautrin to disappear so that they could sneak in and rape women.

Vautrin told Rabe that she wanted him to dispatch some voluntary police from other safety zones to the college to keep public order. Rabe helped and went to negotiate with the Japanese embassy on the issue. As a result, the embassy agreed to send a band of military policemen to the college. But not only did these military policemen eat food that was meant for the refugees, they also used their roles to take advantage of the women. This sent Vautrin into an even greater rage, remarking: "We'd rather guard the college ourselves than let a pack of wolves do it!"

The vulnerable refugees eventually created a volunteer army to fight back against the cruel guards. It was quite clear who was going to win and who was going to lose. Vautrin scared away groups of greedy guards with her characteristic courage and wisdom, making "Ms Hua" well known and liked among the citizens of Nanjing, who said: "If you want to avoid dying in the streets and being raped, then go to Ms Hua." With this, Jinling College once again became a shelter for women and children around the city and the number of refugees taking shelter there rapidly surged to more than 20,000.

But how could they settle and care for such a large number of refugees? Vautrin and her colleagues were overworked and barely even had time to complain about how exhausted they were. All the staff at the college had to work for 20 hours almost every single day. They were often disturbed during the other four hours when they were supposed to be sleeping. This was only the tip of the iceberg of their problems.

On 24 December, a senior officer in the Japanese army, a diplomat from the Japanese embassy and an interpreter arrived. They went to visit Vautrin and asked her to cooperate with them in choosing 100 women out of the refugees at the college to work as prostitutes for the army.

Vautrin was furious about their blatant disregard for the human rights of the Chinese women and she naturally turned them away.

But they were tenacious and warned Vautrin in a threatening manner: "If you can arrange a legal way for our soldiers to satisfy their sexual urges, the harassment here will decrease." What this really meant was: "If you don't do as we say, the college will never enjoy a single day of peace again."

"It's natural for prostitutes to do these things, there's no need to be ashamed," the interpreter told Vautrin.

"Only when they consent to it," snapped Vautrin.

"You can think over our requirements this afternoon," said the senior officer in an arrogant yet irritated tone. He then motioned to the others to follow him out. This was a clear final warning.

This had thrown Vautrin in a dilemma. If she responded to their unreasonable demands, would the prostitutes cooperate? Going to a Japanese military camp was a grave affair; she'd heard about prostitutes going to the camps with the Japanese soldiers but they seldom came back. Most of them were raped or beaten to death. Who'd be mad enough to provide sexual services to these barbarians?

After discussing the matter with her colleagues like Cheng Ruifang, Vautrin saw that her only option was to try to meet their demands. This scene was depicted in *The Flowers of War*, directed by Zhang Yimou. Twenty-one women who had previously worked as prostitutes volunteered and instead of being met with contempt by the other women, they were seen as heroes trying to save the others' lives. Vautrin felt grateful for them, as did the other refugees in the college.

All the refugees respectfully watched the first group of prostitutes getting into the Japanese trucks and being taken away.

But what about the 79 other prostitutes? Were the Japanese soldiers going to pick them out from the other women here? This was exactly what the refugees feared.

Cheng Ruifang was anxious about their safety as the Japanese army's brutality was notorious. All the refugees were openly panicking.

Vautrin stood up and shouted proudly: "As long as I am here, you are all safe!" The refugees, especially the female refugees, stared at her with eyes filled with trust and hope.

However, the women were still terrified about their fates.

"Please trust me everyone," said Vautrin as she consoled the refugees. However, Vautrin herself didn't even believe what she'd just said to them. She was also a vulnerable and unarmed woman. How could she fight back against so many Japanese soldiers?

For Vautrin, every second from that moment was torture.

Just before sunset, the Japanese trucks returned asking for 79 more prostitutes.

"This is impossible!" said Vautrin, refusing to agree.

"You dare say no to the Imperial Japanese Army?" One soldier aggressively pointed his bayonet at Vautrin's nose.

"It's not about me saying no to you, but what we discussed with your general and diplomat. We only agreed to offer you the working women who were willing to provide their services. They've all already gone with you earlier today. I cannot wantonly change the deal I have with your commander," responded Vautrin curtly.

"We're going to kill you one day!" shouted the soldier angrily in Japanese. But there was nothing more they could do, so they left in vain.

A burst of applause suddenly broke out around the campus, with cries calling Vautrin a "miracle worker" and "goddess". Women jumped in joy and many couldn't help crying. They were grateful for Vautrin's hard work to save them and their families.

During the Second Sino-Japanese War, especially in the Japanese occupied areas, life for women was never easy. With now more than 10,000 refugees in the college, many babies were being born there. "Two more babies were born today!" Cheng Ruifang reported to Vautrin. Cheng was the only nurse on campus and she voluntarily delivered the babies. While giving birth is difficult at the best of times, it was made a truly arduous affair in this chaotic refugee camp.

"We have to do everything we can to keep the mothers and babies alive," Vautrin told Cheng. She continued: "Even if there's just half a bowl of congee left, we should give it to a new mother and baby."

"Understood," said Cheng with a nod. To be frank, this was exactly what she'd always done anyway.

Vautrin had never had any children of her own but she was still an incredibly loving mother. She went to see the new mothers and their babies whenever she had a spare moment. She asked the medical workers to take care of them as much as possible but the conditions were often too poor. Cheng reported that over the past 10 days or so, 10 new babies had been born. However, three had died. A further five elder infants had died due to disease.

After hearing the miserable news, Vautrin was distraught and prayed to God to watch over the children.

There was now another problem that more and more woman were complaining about. If they stayed with their husbands at home, the soldiers would rape them and threaten their husbands. But if they ran away to the college then the Japanese soldiers would take their husbands away and accuse them of being Chinese soldiers so they could slaughter them.

"Ms Hua, please help us! What can we do?" sobbed one poor women, kneeling in front of her.

But what could she do? Vautrin felt depressed. If she kept the women in the college, their husbands would be killed. If she let them go back home, then they would definitely be raped by the Japanese soldiers and may even be killed too. Vautrin felt completely lost.

She could hardly stand it any longer. In this desperation, she had an idea. It was a very dangerous idea, but it was an idea nonetheless and much better than just sitting by and doing nothing.

She decided to negotiate with the Japanese embassy. She asked the women who were facing this dilemma to give their names and then she went to negotiate with the embassy, carrying the list of the women and their husbands.

"Will this really work?" Cheng Ruifang wasn't convinced of the plan's success.

"What else can we do?" asked Vautrin.

Everyone shrugged.

"Then this is all we've got," said Vautrin.

"It's too dangerous. You've angered them many times, Ms Hua. You can't go to the Japanese for help!" protested Cheng.

"Since I've already angered them so much, one more time doesn't matter at all. I'm not afraid of them. I'm an American."

Then Vautrin went to the Japanese embassy and visited Fukuda on behalf of all the women who'd complained to her about their problem. Fukuda was impressed: "Ms Vautrin, you really are a goddess to these Chinese people."

Vautrin shook her head and answered: "No, what I've done for them is just my instinct as a woman. I just want to offer my help to these poor women so that they can live with their husbands in safety. Your excellency, you must have a wife. You surely understand the worries of these women in the refugee camp."

"I'll try my best," responded Fukuda. When faced with such a tenacious and selfless American woman, he had no choice but to make a promise to her, which saved thousands of women and their husbands. However, there were still many men being killed under the excuse that they were Chinese soldiers.

Problems in the refugee camp continued to get worse. While Vautrin was busy negotiating with the Japanese embassy, more women were claiming that their husbands or sons were nowhere to be found and they were desperate to know where they were. Women's cries for their lost children and husbands never stopped in the camp, which greatly upset Vautrin as if a knife were being twisted in her heart.

"We have to help them find their husbands and sons," shouted Vautrin, trying to help once again.

"But Ms Hua, how can we help them? There are hundreds, maybe thousands of women who need our help," replied her colleagues. One continued: "Not only do we have to give everyone congee and water every day, we also have to keep an eye on the Japanese soldiers lurking outside. When you went to the headquarters of the International Committee yesterday, two Japanese soldiers broke into the Nanshan building and raped some of the girls in the corridor. We don't have enough energy to help the women that want to find their husbands and sons."

Vautrin pursed her lips while listening to her colleagues. She then said: "I know you're all right, but let's just think about it: all the women and children who've come to us here at the college are helpless and powerless. Our campus is now an isolated island. The refugees can't go out to find their family members all on their own. We all know that if they left the campus they'd be raped and maybe even killed by the Japanese soldiers. This would be the worst outcome for us. We can't tolerate any women being abused here. Now let me ask you something: if you were in their shoes and hiding here without knowing whether your family was dead or alive, would you be worried about them? Would you want to go out and find them? I think the answer is obvious. So let's show we understand. All we can do is try."

No one said anything else. Vautrin then asked Wang, an old member of staff at the college, to collect a list of the women who wanted to find their husbands or sons. The first list was rapidly created and handed over to Vautrin. More than 560 women wanted to find their lost family members.

Japanese soldiers were still robbing, raping and murdering the civilians of Nanjing. However, in order to cover up their crimes, the army had arranged for the crime scenes to be covered up. If they didn't go out to find these people now, then maybe they'd never know what happened to them. Nevertheless, there was no way that so many women could go out in the streets to look for their families without even knowing if they were alive.

Besides, would the Japanese soldiers even let them look? What would happen when the soldiers saw so many women out on the street? Vautrin faced yet another dilemma.

Could she go to the Japanese army for help again?

"Ms Hua, I have to stop you this time! You can't go to the Japanese anymore!" shouted Cheng along with her other colleagues, refusing to let Vautrin return to the lion's den.

"Why? Do you have a better suggestion?" Vautrin asked Cheng. She knew that her colleagues were worried about her but she couldn't see any other solution.

"No, we don't. But Ms Hua, have you ever thought what would happen if you were wounded or even killed by the Japanese? If that happened, what would we - no, we aren't what matters - what would the refugees and their children do?"

"Take it easy, Cheng. The Japanese won't do anything bad to me."

"Then what if they do?"

"My dear Ms Cheng, we are at war. Anything is possible. There are so many what ifs, but it's still worth trying. Cheng, you have a husband and children that you love a great deal don't you? So do these women who've lost their husbands and sons! So why shouldn't we help them?"

"You win, Ms Hua, but..." Cheng Ruifang couldn't help silently crying.

Vautrin stretched out her arms and hugged her, telling her not to worry before saying goodbye and leaving the college in Cheng's hands.

Vautrin waved and then left the campus gate, disappearing into the streets. Fire and smoke smothered the streets and cries and moans accompanied the crackle of the flames.

Thanks to Vautrin's efforts, the Japanese army finally made a small compromise. They allowed Vautrin to help the women find their husbands and sons but they asked for something in exchange: Vautrin had to send people to help bury the dead.

Vautrin had no choice but to accept all of the Japanese army's demands, even the most terrible and humiliating ones. This was the only way that she could help the refugees and it also gave Vautrin more insight into the Nanjing Massacre and the crimes of the Japanese. She recorded the crimes in her diary:

> It's the most miserable thing I've ever seen in my entire life: buses and cars have been toppled over on the sides of the city's streets; charred corpses are scattered all over the road. Military jackets can be seen strewn here and there. All the houses and shops have either been robbed bare or burned down.
>
> — VAUTRIN'S DIARY: 21 DECEMBER 1937

> The Japanese embassy wanted to repair the power station and restore the electricity supply, so Mr Rabe hired 50 employees and sent them to the factory. But later on in the afternoon, 43 of the employees were shot by the Japanese soldiers as they were regarded as former employees of the Chinese government.
>
> — VAUTRIN'S DIARY: 22 DECEMBER 1937

> According to my neighbour in East Court, about 60 to 100 people, mostly young, were sent to a valley south of Jinling Temple on a truck last night. Those

poor men were all shot with machine guns. The Japanese soldiers then put them into a house and set fire to it.

— Vautrin's diary: 23 December 1937

At 4.30 this afternoon, I went to Jinling College. I heard from some women that the Japanese soldiers were picking out some of the male refugees. If they couldn't prove their identities, they were killed.

— Vautrin's diary: 24 December 1937

This morning, I left the campus with the boiled water vendors to help them purchase coal. Out of fear of being arrested or the truck being robbed by Japanese soldiers, they didn't dare go alone. While I was standing in front of the coal vendor for them to finish loading the coal, a woman approached us and told us that she lived in Xiaolingwei, a district located outside of Nanjing and near the stadium. She said that Xiaolingwei had been burned to the ground and completely destroyed by both the Chinese army and the Japanese soldiers. She said that out of her 10 family members, only she, her husband and their grandson were still together. The others, including her two sons, three daughters, a daughter-in-law and a grandson, had been separated from them and were missing.

— Vautrin's diary: 29 December 1937

Tonight, our courier Mr Wei told me his experience in detail. On 14 December, he went to the International Committee in Gulou Hospital to deliver a message. He was stopped by two Japanese soldiers near the hospital. One of the soldiers pushed his bayonet against his stomach and the other pointed a gun at his back. The Japanese soldiers then pulled off his American embassy armband. After that, he was taken to Xiaguan where he was forced to load goods the Japanese had stolen onto trucks. In addition to this, he said that he'd seen thousands of Chinese people, including civilians, soldiers, the elderly and the young being cruelly massacred and that their corpses were scattered everywhere. He was later escorted back to the city to continue working. He said that on the way back to the city, every pond was filled with the corpses of Chinese people and animals.

— Vautrin's diary: 3 January 1938

Vautrin spared no effort in finding the relatives and families of the dead, but this was often in vain. There was good news every once in a while. For example, the mother who'd been looking for her 12 year old daughter had found her by chance and a severely depressed woman found her husband in a safety zone after being separated for more than 10 days. However, this wasn't often the case, and the vast majority of women didn't see their families again. This is just another tragic aspect of the Nanjing Massacre.

"As long as there's even a slither of hope, we'll do all we can to look for their families," insisted Vautrin, continuing to spare no effort in helping refugees find their families. During the search, she saw something that shook her to her very core. On the afternoon of 26 January, she saw a woman she knew in front of a ruined building. The woman asked Vautrin whether she'd heard about the large number of corpses in the pond near the village of Yangjia. She then offered to accompany Vautrin to the pond. When they arrived, Vautrin saw a shocking scene that she recorded in her diary:

> We found charred corpses abandoned on the banks of the pond, along with a couple of tanks of kerosene or oil. The hands of the corpses had been tied behind them with wire. How many corpses were there? Had they been shot with machine guns first and then set alight? I don't know exactly what fate they suffered. In a smaller pond to the west, there were 20 to 40 charred corpses wearing civilian shoes, and they were clearly not Chinese soldiers. Many unburied corpses were left strewn all over the nearby hill.

Devout Christians like Vautrin take telling the truth very seriously and, as such, any who deny the massacre should trust her descriptions.

While helping women look for their husbands and sons, Vautrin still continued to protect thousands of women and children. While Vautrin did all she could to help the victims of the war, she often forgot the fact that she was also a person with needs.

Cheng Ruifang stayed with Vautrin for a long time and she also kept a diary of the events in the college during the massacre. While reading Cheng's diaries, I noticed that Vautrin was mentioned almost every single day. Some of the entries are as follows:

> Today, some Japanese soldiers broke into our college and someone immediately came to inform us. Miss Hua was always the first to act. The Japanese soldiers picked up their pants and ran away as soon as she appeared.
>
> Japanese soldiers came at midday today. They grabbed a schoolgirl and took her behind building number 300 and took off her clothes to rape her. Miss

Hua quickly appeared and scolded them as they ran away in panic. Fortunately, the girl wasn't raped. The place they'd taken her to was full of urine and faeces, which stained the girl's clothes. Are the Japanese soldiers really so lacking in humanity and morality that they can do this without thinking twice about their actions?

Someone on the street turned to us for help because some Japanese soldiers were raping his wife. Hearing the news, Miss Hua quickly ran to the alley where the Japanese soldiers were pinning the woman to the ground. Miss Hua stopped the soldiers from their debauched crimes. They were furious and hit her to get her to stop interfering. However, Miss Hua wasn't easily intimidated and argued with them. They left in indignation. It was obvious that the soldiers hated her. After that, I advised her to be careful and that we couldn't make much difference when faced with the enormous scale of the Japanese army's savagery in Nanjing. She refused to listen.

On top of this, with the pretext of registering refugees to distribute ID cards, the Japanese occupying army came up with a plot to control and repress the Chinese. They also wanted to use the opportunity to capture women seeking refuge in Jinling College.

The registration site came up with a scheme: the women had to take off their clothes whenever the Japanese soldiers commanded them to do so. The soldiers touched them under the pretense of inspecting them. Some even raped women on the spot. The outraged Chinese men accompanying them were immediately shot dead. The women shook with fear, which only further aroused the Japanese soldiers.

The Japanese soldiers had made it clear: those who refused to register would be regarded as traitors who resisted Japan and would therefore be killed.

In order to help the women in the college during registration, Vautrin and Cheng came up with a plan to get the vulnerable women to pretend to be seriously ill so that the Japanese soldiers wouldn't assault them.

The Japanese soldiers were frenzied during the registration but they couldn't lose control because Vautrin watched over them in person and arranged for more than 10 International Committee members, including Rabe, to help preside over the campus registration. She was calm and collected, but the Japanese soldiers took other measures. They selected some women who'd caught their eye, sent them into trucks and said that the imperial army needed them for something.

Vautrin couldn't refuse. The next day, these women were sent back ashamed. Obviously, they had been brutally raped by the Japanese soldiers.

Vautrin talked with Cheng Ruifang about getting these women to pretend to have diseases so that the Japanese soldiers wouldn't dare touch them.

The following day, the Japanese soldiers arrived in a truck to take away some of the women from the college.

"As they're seriously ill, they can't go with you," Vautrin told them in a calm and patient voice.

They didn't believe her. They ordered several women they had previous assaulted to come over and told them to take off their pants. When they saw that their genitals were black and swollen, the soldiers recoiled in disgust and left.

With tears of gratitude in their eyes, the women surrounded Vautrin and kept saying: "Thank God! Thank you Miss Hua!"

> It snowed during the storm and it still hasn't melted. In contrast, just several weeks ago it was as warm as spring. The violets and pansies were blossoming and the spring plum trees were about to blossom. With this acute change in weather, I don't know if there'll be any fruit. This weather makes me even more concerned about the poor who can't afford to buy even the bare essentials. When I think about the future of the poor, I can't help worrying. However, in another sense, it's not all that bad as even the people of the lowest social status and the least-educated understand what the so-called new order in East Asia really means.

This above paragraph is Vautrin's description of the scene at Jinling College on 2 March 1940 when the Japanese army had occupied Nanjing for more than three years. Her diaries tell us of the miserable lives of the citizens of Nanjing under the rule of the Japanese invaders. In these three hard years, Vautrin had done a great deal to help thousands of Chinese women and children.

The Withering of a Flower

14 May 1938 was just another day for most people, but it bore great significance for Vautrin. The Japanese army had occupied Nanjing for six months now. On this date three years later, in 1941, Vautrin also passed away.

It's hard to imagine such a kind-hearted and passionate woman so full of vitality killing herself three years later by turning on a stove gas in her apartment.

She passed away back in the US, in Illinois. She died alone and not even her younger brother went to her funeral. How could Vautrin, who was thought of as a goddess in China, leave this world so depressed and alone?

It was later learned that Vautrin suffered from severe depression. During her last three years in Nanjing, the Japanese subjected her to a horrific assortment of harassment and brutality every day while never giving up on defending the survival and safety of thousands of women and children who had been forced to seek refuge in Jinling College.

On 12 May 1938, Vautrin was sitting in her office preparing schedules for the autumn term for the students under her protection. An old lady called Jiang came to see Vautrin with her daughter. The old lady told Vautrin that her 53 year old son was suffering from lung cancer and he had a wife and son. She said that her other son, who was 33 years old, operated the machines at a grain milling factory and made $50 a month. He had a wife and four children. All nine family members lived on this son's income.

While on their way to cross over to the north bank of the Yangtze to escape the war, they ran out of money and were stopped by Japanese soldiers at the worst possible moment. Her 33 year old son was mistakenly identified as a soldier and stabbed to death. The old lady begged Vautrin to help them, otherwise all of her family would die.

After hearing the old lady's plight, Vautrin felt as if a knife had been plunged into her heart. The old lady knelt in front of her, begging for help.

As soon as she finished accommodating the old lady and her family, someone told Vautrin that something terrible had happened to an old lady called Liu. She lived near a row of three buildings with three sons and two daughters-in-law. Four days ago, two Japanese soldiers broke into her home through a window at night after they had been unable to enter through the front door. The two soldiers asked the old lady to give them her two daughters-in-law, but she refused. The soldiers slashed her torso twice then struck her a third time in the chest. They then raped her daughters-in-law.

"Can you look after them here?" they asked. Vautrin didn't answer straight away as the overcrowded college was already filled with refugees and there was no more room. However, her conscience got the best of her and Vautrin agreed.

14 May 1938 was a Saturday. Vautrin was revered as a goddess and was full of hope and vitality. She died three years later.

Early that morning, Vautrin was busy arranging the schedules of the 250 students at the college, as well as those of the teachers. She expressed her happiness to Cheng Ruifang and her grandson when they came to fetch her to go to church, saying that the students could go back to class the following week.

They returned to the school shortly after 8am. Vautrin found that her dog, Hooley, had passed away after a short but serious illness. Hooley was the third dog that she had lost in three years. He was a little dog, but he was well behaved and always sat by the school gates, as if he was guarding Vautrin. Whenever he saw a stranger, he barked until Vautrin told him to stop. Hooley's death led her to decide that she shouldn't have any more dogs.

She wrote: "Their good fortunes shall come to an end if I continue having them as pets." Does this show the depressed mindset that later led to her suicide?

She never really expressed how she was feeling and instead we have to look to her remarkable achievements: she spared no effort in protecting the poor women and children at the college.

Below are a few extracts from Vautrin's diary:

19 May

Today we helped a woman with five children and gave her five dollars. We also decided to temporarily provide shelter to her two older daughters. She will stay with the three other children by finding something using the five dollars. The son that used to be responsible for the whole family's welfare was caught by Japanese soldiers and he may have been killed. Yesterday, Cheng Ruifang gave a mother with three children five dollars to start a new life after her husband was killed by the Japanese soldiers. After exchanging ideas with Cheng Ruifang, we decided to select 100 desperate women and girls before 1 September to set up a school to teach them handicrafts.

23 May

From 9am to 11.30am, 350 students attended a graduation ceremony for the training classes on the campus. The students from 33 classes demonstrated what they'd learned. With no scores, examinations or diplomas, the graduation ceremony showcased some of the students' creations and people showed genuine interest. The students sang lots of songs and the students of the Chinese language classes translated some excerpts of the classics. Some students told stories and some recited readings from the Bible. A girl, approximately nine years old, showed initiative and told a story. She's been ill for a long time and she couldn't participate in the rehearsals but she still managed to attend the graduation ceremony. The students who've been learning about how to take care of poultry prepared a presentation to showcase what they've learned. I believe that in their later years of life, the women here will tell their stories of their time as refugees at Jinling College.

24 May

We held a meeting, which was attended by the various committees in charge of affairs in the refugee camps. During this meeting, we managed to determine the minimum number of refugees that had to be aided in starting their new lives. Jinling College's quotas are as follows: 32 young homeless and orphaned girls, 672 homeless young girls with no relatives, 237 young homeless and impoverished girls, 127 young homeless women from dangerous areas, 16 homeless widows and seven who are either crippled, blind or dispossessed.

25 May

This morning I spent a large amount of time meeting with refugees. The first group of refugees consisted of a mother who's lost three sons and two other women who've lost two sons. I doubt whether I'd be able to keep living if the same unfortunate thing happened to me. Out of this group, there was one mother who only had one dollar and was trying to make a profit by running a small business. Considering how difficult it is here to make a living, she can't be blamed for selling cigarettes or opium. I've been negotiating the issue of how to accommodate the 1,000 or so refugees if we need to close the six camps with Mills for a long time.

28 May

This morning, I gave six dollars to three mothers who've been left alone after their sons were caught by Japanese soldiers. After meeting me, they have been planning how to make a living. One of them has decided to sell fans, soap and candles. Another woman is going to set up a laundrette. They expressed their sincere gratitude for my help and promised that the money will be used to start their businesses. The money for their relief was donated by some Americans and sent to me by Miss Simpson.

31 May

At 6pm, Cheng treated everyone who's been receiving food relief from building number 400 with a dinner on the balcony of her apartment in the Nanshan building. Mary also joined the party at 8pm. We have to live a normal life for the children's sake. However, I can hardly smile or feel happy when I think about the ongoing battles or the cities being bombed by Japanese planes.

The last entry in Vautrin's diary was written on 14 April 1940 when she was preparing to leave Nanjing for the US. At the very beginning of the entry for the day, she wrote:

I'm going to be exhausted. Although I used to make slow progress in my work, I continued to do it to schedule. But now, in sharp contrast, my hands don't work as well as they did. I would like to be away from my work as soon as possible but I can never stop worrying about the issue of establishing a hands-on class. I occasionally think of a plan to set up such a class, but I could never overcome the difficulty of assigning the scarce teachers available to it.

Exhausted, Vautrin became ill. She couldn't sleep or talk. Talking would cause her to vomit.

With the help of her friends in an American church, she returned to the US on 14 May, 1940. Before leaving Nanjing, Cheng Ruifang and other refugees that she'd helped went to see her off and pray for her in church.

They prayed for Vautrin over and over again as if she were the Virgin Mary and in the eyes of the Chinese people and the citizens of Nanjing, that's exactly how she's seen. Although her body rests in Michigan, her spirit and soul will always remain in China, the land she loved so deeply and helped so much.

When she left China, she said: "Had I 10 perfect lives, I would give them all to China." To this day, "Goddess of Mercy" is engraved on her tombstone.

"Miss Hua", "Vautrin", "Living Buddha" and "Goddess of Mercy" are all different names used to reflect how highly the people of Nanjing think of Vautrin, but there would have been no need for these titles had it not been for the Japanese invaders' atrocities.

While it's important to never forget these crimes, we should never forget the lives of those like Minnie Vautrin who gave so much to help.

7

TRIALS AND TESTIMONIES

The Defence of the Commander-in-Chief vs the Charges of the Presiding Judge

History has shown many times that aggressors and their criminal actions are judged not only morally but also legally. The Japanese invaders were no exception to this and they were put on trial not just for China's sake, but also as a matter of historical record. This is something that those in Japan who deny the massacre have to accept. Whether it's a century or 10,000 years from now, this record of the massacre will never be destroyed or denied by anyone who isn't deluded.

Faced with the unfortunate fact that there are some in Japan, a formerly militaristic country, who deny the Japanese atrocities, including the descendants of those who committed the barbarous acts, it's imperative for China to remind them of what happened at the end of the Second World War. In the last days of the war at the Yalta Conference in 1945, the leaders of the Allied powers made their plans for the final push against the three Axis powers - Germany, Italy and Japan - and their plans for a post-war world. As the war in Europe came to an end, Japan still refused to surrender. The Japanese continued to fight fiercely and were against world peace. Faced with the Japanese refusal to surrender, the leaders of the US, the UK and China clearly declared in the Potsdam Proclamation that: "The full application of our military power, backed by our resolve, will mean the inevitable and complete destruction of the Japanese armed forces and inevitably the utter devastation of the Japanese homeland." Such a forceful and serious warning and declaration didn't have any effect on the heinous Japanese military. They still refused to surrender, continuing to fight and kill civilians and come up with schemes for total war in Japan, planning to sacrifice Japan's entire population in the fight.

Under this difficult scenario, on the morning of 6 August 1945, the US sent a B-29 bomber to drop the first atomic bomb on Hiroshima. Despite this, Japan still refused to surrender.

On the afternoon of 8 August 1945, Molotov and the Soviet government summoned Sato, the Japanese ambassador to the Soviet Union, and informed him that due to Japan's continued refusal to surrender, due to its obligations to the UN, the Soviet Union would be at war with Japan from dawn of 9 August according to the local time in the Far East. Due to the time difference between the Far East and Moscow, this took place just before dawn on 9 August. Therefore, just half an hour later, 1.5 million Soviet soldiers advanced into northeast China at breakneck speed to defeat the Kwantung army, the main Japanese force there. The army collapsed before the Japanese had time to react.

On the same day, the US dropped another atomic bomb on Nagasaki on the Japanese island of Kyushu. Meanwhile, the US expanded their firebombing campaign in Tokyo, the Japanese capital.

On 15 August 1945, the emperor of Japan had no choice but to announce their surrender, which marked the end of its long and aggressive war.

Obviously, Japan had been forced to announce a ceasefire and surrender, rather than willingly own up to its crimes. This left a lasting impact on their failure to approach their criminal history of aggression against China in the following decades. The continued justification or denial of war crimes by some in Japanese society shows a bitter refusal to deal with the past appropriately.

When China argues with Japan about its history and territory, China often refers to the Potsdam Proclamation because it contains two clear-cut stipulations: one proclamation reiterates that the sovereignty of Japan is confined to Honshu, Hokkaido, Kyushu, Shikoku and other islands decided upon in the Potsdam Proclamation; the other states that all criminals, including those who mistreated Chinese captives, must be judged by the law.

There are many issues today in Asia, especially in terms of Sino-Japanese relations, most of which are the result of Japan's deliberate ignorance regarding these two extremely important declarations. As a result, disputes arise between the two countries, so it is important to be clear as to why.

To properly understand, the international situation following the end of the Second World War needs to be explained.

The institutions of the Allied nations and the newly founded United Nations played an active role in judging the crimes committed by Germany, Italy and Japan. During the second half of 1945, apart from having to deal with their own battle scars, the victorious countries implemented measures to deal with Germany, Italy and Japan following their defeat in the Second World War.

European countries were in charge of dealing with Germany and Italy, while the US and China were responsible for dealing with Japan.

The American chief of staff and the supreme commander of the occupying forces, General MacArthur, was responsible for transforming Japan following their defeat. On 19 January 1946, he signed a special announcement judging the Japanese criminals:

> Whereas, the United States and the Nations allied therewith in opposing the illegal wars of aggression of the Axis Nations, have from time to time made declarations of their intentions that war criminals should be brought to justice;
>
> Whereas, the Governments of the Allied powers at war with Japan on the 26th July 1945 at Potsdam, declared as one of the terms of surrender that stern justice shall be meted out to all war criminals including those who have visited cruelties upon our prisoners;
>
> Whereas, by the Instrument of Surrender of Japan executed at Tokyo Bay, Japan, on the 2nd September 1945, the signatories for Japan, by command of and on behalf of the Emperor and the Japanese Government, accepted the terms set forth in such Declaration at Potsdam;
>
> Whereas, by such Instrument of Surrender, the authority of the Emperor and the Japanese Government to rule the state of Japan is made subject to the Supreme Commander for the Allied powers, who is authorised to take such steps as he deems proper to effectuate the terms of surrender;
>
> Whereas, the undersigned has been designated by the Allied powers as Supreme Commander for the Allied powers to carry into effect the general surrender of the Japanese armed forces;
>
> Whereas, the Governments of the United States, Great Britain and Russia at the Moscow Conference, 26th December 1945, having considered the effectuation by Japan of the Terms of Surrender, with the concurrence of China have agreed that the Supreme Commander shall issue all Orders for the implementation of the Terms of Surrender.
>
> Now, therefore, I, Douglas MacArthur, as Supreme Commander for the Allied powers, by virtue of the authority so conferred upon me, in order to implement the Term of Surrender which requires the meting out of stern justice to war criminals, do order and provide as follows:
>
> ARTICLE 1. There shall be established an International Military Tribunal for the Far East for the trial of those persons charged individually, or as members of organisations, or in both capacities, with offences which include crimes against peace.

ARTICLE 2. The Constitution, jurisdiction and functions of this Tribunal are those set forth in the Charter of the International Military Tribunal for the Far East, approved by me this day.

ARTICLE 3. Nothing in this Order shall prejudice the jurisdiction of any other international, national or occupation court, commission or other tribunal established or to be established in Japan or in any territory of a United Nation with which Japan has been at war, for the trial of war criminals.

Given under my hand at Tokyo, this 19th day of January, 1946.

— DOUGLAS MACARTHUR *GENERAL OF THE ARMY, UNITED STATES ARMY SUPREME COMMANDER FOR THE ALLIED POWERS*

After working as a superintendent at the US military academy in West Point in 1919, MacArthur became a commander who led a successful campaign in the Pacific theatre of the Second World War and the famous general who signed the surrender with Japanese representatives on behalf of the UN. The three articles are clear in their aims for bringing the Japanese criminals to justice for their war of aggression. MacArthur was a distinguished officer in the US army and had fought well against the Chinese communist forces in Korea. When he returned home from the Korean war in 1951, he was enthusiastically welcomed by the American public. When his car passed people in the street, they cheered him and displayed a total of 2,850 tons of coloured streamers and confetti - quadruple the amount used to welcome back Eisenhowever. The US Congress approved a motion to honour MacAuthur by casting a special gold medal of honour with his portrait and the following words: "the Protector of Australia, the Liberator of the Philippines, the Conqueror of Japan and the Defender of Korea". Nevertheless, General MacArthur was just a second-class general in the eyes of most Chinese people because he had failed to push back the Chinese general Peng Dehuai. The clarity of the three articles is no surprise considering MacArthur's record as a writer. His autobiography, *Reminisces*, has been used as a textbook by many famous military schools around the world. He was also a passionate orator, confident in the use of five languages: French, German, Italian, Spanish and English. His speech, *Duty, Honour, Country*, has inspired American soldiers and young people for generations:

"Duty, Honour, Country". Those three hallowed words reverently dictate what you ought to be, what you can be, what you will be. They are your rallying point to build courage when courage seems to fail, to regain faith when there seems to be little cause for faith, to create hope when hope becomes forlorn.

Unhappily, I possess neither that eloquence of diction, that poetry of imagination, nor that brilliance of metaphor to tell you all that they mean.

The unbelievers will say they are but words, but a slogan, but a flamboyant phrase. Every pedant, every demagogue, every cynic, every hypocrite, every troublemaker, and, I am sorry to say, some others of an entirely different character, will try to downgrade them even to the extent of mockery and ridicule.

But these are some of the things they do. They build your basic character. They mould you for your future roles as the custodians of the nation's defence. They make you strong enough to know when you are weak, and brave enough to face yourself when you are afraid.

They teach you to be proud and unbending in honest failure, but humble and gentle in success; not to substitute words for action; not to seek the path of comfort, but to face the stress and spur of difficulty and challenge; to learn to stand up in the storm, but to have compassion on those who fall; to master yourself before you seek to master others; to have a heart that is clean, a goal that is high; to learn to laugh, yet never forget how to weep; to reach into the future, yet never neglect the past; to be serious, yet never take yourself too seriously; to be modest so that you will remember the simplicity of true greatness, the open mind of true wisdom, the meekness of true strength.

They give you a temper of the will, a quality of the imagination, a vigour of the emotions, a freshness of the deep springs of life, a temperamental predominance of courage over timidity, an appetite for adventure over love of ease.

They create in your heart the sense of wonder, the unfailing hope of what next, and the joy and inspiration of life. They teach you in this way to be an officer and a gentleman.

And what sort of soldiers are those you are to lead? Are they reliable? Are they brave? Are they capable of victory?

Their story is known to all of you. It is the story of the American man at arms. My estimate of him was formed on the battlefield many, many years ago, and has never changed. I regarded him then, as I regard him now, as one of the world's noblest figures; not only as one of the finest military characters, but also as one of the most stainless.

His name and fame are the birthright of every American citizen. In his youth and strength, his love and loyalty, he gave all that mortality can give. He needs no eulogy from me, or from any other man. He has written his own history and written it in red on his enemy's breast.

But when I think of his patience under adversity, of his courage under fire, and of his modesty in victory, I am filled with an emotion of admiration I cannot put into words. He belongs to history as furnishing one of the greatest examples of successful patriotism. He belongs to posterity as the instructor of future generations in the principles of liberty and freedom. He belongs to the present, to us, by his virtues and by his achievements.

In 20 campaigns, on 100 battlefields, around 1,000 campfires, I have witnessed that enduring fortitude, that patriotic self-abnegation, and that invincible determination which have carved his statue in the hearts of his people. From one end of the world to the other, he has drained deep the chalice of courage.

As I listened to those songs, in memory's eye I could see those staggering columns of the First World War, bending under soggy packs on many a weary march, from dripping dusk to drizzling dawn, slogging ankle-deep through the mire of shell-pocked roads, to form grimly for the attack, blue-lipped, covered with sludge and mud, chilled by the wind and rain, driving home to their objective, and for many, to the judgment seat of God.

I do not know the dignity of their birth, but I do know the glory of their death. They died unquestioning, uncomplaining, with faith in their hearts, and on their lips the hope that we would go on to victory.

Always for them: duty, honour, country. Always their blood, and sweat, and tears, as we sought the way and the light and the truth. And 20 years after, on the other side of the globe, again the filth of dirty foxholes, the stench of ghostly trenches, the slime of dripping dugouts, those broiling suns of relentless heat, those torrential rains of devastating storms, the loneliness and utter desolation of jungle trails, the bitterness of long separation of those they loved and cherished, the deadly pestilence of tropical disease, the horror of stricken areas of war.

Their resolute and determined defence, their swift and sure attack, their indomitable purpose, their complete and decisive victory - always victory, always through the bloody haze of their last reverberating shot, the vision of gaunt, ghastly men, reverently following your password of duty, honour, country.

The code which those words perpetuate embraces the highest moral law and will stand the test of any ethics or philosophies ever promoted for the uplift of mankind. Its requirements are for the things that are right, and its restraints are from the things that are wrong. The soldier, above all other men, is required to practice the greatest act of religious training: sacrifice. In battle and in the face of danger and death, he disposes those divine attributes which his Maker gave when he created man in His own image. No physical courage and no brute instinct can take the place of the divine help which alone can sustain him. However hard the incidents of war may be, the soldier who is called upon to offer and to give his life for his country is the noblest development of mankind.

You now face a new world, a world of change. The thrust into outer space of the satellite spheres and missiles mark a beginning of another epoch in the long story of mankind. In the five or more billions of years the scientists tell us it has taken to form the earth, in the three or more billion years of development of the human race, there has never been a more abrupt or staggering evolution. We deal now, not with things of this world alone, but with the illimitable distances and as yet unfathomed mysteries of the universe. We are reaching out for a new and boundless frontier. We speak in strange terms: of harnessing the cosmic energy; of making winds and tides work for us; of creating unheard synthetic materials to supplement or even replace our old standard basics; to purify sea water for our drink; of mining the ocean floors for new fields of wealth and food; of disease preventatives to expand life into the hundreds of years; of controlling the weather for a more equitable distribution of heat and cold, of rain and shine; of spaceships to the Moon; of the primary target in war, no longer limited to the armed forces of an enemy, but instead to include his civil populations; of ultimate conflict between a united human race and the sinister forces of some other planetary galaxy; of such dreams and fantasies as to make life the most exciting of all time.

And through all this welter of change and development your mission remains fixed, determined, inviolable. It is to win our wars. Everything else in your professional career is but corollary to this vital dedication. All other public purposes, all other public projects, all other public needs, great or small, will find others for their accomplishment; but you are the ones who are trained to fight. Yours is the profession of arms, the will to win, the sure knowledge that in war there is no substitute for victory, that if you lose, the nation will be destroyed, that the very obsession of your public service must be duty, honour, country.

Others will debate the controversial issues, national and international, which divide men's minds. But serene, calm, aloof, you stand as the nation's war guardians, as its lifeguards from the raging tides of international conflict, as its gladiators in the arena of battle. For a century and a half you have defended, guarded and protected its hallowed traditions of liberty and freedom, of right and justice. Let civilian voices argue the merits or demerits of our processes of government: whether our strength is being sapped by deficit financing indulged in too long, by federal paternalism grown too mighty, by power groups grown too arrogant, by politics grown too corrupt, by crime grown too rampant, by morals grown too low, by taxes grown too high, by extremists grown too violent; whether our personal liberties are as firm and complete as they should be; these great national problems are not for your professional participation or military solution. Your guidepost stands out like a tenfold beacon in the night: duty, honour, country.

You are the leaven which binds together the entire fabric of our national system of defence. From your ranks come the great captains who hold the nation's destiny in their hands the moment the war tocsin sounds.

The Long Grey Line has never failed us. Were you to do so, a million ghosts in olive drab, in brown khaki, in blue and grey, would rise from their white crosses, thundering those magic words: duty, honour, country.

This does not mean that you are warmongers. On the contrary, the soldier above all other people prays for peace, for he must suffer and bear the deepest wounds and scars of war. But always in our ears ring the ominous words of Plato, that wisest of all philosophers: "Only the dead have seen the end of war."

The shadows are lengthening for me. The twilight is here. My days of old have vanished - tone and tint. They have gone glimmering through the dreams of things that were. Their memory is one of wondrous beauty, watered by tears and coaxed and caressed by the smiles of yesterday. I listen then, but with thirsty ear, for the witching melody of faint bugles blowing reveille, of far drums beating the long roll. In my dreams I hear again the crash of guns, the rattle of musketry, the strange, mournful mutter of the battlefield. But in the evening of my memory always I come back to West Point. Always there echoes and re-echoes: duty, honour, country.

While I don't want to come across as a huge advocate of MacArthur, the Second World War general's passion is truly inspiring in his love of duty, honour and country. While war in itself is a ruthless affair, it requires passion, both to fight and to end it.

Duty, honour, country. These three words clearly represent the will of the brave individuals who stand up to unjust and aggressive countries.

Justice had to be strict and severe, which was necessary for effectively handling criminals who destroyed so many lives and had brought so much pain. This was to stand up for the dignity of all the innocent victims and nations.

When the Axis powers surrendered, all of the victorious countries that had been so severely damaged by the Second World War set about following their important duty of arresting the war criminals who'd led the war of aggression.

The first arrest warrant to be issued was for Prime Minister Hideki Tojo, which was released by MacArthur on 11 September 1945. At 4pm, an Allied forces squadron leader rushed over to the residence of Hideki Tojo along with a group of American military police.

The first-floor window suddenly opened and a bald man poked his head out, asking the American soldiers in a curious tone: "Why have you come to my house?"

"Are you General Hideki Tojo?" politely asked Lawes, the squadron leader. He explained: "We've been ordered by General MacArthur to bring you to Allied command."

"Sorry, I won't meet with anybody unless my government gives the order," Tojo said. He pulled his head back inside and closed the window. Unsure of what to do, Lawes and the other soldiers heard a gunshot.

Lawes sensed that something was wrong and rushed into the house with the soldiers. They ran up to the first floor only to see Tojo in a short-sleeved jumper slumped in a rocking chair in front of his desk, blood pouring out of his left breast.

"Hurry! Get an ambulance!" Lawes ordered the soldiers to take Tojo down the stairs.

"Sorry it's taking me so long to die. I await the righteous judgment of history," muttered Tojo on his way to hospital. He didn't die and a month later it was clear he was recovering. He was then put in prison.

At the same time, the American military police and armed guards spent every day arresting the criminals the Allied army had asked for in Tokyo and all around Japan. This lasted until the end of 1945. Iwane Matsui, the main criminal responsible for the Nanjing Massacre, was arrested on 19 September. One week earlier, he talked boastfully with American journalists: "I was ordered to be an officer in commanding the Shanghai expeditionary forces and the Japanese central China area army, and led the Battle of Shanghai and the Battle of Nanjing. According to the Potsdam Proclamation, these acts cannot be regarded as war crimes. I have a clear conscience." His limited understanding of the Potsdam Proclamation explains why this slim old man was so furious when the Allied army came to his house to arrest him.

The judgement of the Japanese criminals had to be ruthlessly conducted. This incredibly important trial was to be an arduous affair and although the crimes committed by the Japanese were obvious, all procedures and legal means had to be strictly and precisely followed without any fault, which was essential for the criminals receiving the most severe punishments as well as for upholding justice.

When judging these war criminals, the Chinese and people around the world could refer to a precedent: the Nuremberg trials against the German war criminals in Europe. These trials began on 20 November 1945, prior to the Tokyo trials.

In addition to the concerned staff and judges, many reporters and observers attended the trials, drawing international attention. One reporter described the scene on the first day of the trial:

> It was nearly 10am. Three groups of defence lawyers walked slowly out of the lift one after another and into courtroom 600 - the site of the Nuremberg trials, an expertly prepared international court.
>
> On the bench, four judges from different victorious nations were sat. The judge from the Soviet Union wore brown martial attire and those from the United States, Britain and France wore black robes. In the courtroom, thick grey velvet curtains drooped and covered the autumnal Nuremberg skyline and rows of wooden benches were painted dark. The court reflected a 'gloomy and solemn' atmosphere to the entire world, as described by Justice Jackson.
>
> Twenty-one Nazi war criminals were seated in prisoners' boxes. The public gallery was crowded and 250 reporters took notes rapidly. The entire world was watching.

Nuremberg, a gloomy and solemn series of trials, lasted for a year and sentenced 12 fascist leaders to be hanged and about 10 other criminals to be severely punished. Later, more than 800 key Nazi Party members were sentenced to death. In addition to this, a special judicial taskforce dedicated to looking for Nazis who had committed crimes during the Second World War and had escaped from the Nuremberg trials lasted for several decades.

Hitler committed suicide and could not be judged as a result. However, the Nuremberg trials gave him a thorough and justified judgement.

Japan surrendered later than Germany, making the trial against the Japanese war criminals start later. The experience of the opening of the Nuremberg trials guided and helped the Tokyo trials to some extent. The Tokyo trials featured 818 court sessions, 48,000 pages of court records, 419 witnesses, more than 4,000 documents and 1,213 pages of written judgments. With a scale that exceeded even the Nuremberg trials, this was the trial of the century.

From the beginning, Japan seemed to doubt whether the Tokyo trials were fair or legal.

The Tokyo international tribunal began on 3 May 1946. At the beginning, Keenan, the prosecution attorney general from the US, made a statement to the court, including the Japanese war criminals present, about why judging these criminals was indeed reasonable:

> Honourable president and judges of the International Military Tribunal for the Far East,
>
> As attorney general of the prosecution, I shall provide you with an overview of legal theory, according to which we shall make our prosecution and provide facts to prove that every defendant has committed the crimes recorded in their indictments. This is my responsibility provided by the charter.
>
> We have good reason to say that this trial is one of the most important trials in history. It affects 11 countries present, which have built orderly governments with a population that accounts for half of the world's population; it also matters for other countries and the many unborn generations of all countries because these lawsuits will have a far reaching influence on world peace and safety.
>
> Honourable presiding judge, this isn't just a common trial. We are engaged in a fight where civilised society is steadfastly preventing the whole world from destruction. This trial is just one part of it. The threat to the world comes from the deliberate plans of individuals and small groups rather than the natural course of action. These people seem to be willing to destroy this world so as to satisfy their mad ambitions of world domination. This is an intense line of argument that cannot be described in any other terms when facing these facts.
>
> There is a small group of people in the world, the defendants among them, who are determined to interfere with world affairs and impose their evil wishes on the whole of mankind. They declare war on civilisation. They lay down regulations and implement their policies. They are determined to destroy democracy and its foundations: freedom and respect for individuality. They have decided to get rid of governments that are ruled by the people, owned by the people and enjoyed by the people, thus building a new order under their own definitions. In order to achieve this goal, they have worked with Hitler's Nazis. They are proud of this formal alliance. As listed in the indictment, they worked together, and planned, prepared and waged an aggressive war against democratic countries together.
>
> They are willing to regard human beings as slaves and hostages, which means they see nothing wrong with murdering, conquering and enslaving millions of people. This includes plans of slaughtering the young and old around the world. They don't care if they destroy an entire group of people. It doesn't matter to them whether this causes the flower of youth, including their own children, to wither all too early.

In their minds, treaties, agreements and guarantees are just words and pieces of paper, bearing no influence on their ambitions. They aim to impose their control over the world through force and conquest, regardless of justice. To accomplish this cause, millions of people are killed and national resources are destroyed. Nothing matters except their mad plans of conquering and controlling East Asia and eventually bringing the whole world under their control. This is their main conspiracy.

We are faced with a problem and history has cruelly warned us of the consequences of our civilisation standing by and allowing such atrocities without intervention.

Our era is different to previous eras and everyone is keenly aware of this. Today, tomorrow, and in the future, war is bound to break out again in a more unforgiving way than ever. The wars of today and tomorrow care not for territorial limits. The victims will be the young and the old; armed personnel and civilians. No home, city or small village, will be spared from the destructive power of war.

The answer to this problem requires infinite patience, tolerance and efforts to reach understandings and agreements. We have only taken one aspect of the problem into account. What can we do to fairly and efficiently prevent wars in future by using our powers in this court?

Our aim is to prevent war and deter our enemy. It has nothing to do with such insignificant aims as vengeance and revenge. But we do hope that in these proceedings, these individuals who caused such disaster for so many human beings, will be charged as common criminals and punished accordingly. This may have a deterrent effect on those who see them as role models and seek to start wars in future. This hope can be achieved.

Therefore, our aim has been to reassert the principles that have been widely recognised in these trials. If an officer or an individual in another position worked to start a war of aggression, they should and shall be punished as murderers, bandits, pirates and robbers for centuries to come.

War, or organised murder, is incompatible with justice and the law. Here we advocate that those who plan and start wars and thus destroy millions of lives are equal to those who murder human beings. They are both criminals.

We further advocate that criminals cannot be immune from punishment due to an oath of allegiance to the constitution and laws of their country; nor can they be immune from punishment just by excusing this war that murdered millions of people as following orders. Similarly, they cannot be immune from punishment by claiming that it accords to the laws of their nation, therefore justifying their behaviour.

We believe that the facts and details cited and presented in this court will show that these defendants, who control the government or have had a negative influence on the behaviour of the government, violated the effective laws and obligations to which Japan was bound.

We will undoubtedly prove that these defendants knew that the war they planned and started would lead to the destruction of human life, not only on the battlefield, but also in homes, hospitals and orphanages, and in the factories and farms; the young and the old, the healthy and the sick, men, women and children; they were all sacrificed.

These defendants started wars with and without declaration, and started a war that violates international law and international treaties. A similar lawsuit is underway in Nuremberg and these defendants are sitting in the dock. Although it is clear that their targets were consistent with the defendants in Nuremberg, and they allied with those defendants, we shall pay no attention to them.

So, if our observations are correct, we must make an important decision. This decision may have a decisive effect on whether the human race will continue or end. If this proposition is correct - we suspect that some may believe this to be an exaggeration - there is no doubt that we are in a new and crucial era. For those who require an established precedent to guide this case, we would like to point out that this judgment against a war of aggression is not exactly a new concept. From prehistoric and primitive societies, through the middle ages and until the present, there have always been proceedings to punish the organisers of such aggression.

Keenan looked at Tojo, Matsui and the other criminals and said: "The establishment of an international legal tribunal and allowance for these war criminals to defend themselves and claim they are innocent is a cornerstone of our culture and modern civilisation." Keenan noticed that they gently lifted their heads a little and made eye contact with each other. They were taking slow and heavy breaths and made eye contact with the stern Chinese judges present. Soon the pressure mounted on them again, like a heavy stone had been put on their chests.

Keenan softened his tone, it was now slower and gentler: "Today, we have to stay respectful as we begin our solemn duty. This is a critical case and we have to proceed as such. Just as we in the prosecution have argued, if we cannot do this sincerely and honestly, and if the victors cannot correct things to prevent power from destroying the world, it in itself would constitute an unforgivable crime."

Keenan ended the first part of his moving statement and thanked the court. His touching words had reminded everyone of the importance of the trial, from the prosecution and defence, to the perpetrators and the victims.

No man is an island,
Entire of itself;
Every man is a piece of the continent,
A part of the main;
If a clod be washed away by the sea,
Europe is the less,
As well as if a promontory were,
As well as any manner of thy friends or of thine own were;
Any man's death diminishes me,
Because I am involved in mankind.
And therefore,
Never send to know for whom the bell tolls;
It tolls for thee.

This poem was written by the English metaphysical poet John Donne in the 17th century. The American writer Ernest Hemingway placed it on the title page of his novel *For Whom the Bell Tolls*. This poem's meaning now resonated with Matsui and his criminal cabal, these Nanjing Massacre executioners' minds panicked by the nearing prospect of death. Matsui tried to maintain a calm appearance. The corner of his mouth twisted, although very subtly, but it still didn't escape the eagle eyes of the judges of the military tribunal.

"Mr President, my statement is as follows," began Keenan after spending two days stating the first synthesis report of accusations against the Japanese war criminals, in addition to stating the significance of the trial. The report included five aspects, including the nature of the defendants' guilt, an overview of the juridical logic of the trial, and the legal provisions the defendants had violated. Every word he said was well planned out. He made a strong rebuttal on a legal and factual basis against the opinion held by some that there was a difference between the responsibility of the state for the Japanese war of aggression and the individual responsibility of the war criminals. He said: "Every country has the inalienable right to self-defence, but a war of aggression should not be considered as such. Wars are evil things. The war launched in 1937 should be described as one of the greatest disasters for mankind. This is not an exaggeration. So not only is waging a war a crime, but the principal culprit is a war criminal. However, on a global scale, this is different to a war crime, which violates the laws of war. This is the total accumulation of all evil. Even if a war is fought in the most humane and chivalrous manner, if it is an unjust war, starting it is still a crime. It is a crime against peace." He then bluntly discussed the nature of Nanjing Massacre: "The Japanese army systematically and mercilessly massacred, raped and tortured tens of thousands of prisoners of war, civilians, women and children and indiscriminately destroyed homes and property on a large scale. It was completely beyond any possible military needs. This was the nature of the Japanese occupation of Nanjing. This is now often referred to as the Nanjing Massacre, the likes of which were unprecedented in the history of modern warfare." Keenan then continued: "Nanjing is just one of many cities that were targeted as part of the aggressive plans of the Japanese. The Japanese committed these crimes on an unbelievable scale. These were serious atrocities, which sought to destroy the Chinese people's will to resist their occupation of China."

The legal principle and basis of the trial heavily attacked the Japanese war criminals psychologically. What followed was long and tough to hear in court, and it took more than two years to look back at the worst parts of the war. This legal review of the Japanese crimes forced the people of Nanjing to reopen their wounds.

Who Should Stand Trial?

The Japanese army, which had launched a war of aggression, committed a huge amount of crimes. Who should be brought to stand trial and answer to history? This should have been obvious. However, a series of strange events took place at the International Military Tribunal.

These issues were a result of the US and UK led International Military Tribunal for the Far East, which will be elaborated upon in detail.

All the grisly details of what happened to the victims of the Japanese were now open to the public, despite Japan having spent a lot of time and money trying to whitewash history and cover up its crimes in Nanjing. These crimes were as incredible as they were numerous. The bones of hundreds of thousands of victims were buried deep in the soil. They may have been left to rot, but the Chinese people never forgot their crimes, nor would they let the Japanese forget.

The Tokyo trials across the sea gave the Chinese the opportunity they'd been looking for.

Blood will have blood. It is inevitable, as were China's demands for the Japanese to pay for their crimes.

The retribution for Japan's war crimes should have covered all events from 18 September 1931 – the date of the Mukden Incident - to 2 September 1945 when they announced their formal surrender, during which time the crimes of the Japanese army in China were simply horrific. The International Military Tribunal for the Far East regarded the Nanjing Massacre as one of the key events in the crimes committed by the Japanese, and it appointed Keenan as the attorney general of the prosecution, which also included several Chinese judges. However, the Chinese government didn't quite understand the Anglo-American law adopted in the Tokyo trials and its emphasis on evidence and witnesses. In particular, the testimony of key witnesses can often affect the final outcome of a trial. Chinese civil law on the other hand typically emphasises the role of the judge and ignores the collection of evidence. The Nationalist government headed by Chiang Kai-shek shared the view that it was an indisputable fact that Japan had invaded China and people all over the world had witnessed their crimes. As a result, they considered the Tokyo trials to be a kind of formality. The government was quietly confident that the Japanese war criminals would be sentenced to death. This meant that when the International Military Tribunal for the Far East asked China to send people to participate in the trial, China sent just a small group of jurists. The Chinese jurist Zheng even said: "The Nationalist government thought that it was certain that the victor would punish the vanquished, and the trial was a kind of formality. We didn't need evidence for the crimes. They didn't expect such a strict application of the law regarding evidence."

But the Chinese estimation had been wrong and more focus was placed on evidence with the Tokyo trials being in the hands of the Americans and a group of British jurists.

Keenan, from the US, had a key role in the Tokyo trials. He was the assistant attorney general of the US and an important American representative in the court in Tokyo. Keenan had arrived in Tokyo on 6 December 1945 before MacArthur had established the International Military Tribunal for the Far East.

Keenan, 57, was a graduate of the Harvard law school. In 1933, he served as a special assistant for the Department of Justice. Two years later, he was appointed as the chief of the Department of Justice Criminal Division. He was decisive and merciless, earning the nickname "the demon prosecutor".

The Japanese invaders had acted like demons so it was fitting that they'd be prosecuted by the "demon prosecutor". However, after Keenan arrived in Tokyo, MacArthur clearly pointed out to him: "I have three suggestions for you about the trial. First, try them as soon as possible; second, simplify the reason for prosecuting the Japanese war criminals, focus on the massacre; third, emphasise Pearl Harbor."

Keenan hesitated but nodded in agreement.

What did this mean? Did the International Military Tribunal for the Far East just apply to Americans? China was one of the victors and had been the main battleground in the war against the Japanese. Would the deaths of the 35 million Chinese people in the war be ignored? It wasn't clear. Many strange incidents like this later took place.

The majority of the Japanese army's victims had been Asian. But despite this, the indictment was drafted by the British. The department of public prosecutions and the court essentially consisted of just American and British officials.

The Chinese prosecution arrived in Japan in February 1946. The leader of the group was the famous jurist Dr Mei Ju-ao and the prosecutor was the philosopher Xiang Zhejun.

By the end of February, representatives from 11 countries gathered together, making arrangements about the content and tone of the indictment. The chairman of the committee that had drafted the indictment, the British prosecutor Carr, condescendingly announced: "In view of the large impact of the trial of the Japanese war criminals and the vast amount of work required, the International Military Tribunal for the Far East should make the job as simple as possible. To achieve this goal, the number of defendants should be limited to fewer than 15 people, up to a maximum of 20 people."

"Twenty people? This is ludicrous. The Chinese government alone has listed 33 Class A war criminals. If we follow Mr Carr's suggestion, would the war criminals who've massacred the Chinese just escape punishment?"

"How can we explain this to the Chinese people and government? Twenty people? No! Absolutely not!"

The Chinese prosecutor Xiang Zhejun expressed his sincere dissatisfaction.

"Thirty-three people? You Chinese have too large an appetite! Do you know how many Nazi war criminals were prosecuted in the Nuremberg trials? Twenty-two!" interrupted Carl Bender, a member of the international inspectorate sitting near Keenan and Carr, looking down on the Chinese prosecution.

Xiang Zhejun didn't agree and replied: "Didn't you consider that there may be more Japanese war criminals than Nazi war criminals? Why should we arbitrarily determine how many people to charge first instead of just charging everyone who committed a war crime?"

Bender was silent. He threw up his hands and shrugged as if to question the abilities of the Chinese prosecution. The room went silent.

The Americans now spoke up: "The war in the Pacific broke out because of Pearl Harbor, so the International Military Tribunal for the Far East should severely punish the Japanese war criminals who attacked Pearl Harbor, while any other Japanese war criminals should be dealt with leniently."

The Chinese prosecutors were angry after hearing this absurd argument: "The crimes committed by the Japanese invaders in Asia lasted longer than the Nazis' crimes in Europe. The Japanese committed far worse crimes than the attack on Pearl Harbor, so all Japanese criminals who committed crimes in China and other Asian countries should be punished too!"

"Yes, the attacks on China were bad, but wasn't the attack on Pearl Harbor bad too?" The Americans got up from their chairs.

"The attack on Pearl Harbor cannot be the main focus for prosecution!" The Chinese prosecutors wouldn't budge.

Keenan eventually made a suggestion: "Okay! Okay! Gentlemen, you make some very valid points. However, this case is enormous and incredibly complex and we don't have much time, so we need to limit the number of prosecutions appropriately. War criminals that aren't prosecuted in the first batch will be prosecuted in the second or third batch. Countries can also be authorised by the International Military Tribunal for the Far East to set up independent trials. This would solve the problems you and your countries have. What do you think?"

Although the Chinese prosecutors felt helpless, they still conceded to the compromise.

So, who was to be judged before history at the trial? A new fierce debate broke out once again. On 11 March 1946, Meiji Memorial Hall in Tokyo held an attorney board meeting, held by the Executive Committee. Eleven international prosecution officials gathered to discuss and decide the list of the first batch of Japanese war criminal defendants.

Tojo, the man who had organised the attack on Pearl Harbor, was unanimously chosen to be prosecuted in the first trial. To give this "honour" to Tojo, the American prosecutors prepared a great deal of evidence and witnesses.

All the other countries wanted to try him too, so they had the full support of the prosecution.

The Chinese prosecutor Xiang Zhejun was sitting three seats to the right of the chief prosecutor, Keenan. Although it was a very good position, he seemed anxious and often distracted.

"Now let's start the discussion on Matsui. Chinese prosecutors, please read out your statements," said Keenan, motioning towards Xiang.

"Thank you, chief prosecutor." Xiang hurriedly picked up the statement and began to read.

When he finished reading, Keenan looked around at all of the prosecutors and called out: "Now, could the Chinese witnesses give their testimonies, please."

At that point, the Chinese Nationalist government's military chief minister Qin Dechun, who had already been waiting in the lobby, strode into the hall with a militaristic posture. He appeared in front of all of the international prosecutors. Qin gave a standard military salute. Given the prosecutors' awareness of the Nanjing Massacre, they were eager to hear him speak.

Qin Dechun confidently opened his briefcase and took out a piece of paper on which he'd drafted his testimony. He then read it out like a schoolboy. The content of the speech was well written, with frequent references to the Japanese army's heinous looting, arson, murder and rape. About 10 minutes went by.

Suddenly, an American prosecutor interrupted Qin: "No, no, my dear Chinese prosecutor, this is a court, not a classroom! Please show us the evidence of these crimes! We want evidence, not empty words!"

People in the venue then started to murmur and whisper, echoing the American's sentiments. Xiang and the other Chinese prosecutors looked panicked. How could the Chinese government have sent such a foolish officer? How could the Chinese government appoint this man as its military chief?

Xiang Zhejun's hands shook. He had warned Qin about this in advance. However, Qin was arrogant and said that the Nanjing Massacre was an irrefutable fact, so all he had to do was say a few words and then the criminals would be sentenced to death. Xiang deeply regretted trusting him, but it was too late.

"Mr Qin, have you brought any evidence of specific cases?" Keenan asked.

Qin didn't know what to say and just *ummed* and *ahhed* to himself. The prosecutors from the other countries started laughing.

"The witness has no evidence. Have you come to Tokyo to learn about our atomic bomb?" joked the American attorney.

"You Chinese said the Japanese army massacred the people of Nanjing, but you have no witnesses or evidence. Are you trying to make a mockery of this court?" said another.

The prosecutors were furious and the courtroom descended into chaos once again.

"Gentlemen! Please! Be quiet!" Keenan was visibly annoyed as he motioned for quiet with his hands. He then turned to face Xiang to his right: "Mr Prosecutor, I am truly sorry, but your country hasn't submitted sufficient evidence so we cannot prosecute Matsui for the Nanjing Massacre in the first trial. Please tell your government what has happened as soon as possible. I fully understand that you have suffered from Japanese aggression, and as a representative of your country, I'm sure you'll act accordingly."

Xiang nodded several times; he didn't dare lift his head. He felt ashamed of himself and his country. This was beyond a disgrace. The Japanese invaders had killed so many people in Nanjing, but no one had brought any evidence to make sure that the criminals saw justice. It was an insult and he feared the reaction of his 400 million countrymen.

Xiang didn't know how he could face leaving the courtroom that day.

In the evening, the Chinese representatives gathered in Mei Ju-ao's room in the Imperial Hotel. Everyone angrily shouted about how they interpreted the events, complaining that China was being attacked. Justice Mei sighed deeply.

"How do we correct this? We need to come up with an idea immediately."

"How? We need to return to China to collect evidence as soon as possible."

"Yes, yes. We'll apply to the international bureau for another prosecution. We also need to send someone back to collect evidence immediately."

"Mr Prosecutor, what do you think?" Mei asked Xiang for his opinion.

"I agree. We should send someone to collect evidence immediately," he said.

"I'll go back," volunteered Qiu Shaoheng, 33 years old.

"Good! Shaoheng, your burden is as heavy as Mount Tai. We await your return to Tokyo." Mei and Xiang grasped Qiu Shaoheng's hands in thanks.

They then proceeded to implement their plans. The prosecutors began to diverge between Tokyo and China as Qiu Shaoheng returned to gather evidence. The others were led by Xiang Zhejun to find evidence in Tokyo. After the Allied powers had captured the Japanese capital, they'd found many secret files that proved that the Japanese government had launched a war of aggression. Xiang found a great deal of evidence.

When Qiu returned to China and told the authorities what had happened, the government took the news seriously. Hearing about the need to collect evidence of the Nanjing Massacre, the people of Nanjing immediately volunteered to help. Qiu then returned to Tokyo with plenty of empirical evidence this time.

Meanwhile, the international department of public prosecutions discussed the Chinese problem and felt that they shouldn't ignore an event like the Nanjing Massacre as it may be detrimental to the reputation of the International Military Tribunal for the Far East. They decided that Keenan should go to China personally. Despite the chief prosecutor being busy, he had to do so to try the Japanese war criminals.

Keenan arrived in China on 16 March 1946, a month and a half before the trial. Hawkes, Hurst, Locke, Lee and members of the international inspectorate, which had been set up by the international tribunals, hastily went with Keenan. They first went to Shanghai on an Allied aircraft and then left for Nanjing. Accompanied by the Chinese prosecutor Xiang, they met with more than a dozen witnesses of the Nanjing Massacre. They gathered evidence while they were there and then returned to Tokyo. Although it was short and rushed, their trip was described as "an excellently done job" by the international inspectorate.

On 1 April, the international prosecution office held its last meeting to determine the list of war criminals to be prosecuted. The principal criminal behind the Nanjing Massacre, Iwane Matsui, was listed in the first batch of war criminals to be prosecuted. Xiang was greatly relieved.

There was a month to go until court began in early May. Keenan said the Tokyo trials would be a long and arduous affair. After prosecuting the war criminals listed by the court, each country could continue to collect evidence based on their individual situations in order to judge the war criminals more effectively. The international prosecution office sent out their prosecutor, Laurie, to China.

The American prosecutor Laurie travelled to China and found a lot of new evidence. However, Keenan wasn't satisfied with it. He then sent out his right-hand man, the prosecutor David Nelson Sutton, to conduct further research. On the afternoon of 31 May, Sutton arrived in Shanghai with his assistants, including Lieutenant Luke Lee and Joe Alexander, to focus on investigating the Nanjing Massacre and the Japanese crime of promoting the use of opium in China.

On 3 June, Sutton arrived in Nanjing.

In the United Nations Disaster Relief Organisation (UNDRO) headquarters in China, an American offered Sutton an interesting clue: "There's someone you should find who'd be valuable in the trial. His name is Fitch. When the Japanese army occupied Nanjing, he stayed in the city. He's still working in China."

"Ask the Chinese government for help. We need to meet Mr Fitch immediately and tell him to come with us to Tokyo." The next day, Sutton made an appointment to meet the vice president of the Chinese executive council, Weng Wenhao, and hoped that he'd be able to help transfer Fitch from Kaifeng in Henan to Nanjing.

"Although this could be a little difficult, we'll do what we can to help," chuckled Weng Wenhao, responding to Sutton in English. Fitch was the director of UNDRO in the Henan office. He couldn't leave his post unless there was an emergency.

After talking to Weng, Sutton took an American military plane from the Chinese headquarters to find Fitch in Kaifeng. He then flew him back to Nanjing.

"Testify in Tokyo? It'd be my pleasure! The Japanese did so many wicked things in Nanjing. It's my duty to appear in court," said Fitch immediately after Sutton asked.

"I heard that you did a lot of humanitarian work for the Chinese with some other American professors, doctors and preachers during the Nanjing Massacre. I'd like to give you my sincere thanks for appearing in court to prosecute these war criminals on behalf of the American people and the court," said Sutton as he hugged Fitch warmly.

"You should look for another person, he's very important. He was my secretary when we established the international safety zone. He was responsible for investigating the Japanese crimes and finishing reports."

"Who is he?"

"Professor Smythe."

Sutton was delighted, saying: "I've heard of him. Where is he?"

"He's in Nanjing".

"Good! I'll go and find him at once," Sutton said. He was incredibly pleased, feeling as if he'd unearthed some buried treasure.

When he saw Smythe, Sutton confidently invited him and Fitch to Tokyo, but Smythe refused: "I'm a professor at Nanjing University. I can't leave with you."

Sutton hadn't expected Smythe's reply and his face turned red. He controlled his anger, calming down, and said: "The war against the Japanese not only caused a great deal of damage to China and Asia, but also the US. The attack on Pearl Harbor is just one example. Every one of us is obligated to appear in court as a witness to seek justice for their crimes."

"You're right, and I don't want to abandon this obligation, but I just have so much work to do," Smythe said to the visitors in his characteristic intellectual style. He thought for a moment and said: "I'd be happy to write a detailed report with evidence on the crimes the Japanese committed in Nanjing, which could be used as evidence. Would that suffice?"

"That would be wonderful," Sutton replied. Several days later, Smythe's important testimony was delivered to Sutton.

"Have you tried finding Mr Rabe in Germany? After the Japanese took Nanjing, he was incredibly important and led the International Committee to carry out great work. He's also an important witness," Smythe said to Sutton.

"Things with him are... complicated," said Sutton. He had been discredited as a witness due to his membership of the Nazi Party and had even been called upon during the Nuremburg trials.

"I see. That's a real shame," sighed Smythe.

On 5 June, Sutton found the mayor of Wanping at the time of the Marco Polo Bridge Incident, Wang Lengzhai, through the chief of general staff of the Chinese army. Then, Sutton met Xu Chuanyin. Xu had been a teacher at Jinling College and was willing to appear in court. He also found the survivors Chen Fubao and Shang Deyi on 7 June. On 8 June, Sutton met with Mayor Ma Chaojun and found Lieutenant Liang Tingfang.

On 10 June, they all agreed to go to Tokyo for the prosecution. The official representative, Qin Dechun, had made a fool of himself and now said that he didn't want to go to Tokyo. However, Sutton still wanted him to appear in court, which had been Keenan's idea. Sutton got the chief of general staff, Chen Cheng, to persuade Qin and he eventually reluctantly agreed.

At 10.15am on 12 June, Sutton brought 15 witnesses back from China, including Xu Chuanyin, Liang Tingfang, Shang Deyi, Wu Changde, Chen Fubao, Wang Lengzhai, Bates, Qin Dechun and others. They were transported via Allied military aircraft and left China from Shanghai's Hongwan Airport. They arrived at Houmu Airport in Japan at 4.20pm. They met with other witnesses including John Magee, who'd been found by the international prosecution office and together, they formed the Chinese group of witnesses.

It was a hot Tokyo summer. Strong winds from the sea battered the city, making the people panic. However, there was one place in the city that remained calm and collected: the International Military Tribunal for the Far East.

Iwane Matsui to Be Hanged

There was no doubt that the amount of evidence regarding the Japanese crimes during the Nanjing Massacre would directly influence the outcome of the entire trial, which followed the Anglo-American legal system. On the world stage, China had suffered repeatedly and had felt wronged many times. As for the evidence in the Japanese war criminals' trial, it wasn't that

China didn't have evidence, but that the Chinese government hadn't paid enough attention to the Tokyo trials at the time. The Philippines in contrast had immediately planned and arranged its evidence and the Americans helped to determine keynote speakers and regulations. As a result, the trial on the crimes in the Philippines went well, while China almost let off its only Class A war criminal Iwane Matsui. Prior to the Tokyo trials, China had been incompetent in its search for evidence, proving the incompetence of the government.

In the Second Historical Archives of China, I found an overwhelming amount of evidence regarding the Nanjing Massacre from the citizens of Nanjing several years before 1946. Hadn't this been during the period of Japanese rule? Why had ordinary people dared to discuss Japanese atrocities?

In the period of Japanese rule, Nanjing had been manipulated by the Japanese army, which had established a puppet government. This was the Municipal Committee at first, and then it later became the seat of a national puppet government under the traitor Wang Jingwei. The desperate civilians suffered from cold and hunger, but still persevered, regardless of who was in power. So, during this period, many wrote voluntary reports on what had happened to try to get help, providing evidence regarding the Japanese atrocities during the Nanjing Massacre. I found several texts compiling thousands of people's reports, which provide another level of evidence of what happened in Nanjing.

Selected document 1:
Liu Zhicai's mother was killed
The Nanjing police agency submitted this document to the Nanjing municipal bureau. (11 May 1938)

> Supervisory Nanjing municipal bureau,
>
> This is our report. The fourth police office reported at 6am on the 9th day of this month, that according to the resident of 15 Dongmen Street, Liu Zhicai, at 12pm on the 8th day, a Japanese soldier with a white shirt broke into the resident's house and tried to rape girls. Fortunately, Liu had gone out and hadn't come back. The Japanese soldier then left. At 10pm, the Japanese soldier broke in again through the windows and didn't find anyone. Then, he went into Liu's mother's room and beat her cruelly. Her mother escaped and the Japanese soldier chased her all the way. Liu didn't dare go out at night, and she didn't see her mother the next morning. She went out and found her mother. Arriving at 12 Dongmen Street, she saw her mother lying on the grass with

blood all over her body. She had been dead for a long time. More than 100 yuan had been stolen. They needed to catch the killer. We immediately sent out officials and the police to report to the branch of military police on Yihe Road and rushed to the location of the incident. Injuries on the deceased's face and chest were found after investigation. The wound on the chest was about 10 centimetres long and two centimetres wide. The military police also arrived. Three officials and soldiers and a translator sent out by the Xinjiekou military police helped to investigate. They found out that the murderer was a soldier from the Sata unit of Tagami's troops. Fifty-four yuan and a dagger about 23 centimetres long were found on the soldier. The military policemen helped to deal with the soldier and the money. Liu Zhicai was told to wait for information. This case has been reported and needs to be checked and reviewed by the agency. We are waiting for this information.

Yours sincerely,

— Wang Chunsheng, Chief of police in Nanjing

Selected document 2:
Investigation by Zhu Shou from the Nanjing social department
The report regarding Mrs Tian (née Zhou) being killed by the Japanese army has been submitted. (9 June 1938)

Please transfer this to Mr Wang, the division chief,

This is our report. We are required to investigate the case of the refugee Mrs Tian (née Zhou) of 14 Dayoufang Lane. She is 27 years old and a native of Nanjing. Her husband was a platoon leader and was killed in a refugee zone last year. They have a son, called Huilong. He is nine years old. Their eldest daughter is seven years old. The youngest daughter is Huihu, four years old. Her mother is Mrs Zhou (née Xie), 65 years old. They live together. There are five people in the family living in difficult circumstances. Their relatives are poor and cannot help them. After a thorough investigation, we verified their situation. They are very poor and in need of help.

The situation is truly as described. Please review and check this with the section chief.

Yours,

— Zhu Shou

Selected document 3:
Submitted by Mrs Zhu (née Du) (26 June 1939)

Submitted sincerely to Gao, the mayor of the Nanjing special municipality,

This report is written on behalf of the widow, Mrs Zhu (née Du), 40 years old, native of Nanjing, living at 8 Neitanglangfang, Zhonghua gate.

The widow lives by herself and her two young sons. They live in difficult circumstances and plead for shelter and relief. Her husband once worked in the bamboo business. Unfortunately, he died following an incident. Her two sons are still young and they live in poverty. For the past two years, they have had little to eat and cannot get money and food to survive. They can do nothing but plead with the head of the neighbourhood administration to verify their situation and report it to the senior authorities. They plead for the mayor to help with their living conditions and allow them to have shelter and relief. They would be extremely grateful. By doing this, you will be rewarded by God. They look forward to your response.

On behalf of Mrs Zhu (née Du) and her sons, eight years old and three years old.

— Wo Jingxian, the vice director of the Fourteen Mill neighbourhood administration, second district. Liu Yicai, head of the eighth district administration

Selected document 4:
Submitted by Cai Yuankang (6 November 1940)

Submitted sincerely to the relief committee,

I beg you for shelter and relief to survive. I am a refugee, Cai Yuankang, from Nanjing. I had a shop in Nanjing. Unfortunately, my family went through a series of disasters. When the war began, my sons, wife, parents and daughter-in-law died in the bombing and gunfire. All of our property was robbed. Our house was burned to ashes. However, I escaped. Now I am lonely and unable to make a living. At such an old age, I am constantly sad and worry a great deal. Now, I have become ill. I suffer from cold and hunger every day. I am writing this to make you aware of my situation so you can investigate. Please provide me with shelter and relief. I would be eternally grateful.

Yours,

— The disabled refugee Cai Yuankang. Staying temporarily at 17 Mendong Zhuanlong Lane

Despite the simplicity of these reports, they hold remarkable historical value because they were written by people who in no way seemed to have been forced to testify.

After the Second Sino-Japanese War, the national government tried to contribute to punishing the Japanese for their war crimes. When the task of judging the Japanese war criminals in the Tokyo trials and the Chinese military tribunals began, the Nationalist government launched a thorough investigation of the Japanese crimes in Nanjing. This was the first time that China had launched such an in-depth investigation of the Nanjing Massacre since defeating the Japanese. On 7 November 1945, the Nanjing government accepted the orders of the central government and arranged for 14 institutions and groups, including the municipal government, the KMT party headquarters in Nanjing, the courts and police of the capital, and the Nanjing branch of the Red Cross, to have a joint meeting in a courtroom in the capital. They set up the Nanjing War Crimes Tribunal at the meeting and decided to help the national government's administration to organise and implement the task from top to bottom. When the news spread, the entire city reacted and many civilians went to the municipal government to volunteer to participate in the investigation. Most of them were relatives of victims. Some of them were survivors of the massacre, who'd lived in misery for so many years until the floodgates opened and the pain poured out. Even the normally stern policemen shed tears of sympathy.

"Please calm down. As long as you have information, you can come to us at any time. We shall make sure that no crime goes unpunished."

On this day, Chen Yuguang and Chen Yaodong adopted the positions of chairman and vice chairman of the investigation committee respectively. Xiao Ruoxu then took up the position of secretary general of the Nanjing temporary consultative committee. In addition to all the members of the Nanjing temporary consultative committee and the investigation committee, all the district heads of Nanjing, relevant institutions, groups and representatives joined as members. The number of staff investigating in each district, county and town grew bigger. In order to ensure the investigation was conducted properly, the government was responsible for the city and districts and sent out supervising members to each district and town, being responsible for supervising them and urging others to come forward.

In a few days' time, the Nanjing consultative committee and the Nanjing War Crimes Tribunal made a joint announcement: "In the 26th year of the Republic of China, when Nanjing was occupied, the enemy slaughtered our citizens. We are now investigating the hard evidence. Then, we will provide the evidence to the International Military Tribunal for the Far East for reference. Those murderers will be extradited to Nanjing to be judged and executed. We ask all citizens to cooperate with us in this matter."

The work of the investigative committee was prudent, meticulous and professional. They gave the investigators professional training and were strict in their conduct. Everyone made an oath to the government and the law that the results of their investigations were accurate.

The following investigations went far and wide. Technology was, of course, limited compared to the modern age and the wounds of the citizens of Nanjing were still sore. Vital organisations and living conditions for citizens were chaotic as a blanket investigation was carried out from street to street, from door to door, even going as far as making their own way into houses. This task was carried out for six months from June 1946 and focussed on the cases of the citizens of Nanjing during the occupation. It was said that more than 10,000 families were investigated. There were 2,784 cases that were determined to be used as testimonies. Some cases involved the murders of dozens of people in just one case. Those reports and documents still had to be reviewed by the investigation committee in case of any mistakes. They were then submitted for use at the Tokyo trials and the Nanjing tribunal.

I recently saw the original investigative reports in the Second History Archives of China. These documents are hard evidence for the Nanjing Massacre. As time went on in the investigation, the results it yielded became more and more horrifying. The Nanjing War Crimes Tribunal's work is truly remarkable and essential reading for anyone who still doubts or denies the massacre.

The reports I read used "bao" as a unit, which refers to the lowest-level administrative organisation during the Nationalist government period. Ten households made up one "pai", 10 "pai" constituted one "jia", and every 10 "jia" formed a "bao". The investigative committee sent out at least 40 *bao* level investigation groups to investigate and report on the entire city.

Hard evidence of the crimes committed by the Japanese in Nanjing was found as the investigation went on following the end of the Second Sino-Japanese War. However, this precious evidence didn't reach Tokyo in time. Instead, it was later used in the Nanjing War Crimes Tribunal.

Since the opening of the International Military Tribunal for the Far East on 3 May 1946, the trial had seen fierce accusations and debates with the Japanese war criminals. Although murderers like Iwane Matsui had been imprisoned for a long time, they remained immoral in their conduct. There was still much to be done to make sure that Matsui saw justice and was judged before history accordingly.

After Matsui was sent the legal document accusing him of being a Class A war criminal, as a key criminal behind the Nanjing Massacre, the international military court verified the charges against him face to face in prison. Matsui, a gaunt yet shrewd man, unexpectedly denied the charges. The record of the trial at the International Military Tribunal for the Far East in the American archives is described below, proving the crimes beyond all doubt.

In July 1946, the legal testimonies and arguments in the trials regarding the Nanjing Massacre began. This was one of the key parts of the trial, with fierce debates on both sides.

The president of the tribunal, Webb, appeared in person and presided over the trial.

He began: "Iwane Matsui, how do you plea to these accusations of your crimes?"

Everyone in the court stared at Matsui, who was sat in the dock. He held the materials for his defence and slowly lifted his head, saying: "The contents of the indictment are purely subjective and are not based on fact. As for the actions that were not military in nature, they have been exaggerated a great deal."

The courtroom was alive with murmurs.

Webb banged his gavel, saying: "Order, order!"

The prosecutor immediately raised his hand: "Your honour, I would like to call our witness to the stand."

President Webb agreed.

Sutton called out: "We invite Dr Robert Wilson to testify."

Wilson then appeared in the courtroom and went to the stand.

Sutton asked: "Are you Robert Wilson from Arcadia, California?"

Wilson: "Yes."

Sutton then asked a series of questions for Wilson to answer. He began: "Dr Wilson, when and where were you born?"

Wilson responded: "I was born on 5 October 1906 in Nanjing, China."

"What is your occupation? Where did you receive your education?"

"I'm a surgeon, and I studied at the medical schools at Princeton and Harvard."

"Did you return to China after graduating from medical school? If so, when did you start to practice medicine in China?"

"I went back to China in January 1936. I then worked as a doctor in Nanjing University until August 1940."

"Did you have a close relationship with the Nanjing University medical school? If so, in what capacity?"

"I was a surgeon at Nanjing University Hospital."

"Did all the Chinese doctors and nurses leave the hospital after the fall of Nanjing in 1937?"

Brooks, the court's defence counsel, suddenly interrupted the questioning: "If you'll allow me to interject, I object to asking questions in this way because this form of questioning is too subjective. I request the judge to instruct the prosecution not to ask questions that are too subjective and to ask them objectively."

Webb shook his head gently: "This is just an introductory question, and he's entitled to ask them as such."

Wilson continued to answer the question: "In late November 1937, after the fall of Shanghai, the Japanese troops advanced to Nanjing. The medical care personnel at the hospital came to us and requested us all to leave Nanjing before the Japanese army occupied the city. The reason for doing so was that they'd heard about a lot of incidents in the cities between Shanghai and Nanjing. These cities included Suzhou, Wuxi, Zhenjiang and Danyang. Our staff were afraid that their lives were at risk so they desperately wanted to leave Nanjing. We tried to comfort them and tell them that there would be almost no danger after the fall of Nanjing because of the protection of international law. However, we couldn't convince them and a lot of people left and travelled upstream on the Yangtze River. So only Dr Trimmer - another American doctor - five nurses and I chose to stay, as well as some cleaning staff. Prior to this, there had been a total of 20 Chinese doctors, about 40 to 50 nurses and general practice nurses. They all left Nanjing on 1 December."

Sutton continued with his questioning: "Before the fall of Nanjing, how much had the number of patients at the hospital reduced?"

"When almost all of our staff left the hospital, we had to decrease the number of patients to an incredibly small number. We sent as many patients as possible back home. There were only about 50 patients who didn't have anywhere to go or who were too weak to move."

"After 13 December 1937, did the situation change at all? If so, in what way did it change?"

"The Japanese army moved into the city on the morning of 13 December. On the night of 12 December, all the resistance had stopped. In just a few days the hospital was filled with men and women of all ages, with all sorts of injuries."

Brooks raised his hands to protest once again: "If the court allows it, I object to this form of questioning. I think the court…"

Justice Webb interrupted him: "I can't hear you, say it again with a microphone."

Brooks picked up a microphone and said loudly: "If the court allows, I think this form of questioning should not be warranted. This will affect the judgment of the tribunal. I think the court should understand that the defence would agree that there are always casualties, including women, children and civilians, in war. I propose that this is removed from the record."

"Objection overruled, continue."

Brooks once again protested: "I object once again on the grounds that this is an issue that has no relation to the issue we want to discuss, which is who started the war. I do not see how this question is related to this case."

Justice Webb hit his gavel loudly: "Objection overruled."

The court was in silence once again.

Sutton continued with his questioning: "Doctor, can you talk about the injuries of the patients at your hospital?"

"I can only discuss the injuries of some of the patients that I treated just after the fall of Nanjing. However, I cannot remember many of their names, except for a couple of witnesses sitting here. One case I remember was that a 40 year old woman had come to the hospital after she had sustained a huge wound on her neck; all her neck muscles had been sliced open."

Another defence lawyer, Matisse, raised his hand: "I would like to interrupt the witness's statement. Firstly, what the witness has said is hearsay; secondly, it doesn't have any connection to the question he has been asked. He was asked to describe injuries that he had seen, but this is something that someone told him."

Justice Webb: "Overruled. This is not a valid case of hearsay."

Wilson continued: "By asking the patient, as well as the person who had brought her to the hospital, we knew there was no doubt that this injury had been caused by the Japanese soldiers."

Justice Webb asked Sutton to ask Wilson to discuss other injuries.

Sutton did so.

Wilson described more cases: "A boy, only eight years old, was taken to the hospital. He had a deep wound on his stomach that exposed his organs. The hospital also accepted another patient whose right shoulder had been wounded, apparently caused by a bullet. If the court allows it, I will pass on what he told me. He was the only survivor of a group of people that had been taken to the Yangtze by the Japanese soldiers to be shot and killed one by one. Their bodies were then put into the river, so the actual number of casualties cannot be determined. He pretended to be dead and fled to the hospital at night. His surname was Liang. Another person was a Chinese policeman, who had a deep wound in the middle of his back when he arrived at the hospital. He was also the only survivor out of a group of Chinese people who had been taken away from the city. He had been shot with machine guns and then stabbed with a bayonet. This was a method used by the Japanese soldiers to ensure that all the Chinese had been killed. This man's name is Wu Changde.

"One day, I was in my room for lunch at midday. Suddenly the neighbours ran over to me and told me that several Japanese soldiers were raping women on the table in their room. We immediately rushed over and went to their house. The door had been shut tight and three Japanese soldiers stood in the courtyard with guns in their hands. We rushed into the room and found two Japanese soldiers raping two women. We immediately rescued them and sent them to the refugee camp in Nanjing University. The campus was packed with a large number of refugees who were being protected by the International Committee.

"Later, another man was taken to hospital. A bullet had hit his chin so he couldn't really talk. Two-thirds of his body had been severely burned. He told us what had happened to him. I tried incredibly hard to understand what he was saying. He'd been captured by Japanese soldiers, doused with petrol and set on fire. He died two days later.

"Another man was admitted to the hospital with severe burns covering his entire head and both shoulders. Fortunately, he could speak and told us that he was the sole survivor out of a large number of people. These people had been tied together, doused with petrol and then set on fire.

"We have photos of the cases mentioned above.

"The hospital also admitted an old man who was more than 60 years old. He had a bayonet wound in his chest. He told us that he'd gone to another area of Nanjing to find his relatives after he left the refugee camps. Halfway there, he ran across a group of Japanese soldiers and they stabbed him with bayonets. They thought he was dead and threw him in the gutter. Six hours later, he regained consciousness and was taken to hospital.

"An infinite number of incidents like these happened on 13 December 1937 when Nanjing fell. The hospital had 180 beds and they were all occupied every day during this period."

A wave of depression washed over courtroom, apart from the defendants. Everyone had been shocked by the American doctor's statement.

Sutton asked: "Doctor, were there any other children who were taken to the hospital during this period?"

Wilson answered: "I still remember two other children. One was a girl, seven years old, whose elbow had been seriously injured. You could clearly see the bone. She told us that Japanese soldiers had killed her parents in front of her and she had been slashed and wounded. Another girl was 15 years old, taken to hospital by the priest John Magee. She said that she'd been raped, and the examination confirmed this. Two months later, the girl was sent back to the hospital and was diagnosed with secondary syphilis."

"Did these patients tell you who had caused these injuries?"

"They just said... they all said that they had been injured by the Japanese soldiers."

"Doctor, these two patients, Liang Shangwei and Wu Changde, are they in Japan?"

"I know Liang Shangwei. He was a stretcher bearer in the Chinese army. He's currently in Japan and we came here together to give evidence. Wu Changde, the policeman I mentioned earlier, has also come here."

The atmosphere in the courtroom was emotional and excited. Just as the people present were looking forward to the testimonies of the two Chinese victims Wilson had mentioned, Justice Webb looked at his watch and pounded his gavel: "Let's take a recess until 9.30 tomorrow morning."

It had been a remarkable day for the prosecution. The testimony of the first witness had stifled Matsui's arrogant attitude. People noticed that the thin, old man looked rather less confident than the man who had first appeared in court.

The trial continued the next day. China used Xu Chuanyin, a professor at Nanjing University, as a witness.

The procedures continued as usual. The prosecutor first showed the witness's written material and evidence, and then swore an oath in court to guarantee the accuracy of their testimony. Xu Chuanyin was a university professor and fluent in English. Therefore, McManus, the Japanese legal defence, said: "If I may, I'd like to make a protest. I found out from Mr Levine yesterday that the witness is university educated and fluent in English, so obviously he is a smart man. We object to the use of his sworn testimony. The court should obtain testimonies from witnesses directly."

Justice Webb said: "Mr McManus, I would like to know more about this person. We have not heard his statement. Mr Sutton, please start asking questions so that we can form a judgment."

McManus suddenly raised the written testimony in his hands, looking angry and asked Webb: "You agree to accept the document?"

Xu had submitted a copy of his document to the tribunal before he appeared in court. The document was sent to both the prosecution and the defence to be used to ask questions. Why had the defence lawyer objected so strongly to the document Xu had submitted? The truth is that it was an utterly damning indictment of the Japanese crimes. The testimony is as follows:

The Testimony of Xu Chuanyin

International Military Tribunal for the Far East, File No. 1734, Evidence Files: No. 205

I am Xu Chuanyin, PhD, now living at 7 Emei Road, Gaoloumen, Nanjing, China. I testify as follows.

I am Chinese, aged 62. I received my PhD from the University of Illinois in the US. I have long been teaching in many universities in China and I have worked for the Chinese ministry of transportation for 25 years. My family has been living in Nanjing since 1928.

I was living in the city when the Japanese army occupied Nanjing in 1937. After Nanjing fell into the hands of the Japanese, I stayed there. I was a member of the International Committee in the safety zone and I was responsible for work in the subordinate housing committee. I also served as director general of the international relief committee. I was later president of the Red Cross society after the fall of Nanjing.

I know all about what happened in Nanjing after the Japanese soldiers conquered and entered the city. The Japanese troops entered the city from the south gate. The Chinese troops did not make any real resistance after the Japanese soldiers broke through the walls into the city. After the [Japanese] army entered the city, they brazenly gunned down the civilians. Some civilians were killed just because they were out on the street.

The Japanese soldiers then searched all the houses and robbed food and everything else from the civilians. They also captured all the young men they found, stating that these people had been soldiers in the Chinese army. Then the Japanese soldiers pulled them out of the city or shot them on the spot. I have heard compelling information that the vast majority of people who were later escorted away were shot or massacred on a large scale.

They demanded the right to enter the safety zone to conduct searches and took away a lot of men they found there. I saw them take away a group of people with my own eyes, nearly 1,500 people. According to the information I received, the people taken away were later shot with machine guns and their bodies were thrown into the water. Members of the Red Cross society later found the bodies and buried them.

The Japanese ordered the people to line up orderly under the pretext of issuing "good citizen certificates". If the answers to their interrogations weren't to their liking, or the Japanese soldiers thought someone had been a soldier despite there not being any evidence, the person would be executed on the spot immediately or taken away with groups of men to be shot later.

There was no form of resistance in the city. The Japanese soldiers took away men or executed them under the pretext that they were Chinese soldiers. After these people were cleared away, [the Japanese] began a frenzied massacre of the civilians, raping girls and women, looting and burning property. From 13 year old girls to 70 year old women, none could escape the sexual assaults of the Japanese soldiers. Some were raped many times. Thousands of women were killed by Japanese soldiers after being raped and humiliated. The atrocities happened all over the city and the surrounding areas. I remember a tragic incident with a family at 7 Sin Kai Road in the south of the city. Eleven people in the family were killed.

The Japanese soldiers came to the house and knocked on the door. The grandfather then opened the door. He was shot on the spot and died immediately. His wife, who was 35 or so, went out to see what had happened, but she was also shot a few steps away from her husband. Their daughter, holding a baby, went to investigate. The Japanese soldiers killed both of them. Another two girls in the family, aged 17 and 14, were both unmarried and were killed by the Japanese soldiers after being raped. One girl died on a table, surrounded by a pool of blood, with a stick inserted in her vagina. The other died on a bed, with a water bottle stuck in her vagina. The other five women in the family were also killed. This was everyone the Japanese soldiers had found. After the rest of the family had been killed, one child escaped after hiding nearby for a day and a night.

After the fall of Nanjing, the atrocities continued for almost three months. After that, the rapes and murders weren't as common as they had been at the beginning.

On the third day after the fall of Nanjing, I drove out to investigate the current situation because the Japanese had not consulted us about burials. I saw that there were corpses of civilians lying on the street, in front of doors and inside houses. You could see corpses everywhere. The physical condition of the dead showed that they'd been brutally murdered, and some people's bodies had been dismembered. The Red Cross society buried more than 40,000 civilian corpses. These people had been killed by Japanese soldiers in the city and the surrounding areas after the fall of Nanjing. There were also other organisations helping to bury bodies, but many corpses were later buried by their surviving family members or friends. The day after the Japanese troops occupied Nanjing, there was no resistance in the city of any sort. The Japanese soldiers began to systematically set fire to the city. They drove military vehicles to the entrances of stores, stole all the goods inside and then set fire to them. People's homes were often burned after they were robbed. If the Japanese soldiers could take it, they would.

About 250,000 refugees were staying in the safety zone. Japanese soldiers repeatedly harassed the safety zone and frequently captured groups of girls and women. They were usually killed after being raped by the Japanese soldiers.

In total, there were approximately 25 refugee camps throughout the city. Due to the shortage of foreign citizens, they failed to take care of all the refugees. The most brutal atrocities took place in the refugee camp not far from Nanjing University and the missionaries' residences.

I assisted Magee in shooting footage. The film was taken out of Nanjing by Fitch.

My most optimistic estimate is that 200,000 civilians were killed by the Japanese army in Nanjing and the surrounding areas after they occupied the city and all the resistance had stopped. It is impossible to have any accurate statistics on how many women and girls were raped, how many people were injured or killed, how many buildings were ruthlessly destroyed and burned, and how much property was stolen by the Japanese soldiers.

We repeatedly protested to the Japanese but the Japanese authorities and consulates flatly ignored our protests. We were ordered to get out when we submitted a letter of protest. They didn't take any steps to rectify the situation. There is absolutely no excuse or justification to defend the Japanese soldiers' atrocities. These atrocities lasted for almost three months after the fall of Nanjing, and it gradually stopped later.

During the Japanese occupation, the Japanese acted as badly as possible to gradually destroy the Chinese people's morale. They advocated gambling, prostitution, and selling and smoking opium and narcotics in public, turning the city into the worst place imaginable.

They mercilessly destroyed educational institutions, churches and church buildings, not to mention the YMCA buildings, the Russian embassy and the houses of famous Chinese people.

The Japanese also terrorised the city economically, plundering all the natural resources they could. The Japanese monopolised everything to support themselves and the businesses of those who collaborated with them. On top of that, they didn't allow the Chinese to conduct business. This was more evident in small towns than big cities.

The Japanese soldiers murdered and raped regardless of whether they were occupying a town or a city, sometimes even just a small village. Small villages were often in a worse position because there was no international committee to protect the local civilians against the atrocities of the Japanese soldiers. This was how the Japanese waged war. Nanjing was just one example of many. In Jiangxi and Anhui Provinces, where my hometown

Guichi is located, the Japanese committed similar atrocities as far as I am aware.

The Japanese and its puppet government set up opium dens to allow the public sale of opium and narcotics.

The Japanese implemented psychological warfare to intimidate the Chinese people, cutting off their link with all the wonderful and sacred things they had once had. Even if a child wrote something against the Japanese, the entire family would be responsible and would all be executed. Even if someone in a village said something that even slightly offended the Japanese, the entire village would be completely destroyed, and the villagers would be killed. I know that a lot of these incidents happened. The tragedy that occurred in a village called Tianwangshu, north of the Yangtze near Nanjing, is just one example.

Chinese people had to bow to the Japanese soldiers whenever they saw them. If their behaviour wasn't to their liking, they were quickly and severely punished, or even killed.

I confirm and sign that the above statement is correct.
    6 April 1946.

I declare that I witnessed Xu Chuanyin make the above testimony. He then wrote it down and signed it in front of me on 6 April 1946 in Nanjing.
    Assistant Prosecutor David Nelson Sutton, Tokyo international prosecution.

Xu Chuanyin first swore that he provided the above statements as sworn testimony on 6 April 1946. He guaranteed its authenticity.

I confirm Xu Chuanyin's signature.

The testimonies of the two witnesses, Xu Chuanyin and Wilson, a Chinese man and a foreigner, were hugely successful and greatly encouraged the other Chinese judges and lawyers.

On top of this, Wu Changde, Chen Fubao, Liang Tingfang and other Chinese witnesses then appeared in court along with Bates and others. The court also accepted more than a dozen written testimonies of those who could not appear in court, including Cheng Ruifang, Smythe and other witnesses.

Due to the sufficient amount of evidence, Justice Webb spent the next two days cross-examining Matsui in court. Matsui did whatever he could to avoid justice and deny his crimes. But the court ultimately sentenced Matsui, the chief perpetrator of the Nanjing Massacre, to death by hanging.

The court decision was written as follows:

Matsui was a senior officer in the Japanese army and attained the rank of general in 1933. He had an extensive career in the army, including service in the Kwantung army and in the general staff. Although his close association with those who conceived and carried out the conspiracy suggests that he must have been aware of the purposes and policies of the conspirators, the evidence before the tribunal does not justify finding that he was a conspirator.

His military service in China in 1937 and 1938 cannot be regarded, in itself, as the waging of a war of aggression. To justify a conviction under Count 27, it has been the duty of the prosecution to tender evidence that would justify an inference that he had knowledge of the criminal character of the war. This has not been done.

In 1935, Matsui was listed as retired, but in 1937, he was recalled to active duty to command the Shanghai expeditionary force. He was then appointed commander-in-chief of the central China area army, which included the Shanghai expeditionary force and the 10th army. With these troops, he captured the city of Nanjing on 13 December 1937.

Before the fall of Nanjing, the Chinese forces withdrew and the defenceless city was then occupied. What then followed was a long succession of the most horrible atrocities imaginable, committed by the Japanese army on its helpless citizens. Japanese soldiers committed large scale massacres, individual murders, rapes, looting and arson. Although the extent of the atrocities has been denied by Japanese witnesses, the evidence to the contrary provided by neutral witnesses of different nationalities and unquestionable integrity is overwhelming. This orgy of crime started with the capture of the city on 13 December 1937 and did not cease until early February 1938. In this period of six or seven weeks, thousands of women were raped, upwards of 100,000 people were killed, and an untold amount of property was stolen and burned. At the height of these dreadful incidents, on 17 December, Matsui entered the city triumphantly and remained there from five to seven days. From his own observations and from the reports of his staff, he must have been aware of what was happening. He admits he was told about some degree of misconduct in his army by the Kenpeitai and by consular officials. Daily reports of these atrocities were made to Japanese diplomatic representatives in Nanjing, who in turn reported them to Tokyo. The tribunal is satisfied that Matsui knew what was happening. He did nothing, or nothing effective, to abate these horrors. He did issue orders before the capture of the city to ensure the propriety of conduct of his troops, and he later issued further orders of the same vein. These orders had no effect and he must have known so. It was pleaded on his behalf that he was ill at this time. His illness did not prevent his conducting of military operations nor did it prevent his visiting the city for several days while these atrocities were occurring. He was in command of the army responsible for these events. He knew of them. He had the power as he had the duty to control his troops and to protect the unfortunate citizens of Nanjing. He must be held criminally responsible for his failure to fulfil this duty.

On 23 December 1948, Matsui's life of crime came to an end when he was executed at Sugamo prison in Tokyo.

When sentencing the Class A war criminals like Matsui to be sentenced to death by hanging, Justice Webb, on behalf of the judicial committee of the International Military Tribunal for the Far East, made an independent and lengthy statement in court: "If someone knows or should know that a war is aggressive, but still promotes or participates in the war, there is no rule that can reduce their culpability for the war regardless of their position or status." Webb also stated: "We believe that the death penalty is the only possible punishment for criminals who provoke or start wars and the evil actions that follow as a result."

Webb finally said: "Even though I cannot say that I support all the judgments of this decision, it will most likely achieve the main purpose for their punishment. I have not heard any objections. I cannot say if any sentence is too heavy or too light."

Mei Ju-ao, the Chinese chief justice in the Tokyo trials, also bluntly stated: "The Nanjing Massacre is undoubtedly the biggest Japanese atrocity in the Second World War. It's only marginally less cruel than what Nazi Germany did to the Jews in the Holocaust in places like Auschwitz when compared with the other fascist atrocities in the Second World War." He then gave his opinion of the verdict: "The language used in court has been prudent, and perhaps rather conservative, too... However, it is obvious that the Japanese army acted like a vicious beast. They ignored the law and the tragic fates of hundreds of thousands of my innocent countrymen in Nanjing are obvious for all to see. They suffered under the iron heel of the invaders. These few words in this verdict are nothing more than a snapshot of the nightmare."

History made an unalterable decision about the war criminals who invaded China and killed its people more than 70 years ago. How can anyone today, including the Japanese, ignore this fact?

Matsui's execution wasn't the only consequence of the Nanjing Massacre. At the same time, the Chinese capital of Nanjing also carried out its own trial, which had an unprecedented influence.

Cheering Amidst the Wails of Purple Mountain

I will now describe the stories of two people in Nanjing from 1937 to 1947.

The first arrived and later left. He then came back again before leaving once again, this time for good. This man was Chiang Kai-shek. Chiang moved to Nanjing as president in 1927. He then fled when the Japanese began to invade Nanjing in December 1937. When the Second World War ended, he returned to Nanjing once again as president, but he was ineffective in prosecuting the Japanese criminals who'd thrown him out of the Presidential Palace in the first place.

The second arrived and then left. He then came back to never leave again. This man was Hisao Tani, the Japanese commander of the 6th division and the commander of the main force in the Nanjing Massacre. He had to pay the people of China for his crimes. On the morning of 13 December 1937, he commanded the troops entering Nanjing. He then allowed his army to commit crimes in the city, including burning, looting and raping. They committed horrific sins. Tani later returned to Japan. On 16 October 1946, he was escorted back to Nanjing for trial. At the same time, the Chinese military police also escorted 32 Class B and C Japanese war criminals for trial.

Tani never left Nanjing because he was sentenced to death by Chiang Kai-shek's government and the Chinese people.

As a perpetrator behind the Nanjing Massacre, Tani was escorted back to Nanjing to stand trial. It was an extension of the trials of Japanese war criminals being conducted in Tokyo. As the people of China's trial of the criminals behind the Nanjing Massacre, it attracted a great amount of attention.

When Japan surrendered, according to the Potsdam Proclamation, all the victors, including China, were to proceed with the trial of war criminals. The Chinese government's trials of war criminals were much weaker than those of the USSR and the US. One reason is that Chiang Kai-shek wanted to take revenge on Wang Jingwei. As a result, at the end of the war, the first thing Chiang did was judge the traitors in Wang Jingwei's government. In fact, this almost delayed the trial of the Japanese war criminals in Tokyo.

It's likely that the Chinese government at the time didn't focus on punishing Japanese war criminals due to them being tried on an international level. Therefore, Chiang Kai-shek dealt with traitors like Wang Jingwei instead, while Japanese war criminals were punished through international procedures.

By the end of 1945, the committees the Chinese government had established to handle the war crimes researched the criminals behind the

Nanjing Massacre. They made a list of nearly 60 war criminals and submitted it to the UN war crimes commission. The list of war criminals included Iwane Matsui, Prince Yasuhiko Asaka, Heisuke Yanagawa, Hisao Tani, Kesago Nakajima, Sadao Ushijima, Susumu Fujita and other major commanders of the troops that had invaded and occupied Nanjing. Prince Yasuhiko Asaka, the uncle of the emperor, evaded justice at the war crimes trials. Heisuke Yanagawa and Kesago Nakajima were now dead so they could not be prosecuted. Matsui had been listed as a Class A war criminal in the Tokyo trials. Out of the rest of the list, Hisao Tani was one of the main culprits behind the Nanjing Massacre. He was extradited to Nanjing by the Chinese government to be tried by the Chinese people.

On 1 August 1946, Hisao Tani was extradited to Shanghai, then to Nanjing. He was taken into custody in Xiaoying prison. Reporters from Central Daily News were able to go to the prison to interview Tani after he was extradited to Nanjing. One reporter wrote the following report:

Two Japanese criminals, Hisao Tani and Rensuke Isogai [author's note: *Isogai was the imperial Japanese army chief of staff and governor of Hong Kong*], are no less heinous than Göring, Ribbentrop and other Nazis. As millions of people had awaited, they were finally extradited from Shanghai to Nanjing yesterday at 7am. This gave people the right to prosecute those who had killed so many. It was understandable and it made the criminals regret the massacre.

To introduce the crimes of these devils to our readers, reporters went to Xiaoying prison to visit these criminals yesterday afternoon after 4pm. This was when the criminals were resting. With the help of the translator Mr Chen, I went out into the field where the devils were and joined a group of several people including Hisao Tani. They sat on the grass and talked for nearly half an hour. They pulled the grass as they answered all my questions.

When they were arrested in Tokyo, Hisao Tani was the military commander in Hiroshima. They were extradited from Tokyo to Shanghai by plane. They were put into the Yangpu prison in Shanghai. They'd been in the prison for 60 days until they were extradited to Nanjing today.

When I asked about life in prison, Tani said: "It's the same as ordinary prisoners, but sometimes it's easier." When asked about his family's situation, a smile appeared on his fat bearded face for a while. He said: "I have no son, just two daughters, both of them are married. My two sons-in-law are soldiers. They have all lost their jobs now. My wife has also been in Tokyo for two months. I haven't had any information about them. Their financial situation must be very tough."

"Did you know that Takashi Sakai was sentenced to death?"

"I didn't know that."

"Did you know that Göring, Ribbentrop and a group of German prisoners of war were sentenced to death by hanging the day before yesterday?"

"I didn't know. We haven't had newspapers."

"What do you think about their judgement?"

"I have no hope so I don't have any opinion about them." He then gave a bitter smile.

"Do you want to have a lawyer to defend you in the trial?"

"If possible, I hope to have one."

"Have you prepared to defend yourself?"

"I'm ready for it. But I don't know why I was arrested. I never committed any crimes over the past six years, apart from six months ago. I've only prepared to frankly state what happened in the past." Hearing Tani speak in this way, I couldn't help laughing. The commander was so naive. His bald head was truly forgetful. He didn't even know why he'd been arrested. I'm sure the judge will tell him.

I asked him in another way: "Why did you initially come to Nanjing?"

"I was the commander of the 6th division on 1 August on the 26th year of the Republic of China. I was ordered to depart from Kumamoto via Korea. In late August, a group of three divisions participated in the battle along the Yongding River, which was directed by Yukari. We then moved on to Baoding, Zhengding, and Shijiazhuang. In late September, after receiving a secret order, we went to Taku through the shipping lanes to Bakoupu for a landing combat exercise. We then followed secret orders to attack Hangzhou Bay with the Ushijima division and the Suematsu division, and then made the last successful landing in Jinshan. We then attacked Songjiang and Kunshan, aiming to cut off the Chinese army's retreat. After that, the troops advanced south of Lake Tai. My troops got full access to the city of Nanjing on 13 December." Whenever it came to a successful military campaign, he happily talked without interruption. It was hard for us to imagine the horrors of which this man was capable.

"Now that you're back in Nanjing, what are you thinking?"

He looked down and stayed quiet.

I later went to the military tribunal. Zhang held several pictures, showing piles of dead bodies in Xinjiekou, Shanghai Road, Xiaguan and other places. In the biggest single massacre, 9,000 of our compatriots were shot dead. They had been screaming and groaning. In the refugee shelters in the University of Nanjing, a team of Japanese soldiers announced that former soldiers were to stand on one side so that they could receive severance payment from the Japanese army and be sent home later. Civilians and businessmen were to stand on the other side and they could carry on as usual after they were released. However, everyone who stood on the soldiers' side was shot and then set alight. Only 11 people were left alive. Later, the scars on their bodies would serve as evidence in court. Among this group of monsters was Hisao Tani, sat on horseback with bloodshot eyes that screamed: "Kill them! Kill them!"

It was time for Hisao Tani, the leader of the Japanese soldiers who participated in the Nanjing Massacre, to stand before the Chinese people for trial. When the news came out that the butchers who'd killed hundreds of thousands of Chinese people were being escorted back to Nanjing, the entire city was shocked. People were excitedly spreading the news, especially the families of the victims and witnesses. They were crying but excited and all sorts of people, young and old, went to the prosecutors and courts to be interviewed.

The prosecutor asked a witness: "Are you coming to provide evidence for the Nanjing Massacre?"

"Yes."

"Are you aware that if you make false statements that you will be sentenced to seven years in prison?"

"I am aware."

"Please give your evidence."

Judges and prosecutors at the department of defence military court saw huge numbers of people every day. These people were witnesses and victims of the Nanjing Massacre and their testimonies were extremely valuable and powerful, playing a key role in the trial of the war criminals.

All witnesses had to answer these questions in advance and were told that if they falsified any evidence, they were to be sentenced to a maximum of seven years of imprisonment. After agreeing that they understood the law, they marked the authenticity of their statement with their fingerprint.

No one had any objections. Almost everyone said: "The Japanese killed my family members and almost me. I am here to testify."

According to the court's records, as many as 2,784 pieces of evidence regarding the crimes committed by the Japanese in the Nanjing Massacre were gained through these testimonies of the citizens of Nanjing.

Finally, Hisao Tani, a culprit behind the Nanjing Massacre, was called into court in February 1947, the moment the people had been waiting for.

At 11am, the first witness appeared in court.

The domineering judge Shi Meiyu gave an order: "Call witness Zhou Yiyu to the stand."

The clerk, Shi Yong, led a man into the court.

The judge asked the witness for their name, age, nationality and more basic details.

The witness replied: "My name is Zhou Yiyu. I am 60 years old. I am a resident of Nanjing. My address is 32 Jinshajin, Zhonghua Road."

The judge then asked: "This court has heard that you buried corpses for the Chong Shan Tang Benevolent Association when Nanjing fell into enemy hands. Could you elaborate?"

"We founded the Chong Shan Tang. I was chairman of the board. We buried 112,266 corpses. We printed a table, please allow me to bring it to court tomorrow for reference. There are still a lot of corpses left unburied."

"This court has determined that the public trial for Hisao Tani is scheduled for 6 February at Lizhishe auditorium. Please come to court at that time as a witness and show what the Japanese army did when the city fell into their hands."

The witness agreed.

The judge asked: "When did the Japanese army move into the city?"

"On 13 December, the 26th year of the Republic of China."

"Whose troops moved into the city?"

"Hisao Tani's troops entered Nanjing first, then Nakajima's troops began to move into the city."

"Did you leave town when Nanjing fell into the Japanese army's hands?"

"No, I didn't leave."

"Did they kill any of your family members?"

"No."

"Did you ever witness any Japanese atrocities?"

"I witnessed seven or eight massacres, maybe more."

"How were the victims generally killed?"

"I saw some corpses that had been stabbed from the front right through to the back when I buried them."

"Where did you bury the corpses?"

"Wherever we could. There were bodies everywhere."

"Did they use any other ways to kill their victims?"

"The Japanese also stood outside shelters with people inside. They then shot into the shelters with their guns."

"Were there any workers present to help you bury the corpses?"

"Yes."

"Could you find those workers now?"

"I could. Let me find them and bring them to testify in court on 6 February."

"Were the corpses you buried soldiers?"

"They were all wearing civilian clothing. None wore military uniforms, and there were children, elderly people, men and women among them."

"Which incident do you consider the worst one?"

"I saw a woman who was approximately 50 years old and sold chicken in the Dou Mu Gong food market under the bridge. After being raped by Japanese soldiers, they stuffed rags and other objects into her vagina. She died as a result. It was 16 December of that year."

"After Nanjing fell, when did the largest massacre happen?"

"In the first week after they came into the city. They also set fire to a lot of buildings."

In the following days of 6, 7 and 8 February, Hisao Tani and the witnesses argued face to face in court. On 9 February 1947, Central Daily News reported the events in court:

WASHINGTON
Nanjing War Crimes Tribunal

Yesterday afternoon on 8 February, debates regarding accusations were heard in the Lizhishe auditorium. The criminal behind the Nanjing Massacre, Hisao Tani, was put on retrial. There were about 1,000 in attendance in the court. No seat was left unfilled. Mayor Shen also attended the hearing.

At 2.05pm, the defendant hobbled his way to the stand and was held by a gendarme. After the judge announced that further evidence was to be collected, Hisao Tani raised his hand and requested to speak: "According to what the witnesses have said over the past two days, the crimes tended to occur in the Zhonghua gate area. However, there was fierce fighting there on the 12th and the 13th. There were no civilians in the area. If there were still any civilians left, the Japanese forces would have been forbidden from killing them. In the investigation document, I found that many crimes were committed by Nakajima, but they didn't happen in my own area of combat. Please consider these statements."

The presiding judge immediately cited three events regarding collective massacres:

A) On 16 December, the 26th year of the Republic of China, 57,000 refugees and Chinese soldiers were captured and gathered together in the Mufu mountains. They were driven to Xiaguan where they were killed with machine guns. Their bodies were abandoned in the river. This was the largest massacre.

B) On the 25th, more than 9,000 refugees were also massacred in Xiaguan.

C) On the 16th night, 5,000 refugees were brought from Huaqiao hostel to Xiaguan. They were killed with machine guns. Their bodies were abandoned in the river. The victims who survived the three massacres are able to appear in court to testify.

The judge then brought up the news story about two soldiers who had had a competition to kill the most people, which was published in the *Tokyo Nichi Nichi Shimbun*. One had killed 105 people and another killed 106 people. The judge asked the defendant if he had heard about it. Tani said: "I never heard about this. The collective massacre was committed by the navy and other divisions. It had nothing to do with me. My district was almost abandoned. I swear to God this is true. The judges should not consider me as the culprit of the massacre. If you were to summon the supreme commander to the court you would know the truth."

At this point, the victims Liang Tingfang, Xiang Zhenrong, Chen Baofu, Liu Zhenhan and Ding Hui were scheduled to appear in court alongside other witnesses. These included lonely widows, a mother who'd lost her son, monks and nuns, a silver-haired balding man and a victim who had barely survived. They were from different backgrounds and different ages. However, they said the same thing. They narrated the miserable scenes that they had witnessed. Nevertheless, only the defendant refused to acknowledge the crimes he had committed. He passed the blame to plain clothes officers, saying it was them who'd taken the opportunity to loot the city.

When it was mentioned that they had encouraged their subordinates to rob clothes and antiques in Shijiazhuang and Baoding, and to force themselves upon women, Tani said: "We commanders were too busy giving orders to move south. Committing robbery would have been impossible at the time. Not that we would have done so if it were possible. We never heard of this happening."

After 10 minutes of recess, at 4.20pm, the debate in court began. Firstly, Prosecutor Chen Guanyu made a statement and he then came to a conclusion. His tone was stern and he had a serious attitude. He said: "At the beginning of the first day of the public trial, prosecutors briefly mentioned the massacre. With the evidence provided by witnesses of different ages and from different countries, it can be proven that the Japanese army did indeed commit crimes in Nanjing, including massacres, arson, destruction of property, looting and rape, as seen in the data collected by the Red Cross and other charity groups. The victims of the Nanjing Massacre numbered approximately 480,000 people. The scale of this atrocity is unprecedented in the history of human civilisation.

"This atrocity is a blight on human history and even if there were hundreds of Hisao Tanis to punish, it still wouldn't be enough to undo the shame.

According to more than 2,000 testimonies and the victims in places like the Zhonghua gate, the evidence shows the reality of what happened, and the defendant's evasive behaviour cannot undo this.

"Secondly, the Nanjing Massacre was part of a general attack on major cities, but Nanjing suffered the most for a reason. This was nothing more than an attempt to destroy the national consciousness and undermine Chinese morale in the war. Nanjing was the capital of China. It was the capital of the war effort and the seat of the high command. National zeal was at its highest there. In regard to the killings, all participants, regardless of which division they fought in, should take responsibility for the massacre. Hisao Tani led his troops and arrived at the Zhonghua gate on 12 December. He then entered the city on 13 December. Japanese and Chinese forces were in the city and the defendant here today was a criminal behind this holocaust and cannot escape his responsibility for the crime."

They then discussed the overwhelming evidence. Chen said: "In the three days of this trial, we have seen testimonies collected by the city council and the local court, statistics regarding burials from the Red Cross, European and American reports regarding the aforementioned crimes, records from the safety zone, a film shot by an American pastor, Japanese photographic evidence and more. All of the evidence is reliable. However, the defendant remains unconvinced by the evidence and, to the contrary, only tries to stall and pass the buck with his irresponsible words. Nevertheless, he cannot get rid of his responsibilities so easily."

Chen added that the defendant's arrogant attitude, speech and lack of responsibility cannot be considered as simple deception. In such a colossal and unparalleled tragedy, although there were thousands, maybe millions, of Hisao Tanis who ought to face justice, this would not undo this stain on human history and the pain felt by the people. Tani was to be sentenced to death for his heinous crime.

While the defendant listened to the Japanese interpreter paraphrasing the proceedings, the court orderlies lit a candle. By candlelight, Tani no longer looked as confident in front of the calm men in the dock.

Then began Tani's response. As stubborn as ever, he argued that what happened depended on how you looked it. He denied everything.

Tani then said: "The prosecutor's assertion is completely wrong. It has no basis in fact; the records were faked so they are deliberately artificial. I was incorrectly singled out as being the criminal behind the massacre. I never recognised this." He continued: "Many civilians who have had their lives ruined because of other Japanese troops are taking advantage of this opportunity because it is not easy to get revenge, so they are passing all the crimes onto me. A witness testified in court two days ago and stated that all crimes were committed by other parties.

"These speculations are not grounds for criminal conviction. The perpetrators and the victims should be summoned to appear and speak in court before deciding whether a defendant is guilty of a crime. The unilateral statements do not match the facts and cannot be proven to be crimes. I refuse to receive an unfair judgment based on these errors."

Tani then made various excuses, saying that Chinese undercover units had caused the destruction and that it had been due to a lack of discipline.

On 25 February 25 1947, the debate in court continued. Tani tried to do all he could to deny the accusations and the defence lawyer was also booed.

On 3 March, the military tribunal held another trial and the debate continued. Although Hisao Tani was visibly upset, he continued to argue incessantly and deny his crime. He even said that the trial of the Nanjing Massacre "had no international legal precedent". Chief Justice Shi Meiyu angrily warned Tani not to repeat what he'd just said.

This was the last part of the trial, lasting till 5pm. Chen Guangyu made the closing statement for the prosecution. He argued that the defendant kept repeating nonsense to try to escape justice; he'd said that he supported Sino-Japanese rapprochement yet he enthusiastically led an invasion of China at an age where he qualified for retirement. Tani had also argued that the witnesses had been fake, but how could thousands of cases of victims found by the Nanjing council, international records, reports and photos published in the *Asahi Shimbun* as well as photographs and films of Japanese troops entering Nanjing all be fabricated?

"The evidence is conclusive and there is no point denying it. The defendant has been rude and unreasonable and his crime cannot be forgiven. He should be sentenced to death. Please be reminded that more than 400,000 of our compatriots had no right to speak when they were killed. Although the defendant is 65 now, he should be sentenced to death," said Chen as a thunderous applause roared around the courtroom.

"This unfair trial will damage any hope of improvement in Sino-Japanese relations!" Tani continued shouting.

The trial didn't finish until 7.30pm.

Chief Justice Shi Meiyu slammed down his gavel and declared that court was adjourned. Judgment would be made on 10 March at the Lizhishe auditorium.

The Lizhishe auditorium was a rather famous place in Nanjing. From the west to the east, the buildings were the auditorium, building 1 and building 3, all of which faced the south. In front of building 1, a stone stele had been erected. An inscription of a Chiang Kai-shek quote was written upon it:

> Make yourself a paragon so as to set an example for others;
> Transfer your thoughts to implementing the revolution.

On the afternoon of 10 March 1947, the Lizhishe, which had been set up for Chiang Kai-shek, his students and his party, was used as the courtroom for the trial of the war criminal Hisao Tani. The citizens of Nanjing had gone through so much and had longed for this day for a very long time. As a result, it was extremely crowded in the Lizhishe auditorium. The citizens were eager to see the murderer of hundreds of thousands of people in Nanjing see justice.

The trial began.

Six powerful armed military police brought Hisao Tani into the courtroom. He no longer had the same prestige that he'd had when he first came to Nanjing. His hair was white. He stumbled through the courtroom with his dark eyes suspiciously darting around.

The chief justice Shi Meiyu stood in the middle of the courtroom. Next to him stood the judges, Song Shutong, Li Yuanqing, Ge Zhaotang and Ye Zaizeng. The chief prosecutor Chen Guangyu and Hisao Tani's lawyers, Mei Zufen and Zhang Rende, stood on both sides of the court. There were several interpreters and Chinese and Japanese witnesses.

"I shall now announce the verdict for the trial of the war criminal Hisao Tani," Shi Meiyu shouted as he read. The verdict of the Nanjing War Crimes Tribunal was rather long. In order to allow future generations all over the world, including the Japanese, to see the truth, I have retrieved part of the verdict from the Second Historical Archives of China:

> Hisao Tani allowed his troops to kill captured soldiers and civilians. They raped, robbed, and destroyed property. He is hereby sentenced to death.
>
> Outline of the facts:
>
> Hisao Tani is a confident and courageous general who stands out among the Japanese warlords and he once fought in the Russo-Japanese war. He received many commendations in the Russo-Japanese war. Since the beginning of the Second Sino-Japanese War, he has been the leader of the 6th division. In August 1937, he led his troops to China. Firstly, he fought by the Yongding River, Baoding and Shijiazhuang in Hebei Province.
>
> In November, we lost the battle in Shanghai and we then turned to defend Nanjing. The Japanese warlords made Nanjing a crucial target and gathered their most brutal and elite forces, namely Hisao Tani's 6th division, Nakajima's

16th division, Ushijima's 18th division and Bunshin's 114th division to attack in unison under the direction of General Iwane Matsui.

They were met with fierce resistance by our forces and planned to slaughter people after taking Nanjing as revenge. Tani's 6th division fought as the frontline troops and broke into the Zhonghua gate on the afternoon of 12 December 1937. The frontline troops used rope ladders to climb into the city and then began slaughtering the people inside. The next morning, Tani's 6th division, Nakajima's 16th division, Ushijima's 18th division and Bunshin's 114th division slaughtered people all over Nanjing and then started fires, raped women and stole property. The period between 12 December and 21 December was the most miserable, which was during the 6th division's garrison in the city. More than 190,000 people, including Shan Yaoting, were killed by machine guns in Huashen Temple, outside the Zhonghua gate, Baotai bridge, Qixia Temple, Xiaguan and Straw String gorge. Their bodies were then burned. On top of this, according to a charity organisation, more than 150,000 bodies were buried after sporadic slaughter. The victims added up to more than 300,000 people. Corpses lay everywhere.

The miserable situation is unimaginable. For example, at 1pm on 15 December, 2,000 Chinese military police were captured by Japanese soldiers and brought to the Hanzhong gate. They were shot with machine guns. Those who ran were then buried alive. At 6pm, 5,000 refugees in the Luji Hotel were brought to Zhongshan wharf by the Japanese army to be shot. Their bodies were thrown into the Yangtze River. Only Bai Zengrong and Liang Tingfang survived out of those refugees.

On the night of 18 December, Japanese soldiers tied up 57,418 prisoners with iron wire and brought them to Straw String gorge. All these people were shot. Anyone who survived the gunfire was killed by sword. Finally, they burned the dead bodies with petrol so as to destroy any evidence.

On 12 December, a civilian woman called Xu was beheaded and burned by the Japanese at the Zhonghua gate wharf. On 13 December, the civilian Wei Xiaoshan found that Hisao Tani's men were starting fires; he shouted for help and was killed. On the same day, the monks Longjing and Longhu and the nuns Zhengxing, Denggao and Dengyuan were killed outside of the temple near the Zhonghua gate.

On 14 December, the citizen Yao Jiatong took his family in search of shelter along Zhanlong bridge, which was near the Zhonghua gate. The Japanese soldiers raped his wife and then killed him. His eight year old son and one year old daughter were thrown into the flames because they were crying.

It was very cold from 13 to 17 December. The Japanese soldiers ordered approximately 30 civilians to catch fish in the cold water. Peasants who followed their orders died due to the extreme cold and those who did not were killed anyway.

The Japanese soldiers hanged an old man so as to shoot at him as a target. The old man hanged there dead until the rope broke. Two Japanese military officers had a competition to kill the most people; one of them killed 105 people and the other killed 106, winning the game.

On 19 December, a civilian woman called Xie Shanzhen, who was in her sixties, was killed outside the Zhonghua gate. A plant was inserted into her vagina. These are all inhuman acts. From 12 to 21 December, there were as many as 886 recorded cases of innocent Chinese civilians being brutally killed (attachments A1-A28; B1-B858).

In addition to the aforementioned incidents, there were as many as 378 more cases of people being killed near the Zhonghua gate, including Wang Fuhe, Ke Dacai, Zhuo Lütong, Shen Yougong, Liu Guangsong, Yu Bifu and a woman called Zeng Xiao (attachments A9, 13, 18, 19, 20, 24, 26, 28, B1-370). After the Japanese broke into the city, they criminally raped civilians everywhere to vent their sexual frustrations.

On 16 and 17 December, according to the accounts of the International Committee, which consisted of foreign residents in Nanjing, there were more than 1,000 recorded rape victims. The brutality was unimaginable. For example, on 13 December, a citizen called Taolang was gang-raped and disembowelled. Her dead body was burned.

Mrs Xiao, who was more than nine months pregnant, a 16 year old girl called Huang Guiying, Mrs Chen and a 63 year old country woman were all raped near the Zhongshan gate. Thirteen Japanese soldiers took turns raping a country girl called Ding who couldn't stand it so she shouted for help. She was then stabbed in the stomach and finally died.

Between 13 and 17 December, after raping women near the Zhonghua gate, the Japanese soldiers forced passing monks to rape women too. These monks refused and were then castrated and killed. Some girls were also thrown into the Yangtze after being raped near the Zhonghua gate.

Every woman who stayed in Nanjing lived in great fear and moved to the safety zone that had been established by the International Committee. However, the Japanese army paid no attention to international law and entered these areas at night so as to vent their sexual frustrations. They raped women in the darkness regardless of age.

Although the foreigners protested to the Japanese government on behalf of their international organisations, Hisao Tani turned a blind eye to it and allowed his forces to continue their crimes. Wherever the Japanese went, so did fire and death. Our capital became the target for their horrific exploits. The situation was truly horrifying.

Fires were constantly started near the river. Half of the city was reduced to ash. The value of the damage and loss of both public and private property cannot be evaluated. In just one incident, 10 houses were destroyed in a fire in Xunxiang Lane. Some 100 people, including He Qingsen, Xia Honggui and Mrs Bizhang, became homeless. Houses in Diaoyu Lane, Hubei Street, Changle Street and Shuangjia village were destroyed by fires. The homes of the residents Zeng Younian, Mrs Changxu and Feng Zhaoying were destroyed.

Fires spread all over the city until 20 December; Taiping Street in the city centre was on fire and wasn't put out until the night. All firefighting apparatus was stolen and any citizens who dared to help were killed.

The Japanese forces were also greedy and stole everything including food, livestock, utensils and antiques. At 50 Shibei Street, they stole four cases of rare ancient books from a famous Chinese doctor, Shi Xiaoxuan, as well as more than 2,000 antiques, 400 wooden utensils and 30 more cases of clothes. An innumerable amount of food, livestock, utensils and money was looted from Jiqing Road and Renguan Lane.

In the Red Cross hospital, nurses' property, patients' bedding and refugees' food were also robbed. They also robbed the houses of Douglas Jenkine who worked for the US ambassador, the American teacher Miss Grace Bauer, the German Rabe, Pasteur, Paul and Jameson. These victims all suffered great losses. These kinds of crimes cannot be counted. After Japan's surrender, Hisao Tani was arrested in Tokyo and was brought to Nanjing by our delegation in Japan. He stands accused by the prosecutor.

10 March 1947

— THE SIGNATURES OF THE CHIEF JUSTICE, JUDGES AND CLERKS ARE BELOW.

The moment after the chief justice announced the verdict, the court burst out into cheers and people could be heard crying amidst the thunderous cheers.

The people of Nanjing had gone through so much. They'd lost so many loved ones and had cried and bled themselves dry. Now they finally saw justice.

Nanjing cried. Zhongshan cried. Mochou Lake wept. The Rain Flower Terrace cheered. Zhonghua gate celebrated. Guanghua gate wept.

All of Nanjing was moved that day.

The End of the Trial of the Century and Another Injustice

The date was 26 April 1947. Crowds had gathered by the Rain Flower Terrace in Nanjing.

The Rain Flower Terrace was dubbed "the guillotine" by the people of Nanjing and now all eyes were on it. At 11.30am, Hisao Tani was brought to the Rain Flower Terrace after verifying his identity. Knelt before an audience, after Hong from the 1st guards' regiment of the ministry of defence fired his gun, Hisao Tani, a major criminal behind the Nanjing Massacre, died.

At the same time as Hisao Tani's trial had been conducted, other Japanese war criminals had been tried at the Nanjing military tribunal and executed, including the low-ranking officers Mukai and Noda who'd competed to kill the most people.

As a result, the trials in Tokyo and Nanjing were coming to an end.

However, two years later, on the morning of 27 January 1949, news reported by the Central News Agency shocked China.

"The former Japanese war criminal, commander-in-chief of the China expeditionary army, Yasuji Okamura, has been acquitted by Chief Justice Shi Meiyu after a judicial revision by the war crimes tribunal and the ministry of defence on 26 January." The news caused uproar in China.

The next day, Chairman Mao from the CPC telegrammed the Nanjing Nationalist government and urgently proclaimed: "The former Japanese war criminal, the commander-in-chief of the China expeditionary army, Yasuji Okamura, was a major war criminal in the War of Resistance Against Japanese Aggression. He was acquitted by the military tribunal and the Nationalist government in Nanjing today. The CPC and PLA have proclaimed that this is forbidden. The Chinese people fought hard to win the war at a cost of innumerable lives and property to capture this criminal. We will not allow the Nanjing Nationalist government to arbitrarily acquit him. The Chinese people, all democratic parties, organisations and patriots in the Nanjing Nationalist government should stand up at once to oppose the reactionary Nanjing government who betrayed our national interests by colluding with Japanese fascist warlords. We now warn the gentlemen in the reactionary Nanjing government: you must reconvict Yasuji Okamura and we ask you to stay consistent in what you say and what you do."

The declaration from Chairman Mao and the CPC was incredibly serious, but in reality, it wasn't their decision to make. As a result, the declamation was ineffective.

At the time, Li Zongren took charge of affairs in Nanjing but his power as an interim leader was very limited. He had to follow Chiang's orders, who was in his hometown of Fenghua in Zhejiang Province.

Who was Yasuji Okamura? He was the commander-in-chief of the China expeditionary army as well as the biggest major criminal during the Second Sino-Japanese War, with the longest career during the invasion of China. He came to China during the Russo-Japanese war. He then became the military consultant of the Nanjing warlord Sun Chuanfang. He was also the executioner who impeded the northern expedition army. In 1928, he was assigned as the commander of a Japanese force and joined the internal Chinese conflict as part of the Japanese invasion of Jinan. In 1932, Okamura was vice chief of staff of the Shanghai expeditionary army and took part in the 28 January incident in Shanghai. From 1937 to 1944, he worked as the commander-in-chief of the Japanese 11th army, the Japanese northern China army and the Japanese 6th area army before being promoted to commander-in-chief of the China expeditionary army. It was this army that was responsible for most of the war crimes in China. However, he was released by Chiang Kai-shek and was invited by Chiang in 1950 to Taiwan to provide advice.

Yasuji Okamura was not sentenced to death like Iwane Matsui and Hisao Tani. This was all because of Chiang Kai-shek's policy of being half anti-Japanese and half friendly to Japan.

The reason for Chiang Kai-shek's orders to release Yasuji Okamura was that he got him to promise that the Japanese army wouldn't surrender to the communists but work for the Nationalist government and their forces.

Chiang then used these forces to fight against the CPC for a few years. For most of the time since 1927, Chiang had been hostile to Mao and the CPC. Even during the Second Sino-Japanese War, he still spent a great deal of time taking precautions against and even killing the communists. As president, he was essentially forced to fight against the Japanese and he reluctantly dealt with the war criminals afterwards. If it weren't the Xi'an Incident, Wang Jingwei's betrayal and the patriotism and strong will of the people of China and the communists, who knows when he would have actually decided to fight against the Japanese.

Chiang Kai-shek's policy of being half anti-Japanese and half friendly to Japan put many Chinese people at risk. Not only was it despicable due to the Japanese crimes at the Nanjing Massacre, but if Chiang Kai-shek had actually played a proactive role in fighting at the battle, then the Japanese wouldn't have conquered Nanjing so easily. But he didn't do so and assigned the middling Tang Shengzhi as the commander of the city's garrison. Nanjing had lost the battle before it had even started.

More than 300,000 people in Nanjing were brutally killed by the Japanese soldiers' swords and guns. Their blood dyed the Yangtze and Zhongshan red.

The US government was another key player in the Japanese war criminals being allowed to escape justice. In the following decades, a great deal of the problems that China has faced, including the resentment between China and Japan and the issue of Taiwan, can all be attributed to the US government.

The US supports Taiwanese independence and hasn't forgotten its Cold War mentality, remaining somewhat hostile towards China. After the Second World War, the US wanted China to become an outpost for its defence against the USSR. When the CPC led the Chinese people in establishing the People's Republic of China, the US was incredibly concerned. As a result, it went against the international principles that had been used for handling defeated fascist countries like Japan, such as the Cairo Declaration and the Potsdam Proclamation, which it had once encouraged. Instead, the US convinced the Japanese government to oppose the Chinese government. At the same time, the US supported Chiang Kai-shek in his continued hostility against the CPC.

8

ANOTHER UNRESOLVED INJUSTICE

Where to begin with this long story? The essential injustice is rather simple. Japan not only killed more than 300,000 Chinese in the Nanjing Massacre but also robbed China of unimaginable amounts of wealth during the war. If the value of the stolen loot was calculated, it would have been enough to build several high speed railways or cities, or even to take a poverty-stricken nation out of poverty. This isn't fiction. It actually happened.

You will be aware of this if you've read books like *The Yamato Dynasty* and *Gold Warriors*, written by Stirling Seagrave and Peggy Seagrave, both of whom are famous academics and independent investigators. The couple spent decades investigating the background of the Japanese invasions as well as the Japanese pillaging in China and other Asian countries, helped by agencies that were supposed to uphold justice including the CIA. They concluded that the gold and other precious materials that Japan had taken during the Second World War were worth more than $20 billion, valued according to 1945 currency rates.

In 1945, $100 million would have been enough to build five lines of the Beijing underground. So how much is this amount worth today? Enough to build 20 first class aircraft carriers? However, some historians believe that the figure of $20 billion is just a tiny part of the stolen amount. The wealth that Japan stripped from China from 1895 to 1945 is far greater than that.

Where did this wealth go after the Second World War? It's still a mystery.

It is the US that has to accept responsibility for this.

In 1951, the US and Japan signed the Treaty of San Francisco. One of the peace treaty's most notorious terms was article 14:

> It is recognised that Japan should pay reparations to the Allied powers for the damage and suffering caused by it during the war. Nevertheless, it is also recognised that the resources of Japan are not presently sufficient if it is to maintain a viable economy to make complete reparations for all such damage and suffering and at the same time meet its other obligations. Therefore... the Allied powers waive all reparation claims of the Allied powers, other claims of

the Allied powers and their nationals arising out of any actions taken by Japan and its nationals in the course of the prosecution of the war, and claims of the Allied powers for direct military costs of occupation.

According to this provision, all the victors, including the Chinese who were invaded by Japan for decades, were to give up any claims for reparations due to the Second World War. This was an outrage and the people of China did not agree. However, the US signed the agreement with Japan in private, making fools out of China and the other countries of Asia. The US profited as it would receive wealth that Japan had looted from the countries it had invaded through continuous private tributes to the Americans.

This was a despicable agreement and it made the US much wealthier while also allowing large Japanese enterprises like Mitsubishi, Mitsui and Sumitomo that had contributed to the war machine to avoid paying compensation. These companies had relied on the free source of labour provided by other countries and their prisoners. After the Second World War, these companies quickly became an important pillar in supporting the Japanese economy while also making strong contributions to American economic development and resistance against the communists. It appears that not much has changed.

In the decades after the Second World War, the anger and struggle between the east and the west have never stopped, especially now that China's economy has risen up from the pressure placed upon it by western powers. However, the economy isn't the main issue. The bigger problems are the friction and struggle between systems and ideology. With this in mind, it is clear why the Tokyo trials still left so many problems unaddressed. There was one thing that always perplexed me when writing this book. In Hisao Tani's Nanjing trial, I saw many attachments at the back of the judgment document featuring a great deal of cases about what the Japanese had stolen, such as:

> On 14 December 1937, Shen Xiurong, a merchant who lived at 11 Feng Yousi Street, was still missing. On 10 December, a lot of Japanese soldiers looted furniture and money from Shen Xiurong's house (witnesses: Hua Yunxi; Shen Wangshi).

> On 14 December 1937, the Japanese robbed all of the merchant Wang Jiade's furniture and belongings from their address on Feng Yousi Street (witnesses: Fang Shufu; Wang Hanshi).

On 20 December 1937, the Japanese robbed all valuables from Hu Tingzhen's house, which was located on 1 Mu Jia Lane, Bai Xia Road. They then set fire to Hu's house after they beat his family and abducted Hu Fanshi, who is still missing to this day (witness: Hu Tingzhen).

In December 1937, the Japanese robbed the Chinese doctor Shi Xiaoxuan, who lived at 50 Da Ba Street. They took four boxes of valuable books, more than 2,000 paintings and antiques, 400 pieces of carved wood and more than 30 cases of clothes (witnesses: Shi Xiaoshuan; Zhang Yulin).

Nanjing is a historic city and it had been the capital of China for six dynasties, as well as the capital at the time of the massacre. Today, we shall not discuss how wealthy Chiang Kai-shek was, just the great quantity of antiques that collectors held and the many wealthy citizens among the people of China. Their collections shared the same fate as them when the Japanese occupied their hometowns. They set fire to their homes after they looted them, and often just killed the owners after they forced them to hand over their valuables.

In 1937, the Japanese occupied two of the richest cities in China: Shanghai and Nanjing. How much gold and wealth was looted by the Japanese? Only the Huangpu River could say. I heard from my uncle that his father - my grandfather - had a business partner who had a collection of 300 pieces of porcelain that had been in the family for three generations. They were mostly valuable pieces from the Ming and Qing dynasties. Without exception, all of these were taken by the Japanese, who only left a few pieces of redwood furniture, which could still be exchanged for tens of thousands of silver coins after liberation.

There were some very wealthy families in Shanghai that had thought that if they fled to the French concession, they would be able to take shelter. Many of them still felt unsafe, however, and brought their valuables to Nanjing. Tragically, the capital was captured by the Japanese the next month. These people were unable to flee the capital due to the threat of being cut down by Japanese swords. Where had their savings and treasures gone? Nanjing said nothing, but the people of Tokyo betrayed themselves when they talked about the treasures their soldiers had brought back.

There were two key motivations for the Japanese occupying Nanjing. The first was to demonstrate their power by occupying the capital of China, and the second was due to the extreme wealth in Nanjing as it was the capital and the ancient home of six Chinese dynasties. These factors made Nanjing a target for the Japanese.

When they launched the assault on Nanjing, the Japanese emperor's uncle, Yasuhiko Asaka, was sent to the frontline as the senior commanding officer. After they occupied the city, the Japanese soldiers were busy murdering civilians, setting fire to buildings and raping Chinese women. However, the Japanese emperor and his cronies were busy with their own crimes, robbing the wealth of the Nanjing government and the city's private citizens.

The royal family created an organisation, *Kin no Yuri* (Golden Lily), for this purpose. The actions were conducted by a Japanese *gendarmerie* group with more than a regiment's worth of men. The operations were covertly conducted after they entered Nanjing. They were to seize all Chinese government property, storm the banks' safes, rob the rich, middle class businessmen and their shops, as well as the valuables that professionals kept in their homes. The Seagraves describe in their book *Gold Warriors*: "It is said that, at that stage, the secret *gendarmerie* collected at least 6,000 tons of gold. Historical research on this topic showed that plundered wealth in the official reports was just a fraction of the actual number. In addition, there are numerous Chinese who liked to store small amounts of gold, platinum, diamonds, rubies, sapphires, art, antiques, and so on, which were also stolen. All of these were taken from private residences or rural tombs. The Japanese were thorough in their operations and even removed the gold teeth from corpses." They continue: "The *gendarmerie* busied themselves with looting houses and moving furniture, mirrors and carpets and sending them to Japan by railway. The Golden Lily special detachment of Japanese elite agents had to focus on bank bosses, industry association chiefs, pawnbrokers and gang leaders. All of these people's identities had already been made clear beforehand. Agents controlled these rich people through extortion. If they resisted, death was the only fate that awaited them." This method was very effective and many Chinese businessmen and collectors had to give their gold and treasures to the Japanese to survive.

Ordinary Chinese civilians could only see the slaughter as blood flooded the streets, calling these Japanese murderers "devils". However, they didn't know that the real "devils" were the Golden Lily detachment, who looted in the darkness and flames as they extorted the city's elites. A resident of Nanjing told me something that he had heard from his grandfather. Several troops in the Japanese army didn't usually kill people, but when they saw a good house or a big house, they would surround it with heavily armed soldiers. Then they'd go in and out of the building for a long period of time. Sometimes these Japanese troops would send for several cars to come and transport things, always doing so in secret. "They must have been taking away valuables," the resident said.

Where did the gold and treasure go after the Japanese looted it from China? Of course, they were shipped back to Japan. It was said that after MacArthur's army occupied Tokyo, American soldiers would drive around the ruins and their wheels would sometimes suddenly hit something. They often found dusty gold and silver vessels, and most of them had come from Asian countries like China. Once, an American soldier found a shiny "stone" amidst the ruins and he picked it up, wiped it with his sleeve and found that it was a priceless diamond.

After the Second World War, Japanese politicians and the US occupation force held a secret negotiation. One of the core purposes of the negotiations was to get Japan to reveal the location and quantity of the valuables it had looted. A reason why this was an important factor was that the US was to be given this wealth by the Japanese in return for protection.

After writing this section, I felt a sense of eternal and profound grief because in the decades following the Second World War, the US government received the loot the Japanese invaders had stolen from China and other Asian countries at the cost of justice and responsibility. The US arbitrarily schemed with Japanese right wing elements to move away from the road to recovery from militarism and to remain opposed to the people of China and the other peaceful peoples of Asia. This was a tremendous shame.

It all reminds me of the war criminal Hideki Tojo, who asked two American lawyers to write a final proclamation before his death. The content was all about his will for the US to "protect Japan". Decades after the war, it has been proven that the successive US governments have truly carried out all of Tojo's wishes.

This was a tragic failure on the part of countries like the US to live up to their fundamental moral obligations. China shall not simply forget a crime of this scale that went hand in hand with the Nanjing Massacre.

Winter in 1937 was a nightmare for the citizens of Nanjing. The cold, cloudy and wet weather added more fear to the ancient city. The Japanese army's endless burning, killing and rape terrorised the entire city's defenceless population as even former soldiers hid in terror. At the time, a special Japanese detachment arrived in the city intermixed with the Japanese army. These men did not go to banks or shops, but specifically went to libraries, universities, government agencies and elegant buildings. They stole books, statues of Buddha and Confucian classics whenever they saw them. They were a special detachment that had been sent by the Japanese government to plunder rare

Chinese books and relics. A group of bloodthirsty monks was in this detachment. Before the Japanese occupied Nanjing, the monks travelled throughout China and communicated with various universities, scholars and collectors. This was to learn about the collections of Chinese books and precious cultural relics that they held so that they could forcibly take them in future.

On 13 December 1937, Nanjing was occupied by the Japanese army and this special detachment quickly slipped into the city.

During the first six weeks of the massacre, all of Nanjing was soaked with blood. Everyone, including intellectuals and the wealthy, could only focus on survival, so all their possessions, including gold and silver valuables, seemed insignificant in comparison. I heard from one of the survivors of the massacre that his family had had a large collection. His father was at home one day with three girls and two maids. Japanese soldiers broke into his home to look for women to assault. His father was a traditional teacher who couldn't stand the barbarity of the intruders, so he said to the soldiers: "You're so savage, even worse than pigs or dogs. How can you be so lecherous?" The Japanese soldiers laughed when they heard him shout and said: "You won't let us touch any women, so do you have anything better than women?" The teacher pointed to hundreds of bottles and pendants that were displayed in the house and said: "You can sell these things for money and stay in a brothel forever." The soldiers said: "We need something newer, these old things are really boring." Then they raised their bayonets and destroyed the collection that had taken three generations to curate. They then kicked the old man and shot him. The Japanese soldiers then raped all five of the women there. The Japanese relics detachment were incredibly angry after they found out about the incident and rushed over to the house immediately. They were still able to loot two trucks full of books and cultural relics.

"Things like this happened in the street every day back then," an older resident of Nanjing told me.

This theft was by no means the end of the Japanese aggression. After the special detachment had checked and verified all the cultural relics and valuable books in the city, in the spring of 1938, the Japanese brought more than 1,000 experts and academics to the city from Japan. They came to Nanjing in great numbers and systematically picked valuable objects from the city's vast libraries, colleges, government agencies, temples and other homes of cultural relics. Although the bombing campaign had begun in August 1937 and had lasted for months, and the Chiang Kai-shek administration had prepared for evacuation for months, important national cultural relics and rare books still remained, including the large amount of relics in the Ming Palace. The Chinese army had been busy relocating Chiang Kai-shek's private belongings and the government's confidential materials, so they chose not to protect the city's cultural relics and rare books. This was why the Japanese experts were overjoyed when they saw the vast amount of valuable collections and relics that had remained mostly intact.

The royal crony Prince Tsuneyoshi Takeda was responsible for the transportation and collection of the relics and greedily told his unit of cultural thieves to take everything they could.

Stolen cultural relics and books were classified, numbered, packed up and then put into waterproof boxes. The best ones were transported to Emperor Hirohito's royal palace along with other stolen gold and jewellery. The others were reserved by a range of government agencies and academics, and some were sent to academics and professors in relevant fields.

Throughout the spring and summer of 1938, the Japanese recruited more than 2,300 workers from Nanjing and Shanghai to prepare these collections and cultural relics for shipment. Some were to depart from Shanghai and some were shipped to Japan from Qingdao and Tianjin. Approximately 400 Japanese soldiers were responsible for this task. It has been said that for the shipment of collections stolen from Nanjing to be sent to Shanghai alone, more than 300 trucks were used. This is truly a staggering amount and it marks a colossal loss.

After the Second World War, Chinese academics asked the Japanese to return the collections with the help of the US. However, the Japanese insisted that government policy had had no influence in regard to this and blamed soldiers and officers in order to deny the criminal acts. In fact, after the US forces occupied Japan, they found several stolen book collections and relics from China, but MacArthur turned a blind eye to them because they took a cut of these Chinese treasures. Now we know that the relics and rare books that had been looted from China were stored in the Tokyo Imperial Palace, the Royal Grand Hall, the Yasukuni Shrine, the Tokyo Science Museum, the Tokyo Academy of Fine Arts, Waseda University, Tokyo Imperial University, Keio University and more. At least 17 places were used for storage. The US occupation authorities actually published details on some of the collections of cultural relics that the Japanese had looted from China, with at least three million volumes. Many of them, such as the Song Dynasty manuscripts, were priceless and important relics of human cultural history. Today, the national Japanese library is still the best in Asia because it is full of valuable Chinese books.

Post-war Japanese academics and university professors have used the Chinese books that were stolen from Nanjing and other places in China as primary materials and sources when studying Chinese and Asian culture and history. As a result, following the Second World War, Japan established the East Asia Institute, the Research Institute for Oriental Cultures, the East Asia Research Institute of Endemics and other professional institutions. Academics studied medicine, agriculture, biology, economics, culture, military affairs and other subjects by using Chinese sources to lay a solid foundation for improvements in the academic level of the related industries in post-war Japan.

The Japanese killed more than 300,000 innocent people during the Nanjing Massacre; rare books and relics that the Japanese robbed from Nanjing and other locations in China also destroyed a part of China's national culture. This was a heinous crime. Younger Chinese generations should keep these facts firmly in their minds.

A collector once told me that he had collected Chinese porcelain in Japan from the 1970s to the 1980s, and he saw a large number of Japanese national and civic collections with artefacts that were mostly from China. How did these precious items get to Japan? There was only one explanation: most of them had been stolen when the Japanese army invaded China.

There was one man who played a key role in the notorious Golden Lily operations: Yoshio Kodama, an important figure in the notorious Japanese *yakuza* and underworld. Kodama was dispatched by an important general in the aggression against China, Kenji Doihara, to loot Chinese folk arts and cultural artefacts. Kodama wasn't much to look at with a short and stocky build, but he was a real thug.

When Nanjing was still suffering from the massacre, Kodama took his special detachment dressed in Japanese uniforms to the fertile Jiangnan region, including Suzhou, Wuxi, Changzhou, Zhenjiang, Huzhou, Wuhu and other cities. They threatened local wealthy and powerful Chinese people and forced them to hand over their valuables to the Japanese emperor, threatening to kill them. Most wealthy civilians chose to surrender their prized goods rather than die. Kodama made a huge fortune. It was said that Kodama had stolen so much gold that it made Japanese aircrafts transporting it fall out of the sky. From that point, he only collected rubies, sapphires, ancient works of calligraphy and paintings, which were easy to take back home.

When Kodama came to Nanjing, he was just like Ali Baba after he entered the cave full of treasure. He was moved to tears of joy. Meanwhile, millions of Chinese people also cried, but out of helplessness, bitterness and anger.

The Japanese army's storming of Nanjing was the most severe historical and cultural catastrophe to happen to the ancient city. The crimes against the cultural and material wealth of the city can only be compared to the devastating slaughter of 300,000 of the city's inhabitants. Japan has been able to carefully study every region of China and its history through these Chinese books and artefacts. China was humiliated when its most important cultural and spiritual relics were stolen, which had been with China's ancestors for thousands of years. Instead, they remain withheld by a foreign power. This is a massacre of Chinese culture.

The massacre of Chinese culture differs obviously to the massacre of the citizens of Nanjing. One key difference is the role of the US, which made clandestine deals with Japan to make the Chinese unable to request the return of their gold, treasure and cultural relics, or even to claim for compensation. This eventually allowed post-war Japan to use these huge amounts of money and valuable artefacts to assist in its post-war reconstruction and rapidly develop the country's economy and culture.

As is well known, the long suffering Chinese economy and people's living standards were below the international poverty line for more than 10 years after the Japanese invasion. It wasn't until after decades of the reform and opening up period that the Chinese economy overtook Japan's to be the second largest in the world today. During this period, the Chinese suffered from great difficulties. Why? As China was poor, it had been invaded several times by the Japanese and other countries over the course of half a century from the first Sino-Japanese war to the Chinese victory in the Second Sino-Japanese War in 1945. In contrast, Japan rapidly became the world's second largest economy less than 20 years after the Second World War; even today, their average living standards are still far higher than China's. This wasn't because the Japanese were smarter than the Chinese, but because the defeated war loving nation's state infrastructure, especially the economic system, wasn't destroyed, even though they did face some punishments. When the international situation stabilised following the Second World War, the gold and silver in the Japanese treasury and coffers of the royal family, which had been looted from China and other Asian countries, were continually used to supply the development of their economy, military, culture, education systems and healthcare, while huge construction projects were launched all over Japan. Big companies like Mitsui, Sumitomo and Mitsubishi that had made huge profits from the war did not collapse after it came to an end, but instead received funding from the government to help them once again play a role in the Japanese economic machine with funds stolen from all over Asia. Even today, these large Japanese companies still continue to make money for Japan all over the world. In Europe, the Allied forces demanded approximately $500 billion (value of the US dollar in 1946) in compensation after the defeat of Germany, and the German government later paid tens of billions of dollars in compensation for their massacre of the Jews.

However, the Japanese did not do this. Japan still clings onto its profits from the war, sat atop its bloody stolen diamonds and riches, enjoying a better quality of life in the decades following the Second World War than the countries it robbed. In this well-off position, the Japanese learned from the vast knowledge contained in the Chinese artefacts they stole while also repeatedly discriminating against the Chinese. This should be a real source of national embarrassment for Japan.

However, these factors are not what truly matters. The most important issue that Chinese people cannot bear is that Japan has tried to deny the crimes for which they were convicted by history and international tribunals, challenging China whenever it can. Japan's ambition continues to expand, even trying to take Chinese territory like the Diaoyu Islands.

This is a continuation of the spirit in which the Nanjing Massacre and other crimes were committed. Today, Japan not only opposes China on its own, but it has also encouraged Association of South Eastern Asian Nations member states such as the Philippines and Vietnam to oppose China in the East China Sea and South China Sea disputes.

The US received a huge amount of the gold and treasure that Japan stole from China and it has played a fundamental role in present Sino-Japanese relations. It is important to keep these facts in mind, as well as the key reasons why history has developed as it has. As mentioned earlier, the Americans occupied Japan after the Second World War and were key in the Tokyo trials and the conspiracies at the Treaty of San Francisco, as well as the Treaty of Mutual Cooperation and Security between the United States and Japan. To this day, the US president has insisted that the Diaoyu Islands are included under the scope of the US-Japan security treaty. They also support the Japanese government in increasing their mutual self-defence ties. Japanese right wing elements, egged on by the US, are ever closer to achieving their dream of restoring Japan's military capabilities, which were constitutionally limited following the Second World War.

These aren't the only worrying aspects. The US also supported Japan in retaining its royal family, refusing to charge the royals for war crimes. They also gave up the pursuit of Japanese compensation for the war while ignoring the legitimate rights of China and other Asian countries. There were two reasons for this. One was to enhance their national and political power, while the other was to use Japan as a bastion in Asia in the Cold War. The US wanted to use Japan to fight socialist countries like China and despicably tried to bring them into the conflict.

People have used a plethora of political systems for thousands of years; all countries have the right to choose a path of development that suits their nation and institutions. Socialism and capitalism are not necessarily at odds with each other. They can coexist and the world today is testimony to this. However, the Cold War mentality of the US government has dominated their diplomatic and national philosophy. They are even prepared to ally themselves with despots to share the gold and silver that was looted by Japanese invaders and war criminals to support anti-communist and anti-Chinese forces. The people of China are now becoming more and more aware of this.

This national awakening in China is a great blessing, meaning that the country, which has faced repeated invasions and enslavement, refuses to be a victim like it was during the Nanjing Massacre when the Yangtze River was red with blood. This consciousness is essential for the Chinese nation.

Remembering the pain that China suffered in the past will help to make sure that it never happens again.

BETWEEN MAN AND DEVIL:
THE CONFESSIONS OF THE JAPANESE

Not all Japanese people are evil. A number of Japanese soldiers who participated in the invasion of China have since regretted their actions following the end of the Second World War, during which they acted like monsters and committed countless crimes in China. As a result of these crimes, they were dubbed "devils" by the Chinese people. It was war and warmongers that transformed the Japanese soldiers into devils. This is why the emperor of Japan and the key decision-makers in the Japanese regime under his leadership at the time were blamed for the harrowing Nanjing Massacre during the Japanese invasion.

In Japan now, only a few right wing rulers like Shinzo Abe, the current prime minister who is a prime example of a Japanese person stuck in the Second World War mindset, dare to deny the great crimes Japan committed against China and other Asian countries while also attempting to revive the nation's militarism. What's worse is that rulers like Abe, under the pretext of the pursuit of national prosperity, are trying to steer millions of Japanese towards militarism similarly to what happened in Japan prior to the Second World War. This would have disastrous consequences.

Japanese nationals are by no means guilty. It is fundamentally dangerous and morally bankrupt to allow right wing elements in Japanese society to lead their countrymen down a criminal path as they did during the Second World War. This is because these same nationals are bound to turn into the same devils that their ancestors were when they slaughtered the citizens of Nanjing in December 1937. To prevent this, we need to do all we can to understand both the Japanese history of aggression against China and the Nanjing Massacre.

Two complaints regarding the Nanjing Massacre are currently common among the Chinese people. On the one hand, Japan has never accepted the guilt for the heinous event, while on the other, modern Chinese civilians know very little about the Nanjing Massacre, which had a profound impact on modern Chinese history and the nation.

An astute awareness and understanding of the Nanjing Massacre is essential for the people of China. The Japanese need to be confronted about the massacre so that they truly acknowledge and sincerely confess to the evil crimes that were committed so that both countries can move on from the Second World War together.

The decades of intense diplomatic relations between China and Japan have been partly due to the countries' different views regarding historical events and partly due to a mutual distrust of one another, especially in regard to current affairs and fears for the future. It is widely acknowledged that the Japanese are responsible for this unfortunate situation. However, following the end of the Second World War, especially over the past several decades, Japan has continued in its aggression and has denied its crimes time and time again. This not only worries non-violent people around the world but also the Japanese veterans who participated in the Nanjing Massacre themselves. To some extent, these soldiers were victims of the war too, so their acknowledgement of the Nanjing Massacre and their acceptance of guilt for it are an important part of making sure that the event is never forgotten.

Kazuo Sone, a Second World War veteran born in Shizuoka Prefecture in Japan in 1915, was enlisted at the age of 22 and joined the Shanghai expeditionary army as a lance corporal. He was directly involved in the Shanghai campaign and participated in the Nanjing Massacre, as well as other battles. To me, his repentance for the Nanjing Massacre is incredibly sincere. He is a Japanese man with an impressive sense of introspection. As a veteran of the Second World War and the Nanjing Massacre, Sone's profound reflection is incredibly valuable in informing modern Japanese society about the atrocity as well as serving as a source from which to learn more about Japan as a whole, its military forces and its soldiers.

The Nanjing Massacre and the War was written by a 73 year old Kazuo Sone and published in 1988. In the book, the Japanese veteran objectively expounds the reason for the Japanese war of aggression against China and the Japanese crimes, including the Nanjing Massacre and the mass rape of Chinese women. It is a commendable work that painstakingly details the atrocities. On top of this, it provides an insight into many previously unknown stories about the Japanese invaders. Some of the most valuable sources about the Nanjing Massacre are the works written by the Japanese themselves.

After Japan surrendered, Naruhiko Higashikuni was prime minister of Japan and had to tackle the many post-war issues. He officially admitted that the Japanese invasions of China and other Asian nations had not been for those nations' benefit and he even offered the "repentance of 100 million Japanese as a whole" under pressure from the international community.

Having reflected on their war crimes, a vast majority of Japanese nationals came to a consensus that they had to assume responsibility for waging war against their neighbours and repent for Japan's war crimes. Meanwhile, a campaign was launched among the people of Japan to determine the truth behind the war of aggression. As a result, many came to realise the evil essence of the war. The mysterious veil behind the war of aggression was lifted as Japanese people from all walks of life gradually disclosed war crimes from a wide range of perspectives. As Kazuo Sone said, the barbaric nature of the long and mysterious war of aggression against China suddenly became clear. Japanese nationals now understood that what had been termed as a "holy war" in Japanese propaganda had been conducted to invade its neighbours instead of to bring peace to Japan. It was clear why Japan had fought against China. It had been to enlarge its territory by taking it from others.

Kazuo Sone once said of the Second World War that: "In retrospect, it was impossible to win the war. During the Second World War, we were driven by the mantra of defeating the enemy and we always fought without thinking about the reasons behind the war itself. It was ridiculous that Japan fought the world's largest powers considering we could not even defeat China. It is no wonder that we lost the war."

Japanese soldiers committed many atrocities in China like those seen in the Nanjing Massacre. "Like all my comrades who fought in China, I ended up committing a lot of crimes. I killed innocent and ordinary Chinese people, thinking that I had no choice but to kill them. I even stole food and other possessions from the local residents," writes Kazuo Sone regretfully. He continues: "I also raped women as war trophies and destroyed houses. This was an unimaginable lack of humanity. I always wonder whenever I recall these cruel incidents if the Chinese have forgotten this suffering. No. They have never forgotten."

Yes, he is right, and the Chinese shall never forget about it. A year after the beginning of the reform and opening up period in China, the Chinese-Japanese Friendship Association sponsored a group of Japanese veterans who'd fought in the Second Sino-Japanese War to visit China. When they were in China, they went to many places including the Wusong area of Shanghai, which had been the site of an important battle during the Second Sino-Japanese War. When the Japanese veterans went to Shanghai, Nanjing and other places they had been to during the war against China, tragic scenes showed them the trauma they had caused. Local people gathered to take a look at the foreign visitors out of curiosity when the veterans revisited a village where a fierce battle had taken place almost 30 years earlier. However, when the locals heard the Japanese language, they screamed: "They're Japanese devils!" It terrified the veterans as the locals, who were of a similar age, scowled at them with a mix of hatred and helplessness, just like the many Chinese husbands after they'd found out their wives had been raped.

"Only then did the veterans realise that the suffering during the Second Sino-Japanese War had never disappeared from the Chinese psyche. It brought back memories of the atrocities the veterans had committed, leaving them ashamed of themselves. It pulled open an old wound," writes Sone. He then tells his countrymen: "A modern politician in Japan once said that as the crimes of the Japanese soldiers during the Second World War had happened almost four decades ago, it was all in the past. He then concluded that China was simply attempting to interfere in Japanese internal affairs by discussing the atrocities it had committed in the Second World War. But this is by no means true."

Sone writes: "The Chinese still hold a grudge against the Japanese for the great suffering that the Second Sino-Japanese War inflicted upon them, including their homeland being trampled upon, their possessions being robbed and even destroyed, and their fellow civilians being slaughtered and raped. The Japanese would do well to remember this and veterans like me share this belief." He sincerely told people around the world that whenever a Japanese veteran denied having committed a crime, he must be lying because almost every single veteran stole Chinese crops and livestock in addition to the slaughter and rape.

On 20 June 1987, another Japanese veteran was interviewed by journalists at the *Asahi Shimbun*. When it came to the reason why he had decided to confess to the sins he had committed during the Second Sino-Japanese War, the old man remarked in a harsh but cordial way that he was so old that he could do nothing but lament his previous mistakes. He said that he and his fellow veterans had been forced to kill the Chinese rather than having done so out of a sense of superiority, although this obviously wasn't the case. He added: "Veterans with a sense of humanity have to admit it. I would now like to reveal the essence of the evil during the Second Sino-Japanese War and sincerely make my wish for world peace clear."

In the 1980s, great efforts were being made by leading politicians in both countries to bring bilateral diplomatic relations back to normal. It allowed the regretful Japanese veterans and anti-war protesters to both criticise the Second Sino-Japanese War. As to why, Kazuo Sone says that: "They were among those who had been of the lowest military rank, who knew the reality of the war and hated it most. It is not inappropriate to say this. They were fed up with the war."

People criticised the Second Sino-Japanese War for many reasons, however, Sone knows the true feelings of those people who were caught in the war more than anyone. He writes: "Slaughter, looting, arson and rape are overshadowed by a fear of being stuck amidst artillery fire and machine gun and rifle battles. I have experienced this kind of terror both as a soldier in the Second World War and as a victim of an incendiary bomb dropped by an American B-29. Being massacred is much more terrifying than being caught in the range of an atomic bomb, which I luckily never experienced. As I age, I start to lose my sense of fear but not my sense of guilt."

In his old age, Sone had a profound knowledge of the war crimes. He explained that the Second World War turned almost every soldier who fought in it from a little mouse into a true devil capable of crimes for which they would have been thrown into prison back in Japan.

The former Japanese devil made it clear that what made the war most terrifying was that kind and simple young men were driven to madness and committing cruel crime. He since decided to confess and reflect on the crimes he committed during the Second World War.

On 15 August 1945, Japan's unconditional surrender was announced via a message broadcasted by the emperor. Veterans including Kazuo Sone were relieved because it was the end of the war. Sone recalled: "Despite all the radio static, I realised that the war had ended. The other Japanese were all saying that they'd had enough. We were truly looking forward to the end of the war."

During the early years following Japan's surrender, aversion to war spread among its citizens. Those who had once been worshiped as living gods in the special forces became abhorrent soldiers. In 1946, the so-called "Peace Constitution" was drafted and passed, stating that Japan would renounce war forever and never have any armed forces.

From then on, the people of Japan pursued peace and reconstructed their country. As time passed, however, Japan began to see an increase in right wing power along with militarism. Several decades have passed and some, especially those with ties to key players in the Second World War, have spoken highly of the war while glossing over the Japanese war crimes and constantly trying to glamorise the Second Sino-Japanese War. One example of this was when the Japanese ministry of education changed the description of the war against China from an "invasion" to an "entry", hinting at a renaissance of militarism.

Sone maintains that Japanese rulers ruthlessly controlled Japanese nationals through the use of the law, which was so severe that it's hard to imagine today. Soldiers were obliged to obey the military service law, and if necessary, people were forced into being enlisted, or having their land, property or other possessions requisitioned. People were not permitted to refuse or protest. He is of the opinion that the law deprived nationals of all rights to exist, to know and to speak.

A large number of Japanese people supposedly dismissed Sone's book as fabricated nonsense when it was published. When many academics tried to talk me out of quoting his view, I refused. To begin with, Kazuo Sone is much more detailed in his descriptions than other Japanese veterans who committed many crimes but never repented for doing so. Moreover, he vividly recreated the events of the Second Sino-Japanese War based on his own experiences instead of his imagination. This is in stark contrast to those who aren't brave enough to admit to their crimes. Nowadays, many Japanese insist that the Nanjing Massacre was made up by the Chinese.

It is dangerous for any nation to distort history. To further facilitate the Japanese distortion of history, Japanese leaders have insisted on the importance of the state being able to take control of knowledge at times for the good of the nation, creating the State Secrets Law to do so.

Reluctant to be controlled by a few militarist rulers, veterans like Kazuo Sone, who have lived through the enormous transformations of post-war Japan, questioned the need for enacting the State Secrets Law saying: "Japan is currently a country of peace and safety. But the State Secrets Law is likely to destroy this. Do these militarists want to put Japan in great danger again?" Considering what is going on in Japan today, the anxiety of Japanese veterans like Kazuo Sone is understandable.

It is imperative for the Japanese to gain a profound understanding of the story behind the Nanjing Massacre and the Second Sino-Japanese War as a whole. Sone often reflected on the Nanjing Massacre and in spite of his profound and sincere confession he couldn't get rid of his guilt whenever he thought about the evil he'd committed during the war. But confession does provide some relief. He deserves the respect of all peace loving people for his staunchly anti-war stance after witnessing the horrors of war first hand.

The following is extracted from Kazuo Sone's writing:

How a Devil Was Formed

> I was recruited for the Battle of Shanghai in 1937. I spent my twenties and early thirties in constant combat as a soldier on the frontline.
>
> Soldiers on the frontline were responsible for directly fighting enemies to win the war, and only the wealth of experience we'd gained in battle could

guarantee final victory, so we mostly stayed on the battlefields. We didn't only get better experience as frontline soldiers, but more problems too.

The first issue was human slaughter. It is inevitable for soldiers to kill in battle. However, I killed innocent Chinese people, looted, committed arson and even raped people, all of which are evil acts. Now, in a society of peace and safety, I always regret my crimes.

I sometimes think that if I'd have been born 15 years earlier or later then I'd never have committed any war crimes. I hate war.

[Author's note: *After a physical examination, Kazuo Sone was assigned to the united combat team of the Japanese army. This was the beginning of his career as an active duty soldier, which lasted for about two years during which time he committed crimes.*]

I first walked into the military camp with a mix of concern and anxiety because of an uncertainty about everything there. The severity of the training in the army was beyond any of my expectations. The following day, we gathered at the squadron auditorium where the commander gave us instructions regarding army life. He told us that the Japanese army was bonded together by a mutual love and trust between seniors and juniors in the family of soldiers. He said that their love for each other was just like the love between a father and son. The squadron commander could be trusted like a father and the supervisor could be trusted like a mother. He then convinced new recruits that the second year seniors would kindly help them with daily issues.

I'd previously heard about the harshness of army life but I hadn't really believed it. When I heard the affectionate instructions, I gave a sigh of relief. After a while, however, I realised that what the commander had told us was absolute nonsense. The commander was too senior for new recruits to contact, and the supervisors of similar ranks and the second year soldiers had almost all turned into monsters by then, cruelly manipulating the new recruits at random.

We'd all joined the army in the same way and the new recruits deserved the same treatment as the second year soldiers. But this was never the case. New recruits were forced to get the weapons of the second year soldiers serviced, do their laundry and wipe their shoes. The new recruits were essentially their servants. They had to do all of this in their spare time. That was why the new recruits never had a moment spare.

The reveille would call in the new day for the new recruits. They had to finish making their beds before hurrying to the field for roll call because they had to line up in the order they'd arrived. They hardly had time to wash their hands and were then forced to do morning bayonet training.

They had to finish all of these duties before the assembly call was given.

Otherwise, the officer on duty would scold them: "Didn't you hear that? You're a real idiot!" The latecomers would be beaten by the officer with a fake gun.

After assembling the new recruits, they'd start military training, which was the soldiers' most essential duty. Due to the Mukden Incident, the training aimed to create an army for actual combat, which added to the severity of the military training. Lower ranking officers trained soldiers by strictly conforming to the training principles set out by the senior officers, which were truly difficult, believing that beating the new recruits benefited their training.

Being a new recruit was difficult. Lower ranking officers would encourage their assistant officers to train new recruits under the principle of "punches speak louder than words".

As a result, violence was everywhere. If a recruit didn't perform well, they'd bellow: "Are you incapable of doing as I say?" They would then severely beat them.

After beating the recruit, the officer would ask whether he felt any pain. The recruit would obviously be in great pain, but they were faced with a dilemma. If the recruit answered honestly and said that it hurt, then he'd be beaten again. But if the recruit said no, the officer would beat him and ask him again.

The new recruits had no choice but to allow themselves to be severely beaten by the officers. The lowest ranking soldiers had to do everything the other soldiers said.

Exhausted from an entire morning of rigid training, they had to prepare lunch without a break. They were told to wash dishes after they'd finished the meal. New recruits were always busy, running around like mice.

In the afternoon, recruits would be trained again on the military square and training field. The first thing they were supposed to do after afternoon training was wipe other soldiers' shoes and of course cook dinner. Dinner had been a relaxing occasion back at home, but in the military camp, new recruits weren't given enough time to even taste the food. After getting their food, they had to eat it quickly. The second year soldiers would intimidate them if they didn't.

Before the evening roll call, recruits had to finish cleaning and go over all the weapons as quickly as possible. Only when roll call ended and all the lights had gone out could the new recruits do their laundry. Unlike the simplicity of washing with a washing machine today, washing at that time was a truly uncomfortable affair at a laundry station outside in the snow. The bone-chilling water would leave their hands almost frozen. They could go to sleep after washing.

I slept in a bunk bed smaller than 1.7 metres long with a mattress made from straw. As was often described in military songs, bed was paradise for these unlucky souls and their eyes would water because they were so homesick.

The new recruits' first day had passed. This would have been unbelievable in a normal society but not in the military, where you'd be punished severely for not doing this.

After the war, this became known to everyone when scenes showing violence in the military were recreated in films or on the TV. You always saw scenes in films about military life where senior officers mistreated lower ranking soldiers.

Some believe that these films were made to paint the army at the time as evil, but that is complete nonsense. Punishment using violence was commonplace in the Japanese army since its founding in the Meiji Era, even though it changed somewhat in different periods of the nation's history.

Those with experience of life in a military camp would never forget these memories. Although memories of events may vary from person to person, regardless of who they are and regardless of their age, all of them would have been beaten at some point. You would often hear recollections like: "During the first year in the army, you'd be beaten for no reason. Anyone with experience of army life must have experienced it, even if they didn't hit anyone. If someone says that they were never beaten, they're lying." Violent punishments were commonplace in the Japanese army.

A variety of methods were used to carry out violent punishments, most of which involved being hit in the face. This was known as "slapping" in Japanese military jargon. The different methods of slapping included an open handed slap, a punch with a fist, being beaten with a belt, a leather strip, slippers and more. As young men hit hard, even being slapped with someone's palm was incredibly painful. If someone was slapped with a strip of leather, then they wouldn't be able to stand up due to the pain. The next morning, their face would be swollen and dark purple in colour, no longer looking like a person. It not only affected their appearance as soldiers' mouths would also be so swollen that they couldn't even chew their food. Although these people had been so cruelly and violently punished, they had to lie when they went to the clinic for treatment, saying: "I was clumsy and fell. This was all my fault."

If you were honest and said that you'd been beaten by someone, the attacker would be punished, and in retaliation, he would punish you more severely. Although the medical officers knew these injuries were the result of violent punishment, they would stay silent. They had no choice but to tolerate it and cry themselves to sleep. Of course, I was also slapped and I know the feeling well.

At the time, there were rumours about the army, like you'd be treated well for the first five days, but then you wouldn't be allowed to have any fun. Then after 10 days, you'd be beaten. This may sound like somewhat of an exaggeration, but this was how senior officers treated new recruits.

I was slapped after 10 days or so in the army. Before my enlistment, I had already heard of this kind of punishment and had been aware that there was violent punishment in the army. However, I was incredibly naive and just thought that they wouldn't beat soldiers who didn't do anything wrong. It was the army after all.

Following the evening roll call after 10 days or so, the senior soldiers announced that the soldiers were dismissed. I remember thinking with a sigh of relief: "Today has come to an end at last, thank God." Then a senior soldier walked over to us and said: "New recruits, wait a minute please." Then the senior soldier suspended the dismissal.

The senior soldier was the lowest ranked officer among the other senior soldiers. He got all the new recruits to stand in a line and then stood in front of them and said: "Recruits, don't you know how many days you've been enlisted for? Are you going to be a guest in the army forever? The army has given you food to eat, clothes to wear, and even money to spend. You can't be so ungrateful! I'm here to cheer you all up. Clench your jaws and man up! Everyone wearing glasses, take them off."

They wanted us to clench our jaws so that they wouldn't damage our mouths when they beat us, and they wanted us to take off our glasses so that they wouldn't break them. If anyone was told to do this, it meant that they were going to get slapped. I remember thinking: "I'm finally going to get slapped." I then stood upright and heard a sound getting nearer from the right of me that sounded like someone punching meat. It was very loud and made everyone who heard it sad, making people feel as if they were being beaten themselves. It was my turn. When they hit my cheek, I heard the familiar sound as I saw stars. I felt a burning pain that rushed to my brain, making me dizzy. Even so, I didn't fall over and I tried very hard to stand firm.

I'd always told myself to not allow myself to get upset about such petty things and I tried to cheer myself up, but once I thought "it's finally ended", tears suddenly streamed down my face. I didn't stop crying until I went to bed. I didn't know why I cried so much. At the time, I thought that it was because I'd been beaten without having done anything wrong and felt insulted.

This was the first time I was slapped on the face after joining the army. This was the way it was in collective army life; even those who didn't do anything wrong would get beaten. It was so common because whenever a new recruit made a mistake, all of the soldiers in his unit would be slapped as well. In the army, they called this a "general face slap".

Apart from the physical damage due to these acts of violence, they also punished new recruits mentally. This was a sadistic and predatory form of torture. The methods used somewhat differed from unit to unit, but they were generally very similar. One of the most commonly used methods was "holding the gun". Back then, our rifles were engraved with a 16 petal chrysanthemum badge and they were considered to have been given to us by the emperor. As a result, everyone cherished their rifles and they would be checked after evening roll call to see if they needed maintenance. Those who hadn't sufficiently maintained their rifles were subjected to this form of punishment. During the rifle inspection, those who were found with problems would be singled out as victims and told to raise their guns and apologise to the rifle, saying: "I apologise to the great *sanpachi-shiki hohei-ju* rifle. I, a no good private, have been reprimanded by the senior soldiers because I was lazy and did not do a good job maintaining the rifle. In the future, I will not be so lazy, not just in active service but also in reserve. I swear this to you, please forgive me."

On the surface, this looks fairly insignificant and there wouldn't be anything wrong with it if this was all that happened. However, these poor new recruits experienced a great deal of pain. They had to keep holding the gun for many hours and couldn't change position until they had properly apologised to their guns. However, even if they apologised to the rifle a million times, it couldn't ever forgive them. As time passed, their rifles became heavier and heavier and they began to feel exhausted. An hour later, their arms would be numb. Even so, they weren't allowed to put their guns down.

This was a form of both mental and intense physical torture and it wasn't rare to see men burst into tears. Their faces would then be slapped until they were swollen before being allowed to go.

There was another form of mental punishment known as "hey, brother". This would also be given to those who didn't look after their rifles properly. In this punishment, victims had to look through the sight of their rifle as if it were a window. They would then treat passing soldiers as their "guests", forced to humiliate themselves by saying: "Hey brother, come here, I'm waiting for you."

As the soldiers who passed by knew this was a form of punishment, they wouldn't come over regardless of what they said. The soldiers who were being punished had no choice but to say this to them and sometimes passing soldiers angrily shouted: "What the fuck did you say?" They then slapped the soldier and left without saying anything else. The senior soldier who was on duty would then say: "You let the honoured guests get away!" The senior soldiers acted as if it were a joke, but the new recruits knew it was serious. When forced to do this, men became frustrated and quietly sobbed.

There were other typical forms of mental torture, including one known as "go cycling" and another known as "the bird walks past the valley".

The "go cycling" punishment involved getting soldiers who were being punished to stand between two beds and use their hands to lift up their bodies between them, with both legs spinning in the air as if they were cycling.

Although this wasn't normally a difficult task, this form of torture drained people of their energy. People who were being punished became incredibly tired as their arms were under great pressure. When they couldn't stand it anymore, they cycled slower and slower. Senior soldiers would then mock them, saying: "You can't stop! Speed up! Listen, boy, you better do this seriously!" People who had to do this for long periods of time became very tired and swore profusely. This was a depressing agony for everyone who was subjected to this form of punishment.

Like the "go cycling" punishment, "the bird walks past the valley" punishment also took place on a bed. They got the soldier to lie on their stomach under the bed and to act like a bird whenever they went past the bed. The senior soldiers would then make fun of the recruit and say: "You've got to sing better than that! The birdsong sounds terrible this year, I can't stand it!"

This type of punishment tormented the soldiers mentally rather than physically. We never knew who'd thought of these bizarre punishments. I could provide an endless list of similar punishments. I will give one last example of an unusual punishment, which was called "going for a walk among the soldiers".

This punishment was targeted at those who hadn't properly maintained their boots. As they had been provided to the soldiers by the army, the boots that we wore during the day had to be cleaned and polished in the evenings. The boot check took place after the evening roll call and if soldiers did a bad job, they'd be punished. The preferred method was getting these soldiers to "go for a walk among the soldiers".

They got the soldiers to put their boots around their necks and pretend to be a dog as they crawled on the ground on their hands and legs. They had to go around the entire camp and stop at each door to whine like a dog. They then told all of the soldiers around them: "I'm here to report that I was too lazy to clean my shoes and have been punished by the commander."

If this was all that happened in the punishment, then it wouldn't have been that bad. However, there were always a few bullies who took advantage of any opportunity to torment others. They'd say: "So you didn't clean your boots and you still have time to hang around with nothing to do? Did you have too much to eat? Or was cleaning your boots too boring? If you think it's too boring, tell me and I'll beat it into you." They then beat them until they couldn't stand.

Whenever this happened and the soldier returned to their unit, their face would be covered with blood so we couldn't even tell what they used to look like.

These punishments were by no means unique and were indeed commonplace in the army.

The Japanese Soldiers: Human Killing Machines

[Author's note: *Kazuo Sone understood one thing before joining the army. Japan's army was personally led by the leader of the Japanese. It was the best in the world. Why would there ever be brutal violent punishment? Then he realised why.*]

This culture of violent punishment can be dated back to the early Ming dynasty. At that time, there were many soldiers who'd been born knights and violence was considered to be the best method of training brave soldiers. As common soldiers, we didn't think we actually became brave through violence, but the senior leaders seemed to think that soldiers would only become brave and strong if they went through great hardship. They used the word "tough" to describe savage and considered toughness to be essential to the warrior spirit and the foundation of training soldiers. This seemed to be the original reason for training soldiers through violence.

There's a very good example to illustrate this point. I was a teacher for a long time in a high school after I left the army. The school's military education results were checked by commanders every year. One time, a *shousa*, or a major in English, who was in charge of checking the results said: "Superficially, there seem to have been a lot of improvements in military training, but it doesn't really work. The military training you've been providing is just an imitation of what happens in the army, as if the students were just playing soldier. Only by doing what soldiers do can you understand the skills and spirit needed to be a soldier." What the major meant was not training as seriously as they did in the army was just a waste of time.

The major later talked with me about military education and said: "The aim of military education in a high school is to teach introductory military knowledge so it would be impossible to instil the warrior spirit in them at that point. It would be acceptable if it just helps improve their conduct and performance, but the average person's military education needs to train them into being the excellent soldiers that the army expects. That's why violence is needed." I would like to analyse what the major said here. The army generally expected its soldiers to acquire three characteristics. First, as the army's *raison d'être* was to fight, good soldiers had to be able to fight better than the soldiers of enemy nations. Second, good soldiers had to be taught to have faith that they could overcome whatever hardships came their way. Third, good soldiers had to listen to what their commanders said and do as they said. These three points were essential characteristics for the model soldiers that the army expected. The first two points could be fulfilled through military training and the third point had to be remembered during education.

I would like to talk about obedience in this following section as there was a great deal of violence involved in training obedience. The use of the term military obedience is essentially synonymous with blindly following one's superiors. Lower ranking soldiers had to strictly follow their commanders' orders; if their commander told them to turn right, they'd turn right, if he told them to advance, they'd advance, if he told them to stop, they'd stop. Their only choice was to follow their commanders' orders. Soldiers who blindly followed orders were considered exemplary.

However, soldiers who dared to ask questions were loathed by the army.

I'd like to take this opportunity to explain this a little more. When the Second Sino-Japanese War began, the lower ranking soldiers didn't know why they'd been sent to war. They acted like drones and blindly followed their commanders' orders to advance and fight. They had been conditioned to fight like this for five or six years without knowing when the war was finally going to come to an end. This was how soldiers were trained: to blindly follow orders.

Now, back to the soldiers' training. The army required the soldiers in training that they were checking to be able to serve as regular soldiers for a period of time. The aim of this was to mould the soldiers into the troops the army expected.

These soldiers in training were recruited from a wide range of backgrounds and nationalities across the country, so they belonged to all kinds of positions in society. They included local and national civil servants, average blue and white collar workers, farmers and fishermen, industrial and business workers, actors and performers, part time workers and more.

There was a huge range of people in the army, from the incredibly wealthy to the impoverished, having grown up with differing levels of education and having worked in a plethora of professions. There were soldiers who'd attended college or university and there were some who still hadn't completed their compulsory education. Not only did they differ in terms of education, but they differed in their personalities too. Among them, there were racial supremacists, left wing thinkers, tough recruits and those who couldn't stand the army.

The army was filled with the educated and those who lacked education, the sane and the insane, the gentle and the mean, and so on. It was a rather diverse organisation. It was the army's job to turn these people into the soldiers they expected.

To do this, the first step was to keep the numbers of new recruits to the smallest level possible and then to make everybody the same. Everyone in the group had to be stripped of their identity. This meant that there would be no motivation for some to reach a certain level in the organisation, which was a reason for its success. Using violence was the most effective method for achieving this purpose.

After joining the army, regardless of who the new recruit was, they'd be violently punished in their first year. The same thing happened the next year; violent punishments were used against the new soldiers in the next batch of recruits. This happened every year between the new and senior soldiers. It looked like nothing more than revenge for their own pain, but this practice was vital for moulding the soldiers into the army's expectations. Although this was very cruel, after entering the military, the soldiers' only option was to obey. The soldiers could do nothing to stop it. If they rebelled against their superiors and were found guilty, they would be punished for the disobedience. As a result, most people thought that there was no way you could even think during active service, regardless of how much injustice you faced. They all thought the same way, thinking that it was better to suffer indignity without putting up a protest. Once this idea had been ingrained into the soldiers, they became mindless drones and were under the control of their superiors and would immediately respond to their orders. Model soldiers not only had to fight well and have courage, they had to be blindly obedient.

Military camps were used to transform ordinary people into weapons of war. It took about two years of this process to make a private first class out of a recruit, ending up with troops that were far superior to standard privates.

This is a good opportunity to explain the ranks of the soldiers. When I was a recruit, soldiers were divided into three levels: private, lance corporal and private first class. During the Second Sino-Japanese War, the rank of corporal wasn't used. All newly enlisted recruits were privates. As the training progressed, the best recruits would be promoted to private first class in much less than a year, which is how long it normally took. The most outstanding privates were promoted to this position. As this was the highest possible rank among these soldiers, only a small percentage of people could be promoted to this position. Not only did they have to have an excellent record, they also had to be extremely honourable with an attitude that served as a role model for other soldiers. Therefore, becoming a private first class was seen as a glorious achievement. However, senior officers used this possible promotion as bait to tame soldiers. Soldiers would be more willing to endure humiliation during the beginning of their career in the army because they wanted to be promoted to private first class. Most soldiers endured this pain when they enlisted, but some of them couldn't stand it and committed suicide. I'll introduce a comrade of mine here, let's call him A. A and I joined the army together and we were assigned in the same squadron in the early years, but because he was unable to endure the violent punishment and knew that he couldn't escape, he eventually committed suicide.

A was one of the few intellectuals in the army who'd attended university. He wasn't just intelligent, but also hardworking, so he was considered to be a genius in the army. The superior officer was also fond of him. If he continued like this, he could have become a midshipman and been appointed as a reserve second lieutenant. Although there was nothing wrong with him, because he was an intellectual, he was a bit different from the rest of the soldiers when he spoke. In general, this wouldn't be a problem in normal society, but in the army he was hated by the uneducated senior soldiers. Solely because of this, they hated A and no matter what he said, they'd say he was talking nonsense. He was beaten several times more than the other new soldiers. If the others had been more mature, he might have been able to stand it, but because A had come from a much better background than the environment he found himself in, and because A was afraid, he couldn't tolerate it and decided to leave. Even though A was an intellectual, he was remarkably naive. Although he successfully ran away from the army after the lights had gone out, he had left in military uniform and they had a network of military police and regular police to chase him so he had nowhere to run. It wouldn't be easy to escape them. A understood that even if he could escape, he wouldn't be able to hide anywhere in all of Japan. He then committed suicide in the living room of a seaside fisherman's residence. After his body was found, he was brought back to the camp. He had begun to decompose before being given over to his family. I then saw people become aware of how relentlessness life in the army was. Even when he was just a bag of bones, A's desertion charges didn't leave him. His father walked with slumped shoulders because his son was labelled with the crime forever, a sight that made everyone depressed.

The Excitement of Killing the Chinese

I was in the army when the Marco Polo Bridge Incident took place.

We were doing evening exercises in the country in Aichi Prefecture when we heard about the incident taking place. I was at a camp on the east coast, waiting for the next morning.

As I looked at the lights turning on in the evening, I told myself: "I'll get out of the army soon so I'll tolerate this for now. Then I'll go back home on the train. I can't wait to go back home." I was incredibly depressed. At this point, the squadron headquarters contacted returning soldiers who brought news of the Marco Polo Bridge Incident. They said: "According to the grocery store owner in front of the station, armed conflict took place between the two sides in Beijing. They're still fighting now."

The soldiers were very interested in the news that Japanese and Chinese forces were fighting each other but I didn't think that it was such an important event at the time. I was just thinking that it was at most an insignificant incident where the Japanese were fighting the Chinese slaves. It wasn't a big deal and I thought it'd be swiftly resolved.

At that point, I wasn't alone in thinking this as most people in the army had never thought that they'd go into battle, thinking that even if the fighting lasts for a long period of time, there were a lot of Kwantung army elites in Manchuria, so the domestic army probably didn't need to bother themselves. As a result, we carried on like normal, and at the end of the day's drills, we went back to the barracks. We then just thought that China probably wouldn't deploy any troops, and if they did, the government would send in their troops to foil their plans.

After that, on the way to a business trip to Toyohashi, I saw characters written on several banners in towns and villages, which read: "Best wishes to the soldiers who are following the wishes of the rulers of the country." On the square in front of the station, small Japanese flags waved in wind, seeing the soldiers off to the sound of cheers and military songs, which sounded like angry waves.

Appetite for war was growing in the towns and villages, but the active duty soldiers in the barracks weren't all that eager to go and fight. The officers and soldiers who'd been called up were those who were needed for their special technical skills, as well as forces to supplement the military's transportation capacity. We hadn't expected to be mobilised.

However, by the end of August, the war in the north of China spread to central China, and even Shanghai was ablaze. Not until the middle of August did my division begin to mobilise. High command then began to choose to send active service soldiers into the war and it was decided that we were to be deployed.

We finished the emergency mobilisation and our division began to head for Shanghai. Even at this point, we didn't think we low ranking soldiers had been called up to fight in a major war. We assumed that the navy was acting like a police force in Shanghai, so the army was just being called up for support. We thought that the army was being asked to help because the marines couldn't cope.

When fighting in the war, where the army thought of themselves as heroes for fighting, the soldiers in active service remembered how Japan had taken on great powers like Russia so they believed that China would be no match for them. In a similar vein of arrogance, we thought that the marines just weren't able to cope on their own.

When they left home, many soldiers at the time naively expected it to be like the January 28 incident in 1932, which had come to an end in little more than a month. They thought that this war would be over in a month or so. Even if it did end up taking more time, no one thought it would take any longer than two months. However, this assumption proved wrong after a few days. Chinese troops were heavily fortified near Shanghai at the time, which the Japanese hadn't expected so the Japanese army lost the battle.

The first batch of divisions set sail from Nagoya to the banks of the Huangpu River two days earlier than we had. After a day and a night of fighting in Wusong, they were almost all completely annihilated.

After this battle had taken place, we followed as the second batch of troops and landed in the battlefield. I was the sort of person who felt bad about even killing an insect and I felt sick with sorrow at the thought of seeing such violence up close. But this was not because I was full of compassion and had a strong sense of justice, but because I was rather more timid than most.

Cowards like me were put at the top of the list in conscription inspections to be enlisted as soldiers. The military said that it was one unit with a sole purpose of killing people. Our job was to kill. In order to prepare for the war in peacetime, soldiers had to practice shooting and stabbing people with bayonets. To fully teach soldiers how to kill people, strategic military drills that incorporated these two skills were essential. This is what I experienced when I became a soldier. I spent all day learning how to kill the enemy when I was in active service. My progress was noted and I had performed better than other soldiers, so I became the first to be promoted to private first class. That meant that, as a soldier, I was considered better than others. But this was only true in simulated military drills. Once we were in an actual combat situation, I could hardly be described as a soldier, let alone a private first class. I was useless. When I arrived on the battlefield, I was terrified.

We landed in the same place as the first troops, which was the pier at the end of the Wusong railway. Since the first troops' successful landing, they hadn't been able to advance, so we were near the front.

When we landed, the sound of gunfire being exchanged between our troops and the enemy could be heard. Stray bullets flew past with a whistle and bang.

Because this was the first time I'd ever seen real combat, I was terrified. Bullets brushed past me and hit the ground nearby with a wisp of smoke and dust rising from the dirt. If a bullet hit me, I would have been doomed. Whenever this happened, I became extremely afraid and was unable to calm down, thinking that I was going to die. A pungent smell hung in the air. The soldiers said that the troops that had fought in the battle first were cremating their dead comrades in the square next to the Huangpu River near to where we'd disembarked.

When other troops landed, I went to take a look. It was more like a barbecue than a cremation. Back in Japan, one dead body would have given me nightmares, let alone hundreds of bodies piled up like a mountain. Only a few of the bodies were pulled out and thrown into the roaring flames. Some burned very well and were removed, but the rest were just lightly singed and thrown into the Huangpu River.

I stared blankly at the horrifying scene and heard the voices of the soldiers who were burning the bodies: "Because our squadron was completely wiped out and fewer than 10 people survived, we could never burn all the bodies. We have done our best to cope." I had seen how frightening the war was. Looking around at the scene, I found that many dead enemy bodies had been left there.

We hadn't been the only ones to take heavy casualties during the landing; many enemy soldiers had been killed. The longer I stayed, the more the mountains of dead bodies grew. Dozens, maybe even hundreds, of dead bodies had been piled up and left to rot in the extremely hot weather. It looked like there were bodies filled with gas, which would burst if they were poked. Maggots writhed around their eyes, noses and mouths.

Although I was horrified by the scene, I knew the real horrors were yet to come. Fighting on a battlefield wouldn't be as easy as what I'd experienced in simulated combat because here it was kill or be killed. I would die if I carried on being a coward. I realised that I had to kill and began to worry about my survival. I had seen the brutality when we landed in Wusong and was terrified. The next day, I saw my comrades stab Chinese people to death with their bayonets.

In the army, the weapons soldiers generally used were Type 38 rifles and bayonets. The rifles were used to shoot and kill enemies while bayonets were mounted on the end of the rifles to stab enemies when they got near. Soldiers had been forced to practice their shooting and stabbing skills during training. I had also trained these skills when I was in service and understood exactly how to do it, but it was a different matter to actually stab someone to death.

After landing in Wusong, my squadron moved out very early on and gathered in one corner of Tongji University to rest for the night. The next morning, when our soldiers were on watch, we suddenly heard somebody say that they'd caught a spy and everyone rushed to see what had happened.

As I'd never seen the enemy before, I went out of curiosity. However, the accused spy was an old lady who was 60 or so. At first glance, nobody could imagine how she could ever be a spy as she hobbled down the road. She kept speaking in an unfamiliar language and bowed her head, seemingly begging us: "I am a common woman and have never been a spy. Please let me go." I felt sorry for her and wanted to save her. When I was about to say that there was no way she could be a spy and that they should let her go, I was stopped by the bloodthirsty soldiers around me and couldn't say a word. The soldiers surrounded the old woman and began to discuss how to kill her. While they were discussing the matter, a private first class shouted: "I'd like to kill her with my bayonet."

He looked very young, probably the same age as me. He looked like he had come from a good background and to look at him, you'd think he was a kind man. He did not look like a killer so his words startled me. Not only did he say it, he pushed his bayonet up against the old lady and shouted at her. He pushed it into her heart and its tip went through her, coming out of her back.

The old woman yelled and fell to the ground as her eyes rolled back. I could see the resentment in her eyes and hurriedly looked away.

Although I felt appalled by the murder of this bystander, the killer seemed unperturbed by what he'd done. After kicking the old lady's body into the gutter, he lit a cigarette. I remember thinking that what he'd done was incredibly cruel. But then I thought about it once again and realised it wasn't a matter of morality. He had come here earlier than me and had become a real soldier when he'd fought in battle, while I had no idea what this must have been like. If someone was killed like this in normal society, it would be treated as a heinous crime and punished severely in accordance with criminal law. Moreover, the criminal would be branded a murderer or serial killer, which was common sense for a normal society. However, in battle, killing was normal. These soldiers had been normal civilians in a normal society before being sent off to war. Although these soldiers had already fought in battle, it didn't mean that killing was easy for them.

Soldiers needed to experience war and have their normal psychological processes disrupted in order to learn how to kill someone. The soldiers called this process "making a real soldier from a common man on the battlefield".

The night when the old woman was killed by the private first class, I went to the front and engaged in the war for the first time. The next day, I killed enemies and became a real soldier. Whenever killing was discussed between when I first arrived and my first kill on the battlefield, it was very blunt.

However, I was incredibly ashamed of it. We decided to mount a night raid against the enemy that day. When I recall the time I spent waiting to go on this night raid, I find it very hard to put my complex feelings into words.

I will try to analyse these complex emotions of mine. After we broke into the enemy positions, we launched a bayonet charge to kill them. I felt intense fear. Although I regarded Chinese soldiers as weak and looked down on them, I became frightened when we were actually fighting. When I thought about death, all I could think about was my own survival and wanting to avoid the ridicule of my comrades.

Several other thoughts raced through my mind, but I can't remember much. They made me uncomfortable. Waiting for our orders to advance with such heightened anxiety was agony. I thought that this must be how criminals on death row felt before being executed.

The order to advance was given and we left the Tongji University campus in the direction of a large field in a farm. Enemy bullets flew past us with more and more intensity and it felt like it was raining bullets.

Bullets were hitting the ground when we arrived on the frontline. We crawled forwards, but bullets still showered overhead, barely missing us. Bullets hit cotton plants, which were less than a metre tall. They shattered and fell to the ground, while bullets continued to strike the dirt. If I had been shot by just one of these bullets, I would have died. I remember thinking that even if our destination was hell, I just wanted to get there as soon as possible.

When we arrived at the destination, we had no time to rest and started the assault on the enemy positions. At this phase of the battle, I panicked and no longer wanted to kill the enemy after breaking into their garrisons. I ran around with my bayonet like a boy playing soldier. When I realised that this was a real war and that I was actually in battle, I felt deeply ashamed. In order to save face in front of the other soldiers, I told myself that to be respected, I had to bloody my bayonet.

I looked around and saw five or six enemy corpses scattered on the ground. When I got ready to stab one of them, adopting the stance of an assassin, the body suddenly jumped up and ran away. The soldier had been pretending to be dead. When I went to stab him, he got scared and began to flee. I was as astounded as the fleeing soldier. I was startled when I saw this so-called corpse suddenly get up and run away. The enemy fled and I had failed to do my duty.

I had been successful in learning the killing skills taught in training and I had some of the best skills in my squadron. I thought that it would have been a piece of cake to kill one or two enemies with these skills but I'd failed to do so. After that, I reflected on it and put it down to insufficient preparation for being a real soldier. I was letting my normal mindset coexist with my identity as a soldier. My rational mind feared what a soldier's psychology was capable of, thus hindering my development as a soldier.

Although I hadn't done well, the assault had been a success and the enemy's position had been captured. We stopped the pursuit that night and stayed overnight in the enemy's trenches.

As the first rays of the morning sun lit up the trenches, we could suddenly see everything. Probably due to their hurried retreat, the enemies had left behind their rifles and ammunition, as well the bodies of their dead. When we saw the bodies, we realised that the Chinese soldiers deployed here weren't regular soldiers but people of different ages and backgrounds who'd been put together wearing different coloured clothes, wearing khaki, blue and other colours.

Looking around at the bodies, some were more than 40 years old and may well have been fathers. They wore terrified expressions, which made me sad. Among them, there were several teenage soldiers. Seeing these children's faces, I hoped they were resting peacefully and I felt very sorry for them.

I thought that these people had probably left their wives, children and siblings behind at home and come to fight in battle. They had to have missed them before they died. I felt a great compassion for the dead enemies. When I remembered the soldier that I'd let go, I felt relieved and grateful for not having killed him.

After having breakfast, which I'd brought in a bento box, the order to advance was issued. This wasn't for the whole unit, but just my squadron. We were told to finish off the enemies from last night. It may have just been a small battle, but it was very important for me.

Thanks to it having been dark during the skirmish the night before, nobody had seen me mess up. But as it was now daytime, if I did it again I'd be a laughing stock. I decided to do all I could with the skills I'd learned in training.

But despite my determination, I did exactly as I had done the night before after breaking into the enemies' positions. By the time I realised what I'd done, all the enemies had fled. I thought that the war was going to have come to an end and all I'd have done was aimlessly wave around my bayonet. I began to think how I could save face as I saw an enemy soldier stumbling as he ran away. I thought that God had given me this opportunity to kill him and I had to do it quickly. I thought: "I can't let this good prey go." I was about to stab him as I caught up with him, but failed once again. I normally wouldn't have failed, but because of my anxiety and exhaustion, I didn't seize the opportunity and failed to thrust the bayonet into his body. Despite this, I knew I could do it if I tried again. Just as I was about to do so, I got a stitch. As I struggled to stand up, the soldier got away.

Then another enemy soldier ran over to where I'd fallen a moment ago. He didn't notice me and almost stepped right on top of me, probably because he was so worried after falling behind his comrades. To my surprise, I looked up and he noticed me, staring at me with shining eyes. I looked away and instinctively stabbed him with my bayonet, thinking that he was a threat.

I subconsciously felt the bayonet thrust into his body and I finally came to my senses when I heard a strange sound. I looked at what I'd done and saw that the soldier was almost trying to kill himself as he pushed himself into my bayonet. It had been instinct, as if my body was trying to protect me. I had stabbed him as soon as he'd approached me. When I was about to stand up slowly, the soldier fell down on top of me. I tried to push him away, but I couldn't move.

It was at that point when the soldier's blood sprayed all over me. I felt his lukewarm blood on my skin and felt a burst of energy course through my body like electricity. My paralysis disappeared and a powerful force flooded through my body, making me instantly stronger. I then kicked the soldier off me and stood up powerfully and shouted in celebration. When I recall this feeling, it was as if some power had been transmitted to me and all of my confusing emotions had faded away. I felt like a victorious warrior in the Sengoku Period when I shouted triumphantly.

This battlefield experience is what made me able to commit crimes. I took this as an opportunity to grow and quickly became a so-called "real soldier" who'd proven himself in battle. When I first went to war, I was afraid of enemy fire. But now all of this fear had gone and in contrast, I fell in love with the joy of the adventure. I was also used to killing and felt a great joy when I did so. After this transformation, I was no longer an ordinary man. I had lost my normal mindset and had become a mad soldier.

The More You Kill, the More Praise You Get

As a popular saying went among soldiers on the battlefield: "The benefit of being a soldier is the credit you get after killing someone." These words were said in a somewhat self-deprecating manner. However, in the eyes of their supervisors, the main task for the soldiers who went to fight against their enemies was to kill others. As long as the soldiers went to battle, even if they didn't directly kill someone, they would in some way have indirectly killed someone. As mentioned earlier, soldiers were generally conscripted. Although they looked like soldiers and were called soldiers, they were still human beings like any other ordinary civilian. Even if they put on a military uniform and took up arms, they still weren't a real soldier capable of killing the enemy in battle. But such hesitation had to be eliminated as soon as possible once in battle.

For this reason, in order to make real soldiers out of new recruits in a short period of time, new arrivals on the front would be allowed to experiment on live prisoners by stabbing them. Most of these people were Chinese prisoners of war as well as some local residents. Stabbing people like this was regarded as a shortcut for transforming new arrivals into real soldiers. It was cruel to use people for target practice but it was also a stressful experience for the new soldiers.

Those of us who'd landed in Wusong had fought in the war from the moment we'd arrived and had had no time to practice. But after the Battle of Shanghai, some new recruits from Japan adopted this method to practice killing. I saw new soldiers stab living targets several times in the war and I still remember how the scene first looked when we made our way to Nanjing.

My unit was always the first on the frontline during the Battle of Shanghai so we lost more than half of our soldiers as well as large amounts of weapons. As a result, we were arranged to be second on the frontline in the march to Nanjing. However, this still wasn't easy because we had to always keep a certain distance between us and the frontline troops to be able to help when we were needed.

We departed Wuxi in the morning and en route to our next destination, we entered a village to rest and found that a group of soldiers we didn't know had arrived there earlier. These soldiers were busy doing something. They had put up several stakes in the square and tied dozens of local residents to them. I knew what was going to happen next. These living targets were villagers who had no time to run away, among whom there were elderly people, women and teenagers. There was no need to ask for the reasons. This wasn't happening to the villagers because they'd committed any crimes, but because new arrivals needed to practice stabbing living people. Standing by these living targets was a group of young soldiers waiting for their orders. Although they looked the same as the other soldiers, upon closer inspection they were very young. It was obvious that they weren't "real soldiers", and were just new recruits being sent to the frontline. We could tell from their new uniforms that they'd never fought in battle. They seemed to behave like normal civilians. Judging from this, these new soldiers were going to advance to Nanjing and join the troops at the front there. They were being trained to stab living people as if they didn't do it, they'd never be accepted by the "real soldiers". Several minutes later, everything unfolded as I had expected.

The new recruits secured their bayonets under the orders of the private first class and stood directly in front of their victims. Even though they had learned stabbing techniques during their training in Japan and had stabbed a scarecrow to prepare for war, it was totally different to stabbing a real person. As they stood in front of their targets and held their bayonets with both hands, it was obvious they were unwilling to stab them. Their bodies were stiff and frozen from worry and their faces were even paler than their victims.

When their commander gave the order, they had no choice but to muster all their courage and stab the victims with a shout. But they didn't move in time with the order. On the contrary, they nervously ran up to their victims and stabbed them as they shook with fear.

Stabbing someone like this doesn't directly pierce their heart and therefore it doesn't instantly kill them. The injuries inflicted by the new soldiers were doing nothing more than torturing the villagers to death. Every time they stabbed their victims, they let out a bloodcurdling scream due to the intolerable pain. Their blood flowed out and dyed their bodies a deep crimson, making the victims look even more nightmarish. As a result, the recruits hesitated to stab them again. They were so frightened by their screams and the red blood that they stabbed them with less and less force. The private first class then shouted: "Don't hesitate! Or the *Shinajin* slaves will joke about you! End their lives quickly!" They had no choice but to chaotically stab them as bravely as they could. I speculate that there are two reasons why the soldiers then did this. First, they were afraid of being scolded by their supervisors. Second, they wanted to end all the screams, the blood and the suffering of the victims. The new recruits blindly stabbed the bodies. They were relieved when they saw them fall down weakly. The colour returned to the recruits' faces.

This was the first incident like this that I saw en route to Nanjing. Of course, there were some calmer soldiers among the new recruits who did exactly as they'd learned in training. However, these were few and far between and most new recruits were terrified of killing the person in front of them. That being said, they quickly became true soldiers thanks to this experience. Although this was brutal, a soldier's main task was to kill people in battle, which explained why they did this. Once a soldier was sent off to war, they first had to learn how to kill. After they were able to kill without hesitation, they were recognised as a real soldier by their comrades and would hold their heads high.

There are many reasons why the Japanese soldiers killed people but a key reason is that soldiers who killed enemies in battle would be rewarded and honoured. Killing was seen as glorious. The proof of this was in the popular saying: "The benefit of being a soldier is the credit you get after killing someone."

Once soldiers developed the courage to fight in the war, they'd become interested in killing. Naturally, battlefields were the perfect place for them to explore this fascination. Here, there were no troublesome ethical or moral quandaries and there were no national regulations in effect that could control the killing, so people got away without punishment even though they'd stabbed someone who'd surrendered or had shot innocent civilians. The more someone killed, the more they earned. But for victims, the result was the reverse. All this led to a sense of numbness and a lack of care about the crimes being committed. Instead, soldiers began boasting: "I've killed two or three *Shinajin* slaves."

In the Nanjing Massacre, the killers were people who'd been recently enlisted into the army and had transformed from ordinary humans into "real soldiers". These new recruits I met en route to Nanjing got the courage to kill by practicing stabbing people many times. Several days later, they joined the more experienced soldiers and carried out the Nanjing Massacre together.

The Nanjing Massacre saw large numbers of Chinese people being killed by Japanese soldiers after they occupied Nanjing in December 1937. We soldiers called it the Nanjing Brutality. This wasn't the official name, it was just what some soldiers called it. It earned this name not just because of the slaughters in Nanjing, but also because of the brutal crimes the soldiers committed on their way from locations near Shanghai to Nanjing, which included crimes that terrorised the locals, like looting, arson and rape.

I think it's time that I discuss the massacre. I was in the second line troops, as I mentioned earlier, and had joined the battle with the frontline troops after crossing through the mountains but we didn't fight in any major battles before the fall of Nanjing. We then approached the outskirts of Nanjing, which were in chaos, and finally settled down outside of the city. Because of this, I didn't participate directly in the massacre but saw where Chinese people had been killed by other troops. If I say that the unit I was in didn't participate in this brutal massacre, then some may think we were rarely well behaved. However, this wasn't actually the case. We did everything the others did in the massacre, such as killing civilians, looting property, burning houses and raping civilians. We were no less brutal than the others. There was no one left when we arrived in some areas. Later, we heard news that the people had all been killed by other soldiers. That's why we didn't participate in the massacre. There were no soldiers left. Even if we wanted to kill someone, there was no one left. At the time, we felt bored but I now feel lucky when I recall this.

The massacre in Nanjing and its outskirts lasted for at least 10 days. My unit was transferred to the north of Jiangsu Province on 20 December. I believe that the massacre was still going on when we left. When I walked around the area, there was evidence of mass murder everywhere with large piles of corpses. You'd even occasionally see a mountain of dead bodies.

As I'd landed in Wusong, I'd seen many dead bodies in the Battle of Shanghai. This meant that seeing 50 or 100 dead people didn't really bother me. However, I was astounded by the amount of killing in the Nanjing Massacre. No words can describe this horrible event, and all I can say is that it killed a huge number of innocent people. I also saw many sites where people were being massacred but I can only bring myself to write about one of them.

It happened a few days after we settled down outside of Nanjing. On my way back to the outpost from Xiaguan, I saw a scene straight out of hell. I vaguely remember that it took place in a square, about four to five miles away from eastern Xiaguan with the Yangtze River running to the north. The Japanese massacre in the square was truly hell on earth.

I didn't know which division the soldiers committing the massacre belonged to, nor did I know the name of their unit. All I know is that they had northeastern Japanese accents. That's one of the few details about them that I can still remember, but I'll never forget the hellish scene.

I didn't see it begin but according to soldiers who'd been watching from the beginning, the massacre had started at 9am. Several machine guns had been set up throughout the square, ready to open fire. About 100 Chinese people had been brought there and were standing in a row with the Yangtze behind them. It was a mix of soldiers and civilians, all wearing different types of clothes. There was a wide range of ages among the Chinese captives, from children to the elderly, roughly aged between 15 or 16 to 60. Under the commander's orders, the machine guns opened fire in unison, firing bullets at the people who were stood in a row. The sound of gunfire and people's screams made the square descend into chaos for a while. However, after just five minutes, it became quiet again. Even if any of the Chinese had tried to escape, it would have been almost impossible for them to survive as the Yangtze was behind them and the guns were firing at them from a short distance in the exposed square. The captives' corpses fell down on the ground in an uneven line. After shooting this batch of prisoners, another similarly sized group of Chinese people was brought over. When they entered the square, they were ordered by the Japanese soldiers to throw the bodies that had fallen on the ground into the river. After they finished, they were shot as well. Countless Chinese people were shot dead this way in this production line of death.

This is what the soldiers who'd been watching had told me. What I saw with my own eyes was the massacre approaching an end. The blood of dead Chinese people had accumulated into pools. I could see countless corpses floating in the Yangtze.

Although I had no idea exactly how many Chinese people had been killed on this square, I estimated that 10,000 people had been slaughtered judging by the method of execution and the amount of time they'd spent killing. In addition to these huge scale massacres, massacres of hundreds or thousands of Chinese people took place in areas of Nanjing captured by the Japanese army.

It took 103 days for my unit to capture Nanjing after landing in Wusong. This period showed me how horrible the war was. When I was in the war, I didn't pay much attention to the events but I now get goose bumps whenever I think about it to this day.

People who'd fought in the battle around Nanjing talked about how horrible it was, having to fight artillery, machine guns and riflemen. I was often told how the soldiers had expected to die themselves whenever they saw other soldiers around them getting injured or killed, which made them even more terrified.

I knew exactly how this fear felt. When the Japanese army landed in Wusong, I fought on the frontline, passing through tens of thousands, or even hundreds of thousands, of bullets and bombs along the way. I couldn't believe that none of them hit me. Dozens of the soldiers who'd left Japan with me had died. They died just two or three days after reaching the front line. We wouldn't have lost so many young lives if the war had never happened. They could have had their entire lives ahead of them, enjoying life and passing away like normal people. The surviving family members of the young soldiers who died were distraught, which was another aspect of how horrible the war was. Whenever I think of war, the first horrible effect that comes to mind is how people are twisted, becoming violent and cruel.

Men who had been kind civilians before joining the army had turned into monstrous killers in just 100 days of fighting on the frontline. It is these men who were able to conduct huge massacres like those seen in Nanjing. Apart from a few career soldiers, most of the officers and soldiers had been normal civilians before joining the army, ranging from policemen, lawyers, teachers who cared for the country's young, monks who preached Buddhism, shrine workers who served the gods, and role models from all sorts of sectors.

Kind as these civilians had previously been, they committed the most heinous crimes imaginable in the war. They first began by learning to kill people, then massacred poor soldiers begging to surrender, looted the property of locals, randomly slaughtered innocent civilians and set fire to whatever building they pleased. Whenever Japanese soldiers ran into young women, they'd rape them. They would never have committed these major crimes in normal society.

The mad war was to blame for these brutal crimes. What happened to the Chinese victims is heartbreaking but what happened to the twisted Japanese soldiers is also a tragedy.

Some people today, and some of those who were far removed from the war, believe that the Nanjing Massacre was just a one off incident, but this isn't true. Incidents like this happened too often to be counted in the war in China following the Nanjing Massacre, ranging from small crimes to large scale massacres.

As the invasion of China expanded, the violence grew. Some of the Japanese armies in China adopted the Three Alls policy: kill all, loot all and burn all. In this policy of total war, it wasn't just Chinese soldiers who were targeted as civilians were also killed by the Japanese army. Valuable property and food that belonged to the residents was stolen. Even their houses were burned down. As a result, by the time the soldiers had finished their operations, towns were rendered unliveable with their residents massacred and their houses burnt down.

I was also told that Japanese troops committed genocide in some areas. According to the Japanese soldiers who had participated in these incidents, it was likely the result of the Three Alls Policy too. For the Japanese army, it was seen as a good thing when residents lived in areas where they were operating as they would kill all of them. After some Japanese operations, elderly people and infants were killed. Not even cats and dogs were left alive.

The soldiers engaged in these brutal operations had been normal law-abiding civilians, but they were now able to kill without hesitation. It had nothing to do with their personality or level of education.

Below is a good example of how the Japanese soldiers acted in battle. It is from the diary of a private first class who was involved in the battle to take Nanjing. He belonged to the 23rd capital infantry division and had come from Miyazaki Prefecture. It was published by the *Asahi Shimbun* on 5 August 1984:

We've been bored recently so to kill some time we took some innocent Chinese civilians and buried them alive, pushed them into fires and beat them to death with bats. It was good fun and we enjoyed it. We even killed the Chinese who'd surrendered. Today, we pushed some other Chinese people on the ground and almost beat them to death. We then threw them into a ditch, set fire to their heads and they died in agony. As we had nothing else to do, we enjoyed it a lot. However, back in Japan, it would have been a very serious incident and as bad as killing cats and dogs.

There is no way that this diary extract has been fabricated. Soldiers wrote in their diaries about what they'd experienced, what they'd seen and what they'd been thinking about. Back then, many brutal crimes were committed by the Japanese army. I wasn't an exception. During my three years of fighting in battles both big and small in China, I committed brutal crimes that would not have been allowed in normal society. I killed, looted, burned and raped. When I recall what I did, I wonder how I could have been so brutal, which makes me scared of the monster who lies hidden within.

Matters of Ghosts and Dialogues Between Men

It has been more than 70 years since the Nanjing Massacre took place. The total number of people the Japanese army killed has been the biggest cause for argument between China and Japan. In the years when the Japanese were able to reflect on their war crimes more positively, they seemed to accept the judgment that they had killed "more than 200,000" in Nanjing as stated at the Tokyo trials. However, in recent years a rather large group of Japanese politicians and right-wing elements have openly argued that the Nanjing Massacre was "a lie invented by the Chinese". It was this impudence that truly enraged the Chinese people. The Nanjing Massacre has therefore become a controversial area of historical debate. Kazuo Sone discussed his general views on the Nanjing Massacre:

> When the Japanese army swarmed into Nanjing after a string of victories, the attacking Japanese army and the defending Chinese army were both in states of chaos and confusion. The massacre took place under those circumstances. Due to this, the Japanese army did not have the energy to investigate how many people they had killed, nor did the Chinese.
>
> I do not want to deny the figure of more than 300,000, which was proposed by the Chinese in the Nanjing trials. But personally, I don't believe that this figure is accurate because their national government had been transferred to Wuhan before Japan occupied Nanjing. Nanjing was in anarchy by the time the Japanese army occupied it.
>
> Only junior officials, Nanjing garrison troops and the poorest citizens stayed there. As they were the targets of the massacre, they ran desperately for their lives and nobody investigated the number of people killed. Even though the figure was investigated, the results wouldn't be accurate in such chaos. In addition to the charity organisations that buried the corpses, Japanese officers and soldiers dealt with the corpses themselves, burying them in trenches, burning them with petrol, throwing them into the Yangtze and various other methods of disposal. These practices were specified in the diaries and statements of the Japanese soldiers who participated in the massacre.
>
> The Japanese army flooded into Nanjing in great numbers from all directions and caused a great deal of chaos when they approached the city. The frontline troops competed with each other, going out of control and causing

bitter and bloody conflicts along the way. These troops couldn't contact headquarters and team leaders made arbitrary decisions. Without instructions from headquarters regarding the disposal of the surrendering Chinese officers and soldiers, they arbitrarily had them killed and disposed of, failing to accurately report it after the event.

The Japanese troops near Nanjing made erratic decisions and killed a multitude of Chinese people. The high-ranking commanding officers knew it but didn't stop the excessive massacre, pretending to know nothing about it. This was my experience back then. When the Japanese army occupied Nanjing, the Japanese military authorities didn't know the reality of the massacre of the Chinese by their subordinates. Decades later, someone proposed that 50,000 Chinese had been killed for some reason that remains unknown and alien to me.

Some Japanese people objected to the figure proposed by China and its allies, and they tried to downplay it. While this is understandable, their sins would not be undone by a reduced figure. The tragedy of a massacre cannot simply be defined by its death toll, with 300,000 being a massive massacre, 200,000 a moderate massacre or 50,000 a small massacre.

Although I have said so much about the Nanjing Massacre, I cannot know or even speculate how many Chinese people were killed. I can just say that an uncountable number of Chinese people were killed in this unprecedented massacre. The usually discussed figures are 300,000, 200,000 or 50,000, and these Chinese were killed near Nanjing. But if the Nanjing Massacre is judged on a larger scale, the figure goes far beyond any of these estimates.

I think that the Nanjing Massacre began when the Japanese army set out from near Shanghai to attack Nanjing. The crimes of the Nanjing Massacre, as mentioned by the soldiers in the local area, occurred from the period when they set off near Shanghai and continued after they arrived in Nanjing.

On the way to Nanjing, the officers and soldiers manifestly committed many atrocities, killing beyond the scale expected in usual combat, robbing grain the citizens had stored for winter, burning the commoners' houses and raping women. Although they were collectively called atrocities, many people were killed in this process. If such figures are added to the total number of those killed in the Nanjing Massacre, the figure may well be greater than assumed.

After the Nanjing Massacre was brought to the attention of Japanese nationals after the Second World War, there was a statement as follows: "The so-called 'Nanjing Massacre' was invented by the Allied countries to fabricate Japanese war crimes."

The reason for this is that back then, most Japanese nationals hadn't heard anything about the massacre when the Japanese army had occupied Nanjing. The first they'd heard of it was at the Allied powers' Tokyo trials. The Nanjing Massacre was subsequently discussed in the trial. Senior General and Commander Iwane Matsui had been in charge of the troops in central China when the massacre had occurred. He was found to have been responsible for it and was sentenced to death. Ordinary Japanese nationals now knew what had happened.

The Tokyo trials took place in August of the 21st year (1946) of the Showa period, 10 years after the Nanjing Massacre. The Japanese nationals had had no knowledge of this over that long period and it was beyond comprehension to the people of Japan at that time. But this is understandable, given the situation in Japan back then.

Before its defeat in the Second World War, Japan had an oppressive political system where rulers had a degree of power unimaginable to modern people. The freedom of expression of ordinary Japanese nationals was rigorously restricted and they did not have the right to be informed. After the wartime system was implemented, the National Mobilisation Law further strengthened national control over the freedom of expression. In addition to this, there were the Public Security Preservation Laws, the National Defence and Security Law, the Military Plan Law, the Dangerous Document Temporary Prohibition Law, acts by the Ministry of War and Ministry of Foreign Affairs, and many more oppressive laws. Therefore, Japanese nationals were tightly controlled. Reports by newspapers and broadcasting stations were put under tight controls and could not report on reality.

For example, the air raids launched by the American military towards the end of the war caused heavy losses but the government did not allow any reporting of information regarding the afflicted areas, the number of victims and which houses had been destroyed for the reason that such information would provide the enemy with data to judge the effectiveness of the attack. Although Japanese people can discuss war freely now, if they condemned the war back then, they would have been condemned as 'pacifists'. It was the power of politics that made people do this. It was all well and good to just be condemned, but they could also be branded as 'traitors' or 'non-nationals' and be punished according to criminal law.

When the Japanese invaders marched towards Chinese territory after the Marco Polo Bridge Incident, the Japanese government declared that it would "punish tyrannical China to force the national government to reflect" and proposed a "holy war for peace in Japan" in an attempt to beautify the war. Therefore, anything unfavourable regarding the Japanese army was not allowed to be reported on for the Japanese public.

It was, of course, unfavourable for the army to have slaughtered the Chinese in Nanjing. If their nationals knew the reality, the prestige of the Japanese army would have been damaged, which would go against the original aims of the "holy war" and become an excuse to condemn the war.

The leaders of the government and the army adopted whatever measures they could to keep their nationals in the dark about the Nanjing Massacre. First, to prevent any reporting or disclosure of information, they increased restrictions through inspections. For this reason, the special reporters and news photographers dispatched by newspaper offices to the front were deprived of the freedom of reporting the facts. Although many reporters were in the army during the battle in Nanjing, they could not report on or take photographs of the facts.

There is further evidence for the massacre. Identical articles on the fighting in Nanjing were published by all newspaper offices. They all talked about the brilliant achievements of the attacking army and the military accomplishments of the imperial officers and soldiers. Not a single word about the massacre was published in any articles, news reports or films. Corpses were scattered and piled up everywhere around Nanjing following the massacre, but they were not shown in films.

Even if the reality had been recorded in articles or photographs, they would have been detained during examinations. In this way, any information unfavourable towards the army would be seized and only the 'glorious military accomplishments' of the forces occupying Nanjing would be reported to Japanese nationals. The citizens trustingly accepted the news, parading and waving banners during the day and lighting lanterns during the evening to celebrate the Japanese occupation of Nanjing, getting drunk to celebrate the victory. Even if they had known that so many Chinese people had been killed, they would have thought of it as a military achievement back then.

On the one hand, the army strictly prevented any reporting to the nationals of anything bad they had done at the front; on the other hand, they rigorously forbade the soldiers at the front from disclosing any information. After the Battle of Nanjing came to an end, some veterans were gagged when they returned home. I returned to Japan in the autumn of the 15th year of the Showa period. When I was about to leave my unit, I was warned: "Even if you are dismissed after you return to your hometown in Japan, you should protect the honour and sense of pride of our soldiers. You should never disclose anything that damages the honour of the imperial army to anyone else."

The wording was difficult to understand. In brief, it means: "Even if you return to Japan and leave the army, you should never mention anything bad the Japanese army has done in the war."

I left the army and returned home after that. But I faithfully abided by the army's wishes and did not mention anything to the outside world. Although someone who knew something about the Nanjing Massacre came to ask me about it, I just replied "I don't know" and ignored them. Although it was despicable, we could not fight against it and had to obey. At that time, I thought it wiser to stay silent than to be beaten for saying something unwelcome.

The division I belonged to was mobilised back in late August 1937. The majority of the force were lower ranking soldiers who had recently joined the army. After mobilisation, we marched to the frontline in late August before advancing and capturing Nanjing about three months later. To put it another way, normal people who had been part of normal society before the war committed a terrifying massacre after three months of fighting. I want to find out why.

We didn't carry out extremely brutal attacks when we first arrived in Shanghai, partly due to the close and intense fighting in the city, but mostly because of our aim of protecting the Japanese citizens there and protecting their rights and interests. We also clung onto the hope that the fighting in Shanghai would be the end of our mission.

This hope turned into despair when we advanced to take Nanjing. As the capital of Chiang Kai-shek, the city of Nanjing was expected to be well defended. Strong resistance would lead to a fierce battle between the two sides and I thought about the possibility of my death. Even if I could avoid death, I still didn't know when the war was going to end. It was because of the strong hope that the fighting would swiftly come to an end that the subsequent despair was so strong.

One of the reasons behind the brutal crimes was that the Japanese soldiers felt a strange rage towards the Chinese people. To make Chiang Kai-shek surrender, the Japanese army captured Nanjing, where his government was located. As a result, the middle ranking officers who'd led the soldiers were in high spirits.

The major I knew who'd acted as a main leader told his officers and soldiers: "In order to make Chiang Kai-shek surrender, just capturing Nanjing isn't enough. We have to do all we can to make the Chinese people panic. You shall accomplish this by killing every Chinese person you find, including civilians. You should loot, rape and even start fires."

I had a friend who had been in north China for a while. He had been enlisted in the 10th army, which had landed in Hangzhou. He said that officers and soldiers in the 10th army also acted this way. As they were approaching Nanjing, an order from above apparently stated: "Chinese people shall not be allowed to be uncontrolled. Everyone, including farmers, workers, women and children, should all be killed."

He said that with an order like this, every time they found a Chinese person, whether they were a soldier or a civilian, they'd kill them without hesitation. Every time they ran into a woman, whether they were married or not, they would rape them before killing them, but it wasn't as simple as stabbing them with a bayonet. They'd hit them with a bat. Their blood would spray out like hot spring and they died. As the Chinese were wearing cotton clothing and had been bound with iron wire, it took a long time to burn them.

As a result, the assault and capture of Nanjing descended into madness, which I think was one of the contributing factors for the massacre. This was already enough to mean that the coming operations would be brutal, but levying grain made it even worse, just like pouring oil on a fire.

I'd be repeating myself if I were to explain requisition all over again, but I'll just briefly mention here another reason behind the Nanjing Massacre. We would rob local households in the name of requisition, but we were doing nothing more than acting like bandits. By doing so, the lower ranking soldiers lost their morality and now acted like marauders. This was another reason that led to the brutal violence. However, there were still other smaller factors as well.

Before we went to war in Shanghai, we were incredibly naive and thought that the war was going to be easy because they were "just Chinese". We hadn't expected such strong resistance from the enemy, which dragged into a long and brutal war. It took us more than 70 days to capture a small city like Shanghai, with our casualties reaching at least 40,000. We no longer thought of them as "just Chinese", but "damned Chinese".

Lower ranking soldiers in the Japanese army were full of complaints. First came the wide gap in rank and respect, which allowed generals to act like nobility while soldiers were treated like slaves. Next, soldiers were required to obey all orders, regardless of how unreasonable and insulting they were. Once on the battlefield, the low ranking soldiers, who'd been oppressed and tormented, finally found someone weaker than themselves: the Chinese. They took out all of their frustrations on them.

Like all other battlefields, once on the frontline, there was just a fine line between life and death. You never knew what was going to happen tomorrow. You didn't talk about tomorrows. It was common to hear that someone you'd been happily chatting to a few minutes ago was dead. Under these circumstances, lower ranking soldiers chose to eat, drink and be merry. All they wanted was good sleep, delicious food and sex with women.

This is all everyone in battle wanted and while some could have these luxuries, others could not. In China, because of the belief that you could do anything to the Chinese, robbing and raping were allowed. All that was missing was good sleep. As the residents didn't dare complain that their livestock had been stolen or that they'd been raped, the Japanese soldiers became more arrogant, committing more crimes as a result, which were becoming ever worse. Although not every soldier did it, most were violent against the Chinese.

When I was on the frontline, a local interpreter once complained to me: "We've been extremely frustrated as the Japanese have tried to make us obey through violence. The more violent Japan is, the more apathetic we become. We'd be distraught if this behaviour continues in the war." As the interpreter had said, violence was used as a weapon by the Japanese army to force the Chinese to obey.

I felt that the use of violence in this way was very similar to how middle and higher ranking officers in the Japanese army would make lower ranking soldiers obey. I believe that this was a factor that may have contributed to the Nanjing Massacre. As I reflect on the incident, I can't deny that I also behaved brutally. When I look back at it now, I did these things impulsively without any consideration of whether they were right or wrong, kind or evil. However, upon further reflection, the reason that I was able to be so brutal was because, deep down, I looked down on the Chinese, buying into the common belief that you could do anything you liked to them.

At first, I was hesitant in acting brutally against the Chinese, but as I spent more time at war this hesitation was somehow replaced by an idea that became stronger and stronger, that the Chinese didn't matter at all and that I should just do whatever I liked. When I brutally tortured the Chinese during the war, I didn't think about whether it was right or wrong at all.

If I had to give one reason behind the Japanese brutality in the war against China, I'd say that Japan's hatred of the Chinese was fundamentally to blame. This hatred hadn't just come out of the blue during this war. Instead, Japan's hatred of the Chinese had been cultivated as early as the Meiji period.

Kazuo Sone, an ordinary Japanese veteran who took part in the invasion of China, wrote the above analysis in his sixties, decades after the war. His analysis largely contains a great deal of truth about the incident as well as confessions to his own crimes. It provides a clear analysis of Japan's views of China and how war had turned ordinary Japanese men into murderous and raping monsters. It would be a good idea for the people of modern Japan to reflect on their past like a mirror. There are in fact quite a few veterans like Sone who wrote about their experiences in the war and who they became.

Some of the soldiers and officers who participated in the Nanjing Massacre enjoyed peaceful lives when they returned to Japan. As their humanity reawakened, their consciences were appalled by the crimes they had committed during the invasion of China. However, due to Japan's tendency to ignore the sins of its past, few people have risen up to tell the truth. Their inner conflicts between brutality and humanity became more ferocious as they got older, so eventually, people like Sone stood up bravely to tell the public what had really happened. The inner conflicts in the Japanese veterans who participated in the Nanjing Massacre serve as further evidence of the Japanese crimes, showing just how shocking the events really were.

Kazuo Sone once provided an incisive insight into his mentality: "I have stated that the Nanjing Massacre indeed happened, for as a soldier at the time, I was involved in the invasion of Nanjing and committed violent and brutal crimes. I saw the massacre with my own eyes and even took part in the brutality. Many other soldiers who also participated in the war are still alive. Although they have first hand knowledge of the truth of the Nanjing Massacre, they don't want to say what really happened because they want to avoid the painful memories. I believe that the deliberate denial of the Nanjing Massacre results from a desire to cover up the stain of Japan's military past and this is why the truth has been distorted. But instead, the Nanjing Massacre remains a stain on Japanese history and it cannot be easily removed. I believe that instead of distorting what really happened, we should confess to our sins and reflect on them, allowing future generations to learn from our mistakes. This is why I wanted to reveal what I saw and my experiences of the event. The descriptions are based on what I, a soldier at the time, experienced, heard and saw with my own eyes during the Nanjing Massacre when fighting in the Japanese invasion of China. I have also written about it out of a sense of redemption and because of my conscience."

Junji Ide, who was a sergeant in the Japanese army's air force at the time, also hit the nail on the head: "The stupid discussion on whether it happened or not should be put to an end because it was indeed true as a huge number of soldiers from both China and Japan witnessed it. Let's leave the historians [to deal with] the issue of how many were killed in the Nanjing Massacre and whether it was thousands or hundreds of thousands of people. I think we should face the fact that humans can be divine but also demonic. We have two opposite sides. What we should remember is that war is the chief culprit for turning humans into demons, and the turmoil and destruction caused by the Nanjing Massacre is excellent testimony to this. It should remain as a lesson for us to learn from and as a subject for ongoing discussion."

The Japanese soldier Kenzo Okamoto put it rather more bluntly: "It's complete bullshit if someone denies the Nanjing Massacre because I was there." He talked about what happened to the Chinese during the Nanjing Massacre: "If we resisted the order to kill in war, then we'd risk being killed by others. But in a situation like this, soldiers wouldn't have shot people if they'd even had just a shred of humanity. The shootings were conducted by the shooting division, while our division was responsible for guarding the deployments. It wasn't just men who were killed, but women and children too, even children under 10 years old. This was a complete massacre."

Some Japanese veterans have revealed and astutely analysed the ferocious crimes committed by a great number of their former comrades in the Nanjing Massacre, considering their own experiences and feelings.

Kazuo Sone further explained the crimes: "The Battle of Shanghai had been a very fierce battle so we all expected a similar fight when we assaulted and occupied Nanjing, thinking that many of us were going to die. Although our morale was very high, we didn't really know what we were fighting for at the time. We had become lost in the darkness. We didn't know how many of us were going to become casualties and as we all believed that we'd be wounded or killed in the future, we gave up on hope. With the order to go to Nanjing, our reason for fighting became clearer and everyone in the army became less anxious. Since the beginning of the assault and capture of Nanjing, lower ranking soldiers had already been irritable, but a later desire to get revenge made things worse. Even without orders to loot, they'd have committed atrocities on their own will, but with the order to rob grain from local residents, soldiers lost all sense of guilt and were no different to bandits. They became an army of bandits, raping every woman they saw and using violence against anyone who opposed them."

Another Japanese veteran, Ikuo Kō, said: "Because the leaders of the military thought that the Chinese were pigs, they gave orders like: 'Kill all Chinese, including the women and children, and burn down all their homes' (from *Tales of the National Army's Battles* by Takashi Hiramatsu). This led to the guaranteed outcome of lower ranking soldiers raping, robbing and committing crimes. Since they didn't even care about massacres, robbing became the norm. Everything the invaders robbed was seen as a trophy."

Hisashi Nakano, who once served as a squadron leader in the 23rd wing of the 6th infantry division, confessed his crimes in writing on 26 August 1954: "Back then, the spirit that motivated me to go to the Chinese capital of Nanjing was that the only way to demonstrate the might of the emperor to the entire world was to wipe out all of the Chinese patriots who opposed Japan. It would benefit Japan and also show the entire world Japan's superiority. Only by doing this would I attain the highest honour of being a

Japanese soldier and set an example for Japanese civilians. As I committed terrible crimes along the way, another idea in the back of my mind was that to facilitate Japanese rule over China, after invading Nanjing, Chinese patriots fighting against the Japanese army in the area had to be annihilated so as to force Chiang Kai-shek to surrender. With these thoughts in my mind, when I committed the crimes I mentioned earlier, I thought that what I was doing was sacred and just."

One Japanese veteran became an artist after the war. His left arm had been injured during the fierce fighting against the Chinese army. He was a warrant officer back then, described as "a hero" on the battlefield, but from the Chinese perspective, he was just another executioner with a blade that been "shortened by nearly 16cm" from use (*Truth of the War in Nanjing: Kumamoto's 6th Division War Stories, Collection of Historical Materials from the Nanjing Massacre*, vol. 6, p. 77). This Japanese veteran later wielded a paintbrush with the same hand he'd once used to hold a bloody knife. When he later looked back at the war, he said: "The war was miserable, regardless of whether you liked it or not, you had to choose between being killed and killing someone else. I killed people because I would be killed if I didn't." He later gave his own insights into his participation in the Japanese army: "I hated the community with its different ranks, which is why I now enjoy my precious freedom so much; during the long war, kind people were going to be killed. That is how war works."

After analysing the mindset of the Japanese soldiers who were involved in the massacre, we can come to a conclusion: an ideology of national invasion and expansion plays a key role in turning ordinary men into monsters. The commanders who turned ordinary civilians into barbaric invaders should be blamed first. With these conditions and a thirst for victory, it was inevitable that the invaders would act with brutality.

Born on a relatively small archipelago nation, the Japanese were unsatisfied with enjoying what they had on their islands. As a result, they looked overseas to expand their borders, continuously chasing more wealth and prosperity. Invasion and expansion therefore shaped the nation's identity.

But why couldn't this nation abandon this expansionist path, especially after it became wealthy and strong?

John Toland, a renowned American writer, wrote about Japan's national character: "Japan is a nation unlike any other in the world. Everything it does is the opposite to the norm. Usually, people like cooked food while the Japanese like it raw. Usually people like to lie down or sit, while the Japanese prefer to kneel. Therefore, the Japanese had a unique way of expressing love, for instance, in Nanjing, in order to show his love for the local residents,

Matsui inspired his demonic soldiers to set houses on fire, slaughter the innocent, rape women and rob shops and residents."

I think that John Toland's remarks make sense, and understanding the roots of the Japanese nation is essential for China. While this is indeed crucial, I also believe that the Chinese need to better understand their own history and identity to ensure that tragedies like the Nanjing Massacre never happen again.

ABOUT THE AUTHOR

He Jianming is a well-known Chinese reportage writer. More than 50 of his literary works have been published, with most of them being in the reportage genre. He is the vice president of the Chinese Writers' Association and is well regarded, as shown by his extensive awards, including the Lu Xun Literature Prize, the National Excellent Reportage Prize and the Xu Chi Reportage Prize. In addition to novels, he has written scripts for films and TV, including *Westbound Convict Train* and *National Action*. Other works by He Jianming include *The Country*, *Fidelity and Betrayal* and *Fundamental Interests*.

ABOUT ACA

We hope He Jianming's extensive and often moving account has helped to shed some light on what happened in Nanjing in 1937.

ALAIN CHARLES ASIA publishes an exciting range of China-focused non-fiction. From the soaring highs and grim lows of China's tumultuous history to the vivid life stories of its major and minor players, ACA has books for anyone eager to learn more about this vast, diverse nation.

To let us know what you thought of this book, or to learn more about the eclectic selection of titles we offer, find us online. If you're as passionate about books as we are, then we'd love to hear your thoughts!

alaincharlesasia.com
@aca_pub